The Triumph of Grace

Literary and Theological Studies in
Deuteronomy and Deuteronomic Themes

Daniel I. Block

CASCADE *Books* • Eugene, Oregon

THE TRIUMPH OF GRACE
Literary and Theological Studies in Deuteronomy and Deuteronomic Themes

Copyright © 2017 Daniel I. Block. All rights reserved. Except for brief quotations in critical publications or reviews, no part of this book may be reproduced in any manner without prior written permission from the publisher. Write: Permissions, Wipf and Stock Publishers, 199 W. 8th Ave., Suite 3, Eugene, OR 97401.

Cascade Books
An Imprint of Wipf and Stock Publishers
199 W. 8th Ave., Suite 3
Eugene, OR 97401

www.wipfandstock.com

PAPERBACK ISBN: 978-1-4982-9265-8
HARDCOVER ISBN: 978-1-4982-9267-2
EBOOK ISBN: 978-1-4982-9266-5

Cataloguing-in-Publication data:

Names: Block, Daniel I.

Title: The triumph of grace : literary and theological studies in Deuteronomy and deuteronomic themes / Daniel I. Block.

Description: Eugene, OR: Cascade Books, 2017 | Includes bibliographical references and index.

Identifiers: ISBN 978-1-4982-9265-8 (paperback) | ISBN 978-1-4982-9267-2 (hardcover) | ISBN 978-1-4982-9266-5 (ebook)

Subjects: LCSH: Bible. O.T. Deuteronomy—Criticism, interpretation, etc.

Classification: BS1275.52 B57 2017 (print) | BS1275.52 (ebook)

Manufactured in the U.S.A.   11/03/17

"Daniel Block, in *The Triumph of Grace*, demonstrates why he is considered one of the premier Old Testament theologians of this generation. Lucid, thoughtful, engaging, and persuasive, Block brilliantly illuminates for his readers the theme of God's amazing grace in the Book of Deuteronomy. Scholars, pastors, and laypeople alike will be blessed and helped as they work through this significant volume. It is a joyful privilege to recommend this outstanding work."

—**David S. Dockery**, President, Trinity International University

"By his own testimony, Dan Block has been 'marinating' in Deuteronomy for over twenty years. This volume completes a trilogy of his essays on this important book. Like the previous books, the present one is—not unlike Deuteronomy itself!—a collection of things old and new, including seven previously unpublished studies that cover Deuteronomy and: education, the book's genre/message, covenant, Sabbath, prayer, the fear of the Lord, and the 'prophet like Moses.' Although these studies will not convince everyone, Block has covered immense ground, providing us with much food for thought—especially for those of us who understand Deuteronomy as Holy Scripture. I, for one, hope Block continues 'conversing with Moses' for years to come."

—**Brent A. Strawn**, Professor of Old Testament, Emory University

"What a precious resource this is! There are few who have immersed themselves in 'the gospel according to Moses' like Dan Block, and fewer still who have matched his scholarship (which is careful and creative in equal measure), warmhearted generosity, and overwhelming desire to live and communicate the gospel of the Lord Jesus Christ in Deuteronomy with integrity and rigor. This collection is another hugely valuable contribution to Block's already rich body of writing on Deuteronomy. These essays encapsulate the humble brilliance of his approach, modeling as they do academic rigor and a profound commitment to apply the Scriptures to the life of the church, family, and society. This book is, at every level, reflective of the triumph of grace which its title proclaims."

—**J. Gary Millar**, Principal, Queensland Theological College, Brisbane, Australia

"This remarkable book eloquently demonstrates that Deuteronomy proclaims the gospel of divine grace that is embodied and reaches its ultimate triumph in the New Testament. Block shows masterful sensitivity to all levels of the text and to intertextual relationships. He solves interpretive problems and overturns misconceptions while uncovering details of meaning and literary artistry that converge to carry themes of soaring theological significance. The chapter on rediscovering the gift of Sabbath rest is a jewel."

—**Roy E. Gane**, Professor of Hebrew Bible and Ancient Near Eastern Languages,
Seventh-day Adventist Theological Seminary, Andrews University

"Aptly named, *The Triumph of Grace* contains the most profound and comprehensive collection of Daniel Block's articles to date. Whether studied individually or as a coherent whole, the articles reflect exemplary scholarship marked by sound methodological inquiry, passionate engagement with the text, and a refreshing tone of humility. Further, this collection brings synthesis of scholarship to a new level, inviting readers to follow the implications of understanding Torah as grace into the New Testament—specifically, Galatians."

—**Rebekah L. Josberger**, Associate Professor of Hebrew and Old Testament,
Multnomah Biblical Seminary

The Triumph of Grace

This book is dedicated to my friends
in the Veritas Adult Community Group
of College Church, in Wheaton, Illinois.

For seven years, you have endured my instruction
on the gospel according to Moses and inspired me with
your hunger for the life-giving word of God.

In your daily lives, may you all experience the triumph
of God's grace—the same grace that Moses proclaimed in
his farewell addresses to his own congregation
within sight of the promised land more than 3,000 years ago.

Contents

List of Figures | ix
List of Tables | xi
Preface | xiii
Acknowledgments | xvii
Credits | xxi
List of Abbreviations | xxiii

1   Deuteronomy: The Heart of Theological Education in the First Testament | 1

2   "That They May Hear": Biblical Foundations for the Oral Reading of Scripture in Worship | 19

　　Appendix A: A Liturgical Reading of Israel's National Anthem (Deuteronomy 32:1–43) | 35

3   "Do You Hear What I Hear?" Reflections on the Genre and Message of Deuteronomy | 36

4   Covenance: A Whole Bible Perspective | 60

5   Deuteronomic Law | 89

6   In the Tradition of Moses: The Conceptual and Stylistic Imprint of Deuteronomy on the Patriarchal Narratives | 105

7   "A Place for My Name": Horeb and Zion in the Mosaic Vision of Israelite Worship | 126

8   "What Do These Stones Mean?" The Riddle of Deuteronomy 27 | 152

9   "The Meeting Places of God in the Land": Another Look at the Towns of the Levites | 177

10 "O Day of Rest and Gladness": Rediscovering the Gift of Sabbath | 198

11 The Patricentric Vision of Family Order in Deuteronomy | 225

12 Wrestling with God: A Study on Prayer in Deuteronomy | 240

13 How Can We Bless YHWH? Wrestling with Divine Violence in Deuteronomy | 264

14 The Fear of YHWH: The Theological Tie that Binds Deuteronomy and Proverbs | 283

15 All Israel Will Be Saved: An Examination of Moses' Eschatological Vision in Deuteronomy | 312

16 The Spiritual and Ethical Foundations of Messianic Kingship: Deuteronomy 17:14–20 | 335

17 A Prophet Like Moses: Another Look at Deuteronomy 18:9–22 | 349

18 Hearing Galatians with Moses: An Examination of Paul as a Second and Seconding Moses | 374

Bibliography | 405

Index of Modern Authors | 439

Index of Selected Subjects | 445

Index of Biblical References | 449

Index of Ancient Extracanonical Literature | 503

Figures

Figure 1.1: The Dimensions of Divine Expectation (Deuteronomy 10:12—11:1) | 11
Figure 1.2: A Schematic Portrayal of the Location and Function of the Levitical Towns | 12
Figure 1.3: The Deuteronomic Formula for Life | 14
Figure 3.1: The Structure of the Book of Deuteronomy | 40
Figure 4.1: God's Irrevocable Covenant Commitment | 62
Figure 4.2: A Synopsis of the Cosmic and Israelite Covenantal Triangles | 65
Figure 4.3: The Evolution of the Israelite Covenant: A Sheep's Eye View | 66
Figure 4.4: The Evolution of the Israelite Covenant: A Bird's Eye View | 66
Figure 4.5: The Place of Sinai/Horeb in the Plot of the Pentateuch | 68
Figure 4.6: The Growth of Israel's Constitutional Tradition | 74
Figure 4.7: The Relationship between Physical Israel and Spiritual Israel as Perceived by Moses and Jeremiah | 80
Figure 4.8: The Expansion of the Covenant Community in the New Testament | 81
Figure 4.9: The Role of Adam/Humanity in the Cosmic Administrative Order | 85
Figure 4.10: The Role of the King in Israel's Administrative Order | 87
Figure 4.11: The Role of Jesus Christ in the Eschatological Cosmic Administrative Order | 88
Figure 6.1: The Place of Sinai/Horeb in the Plot of the Pentateuch | 125
Figure 7.1: The Syntactical and Discourse Structure of Deuteronomy 4:9–10 | 130
Figure 8.1: A Hebrew-English Synopsis of Deuteronomy 27:1–8 | 158
Figure 8.2: A Synopsis of Deuteronomy 27:2–3 and 27:4–8 | 159
Figure 8.3: The Location of Mounts Gerizim and Ebal | 164
Figure 8.4: The Completion of the Israelite Covenantal Triangle | 169
Figure 8.5: The Right and Wrong Roads to Ebal | 176
Figure 9.1: The Locations of the Levitical Towns | 179

Figure 9.2: The Expanding Pastureland (מגרש) | 181

Figure 9.3: A Schematic Portrayal of the Location and Function of the Levitical Towns | 194

Figure 10.1: Concentric Gradations of Holiness | 204

Figure 10.2: The Growth of Israel's Constitutional Tradition | 210

Figure 10.3: The Dimensions of the Decalogue | 211

Figure 10.4: God's Irrevocable Covenant Commitment | 215

Figure 10.5: The Sacred-Clean-Unclean-Abominable Continuum | 222

Figure 10.6: The Relationship between the Cosmic and Israelite Covenants | 223

Figure 11.1: The Patricentric Ideal and the Reality in Ancient Israel | 230

Figure 13.1: The Sacred-Clean-Unclean-Abominable Continuum | 272

Figure 14.1: The Semantic Spectrum of ירא Words in Deuteronomy | 286

Figure 14.2: The Dimensions of Divine Expectation (Deuteronomy 10:12—11:1) | 293

Figure 15.1: The Israelite Covenantal Triangle | 316

Figure 15.2: The Relationship between Physical and Spiritual Israel as Perceived by Moses and Jeremiah | 328

Figure 17.1: A Colometric Synopsis of Deuteronomy 18:9–22 | 362

Figure 18.1: The Semantic Spectrum of ירא Words in Deuteronomy | 395

Tables

Table 1.1: The Structure of Deuteronomy 10:12–11:1 | 8

Table 1.2: The Importance of Hearing the Torah | 14

Table 3.1: The Textual Evolution of the Shema (Deuteronomy 6:4–5) | 43

Table 3.2: A Synopsis of the Textual Variations of Deuteronomy 32:43 | 44

Table 7.1: Horeb and Zion: A Comparison | 144–45

Table 8.1: The Relationship between Deut 11:26–32 and 26:16—29:69[29:1] | 155

Table 8.2: The Structure of Deuteronomy 27 | 156

Table 10.1: A Synopsis of the Sabbath Command in Exodus and Deuteronomy | 212–13

Table 12.1: A Synopsis of Moses' Argumentation in His Intercessory Prayers | 249

Table 12.2: A Synopsis of Moses' Prayers in Deuteronomy | 258–59

Table 14.1: The Root ירא in the Book of Deuteronomy | 285

Table 14.2: The Importance of Hearing the Torah | 297

Table 14.3: The Root ירא in the Book of Proverbs | 304

Table 17.1: The Parallel Structures of Deuteronomy 18:9–13 and 14 | 363

Table 17.2: Moses' and YHWH's Promises of a Prophet Like Moses | 367

Table 18.1: The Structure of Biblical Prophetic Appointment Accounts | 381

Table 18.2: Elements of a Prophetic Call in Galatians 1:15–16 | 382

Table 18.3: The Structure of Deuteronomy 10:12–11:1 | 391

Table 18.4: The Importance of Hearing the Torah | 395

Preface

BELIEVE IT OR NOT, five years have passed since the publication of my two volumes of essay collections on the book of Deuteronomy, *How I Love Your Torah, O LORD: Studies in the Book of Deuteronomy* (Eugene, OR: Wipf & Stock, 2011), and *The Gospel according to Moses: Theological and Ethical Reflections on the Book of Deuteronomy* (Eugene, OR: Wipf & Stock, 2012). In the meantime, my commentary on *Deuteronomy*, NIVAC (Grand Rapids: Zondervan, 2012), has also seen the light of day. But the conversations that Moses and I had for more than two decades continue, and with remarkable effect. Earlier impressions of Moses as a paradigmatic pastor-teacher (Eph 4:11) have been reinforced, and his enthusiasm to proclaim a gospel of grace have energized my own work.

To many Moses is a dour, if not angry figure. Indeed, I have found it impossible to find an image, either sculptured or painted, of the man with a smile. Most commonly he is portrayed as shaking his finger at people or holding the tablets of the covenant above his head as he prepares to smash them. The cover on *The Gospel according to Moses* was the most benign image we could find. However, by having him hold a copy of the stone tablet, Michelangelo still presented him as primarily a man of law rather than grace.

The reasons for this negative image may be readily recognized. Having visited with and been inspired by Christians all over the world, the North American church exhibits a profoundly Pauline character. Indeed, it is so Pauline in some quarters that ministers seem to feel uncomfortable preaching from the Gospels, which represent a different genre of biblical literature than the doctrinal and propositional epistles of Paul. More specifically, Paul's repeated negative comments concerning the law have provided the lenses through which the rest of Scripture tends to be interpreted—which accounts for Martin Luther's dismissal of the epistle of James as a "strawy epistle." The dark lenses that Paul's statements on the law have given us prevent us from seeing the grace of God in texts that are pejoratively labeled "The Law," namely the first five books of the First Testament. Oh, we salvage some grace in the narratives of Genesis, by seeing Abraham as a man of faith apart from the law, but once we get to Exodus 19, either the law eclipses the sun or our lenses filter out the grace rays.

Recently at a men's gathering I read orally a large swath of text from YHWH's provision of a range of sacrifices in Leviticus 4:1—6:7. I then asked those gathered if they had heard the gospel anywhere. The room was silent. Because they did not expect to hear the gospel, they were quickly bored with the details of the sacrifices, frustrated that we should even be reading this, and feeling sorry for the Israelites who were saddled with these laws. How could those poor folks ever remember all these details? Their ears were not attuned to hear the glorious gospel proclaimed no fewer than ten times as the climax of each paragraph: "The priest shall make atonement on their behalf and they will be forgiven!" (4:20, 26, 31, 35; 5:6, 10, 13, 16, 18; 5:26[6:7]). The sacrifices represent concrete symbols of the triumph of divine grace over human rebellion and the dysfunction this has created between God and humanity.

Deuteronomy often evokes the same response. The name of the book itself (*deuteronomos*, "Second Law") blinds hearers to the gospel that is proclaimed from beginning to end. This *tôrâ* is to be heard that people might learn to fear Yhwh, that they might walk in grateful obedience to his will, that they might live! Deuteronomy reminds us over and over that Israel's story represented the triumph of divine grace over oppressive external forces (the Egyptians), that Yhwh's call to covenant relationship is all of grace, that their ongoing fellowship with him is rooted in grace, and that—even though their future failure seems inevitable, Yhwh's grace will triumph in the end (4:20–31; 30:1–10). The nation's judgment cannot be the last chapter of their story.[1]

Since Israel's life in the land and in covenant relationship with Yhwh was to be paradigmatic of the ultimate destiny of humanity and the cosmos, Yhwh's grace to Israel was paradigmatic of our own experience. Israel's story provided the vocabulary with which to describe the incarnation and the glorious divine plan of redemption for humankind and all creation (Matt 1:21). The One who lavished his grace on Israel is none other than the One who took on human flesh, and in so doing embodied the grace and faithfulness (Greek, χάριτος καὶ ἀληθείας; Hebrew חֶסֶד וֶאֱמֶת) that Moses could only mediate through proclamation (cf. John 1:14). But it was the same grace. The contrast between ancient Israel's experience and that which the New Testament makes available was not between law and grace, but between *mediated* grace and *embodied* grace. Like the anthem that concludes Moses' pastoral instruction preserved in the book of Deuteronomy (chapter 32), the book of Revelation paints a brilliant picture of the ultimate cosmic triumph of divine grace.

Although the essays in this volume are not all equally focused on the triumph of divine grace, they reflect the trajectory of my ongoing research in Deuteronomy and Deuteronomic themes. While the theological trajectory of the studies is consistent, this volume does not attempt to develop a single theme in a coherent and smoothly flowing sequence. Nor are the essays composed in the same linguistic register. Some are written for the general population, with minimal footnotes and minimal technical details. Others involve detailed analysis of exegetical minutiae. Two-thirds of the essays were written for publication elsewhere, and with the gracious permission of editors and publishers, are republished here to enhance their accessibility for interested readers. The remaining

---

1. I am well aware of and deeply grateful for Paul A. Barker's excellent study, *The Triumph of Grace in Deuteronomy: Faithless Israel, Faithful Yahweh in Deuteronomy*, Paternoster Biblical Monographs (Eugene, OR: Wipf & Stock, 2007). However, the correspondence in title is purely coincidental, and readers familiar with his work will quickly recognize that our purposes and the content of our respective volumes differ significantly.

third have either been inspired by invitations to present papers at conferences or represent fuller discussions of shorter essays prepared for other purposes.

As in the previous volumes, the studies here have all been edited for style and format to produce a stylistically coherent volume in accordance with the standards of Wipf & Stock Publishers. Among other distinctive features, this means that all references to secondary literature in the footnotes appears in sharply abbreviated form. A full bibliography is provided at the end. The articles themselves are generally concerned with broad hermeneutical and theological issues raised by Deuteronomy and with themes that concern the composition. They exhibit a considerable range in focus, involving introductory considerations of the genre and nature of the book, Deuteronomy's relationship to other Pentateuchal texts, its contribution to broad biblical theological themes, closer looks at particular texts, ethical and spiritual implications of its teachings, and concluding with a daring foray into the relationship of Moses and Paul.

Each essay in this collection was written to stand on its own. Since they arise from a twenty-year conversation with Moses, and were originally presented orally and in print in widely different contexts, readers of the entire volume may notice some repetition within this volume, and repetition of ideas developed in the earlier volumes published by Wipf & Stock: *How I Love Your Torah, O LORD! Studies in the Book of Deuteronomy* (2011), and *The Gospel according to Moses: Theological and Ethical Reflections on the Book of Deuteronomy* (2011). Because we cannot assume that readers of this book will have easy access to the earlier collections, we do so unapologetically. As my father—who was a rather effective preacher—used to say, "If it's worth saying once, it's worth saying twice." Commitments to the publishers of the earlier versions of the essays included here have precluded eliminating redundancies with cross references and summary statements when material presented earlier resurfaces.

Unless otherwise indicated, generally the English translations of biblical texts are my own. I have tried to be consistent in rendering dates according to contemporary scholarly convention as BCE ("before the common era") and CE ("common era"), which Christians may also interpret as "before the Christian era" and "Christian era," respectively.

The presentation of the divine name—represented by the Tetragrammaton, יהוה—is a particular problem for scholars. The practice of rendering the divine name in Greek as κύριος is commonly carried over into English translations as "LORD," which reflects the Hebrew יהוה, and distinguishes it from "Lord," which reflects Hebrew אֲדֹנָי. But this creates problems both in hearing and in interpretation, for the connotations and implications of referring to someone by name or by title are quite different. Traditionally, when rendered as a name, English translations have vocalized יהוה as "Jehovah," which apparently combines the consonants of יהוה with the vowels of אֲדֹנָי. Today non-Jewish scholars generally render the name as "Yahweh," recognizing that "Jehovah" is an artificial construct. But "Yahweh," a scholarly convention, is equally—if not more—artificial that Jehovah. Grateful that Yhwh expressly revealed his name to his people and invited them to address him by name (e.g., Exod 3:13–15), but recognizing the uncertainty of its original vocalization and in deference to Jewish sensibilities regarding the name, in this volume the divine name is rendered simply with the English letters of the tetragrammaton, Yhwh (except in direct quotations of English versions or secondary authors).

On a related front, since the publication of the previous volumes, in my writings I have to a large extent stopped referring to the Bible that Jesus and the apostles possessed as the Old Testament. What we call something matters. The expression "Old Testament" contributes to and fosters the dismissive disposition toward the Hebrew Bible that prevails in Western Christianity. It connotes unfortunate notions of antiquity and out-of-dateness, as if God's earlier revelation has been supplanted and rendered obsolete by later revelation. Observing that we have inherited the phrase from the patristic period, John Goldingay rightly questions it, "because it . . . suggests something antiquated and inferior left behind by a dead person."[2] Although the reference is not to the First Testament, when the book of Hebrews compares the previous covenant with the later one, he speaks of them as "first" (ἡ πρώτη διαθήκη) and "new" (ἡ διαθήκη καινή) covenants, respectively (Heb 9:15). We would gain a better understanding of the relationship between the testaments if we called the Old Testament the First Testament and then viewed the New Testament as the completion or fulfillment of the first, rather than its replacement. Thus, throughout this book, I will use "First Testament" for the former Scriptures, the Hebrew Bible.

Readers will notice that biblical references are often given with alternate references in square brackets (e.g., 13:4[3]; 28:69[29:1]; etc.). This signals that the versification in the original Hebrew differs from our English translations. In these cases, the Hebrew verse number is given first, and the corresponding English number is bracketed. Unless otherwise indicated, all English translations offered are my own.

Behind the voice of Moses in the book of Deuteronomy we hear the voice of Yhwh, for Moses repeatedly declares that all his instructions were given as Yhwh his God had charged him. But Yhwh, the God of Moses and Israel, is incarnate in Jesus Christ.[3] When Moses speaks of Yhwh, he speaks of Jesus (cf. Luke 24:44). Deuteronomy was not only Jesus' favorite book in the New Testament (judging by the frequency of quotations); he also stands behind the Torah left for our meditation and nurture by Moses.

Although I do not expect all who read my essays to agree with me on all points of interpretation, I pray that my delight in the grace of God as revealed and recounted in the Torah of Moses will be contagious, and that readers will grasp the life-giving and life-transforming Torah of Yhwh. Knowing that grace will triumph in the end we live with optimism and hope. May the gospel of grace proclaimed by Moses—which is the word of Christ—dwell in us richly, filling our hearts with gratitude to God, leading us in paths of righteousness, and inspiring us to sing to one another with psalms, hymns, and spiritual songs (cf. Col 3:16).

---

2. See Goldingay, *Israel's Gospel*, 15.

3. Cf. Rom 10:13; 1 Cor 1:31; 2:16; 2 Cor 10:17; Phil 2:10–11. For further discussion of this matter, see Block, "Who do Commentators Say 'the Lord' Is?" 173–92.

Acknowledgments

I HAVE BEEN IMMERSED in the study of the book of Deuteronomy for more than thirty years. Over the course of these decades I have been challenged, inspired, frustrated, and corrected by many scholars who have been involved in parallel pilgrimages. Rarely may contemporary communicators be credited with a new discovery. The same is true in biblical studies. Like most scholars, I hold to some idiosyncratic views concerning the meaning of many biblical texts and ideas. While I may sometimes sound passionate about my interpretations, I must emphasize that everything I write is in soft lead pencil, subject to modification, revision, correction, and even rejection, as more data become available, and as we discuss these issues in communities of faith and scholarship. In identifying those mortals who have aided and inspired me along the way pride of place must go to Moses himself, as well as to those who collected, organized, and edited his farewell addresses on the Plains of Moab. In preserving the spirit of Moses, they have proved themselves prophets like Moses, raised up by Yhwh. Throughout my pilgrimage his voice has been ringing in my ears,

But I must acknowledge my deep indebtedness to students and teachers of Deuteronomy who have gone before, and to peers and colleagues in the disciplines of biblical and theological studies, many of whom gather annually as members of professional societies: Evangelical Theological Society, Institute for Biblical Research, Society of Biblical Literature. The input I have received in response to papers I have presented has been most helpful. I also acknowledge the influence of students who have walked with me as I have walked with Moses. In addition to undergraduates and graduate students in this country and in Canada, I have had the inestimable privilege of sharing Moses' message of grace in international educational settings in Moscow, Copenhagen, Athens, Singapore, Hong Kong, Australia, Kenya, and Colombia. Not only have students' interest all over the world inspired me, but in each context, they have offered keen insights to which my North American eyes are blinded.

I am deeply grateful for support of faculty colleagues at Wheaton College and student assistants who have read my work and encouraged me along the way. Some of these are acknowledged in footnotes to the essays included here. Many assistants have performed mundane tasks for me, scouring databases and libraries for secondary materials that might aid in our interpretation, or proofreading drafts for factual errors and stylistic infelicities. Specifically, for this project I must acknowledge the assistance of

Michelle Knight, who edited many of the essays presented here for Wipf & Stock style. Along the way, Carmen Imes, Austin Surls, Daniel Lanz, and Franklin Wang have also offered helpful service in proofreading my work and offering wise counsel as individual essays were being formulated.

Since many of the essays in this volume have been published elsewhere, I must express my deep gratitude to editors of journals and books and publishers of all things printed for their grace and willingness to let us reprint what they had made available earlier. In keeping with our promise, we have acknowledged the original place of publication on a separate page below, as well as at the beginning of each reprinted article. The versions presented here retain the essence of each original publication. Naturally, to produce a coherent volume and to follow the stylistic standards of Wipf & Stock Publishers, we have had to modify these essays stylistically—some more than others. Where needed, I have corrected errors of substance or form in the original. But readers should find no dissonance between the present forms of these essays and the original publications. Special thanks are due to Robin Parry, Christian Amondson, and Brian Palmer, for their patience with me and their enthusiasm for this project and the efficiency with which they have handled all the business and editorial matters, and to Calvin Jaffarian, my typesetter at Wipf & Stock. It is a special delight to work with this publisher and its staff, because their primary goal is to make available to the public the ideas that fuel the passions of authors.

I am grateful to the administrators and my faculty colleagues at Wheaton College, for the unwavering institutional support and encouragement they offer, not only by creating a wonderful teaching environment, but also for providing the resources for our research. Special thanks are extended to Bud Knoedler and his dear late wife Betty, who have given so generously to underwrite my professorial chair for the past decade. It is a distinct divine grace to know them not only as supporters of Wheaton College, but also as personal friends. I am grateful for their prayers over the years. I eagerly also acknowledge Ellen, מַחְמַד עֵינַי,[1] "the delight of my eyes," who has stood by me as a gracious friend and counselor for more than fifty years. Without her love and wisdom, the work represented here would either never have been finished, or it would have taken a very different turn.

I conclude my accolades with a note about the folks to whom this book is dedicated, my friends and fellow pilgrims in the Veritas Adult Fellowship Community at College Church in Wheaton. For seven years, we have walked together through the book of Deuteronomy. Really? Seven years? Admittedly, we do not generally meet in the summer, and during the school year I am often away on other assignments, but yes, it has taken us seven years to mine this treasure. When we stop to think, this seems appropriate, since in the Scriptures the number seven plays such a formative role in measuring time: the 6 + 1 weekly rhythm, the Sabbatical years, climaxing in the Year of Jubilee (the fiftieth year, following the seventh heptad of years). The fact that we are surprised by how long we have spent in Deuteronomy is a symptom of the problem that exists in our churches. As a matter of course, pastors often preach through Paul's epistles line by line and verse by verse, spending years in Galatians and Romans, with which we are much more familiar,

1. See Ezek 24:16.

and which are actually short books in comparison with the Torah of Moses. Why should we not do the same with a book like Deuteronomy, which is equally dense theologically, equally practical ethically, and equally inspiring homiletically?

Over the years, I have taught the book of Deuteronomy many times in educational settings. But these courses have always been constrained by semester schedules, and academic goals, some of which are determined by crediting institutions. There is something delightfully liberating about working without these restrictions, about each week seeing how far we can get and how deep we can go, about taking time to discuss broader theological questions raised by the texts, and especially about wrestling with how Deuteronomy is our [Christian] Scripture.

I have been inspired by the sustained attention the Veritas folks have given to this book. There is no greater joy than to see people's eyes light up from discoveries in places where our expectations are so low. But the theological and hermeneutical ruts are deep. Having been indoctrinated with pervasively misonomistic teaching in the evangelical church, many prefer a truncated canon, consisting primarily of Romans and Galatians. The questions the Veritas folks have asked over the years have been probing, but their demand to grasp the relevance of biblical laws for everyday life has inspired me all along the way. Sometimes the expressions on their faces communicate incredulity, sometimes consternation, and sometimes joy. It has been a rare treat to work with people who love the Lord and who treasure his word so deeply. I am deeply grateful for their patience and their encouragement since we joined this blessed "fellowship of the gospel."

Finally, we must give praise to God. Unlike others who serve gods of wood and stone, that have eyes but don't see, ears but don't hear, and mouths but don't speak, we serve a God who speaks. In ancient times, he spoke through the mouths of his servants the prophets, especially Moses, but he has spoken more recently and even more clearly in the person of Jesus Christ his Son (Heb 1:1–2), the perfect and full embodiment of grace and truth (John 1:16–17). To him be all the praise and glory.

Credits

I hereby gratefully acknowledge permission by editors and publishers to reproduce stylistically modified versions of articles that have appeared elsewhere:

Chapter 2: "'That They May Hear': Biblical Foundations for the Oral Reading of Scripture in Worship," was previously published in *Journal of Spiritual Formation & Soul Care* 5/1 (2015) 5–23, with an Appendix, "A Dramatic Reading of the Book of Ruth," 24–34.

Chapter 5: "Deuteronomic Law" was previously published in *The Oxford Encyclopedia of the Bible and Law,* edited by Brent Strawn; 2 vols. (Oxford: Oxford University Press, 2015), 1:182–95.

Chapter 6: "In the Tradition of Moses: The Conceptual and Stylistic Imprint of Deuteronomy on the Patriarchal Narratives," was originally composed for publication in *Exploring the Composition of the Pentateuch*, edited by L. S. Baker, Jr., Kenneth Bergland, Felipe Masotti, and Rahel Schafer (Winona Lake, IN: Eisenbrauns, forthcoming).

Chapter 7: "'A Place for My Name': Horeb and Zion in the Mosaic Vision of Israelite Worship," was previously published in *The Journal of the Evangelical Theological Society* 58 (2015) 221–47.

Chapter 8: "'What Do These Stones Mean?'" The Riddle of Deuteronomy 27," was previously published in *The Journal of the Evangelical Theological Society* 56 (2013) 17–41.

Chapter 9: "'The Meeting Places of God in the Land': Another Look at the Towns of the Levites," was previously published in *Current Issues in Priestly and Related Literature: The Legacy of Jacob Milgrom and Beyond*, edited by Roy Gane and Ada Taggar-Cohen; Resources for Biblical Study 82 (Atlanta: Society of Biblical Literature, 2015), 93–121.

Chapter 11: "The Patricentric Vision of Family Order in Deuteronomy," was previously published in *Marriage, Family and Relationships: Biblical,*

Doctrinal and Contemporary Perspectives, edited by Thomas A. Noble, Sarah K. Whittle, and Philip S. Johnston (Nottingham, UK: InterVarsity, 2017), 11–29.

Chapter 13: "How Can We Bless YHWH? Wrestling with Divine Violence in Deuteronomy," was previously published in *Wrestling with the Violence of God: Soundings in the Old Testament*, edited by M. Daniel Carroll R., and J. Blair Wilgus; BBRSup 10 (Winona Lake: Eisenbrauns, 2015), 39–50.

Chapter 15: "All Israel Will Be Saved: An Examination of Moses' Eschatological Vision in Deuteronomy," was previously published under the heading, "The Doctrine of the Future in Moses: 'All Israel Shall Be Saved,'" in *Eschatology: Biblical, Historical, and Practical Approaches*, Festschrift in honor of Craig Blaising, edited by D. Jeffrey Bingham and Glenn R. Kreider (Grand Rapids: Kregel, 2016), 107–34.

Chapter 16: "The Spiritual and Ethical Foundations of Messianic Kingship: Deuteronomy 17:14–20," was originally written for publication in *The Moody Handbook of Messianic Prophecy*, edited by Michael Rydelnik and Edwin A. Blum (Chicago: Moody Publishers, forthcoming).

Chapter 18: "Hearing Galatians with Moses: An Examination of Paul as a Second and Seconding Moses," was originally composed for publication in *Sepher Torath Mosheh: Studies in the Composition and Interpretation of Deuteronomy*, edited by Daniel I. Block and Richard L. Schultz (Peabody, MA: Hendrickson, 2017), 338–74.

Abbreviations

AHw	*Akkadisches Handwörterbuch*. Edited by W. von Soden. 3 vols. Wiesbaden: Harrassowitz, 1965–81
ANEP	*The Ancient Near East in Pictures Relating to the Old Testament*. Edited by J. B. Pritchard. Princeton: Princeton University Press, 1969
ANET	*Ancient Near Eastern Texts Relating to the Old Testament*. Edited by James B. Pritchard. 3rd ed. Princeton: Princeton University Press, 1969
BCE	Before the Common Era [or Before the Christian Era]
CAD	*The Assyrian Dictionary of the Oriental Institute of the University of Chicago*. Chicago: Oriental Institute, 1956–2011
CD	Cairo Damascus Document
CE	Common Era [or Christian Era]
CL	Cognitive Linguistics
COS	*The Context of Scripture*. Edited by W. W. Hallo. 3 vols. Leiden: Brill, 1997–2003
CSB	Christian Standard Bible
CT	Hebrew consonantal text
D	Deuteronomy, or Deuteronomist, the designation given by scholars to the supposed source underlying the Pentateuch that exhibits the style and theological perspective of Deuteronomy.
DC	Deuteronomic [Law] Code
DCH	*Dictionary of Classical Hebrew*. Edited by D. J. A. Clines. Sheffield, UK: Sheffield Phoenix, 1993–2016
DH	Deuteronomistic History
DNWSI	*Dictionary of the North-West Semitic Inscriptions*. Jacob Hoftijzer and Karen Jongeling. 2 vols. Leiden: Brill, 1995

E	Elohist, the designation given by scholars to the supposed source underlying the Pentateuch that prefers to refer to God as Elohim
EA	El-Amarna tablets. According to the edition of J. A. Knudtzon. *Die El-Amarna-Tafeln mit Einleitung un Erläuterungen*. Leipzig: J. C. Hinrichs, 1908–15. Reprint, Aalen: Otto Zeller, 1964. Supplemented in A. F. Rainey, *El-Amarna Tablets 359–379*. 2nd ed. AOAT 8. Neukirchen-Vluyn: Neukirchener Verlag, 1978.
ESV	English Standard Version
GKC	*Gesenius' Hebrew Grammar*. Edited by E. Kautsch. Translated by A. E. Cowley. 2nd ed. Oxford: Clarendon, 1910
HALOT	L. Koehler, W. Baumgartner, and J. J. Stamm, *The Hebrew and Aramaic Lexicon of the Old Testament*. Translated and edited under the supervision of M. E. J. Richardson. 4 vols. Leiden: Brill, 1994–99
HCSB	Holman Christian Standard Bible
IBHS	B. K. Waltke and M. O'Connor. *An Introdution to Biblical Hebrew Syntax*. Winona Lake, IN: Eisenbrauns, 1990
J	Yahwist/Jahwist, the designation given by scholars to the supposed source underlying the Pentateuch that prefers to refer to God as YHWH/Yahweh.
JEDP	Scholars' acronym for the hypothetical Yahwist, Elohist, Deuteronomic, and Priestly sources of the Pentateuch.
JSFSC	*Journal for Spiritual Formation & Soul Care*
LSJ	H. G. Liddell, R. Scott, and H. S. Jones. *A Greek-English Lexicon*. 9th ed., with revised supplement. Oxford: Oxford University Press, 1996
LXX	Septuagint, the early Greek translation of the Hebrew Bible.
MT	Hebrew text with Masoretic vocalization
NAS	New American Standard Version
NC	New Covenant
NIDNTT	*New International Dictionary of New Testament Theology*. Edited by Colin Brown. 4 vols. Grand Rapids: Zondervan, 1975–78.
NIV	New International Version
NJPSV	*Tanakh: The Holy Scriptures*. The New Jewish Publication Society Version. Also known as TNK.
NLT	New Living Translation
NRSV	New Revised Standard Version
P	The designation given by scholars to the supposed source underlying the Pentateuch that exhibits special interest in priestly issues.

ABBREVIATIONS

PH	Hebrew text in Phoenician script
PN	Patriarchal narratives
TLOT	*Theological Lexicon of the Old Testament*. Edited by E. Jenni, with assistance from C. Westermann. Translated by M. E. Biddle. 3 vols. Peabody, MA: Hendrickson, 1997.
VL	Hebrew text with vowel letters
WUNT	*Wissenschaftliche Untersuchungen zum Neuen Testament*

1

Deuteronomy

The Heart of Theological Education
in the First Testament

Introduction

THEOLOGIANS, CHURCH HISTORIANS, AND biblical scholars perceive "theological education" differently. The burden of this essay is to consider, define, and describe theological education as it was conceived and perceived in the Hebrew Bible. But this task is daunting, for several reasons.

First, the literature of the Hebrew Bible (our only resource for establishing a First Testament perspective on theological education) spans a wide range of genres (historiography, genealogies, hymnody and poetic lament, prophecy and apocalyptic, and wisdom texts—which many understand by definition to be educational in intention).[1] While "the fear of YHWH" is a common goal of all these writings, the means of achieving that goal varies from genre to genre.

Second, since the composition of the books that make up the Hebrew Bible spanned more than a millennium,[2] the theology that was taught evolved progressively with additional revelation, and the forms of education changed as the nation of Israel evolved from a migratory clan of patriarchs, to a nation on the march out of Egypt and

---

1. Note especially Ansberry, *Be Wise, My Son, and Make My Heart Glad*. Ansberry argues that Proverbs is cast as a curriculum for young men preparing for responsible adulthood in positions of power. The recurring refrain, "The fear of YHWH is the first principle of wisdom" (i.e., "Wisdom 101"; Ps 11:10; Job 28:28; Prov 1:7; 9:10; 15:33; Eccl 12:13) reminds hearers of the fundamental theological underpinnings of wisdom. Although scholars often treat First Testament wisdom literature as essentially secular, this statement assumes that a faith commitment to the God of Israel who has revealed himself through particular saving acts is a prerequisite to seeing reality as it truly is and living accordingly.

2. Taking at face value the inner biblical witness of texts like Deut 31:9–13, the *terminus a quo* (earliest possible date) for the composition of documents that were incorporated into the Pentateuch would date to the early part of the second half of the second millennium BCE (depending on whether one adopts a fifteenth century date for the exodus, as do many American evangelicals, or an early thirteenth century date, as do most British evangelicals). The *terminus ad quem* (latest possible date), would depend on the dates assigned to books like Malachi and Chronicles (ca. mid- to late fifth-century BCE) or when the latest psalms included in the Psalter were composed (third to second century BCE). On the latter, see G. Wilson, *Psalms*, vol. 1, 13.

through the desert, to a loose tribal confederacy in the period of settlement, to a united monarchy with intellectual, spiritual, and political influence emanating from Jerusalem, to a divided kingdom with the education of Judah continuing to be based in Jerusalem, and finally to the Persian period after the exile when the remnant of the nation occupied a small space in and around Jerusalem. Meanwhile in the northern kingdom of Israel religious education was separated geographically from political power, the former emanating from Bethel and Dan and sanctuaries scattered throughout the land and the latter emanating from Samaria in the heart of Ephraim.

Third, over time and space the institutions charged with the theological education of the citizenry changed. In earliest times this will have been largely in the hands of household and clan leaders, but the constitutional documents of the Pentateuch place formal responsibility in the hands of the Levitical priesthood (Deut 33:9–10) and provide for Levitical towns throughout the land. These were intended to function as bases of education for the people, and may have provided the antecedents for the synagogues that sprouted throughout the land in the periods of Persian and Greek domination.[3]

Fourth, the sheer bulk of the Hebrew Bible thrusts us into a veritable library of literary resources and complicates efforts to try to condense First Testament teaching on the subject in one short essay.[4] For these and other reasons, this essay represents only a preliminary and summary foray into a much broader subject.

Considering these four factors, for my exploration of the nature and goals of theological education I will focus on the book of Deuteronomy. This is an appropriate place to begin for several reasons. First, regarding form, genre, and intention, this book is the most didactic in the entire Hebrew Bible. Second, contrary to popular opinion, which views Moses' role in the book as a legislator,[5] both the narrator and Moses himself viewed his role primarily as that of a pastor-teacher.[6] Indeed, the opening line explicitly characterizes the contents of the book not as "statutes and judgments" (חֻקִּים וּמִשְׁפָּטִים),[7]

---

3. On which, see chapter 9, "'The Meeting Places of God in the Land,'" below pp. 192–213.

4. By word count, the Hebrew [and Aramaic] Bible consists of 300,000 to 420,000 words, depending on whether lexemes that involve prefixed particles (e.g., articles or prepositions) are considered separately. For the statistical lexical data, see *TLOT* 3.1444–45.

5. Note the titles of books like, Murdock a.k.a Acharya S, *Did Moses Exist?*; Keneally, *Moses the Lawgiver*; Leibert, *The Lawgiver*; William M. Taylor, *Moses: The Law-Giver*.

6. The only role the book explicitly ascribes to Moses is that of "prophet" (נָבִיא, Deut 18:15; 34:10). The verbs used by the narrator to describe his speech actions include "to say" (אָמַר, 1:5; 31:2; 32:6), "to speak" (דִּבֶּר, 1:1; 4:45; 27:9; 31:1; 32:44, 45); "to summon" (קָרָא, 5:1; 29:1[2]; 31:7; "to teach" (לָמַד, 31:22); "to bless" (בֵּרֵךְ, 33:1); "to set" [the Torah before the people] (שִׂים, 4:44). Only thrice (and not until after the bulk of the second address) does Moses "charge/command" the people (27:1; 31:10, 25). For full discussion, see Block, "Will the Real Moses Please Rise?" 76–82. Moses characterizes his first address as teaching (לָמַד) as well (4:1, 5, 9, 14) and he casts the people as "learners" (4:10). Verbs used for the second address include "to say" (אָמַר, 1:5; 31:2; 32:6), "to speak" (דִּבֶּר, 5:1); "to teach" (לָמַד, 6:1), while the people are "to learn" (לָמַד) from him (5:2–5), though the tone of the second (5:1–11:332) and third addresses (12:1—26:19; 28:1–68) is entirely pastoral and sermonic. For full discussion, see ibid., 82–101.

7. When מִשְׁפָּטִים is used of "judgments," it does not refer to legal precedents established by some court, but to divine judgments concerning the appropriate conduct of the parties to the covenant YHWH made with Israel.

but as "the words that Moses spoke to all Israel" (הַדְּבָרִים אֲשֶׁר דִּבֶּר מֹשֶׁה אֶל־כָּל־יִשְׂרָאֵל). The speeches that follow represent Moses' farewell pastoral addresses to his congregation, before they crossed the Jordan and before he went to his eternal reward. Third, Deuteronomy casts Moses' speeches in this book as "instruction," rather than law (1:5; etc.). The Hebrew word, תּוֹרָה, does not mean "law." This is a didactic, rather than legal, expression, derived from the hiphil form of ירה, meaning "to teach." To be sure, the book contains statutes and ordinances, but they play a subordinate role in the book, always being presented in support of the larger pedagogical and homiletical goals. Fourth, since Moses' addresses in Deuteronomy establish the theological and pedagogical bar for the entire Scriptures, both First and New Testaments,[8] if we grasp the perspectives of this book, we will have grasped the Hebrew Bible's understanding of theological education.

The Goals of Theological Education in the First Testament

The goal of Moses' theological education is declared in Deut 26:19: if Israel will stay true to YHWH and the commission to which he has called them, he will set them high above all the nations "in praise, fame, and honor" (תִּפְאֶרֶת, שֵׁם, תְּהִלָּה) and they will be recognized as "a holy people belonging to YHWH" (עַם קָדֹשׁ לַיהוה). How this happens is clarified in 28:1–14: if Israel will be faithful to YHWH he will bless them abundantly and all the nations will be in awe of them, knowing that they are called by YHWH's name—that is, they belong to him (vv. 9–10). Moses had alluded to this earlier, when, with language reminiscent of later wisdom writers, he had declared:

> [Observe the commands of YHWH diligently], "for that will demonstrate your wisdom and discernment in the sight of other peoples, who on hearing of all these ordinances will say, 'Wow! This great nation certainly is a wise and discerning people.' For what great nation is there that has a god as close at hand as YHWH our God is whenever we call upon Him? Or what great nation has ordinances and judgments as righteous as this entire Torah that I am presenting to you this day? (Deut 4:6–8)

In characterizing the Torah as unequaled in its righteousness (צַדִּיקִם) Moses introduces one of the most significant theological notions in the book, represented by the root צדק. In Deuteronomy "righteousness" speaks of conformity to an ideal and objective standard, in this case established by God in his covenant. We should not be surprised if the climactic song—Israel's national anthem—should ascribe to YHWH himself the attributes of "faithful" (אֱמוּנָה), "righteous" (צַדִּיק), and "true" (יָשָׁר), for his ways are always consistent with his covenant commitments and he never deviates from that course

---

8. This includes retroactively the narratives of Genesis and Exodus, on which see chapter 6, "In the Tradition of Moses, below, pp. 105–25. Unless otherwise indicated, when later books refer to "the Torah of Moses" (תּוֹרַת מֹשֶׁה) or "the book of the Torah" (סֵפֶר הַתּוֹרָה), the expression refers minimally to the speeches of Moses contained in the book of Deuteronomy (e.g., Josh 1:8; 1 Kgs 2:3), and maximally to Deuteronomy as a book (2 Kgs 23:8–20; Neh 8; Ps 1:2; Mal 3:22[4:4]), rather than the Pentateuch as we have it. By New Testament times the designation, הַתּוֹרָה (Greek ὁ νόμος) had come to identify the Pentateuch, as distinct from the Prophets and the Writings. Cf. Luke 24:44.

(32:4).⁹ The divine righteousness provides the background for Moses' ethical watchword for his people in 16:20: "Righteousness, righteousness you shall pursue" (צֶדֶק צֶדֶק תִּרְדֹּף), and this is what is credited to the faithful when they, with gratitude for divine grace, live (6:25; 24:13; 25:15;), worship (33:19), and govern (1:16; 16:18–19; 25:1) according to the revealed will of God. The mark of a theologically educated people (חָכְמָה וּבִינָה, 4:6) is a righteous community living by righteous standards revealed by a righteous God.

The Provisions for Theological Education in the First Testament

How were these goals for theological education to be achieved in ancient Israel? Deuteronomy provides three answers to this question, depending on the target audience. An examination of the contexts in which words like "to teach" (לִמַּד) and "to learn" (לָמַד), "to test" (נִסָּה), "to discipline/train" (יִשֵּׁר), and "to [come to] know" (יָדַע) occur, reveals that the strategies for education change as we move from the exodus generation, to the present generation gathered on the Plains of Moab, and ultimately to future generations.

Moses' Vision of Theological Education for the Past (Exodus) Generation

The picture of the spiritual state of Israel at the time of the exodus is as dire in Deuteronomy as in the narratives of Exodus and Numbers. After 400 years in Egypt, Abraham's descendants seemed to have lost both the memory of and contact with the God of their ancestors. If YHWH rescued them from their slavery and was about to grant them the land of Canaan, these actions had nothing whatsoever to do with merit. This probably explains why YHWH deliberately staged the events associated with the exodus and his revelation at Sinai as he did. Because they had no knowledge of him, he multiplied the signs and wonders to teach them theological lessons they would never forget.[10]

Moses recalled the educational function of these events in several places in Deuteronomy. Structuring his historical recollections in chapter 4 in the reverse order of Israel's actual experience, he ended his first address by highlighting the educational significance of those formative experiences. As an intensely educational enterprise, in 4:32–33 he invited his hearers to engage in the most thorough educational exercise imaginable: to research exhaustively all the historical and literary resources on earth to see if they could find any precedents or counterparts to YHWH's rescue of Israel from Egypt. Assuming a negative answer, redundantly he added the pedagogical goal of these mighty acts:

---

9. The significance of the litotic third of four attributes: "without fault" (אֵין עָוֶל).

10. Although the revelatory function was also intended for Pharaoh (Exod 8:6, 18[10, 22]; 9:14, 29), this significance for the Israelites is also highlighted in Exodus (10:2; 11:7). For full discussion of the revelatory significance of the events associated with the exodus and the implications of this revelation for understanding the divine name (YHWH), see now Surls, *Making Sense of the Divine Name in the Book of Exodus*.

"You were shown *these things* so that you would know (יָדַע) that YHWH is God; there is no other besides him" (4:35).

"Today, you should recognize (יָדַע) and fix in your mind (הֲשֵׁבֹתָ אֶל לְבָבֶךָ) that YHWH is God in heaven above and on earth below; there is no other" (4:39).

In the final statement of this address (v. 40) Moses declared that the Israelites would demonstrate that they had got the point of these magnificent divine acts (the passing grade) if they gratefully and joyfully lived according to the revealed will of their gracious Suzerain and Redeemer (cf. 28:47)—for which YHWH promised abundant blessing.

The Israelite response was not long in coming. In Moses' addresses, he recalled a series of events that proved the Israelites had miserably failed the divine instructional agenda. Contemplating the grounds for YHWH's giving them the land of Canaan, in chapter 9 he declared emphatically that it had nothing to do with Israel's righteousness (צְדָקָה), the goal of the educational enterprise (vv. 3–6). On the contrary, within months of their rescue from Egypt and weeks of having signed on to the covenant, while they were still at Horeb their worship of the golden calf proved that they had failed the course (9:7–21; cf. Exod 32). But this was not an isolated event; without going into detail Moses simply named the locations of other failed examinations: Taberah (cf. Num 11:3), Massah (Exod 17:7), Kibroth-hattaavah (Num 11:34). In each case the intervention of Moses had staved off the threatened and deserved consequences of the people's rebellion.

Overlooking the chronological order of events, in his first address Moses had described in detail the final proof of the exodus generation's performance in the course YHWH was trying to teach them. Poised to enter the promised land, at Kadesh-barnea they failed their final examination (Deut 1:19–46). The people accepted the scouts' report that Canaan was indeed a desirable land, but they shrank back in unbelief. Despite YHWH's promise to fight for them as he had in Egypt (v. 30), his provisions in the desert ("as a man cares for his son"; v. 31), his constant presence with the fire and cloud, and his guidance throughout their travels (v. 33), to unbelieving minds YHWH's grand plan of redemption and land had become a diabolical plot to destroy the Israelites (27–28). In Moses' assessment, they were judged to be stubborn and rebellious against YHWH their God (v. 26): "Despite [all] this evidence [דָּבָר], you refused to trust in YHWH your God" (אֵינְכֶם מַאֲמִינִם בַּיהוה אֱלֹהֵיכֶם, v. 32). They had obviously failed the course. Infuriated by their failure, YHWH, their divine Teacher, sentenced that entire generation (except for Caleb and Joshua) to death in the desert, and promised to fulfill his promises to their children (vv. 34–40), whose interests the exodus generation had ostensibly but faithlessly sought to protect (Num 14:3, 31).

Moses' Vision of Theological Education for the Present (Conquest) Generation

Most of the Israelites standing before Moses on the Plains of Moab were born after the Israelites left Horeb. This meant they had not been witnesses to the signs and wonders associated with the exodus or the awesome theophanic revelation at Horeb.[11] Neverthe-

---

11. Those sentenced to death in the desert for unbelief included all males who were twenty years

less, for rhetorical purposes Moses occasionally spoke as if they had all experienced both the deliverance (4:32, 34, 37; 6:21–23; 7:19; 29:1–2[2–3]) and the awesome revelation (4:9–14, 33, 36; 5:1–5; 6:24; 9:8–21; 18:16), and should therefore have learned the lessons their parents had failed to grasp. But Moses also referred to the instruction YHWH had been giving this generation since they left Horeb. Chapter 8 is particularly significant in this regard. YHWH had brought the people through the barren desert and fed them manna, to humble (עָנָה) and test (נָסָה) them, to prove (יָדַע) what was in their hearts, and to teach (הוֹדִע) them that people do not live by the food they ingest through their mouths, but by whatever YHWH's mouth egests (8:2–4).[12] Moses highlighted the divine educational purposes in v. 5: "Therefore, know in your mind (וְיָדַעְתָּ עִם לְבָבֶךָ) that YHWH your God has been disciplining (יָסַר) you just as a man disciplines (יָסַר) his son." Like the references to "wisdom" (חָכְמָה) and "understanding" (בִּינָה) in 4:6, this is the sort of language we expect in overtly instructional books like Proverbs (Prov 1:2–7).

However, despite Moses' references to YHWH trying to educate the present generation directly, the book of Deuteronomy itself embodies his own pedagogical agenda, which, incidentally, did not begin on the Plains of Moab. The preamble to the book (1:1) suggests that Moses had been engaged in teaching the people all along the way from Mount Horeb. Perhaps analogous to Jesus' Sermon on the Mount (Matt 5–7), this book provides a structured distillation of his teaching (תּוֹרָה, Deut 1:5), "according to all that YHWH commanded him [to speak] to them" (1:3).

As noted at the outset, the book characterizes Moses primarily as a "teacher," and the Hebrew word תּוֹרָה means "instruction," not "law." The semantic range of the word in Deuteronomy corresponds exactly to the range of the Greek words διδασκαλία or διδαχή, both of which mean "teaching, instruction."[13] The appropriateness of this designation for Moses' addresses is reflected in the nature of material found in the book: historical recollections (1:6—3:22), personal anecdotes (3:23–29), impassioned appeals for self-watch (4:1–31), calls for reflection (4:32–40); recitation of a sacred text (5:1—6:3); exposition of the first principle of covenant relationship (6:4—11:32); invitations to the presence of God (12:1–14; 14:22—16:17; 26:1–15), promises of blessing as a reward for fidelity (7:12–16; 11:13–25; 28:1–14) and stern warnings against defection (12:28—13:19[18]; 28:15–69[29:1]; 29:1–28[2–29]); invitations to delight in life itself through dietary provisions (12:15–28; 14:1–21); provision of administrative institutions to ensure the promotion of righteousness (16:18—18:22); instructions regarding a wide range of ethical situations (19:1—25:19); promises of a future when the covenant relationship will be in full force (30:1–20); a national anthem (32:1–43); and a blessing for the tribes (33:1–26).

---

of age or older at the time the covenant was ratified at Horeb (Exod 38:26; Lev 27:3–5) and had been registered as warriors in preparation for the conquest of Canaan (Num 1:3, 18–45; 14:29; 26:2, 4; 32:11). Except for Caleb and Joshua, the oldest in Moses' audience would now have been almost sixty years of age.

12. The Hebrew expression, כָּל מוֹצָא פִי יהוה, translates literally, "all that exits the mouth of YHWH." While most assume these are the commands he gives (cf. 6), the expression is vague and could also mean his verbal pronouncement of life ("Live!" cf. Ezek 16:6; 1 Pet 1:23), or his life-giving breath/Spirit (cf. Gen 2:7; Ezek 36:26–27).

13. Cf. Block, "Will the Real Moses Please Rise," 79–80.

The didactic contents of the book are reinforced by his rhetorical style, which includes (1) hortatory appeals to "listen,"[14] "guard yourselves,"[15] "know [therefore],"[16] "remember,"[17] "lest you/do not forget";[18] be diligent in obedience,[19] adopt the right attitude, especially to love and fear YHWH,[20] be committed to YHWH with one's entire heart/mind (לֵבָב) and being (נֶפֶשׁ, 6:5; 10:12; 11:13, 18), to circumcise one's heart/mind, and to stop stiffening the neck (10:16). Additional rhetorical features include numerous positive and negative motive clauses,[21] and triadic constructions (e.g., 6:4–9), appeals to and quotations of divine speech,[22] recollections of past events,[23] and the imaginative anticipation of future scenarios, complete with hypothetical interlocutors and prescribed responses.[24] Moses' second address reaches an artfully and pedagogically crafted crescendo in 10:12—11:1 (Table 1:1, below, page 8).

This is neither the stuff of law, nor a mere deontological call to obedience to the law. Moses' concern here was not legal, but personal, spiritual, didactic, and pastoral; he appealed for undivided devotion to YHWH demonstrated in acts of piety and fidelity to him and covenant commitment to one's fellow citizens.

This didactic/pastoral tone is maintained in the third address (chapters 12–26),[25] which is often misidentified as "the Deuteronomic Law Code." However, chapters 12–26 also include some new features. Moses' (and YHWH's) pastoral sensitivity toward the people is reflected in his response to their desires, expressed particularly with the phrase, "your personal desire" (אַוַּת נַפְשְׁךָ). With remarkable magnanimity, in 12:15 Moses opened the door to the consumption of meat away from the central sanctuary as wide as he can:

14. שְׁמַע יִשְׂרָאֵל, 4:1; 5:1; 6:4; 9:1.

15. הִשָּׁמֶר/נִשְׁמַרְתֶּם, 2:4; 4:9, 15, 23; 6:12; 11:16; 12:13, 19, 30; 15:9.

16. וְיָדַעְתָּ, 4:39; 7:9; 8:5; 9:3, 6.

17. זָכַרְתָּ/זְכֹר, 5:15; 7:18; 8:2, 18; 9:7; 15:15; 16:3, 12; 24:9, 18, 22; 25:17; 32:7.

18. פֶּן תִּשְׁכַּח/אַל/לֹא תִשְׁכַּח, 4:9, 23; 6:12; 8:11 (cf. v. 14); 9:7; 25:19.

19. וְשָׁמַרְתָּ לַעֲשׂוֹת and variations, 5:1, 32; 6:3, 25; 7:12; 8:1; 11:32; 12:1, 13, 19, 28, 30; 13:1[12:32], 19[18]); 15:5, 9; 16:12; 17:10, 19; 19:9; 23:10, 24 [9, 23]; 24:8; 26:16–18; 28:1, 9, 13, 15, 45, 58.

20. אָהֵב, "love," 6:5; 11:1, 13; יָרֵא, "fear," 6:2, 24; 10:12, 20. In the third address, see 13:4, 11[3, 10]; 14:23; 17:13, 19; 19:20; 21:21; 25:18; 28:58; 31:12–13.

21. Positive: 5:33; 8:1; 11:9; 12:25, 28; 13:18[17]; 14:23, 29; 16:20; 17:19–20; 22:7; 23:21[20]; 24:19; 25:15. Negative: 6:12, 15; 7:22, 25; 8:11–12, 17; 9:28; 11:16; 12:13, 19, 30; 15:9; 19:6; 20:5–7; 22:9; 25:3.

22. Apart from the Decalogue, Moses quotes divine speech in 5:28b–31; 9:12–14; 10:1–2, 11; 17:16.

23. Deut 5:2–33; 6:16; 8:2–4, 14–16; 9:6–10:11; 11:2–6. Although Moses did not claim to function as an intercessor for the assembly on the Plains of Moab, in 9:7–10:11 he recalled in considerable detail an earlier event at Horeb (the golden calf incident), when he had wrestled with YHWH for forty days and nights on the people's behalf. While his intercession then involved deprivation—forty days and nights without food and water (9:9, 18, 25)—unlike the narrative in Exod 32:30–33, Moses did not recount that he had offered to make atonement for the people's sin by having his own name blotted from YHWH's book, if only he would forgive (and take back) his people.

24. Deut 6:20–21; 7:17–18; 8:17–18; 9:4–5; 12:20; 15:9; 17:14; 18:21; 20:3; 26:3, 5–10, 13–15.

25. Judging by 11:26–32, which looks like a formal conclusion (like 30:11–20), and 12:1, which exhibits qualities of a title (like 1:1), the lack of a prose note separating the two parts (like 4:41—5:1a and 28:69—29:1a[29:1–2a]) suggests the person responsible for the present shape of the book has combined what may have been presented as two separate addresses, consisting of chapters 5–11 and 12–26 + 28 respectively.

Table 1.1
The Structure of Deuteronomy 10:12–11:1

The Key Theological Question	So what does YHWH your God ask of you? (10:12a)		
		The Basis of the Requirements	
The Answers	The Requirements	YHWH's Transcendent Status	YHWH's Gracious Presence
The First Answer (10:12b–15)	You shall fear YHWH your God, walk in all his ways, love him, and serve YHWH your God with all your heart and with all your being, and keep the commands and ordinances of YHWH, which I am commanding you today for your good. (10:12b–13)	Look, to YHWH your God belong heaven and the heaven of heavens, the earth with all that is in it. (10:14)	Yet YHWH set his heart in love on your fathers and chose their offspring after them, you above all peoples, as you are this day. (10:15)
The Second Answer (10:16–19)	Circumcise therefore the foreskin of your heart, and be no longer stubborn. (10:16)	For YHWH, your God, is God of gods and Lord of lords, the great, the mighty, and the awesome God. (10:17a)	... who is not partial and takes no bribe. He executes justice for the fatherless and the widow, and loves the sojourner, giving him food and clothing. Love the sojourner, therefore, for you were sojourners in the land of Egypt. (10:17b–19)
The Third Answer (10:20–22)	You shall fear YHWH your God. You shall serve him and hold fast to him, and by his name you shall swear. (10:20)	He is your praise. He is your God, who has done for you these great and terrifying things that your eyes have seen. (10:21)	Your fathers went down to Egypt seventy persons, and now YHWH your God has made you as numerous as the stars of heaven. (10:22)
The Summary Answer to the Question	You shall therefore love YHWH your God and keep his charge, his ordinances, his judgments, and his commands always. (11:1)		

> Go ahead, slaughter and eat meat in any of your towns, as much as you desire, in keeping with the blessing of YHWH your God that he has given you. The unclean and the clean may eat of it, like they eat the meat of the gazelle and the deer.

This tone continues in verses 20–23. In 14:24–26 Moses made it as convenient as possible for people who lived far from the central sanctuary to bring the tithes of their crops, permitting them to bring the equivalent value in silver shekels, and then extended the same magnanimity to Levites in 18:6–8.

Although the expression, "your personal desire" (אַוַּת נַפְשְׁךָ), is missing in 17:14–15, Moses acceded to the people's wish for a king with equal sympathy. This last permission is granted within the context of a series of official appointments (judges, 16:18–19; priests, 18:1–8; prophets, 18:9–22), but none of these texts is cast in the form of a law or as legal guidance for officials to appeal to in prosecuting cases.[26] These are instructions for the people, regarding leadership, that they might understand the appointed leaders' roles, but even more importantly, that they might all assume responsibility for pursuing "righteousness, only righteousness" (צֶדֶק צֶדֶק, 16:20) in the land.[27]

The didactic and pastoral nature of chapters 12–26 is suggested by the literary units that frame this large section. While commentators and translations often refer to 12:2–14 as "the altar law," this text actually never mentions an altar. This label obscures the exciting provisions for worship Moses announced here. If we translate the critical verbs in verses 5–14 modally, rather than as imperatives ("There you may come, and there you may celebrate, and there you may eat in the presence of YHWH"), the passage takes on a different flavor. This is not an imposed legal ordinance, but an invitation to an ongoing relationship with YHWH through feasting and fellowshipping in his presence.[28] The same is true of the "Little Creed" that concludes the third address (26:1–15). These are the farewell instructions of a pastor-teacher about to leave, pleading with his congregation never to forget YHWH's saving and providential grace, and never to forget the economically marginalized in the community.

Moses ended his third address with a passionate appeal to fidelity, describing again Israel's privileged role as YHWH's people and the conditions necessary to enjoy the benefits that come with the role (26:16–19; 28:1–14), and then with severe warnings against infidelity (28:15–68). Like chapters 12–26, chapter 28 is driven by compassionate pastoral concerns, setting before the people two ways: the way of life through joyful obedience to YHWH (vv. 1–14), and the way of death through disobedience and persistent rebellion against YHWH (vv. 15–58). With reference to the curses Brent Sandy rightly observes, "This was language designed to get the hearers' attention, to warn of serious

---

26. On which, see Berman, "The History of Legal Theory and the Study of Biblical Law," 19–39.

27. Most commentators and translations mistakenly render the phrase "justice only justice," but this gives the expression too legal a flavor and obscures the wide-ranging scope of the instructions that follow.

28. See my full discussion in "The Joy of Worship," in *How I Love Your Torah, O LORD!*, 98–117.

consequences, to arouse fear, to imagine what it would be like to be sinners in the hands of an angry God."[29]

From the golden calf incident at Horeb and the Israelites' refusal to enter the promised land from Kadesh-barnea we know that the exodus generation did not do well in YHWH's educational program. How did their children fare, that is, the generation standing before Moses on the Plains of Moab? Moses' interim assessment suggests that they had passed the course. In Deut 4:3–4 he alluded to a recent test of their faith at Baal-Peor. There was no need to specify the nature of the test, since it was still fresh in the peoples' minds—though his comment that those who stood before him had held fast (דָּבַק) to YHWH their God recognizes that it involved the supreme command: "You shall have no other gods besides me" (5:6–7). The narrative of Num 25:1–5 confirms this conclusion. In that instance, there were obviously some who had failed the test and suffered divine judgment for it. In a remarkable rhetorical move, in Deut 5:1–5 Moses dismissed the exodus generation as irrelevant, and transported this generation back in time and space to Horeb, declaring that YHWH had actually made the covenant there with them. He reported that YHWH had commended them for their response to the awesome revelation, though he also hinted that the disposition they had displayed there might not endure (5:28–29). Indeed, Moses' enigmatic statement in 12:8 suggests that even as he spoke, some were going off course.

However, the most serious indication of a problem with this generation comes in chapter 31, where both YHWH (vv. 16–18) and Moses (vv. 27–29) anticipated that as soon as Moses' personal restraining influence was removed, the people will rush into apostasy. Instead of appointing a prophetic leader to replace Moses, YHWH dictated a song that was to be heard from the people's lips in perpetuity, reminding them of YHWH's past favors, warning against the fearful consequences of spiritual recidivism, and promising Israel's ultimate return (32:1–43).[30]

Moses' Vision of Theological Education for Future Generations

That Moses perceived his addresses on the Plains of Moab as having binding authority for future generations is clear from the outset. On the one hand, he declared his Torah to be totally and irrevocably normative (4:2), and on the other, he provided a host of means by which the memory of YHWH's saving actions and his revelation could be remembered and transmitted from generation to generation:

1. Adults were to take advantage of every "teachable moment" to instruct their children in the Torah (6:7; 11:19–20).[31]

---

29. Sandy, *Plowshares & Pruning Hooks*, 89.

30. On which, see Block, "The Power of Song," in *How I Love Your Torah, O LORD!*, 162–88.

31. Deut 4:9–10; 6:7, 20–25; 11:20; 32:46–47. These texts are addressed to heads of households, but this did not mean that only biological or adoptive parents would be involved in the educational enterprise. As envisioned by Deuteronomy, within the community, which was based largely on family and clan relationships, the education of the children would be a "village" responsibility.

2. The heart of Israel's historical and theological traditions were cast in forms easily memorized and recited: (a) YHWH had cast the Decalogue in ten "words," one for each finger on two hands (5:6–21); (b) Moses captured the essence of Israelite faith in the two-sentence Shema (6:4–5); (c) He prescribed responses to children's expressions of curiosity regarding the function of Israel's laws in creedal-like form (6:20–25; (d) He captured the heart of Israelite faith in a catechetical question and five part answer, one for each finger of the hand (fear YHWH, walk in his ways, love him, serve him whole-heartedly, keep his commands [10:12–13]; Fig. 1.1), and then fleshed it out more fully in three doxological scenarios (10:14—11:1):[32]

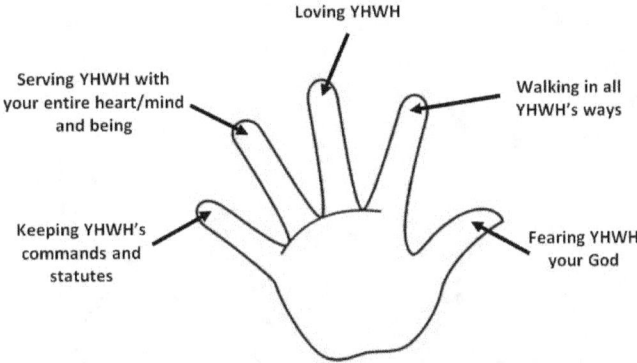

Figure 1.1
The Dimensions of Divine Expectation
Deuteronomy 10:12—11:1

(e) Moses preserved the heart of Israel's history in a "small creed" to be recited whenever the offering of first fruit was presented at the central sanctuary; (f) YHWH reminded the Israelites of his grace in their history, his warning against apostasy, and his promise to restore the nation after judgment in the nation's national anthem (32:1–43).

3. Through participation in the national festivals (Passover, Weeks, Booths) three times a year all Israel was to gather at the central sanctuary to refresh their memories of YHWH's acts of salvation and covenant (16:1–17).

4. Moses placed responsibility for the administration of righteousness in the hands of the people, particularly the elders (16:18–20).

5. He highlighted the appointment of Levitical priests to perform ritual acts associated with the Tabernacle/Temple (10:6–9; 18:5), to serve as custodians of the Torah (31:9–13; cf. 17:18–20), and to teach Torah in Israel (33:8–11). Practical provision for this responsibility is symbolized by the 48 Levitical towns, where the Levitical priests would live and from which they would go out to the villages in their varied pastoral ministries (Fig. 1.2).[33]

---

32. On the form and function of 10:12—11:1, see Block, "In Spirit and in Truth," in *The Gospel according to Moses*, 290–97, idem, *For the Glory of God*, 268–79.

33. On the nature and function of Levitical towns in ancient Israel, see chapter 9, "'The Meeting

Figure 1.2
A Schematic Portrayal of the Location and Function of the Levitical Towns

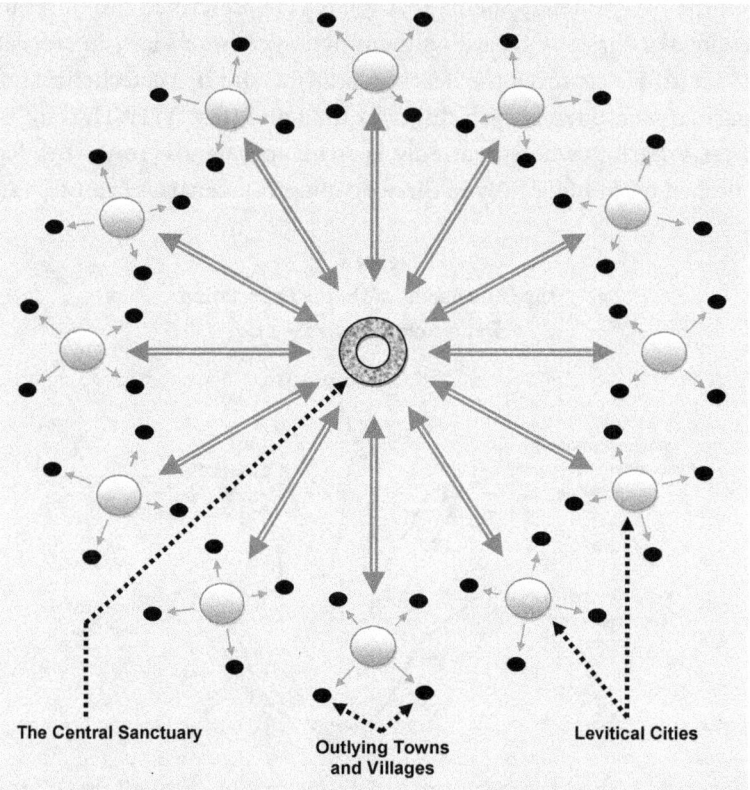

The Central Sanctuary   Outlying Towns and Villages   Levitical Cities

6. He promised that YHWH would raise up prophetic successors who would provide constant witness to the presence and voice of God in Israel's midst (18:15–22).

7. He approved a model of covenant righteousness in the person of the king, whose primary role would not involve leading the people in battle, administering justice, or building a temple for YHWH, but reading and living the Torah in the midst of the people.

8. He provided permanent concrete witnesses to YHWH's gracious acts on Israel's behalf in a variety of forms: (a) the Decalogue on tablets of stone (4:13; 10:1–5); (b) Og's bed in Rabbah (3:11); (c) the pillars at Ebal (27:1–8).

9. He promised that in the future, when YHWH had given rest to the people in the land, he would choose a place to affix his name.[34] Through the voice of Moses YHWH invited his people to come there regularly and often to "see his face" (31:11; cf. 16:16), hear the Torah read (31:11) and thereby learn to fear YHWH (14:23;

Places of God in the Land," below, pp. 177–97.

34. The "chosen place formula" occurs twenty-one times in Deuteronomy: 12:5, 11, 14, 18, 21, 26; 14:23, 24, 25; 15:20; 16:2, 6, 7, 11, 15, 16; 17:8, 10; 18:6; 26:2; 31:11. For variations/echoes of the formula in later writings, see Josh 9:27; 2 Kgs 21:7; 23:27; Jer 7:12; Ezra 6:12; Neh 1:9.

31:9–13), celebrate the three annual pilgrimage festivals,[35] present their offerings and recall YHWH's saving and providential grace (26:1–11), demonstrate their covenant commitment to YHWH horizontally by gifts of charity to the marginalized (26:12; cf. 10:12–22), celebrate communal solidarity with children, servants, the Levites, and aliens (12:12; 14:27–29; 16:11), and even to settle legal disputes before the Levitical priest/judge (17:8–13). This was also the place where the people would observe Levites serving in the name of YHWH, standing before him, and receive their blessing in his name (10:8; 18:6–8).[36]

10. Moses provided a written record of his teaching on the Plains of Moab in the form of "this Document of the Torah" (סֵפֶר הַתּוֹרָה הַזֶּה),[37] or "the Document of this Torah" (סֵפֶר הַתּוֹרָה הַזֹּאת, 28:61). Of all Moses' provisions for the education of future generations, this one was the most significant, for it provided for the people to hear the voice of Moses in perpetuity, long after he had departed the scene. This subject demands further comment.

In Deut 31:9–13 the narrator summarizes the circumstances of the writing of the Torah and its future use in Israel's life and worship:

> [9] Moses wrote down this Torah and handed it to the priests, the sons of Levi, who carried the ark of YHWH's covenant, and to all the elders of Israel. [10] Then Moses charged them, "At the end of every seven years, at the appointed time in the year when debts are cancelled, during the Festival of Booths, [11] when all Israel assembles in the presence of YHWH your God at the place he chooses, you shall read this Torah aloud before all Israel. [12] Assemble the people—men, women, children, and foreigners who live within your gates—so that they may hear and learn to fear YHWH your God and observe all the words of this Torah by doing them. [13] Then their children, who are uneducated/uninformed,[38] will hear and learn to fear YHWH your God as long as you live in the land you are crossing the Jordan to possess.

This paragraph grasps the essence of the theological educational process envisioned by Moses and highlights the critical role the Torah was to play. Based on this and other

---

35. Passover (16:1–8), Festival of Weeks (Pentecost, 16:9–12), Festival of Booths (16:13–17; 31:9–13).

36. On the place of the place in Deuteronomy's vision of worship, see chapter 7, "A Place for My Name": Horeb and Zion in the Mosaic Vision of Israelite Worship," below, pp. 126–51.

37. Deut 29:20, 26[21, 27]; 30:10; 31:26. Traditionally the expression has been translated as "this book of the Law," which is wrong on two counts. First, סֵפֶר cannot mean "book," since books as we know them were not invented until a thousand years later. The word means written text, which would probably have been inscribed on specially treated sheepskin scrolls. Second, as we have already notes, the Hebrew word תּוֹרָה, "instruction," does not come from the court or the legislature, but from the world of education.

38. Hebrew אֲשֶׁר לֹא יָדְעוּ, "who do not know," is cryptic, lacking a direct object. Most translations supply something like "it" (ESV, NRSV) or "the/this law" (HCSB, NIV). NJPSV reads, "who have not had the experience."

texts, we may summarize the educational process as follows: *Read that they may hear, that they may learn, that they may fear, that they may obey, that they may live.*" (Fig. 1.3):

Figure 1.3
The Deuteronomic Formula for Life

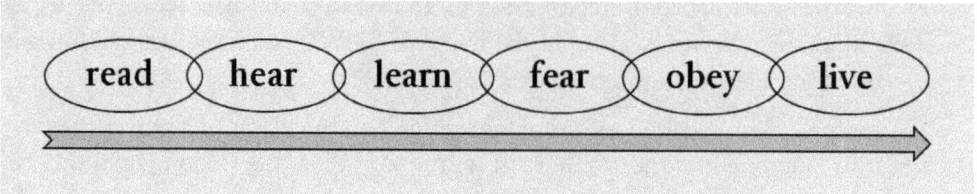

We have encountered this formula earlier in Deuteronomy (See Table 1.2). Although no single text contains all the elements, remarkably the most complete version occurs in 17:19–29, which presents the king as a model of covenant righteousness. This "charter for kingship" prohibits the king from using his office for personal advantage, and calls on him to read the Torah *for himself*. Through this exercise he will learn to fear YHWH, remain humble, stay on course in his obedience to YHWH, and ultimately enjoy a long tenure on the throne. For ordinary citizens the equivalent reward for obedience would simply be a long full life.

Table 1.2
The Importance of Hearing the Torah

Reference	Reading	Hearing	Learning	Fearing	Obeying	Living well
1. 4:10		✓	✓	✓		
2. 5:23–29		✓		✓	✓	✓
3. 6:1–3			✓	✓	✓	✓
4. 17:13		✓		✓	✓	
5. 17:19–20	✓	[✓]	✓	✓	✓	✓(?)
6. 19:20		✓		✓	✓	
7. 31:11–13	✓	✓	✓	✓	✓	[✓]

But how does hearing the Torah promote "fear" that yields obedient living and is rewarded with life? The answer is found in part in recognizing the breadth of meaning of the Hebrew word יָרֵא. It frequently means "to be afraid," but in Deuteronomy it is also used of "trusting awe" or "awed trust," in place of אֱמוּנָה, "to trust in" someone.³⁹ The word often occurs as a prelude to obedience and righteous living,⁴⁰ but its significance for theological education is evident particularly in the sequence of verbs listed above and illustrated in Table 1.2. For our purposes the fifth and seventh texts, which involve encounters with YHWH through hearing the written Torah read, are especially significant.⁴¹ Whereas Israel's encounter with YHWH at Horeb had terrified the people (4:9–14, 36; 5:5, 23–33; 18:16), Deuteronomy portrays worship at the place where YHWH would establish his name as confident, intimate, and celebrative.⁴²

If "the Torah" (i.e., Moses' addresses in Deuteronomy) is viewed primarily as "law," as many assume, hearing "the law" could evoke fear of negative consequences, analogous to the effect of hearing verdicts in criminal cases (13:12[11]; 17:13; 19:20; 21:21). However, if we understand הַתּוֹרָה as "instruction," whose goal was the promotion of יָרֵא in the sense of "faith, trust" (Paul's *pistis*), then its significance for this discussion is readily apparent.

But how does hearing the Torah promote faith in YHWH? This essay cannot offer a full discussion of the issue, but we may begin by observing Deuteronomy's characterization of YHWH.

First, Deuteronomy portrays YHWH in gloriously transcendent terms, pointing to a trustworthy deity. By itself this image could evoke fright/awe, but in context it is intended to promote confidence and trust (cf. Isa 40:12–31). The concluding "Song of YHWH" opens by ascribing greatness (גֹּדֶל) to him (Deut 32:3), a theme that had been declared in earlier doxological descriptions.

7:21 YHWH your God is in your midst, a great and awesome God.

10:1 YHWH your God is God of gods and Lord of lords, the great, the mighty, and the awesome God.

28:5 That you may fear this glorious and awesome name, YHWH your God.

YHWH's transcendent power and glory were demonstrated particularly through the "signs and wonders" performed against the Egyptians (4:34; 10:21; 26:8) and for Israel's benefit.⁴³

---

39. The biblical roots of Deuteronomy's use of יָרֵא to mean "trusting awe," may be traced back to Abraham's proof of his faith in the sacrifice of Isaac (Gen 22:12; cf. v. 1). For full discussion, see chapter 14, "The Fear of YHWH: The Theological Tie that Binds Deuteronomy and Proverbs," below, pp. 283–311; and chapter 18, "Hearing Galatians with Moses: An Examination of Paul as a Second and Seconding Moses," below, pp. 374–404.

40. Deut 5:29; 6:2; 8:6; 10:12–13; 13:5[4]; 17:19; 28:58; 31:12.

41. In the first three the sound of YHWH's voice accompanied by awesome theophanic visual phenomena at Horeb evoked severe fright in the people. The fourth and sixth cases involve warnings against disregarding the divinely rendered decisions in criminal cases (17:13) or repeating the crime (19:20).

42. Signaled by the verb שָׂמַח, in 12:7, 12, 18; 14:26; 16:11, 14–15; 26:11 (cf. Lev 23:40). On the contrast between Israel's one-time encounter with YHWH at Horeb and Israel's regular meetings with him at the central sanctuary, see chapter 7, 'A Place for My Name': Horeb and Zion in the Mosaic Vision of Israelite Worship," below, pp. 126–51.

43. Deut 11:2–7 includes YHWH's care for the Israelites in the desert and his punishment of

Second, the Torah portrays YHWH in graciously personal terms. Although explicit verbal characterizations of YHWH as gracious in Deuteronomy are rare,[44] Israel's confidence in future restoration after judgment was based on his compassionate character (4:31), and his change of heart toward his wayward people (32:36). But Moses laced his recollections of past events with stories of divine grace: YHWH loved the ancestors and elected their descendants for his favor out of all the peoples on earth (4:37; cf. 7:6–7; 10:15; 14:2); he rescued his people from Egypt (4:32–40; cf. 5:6 et passim); he invited Israel to assembly in his presence at Horeb and established his covenant with them there (4:9–31; cf. 5:2–3); he revealed his will to Israel (4:1–8; cf. 5:1–22; 6:20–25; 30:11–20); he spared Israel and renewed the covenant at Horeb (9:19, 25—10:5); he cared for Israel in the desert (1:31; 8:1–5); he gave them a fruitful homeland (1:7–8; 6:10–11, 23; 8:7–10; 11:9–12; 26:9, 15; 27:3; 32:13–14); he provided leadership in the forms of king (17:14–20), prophets (like Moses; 18:9–20), and Levitical priests (10:8–9; 18:1–8; 21:5; 33:8–11); he confirmed the covenant with the present generation in Moab (26:16–19; 27:9; 28:69[29:1]; 29:11[12]; etc.); he invited Israel to worship and celebrate in his presence (12:1–14; 14:1–21, 26; 16:11–14; 26:1–11); and he desired Israel's well-being (11:18–25; 12:7, 18; 15:10; 23:21[20]; 28:1–14; 30:11–20). Even threats of punishment represent overtures of grace, reminding the people how passionately YHWH treasured his relationship with them and warning in advance of the consequences of apostasy. Hearing the Torah would remind the people of all these graces, hopefully evoking in them not only fear in the sense of fright and awe, but especially the sense of confidence in the one who had chosen them to be his treasured people.

Third, the Torah portrays YHWH as faithful to his word. The exordium to the "Song of YHWH" (chapter 32) begins by proclaiming YHWH's greatness (32:3), but the next strophe (v. 4) focuses on his faithfulness:

> The Rock, his work is perfect;
> See, all his ways are justice.
> A God of faithfulness and without fault,
> Righteous and upright is he.

Earlier in 7:9 Moses had celebrated this faithfulness doxologically:[45] "YHWH your God is God, the faithful God who maintains covenant loyalty with those who love him and keep his command, to a thousand generations." While this summary declaration is covenantal from beginning to end, the Torah of Deuteronomy proclaims the faithfulness of YHWH with repeated reminders of how he has kept the promises associated with his covenant made with the ancestors, established with their descendants at Horeb,[46] and renewed with this generation:[47] (a) YHWH has multiplied the

---

Dathan and Abiram among "all the great acts of YHWH that he executed" (כָּל מַעֲשֵׂה יהוה הַגָּדֹל אֲשֶׁר עָשָׂה). Cf. Exod 15:11.

44. The root חֵן occurs only in 24:1, which notes its absence in a man who has a needy wife.
45. Cf. Exod 34:6; Ps 86:15.
46. Cf. Gen 17:6–8; Exod 6:2–8; 19:4–6; Deut 4:9–31.
47. On "the covenant with the fathers," see Hwang, *The Rhetoric of Remembrance*, 178–232.

population like the stars of the sky;[48] (b) as predicted in Gen 15:13, after centuries in a foreign land, ending in slavery, YHWH rescued them from their oppressors;[49] (c) now, after the failure of the exodus generation (Deut 1:35; 4:25), YHWH is about to deliver the promised land of Canaan into their hands.[50] But YHWH's fidelity to his word is also reflected in his oath, with which he guarantees the fulfillment of the imprecations built into the covenant for his people's infidelity (11:13–28; 28:1–69[29:1]). Moreover, building on Lev 26:40–45, Moses declared that however horrendous the punishment for rebellion might be (4:26–28; 28:15–68; 29:19–27[20–28]), the judgment would not be the last word. With compassionate heart and true to his commitments YHWH would bring his people back from exile and reestablish them in the land promised to the ancestors (4:30–31; 30:1–10; 32:43). The Israelites may soon forget their commitments by going after other gods (4:23; 6:12; 8:11, 14, 19; 31:16–18, 26–29), but YHWH would never forget his covenant (4:31). YHWH hereby guaranteed his people's future with his promise (32:36–43) and his oath.[51]

Why is hearing the Torah in community so important? In addition to stimulating reverent and trusting awe (יָרֵא), hearing the reminders of YHWH's compassion toward his people in the past and his declarations of his faithfulness to his words, his covenant, and his people in the future should evoke in hearers the faith that Abraham exhibited in Gen 15:6 and 22:1–12. Since this confidence in YHWH represents part of the fuller meaning of יָרֵא, "to fear, demonstrate trusting awe," in Deuteronomy, hearing the Torah would be critical for maintaining Israel's faith. At the festival of Sukkoth the priests were to "read" the Torah that the people might "hear," that they might "learn" to "fear" (i.e., trust) YHWH, that they might "obey," that they might "live" (Deut 31:9–13).[52] We now understand why the five markers of Israel's identity in Deut 10:12–13 begin with "fear/trusting awe," and then move successively through walking in the ways of YHWH, demonstrating love for him, whole-hearted and full-bodied service, and finally to obedience to the commands. Borrowing from Deuteronomy, the wisdom writers had it right: The fear of [trusting awe in] YHWH is the first principle of wisdom; and knowledge of the Holy One is understanding (Prov 9:10).[53]

And now we also understand the conclusion to the book of Malachi, and indeed to the First Testament.[54] In a series of oracles from the Persian period responding to the absence of fear/trust in YHWH in the restored community in Jerusalem, Malachi

---

48. Deut 1:10; 10:22; 26:5; cf. Gen 15:5; 22:17; 26:4.

49. Deut 4:37; 5:6; 6:12, 21–23; 7:8; 8:14; 13:6, 11[5, 10]; 26:6–8.

50. References to the covenant oath involving the land occur a dozen times in the book: 1:8, 35; 4:21; etc.

51. Cf. the references to "a covenant . . . with an oath" in 29:11, 13, 20[12, 14, 21].

52. This sequence reinforces Nahum Sarna's contention (*Exodus*, 75) that "faith" in the Hebrew Bible "refers to trust and loyalty that find expression in obedience and commitment."

53. For further discussion, see chapter 14, "The Fear of YHWH: The Theological Tie that Binds Deuteronomy and Proverbs," below, pp. 283–311. On "fear" and its relation to wisdom, see also Moberly, *Theology of the Old Testament*, 265–77.

54. As arranged in LXX and all Christian translations. The Hebrew Bible concludes with 2 Chronicles.

prescribed a remarkable solution: "Remember the Torah of Moses my servant whom I charged at Horeb [to teach] ordinances and judgments for all Israel" (Mal 3:22[4:4]).[55] Let the reeducation program begin.

Conclusion

At the outset of this essay I suggested that Deuteronomy establishes the paradigm of theological education for the entire First Testament. This is true with respect to both its content and its pedagogical strategy. The importance of these two elements is reflected in Judg 2:7–12:

> The people [of Israel] worshiped YHWH throughout Joshua's lifetime and during the lifetimes of the elders who outlived Joshua. They had seen all YHWH's great works that he had done for Israel. Joshua ben Nun, the servant of YHWH, died at the age of 110. They buried him in the territory of his grant of land, in Timnath-heres, in the hill country of Ephraim, north of Mount Gaash. That whole generation was also gathered to their ancestors. After them another generation rose up who did not know YHWH or the works that he had done for Israel. The Israelites committed *the* evil in YHWH's eyes; they worshiped the Baals and abandoned YHWH, the God of their fathers, who had brought them out of Egypt.

Obviously all the agents and institutions responsible for spiritual nurture of the people provided by the Torah of Moses had failed: parents stopped teaching Torah to their children; the Levitical priests failed in their pastoral duties; if the national festivals were remembered at all, they must have become perfunctory observances; the national anthem was forgotten; the memorial objects and places were neglected. It is no wonder that YHWH's ire was raised.

The Torah of Moses represents the heart of Hebrew Bible; this was the treasure that priests were to teach, and model,[56] that psalmists praised,[57] to which the prophets appealed,[58] by which faithful kings ruled,[59] and righteous citizens lived (Ps 1). In short, the book of Deuteronomy provides the theological base for virtually the entire First (and New) Testament and the paradigm for much of its literary style. May we in our day discover anew in the book of Deuteronomy the divinely breathed, hence living and transforming Scripture of which the apostle Paul, the New Testament Moses, spoke in 2 Tim 3:16. And like Paul, may we find in the "Book of the Torah of Moses" a sure and effective instrument of teaching, reproof, correction, training in righteousness, and equipping for every good work to the glory of God.

---

55. Malachi echoes Deut 4:1 and 4:14). Cf. also 6:1.
56. Deut 33:10; 2 Chr 15:3; 19:8; Mal 2:6, 9; cf. Jer 18:18; Ezek 7:26; Ezra 7:10.
57. Ps 19:7–14[6–13]; 119; etc.
58. Isa 1:10; 5:24; 8:20; 30:9; 51:7.
59. 1 Kgs 2:2–4; 2 Kgs 14:6; 22:11; 23:25.

2

"That they may hear"

Biblical Foundations for the Oral
Reading of Scripture in Worship[1]

Introduction

IF TRUE WORSHIP INVOLVES reverential human acts of submission and homage before the divine Sovereign, in response to his gracious revelation of himself and in accord his will, how does God reveal himself to worshipers?[2] While we do not exclude the possibility that God can and does reveal himself to individuals or groups of people in other ways (providential experiences, dreams, visions, oracular inspiration), as a norm knowledge of God himself and of his will is gained through the written record of past revelation. And this includes the revelation of Jesus Christ. Through the incarnation in Christ God has revealed himself in all his glory and grace (John 1:14–18; 14:9). Nevertheless, the only normative access even to that revelation is found in the Scriptures. In Scripture, produced by inspired human authors, we hear the authoritative voice of God revealing the mind of God. If worship is indeed an engaged response to God's revelation, then ensuring that formal worship actually introduces worshipers to God and gives them a revelation of him is the highest priority.

The chancels of many older, traditional Reformed and Lutheran church buildings reflect the importance of the word in worship by including two pulpits: a larger pulpit—often raised above the people—from which the word was read and proclaimed, and a smaller pulpit from which other aspects of the service were performed.[3] By contrast, many evangelical churches today diminish the role of the Scriptures in worship by: (a) drastically reducing or eliminating the reading of Scripture; (b) replacing sustained expo-

---

1. This is a stylistically modified version of an article previously published in *Journal of Spiritual Formation & Soul Care* 5/1 (2015): 5–23, with an Appendix, "A Dramatic Reading of the Book of Ruth), pp. 24–34. I am grateful to the editors of the journal for their kind permission to republish it here.

2. For full development of this thesis on worship, see Block, *For the Glory of God: Recovering a Biblical Theology of Worship for the Church*.

3. For a dramatic description of an event involving the former in Puritan New England, see Herman Melville's, *Moby Dick*, 33–35.

sition of the Scriptures with short topical homilies; (c) replacing pulpits that highlighted preachers' roles as spokespersons for God with nondescript and transparent stands to make the preacher more visible to the congregation; (d) substituting hymns steeped in the language and theology of Scripture with jaunty jingles that on the surface appear scriptural but are little more than slogans and sound bites, empty of biblical meaning to many who sing them.

The purpose of this essay is to explore the biblical basis for the public reading of Scripture. However, before we address that topic, we must consider private Bible reading as a means of grace and personal spiritual nurture. Fortunately, this is where much of the reading of Scripture today begins, but unfortunately this is also where much of it ends.

Reading Scripture in Personal and Private Worship

Because the Psalms express how humans feel toward God and they speak to every emotion, most Christians find their inspiration for personal reading of the Scriptures in the Psalms, and rightfully so. Psalm 1 opens the Psalter by encouraging readers to find their delight in the Torah of YHWH and to meditate on it constantly,[4] and promising life and well-being for those who do so, in contrast to the judgment that awaits the wicked. The celebration of Torah reading climaxes in the Torah Psalms 19:7–14[6–13] and 119, both of which may be interpreted as "meditations" (הֶגְיוֹן) as called for by Psalm 1:2. These Torah Psalms speak of individual and private reading of the Torah, as opposed to liturgical events involving the assembled community of faith.[5] Obviously this does not exclude their use in corporate worship, for what is true for the individual is also true for the group, and private meditation on the Torah prepares one for hearing it in worship.

On the surface, Psalm 1 seems to be addressed to everyone. However, strictly interpreted, the "blessed man" who "walks in the counsel," "stands in the path," and "sits in the seat" (Ps 1:1) is not "everyman," but a high official, perhaps a prince who aspires to the throne—which accords with the royal nature of Psalm 2. Indeed, some argue that the entire Psalter is a Davidic/royal document,[6] in which case Psalm 1 orients a royal reader on how to read the Torah. Although Psalm 1 echoes Josh 1:7–8, its inspiration derives from Deut 17:14–20, where Moses emphasizes that far from being preoccupied with normal royal concerns (military leadership, administration of justice, and temple construction), Israel's king was to concern himself with the Torah. By this interpretation, Psalm 1 instructs a king or prince how to read the Torah for himself to nourish his soul, offer guidance for life, and secure success for his reign. However, since the king was to model covenant righteousness for all God's people, ultimately it offers any reader insight into how to read the Torah.[7]

---

4. "Day and night" functions as a literary merism, meaning "all the time."

5. So also 37:31; 40:9[8]; 89:31[30]; 94:12. A similar individualistic emphasis is evident in references to the "Torah" in Proverbs (28:4, 7, 9; 29:18) and the allusion to the Torah in the charge to the reader to "fear God and keep his commands" in the postscript to Ecclesiastes (12:13–14).

6. Waltke, with Yu, *An Old Testament Theology*, 873–74; cf. Grant, *The King as Exemplar*.

7. However, we must caution against an anachronistic interpretation of these texts. In biblical times literacy of the masses cannot be assumed, and few had ready access to copies of the Scriptures

As the prologue to the Psalter, which is a collection of prayers, laments, and hymns to be used in worship, Psalm 1 suggests that for the king at least true and authentic worship is nurtured by and results from daily and constant delight in hearing the voice of God in the Torah. While the communal Psalm 95 notes that those who worship in spirit and truth do not resist the word of God when he speaks (vv. 7c–11), Psalm 1 speaks of delighting in and meditating on the Torah of YHWH day and night, which means constantly practising the presence of God. In the Torah, they hear his voice, instructing, inspiring, challenging, and directing them.

Some interpret "the Torah of YHWH" as "the Law," that is, the Pentateuch, as opposed to "The Psalms" and "the Prophets" (Luke 24:44), However, it is doubtful the word *tôrâ* (תּוֹרָה) functioned this way when the psalm was written. Many interpret the word narrowly as "law" (Greek ὁ νόμος). However, apart from the gospel narratives of the Pentateuch in which the law is embedded, the law becomes a burden to be borne, rather than a cause for delight. Some interpret "the Torah of YHWH," broadly as Scripture,[8] all the inspired writings of the First Testament, perhaps even the New Testament. While the word is often used of "instruction" generally, many texts announce judgment and call for lamentation and confession, rather than celebration. Furthermore, "the Torah of YHWH" (תּוֹרַת יהוה) never carries the generic sense of "instruction"; it always refers to teaching received from God,[9] which Psalms 19 and 119 associate with specific expressions, like "commands" (מִצְוֹת), "ordinances" (חֻקִּים), "judgments" (מִשְׁפָּטִים), "[covenant] stipulations" (עֵדוֹת), "precepts" (פִּקּוּדִים), and "word" (אִמְרָה) preserved in the Pentateuch. Viewing "the Torah of YHWH" as a reference to the Psalter itself, some understand Ps 1:2 to exhort readers to meditate on the Psalter as Scripture, and to find there divine guidance and inspiration in the life of faith.[10] This is how many Christians treat the Psalms.[11] Neglecting—or worse rejecting—the rest of the First Testament, especially the constitutional materials of the Pentateuch, they find great inspiration in the Psalms and elevate this book above the rest of the First Testament. However, not only do the Scriptures not support this approach, but it also flies in the face of Jewish tradition, which ascribes the Torah (Pentateuch) unrivaled authority within the Bible.

In the end, it seems best to see in "the Torah of YHWH" (Ps 1:2) a reference to the book of Deuteronomy. Not only is the vocabulary of Psalm 1 thoroughly Deuteronomic,[12] but also few of the psalms are cast as instruction. The direction of speech tends to be upward to God, rather than downward from God. Just as Josh 1:7–8 opens the second part of the Hebrew Bible (*Nebi'im,* Prophets) with an exhortation to meditate on the Torah

---

before the invention of the printing press.

8. Wilson, *Psalms 1,* 96.

9. Exod 13:9; 2 Kgs 10:31; 1 Chr 16:40; 22:12; 2 Chr 12:1; 17:9; 31:3–4; 34:14; 35:26; Ezra 7:10; Neh 9:3; Isa 5:24; Jer 8:8; Amos 2:4.

10. Childs, *Introduction to the First Testament as Scripture,* 513–14.

11. Symbolized by the inclusion of the Psalms at the back of Gideon New Testaments.

12. For אַשְׁרֵי, "blessed," see Deut 33:29; for the notion of choosing between the ways of blessing and retribution, see Deut 11:26–28 and 30:15–20; the word תּוֹרָה as authoritative teaching agrees perfectly with Moses' role as pastor-teacher in Deuteronomy. See further, Block, "Will the Real Moses Please Rise," 68–103.

(i.e., Moses' speeches in Deuteronomy), so Psalm 1 opens the third part with a similar challenge. The last verses of Malachi reinforce this canonical stitching with its own prophetic exhortation to Torah piety. This does not mean the psalmists were not inspired or that the Psalms are not Scripture in the full sense of the word.[13] It means rather that we should read the psalms that follow as prayers and hymns that teach believers how to respond to the Torah, learning the righteousness called for by God in his covenant with his people and applying it to every conceivable circumstance of life. In the end, whether "the Torah of YHWH" refers narrowly to the speeches of Moses in Deuteronomy (which seems most likely) or more broadly to the five books of the Pentateuch, the Torah involves much more than law; its laws are all embedded in narratives of divine grace. The Decalogue itself begins with Gospel: "I am YHWH your God who brought you out of the land of Egypt, out of the house of slavery." This is the Gospel on which the Israelites were to meditate day and night.

The disposition of the psalmists toward the Torah is remarkable. Whereas not a single person in the First Testament ever says he or she loves (אָ֫הַב) God,[14] seven times in Psalm 119 the psalmist declares with unembarrassed enthusiasm that he loves (אָהַב) the Torah and the commands of YHWH (vv. 97, 113, 119, 127, 159, 163, 165). If the Torah Psalms remind worshipers that hearing the Torah should be their highest delight, they also suggest to Christians that if they will not treasure the Torah as authoritative Scripture, they have no right to seek inspiration from the Psalms. Judging by the explicit quotations and allusions in the Gospels and in the Epistles, Deuteronomy was the favorite book of the First Testament for Jesus and Paul, and so it should be for us. Herein lies the heart of biblical revelation.

Reading and Hearing Scripture in Public Worship in the First Testament

When I teach biblical courses, in preparation for class I regularly require students to read the texts we are studying aloud in preparation for class. I do this for four reasons: (1) pedagogically, the more senses we engage in our learning exercises the better the learning; (2) the Hebrew word for "read," קָרָא, means literally "to cry out, call" audibly so someone will hear;[15] (3) because so much of Scripture is presented as speech it is helpful to hear these utterances as actual voices; (4) in the ancient world all sacred texts were written to be read orally and heard by an audience. If this was true of other texts, it is especially true of our Scriptures. Because they are inspired by the Holy Spirit of God (2 Tim 3:16–17; 2 Pet 1:20-21), in hearing the Scriptures read we hear the voice of God himself.

So far, our discussion has involved reading Scripture for personal nurture and study. But what do the Scriptures say about their public reading in corporate worship?

---

13. The New Testament writers clearly recognized the psalmists as inspired: Acts 1:16; 2:25, 34; 4:25; Rom 11:9; Heb 4:7.

14. In the Hebrew Ps 18:2[1] and 116:1 do not contradict this statement.

15. The word for "meditate" in Ps 1:2 actually refers to making audible sounds: the cooing of doves (Isa 38:14; 59:11; Nah 2:8); human declarations (Isa 59:3, 13; Ps 35:28; 37:30; 71:24; 115:7; Job 27:4; Prov 8:7; 15:28).

I begin answering the question by observing how the Scriptures were actually used in worship in the First Testament.

The covenant ratification procedures at Mount Sinai recounted in Exodus 19–24 involved one extended service of worship.[16] When the service began the Israelites did not yet have a Scripture to read—the worship began with YHWH speaking directly and orally to the people (Exod 20:1–17)—but by the time it was over they possessed at least two "scriptural" documents, the "words of YHWH" and "the Book of the Covenant" (Exod 24:3–4, 7–8).[17] These Moses transcribed and read before all the people as part of the covenant ritual, after which they declared in unison for the third time, "All that YHWH has spoken we will do, and we will listen!" (Exod 24:7; cf. 19:8; 24:3). Later YHWH would provide his own copy of this "scripture," the Decalogue ("Ten Words") inscribed in tablets of stone with his own finger (Exod 24:12; 31:18; 34:28). When Moses led the new generation of Israelites in renewing the covenant on the Plains of Moab, he began his second address by reciting the Decalogue in its entirety (Deut 5:6–22), before offering his sermonic exposition (chapters 6–26). Although Jewish tradition suggests the Decalogue was regularly read at Shabuoth (Festival of Weeks) three months after the Passover celebration of the Exodus (Exod 18:1),[18] none of the constitutional documents from Sinai[19] calls for their regular and repeated oral reading in worship.

However, matters change when we get to the Torah of Moses, that is, the book of Deuteronomy. In Deut 27:1–8 Moses prescribes a curious ritual involving the Torah to be performed as soon as the Israelites have crossed the Jordan. Reminiscent of the covenant rituals at Sinai, between Mounts Gerizim and Ebal they are to build an altar of uncut stones for whole burnt offerings and fellowship offerings. Then they are to erect pillars, smear them with plaster, and instead of reading the Torah to the people, as a covenantal act apparently incorporating the land as a vital partner in the covenant involving YHWH, the people, and the land, the Levitical priests were to write all the words of this Torah on the plastered stones.[20] Moses' prescriptions leave no hint of an oral performance; apparently, the actions involved in this one-time event (that is, vv. 1–8) were to be performed silently.

In this respect, the ritual at Ebal and Gerizim presents a sharp contrast to the regular oral reading of the Torah that Moses prescribes in 31:11–13. Having transcribed his addresses, Moses handed the Torah documents (presumably the three addresses written on separate scrolls) to the elders and Levitical priests. Deuteronomy 17:18 and 33:9b–10a suggest that in addition to their other roles, the Levites served YHWH and Israel as the authorized custodians of Torah. Unlike the king, who was to read the Torah for himself

---

16. Note the repeated references to "serving" (עָבַד) YHWH in anticipation of this event: Exod 3:12; 4:23; 7:16, 26[8:1]; 8:16[20]; 9:1, 13; 10:3, 7, 8, 11, 24, 26, 12:31.

17. The former expression, דִּבְרֵי יהוה, probably refers to the Decalogue (Exod 20:2–17), while the latter apparently refers to the "judgments" (מִשְׁפָּטִים) listed in 21:1—23:19.

18. See Weinfeld, "The Decalogue," 12–15.

19. The Decalogue (Exod 20:2–17), the Book of the Covenant (Exod 21:1—23:19), the manual on worship (Lev 1–16), the Instructions on Holiness (Lev 17–26).

20. On the nature and significance of this ritual, see further, Block, *Deuteronomy*, 624–29; also chapter 8, "What do These Stones Mean?" below, pp. 153–76.

(Deut 17:18–19), the Levitical priests were charged with reading it to all the people every year at the Festival of Booths (Sukkoth; 31:10). The importance of this ritual is reflected in the chain of actions and responses the reading of the Torah would trigger:[21]

Reading   Hearing   Learning   Fearing   Obeying   Living

In the long run, Israel's very life depended on hearing the Torah, for how could they live, if they did not obey YHWH? How could they obey, if they did not fear him? How could they fear him if they did not learn the Torah? How could they learn the Torah, if they did not hear it? And how could they hear it if no one would read it to them? Remarkably, from now on the reverential fear that the vision and sound of YHWH's glory had produced at Sinai (Exod 20:20; cf. Deut 4:10) would be produced by hearing the Torah! Through hearing Scripture, the people would encounter God.[22]

Israel's history of listening to the Torah was a history of failure. The generation that succeeded Moses and Joshua did not know YHWH, nor his magnificent actions on Israel's behalf (Judg 2:10), presumably because the Levites failed to read the Torah to them. In the days of Eli the "word of YHWH" was "scarce" (1 Sam 3:1). The people's religious fervor may have been kindled by David's leadership, but the flame was short-lived. Indeed, Israel's Scriptures were so neglected that, when Josiah's men found a Torah scroll while refurbishing the Temple, Shaphan the scribe seems not to have recognized it (2 Kgs 22:10). In direct violation of the Torah, centuries earlier, Solomon had set the nation on a course of apostasy that led to their ruin and exile in 586 BCE, exactly as the Torah had predicted (2 Kgs 23:8–20; cf. Deut 28:15–68).

One might have hoped that when the exiles returned from Babylon in 539 BCE they would have learned their lesson, and that the Levites would have been more conscientious in reading the Torah to the people. However, the book of Malachi suggests that within a generation, the people in Jerusalem suffered from the same lack of fear of YHWH that had plagued their predecessors. While the exile weaned them of idolatry, other symptoms of the old spiritual malaise remained: cynicism toward YHWH and his love (Mal 1:2); contempt for all things sacred (1:6–12); boredom in worship (1:13); refusal to fulfill vows (1:14); intermarriage with idolaters (2:10–12); infidelity in marriage covenants (2:13–16); cynicism toward YHWH and his justice (2:17); moral and spiritual crimes (sorcery, adultery, adultery, false oaths (3:5a); oppression of the economically marginalized (3:5b); tight-fistedness in relation to tithes and offerings to YHWH (3:8–9); and cynicism toward YHWH and his relationship to his people (3:13–15). Malachi blamed the absence of reverence toward God on the priests (Mal 2:1–9). Instead of teaching the Torah with integrity and modeling fear of YHWH by walking in his ways, the Levites had turned aside from the way. Instead of instructing truth, the Levites caused many to stumble by teaching the people what they wanted to hear. Because they had corrupted the covenant and their office the fear of God was lacking in the land. As the solution to the fundamental problem of the lack of fear, Malachi challenged

---

21. For variations of this formula, see Deut 5:23–29; 6:1–3; 17:13; 17:19–20; 19:20.

22. Moses will reinforce the importance of access to the revelation of God by means of his word in 30:11–14.

the people: "Remember the Torah of my servant Moses, the statutes and ordinances that I commanded him at Horeb for all Israel" (Mal 3:22[4:4]). The vocabulary, the reference to Moses, and the identification of the mountain as Horeb[23] suggest he had in mind primarily the book of Deuteronomy, which had repeatedly declared the recipe for life (e.g., 31:11–13): the key to life is obedience; the key to obedience is reverent awe before YHWH; and the key to reverent awe is hearing the Torah.

Whether or not Ezra knew Malachi, his personal disposition toward the Torah was correct: he committed himself to studying the Torah of YHWH, applying its teaching to himself, and then teaching it comprehensively in Israel (Ezra 7:10). Nehemiah 8 illustrates how he fulfilled the last commitment in a communal worship context. Responding to the people's hunger (v. 1), Ezra mounted the podium and opened the Torah scroll, and all the people rose. This gesture was not incidental. They had come for an audience with God, and, as had been the case at Sinai, the people rose when he was about to speak.[24] In response to hearing the voice of God in the reading and interpretation of the Scriptures,[25] the people wept. However, Nehemiah encouraged them to celebrate because they understood the words they had heard (Neh 8:9–13). Indeed, they were so eager to hear the Torah that Ezra read from it every day for seven days during the Festival of Booths (Neh 8:13–18). Twenty-four days after the first reading of the Torah (Neh 8:2) the religious exercises climaxed with a penitential liturgy (Neh 9:1—10:39) that included lamentation (fasting, sackcloth, dirt on their heads; 9:1), separation from all non-Israelites (9:2a), verbal confession of their own and their ancestors' sins (9:2b), more reading from the Torah for three hours (9:3a), three hours of confession and prostration (9:3b), loud crying out to YHWH (9:4), extended blessing and praise of YHWH (9:5–39), renewing the covenant, and recommitment to the proper worship of YHWH (9:38b–39), culminating in the purifying of the community. With these images of the community in Jerusalem at worship the First Testament closes, creating hope in readers that hereafter the people would faithfully serve YHWH as spelled out in the Torah. However, when the curtain rose again four hundred years later, the people we meet were indeed committed to Torah, but they seem to have lost its heart (cf. Matt 23:23; Luke 11:42); commitment to the Torah had eclipsed commitment to YHWH.[26]

So far, our discussion of the Scriptures in First Testament worship has involved only the Torah. It is difficult to determine the extent to which the rest of the Scriptures were used in worship. The prayer of the prophet in Jonah 2 suggests that true believers were steeped, not only in the Torah, but also in many of the psalms, particularly those that had been written by David and those he commissioned to lead in Temple worship: Asaph, Heman, Ethan. Nevertheless, the internal evidence of the psalms offers little help

---

23. Deuteronomy always refers to Mount Sinai as Horeb.

24. At Sinai, the people rose at the sound of the trumpet to signal the arrival of the Great King (Exod 19:16–17). In a formal audience with a superior it would have been rude and disrespectful to sit. Cf. Ezek 2:1.

25. Whereas the Torah was written in Hebrew, the people returned from exile speaking Aramaic.

26. The rabbis asserted that if one were to choose between abandoning God and forsaking the commands, the former was preferable. For these texts, see *Yerushalmi Hagigah* 1:7; *Eikhah Rabbati Proem* 2; *Pesikta de-Rav Kahana* 15. See further, Tigay, "Parashat Terumah," 141–147.

in establishing how they were used in the cult. Royal psalms (2, 45, 72, 89, 110, 132) were probably read during liturgies celebrating the founding of the dynasty or in festivities inaugurating a new king. Divine royal psalms (47, 93, 95–99) celebrated the kingship of YHWH.[27] Individual laments (3–7, 22, 51), which seem to have arisen out of personal experiences, were adapted for cultic use. Communal laments (44, 80), individual and communal hymns (many of which call the assembly to praise YHWH (33, 66, 100, 105, 146–150), and songs of thanksgiving (תּוֹדָה) praising God for specific acts (67, 75, 107, 136), may well have been composed for corporate worship. The "songs of Zion" celebrate YHWH's choice of Zion as the place for his name to be established (46, 48, 76, 84, 87, 122). Some psalms suggest they were recited as antiphonal dialogues (15, 24, 50, 81, 95, 115, 121, 132); others are associated with processions (48), covenant renewal rituals (50), or festivals (81). Intertextual connections within the prophets suggest they were aware of each other's works.[28] However, the First Testament provides no evidence for the use of prophetic writings in corporate worship. For this development, we must look to the intertestamental period.

Reading and Hearing Scripture in Synagogue Worship

Whatever the origins of the synagogue, the primary goals of Jewish worship were to praise God and educate the people. The latter was achieved by hearing the Scriptures and a sermon that would follow. In these gatherings, the reading would focus on the Torah.[29] Indeed the people often treated the Torah scroll like others treated monarchs, icons, or idols.[30] Perhaps inspired by declarations of love for the Torah in Psalm 119, after the destruction of the Temple and the loss of the Ark of the Covenant, the Torah took the place of idols as the symbol of God's presence. Through the reading and study of the Torah people had access to God.[31]

In synagogue services, at the appropriate time the "attendant" would retrieve the Torah Scroll from the ark and hand it to a reader. Without taking his eyes off the scroll, the reader would read, while a translator rendered the Hebrew in the vernacular. According to Babylonian custom, the Torah would be read through in one year; according to Palestinian custom, this was done every three years. Worshipers celebrated the completion of the reading of the Torah with great joy. At least from the time of persecution prior to the Hasmoneans, after reading the assigned portion of the Torah, the Scroll would be returned to the ark and a portion of the Prophets (Haftarah) would be read.[32] Since the prophets were not revered as highly as the Torah, it was permissible to skip verses when

27. Although scholars often associate these with the New Year, evidence for a New Year festival in the First Testament is lacking.

28. Jeremiah quoted Micah (Jer 26:18); Daniel read the prophecies of Jeremiah (Dan 9:1–2); Isaiah and Micah cited the same poem (Isa 2:1–4//Mic 4:1–3); Ezekiel 34 expands on Jer 23:1–8.

29. For a helpful study of the use of the Scriptures in early Jewish worship, see Graves, "The Public Reading of Scripture in Early Judaism," 467–87.

30. See further Tigay, "Parashat Terumah," 141–47.

31. Thus Tigay, ibid.

32. In Luke 4:16–20 Jesus probably read a Haftarah from Isaiah.

reading. In addition to these readings in regular worship, on festival days certain books would be read: at Passover, the Song of Songs; at Pentecost/Shabuoth, Ruth; at the commemoration of the destruction of the Temple, Lamentations; at the Festival of Booths/Sukkoth, Ecclesiastes; at Purim, Esther. Qumran evidence suggests that the Psalms were also used widely in worship.

In Luke 4:16–20 we observe Jesus reading Scripture in the synagogue in Nazareth on the Sabbath. Whether the rabbis in Nazareth assigned Isa 61:1–2 to him or if he chose it on his own, when he stood to read and was handed the Isaiah scroll he appears to have taken complete charge. Having read the text, he handed the scroll back to the attendant, sat down, and with all eyes fixed on him, he offered his own straightforward interpretation: "Today this Scripture is fulfilled in your hearing." Although Jesus made it his practice to teach in the synagogues (Luke 4:14–15), we do not know if he ever read the Scriptures in the Temple or at other gatherings prepared by the religious leaders.

Reading and Hearing Scripture in Public Worship in the New Testament[33]

The Gospels provide little information on how the early church used the Scriptures in worship.[34] Apart from Jesus' teaching in Jewish synagogues, his ministry occurred largely in non-cultic contexts. As a traveling rabbi, he shared with all the good news of the Kingdom of God, declaring to his band of disciples that he had come to fulfill the Torah and the prophets. While his utterances will all have been laced with First Testament Scriptures, he apparently offered his most comprehensive exposition during a post-resurrection conversation with two disciples traveling from Emmaus to Jerusalem (Luke 24:13–33). However, this account provides a paradigm for later Christian preaching, rather than the public reading of Scripture. Otherwise the Gospels provide few hints of the reading of the Scriptures in Christian worship.

In the book of Acts, the apostles' use of the Scriptures depended upon the context. For audiences of unconverted people they proclaimed that this is the age of fulfillment—the prophecies and the hope of Israel have been realized.[35] This fulfillment is demonstrated in the life, death, and resurrection of Jesus the Messiah;[36] through his resurrection Jesus Messiah/Christ is exalted as Lord.[37] Since God's favor toward the church as the new covenant community is demonstrated in the pouring out of the Spirit,[38] people should

---

33. For introductory discussion see especially Martin, *Worship in the Early Church*, 66–77, and Old, *The Reading and Preaching of the Scriptures in the Worship of the Early Church*, vol. I, *The Biblical Period*, 111–250.

34. The curious note, "Let the reader understand," inserted in Matt 24:15 and Mark 13:14 may be addressed to the person reading the Gospel (as Scripture) to the congregation. Cf. Stein, *The Synoptic Problem*, 43.

35. Acts 2:16; 3:18, 24; 10:43; 13:17–41; 18:27–28.

36. Acts 2:24, 30, 32, 33; 3:15; 5:30; 10:37–39; 17:2–3; 18:31.

37. Acts 2:33–36; 3:13; 4:11; 5:30.

38. Acts 2:17–21; 5:32; cf. 8:14–24; 10:44–48; 19:1–7.

repent and receive forgiveness, the gift of the Holy Spirit, and the assurance of salvation.[39] In Acts 8:26–38 Philip's preaching of Jesus was based on Isaiah 53, which the Ethiopian eunuch had been reading for himself.

The use of the Scriptures by those who gathered as believers is less clear. Devoting themselves to fellowship, breaking bread, and the apostles' teaching (τῇ διδαχῇ τῶν ἀποστόλων; Acts 2:42), the apostles apparently read the Scriptures systematically and offered their interpretation in the light of the death, resurrection, and ascension of Christ Jesus (cf. 5:28; 13:12).[40] Acts 17:10–15 portrays the Berean brothers receiving the word of Paul and Silas eagerly and carefully studying the Scriptures to see if what they proclaimed accorded with the written revelation. Acts 18:24–26 characterizes Apollos as an eloquent Jew, with a strong grasp of the Scriptures who taught accurately concerning Jesus. In Acts 15:1–21 the Scriptures provided the basis for solving critical questions in the life of the church. Converts from Judaism appealed to Moses to demand circumcision by all, but James quoted the prophets to argue that Gentiles are included (as Gentiles) in the new covenant community.

Although Paul defines the basic stance of the apostles regarding the authority and power of the Scriptures in 2 Tim 3:15–17, this text says nothing about the reading of the Scriptures when the community of faith gathered in worship. The Epistles envision the Scriptures being used in several different ways. When Paul explicitly charged Timothy to read the Scripture publicly, to exhort, and to teach (1 Tim 4:13), he had in mind primarily the First Testament, though as a student of the Pharisee Gamaliel (Acts 22:3), he will have emphasized the Torah. Most of Paul's epistles are addressed to Gentile churches. The abundance of citations and allusions to the First Testament suggest that systematically reading the First Testament Scriptures was a high priority wherever churches were planted; otherwise the allusions would have had no rhetorical or theological force.

The First Testament Scriptures were soon supplemented by a growing corpus of New Testament writings. Paul assumed the Colossian Christians would read his letter at their gatherings, and he charged them to have it read in the Laodicean church as well. Conversely, he also encouraged the Colossians to read his letter to the Laodiceans (Col 4:16). Elsewhere the apostle adjured the Thessalonians by the Lord to have this letter read to all the brothers (1 Thess 5:27). Second Peter ends with a curious reference to Paul's letters, some of which were obviously familiar to the addressees: "This is what our beloved brother Paul also wrote to you with the wisdom God gave him—speaking of these things in all of his letters. Some of his comments are hard to understand, and those who are ignorant and unstable have twisted his letters to mean something quite different, just as they do with other parts of Scripture" (2 Pet 3:15–16, NLT). In Rev 1:3 John pronounced a special blessing for "the one who reads aloud the words of the prophecy"

---

39. Acts 2:38; 3:19; 10:43; 15:8.

40. The New Testament distinction between preaching and teaching (Matt 4:23; 11:1; Eph 4:11; 1 Tim 2:7; 2 Tim 1:11; 4:2–4) seems to have had less to do with the passion or energy of the messenger than with the state of the audience. Whereas preaching was geared to unbelievers, in the assembly of God's people, the aim of instruction was to equip the saints for ministry and to build up the body of Christ (Eph 4:12). However, sometimes terms were used interchangeably (Mark 1:14–15, 31, 38–39), and the apostolic witness to Christ in Acts is described as both "preaching" and "teaching" (5:42; 28:31; Col 1:28).

and "those who hear and who keep what is written in it." Undoubtedly the only Scripture most early Christians had was what they heard read orally by a lector. Describing worship near the middle of the second century, Justin Martyr wrote, "The memoirs of the Apostles and the writings of the prophets are read as long as time permits. Then, when the reader has ceased, the president gives verbal instruction and invitation to the imitation of these good things. Then we all rise together and pray."[41]

In addition to hearing the Scriptures read, early Christians were encouraged to sing or recite the Psalms to each other (1 Cor 14:26; Eph 5:18–19; Col 3:16). These may have been the Psalms of the First Testament put to new melodies by Christians, or Christian odes patterned after the Psalter and other songs embedded in First Testament narratives and the prophets. James' call for the cheerful to sing praises (הָלֵל songs) in 5:13 may also refer to odes based on the Psalter.

Implications for the Use of the Scriptures in Worship Today

Although the Scriptures do not actually prescribe *how* we should use them in Christian worship today, a biblical theology of worship demands *that* evangelicals devote more time and attention to reading them in communal worship than is currently practised. When Christians gather to worship, they heed God's invitation to an audience with him. In an audience with a superior, what the superior has to say to those gathered before him is always more important than what those who have gathered have to say to the superior (Eccl 5:1–7). The Scriptures represent the normative means by which God reveals himself to us, and provide the only sure foundation of belief and practice. Therefore, it is imperative that reading the Scriptures be given the highest place in worship. But how may this be done in the modern context?

First, evangelicals must rediscover that in hearing the Scriptures worshipers hear the voice of God. With the Reformers, we should highlight the place of preaching in Christian worship, but we must remember that the Scriptures were not written primarily to be preached; they were written to be heard. Indeed, the Scriptures represent the original sermons of God's inspired prophets and apostles, and the narratives of Judges, the prophecies of Ezekiel, the Gospel of Mark, and the Epistle of James come to us as truly inspired preaching. Exposition may be needed to render the text understandable for modern hearers, but human interpretations are always flawed and subject to revision. Only the word of YHWH stands forever (Isa 40:8; cf. Ps 33:11) and only the Scriptures have ultimate authority. The more layers of human interpretation there are between the text and those who have come for an audience with God, the more muted and muffled the voice of God may be.

Second, evangelicals need to rediscover the transforming power of Scripture. The transforming power of the Scriptures is assumed in Moses' charge to the Levites to read the Torah that the people may hear that they may learn to fear that they may walk in his ways that they may live (Deut 31:9–13). Elsewhere Moses declared (and Jesus reiterated)

---

41. Justin Martyr, *First Apology*, 67.

that people do not live by physical food, but by whatever comes from the mouth of God (Deut 8:3; cf. Matt 4:4). On the surface, this statement refers to the breath of God,[42] but the prophets interpreted it as a reference to his Spirit that he puts within his people (Ezek 36:26–28), or the Torah (Jer 31:33–34) and the fear of YHWH that he puts in their hearts (Jer 32:38–41), energizing them to practice covenant righteousness and flourish in their relationship with him. According to the author of Hebrews, "The word of God is living and active; it is sharper than any two-edged sword; it pierces and divides soul from spirit, and joints from marrow; it is able to judge the thoughts and intentions of the heart" (Heb 4:12). Peter also declares its life-giving power: "For you have been born again, not of seed that perishes, but that is imperishable, that is, through the living and enduring word of God" (1 Pet 1:23). With Paul, we need to recognize that people are not changed by clever arguments or persuasive rhetoric, but by the Holy Spirit, the power of God, and the wisdom of God, which is embodied in his word (1 Cor 1–3). Because the Scriptures are God-breathed (θεόπνευστος) they are effective in instructing, reproving, correcting, training in righteousness, producing men and women of God who are thoroughly equipped for every good work (2 Tim 3:16–17).

Despite creedal affirmations of high views of Scripture, the relative absence of Bible reading is one of the marks of contemporary evangelical worship and symptomatic of a very low view of Scripture. At best the Scriptures are read piecemeal and impatiently, that we might get on with the sermon—which is what people have come to hear. At worst, we do not open the Scriptures at all. Driven by the spirit of this age, we dismiss reading the Scriptures as a fossil whose vitality and usefulness died long ago. Consequently, displacing the voice of God with the foolish babbling of mortals, we foreclose the possibility of true worship. And we wonder at people's ignorance of the Scriptures (cf. Amos 8:11–14) and their lack of spiritual fervor.

Third, evangelicals must rediscover the joy of a catholic reading and hearing of Scripture. Hearing Scripture in worship is a communal enterprise, intended for full participation with our contemporaries, and in communion with the saints who have preceded us, and those in far off corners of the globe. Oliver O'Donovan has aptly asserted,

> All serious reading of the canonical text has in view the catholic horizon. It is not because the church of the past bequeathed us a different text from that which it inherited, but because it shares a text with us, that we can read in hopeful anticipation that the insights of one generation and another will complement each other. Good interpretation catches the echo of the text as it bounces off different surfaces. So the readings of the past are a proper test of our readings, challenging us to demonstrate our care, good faith, and self-abnegating attention. And that, too, the Reformers knew very well.[43]

As a corollary, we must rediscover that in praying the Scripture we express ourselves in forms pleasing to God and identify with God's people from ages past and from around the world. The prayer the Lord taught his disciples serves as a beautiful paradigm

---

42. Cf. Gen 2:7; Eccl 12:7; Job 34:15; Ps 104:29–30.
43. O'Donovan, "The Reading Church: Scriptural Authority in Practice."

for all, and the Aaronic benediction of Numbers 6 is obviously divinely ordained. But like Jonah (Jonah 2) and Jesus (e.g., Matt 27:46; Mark 15:34), we should be so steeped in the Scriptures that when faced with severest crises or most thrilling joys we find strength and inspiration through fellowship in the sufferings and delights of God's people in history and around the world. Blessing others and praising God with forms employed in the Scriptures stifles the drive to impress others and the idolatry of novelty.

As a second corollary, we must rediscover the blessing derived from singing Scripture. Godly people express themselves in godly song. But this involves more than the vacuous repetition of snippets derived from Scripture. We are scarcely singing Scripture if we simply put the opening or closing verse of a Psalm to music but remove the heart of the Psalm, which celebrates God's transcendent character and his immanent grace with profound theological voice. When we sing entire biblical texts, we nourish ourselves with solid and healthy food rather than with empty calories.

As a third corollary, we must rediscover the fellowship and joy of spontaneous and planned sharing of Scripture. In 1 Cor 14:26 Paul calls on believers to edify and encourage one another with a psalm or teaching or a revelation. When I was a doctoral student at the University of Liverpool, we met every Sunday for fellowship around the Lord's Table. I always came away inspired by the spontaneous testimonies of the truth of Scripture expressed by ordinary folks reading biblical texts and singing profoundly biblical songs.

Fourth, evangelicals must rediscover the importance and nature of expository preaching. Since true worship involves the response of believers to the self-disclosure of God, worship leaders must devote their energies to giving worshipers an ever-clearer vision of God. Because this vision of God comes primarily from his word, we do well to follow the model of Ezra (Ezra 7:10), carefully studying of the whole counsel of God, scrupulously applying it to our own lives, and forthrightly proclaiming its message. Through the preaching of the word God's people are nourished, edified, transformed, equipped, and energized for divine service. However, authoritative preaching always subordinates the sermon to the Scripture. What God has to say to the preacher and the congregation directly is by definition more important than what the preacher has to say: let the voice of God be bold and clear, but let the voice of the human mouthpiece be subdued and modest.

Fifth, evangelicals need to rediscover the lost art of expository reading of Scripture. If interpreting Scripture is both an art and a skill,[44] this is equally true for the public reading of Scripture, for in so doing we represent the voice of God to the people. By "expository reading" I mean reading biblical texts so that their message is heard and the transforming power of the word is released. This will not happen if the words of Scripture come from the lips of one who is spiritually disconnected from the text, who has no passion to communicate the life-giving word of God, and who reads badly. Expository/expositional reading requires both an aesthetic appreciation for the Scriptures as literature and discipline in the performance of the verbal act. The following suggestions should aid hearers in grasping the meaning of Scripture, being inspired by its message, and being transformed by its power.

---

44. See the helpful volume edited by Davis and Hays, *The Art of Reading Scripture*. The concern of the book is not the art of public reading of Scripture, but the art of interpreting Scripture.

a. *Devote more time to reading Scripture.* Instead of reading a verse or two from the Psalms as a quick call to worship or a short text from Paul as the preface to the sermon, people need to hear large blocks of Scripture as coherent literary and aural wholes. While the chapter and verse divisions are helpful for navigating biblical texts, they invite us to treat the Scriptures as fragments and hinder hearing biblical texts as they were intended to be heard. In some ways the early church did well in developing lectionaries to guide pastors in selecting Scriptures to read before the assembly, especially in their regular inclusion of First Testament texts.[45] However, like chapter and verse divisions, these lectionaries tear biblical texts into fragments and remove them from their broader contexts. For practical reasons, we may need to break up larger books into smaller segments, but this should not obscure the fact that texts like Deut 4:44—26:19 were preached and transcribed as single coherent wholes.[46] Paul wrote his epistles to be heard in one reading; the same is true of the book of Revelation. The books of Psalms and Lamentations, and perhaps some prophetic books may be read piecemeal because they consist of collections of originally independently delivered and composed utterances. However, sermon series on Abraham should begin with the oral reading minimally of 11:27—25:11 in its entirety, and a series on Ephesians should begin with the oral reading of the entire book. If we hesitate to do so for fear the congregation will not tolerate it, we have created the problem ourselves with our bad reading. Even five verses read badly may be too much.[47]

b. *Promote an atmosphere of reverence when reading the Scriptures.* In the First Testament people invited to an audience with God stood in awe before him and waited eagerly for him to speak (Exod 19:17; Neh 8:5). While it is good and right to fall on our faces in submission and homage before God when we enter his presence (Ps 95:6), when he speaks he bids us rise (Ezek 1:28—2:1). We promote reverence and awe before God by having the congregation stand, and formally inviting the people to hear his word.

c. *Develop expository reading skills.* Meaningful reading demands focus and discipline. When asked to read Scripture in worship, we might increase our effectiveness by asking a series of questions regarding our reading:[48]

---

45. On the Jerusalem lectionary in the fifth century, see Old, *The Reading and Preaching of the Scriptures in the Worship of the Christian Church*, vol. 2, *The Patristic Age*, 135–66; on the Syriac lectionaries, see ibid, 277–95.

46. Although a narrative interlude is lacking, on literary and discourse grounds, it is possible that 4:44—11:32 and 12:1–26:19, 28:1–69[29:1] represent discreet addresses.

47. On January 24, 2010, at St. Andrew the Great Church in Cambridge, UK, in preparation for the sermon on worship we heard 1 Chr 13:1—16:43 read orally with inspiring force. On the Monday of Holy week, April 12, 2009, in the Wheaton College Chapel, we participated in a moving chapel service involving an opening song, "To God be the Glory," expository reading of John 12:1–19, a hymn ("Hosanna Loud Hosanna"), prayer by the Student Chaplain, another hymn ("Our Great Savior"), expository reading—without comment—of John 12:20–36a; 13:1–38; 18:1—19:30 (from NLT), a third hymn ("Lift High the Cross"), and the benediction. The reading of Scripture lasted twenty-two minutes, but it left 1800 undergraduate students in awe; any commentary would have trivialized a very sacred moment.

48. These questions are adapted from McComiskey, *Reading Scripture in Public,* 19. For additional

- Do I read at a pace that allows hearers reader to grasp the message of the passage?
- Do I stumble frequently in the reading?
- Do I make a conscious effort to help the hearer catch the proper emphases in the passage?
- Do I pause sufficiently in the reading?
- Do hearers sense my conviction of the importance and value of this passage?
- Do I read with sincerity?
- Do I consciously complement the aesthetic and literary features of the passage by reading with appropriate tonal shading?
- Do I reflect the emotion inherent in the passage? Laments (Psalm 137) should be read differently than celebratory odes (Psalm 98); prophetic announcements of woe (Isa 5:8–30) should be distinguished from promises of hope (Isa 40:1–11); comedic narratives (Judg 3:15–25) should not be read like accounts filled with pathos (Gen 22:1–19).

Since reading Scripture is a communal expression of worship, there is no reason why ministerial professionals should monopolize the exercise. In addition to engaging the congregation in responsive readings, lay people should be involved regularly in the reading—provided they exhibit appropriate spiritual, artistic, and literary qualifications.

d. *Develop creative ways of communicating Scripture.* In the Scriptures, we find a cornucopia of types of texts. Nothing about them demands that they all be read as monologues. Some psalms lend themselves to antiphonal reading (Ps 136). Poetic texts that obviously involve multiple voices may be read by several individuals or combinations of individuals and groups.[49] Since by definition Hebrew narratives are driven by dialogue, many may be effectively presented as dramatic readings.[50]

Finally, in addition to rediscovering the delight of public reading of Scripture, evangelicals must rediscover the burden of the enterprise. To stand before people who have come for an audience with God and to function as God's voice-box is an awesomely sacred task, calling for careful spiritual preparation. Ezra established the pattern of internal preparation by setting his heart/mind to study the Torah, to apply it in his own life, and to teach it in the assembly of God's people (Ezra 7:10). To set one's heart means adopting a stance of humble reverence and awe before the text as one reads it in private and as one reads it to the people. The early fifth-century theologian, John Cassian, grasped the importance of Ezra's commitment:

---

recent resources, see Schmitt, *Public Reading of Scripture: A Handbook*; McLean and Bird, *Unleashing the Word: Rediscovering the Public Reading of Scripture*.

49. For a multi-voiced liturgical reading of Israel's national anthem (Deut 32), see Appendix A below.

50. By dramatic reading I mean having different people read the direct speech uttered by characters in the text. For an example involving the book of Ruth, which I have used with very satisfying effect on several occasions in preparation for a sermon series on Ruth, see "Appendix A: A Dramatic Reading of the Book of Ruth," in *JSFSC* 5 (2012): 24–34; republished in Block, *Ruth: The King is Coming*, 263–71.

> It is impossible either to know or to teach that of which one has no experience. For how can we pass on what he is in capable of perceiving? And if he is presumptuous enough to teach, his words will come to the ears of those listening to him as being worthless and useless. He will not reach their hearts. He will be betrayed by his lack of practical experience and by his own fruitless vanity. For his words come but from the emptiness of his arrogance.
>
> The fact is that it is impossible for an unclean soul to acquire spiritual knowledge, no matter how hard it labors at the reading of the Scriptures. No one pours some rare ointment or the best honey or a precious liquid into a foul and filthy container. A jar once shot through by evil smells will more easily contaminate the most fragrant myrrh than receive from it some sweetness or capacity to please. Purity is corrupted more speedily than corruption is made pure. So it goes with the container which is our heart.[51]

By standing before the Scriptures with reverent awe we open ourselves to the transforming work of the Spirit who breathed the word of God in the first instance. Without the Holy Spirit there is no delight in the Word, no proper interpretation of the Word, and no transformation by the Word. When we stand before God's people they need to see the embodiment of the Scriptures' power. Commenting on the *Hymns on Paradise* by the fourth century Syriac theologian, Ephrem, H. O. Old observes that to interpret Scripture spiritually "is to stand before the presence of God in awe and wonder and, hearing his Word, to be transformed by that Word in the image of the Son of God."[52] If this would happen to those gathered to worship in the presence of God, it must first happen to those who speak for God in the assembly.

> Breathe on me, Breath of God,
> Fill me with life anew,
> That I may love what Thou dost love,
> And do what Thou wouldst do.
>
> Breathe on me, Breath of God,
> Until my heart is pure,
> Until my will is one with Thine,
> To do and to endure.
>
> Breathe on me, Breath of God,
> Till I am wholly Thine,
> Until this earthly part of me
> Glows with Thy fire divine.
>
> Breathe on me, Breath of God,
> So shall I never die,
> But live with Thee the perfect life
> Of Thine eternity.[53]

---

51. John Cassian, *Conferences* 14.14, pp. 168–69. I am grateful to Tom Schwanda for drawing this text to my attention.

52. Old, *The Patristic Age*, 259–60.

53. Composed by Edwin Hatch in 1878, this prayer for renewal was intended to be used as a hymn in services of ordination for clergy.

Appendix A: A Liturgical Reading of Israel's National Anthem

(Deuteronomy 32:1–43)[1]

Verses	Content	Speaker
1–3	Introduction	Leader of the Service
4	Creedal Affirmation	Congregation
Pause		
5–6	Summary Declaration of the Indictment	Leader of the Service
7	Call to Remember YHWH's Grace	Leader of the Service
8–14f	Recitation of YHWH's Grace	Men
14g–18	Declaration of the Indictment of the People	Leader of the Service
Pause		
19–20a	Declaration of YHWH's Sentence	Leader of the Service
20b–27c	Recitation of YHWH's Judgment Speech	Man, Representing the Priest or Cultic Prophet
27d–e	Declaration by the Nations	Appointed Man in the Assembly
28–29	Description of the Nations	Man, Representing the Priest or Cultic Prophet
30	Question Asked of the Nations	Leader of the Service
31	Declaration of the Israelites	Congregation
32–35	Recitation of YHWH's Description of Israel's Enemies	Man, Representing the Priest or Cultic Prophet
Pause		
36–37a	Declaration of YHWH's Commitment to His People	Man, Representing the Priest or Cultic Prophet
37b–38	Recitation of Israel's Challenge to the Nations	Congregation
39–42	Recitation of YHWH's Judgment Speech Against the Nations	Man, Representing the Priest or Cultic Prophet
43	Concluding Summons to Praise	Congregation

1. This is an adaptation of Thiessen's proposal in "The Form and Function of the Song of Moses," 407–24.

3

"Do you hear what I hear?"

Reflections on the Genre and Message of Deuteronomy

Introduction

AMONG LAY PEOPLE AND still among many theologians and biblical scholars the book of Deuteronomy is interpreted primarily as a legal document, a law book. The book offers some support for these perceptions. First, the name "Deuteronomy," which goes back to the Septuagint's τὸ δευτερονόμιον, "second law," suggests a legal document, and since Moses was the primary hand behind the book, it seems natural to view him as a lawgiver. Second, critical junctures in the book invite readers to expect legislation, as in 4:1a, "And now, Israel, listen to the statutes (הַחֻקִּים) and the judgments (הַמִּשְׁפָּטִים) that I am teaching you."[1] The frequent association of these expressions with the verb "to command" (צִוָּה),[2] Moses' assembly of the people to proclaim divine decrees,[3] and his promulgation of instructions that do in fact have a legal flavor, particularly in chapters 19–25, reinforce this impression.

The fact that in the ancient world covenant writs functioned as formal legal documents seems to reinforce the interpretation of the book of Deuteronomy as law. Since the discovery of Hittite and Assyrian treaty documents, the book's covenantal features have been widely recognized. These features include its frequent explicit references to the covenant (בְּרִית) between YHWH and his people, its covenantal vocabulary ("love," "treasured people," "vassal," "suzerain," etc.), and its covenantal structure. While these features help us understand the theological trajectory of the book, ultimately this is not a covenant document like the Assyrian and Hittite documents that have been unearthed.

The questions we need to ask are: "How does the book present itself? What did the person or persons responsible for the final form of the book think they were producing? And what did Moses think he was was doing when he wrote 'the words of this Torah on a scroll in their entirety' (דִּבְרֵי הַתּוֹרָה־הַזֹּאת עַל־סֵפֶר עַד תֻּמָּם)," ordered the Levites in who took care of the ark of the covenant to place the document beside the ark as a witness

---

1. Cf. Deut 4:5, 45; 5:1, 31; 6:1, 20; 7:11; 8:11; 11:1, 32; 12:1; 26:16; 30:16.

2. Deut 6:2; 8:11; 10:13; 28:15, 45; 30:16.

3. With the root קָהַל, "to assemble": Deut 4:10; 5:22; 9:10; 10:4; 18:16; 31:12, 28, 30; with the root קָרָא, "to summon": 5:1; 29:1[2]; 31:7.

(31:24–26), after he had charged them to read it aloud to the entire congregation of Israel every seven years when they gathered at the central sanctuary to observe the festival of Booths (Sukkoth, vv. 9–13). It is doubtful that if they heard Moses' addresses read orally with the clarity, passion, and force commended by the text itself, they would have characeized the book as a law book and the speaker as a legislator. Then what would they have heard? The thesis of this essay is that among other features, they would have recognized the text that was read as Scripture, and the message that they heard as gospel. I shall develop these two subjects separately.

Deuteronomy as Scripture

When exploring the notion of Deuteronomy as Scripture we need to consider three issues: (1) Deuteronomy as Scripture in Deuteronomy; (2) Deuteronomy as Scripture in the First Testament; (3) Deuteronomy as Christian Scripture in the New Testament and for the church. I shall consider each briefly.

The Torah of Moses as Scripture in Deuteronomy

This question is complex, touching not only on how the book of Deuteronomy was produced, but also on how the final form is cast. Although what the Levites did with the document that Moses produced differed starkly from other documents used in the production of other biblical books, the genesis of the book of Deuteronomy as Scripture was probably not very different from the way later prophetic books were produced. Elsewhere I have suggested that the prophetic books of the First Testament grew through several discreet phases:[4]

1. The prophetic event: the prophet receives his message from God.
2. The rhetorical event: the prophet transmits that message to his/her audience.
3. The transcriptional event: the oracle is committed to written text.
4. The narratorial event: the account of the circumstances of the prophetic event are added to the transcribed oracle, creating a complete literary unit.
5. The compilation event: the literary units are gathered.
6. The editorial event: the collection is organized and the individual oracles are stitched together by means of connective and correlative notes, resulting in a more or less coherent book.
7. The nominal event: a formal heading is added to the book, identifying the prophet, the circumstances of ministry, and genre of the collection (e.g., Ezek 1:1–3).
8. The updating process.
9. The transmission process.
10. The "canonicling" event.

---

4. On Ezekiel, see Block, *Ezekiel Chapters 1-24*, 17–23; on Isaiah, see idem, "Binding Up the Testimony," 293–303. In this treatment, I have expanded on ##8 and 9 and added #10.

While critical scholars put little stock in the reliability of the internal evidence of biblical books, no book in the Hebrew Bible offers as much information on its own composition as Deuteronomy. Space limitations preclude a detailed examination of these factors in the production of Deuteronomy as a book,[5] but each deserves brief comment.

The narrator alludes to *the prophetic event* in 1:3: Moses spoke "to the Israelites *just as YHWH had commanded him* to speak to them" (1:3), which accords with Moses' own statements like "See, I have taught you ordinances (חֻקִּים) and judgments (מִשְׁפָּטִים), *as YHWH my God commanded me* that you may do them in the land that you are entering to take possession of it." (4:5; cf. 4:14 [at Horeb]; 6:1). His awareness of speaking to the Israelites as YHWH had commanded him, distinguishes Moses from false prophets, who claim to have experienced a prophetic moment, but to whom YHWH had never given a prophetic word to pass on (18:15–22). Moses' own prophetic experience underlines the authority of his utterances in Deuteronomy; YHWH has put his words in Moses' mouth (cf. 18:18). The most dramatic prophetic moment in the book apparently involved Moses and Joshua in the tent of meeting, where YHWH appeared in a pillar of cloud, and, after declaring his pessimistic view of Israel after the imminent death of Moses, apparently dictated the song recorded in chapter 32 (31:14–22).

As for *the rhetorical event*, Deuteronomy purports to recount a series of rhetorical events, involving three or four formal addresses (1:6—4:40; 5:1b—11:32; 12:1—26:19 and 28:1—69[29:1]; 29:1[2]—30:20), the public recitation of a song [national anthem] (32:1–43), and a concluding benediction for all the tribes (33:1–29). In contrast to an earlier experience at Horeb, when YHWH had charged Moses to assemble the people so he could speak to them directly (4:10–13), in this book we find Moses carrying out his assigned pedagogical role preparing the people for entrance into the promised land in fulfillment of the divine charge at Horeb (4:14; 5:31).

However, these texts imply two rhetorical events, the first at Horeb, where Moses transmitted to the people the statutes and judgments that represented the terms of the covenant just as YHWH had revealed them to him (4:9–13), and the second, on the Plains of Moab, where he instructed the people in the principles of covenant righteousness, based upon the revelation at Horeb, but in anticipation of their imminent entry into the land. The formality of the rhetorical moment is suggested both by the narrator's comments at the beginnings of the second and fourth addresses: "And Moses summoned all Israel and said to them" (וַיִּקְרָא מֹשֶׁה אֶל־כָּל־יִשְׂרָאֵל וַיֹּאמֶר אֲלֵהֶם, 5:1; 29:1[2]), and by Moses' own appeals for attention (שְׁמַע יִשְׂרָאֵל, 5:1; 6:4; 9:1; cf. also 4:1; 20:3; 27:9) and response (10:12–11:1; 11:26–28; 30:15–20), as well as the ubiquitous references to "today" scattered throughout the book.[6]

Within the narrative framework of the Pentateuch, the Decalogue is cast as Israel's first Scripture. However, the original document was apparently not created either for public display or for public reading; it was stored in the Ark of the Covenant in the Holy

---

5. Although I did not set out to answer these specific questions, my first foray into this issue was inspired by the work of Sonnet, *The Book within the Book*.

6. Deut 1:10; 2:22, 25; 3:14; 4:4, 8, 26, 39, 40; 5:1, 3; 6:6; 7:11; 8:1, 11, 19; 9:1, 3; 10:8, 13; 11:2, 4, 8, 13, 26, 27, 28, 32; 12:8; 13:19[18]; 15:5, 15; 19:9; 26:16, 17, 18; 27:1, 4, 9, 10; 28:1, 13, 14, 15; 29:3, 9, 11, 12, 14, 17[4, 10, 12, 15, 18]; 30:2, 8, 11, 15, 16, 18, 19; 31:2, 21, 27; 32:46, 48; 34:6.

of Holies and was inaccessible to anyone, except YHWH himself. The Decalogue was inscribed on two tablets, of stone (4:13; 10:4), both of which would have been inscribed with the identical text. Presumably one copy functioned as YHWH's copy reminding him of his covenant commitment to Israel, while the other copy functioned as Israel's copy, and in keeping with ancient Near Eastern custom, was deposited in his presence as the divine guarantor of Israel's fidelity to their covenant commitments to him.[7] Cast as "Ten Words" corresponding to the digits on one's hand, this text was easily memorized, but as a written document, apparently its function as Scripture applied primarily to YHWH. The textual modifications from Exod 20:1–17 found in Deut 5:6–21 suggest that Moses began his second address by reciting rather than reading the Decalogue. Earlier narratives had spoken of a second scriptural document, that is, the Covenant Document (סֵפֶר הַבְּרִית, Exod 24:7).[8]

While Leviticus and Numbers provide no clues regarding the time and circumstances when the ordinances they contain were committed to writing, the word, סֵפֶר, "written document," appears repeatedly in Deuteronomy (17:18; 28:58, 61; 29:19, 20, 26[20, 21, 27]; 30:10; 31:24, 26). The expression alludes to the *transcriptional event* involving the speeches contained in this book, identified specifically as "this Torah" (17:18; 28:58, 61; 29:20[21]; 30:10; 31:24, 26). While the contents of this Torah are not explicitly defined, based on 31:9, 26, this document was considered Scripture from the outset—as was the Song (32:1–43), which was apparently added to the Torah (31:19, 22). We may only speculate concerning the transcription of the "Song of YHWH" (chapter 32), and Moses' final benediction of the tribes (chapter 33). Although these are both cast as oral proclamations, as literary documents they are extremely sophisticated.

When exploring the circumstances of *the narratorial event* (the addition of narrative introductions and conclusions to individual utterances), the book presents interesting possibilities. As noted earlier, the pattern of alternating speeches and narrative comments raises the question whether the book contains three or four of Moses' addresses, and whether 1:1–5 originally functioned as the introduction to the first address, or whether 1:1–4 belong to *the nominal event* (when the book as a whole was "named"), and 1:5 alone introduced the address. If the latter is the case, then, rather than 4:44–45 functioning as an awkward double heading to the second address, 4:44 functions as a colophonic conclusion to the first address, answering to 1:4.[9]

---

7. For further discussion and brief bibliography, see Block, "Reading the Decalogue Right to Left," 34–35 = "the Decalogue in the Hebrew Scriptures," 12–13. The reciprocal nature of the commitments is reflected in the distinctive grammatical construction of 26:16–19, on which see briefly Block, *Deuteronomy*, 613–617, and in greater detail, Guest, "Deuteronomy 26:16–19 as the Central Focus of the Covenantal Framework of Deuteronomy."

8. Exod 24:7 suggests the דִּבְרֵי יְהוָה (the words of YHWH") are distinguished from הַמִּשְׁפָּטִים ("the judgments"). The former expression apparently refers to the "Ten Words" while the latter refers to the stipulations preserved in Exod 21:1—23:19, though some begin the סֵפֶר הַבְּרִית ("covenant document") as early as 20:22.

9. Analogous to 28:69[29:1], which in our view concludes the preceding address.

Figure 3.1
The Structure of the Book of Deuteronomy

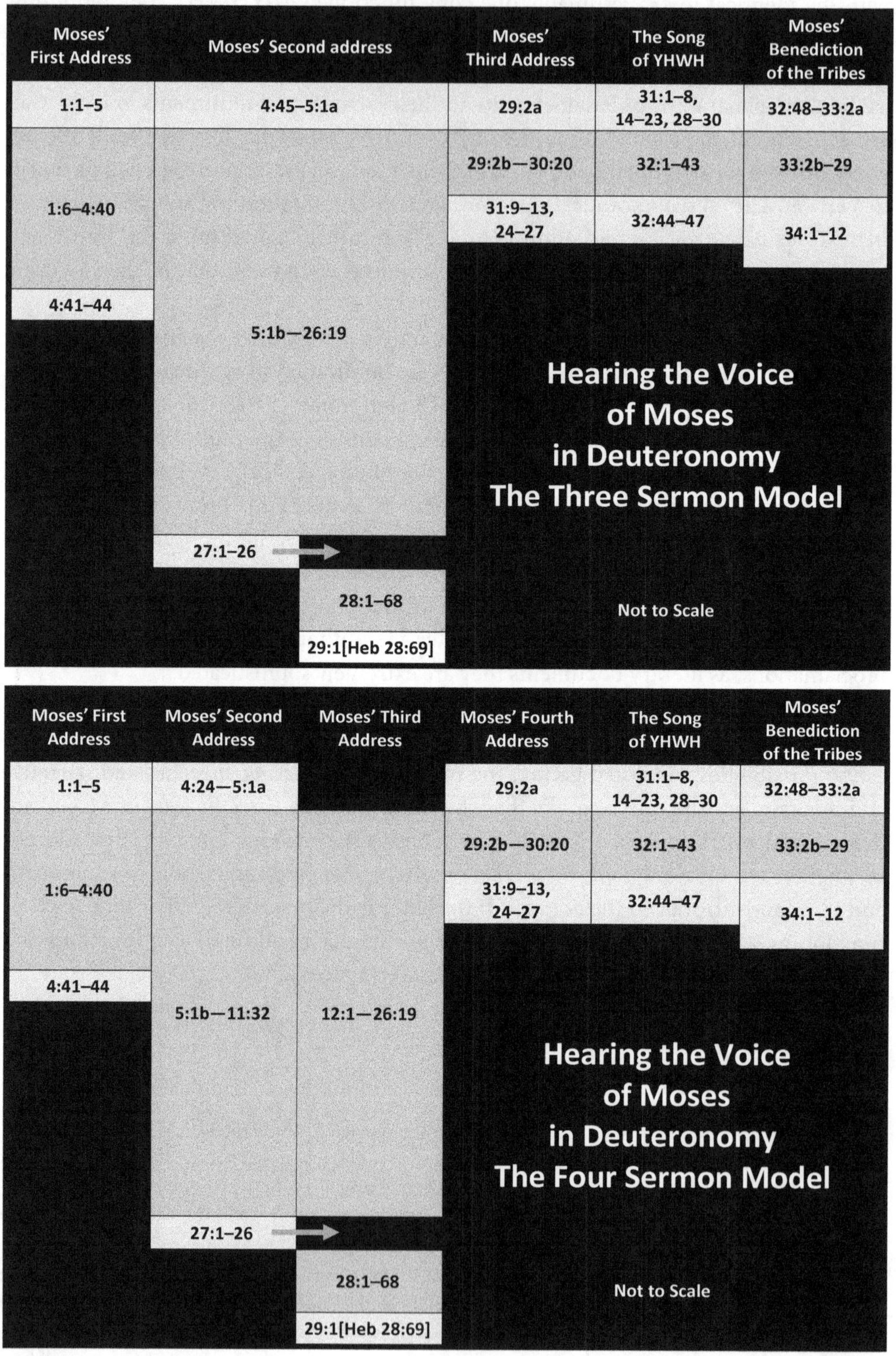

Hearing the Voice of Moses in Deuteronomy — The Three Sermon Model (Not to Scale)

Moses' First Address	Moses' Second Address	Moses' Third Address	The Song of YHWH	Moses' Benediction of the Tribes
1:1–5	4:45–5:1a	29:2a	31:1–8, 14–23, 28–30	32:48–33:2a
1:6–4:40	5:1b—26:19	29:2b—30:20	32:1–43	33:2b–29
		31:9–13, 24–27	32:44–47	34:1–12
4:41–44	27:1–26			
	28:1–68			
	29:1[Heb 28:69]			

Hearing the Voice of Moses in Deuteronomy — The Four Sermon Model (Not to Scale)

Moses' First Address	Moses' Second Address	Moses' Third Address	Moses' Fourth Address	The Song of YHWH	Moses' Benediction of the Tribes
1:1–5	4:24–5:1a		29:2a	31:1–8, 14–23, 28–30	32:48–33:2a
1:6–4:40	5:1b—11:32	12:1—26:19	29:2b—30:20	32:1–43	33:2b–29
			31:9–13, 24–27	32:44–47	34:1–12
4:41–44		27:1–26			
		28:1–68			
		29:1[Heb 28:69]			

Whether or not Deut 1:1–5 originally headed only the first address or was composed as an introduction to the book as a whole, in its present form it identifies: (1) the genre of the work ("These are the words that Moses spoke" [אֵלֶּה הַדְּבָרִים אֲשֶׁר דִּבֶּר מֹשֶׁה]; "this Torah" [הַתּוֹרָה הַזֹּאת]), (2) the historical and geographic context (in Moab beyond the Jordan; forty years after the exodus from Egypt and after the defeat of the Transjordanian Amorite kings), (3) the addressee (all the people of Israel), (4) the authority of the speeches that follow (Moses spoke as YHWH had commanded him), and (5) the illocutionary goal (to put into effect this Torah, that is the covenant relationship represented by this Torah).[10]

Any comments we make concerning *the compilation event* (when these speeches were collected) and *the editorial event* (when they were put in their present order) are speculative. The speeches of Moses that make up most of 1:6—30:20 obviously represent the core of the present book of Deuteronomy. However, there is some question whether the present record includes all of the addresses Moses delivered on the Plains of Moab, or if these have been selected and deliberately arranged according to ancient Near Eastern treaty structure.[11] While the first and last addresses (1:6—4:40 and 29:1[2]—30:20, respectively) are complex, they seem to represent discreet speeches. The issues are more complicated in the large central section, which is framed by narratorial comments (4:45—6:1a and 28:69[29:1]). However, although a narratorial comment is lacking between chapters 11 and 12, 11:26–32 looks like a formal conclusion to the preceding (cf. 30:15–20), and 12:1 looks like a formal introduction to what follows. It seems likely that two originally separate addresses have been combined to create the heart of the "Torah of Moses." The issues are further complicated by chapter 27, which appears as a narrative textual "erratic" inserted between chapters 26 and 28 and interrupting the otherwise natural flow from 26:16–19 to 28:1–14. Chapter 27 consists of three separate short speeches, the first (27:1–8) and last (27:11–26) of which pertain to a ritual the Israelites are to perform on Mounts Gerizim and Ebal, apparently as soon as they have crossed the Jordan (cf. 11:29–31). The short middle speech (vv. 9–10) provides commentary on the current proceedings supervised by Moses.

Although 1:5 and 4:44 seem to function as the frame for the first address, 1:1–4 reflects the *nominal event*. The reference to the place of the present assembly as "beyond the Jordan" (1:1–4), as well as post-Mosaica embedded in parenthetical notes[12] and the chronological and geographical notes, the account of the death of Moses (34:1–8) and especially the retrospective comment that no prophet like Moses had appeared in Israel (34:9–12) suggest the *book* of Deuteronomy was produced a long time—perhaps centuries—after these addresses were delivered. Assuming the speeches have historical roots, it is conceivable that when the Israelites crossed the Jordan, in their "brief cases" they carried a compilation of "files" that eventually provided the raw materials for the book. Contra Juha Pakkala[13] and many others, who argue that the earliest elements of Deu-

---

10. For discussion and bibliography, see Block, *Gospel according to Moses*, 78 and 258.

11. See further, below.

12. Deut 2:10–12, 20–23, 3:9, 11. Note especially the reference to the conquest of the promised land as a past event in 2:12.

13. Pakkala, "The Date of the Oldest Edition of Deuteronomy," 388–401. However, each of his

teronomic law derive from the Persian period, the content and specific chronological and geographical evidence suggest this might have happened during the transition from tribal to royal rule, perhaps begun in the context of David's reforms of temple worship and completed in the early years of Solomon's tenure. Hosea's significant dependence on Deuteronomy suggests that some form of the book existed in the eighth century BCE.[14] The scroll that Josiah's men found in the temple in the late seventh century BCE (2 Kgs 23:1–20), was probably the book of Deuteronomy.

However the book may have evolved, Deut 31:9–13 confirms that the transcript of Moses' Torah (i.e., his speeches) was to be treated as Scripture from the beginning. Moses' earlier warning in 4:1–2 (cf. 13:1[12:32]) not to add a word to or substract a word from what he taught the people orally suggest a sort of canonical status for his oral proclamation long before we have heard about a written document (which appears for the first time in 17:18–19). The canonical status of the written document is demonstrated by Moses' charge to place it next to the Ark of the Covenant inside the Tabernacle, and his prescription for its reading in its entirety before all the people every seven years at the Festival of Sukkoth (Booths). In his blessing of the tribe of Levi, Moses formally declared the Levites the custodians of the Torah in Israel (33:9–10). Presumably their responsibilities included teaching Torah to the people in their Levitical towns and in the surrounding villages and towns.[15]

Whatever its form and style, the present Hebrew version of the book that we commonly read looks quite different from what the original document must have looked like, not to mention the shape of the transcribed version of his addresses that Moses purportedly produced. Over time Deuteronomy has obviously been *updated* with respect to font, and probably also with respect to the Hebrew style. The former may be illustrated by tracing the evolution of the Shema (6:4–5) over time, with the earliest versions at the bottom and the latest version at the top (Table 3.1). Prior to the intertestamental period, northwest Semitic texts were written with a cursive Phoenician style alphabetic script (PH).[16] Whether Moses or someone else transcribed his speeches, he would have used an early version of this cursive script, and the scroll found by Josiah's men would have been a later form, much like the one illustrated here. The square Aramaic script was adopted several centuries before New Testament times, but the earliest versions would have been purely consonantal (CV), without vowels to aid in pronunciation. Eventually vowel letters were added to signify long vowels (VL), and ultimately, nine or ten centuries after Christ the vowel points were added by scribes called Masoretes (MT) to ensure correct reading in synagogue worship.

---

arguments is more naturally accounted for by a pre-monarchic provenance.

14. Whereas critical scholars generally assume Hosea antedated and underlies Deuteronomy, Carsten Vang has recently argued convincingly that the direction of influence was the opposite. See Vang, "When a Prophet Quotes Moses," 277–303.

15. On which, see chapter 9, "'The Meeting Places of God in the Land,'" 93–121; below, pp. 177–97.

16. On the significance of the invention of the alphabet and the reproduction of the Torah as text for Israel's intellectual and spiritual formation, see Berman, *Created Equal*, 108–33.

"DO YOU HEAR WHAT I HEAR?"

Table 3.1
The Textual Evolution of the Shema
Deuteronomy 6:4–5

MT	⁴שְׁמַע יִשְׂרָאֵל יְהוָה אֱלֹהֵינוּ יְהוָה אֶחָד׃ ⁵וְאָהַבְתָּ אֵת יְהוָה אֱלֹהֶיךָ בְּכָל־לְבָבְךָ וּבְכָל־נַפְשְׁךָ וּבְכָל־מְאֹדֶךָ׃
VL	שמע ישראל יהוה אלוהינו יהוה אחד ואהבת את יהוה אלהיך בכל לבבך ובכל נפשך ובכל מאדך
CT	שמע ישראל יהו אלהן יהו אחד ואהבת את יהו אלהך בכל לבבך ובכל נפשך ובכל מאדך
PH	(Paleo-Hebrew script)

As for language, the present text of Deuteronomy exhibits close resemblance to the book of Jeremiah, which represents late seventh century Jerusalem dialect Hebrew. Although the evolution of the Hebrew language is not clearly documented, if Moses and Jeremiah had ever met they would have struggled as much to have a meaningful conversation as we would if Geoffrey Chaucer should appear today. Like modern English translations, it appears that the language of Deuteronomy was updated over time to ensure clear understanding by lay people as it was being read in worship.

Hereafter changes in the text of Deuteronomy become part of the *transmission process*, and their resolution becomes part of the text critical process. The Song of YHWH in chapter 32 provides several illustrations of the issues represented here. Some English translations of verse 8 follow the Masoretic text in rendering the last phrase as "according to the number of the sons of Israel," which reflects Hebrew לְמִסְפַּר בְּנֵי יִשְׂרָאֵל (NIV, cf. CSB, NKJV). However, most render the phrase, "according to the number of the sons of God, which reflects the Greek LXX, κατὰ ἀριθμὸν ἀγγέλων θεοῦ, and two fragmentary readings from the Qumran scrolls, בני אלים, "sons of God."[17] The last verse of the Song (v. 43) provides an even more interesting study, since the ancient manuscripts reflect three different textual traditions (Table 3.2). While the message is not affected fundamentally by the variations in readings, many scholars have wrestled with the significance of these differences, and whether we are able to establish which of them is original.[18]

---

17. For discussion of the text critical issues involved, see Block, *Gods of the Nations*, 25–32; McCarthy, *Deuteronomy*, 140*–41*.

18. For discussion, see Block, "The Power of Song," 185–88; McCarthy, *Deuteronomy*, *152–54. It is striking that Paul's citation as authoritative written text of the third line of v. 43 in Rom 15:10 corresponds to the Septuagint version.

Table 3.2
A Synopsis of the Textual Variations of Deuteronomy 32:43

Masoretic Text	Qumran Fragment	Septuagint
	Celebrate, O heavens with him	Celebrate, O heavens with him
	and bow down to him all gods.	and bow down to him, all sons of God.
Celebrate, O nations, with his people.		Celebrate, O nations, with his people.
		And let all the angels of God strengthen themselves.
See, the blood of his servants he will avenge;	See, the blood of his sons he will avenge;	See, the blood of his sons he will avenge;
and take vengeance on his enemies.	and take vengeance on his enemies	and avenge and take vengeance on his enemies.
	He will pay back those who hate Him;	He will pay back those who hate Him,
He will atone for his land and people.	and atone for the land of his people.	and atone for the land of his people.

The Torah of Moses as Scripture in the First Testament

The incorporation of Deuteronomy into the Hebrew canon of Scripture we may term the *canonicling event*. It seems that the entire Pentateuch as we have it was composed as a single continuous narrative. The division of this large document into five scrolls (presently books) was a matter of convenience. Parchment scrolls made of sheep- or calfskins are very heavy and difficult to manipulate.[19] Although by New Testament times the designation "The Torah" (הַתּוֹרָה, Greek ὁ νόμος) applied to the entire Pentateuch, originally סֵפֶר הַתּוֹרָה (the Torah scroll) designated only the speeches of Moses in the book. However, the title was extended to the book of Deuteronomy (2 Kgs 22:8; Neh 8:1), and eventually applied to the first five books as a whole. Given the homiletical and pastoral nature of Deuteronomy, the narrative nature of almost all of Genesis and one half of Exodus and Numbers, we recognize now the infelicity of the scribes who translated the Pentateuch into Greek and consistently rendered the term תּוֹרָה as νόμος, "law." Greek διδαχή and διδασκαλία, both of which mean "teaching, instruction, doctrine," capture the genre of the book of Deuteronomy much better than νόμος. The contents represent prophetic preaching at its best.

The time and circumstances in which the Pentateuch was produced as a single continuous literary document remain a mystery. Since the book of Deuteronomy brings the biography of Moses to a fitting conclusion, and since the Tetrateuch (Genesis–Numbers) contains many "deuteronomisms,"[20] this could have happened at the end of the process

---

19. The oldest complete Torah scroll in existence (ca. 1155–1225 CE), owned by the Bologna University Library and recently studied by Mauro Perani, is 120 feet long and 25 inches high, and made up of 58 sections of soft sheepskin leather. For brief report of its discovery, see http://news.nationalgeographic.com/news/2013/05/130530-worlds-oldest-torah-scroll-bible-bologna-carbon-dating/.

20. On the "deuteronomisms" in the patriarchal narratives, see chapter 6, "In the Tradition of Moses," below, pp. 105–25.

when Deuteronomy as a book was created. Nevertheless, it seems that in pre-exilic and into the Persian era the designation *the Torah* applied primarily to the book of Deuteronomy, and that its extension to the rest of the Pentateuch was a later development.

This conclusion is reinforced when we examine how expressions like סֵפֶר תּוֹרַת הַשֵּׁם, "the book of the Torah of Moses";[21] סֵפֶר מֹשֶׁה, "the book of Moses";[22] תּוֹרַת מֹשֶׁה, "the Torah of Moses";[23] סֵפֶר תּוֹרַת־יְהוָה בְּיַד־מֹשֶׁה, "the book of the Torah of YHWH by the hand of Moses";[24] and דְּבַר־יְהוָה בְּיַד־מֹשֶׁה, "the words of YHWH by the hand of Moses";[25] are treated in the rest of the First Testament.

That Deuteronomy was recognized as authoritative scripture in ancient Israel is most obvious in the "deuteronomistic history," where the book provides the interpretive grid for assessing Israel's history from the people's entrance into the promised land to their expulsion from the same. The influence of Deuteronomy is evident on almost every page. Although scholars differ both in their assessments of the historical reliability of the account and in their explanations for the origins of the סֵפֶר הַתּוֹרָה, "the Torah document" that Josiah's men found in the temple (2 Kgs 22:8, 11; 23:24), all agree that within the narrative world of 2 Kings this document was some form of the book of Deuteronomy, rather than the entire Pentateuch. The document provided the impetus for the extension of Josiah's reform beyond Judah's borders into the Assyrian province of Samaria.

In the past, critical scholars have often associated Ezra's reading of the סֵפֶר תּוֹרַת מֹשֶׁה, "the document of the Torah of Moses," in Neh 8 with the origins of the Pentateuch. However, it is doubtful the expression refers to the entire Pentateuch. First, the text notes that Ezra read from dawn to noon (v. 3), which is a reasonable time within which to read Deuteronomy (with some commentary), but obviously insufficient to read the entire Pentateuch. Second, the reading was explicitly linked with the Festival of Sukkoth (8:13–18), which is precisely what Deuteronomy had prescribed in 31:9–13.

It also seems most likely that the psalmist's characterization of the "privileged man" (אַשְׁרֵי־הָאִישׁ) in Ps 1:1–2 is rooted in Deuteronomy:

בְּתוֹרַת יְהוָה חֶפְצוֹ	In the Torah of YHWH he delights,
וּבְתוֹרָתוֹ יֶהְגֶּה יוֹמָם וָלָיְלָה	and in his Torah he meditates day and night.

Some interpret הַתּוֹרָה here as the Pentateuch, as opposed to "The Psalms" and "the Prophets" (cf. Luke 24:44); others understand the word narrowly as "law" (Greek ὁ νόμος), finding here a reference to the 613 laws of the Pentateuch, as identified by the Jewish scholar Maimonides. Some view תּוֹרַת יְהוָה, "the Torah of YHWH," broadly as Scripture,[26] that is all the inspired writings of the First Testament, if not also including

21. Josh 8:31, 32; 23:6; 2 Kgs 14:6; Neh 8:1.
22. Neh 13:1; 2 Chr 25:4; 35:12.
23. 1 Kgs 2:3; 2 Kgs 23:25; 1 Chr 23:18; 30:16; Ezra 3:2; 7:6; Dan 9:11, 13; Mal 3:22[4:4].
24. 2 Chr 34:14, 15.
25. 2 Chr 35:6.
26. For example, Gerald Wilson (*Psalms 1*, 96) argues that תּוֹרָה "implies the traditional commandments of God in the Torah—commandments Israel is expected to obey—as well as the life-giving

the New Testament. Although the word תּוֹרָה is often used of "instruction" generally, the expression תּוֹרַת יְהוָה, "the Torah of YHWH," is never used in the generic sense of "instruction"; it always refers to the covenantal revelation and/or the book of Deuteronomy.[27] Indeed, in the *Torah* Psalms 19 and 119, the word is used in the very specific sense of the revealed will of God—alongside other expressions (מִצְוֹת, "commands"; חֻקִּים, "ordinances"; מִשְׁפָּטִים, "judgments"; עֵדֹת, "[covenant] stipulations"; פִּקּוּדִים, "precepts"; אִמְרָה, "word") embodied in the Pentateuch.

Some interpret תּוֹרַת יְהוָה, "the Torah of YHWH," as a reference to the Psalter itself, in which case Psalm 1:2 exhorts readers to meditate on the Psalter as Scripture, and to find here divine guidance and inspiration in the life of faith.[28] While rarely admitted, this is how many Christians treat the Psalms,[29] even elevating the Psalter above the rest of the First Testament. Probably under the influence of the composite Pentateuch ("Five Books"), the Psalter consists of five books, each of which ends with a doxology (1–41, 42–72, 73–89, 90–106, 107–150). However, to place the Psalter above the Torah is without warrant in the Scriptures and flies in the face of Jewish tradition, which views the Torah (Pentateuch) as having unrivaled status and authority within the Hebrew Bible. In the end, it seems best to interpret תּוֹרַת יְהוָה, "the Torah of YHWH," in Psalm 1 as the book of Deuteronomy,[30] for several reasons.

First, the elements of Psalm 1 that scholars have attributed to wisdom influence may all be derived from Deuteronomy. The vocabulary is Deuteronomic (אַשְׁרֵי occurs in Deut 33:29); the notion of choosing between two ways, the way of blessing and the way of retribution, is explicit in Deut 11:26–28 and 30:15–20; the use of the word תּוֹרָה as authoritative divine revelation is most at home in Deuteronomy; the didactic/teaching tone of the psalm accords perfectly with the genre of Deuteronomy, which is cast as Moses' final pastoral addresses to his people.

Second, regarding genre, few psalms in the Psalter fit the category of תּוֹרָה, "Torah," that is, "authoritative instruction," given by a superior to inferiors (God to human beings; parents to children; teachers to students). Most represent personal or communal responses to the ways of God, and the direction of speech tends to be upward to rather than downward from God.

Third, in Psalm 1 we hear clear echoes of YHWH's exhortation to Joshua in Josh 1:8, which in turn echoes Deut 17:14–20, which admonishes future kings to read the Torah for themselves and to embody its righteousness in their conduct. The statement in Joshua appears at the beginning of the Prophets section of the Hebrew Bible, suggesting that those responsible for the Psalter particularly and the third division of the Hebrew

---

guidance God gives elsewhere in Scripture."

27. Exod 13:9; 2 Kgs 10:31; 1 Chr 16:40; 22:12; 2 Chr 12:1; 17:9; 31:3–4; 34:14; 35:26; Ezra 7:10; Neh 9:3; Isa 5:24; Jer 8:8; Amos 2:4.

28. Childs, *Introduction to the Old Testament as Scripture*, 513–14.

29. Symbolized by the inclusion of the Psalms at the back of Gideon New Testaments.

30. Cf. Patrick Miller, who suggests, "[F]or the Psalter, the *law is Deuteronomy*" (italics his). "Deuteronomy and the Psalms," 11.

Bible generally sought to highlight adherence to the Torah as the key to whatever issues the following books would raise.³¹

This does not mean the psalmists were not inspired, that the psalms do not contain the truth of God, or that the Psalms are not Scripture in the full sense of the word.³² It suggests that rather than interpreting the psalms as Torah in the same sense as Deuteronomy and the Pentateuch, we should read them as prayers and hymns that guide the believer in responding to the Torah, learning the righteousness called for by God in his covenant with his people, and applying it to every conceivable circumstance of life. If the entire Psalter is a Davidic/royal document, as some have argued,³³ David was the embodiment of covenant righteousness as advocated by the Deuteronomic Torah. In that case Psalm 1 specifically offers a royal reader guidance on how to read the Torah.³⁴ In Ps 1:2–3, the call to meditate (הָגָה) in the Torah of YHWH "day and night" and the promise of success for those who do (הִצְלִיחַ) clearly echo Josh 1:8. Even though the Scriptures never treat Joshua as a king, in the latter text YHWH recognizes his role as leader of the nation and applies to him the instructions for a king provided by Moses in Deut 17:14–20.

Remarkably, the Deuteronomic Torah is the only part of the Pentateuch for which the First Testament provides any instructions for its liturgical use: it is to be read regularly before the entire community.³⁵ The 150 psalms that follow Psalm 1 reflect responses of persons for whom Torah-reading was the staple of life (cf. Psalm 119). In short, the book of Deuteronomy is the heart of the Torah, which priests were to teach and model,³⁶ which psalmists praised,³⁷ to which the prophets appealed,³⁸ by which faithful kings ruled,³⁹ and righteous citizens lived, and by which prophetic authors assessed Israel's spiritual condition. This book provides the theological base for virtually the entire First Testament and the paradigm for much of its literary style.

---

31. This canonical stitching with exhortations to Torah piety is reinforced in the last verses of Malachi (3:22[4:3]), which call the people back to the Torah of Moses. Sailhamer (*The Meaning of the Pentateuch*, 56) speaks of "canonical seams."

32. The New Testament writers clearly recognized the psalmists as inspired: Acts 1:16; 2:25, 34; 4:25; Rom 11:9; Heb 4:7.

33. See Waltke, "Canonical Process Approach to the Psalms," 3–19; idem, *Old Testament Theology*, 872–74.

34. The "blessed man" who "walks in the counsel," "stands in the path," and "sits in the seat" (Ps 1:1), is not "everyman," but a high official, if not a prince in line for the throne.

35. In keeping with Deut 17:18–20 and Josh 1:8, Psalm 1 seems to address primarily a royal reader, presenting the prince/king instructions on how to read the Torah for himself and thereby nourish his own soul, offer him guidance for life, and secure the success of his tenure. On which see, Grant, *King as Exemplar*.

36. Deut 33:10; 2 Chr 15:3; 19:8; Mal 2:6, 9; cf. Jer 18:18; Ezek 7:26; Ezra 7:10.

37. Pss 19:7–14[6–13]; 119; etc.

38. Isa 1:10; 5:24; 8:20; 30:9; 51:7.

39. 1 Kgs 2:2–4; 2 Kgs 14:6; 22:11; 23:25.

The Torah of Moses as Scripture in the New Testament

Although the shadow of Isaiah 53 hovers over the entire New Testament, no First Testament book is as fundamental to the New Testament as Deuteronomy. We recognize its influence in references to "the νόμος (usually translated "Law") of Moses,"[40] "Moses" used as a substitute for ὁ νόμος (usually translated "the Law"[41] "the book of Moses,"[42] Moses' "writings,"[43] vaguer references to laws that Moses commanded,[44] statements like "Moses wrote,"[45] "Moses says,"[46] and "customs that Moses delivered to us."[47] Although Jesus himself frequently referred to Moses as a recognized authority in Jewish tradition and as an authority behind his own teachings, remarkably of the fifty occurrences of the word, γραφή, only one (1 Tim 5:18) cites or alludes to Deuteronomy.[48] This does not mean Deuteronomy was not taken seriously; rather it means that all the writings in the Hebrew Bible were assumed to be normative Scripture. By New Testament times the word ὁ νόμος (= הַתּוֹרָה) often identified the Pentateuch as a whole.[49] However, most scholars are aware that Jesus quoted or alluded to Deuteronomy more frequently than to any other book in the Pentateuch or elsewhere in the First Testament. Indeed, it has been convincingly argued that "Deuteronomy provides a definitive lens through which Israel's scriptures represent the revelation received at Sinai."[50] This is evident in specific references to "The Supreme Command,"[51] and also in texts like Mark 10:19, which, while ostensibly citing the Decalogue, unexpectedly inserts "Do not defraud" (μὴ ἀποστερήσῃς). Although the Greek word ἀποστερέω occurs only twice in the First Testament,[52] in Mark 10:19 the expression apparently is shorthand for failure to seek the interests of others, especially the marginalized and vulnerable, which receives scant attention in the Decalogue, but is fundamental to Deuteronomic law.

---

40. Luke 2:22; 24:44; John 7:23; Acts 13:39; 15:5 (cf. "the manner of Moses" in v. 1); 28:23; 1 Cor 9:9; Heb 10:28.

41. Luke 16:29, 31; 24:27; John 5:45, 46; Acts 6:11; 21:21; 26:22; 2 Cor 3:15.

42. Mark 12:26.

43. John 5:47.

44. Matt 8:4; 19:7, 8; 22:24; Mark 1:44; 7:10; 10:3, 4; Luke 5:14; John 8:5; Acts 6:14.

45. Luke 20:28, referring to Deut 25:5.

46. Rom 10:5, 19.

47. Acts 6:14.

48. "For the scripture says, 'You shall not muzzle an ox while it is treading out the grain,' and, 'The laborer deserves to be paid.'" In 1 Cor 9:9 the source is called τῷ Μωϋσέως νόμῳ, "the Torah of Moses."

49. Note especially texts that juxtapose "the Law" and the Prophets": Matt 5:17; 7:12; 11:13; 22:40; Luke 16:16; 24:44; John 1:45; Acts 13:15; 24:14; 28:23; Rom 3:21.

50. Thus Stark, "Deuteronomy as an Intra-Canonical Lens for Appropriating Sinaitic Revelation as Christian Scripture," paper present to the Institute of Biblical Research, Baltimore, MD, November 22, 2013.

51. Deut 6:4–5 is cited in Matt 22:37; Mark 12:29-32; Luke 10:27.

52. Exod 21:21, of withholding conjugal rights from a wife; Mal 3:5, of withholding wages from a hired hand.

While many other specific texts exhibit a deuteronomic flavor,[53] the tone and style of epistles like James, 1 Peter, and 1 John are replete with echoes and allusions to Deuteronomy. One could even argue that Pauline books like Romans and Galatians, which on the surface seem so critical, if not dismissive, of the law, are imbued with the Mosaic spirit found in Deuteronomy and seek to recover that spirit for a Jewish world that, while ostensibly hallowing and preserving the law, had actually lost its spirit.[54] Jesus characterized the problem as tithing mint and dill and cumin, while neglecting the weightier matters of the Torah, that is, "justice and mercy and faithfulness" (Matt 23:23; cf. Deut 10:12—11:1). Paul speaks figuratively of Israel being stuck at Sinai, when they should have been celebrating in the presence of God in Jerusalem (an allusion to the place of the divine presence that he had chosen and stamped with his name). And Paul's appeal for whole-hearted and full-bodied commitment to God in Rom 12:1 is thoroughly Deuteronomic (cf. Deut 6:4–5; 10:12—11:1).

In what sense then is Deuteronomy Christian Scripture? Obviously not in a theonomic sense, calling Christians in every corner of the globe to recreate the world of ancient Israel. Like antecedent constitutional materials, Deuteronomy is indeed about boundary markers, but like the Jews of Jesus' and Paul's day, we miss the point if we remain fixated with the external markers and forget the community more generally that Deuteronomy seeks to create. This is the world that Jesus embodied and that he sought to build in his disciples, a society governed less by law than by fundamental covenant commitments; a world that lives by the Supreme Command in both its vertical and horizontal dimensions: "You shall demonstrate covenant commitment to the LORD (read YHWH) your God by always acting in his interest, and to your fellow human beings by always acting in their interests" (a paraphrase of Matt 22:37–39; Mark 12:30–31; Luke 10:27). Thus, laws about parapets (Deut 22:8) and stoning rebellious sons (21:18–21) are not fundamentally concerned about architectural design and punitive precision but about the well-being of all who enter my house, and the health of the domestic environment, where children abandon their self-interest and commit themselves not only to respecting their parents but also to the collective well-being of the home. Deuteronomy sought to create in Israel a paradigmatic community, a microcosm of Eden, and a visual witness to the world of what grace can accomplish (cf. 26:19). Since that was the world that Jesus inaugurated, and that is the world to which I belong, Deuteronomy remains for me my Scripture.

Individual psalmists and those who compiled the Psalter would have been appalled by contemporary American Christianity, which happily appends the Psalter to the Gideon New Testament, but refuses not only to read the Torah of Moses, but more seriously,

---

53. Like the Lord's prayer in Matt 6:9-13; Luke 11:2-4: "Our Father in heaven (cf. Deut 14:1); "Give us this day our daily bread" (cf. Deut 8); "Forgive us our debts" (ὀφείλημα occurs in the First Testament only in Deut 24:10); "Lead us not into testing" (cf. πειρασμός in Deut 6:16); "the evil" (τοῦ πονηροῦ translates הָרַע, which in Deuteronomy and the deuteronomic writings generally means violation of the Supreme Command, i.e., going after other gods); "yours is the kingdom, the power, and the glory" (cf. Deut 4:32–40; 26:19).

54. Cf. the rabbinic quotation, "Would that they would abandon Me but keep My Torah." For further comment on the citation, see below, p. 56, n. 57. For early visual portrayals of the relationship between Moses and Paul, see below, pp. 403–404.

to live by the Torah of Moses. If Christians will not accept the book of Deuteronomy as their authoritative Scripture, they have no right to claim the Psalms, which teach us how to read the Torah.

Deuteronomy as Gospel

The common mislabeling of the fifth book of Moses as "the second law" (Latin, *deuteronomium*) and the primary speaker in the book as a lawgiver, has had unfortunate consequences in the history of interpretation. To be sure, some have recognized the book as a series of prophetic, liturgical, and military orations.[55] Others have acknowledged that as Torah the book is not primarily law, but a program of catechesis, intended to educate or socialize "a new generation in the community's tradition."[56] Dennis Olsen assumes correctly that the book was intended to provide the basis for the identity and life of the community that survived the exile. However, even if the book as we have it was produced later, the book itself wants us to read it as oral and transcribed speeches by Moses intended to provide the basis for the identity and life of the community that crossed the Jordan River many centuries earlier. Deuteronomy is much more than a manifesto on polity or a legal code establishing the boundaries of Israel's behavior. It is above all a pastoral manifesto for a community of faith whose identity and status are summarized in 14:1–2: "Sons you are to YHWH your God.... You are a people holy to YHWH your God, and YHWH has chosen you out of all the peoples who are on the face of the earth to be his people, his treasured possession" (14:1–2). In 26:10 Moses declared YHWH's intention for Israel: to "set you high above all nations that he has made, for [his] praise, fame, and honor; and that you shall be a consecrated people to YHWH your God." And Moses summarized the required ethical response in 10:12–13:

> And now, Israel, what does YHWH your God require of you, but to fear YHWH your God, to walk in all his ways, to love him, to serve YHWH your God with all your heart and with all your soul, to keep YHWH's command and his ordinances, which I am commanding you today for your good?

This is not law; this is pastoral exhortation arising from gospel! Deuteronomy presents Moses first and foremost as Israel's pastor, passionate in keeping the gospel ever before his congregation, and passionate in his call for unconditional and unqualified devotion to their Redeemer. Obviously, he could not anticipate every conceivable ethical or spiritual situation that the people would encounter in Canaan. Therefore, he tried to instill in his people a theological and theocentric world view, a way of thinking that guarantees that every decision arises from a covenant commitment to YHWH and to one's fellow citizens,[57] and thereby ensure the success of Israel's mission as agent of divine grace to the nations.

---

55. See "The Orations," in Weinfeld, *Deuteronomy and the Deuteronomic School*, 10–58.

56. As catechesis, it is (1) theologically centered, (2) humanly adaptable, (3) form-critically inclusive, (4) socially transformative, and (5) communally oriented. Thus Olsen, *Deuteronomy and the Death of Moses*, 7–14.

57. This is the reverse of the rabbinic text that has a Rabbi quoting God as saying, "Would that they would abandon Me but keep My Torah.... For if they had abandoned Me but kept My Torah, then in

When considering the genre and message of Deuteronomy, this is the subject that has had the most profound influence on me and my reading of all of Scripture. But this is the topic that catches most American evangelical Christians by surprise and meets the most resistance. Having been subjected to centuries of anti-Moses rhetoric, rooted either in the law-gospel antithesis of Luther or in the misonomistic stance of dispensationalism, we are taught that the primary function of God's law is to show us that we are sinners. Our inevitable failure to keep the law drives us to the cross of Christ to seek forgiveness. While there is a measure of truth to this, to view this as the default perspective on Deuteronomy is to create a caricature of the law that Moses would not have recognized, and creates serious tension not only with this book, but also with texts like Psalm 1:1–3:

> Blessed are those who do not walk in the counsel of the wicked,
> nor stand in the way of sinners, nor sit in the seat of scoffers;
> but whose delight is in the *tôrâ* of YHWH,
> and on his *tôrâ* they meditate day and night.
> They are like a tree planted by streams of water
> that yields its fruit in its season, and whose leaf never withers.
> In everything they do, they prosper.

And we are even more embarrassed by Psalm 19:7–14[6–13], which speaks of the law as a restoring agent for the soul, causing enlightenment, and bringing great joy to the heart, or Psalm 119, a complex 176-verse acrostic that celebrates God's grace in giving the law. And we cannot understand the psalmist, who declared unashamedly: "Oh how I love your *tôrâ*! It is my meditation all the day." Remarkably, whereas no one in the First Testament had the *chutzpah* to tell God he/she loved him,[58] without restraint ten times in this *Ode to Torah* the psalmist declares his love for the "law."[59]

This is the normative view of the law in the First Testament. In fact, the First Testament provides no hint of the *misonomism* that characterizes much evangelical preaching. And if Paul really felt toward Moses and the law what people take him to say, he should have been stoned as a violator of divinely revealed truth, *à la* Deut 13 and Gal 1:8. When we remove the sinister lenses from our glasses and read the book of Deuteronomy without reference to Jesus' and Paul's polemics against the Judaisms of their day we find it to be a Gospel book from beginning to end.

Resistance to finding Gospel in Deuteronomy begins with the use of the word itself. In some circles the word is so tied to the New Testament Gospel, which focuses on the redeeming work of Christ,[60] that efforts to apply it to other contexts lead to charges of

---

the course of their study of the Torah, the yeast that is in it would have brought them back to Me." As translated by Neusner, in *The Treasury of Judaism*, 77.

58. The verb אָהֵב, "to love, to demonstrate covenant commitment," never occurs with a first person subject and YHWH/God as the object.

59. Psalm 119:47, 48, 97, 113, 119, 127, 140, 159, 163, 167; cf. also v. 165.

60. The word εὐαγγέλιον, "good news," occurs at least 75 times in the New Testament, and is explicitly associated with Jesus Christ dozens of times (e.g., Rom 1:1; 2:16; 15:16; 16:25; 1 Cor 4:15; 9:12; 2 Cor 4:4; 10:14; Gal 1:6; Eph 3:6; Phil 1:27; 1 Thess 3:2; 2 Thess 2:14; 2 Tim 1:10; 2:8), but we note especially expressions like "τὸ εὐαγγέλιον τοῦ Χριστοῦ, "the Gospel of Christ" (Rom 15:19; 2 Cor

a low Christology. The word group represented by the Greek noun εὐαγγέλιον and the verb εὐαγγελίζω occurs more than two dozen times in the First Testament, and is often used of tidings messengers deliver.[61] Usually the verb translates the finite Hebrew verb בשר (piel), while the noun translates the participle, מְבַשֵּׂר/מְבַשֶּׂרֶת, "one who proclaims [good] tidings.[62] To be sure, this word never occurs in Deuteronomy, but we should beware of the lexical fallacy of arguing that a concept is absent because the technical language is missing. The English word "gospel" derives from Anglo Saxon *god + spel[l]*, meaning "good story," though in common usage this is often interpreted more specifically as "God's story," and then narrowed to redemptive historical contexts meaning the story of salvation that climaxes in and focuses on Christ. Assuming the plain sense of the word, *gospel* ("good news") pervades the book of Deuteronomy from beginning to end, and we may characterize Moses' role as that of a מְבַשֵּׂר, that is, a εὐαγγελιζόμενος, "herald of good news." But in the case of Deuteronomy, even the mistaken understanding of the word applies, for the gospel that Moses proclaims is "God's story"; his focus is on all that YHWH has done for Israel.

We could explore many dimensions to Moses' gospel, but I shall focus on three, all of which are summarized in chapter 4. At the end of his first address, Moses presents the gospel in the reverse order of Israel's experience and their encounters with YHWH: The revelation of the Torah as Gospel (vv. 1–8); the covenant as Gospel (vv. 9–31); and salvation from Egypt as Gospel (vv. 32–40). I shall reverse these and treat the gospel according to Deuteronomy in the order that the Israelites participated as beneficiaries in "God's story."

Salvation from Egypt as Gospel

The Vocabulary of Salvation

While the book of Deuteronomy employs a variety of expressions to talk about Israel's salvation from Egypt, the infrequency with which the verb הוֹשִׁיעַ, "to save," is used of God's past rescue of his people is striking. Deuteronomy 20:4 uses this word to promise YHWH's future deliverance of Israel from her enemies when they go out to battle,[63] but in the covenant curses it occurs negatively: if Israel persists in rebellion, YHWH will send in the enemies to destroy her and then there will be no one—not even God—to "save" her (28:29, 31).[64] The root is used of YHWH's salvation of Israel from slavery in

---

2:12; 9:13; Gal 1:7), and τοῦ εὐαγγελίου Ἰησοῦ Χριστοῦ, "the Gospel of Jesus Christ" (Mark 1:1), and τῷ εὐαγγελίῳ τοῦ κυρίου ἡμῶν Ἰησοῦ, "the Gospel of our Lord Jesus" (2 Thess 1:8).

61. εὐαγγέλιον: 2 Sam 4:10; εὐαγγελία: 2 Sam 18:20, 22, 25, 27; 2 Kgs 7:9; εὐαγγελίζω, "to declare good news," 1 Sam 31:9; 2 Sam 1:20; 4:10; 18:19–20, 26, 31; 1 Kgs 1:42; 1 Chr 10:9; Ps 39:10; 67:12; 95:2; Joel 3:5; Nah 2:1; Isa 40:9; 52:7; 60:6; 61:1; Jer. 20:15.

62. Piel verb: 1 Sam 4:17; 31:9; 2 Sam 1:20; 4:10; 18:19–20, 26; 1 Kgs 1:42; 1 Chr 10:9; 16:23; Ps 40:10[9]; 96:2; 96:2; Isa 40:9; 52:7; 60:6; 61:1; Jer 20:15; piel participle: Isa 40:9; 41:27; Ps 68:12[11]; Nah 2:1; a singular hithpael verb, יִתְבַּשֵּׂר, "to receive good news": 2 Sam 18:31.

63. The same notion is expressed in 23:16[15], though with a different verb, נצל, "to snatch, rescue."

64. In 22:27 the same expression, וְאֵין מוֹשִׁיעַ, "and there is no one to rescue," is used of the helpless state of a woman raped out in the field.

Egypt only twice, and that in the poems at the end of the book. "The Song of YHWH" [often mislabeled "the Song of Moses"], which is cast as a sort of national anthem,[65] describes Israel's ungrateful response to YHWH's past graces as follows:

> But Jeshurun grew fat, and kicked;
> > you grew fat, stout, and sleek;
> then he forsook God, who made him,
> > and scoffed at the Rock of his salvation (32:15).

The parallelism suggests that the moment of Israel's salvation (יְשֻׁעָתוֹ) was the moment of her creation, and highlights God's role in her birth. Israel owed her very existence to the creative and saving work of God. Even more impressive is the note that Moses sounds as he concludes his blessing of the tribes:

> How privileged (אַשְׁרֶיךָ) are you, O Israel!
> Who is like you, a people *saved* (נוֹשַׁע) by YHWH,
> > the shield of your help,
> > and the sword of your triumph!
> Your enemies shall come fawning to you,
> > and you shall tread upon their backs (33:29).

We observe Israel's privileged status as the object of YHWH's saving acts in Moses' addresses. On six occasions, he speaks of YHWH's saving acts metaphorically as acts of redemption (7:8; 9:26; 13:6[5]; 15:15; 21:8; 24:18).[66] Hebrew speaks of redemption with two principal verbs, גָּאַל and פָּדָה. The former is a kinship term, whose cognate noun (גֹּאֵל) identifies a kinsman responsible for the economic and well-being of a relative, and who intervenes on the latter's behalf, especially when he/she is distress and cannot help himself/herself.[67] But all the texts cited above all use פָּדָה, which seems more formal, and more specifically related to redemption through the payment of a ransom. As elsewhere, in Deuteronomy the action involves YHWH's gracious act of securing Israel's release from the slave house of Egypt and the strong hand of Pharaoh.[68]

In Deut 20:1 Moses speaks of YHWH's salvation of Israel as "bringing her up" (הֶעֱלָה) from Egypt. The language is geographical. In comparison with the land of Canaan, which is dominated by a mountainous ridge that runs from north to south, Israel's home in Egypt in the Nile delta was barely above sea level. This verb represents the reverse of יָרַד, "to go down," which is used regularly of the journey from Canaan to Egypt (10:22; 26:5). Whereas the family of Jacob had made their own way down to Egypt four centuries earlier (albeit with YHWH's blessing and presence, Gen 46:3–4), this verse highlights that their return was the result of a divine act—YHWH brought them up,

---

65. See Block, "The Power of Song," 162–84.
66. The word is used similarly in Mic 6:4; Ps 78:42; 2 Sam 7:23 = 1 Chr 17:21; Neh 1:10.
67. For a discussion of the functions of a גֹּאֵל and further literature see Block, *Ruth*, 147–48.
68. References to Israel's slavery occur in 7:8; 13:6[5]; 15:15; 24:18.

By far the most common expression for YHWH's salvation is "He brought you out" (הוֹצִיא), which occurs more than twenty times in the book.[69] But from where did YHWH bring Israel out? The book identifies the place by name as "Egypt" or "the land of Egypt" in eighteen of these references,[70] simply as "the land" once (9:28), "the house of slaves" or "slave cage" (בֵּית עֲבָדִים) six times,[71] and "the iron smelter" (כּוּר הַבַּרְזֶל) once (4:20).[72] Although later Israelites may have perceived Egypt primarily as the instrument of their bondage, things had not always been this way. On the contrary, Jacob and his family had "descended" to Egypt as most-favored guests of the royal court, and because of their ties to Joseph, the prime minister, had been settled in a most desirable region of the country. Egypt's role was to serve as an incubator for Israel, a context in which a handful of people (seventy, Exod 1:5) could grow into an innumerable host (Deut 10:22). Only when, in the providence of God, it was time for Israel to "be born," to emerge as a separate people from Egypt did YHWH change the Egyptians' hearts to oppress them (Exod 1:1–4; 2:23–24; Ps 105:25).

The Commemoration of Israel's Salvation

The importance of the theme of Israel's salvation for the overall message of Deuteronomy is reflected not only in the forty plus vocabulary references to the event, but also in the prominence given to it in key creedal type statements in the book. We have already noted that the final blessing of the tribes ends with Israel's declaration of their own identity: They are "a people saved by YHWH" (עַם נוֹשַׁע בַּיהוָה, 33:29) and YHWH is Israel's Savior God, "the Rock of their salvation." The basic covenantal document, the Decalogue, opens with the divine self-identification: "I am YHWH your God, who brought you out of the land of Egypt, out of the house of slavery" (5:6).

In Deut 6:20–25 Moses introduces what some identify as Israel's family catechism. In response to a son's question concerning the significance of the laws and regulations associated with the covenant, Moses prescribes a response that highlights Israel's salvation. In fact, in keeping with the paradign established by Decalogue, he cannot answer the young lad's question about the law without first talking about their salvation. Moses expands on this statement in chapter 26:2–10, where, in another creedal type statement, Moses instructs the people on how to express their gratitude at the time of harvest:

> A wandering Aramean was my father. And he went down into Egypt and sojourned there, few in number, and there he became a nation, great, mighty, and populous. ⁶And the Egyptians treated us harshly and humiliated us and imposed on us hard labor. ⁷Then we cried to YHWH, the God of our fathers, and YHWH heard our voice and saw our affliction, our toil, and our

---

69. Deut 1:27; 4:20, 37; 5:6, 15; 6:12, 21, 23; 7:8, 19; 8:14; 9:12, 26, 28a/b, 29; 13:6, 11[5, 10]; 16:1; 26:8; 29:24[25].

70. The only exceptions are 6:23; 7:19; 9:28, 29;

71. Deut 5:6; 6:12; 7:8; 8:14; 13:6, 11[5, 10]; cf. Exod 13:3, 14; 20:2.

72. Isa 48:10 speaks of Israel's experience in exile as a "furnace of affliction." The present expression occurs as a metaphor for the Egyptian oppression elsewhere in 1 Kgs 8:51 and Jer 11:54.

oppression. ⁸And YHWH brought us out of Egypt with a mighty hand and an outstretched arm, with great deeds of awe/terror, with signs and wonders. ⁹And he brought us into this place and gave us this land, a land flowing with milk and honey. ¹⁰And look, now I bring the first of the fruit of the ground, which you, O YHWH, have given me.

Even in the excitement of harvest celebrations, the Israelites were not to forget that from start to finish, their story is a story of divine grace.

The Manner of Israel's Salvation

The references to Egypt as a "house of slaves" and a "furnace of iron" in Deuteronomy hint at the grip that Egypt held on the Israelites. However, the family catechism in 6:21–22 had recognized that the Israelites were not slaves to the Egyptians generally, but specifically to Pharaoh.

> We were Pharaoh's slaves in Egypt. And YHWH brought us out of Egypt with a mighty hand. And YHWH showed signs and wonders, great and grievous, against Egypt *and against Pharaoh and all his household*, before our eyes (6:21–22).

This is reiterated several times in the book (7:8; cf. v. 18; 11:2–4; cf. 29:1[2]; 34:11). The Israelites were slaves to the most powerful ruler on earth, the Pharaoh, whom Egyptians believed to hold "a divine office that was derived from the realm of the gods and was part of the divinely ordained world."[73] This meant that any challenge to Pharaoh was a challenge to the power of the Egyptian gods. But it also meant that a victory over Pharaoh would signal a victory over the gods of Egypt, a fact remembered in Exod 12:12 and Num 33:3–4. However, the most dramatic and detailed portrayal of Israel's salvation is found in Deut 4:32–40.

In this carefully crafted paragraph, Moses gives his people a carefully crafted lesson in history (vv. 32–34, 36–38), theology (vv. 35, 39), and ethics (v. 40). First, history teaches that through incredible acts of power and in fulfillment of his promise to the ancestors YHWH rescued his people from the bondage of Egypt. Second, this yields Israel's foundational theological conviction: YHWH, the God of Israel is not only greater than all the gods (cf. 10:17); he is the only God. Finally, as beneficiaries of YHWH's gracious saving actions, responding to this gospel, and devoted to the only God, living according to his revealed will was both the logical and the necessary way of demonstrating gratitude for the saving grace that YHWH had lavished on them.

---

73. Thus Leprohon, "Royal Ideology and State Administration in Pharaonic Egypt," 274. See also Bonhéme, "Kingship," 242–43.

The Grounds of Israel's Salvation

As already suggested, Moses highlights Israel's salvation as an act of divine grace by regularly speaking of Israel's salvation (in the past tense) before he speaks of Israel's obligations to keep the law. But he reinforces this notion by expressly excluding Israel's merit as grounds for YHWH's actions on their behalf. In 7:6–9 he eliminates Israel's candidicy for his favor on the grounds of declares of natural qualifications: he did not choose them because they were impressive for their size or significance in the international environment. In fact, they were the least significant (מְעַט) of all the the peoples. His election and salvation of Israel was an act of sheer grace grounded in YHWH's singling them out as the objects of his affection,[74] his prior covenant commitment (Hebrew אָהַב, "love," v. 8). To ward off later temptation to claim credit for their prosperity within the land promised to Israel by virtue of their own skill or power, in 8:11–18, Moses declares that the ability to achieve any economic success is itself a prior divine gift (v. 18). Finally, and most emphatically, in the following chapter, in an impressive disputation speech, Moses answers the argument that YHWH's favors, including the gift of the land of Canaan as their national grant, were rewards for Israel's superior moral righteousness (צְדָקָה) or integrity (יֹשֶׁר, 9:5–6). To the contrary, he develops in detail the counter thesis that, although the impending conquest of the Canaanites constitutes divine punishment for the latter's wickedness (רִשְׁעָה) from the beginning YHWH's own people have proved their demerit: they are "a stiff-necked people" (עַם־קְשֵׁה־עֹרֶף, vv. 6, 13), they have provoked YHWH (הִקְצִיף, vv. 7, 8), they are rebellious (מַמְרִים, v. 7), they are corrupt (שִׁחֵת, v. 12), they are sinners (חָטָא, v. 16), they commit evil (עָשָׂה הָרַע, v. 18), and with their actions they provoke YHWH's intense fury (vv. 18–22). So much for salvation based on merited favor!

Covenant Relationship with YHWH as Gospel

The twenty-eight ccurrences of the word בְּרִית, reflect the importance of the notion of "covenant" in Deuteronomy.[75] But Moses reinforces this notion by the way he speaks of YHWH and his relationship with Israel. More than 300 times he identifies of YHWH as "your God" (ca. 50 singular; 250 plural), and another twenty-two times as "our god." Obversely, Moses frequently identifies Israel as "your people" (9:26, 29; 21:8; 26:15) and "his people" (29:12[13]; 32:9, 36, 50; 33:3, 7). Beyond this, he employs a series of expressions that highlight Israel's special relationship with the YHWH. They are his "special possession" (עַם נַחֲלָה, 4:20; 9:26, 29), his "allotted possession" (חֶבֶל נַחֲלָתוֹ, 32:9), a "holy/sanctified people belonging to YHWH" (עַם קָדוֹשׁ אַתָּה לַיהוָה, 7:6; 14:2, 21; 26:19; 28:9), his "chosen people," selected from all the peoples of the earth (בָּחַר, 4:37; 7:6–7; 10:15; 14:2), that they might be high above the nations for the praise, honor, and glory of God (26:19); his "sons" (בָּנִים, 1:31; 8:5; 14:1); his "treasured people" (עַם סְגֻלָּה, 7:6; 14:2; 26:18;

---

74. On the significance of חָשַׁק, see now Levenson, *The Love of God,*" 38–42. Levenson translates the word as "take a passion to" (p. 41).

75. Deut 4:13, 23, 31; 5:2, 3; 7:2, 9, 12; 8:18; 9:9, 11, 15; 10:8; 17:2; 28:69a, 69b[29:1a, 1b]; 29:8, 11, 13, 18, 20, 24[2a, 1b, 9, 12, 14, 19, 21, 25]; 31:9, 16, 20, 25, 26; 33:9.

cf. 1 Pet 2:9–10). Israel was graciously chosen for this privileged status by YHWH. This people may have been small and insignificant by international standards (7:7), but they were was a chosen diamond, claimed by YHWH as his special treasure, whom he identified affectionately as יְשֻׁרוּן (Jeshurun), "[my] straight one" (32:15; 33:5, 26).

The notion of covenant is so pervasive in Deuteronomy that it has determined the structure of the book. Ancient treaties governing international relations typically consisted of a preamble, historical prologue, stipulations, document clause, blessings and curses, and an appeal to covenant witnesses. Although Deuteronomy is cast as a series of farewell addresses by Moses to his congregation, these speeches are arranged to match this treaty structure: preamble (1:1–5); historical prologue (1:6—4:44); general stipulations (4:45—11:32); specific stipulations (12:1–26:19); provisions for a written copy of the covenant document (4:13; 5:22; 10:1–4; 31:9–13); blessings and curses (28:1—69[29:1]); and appeal to witnesses (4:26; 30:15–20; 31:28). These treaty features highlight the covenantal significance of the book of Deuteronomy.[76] YHWH is the great king (33:5) and Israel is his vassal. Indeed, Berman has argued that Deuteronomy—along with Exod 19–24—considers each individual Israelite a royal vassal of YHWH.[77] However, unlike other international suzerain-vassal relationships of the day, the Israelites did not become YHWH's vassal by being conquered and beaten into submission (as in the Mesopotamian counterparts). She became his vassal through his gracious act of liberation from those who held them in bondage, and his invitation to them to be his covenant people. And her status as vassal was not a humiliation for them, but an honor: they were drawn to YHWH himself, called to a personal relationship with him, and exalted high above the nations as trophies of divine grace, that the world might give praise, honor and glory to their Redeemer (26:10; 28:1, 9).

Although the notion of covenant pervades the entire book, the covenant itself is the focus of attention in five texts: 4:9–31; 5:1–33; 9:1–10:11; 29:1–27[2–28]; 31:1–29). Aware of Israel's apparently inevitable apostasy and rebellion against YHWH, Moses provided two specific means of grace to keep the people on target: a written copy of the Torah (his expositions of covenant relationship, vv. 9, 25, 26), and a national anthem (cf. vv. 16–20), which should be perpetually on their lips, reminding them of YHWH's past grace. In chapter 4 Moses summarizes the grace of covenant past (vv. 9–14), the grace of covenant present (vv. 15–24; cf. v. 20), and the grace of covenant future (vv. 25–31). If in the future, Israel abandons YHWH, forcing him to impose on them the covenant curses, this will not be the end of their story; YHWH's covenant grace will ultimately triumph (4:31; cf. 30:1–10).

---

76. On the relationship of Deuteronomy to ancient treaties, see Kitchen, *Reliability of the Old Testament*, 283–94; Zehnder, "Building on Stone?"; Thompson, *Deuteronomy*, 14–21; Berman, *Created Equal*, 28–40.

77. Ibid., 40–44.

The Law as Gospel[78]

We do well to begin our reflections of "the law as gospel" with the question Moses anticipated future generations of children would ask of their parents in Deut 6:20: "When your son asks you in time to come, 'What is the meaning of the covenant stipulations and the ordinances and the judgments that YHWH our God has commanded you?'" The answers people give to this question in our day vary. For some the laws have no meaning and they make no sense, in part because of the spiritual and cultural distance between us and the world of ancient Israel.[79] For some the laws offer modern readers a helpful window into the society of ancient Israel. Readers familiar with the Near Eastern legal world of the second millennium, BCE, might even conclude that these laws represent a significant advance on those found in the Law Code of Hammurabi, king of Babylon in the eighteenth-century BCE. For many the laws represented a heavy burden Israel was required to bear, a burden from which the work of Christ would deliver them. However, this last view raises serious theological questions. How and why would God rescue the Israelites from the burdensome and death-dealing slavery of Egypt (cf. Exod 20:2) only to impose upon them an even heavier burden of the law, which they in any case were supposedly unable to keep, and which would sentence them to an even more horrible fate—damnation under his own wrath? Viewed this way the exodus turns out not to be such a good deal after all. Finally, many today view the law as the way of salvation for Israel. Whereas in the New Testament people are saved by grace, under the Old Covenant people were saved by keeping the law. I actually still hear people state this position, despite strong Pauline statements to the contrary (see below). Our challenge is to see how Deuteronomy answers this question. To do so we focus on two texts, 4:1–8 and 6:20–25.

Deuteronomy 4:1–8

The answer this short paragraph offers shocks some readers today. Here Moses declares that knowledge of the will of God is the supreme privilege of the covenant people of God. After noting that the Torah that he is teaching is normative and canonical by definition (vv. 1–2), and that obedience to the Torah that he is teaching is the key to life (vv. 3–4), he declares that possession of the Torah makes Israel the envy of the world (vv. 5–8). Unlike the gods of the nations, Israel's God hears them when they talk to him, but he has also spoken to them, and revealed his will in glorious and gracious detail. Indeed, given this fact, as we read both Exodus-Leviticus and Deuteronomy, we should grasp that the greater the detail of the divine prescriptions, the more blessed the gospel, for the less it leaves to chance, guesswork and experimentation.

---

78. For fuller discussion of this subject, see Block, *How I Love Your Torah, O LORD!*, 1–20.

79. E.g., Lev 19:19: "You shall keep my statutes. You shall not let your cattle breed with a different kind. You shall not sow your field with two kinds of seed, nor shall you wear a garment of cloth made of two kinds of material."

Deuteronomy 6:20–25

Returning to the question of the young lad in 6:20, this paragraph offers a remarkable perspective on the law. We might note five dimensions of law as gospel. First, YHWH revealed his law within the context of Israel's experience of divine grace in salvation, and within the context of the divine fulfillment of the promise of land first given to the patriarchs (6:21–23). Second, obedience to the revealed will of God is linked to the fear (trusting awe) of YHWH (v. 24a). Third, the law was given for Israel's good (טוֹב, v. 24b). Fourth, the law was given to maintain Israel's life (חָיָה, v. 24c). Fifth, if Israelites respond to YHWH's gracious salvation with fear and obedience they will be declared righteous (צְדָקָה will be ascribed to them, v. 25).

This is the good news the psalmists celebrated in Psalms 1, 19, and 119. Unlike their idolatrous neighbors, who did not know their gods personally, who had received no revelation of their gods' will, and who never knew if their efforts to placate the gods actually achieved their desired effect,[80] the Israelites were uniquely privileged to know their God by name, and to know the boundaries of righteous and unrighteous behavior, and when they sinned, to know that when offered with contrite hearts, in faith, and according to the revealed will of YHWH, they could celebrate the joy of forgiveness (Ps 32). This Torah is near; it is not far away, that someone needs to fetch it. Nor is it inscrutable or impossible to keep (Deut 30:10–14).

Having freed his chosen people from slavish vassalage to Egypt and claimed them as his own vassals, YHWH did not lay on their shoulders a burden he knew would be so heavy no one could carry it. That is not grace. That is tyranny and deceit. In Deuteronomy, to have received the revelation of God's will for his people was a supreme privilege—and the more detailed the revelation the greater the privilege. The Israelites had been liberated from the bondage of Egypt that they might become YHWH's privileged vassals, serving the heavenly King; indeed they were adopted as sons of the living God (cf. 14:1). It is no wonder then that after four decades of reflection on the significance of the incarnation, the Apostle John could write, "And from his fullness we have all received, grace upon grace (or one grace after another). For the Torah was given through Moses (διὰ Μωϋσέως ἐδόθη); grace and truth happened through Jesus Christ" (διὰ Ἰησοῦ Χριστοῦ ἐγένετο; John 1:16–17). The contrast here is not between law and gospel, but between two climactic demonstrations of grace: mediated grace represented by the Torah and embodied grace, represented by Jesus Christ. The Torah was gospel indeed.

Israel's very existence in ancient times signaled the triumph of YHWH's grace. And it would be the same grace that would triumph in the final chapter of Israel's story; after deserved judgment for a history of rebellion against their gracious Suzerain, YHWH's grace would prevail again and he would restore them to full relationship with himself (4:31; 30:1–10). This is the gospel according to Moses.

---

80. Contrast this with the plight of the author of "A Prayer to Every God," in *ANET*, 391–92. For the text of the prayer and brief discussion, see Block, *How I Love Your Torah, O LORD!*, 8–11; idem, *The Gospel according to Moses*, 124–27.

4

Covenance

A Whole Bible Perspective[1]

Introduction

A COVENANT IS A formally confirmed agreement between two or more parties that creates or governs a relationship that does not exist naturally.[2] Normally parents need not formalize their relationship with biological children; the relationship is established by birth—though conceivably, if parent and child should be estranged, at some point the relationship could be reestablished through a "covenant like" procedure. By contrast, in many societies adults may establish a relationship with a person who is not their child biologically through a formal ceremony of adoption. Through this "covenant" ritual the parents claim the child as their own and commit to caring for it.

Covenants typically involve solemn commitments establishing the privileges and obligations that attend agreements. As is well known, the Scriptures know of two kinds of covenants: "parity covenants" between parties of equal social status, and "disparity covenants" between parties of unequal status. Marriage relationships are considered covenantal: two unrelated persons commit to each other and to the long range goal of establishing a new family (Prov 2:17; Mal 2:14). In the patricentric worlds of the Bible economically the husband was considered the head of the household (בֵּית אָב, "a house of the father").[3] However, the Song of Songs suggests that within the context of sexual relations, the relationship was quite egalitarian.[4]

In the ancient world political relationships were often established and governed by covenants/treaties, involving heads of clans or rulers of realms. These could involve "parity"

---

1. This is an expanded version of a paper presented to the Evangelical Theological Society in Baltimore, November 2013.

2. The term "covenant" derives from an Old French verb *covenancier*, "to settle or contract." The *Oxford English Dictionary* (585) defines "covenant" as "a mutual agreement between two or more persons to do or refrain from doing certain acts; a compact, contract, bargain; sometimes, the undertaking, pledge, or promise of one of the parties."

3. On which see Block, "Marriage and Family in Ancient Israel," 40–52.

4. On which see Davidson, *The Flame of Yahweh*, 569–78; Davidson, "Theology of Sexuality in the Song of Songs," 1–19.

or "disparity" relationships. Gen 31:43–55 illustrates the former. By means of a covenant ritual, Laban formally acknowledged his son-in-law Jacob as his social and economic peer. Second Kings 16:7 illustrates the latter. King Ahaz of Judah expressly acknowledged that he was the "vassal" (עֶבֶד) and "son" (בֵּן) of Tiglath-Pileser III, the emperor of Assyria. This obviously involved a "disparity," that is, a "suzerain-vassal" relationship.

While the notion of "covenant" dominates the Scriptures from Genesis to Revelation, it is presented in a profoundly theological, rather than economic or political sense, involving the infinite God and finite parties whom he invites to covenant relationship with himself,[5] and whose members he encourages to treat each other as coequal beneficiaries of these covenants. In the Scriptures all covenants involving God are fundamentally monergistic suzerain-vassal pacts: God initiates the covenant; God chooses the covenant partner; God declares the terms; God determines the consequences for the subjects, depending on their response to him and his revealed will (blessing for fidelity; curses for rebellion); and God identifies the sign of the covenant (rainbow, Gen 9:12–17; circumcision, Gen 17:9–14; seventh-day Sabbath, Exod 31:15–17). Accordingly, these covenants are always identified as "my/his covenant" or "God's covenant with X," rather than "our covenant," "Israel's covenant," or "X's covenant with God." YHWH's covenant partners are never in a position to negotiate either the terms or the consequences specified; their only option is to accept or reject the relationship.

Biblical covenants have long been classified either as "unconditional and irrevocable covenants of grant" (Abrahamic, Davidic), and "conditional and revocable covenants of obligation (Israelite)."[6] However, they all exhibit signs of both irrevocability and contingency. The repeated use of the word "eternal" (i.e., irrevocable, Hebrew עוֹלָם) in association with the covenants guaranteed their perpetuity irrespective of the response of the vassal partner. God would never retract his commitments. Nevertheless, as in any relationship, the extent to which covenants achieve their goals is always contingent on the response of the vassal partners, who retain freedom at every stage to keep the covenants or to violate them (cf. Exod 19:4–6). The consequences of these divergent courses are built into the covenant, either implicitly or explicitly. Even in the pre-covenant world of Eden, the alternative effects of human response are symbolized respectively by the Tree of Life—representing the divine ideal—and the Tree of the Knowledge of Good and Evil—representing the curse for rebellion by the vassal.[7] In the Israelite covenant, the alternative effects are spelled out in detail in the blessings and curses (Lev 26; Deut 28).

---

5. While the former appears unprecedented in the ancient world, some have seen hints of analogues in a fourteenth–thirteenth-century BCE Hurrian hymn to El. Among other names, he is addressed as 'el brt and 'el dn ("El of the covenant" and "El of the Judgment," respectively). On which, see Mulder, "Baal-Berith," 141–42; Lewis, "Baal-Berith," 1.550–51. While the covenantal nature of YHWH's relationship with Israel as a people seems unprecedented in the ancient world, the relationships between deities and kings was sometimes perceived as covenantal, especially if one regards the word סְגֻלָּה, "treasured possession," and its cognates (Akkadian sikiltu; Ugaritic sglt) as covenantal. For discussion of this expression, see Davies, *A Royal Priesthood*, 51–55.

6. This view is represented especially by Weinfeld, "The Covenant of Grant," 184–83; Weinfeld, *Deuteronomy and the Deuteronomic School*, 74–91.

7. This is the traditional and prevailing interpretation. For a recent proposal that the two designations refer to a single tree, see Wyatt, "A Royal Garden," 19–22.

In the Davidic covenant they are hinted at with God's threat to discipline the descendant of David without spelling out the reasons (2 Sam 7:14; cf. Ps 132:12).

However, the imposition of the curses would not signal the termination or cancellation of the covenant. Rather, as Daniel recognized (Dan 9:1–19), because punishments for infidelity were built into the covenants, the experience of the curses meant that the terms of the covenant were actually being fulfilled to the letter. Objectively the covenant remained in force in perpetuity, irrespective of human response, though subjectively, the mission envisioned for the vassal and enjoyment of the benefactions promised by the covenant depended upon the vassal's faithful fulfillment of the Suzerain's charge (Fig. 4.1).

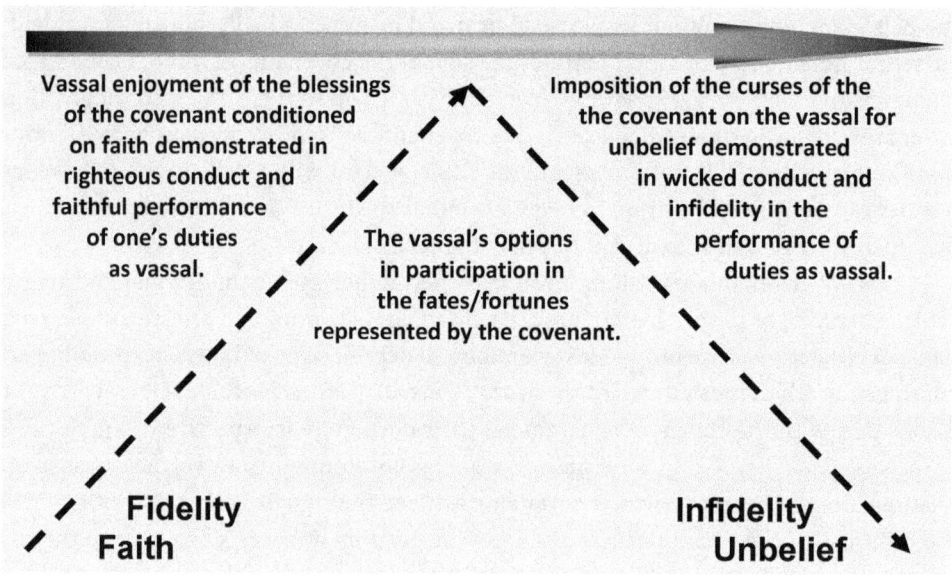

Figure 4.1
God's Irrevocable Covenant Commitment

The notion of "covenance"[8] represents the heart of all biblical revelation,[9] and the "covenants" themselves provide the skeleton for that revelation.[10] Scholars disagree on the number of covenants found in the Hebrew Bible, and on how they should be categorized.[11] Since God's covenants are all irrevocable and the effectiveness of all de-

---

8. I have coined this neologism to reflect the notions of covenant and covenant making/breaking in the abstract. The word is sometimes used in real estate contexts in association with "governance" (see http://livingnewstories.com/keyword/housing-intentional-living/governance-covenance), but is absent in the sense used here from both the *Merriam-Webster Dictionary* and the *Oxford English Dictionary* (cf. p. 1484).

9. For discussion of the notion and place of "covenant" in Hebrew Bible theology, see Barton, "Covenant in Old Testament Theology," 23–38.

10. This has been clearly demonstrated most recently by Gentry and Wellum, in *Kingdom through Covenant*.

11. Reformed scholars often recognize two types: the covenant of works (pre-fall) and the covenants of grace (post-fall). See Robertson, *The Christ of the Covenants*, 54–57. McComiskey, *The Covenants of Promise*, distinguished between promissory (Abrahamic, Davidic) and administrative covenants. Until recently many have recognized conditional covenants of obligation (e.g., Mosaic),

pends upon the fidelity of the human covenant partner (the divine Suzerain is always faithful to his covenant commitments), the categories of conditional and unconditional covenants are best abandoned.[12] It seems best to recognize three types of covenant: the cosmic covenant (Gen 9), the Israelite covenant (Abrahamic, Israelite, New [Renewed]), and administrative (royal) covenants (Noachian, Davidic). I grant that my approach is idiosyncratic, but the biblical descriptions are sufficiently vague and ambiguous to invite more than one approach. I offer this presentation as a contribution to a lively on-going discussion.

The Cosmic Covenant

The data are least complete for the cosmic covenant, often mistakenly identified as the Noachian or Noahic covenant.[13] The cosmic covenant first surfaces in Gen 6:18, where YHWH declared to Noah that after the Deluge he would establish his covenant with Noah.[14] This text is vague on the identity of the covenant partner. To be sure YHWH identified it as "my covenant" (בְּרִיתִי), and he declared that he would establish it "with you" (אִתָּךְ). But the latter does not require that we identify Noah as the covenant partner; in keeping with his role as the heir to Adam, YHWH may look to him as the covenant mediator/administrator, that is, the one through whom the cosmic covenant would be established and who would supervise its implementation.[15] Based on the use of the hiphil verb, הֵקִים, some argue that this was not a new covenant, but the confirmation of a covenant that underlies Gen 1–3.[16] That the term בְּרִית does not occur in Gen 1–3 does not seriously jeopardize this interpretation—a concept may be present even if the technical vocabulary is lacking. However, it is unlikely on two other grounds. First, it exaggerates the distinction between two idioms, הֵקִים בְּרִית and כָּרַת בְּרִית, lit., "to cut a covenant." Admittedly the former usually refers to "upholding a commitment or promise already in place,"[17] and the latter usually involves the creation of a new covenant relationship. However, sometimes the two expressions are used interchangeably.[18]

---

and unconditional covenants of grant (Abrahamic, Davidic).

12. For refutation of Weinfeld's position, see Knoppers, "Ancient Near Eastern Royal Grants and the Davidic Covenant," 670–97. On the Israelite covenant as a covenant of grant, see Davies, *Royal Priesthood*, 178–88.

13. See further below.

14. In Gen 6:8 the narrator had identified Noah as the special object of YHWH's grace within the context of an utterly corrupt humanity (6:1–5, 11–13), and in 6:9 and 7:1 characterized him as a man of extra-ordinarily spiritual and moral qualities.

15. Analogous to Moses' role in the Israelite covenant. See Exod 19–24. The only hint at the Israelite covenant being a "Mosaic" covenant is found in Exod 34:27, where YHWH declared, "I have made a covenant with you and with Israel." See further below.

16. See Gentry in *Kingdom through Covenant*, 155–61; following Dumbrell, *Covenant and Creation*, 15–26.

17. Gentry, *Kingdom through Covenant*, 475.

18. In Deut 28:69 כָּרַת בְּרִית is used of a covenant renewed. In Ezek 16:60, 62 הֵקִים בְּרִית applies to the covenant that YHWH will establish with his people after the judgment; in 34:25 and 37:26, the same event is identified with כָּרַת בְּרִית; contra Gentry [ibid.], who maintains that the latter involves

More seriously, this interpretation contradicts the definition of covenant, which involves the formalization of a relationship that does not exist naturally.[19] Inasmuch as God declared the world that he had made "very good" (טוֹב מְאֹד, Gen 1:31), the pre-fall world and its inhabitants needed no covenant for their operation according to the divine plan; the relationship between Creator and the world was established by the act of creation. This does not mean that the creation accounts lack elements that would later be picked up and built into covenantal arrangements;[20] in a post-fall world, where natural relations had all been compromised, a covenant was required to reestablish a semblance of pre-fall conditions. Even so, it is still possible that הֵקִים בְּרִית in 6:18 alludes to an earlier covenant that God made with Adam or creation—perhaps as Adam was leaving the garden. It is difficult to explain YHWH's acceptance of Abel and his sacrifice (4:4), people's apparently effective calling upon God by what would later be recognized as his covenant name, YHWH (4:26), Enoch's walking with God (5:22–24), and the characterization of Noah as a righteous man (אִישׁ צַדִּיק),[21] apart from some gracious divine provision for continued relationship with fallen humanity as Adam and Eve departed the garden. Inasmuch as that would involve a relationship that did not previously or naturally exist, that relationship could, indeed may have been covenantal. However, since the narratives do not use covenantal language before 6:18, we should not press this issue, and should certainly not impose a covenant on Gen 1–2.

YHWH did not specify the terms of the cosmic covenant first alluded to in 6:18 until the judgment had passed and only Noah and his family remained of the human population. In principle, the cosmic covenant of Gen 9 sought to recover a semblance of the relationships that existed between himself and his creation prior to Gen 3, as well as the relationships between other creatures and human beings, his vice-regents (9:1–7).[22] Accordingly YHWH promised never again to destroy the earth or its living inhabitants (9:8–11), declared verbally his irrevocable commitment to the earth and its creatures (note בְּרִית עוֹלָם, 9:16), and identified the rainbow as a "sign of the covenant" (אוֹת הַבְּרִית), visible to the creatures but ultimately as a reminder for himself of his covenant commitments (9:12–17). The prophets occasionally alluded to this covenant (Isa 54:9–10; Jer 31:35–37), which provided the basis for their vision of the ultimate

---

a covenant that did not exist previously). However, it is clear from the echoes of Lev 26:4–13 in Ezek 34:25–30 that the covenant involves the realization of the ideals of the ancient Israelite covenant. See further, Block, *Ezekiel Chapters 25–48*, 303–7.

19. For detailed repudiation of this distinction between the two idioms, see Williamson, *Sealed with an Oath*, 70–75; idem, "Covenant," 142–43; Day, "Why Does God 'Establish' rather than 'Cut' Covenants," 98–102.

20. Adam and all living things as vassals of God, the prominence of divine "blessing" (1:22, 28; though these blessings are not contingent on the vassal's behavior), vassal obligations (for all creatures being fruitful and filling the earth, for humanity to subdue and rule the earth [1:28], to "serve and guard" the garden [2:15]), the trees in the garden as symbolic representations of covenant blessings (Tree of Life) and curses (Tree of the Knowledge of Good and Evil; 2:9).

21. In the Hebrew Bible the word group based on צדק involves fundamentally dispositions and actions in keeping with the ideals of an established standard, represented by divine covenants after Gen 3.

22. On which see further below.

eschatological recreation of the cosmos. In the future YHWH would create new heavens and a new earth, when the effects of sin would be permanently removed and peace and righteousness would reign (Isa 65:17; 66:22; 2 Pet 3:10–13).

God's cosmic covenant receives only limited explicit attention in the New Testament. However, hints of it underlie a few texts. John 3:16 sets the context of Jesus' incarnation with cosmic covenantal language: "God demonstrated his covenant commitment to ("loved") the world (ὁ κόσμος) by giving his one and only son that all who believe in him might not perish but have eternal life." In Rom 8:20–22 Paul anticipated the ultimate liberation of all creation in fulfillment of the cosmic covenant. Scholars have rightly recognized that Peter's vision of the cosmos' future in 2 Pet 3:10–13 did not involve the annihilation of the present order, but its transformation and recreation so that in the new heavens and the new earth righteousness will finally and permanently dwell. Indeed, the eternality of the cosmic covenant demands that humanity's final abode be earthly, rather than heavenly, for like the other creatures, human beings were created to be earthlings. The book of Revelation paints the final state in dramatic and colorful terms, envisioning the cosmos as a holy city, where the triadic covenant relationship involving God, the earth, and all its inhabitants live in perfect covenantal *shalom* (שָׁלוֹם; Rev 21:1–4).

The Israelite Covenant

Although God renewed his relationship to the cosmos in Genesis 9, this did not solve the fundamental problem of human sin and the consequent curse on the world (Gen 8:21; 9:5–6). Driven by his commitment to the world and by the grace of his heart God called out a people through whom the curse would be lifted and his blessing guaranteed. The mission of this people was to oversee a microcosm of the cosmic covenant relationship and be the agent by which the latter would be fully restored. Instead of a triangular relationship involving God, the earth, and all living creatures, this covenant involved God, identified by name as YHWH, Israel, and the land of Canaan (Fig. 4.2).

Figure 4.2
A Synopsis of the Cosmic and Israelite Covenantal Triangles

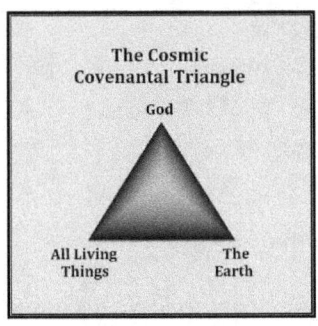
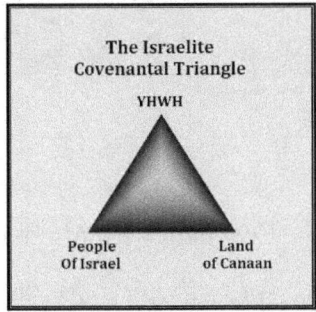
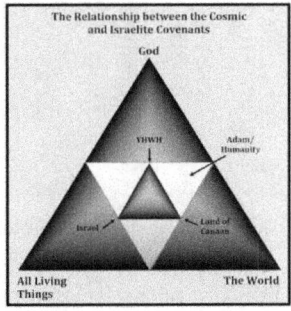

But this was both a communal and a fundamentally missional covenant whose dimensions and terms were revealed in a series of discreet phases, beginning with the Abrahamic covenant, and ending in the Hebrew Bible with the New Israelite covenant in Jeremiah 31 (Figs. 4.3 and 4.4).

Figure 4.3

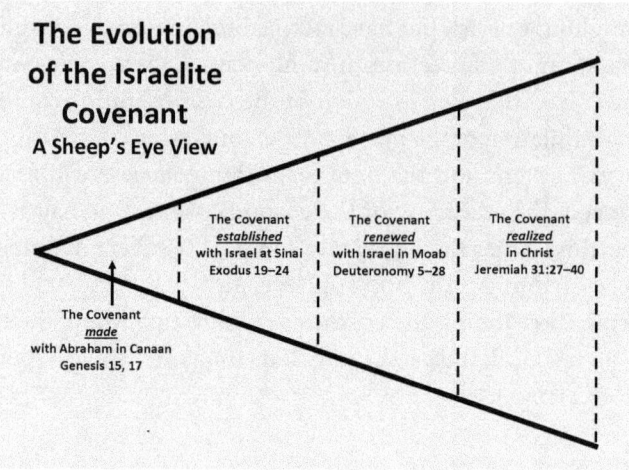

Figure 4.4

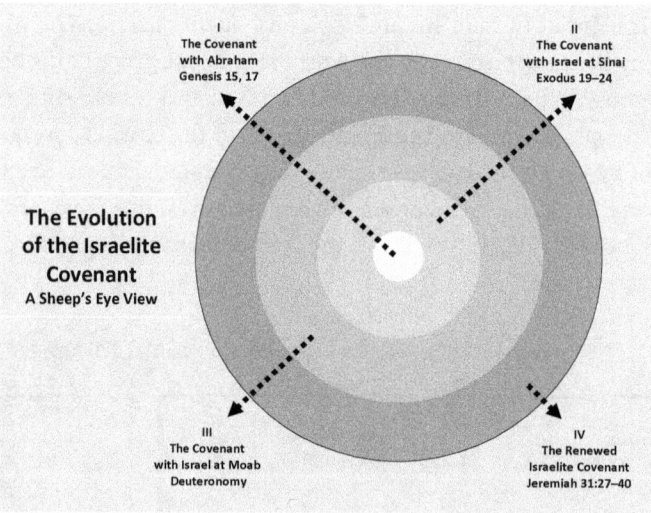

Phase 1: The Initiation of the Covenant with Abraham in Canaan

The story of the Israelite covenant began with God's call to Abraham to leave his homeland in Mesopotamia and head for the land of Canaan, where his descendants would become a great nation, and become agents of blessing to the world (Gen 12:1–3). In Canaan

YHWH formally entered into an irrevocable covenant with the Patriarch (בְּרִית עוֹלָם, Gen 17:7, 13, 19), through a two-part procedure described in Gen 15 and 17 respectively.[23] The benefactions promised within this covenant are well-known. YHWH/El Shadday, who would be the personal God of Abraham and his descendants (17:7; 26:24; 28:13; 46:3–4), promised (1) his presence and protection (12:3; 26:3, 24; 28:14–15; 46:4); (2) innumerable progeny who would become a great nation (12:1; 13:16; 15:5; 17:4–6; 18:18; 22:17; 26:24; 28:14; 35:11; 46:3); (3) kings among their descendants (17:6, 16; 35:11; cf. 22:17); (4) the land of Canaan as their homeland (13:15, 17; 15:7–21; 26:4; 28:13; 35:12); and (5) a mission as God's agent of blessing to the world (12:2; 18:18; 22:18; 26:4; 28:14). While Abraham was in a deep sleep God bound himself by oath to Abraham and his descendants. In a vision Abraham observed a torch passing between the two halves of the slaughtered animals in Gen 15:1–21 as a symbolic declaration of the irrevocability of the covenant that YHWH "cut" with the Patriarch and his heirs.

Many characterize this ['Abrahamic'] covenant as unconditional. However, it is clear that the success of the mission to which Abraham and his descendants were called would depend on their fulfilling certain obligations/prerequisites: (1) specific obedience to God's commands (12:1, 4; 22:1), and general conformity to his will (26:6); (2) faith/trusting awe (Gen 15:6; 22:12); (3) demonstrating acceptance of the covenant through the circumcision of all the males (17:9–14, 22–27); (4) a blameless life (תָּמִים, 17:1); keeping the covenant (שָׁמַר הַבְּרִית; 17:10, 11); (5) "keeping the way of YHWH by doing righteousness and justice" (צְדָקָה וּמִשְׁפָּט, 18:19); and (6) accepting their mission by entering the presence of God (17:1).

Although God promised to confirm (הֵקִים) this covenant with Abraham's descendants the narratives portray the patriarchs as experiencing the covenantal benefactions only in small measure. However, even though the statutes and ordinances associated with Sinai had not yet been revealed, it is clear the author of the patriarchal narratives perceived him as the embodiment of covenant righteousness as expounded by Moses in the book of Deuteronomy.[24]

Phase 2: The Confirmation of the Covenant with Abraham's Descendants at Sinai

The second phase in the evolution of this covenant transpired four centuries later, when YHWH established his covenant with Abraham's descendants, the Israelites, at Mount Sinai. Although most distinguish the Israelite covenant from the Abrahamic covenant, the Pentateuch offers many reasons for treating them as one and the same. The seed planted with the patriarchs comes to full bloom with their descendants.

23. Williamson (*Sealed with an Oath*, 77–93) and Alexander ("Genesis 22 and the Covenant of Circumcision," 17–22), ill-advisedly interpret these texts as involving separate covenants. See further, Gentry, *Kingdom through Covenant*, 275–80. The two phases correspond to the two-part sprinkling ritual in Exod 24:6–8, through which God and his covenant partner respectively bound themselves to the other party.

24. For detailed discussion of this notion, see chapter 6, "In the Tradition of Moses," pp. 116–38, below.

First, in Gen 17:7 YHWH promised to incorporate Abraham's descendants in the covenant: "I will establish (הָקִים) my covenant between me and you and your offspring after you throughout their generations as an everlasting covenant, to be God to you and to your offspring after you." Although the promises associated with the covenant were reiterated to Isaac (Gen 26:2–5, 24) and Jacob (28:13–15; 35:10–12; 46:3–4), and although centuries later YHWH declared to Moses that he had established his covenant with them (הֲקִמֹתִי אֶת־בְּרִיתִי אִתָּם), mentioning Abraham, Isaac, and Jacob by name (Exod 6:4), remarkably the ancestral narratives never recount a covenant renewal ritual. Nor do they ever speak again of the relationship between YHWH and these men as a בְּרִית, let alone use the expression, "establish the covenant" (הָקִים הַבְּרִית).[25] Therefore, it seems best to interpret 17:7 as anticipating the ceremony involving Abraham's descendants on Mount Sinai many centuries later.[26]

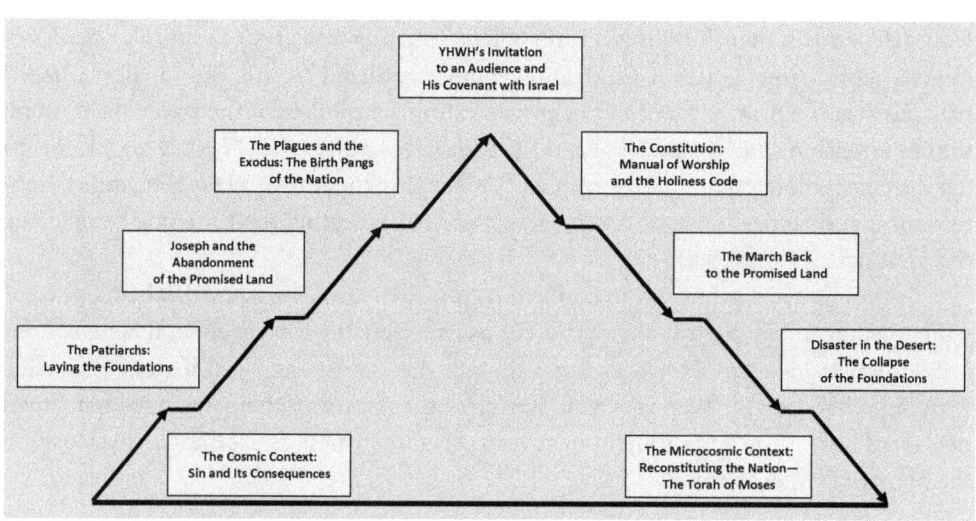

Figure 4.5
The Place of Sinai/Horeb in the Plot of the Pentateuch

Second, YHWH "knew" the time had come to fulfill his covenant promises to Abraham. when he heard the groaning of the Israelites under the Egyptian oppression. The absence of an object for the verb וַיֵּדַע in Exod 2:25 invites readers to fill in that lacuna:

> After a long time the king of Egypt died, and the people of Israel groaned because of their slavery, and they cried out for help. Their cry for rescue from slavery came up to God. And God heard their groaning, and he remembered

---

25. Unlike 11Q29:10, which speaks of "a covenant that I made with Jacob at Bethel." For discussion of this text, see Swanson, "'A Covenant Just Like Jacob's,'" 273–86. However, note that later Lev 26:42 speaks of "my covenant with Jacob, and . . . my covenant with Isaac and my covenant with Abraham." After chapter 17, in Genesis the narrator uses the word בְּרִית exclusively for agreements between human beings: between Abraham and Abimelech (21:27, 32), Isaac and Abimelech (Gen 26:28), and Laban and Jacob (31:44).

26. On Mount Sinai as the focal point of the Pentateuch, see Fig. 4.5. Everything prior anticipates Mount Sinai; everything thereafter is in the light of Sinai. Cf. Jacob Milgrom's portrayal of the structure of the Hexateuch in *Numbers*, xvii–xix.

his covenant with Abraham, Isaac, and Jacob. God saw the people of Israel—
and he knew . . . (Exod 2:23–25).

What did God know? A significant part of the answer is that God knew it was time to rescue Abraham's descendants from slavery and to deliver the land of Canaan into their hands according to his covenant promise made 400 years earlier (Gen 15:13–21).[27] However, Exod 6:4–7 suggests that their groaning also triggered YHWH's memory of his covenant promise to make the "sons of Israel" his covenant people. The modified covenant formula in verse 7 recalls Gen 17:7.

Third, while many interpret "my covenant" (בְּרִיתִי) in Exod 19:5 as a prospective allusion to the covenant rituals about to transpire on the mountain, it probably refers to the covenant that YHWH had previously made with Abraham. John Davies rightly observes that the abrupt introduction of the covenant with the pronominal suffix implies "that the covenant is identifiable and familiar to the recipient of the message (if not to the reader)."[28] According to William Dumbrell, the statement suggests that "the Sinai revelation may in fact be further specification of an already existing relationship," and that what transpires in the following chapters points to the fulfillment of the patriarchal covenant.[29] The expressions, "to listen to my voice" (שָׁמַע בְּקֹלִי) and "to keep my covenant" (שָׁמַר בְּרִיתִי) in 19:5 reinforce this interpretation. Both phrases occur twice in the Abraham narrative. In Gen 22:18 and 26:5 YHWH credited Abraham with "listening to my voice." The use of "to keep my covenant" in Gen 17:9–10 is even more striking, since these are the only occurrences of the idiom prior to this statement:

> Then God said to Abraham, "As for you, *you must keep my covenant*, you and your descendants after you for the generations to come. This is my covenant with you and your descendants after you, *the covenant you are to keep*: Every male among you shall be circumcised. (NIV; emphasis mine).

Apparently in Exod 19:5 YHWH deliberately employed vocabulary that he had used earlier when he had promised to "establish" his covenant (Gen 17:7), and in which he had repeatedly declared that the relationship he had with Abraham he would transfer to his offspring.[30] The descendants of the Patriarch collectively and individually were to emulate their great ancestor. This link heightens the significance of the events at Sinai. Not only would the descendants of the patriarchs, the "sons of Israel," be incorporated into the covenant YHWH made with Abraham, but in bestowing on them the "grant

---

27. Exod 2:25 contains the first reference to the covenant since Gen 17.

28. Davies, *Royal Priesthood*, 49.

29. Dumbrell, *Covenant and Creation*, 81.

30. Various forms of the collocation, "you and your seed," occur five times in Gen 17:7–10. Concerning the link between Exod 19:5 and Gen 17:9, Walter Groß (*Zukunft für Israel*, 130) writes: "Wenn man fragt, von welcher *Berit* hier in Ex 19,5, der feierlichen Eröffnung der Sinai-Perikope, als bereits bestehend und zu bewahren, die Rede sein kann, so kommt ohnehin nur die priesterschriftliche *Berit* mit Abraham und seinen Nachkommen in Gen 17 in Frage, falls man nicht annehmen will, hier werde die *Berit*, die erst in Ex 24 geschlossen wird, antizipiert."

of royal priesthood"[31] YHWH formally commissioned his people to fulfill Abraham's mandate of being a blessing to all the nations of the earth as specified in Gen 18:18–19:

> Abraham will surely become a great and powerful nation, and all nations on earth will be blessed through him. For I have singled him out that he might direct his children and his household after him to keep the way of YHWH[32] by doing righteousness and justice (צְדָקָה וּמִשְׁפָּט), so that YHWH may fulfill his promises to Abraham.

Furthermore, through the revelation at Sinai the Israelites would learn concretely what it means to "walk before YHWH and be blameless" (Gen 17:1).

Many additional clues suggest that the Hebrew Bible views the Abrahamic and Israelite covenants as organically unified. First, as is true of the Abrahamic covenant, the Hebrew Bible repeatedly speaks of the eternal (i.e., irrevocable) quality of the Israelite covenant. The eternality of the covenant made with Abraham is emphasized in the Patriarchal Narratives with expressions like בְּרִית עוֹלָם (Gen 17:7, 13, 19; cf. 9:16) and assurances that specific promises have eternal force "to your seed forever" (עַד עוֹלָם, Gen 13:15; 17:8; 48:4; Exod 32:13; Ps 105:8–10; 1 Chr 16:15). However, the same kind of language is used of the Israelite covenant. Note especially the following texts:

> Exodus 31:16–17
>
> Therefore the people of Israel shall keep the Sabbath, observing the Sabbath throughout their generations, as an eternal/irrevocable covenant (לְדֹרֹתָם בְּרִית עוֹלָם). It is a sign forever (אוֹת הִוא לְעֹלָם) between me and the people of Israel that in six days YHWH made heaven and earth, and on the seventh day he rested and was refreshed.

> Leviticus 24:8
>
> Every sabbath day he shall set it in order before YHWH continually; it is an everlasting covenant (בְּרִית עוֹלָם) for the sons of Israel.

> Judges 2:1
>
> I brought you up from Egypt and brought you into the land that I swore to give to your fathers. I said, "I will never break my covenant with you. . ."

> Psalm 111:2–9
> Great are the works of YHWH,
> studied by all who delight in them.
> Full of splendor and majesty is his work,

---

31. Davies' expression. See *Royal Priesthood*, 60–102.

32. "They shall keep the way of YHWH by doing righteousness and justice" (וְשָׁמְרוּ דֶּרֶךְ יְהוָה לַעֲשׂוֹת צְדָקָה וּמִשְׁפָּט) functions as shorthand for all that YHWH asks of his people as summarized in Deut 10:12–13 and laid out in the Sinai revelation and Moses' exposition thereof in the Deuteronomic Torah. This present idiom occurs elsewhere in deuteronomic texts (Judg 2:22; 2 Sam 22:22; cf. also Ps 18:22[21]; 37:34; Mal 2:9; cf. Job 23:11; Prov 8:32). However, the more common form of the first idiom is "walking in the way of YHWH," rather than "keeping the way."

and his righteousness endures forever.
He has caused his wondrous works to be remembered;
YHWH is gracious and merciful.
He provides food for those who fear him;
he remembers his covenant forever (יִזְכֹּר לְעוֹלָם בְּרִיתוֹ).
He has shown his people the power of his works,
in giving them the inheritance of the nations.
The works of his hands are faithful and just;
all his precepts are trustworthy;
they are established forever and ever,
to be performed with faithfulness and uprightness.
He sent redemption to his people;
he has commanded his covenant forever (לָעַד לְעוֹלָם).
Holy and awesome is his name!

Isaiah 24:4–5
The earth mourns and withers;
the world languishes and withers;
the highest people of the earth languish.
The earth lies defiled under its inhabitants;
for they have transgressed the instructions,
violated the statutes,
and broken the everlasting covenant (בְּרִית עוֹלָם).

Isaiah 54:4–10
Fear not, for you will not be ashamed;
be not confounded, for you will not be disgraced;
for you will forget the shame of your youth,
and the reproach of your widowhood
you will remember no more.
For your Maker is your husband,
YHWH of hosts is his name;
and the Holy One of Israel is your Redeemer,
the God of the whole earth he is called.
For YHWH has called you
like a wife deserted and grieved in spirit,
like a wife of youth when she is cast off, says your God.
For a brief moment I deserted you,
but with great compassion I will gather you.
In overflowing anger for a moment
I hid my face from you,
but with everlasting covenant faithfulness (חֶסֶד עוֹלָם)
I will have compassion on you,"
says YHWH, your Redeemer.

> "This is like the days of Noah to me:
> as I swore that the waters of Noah should no more go over the earth,
> so I have sworn that I will not be angry with you,
> and will not rebuke you.
> For the mountains may depart
> and the hills be removed,
> but my steadfast love shall not depart from you,
> and *my covenant of peace shall not be removed*,"
> says YHWH, who has compassion on you.

Jeremiah 31:35–37

> Thus says YHWH, who gives the sun for light by day
> and the fixed order of the moon and the stars for light by night,
> who stirs up the sea so that its waves roar—YHWH of hosts is his name:
> "If this fixed order departs from before me," the declaration of YHWH,
> "then shall the offspring of Israel cease from being a nation before me forever."
> Thus says YHWH:
> "If the heavens above can be measured,
> and the foundations of the earth below can be explored,
> then I will cast off all the offspring of Israel for all that they have done,"
>   the declaration of YHWH.

As in the Isaiah text, here Jeremiah attaches the certainty of the cosmic order (as guaranteed in the Cosmic Covenant) to the Israelite covenant. When Ezekiel describes YHWH's future "covenant of peace" (בְּרִית שָׁלוֹם), which he also characterizes as an "eternal/irrevocable covenant" (בְּרִית עוֹלָם, 16:60; 36:26), he not only identifies at as the covenant that he remembers "from the days of your youth" (i.e., at Sinai), but in 34:25–30 he also deliberately echoes the blessings built into the Israelite covenant in Lev 26:4–13.[33]

Second, the narrator of Genesis recounts many patriarchal events through the lens of the Exodus[34] and Deuteronomy,[35] but Gen 26:4–5 is especially striking. Here YHWH expressly credited Abraham with fidelity to the stipulations of the covenant as revealed at Sinai and as expounded by Moses in Deuteronomy:

> I will make your offspring as numerous as the stars of heaven, and will give to your offspring all these lands; and all the nations of the earth shall gain blessing for themselves through your offspring, because Abraham *listened to my voice and kept my charge, my commands, my statutes, and my instructions.*

---

33. For discussion, see Block, *Ezekiel Chapters 25–48*, 303–6.

34. E.g., YHWH's adaptation of the self-identification formula in Gen 15:7, "I am YHWH, who brought you out from Ur of the Chaldeans to give you this land to possess."

35. For discussion of the tight links between Deuteronomy and the Patriarchal Narratives, see my essay below, "In the Tradition of Moses." While we question their explanations for these features, recently several critical scholars have highlighted Deuteronomic features in the Patriarchal accounts. See especially Blum, *Die Komposition der Vätergeschichte*; Blum, *Studien zur Komposition des Pentateuch*; Blenkinsopp, *The Pentateuch*; Carr, *Reading the Fractures of Genesis*.

The four expressions, מִשְׁמַרְתִּי מִצְוֺתַי חֻקּוֹתַי וְתוֹרֹתָי, occur only here in Genesis and seem strangely out of place. They are much more at home in the contexts of the Sinai revelation and especially the speeches of Deuteronomy. Apparently in YHWH's (and the author's) mind, Abraham had fulfilled the righteousness called for by the Israelite covenant, despite the total absence of any record of these stipulations—except the ordinance of circumcision called for in Gen 17. In his thorough discussion of "The 'Fathers' and the Divine-Human Covenant in Deuteronomy," Jerry Hwang has demonstrated that this blending of Abrahamic and Israelite covenants is fundamental to the theological rhetoric of Deuteronomy, which

> conceives of Israel in all its generations as a corporate entity that is bound to a single covenant that YHWH made with the "fathers," which is a symbolic group that minimally includes the patriarchs but also expands to include other groups, depending on the chronological horizon occupied by the audience of the book."[36]

How then should we understand the relationship between the Abrahamic and Israelite covenants? In the Israelite covenant, God fulfills the covenant promise he made to Abraham in Gen 17:7, that he would establish his covenant with him *and his descendants after him throughout their generations as an everlasting covenant to be God to Abraham and to his descendants after him.* By revealing the stipulations of this covenant in great detail, YHWH concretized and fleshed out the covenant made with Abraham. In his grace, YHWH committed himself to Israel ("I will be your God") and took Israel as his covenant partner ("You shall be my people") in a marriage from which there would be no divorce. In the future he may indeed suspend the benefits of the covenant (Lev 26:14–39; Deut 28:15–68), but this would not compromise the integrity of the covenant itself, nor could this be the last word. Ultimately, when Israel's heart is circumcised (Lev 26:41; Deut 30:6), she comes to her senses, and repents of her rebellion (Lev 26:41; Deut 4:30; 30:6–10), then God will bring her back to the land he promised the ancestors and renew his covenant relationship with them. Israel's exile cannot mean the end of her relationship with YHWH (cf. Ezek 34:25; 36:22–32; 37:15–28). All of these eventualities are built into the covenant itself. In YHWH's own words, "I am YHWH; I have spoken; I will act accordingly."[37]

Having reiterated that circumcision was to continue as the mark of God's covenant people (Exod 12:43–49; cf. Lev 12:3),[38] in fulfillment of God's promise in Gen 17:7, at Sinai God formally made the people of Israel his own and bound himself by covenant

---

36. Hwang, *The Rhetoric of Remembrance*, 232.

37. YHWH's original covenantal commitment to Israel is expressed in the oft-repeated clause, אֲנִי יְהוָה דִּבַּרְתִּי וְעָשִׂיתִי, "I am YHWH; I have spoken, and I will act." In neither judgmental nor restoration contexts does this formula refer primarily to the prophet's present utterance; rather it refers to YHWH's ancient covenantal word—both blessing and curse—that he is duty bound to keep; he is YHWH! Variations of the formula occur in Ezek 5:13, 15, 17; 17:21, 24; 21:22, 37; 22:14; 24:14; 26:14; 30:12; 34:24; 36:36; 37:14.

38. However, note that Moses never speaks of physical circumcision as an identity marker in Deuteronomy. For further discussion of this issue, chapter 18, "Hearing Galatians with Moses: An Examination of Paul as a Second and Seconding Moses," below, pp. 374–404.

irrevocably to Abraham's descendants. Through the covenant ratification ritual (Exod 24) he confirmed his commitment to being their God (Exod 20:2; 11:24; Lev 26:12); he engaged them in the mission of blessing the world first announced to Abraham (Exod 19:4–6); he reiterated his promise to give them the land of Canaan (Exod 6:4–8; 23:20–33; Lev 14:34; 25:38); and he graciously revealed to them in detail what he meant when he credited Abraham with obeying him, keeping his charge, his commands, statutes and instructions (Gen 26:5).[39] YHWH declared his eternal commitment to Israel verbally, and, as he had done in the case of the cosmic covenant (the rainbow; Gen 9:13–16), he gave his covenant people the Sabbath as a gift and an eternal sign of his commitment to them (Exod 31:16–17; Lev. 24:8).[40] Perhaps even more impressively, analogous to the torch passing between two parts of a slaughtered animal in Gen 15, by having when Moses sprinkled the "blood of the covenant" on the altar (Exod 24:6) YHWH bound himself dramatically and irrevocably to Israel.

**Figure 4.6
The Growth of Israel's Constitutional Tradition**

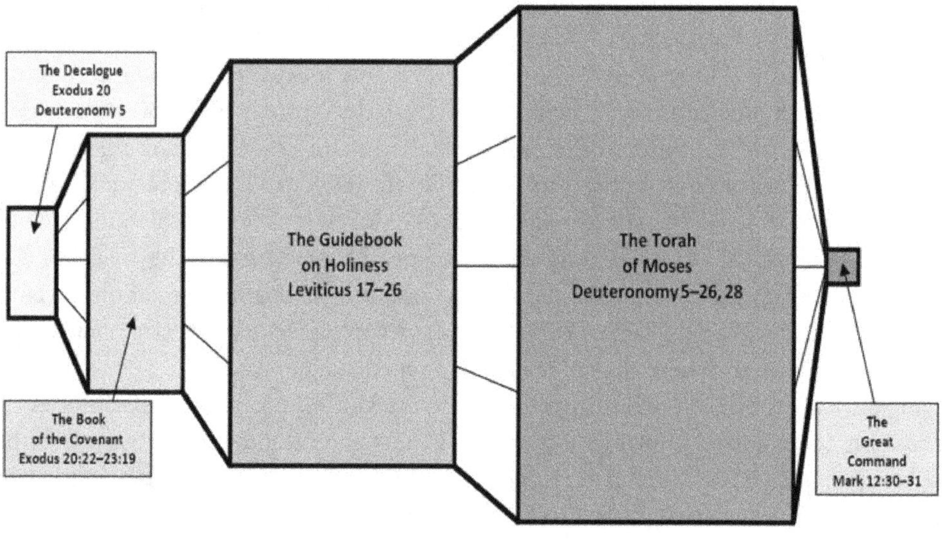

Furthermore, the function of one of the two "tablets of the covenant" (לוּחֹת הַבְּרִית) inside the Ark of the Covenant (Deut 9:9–15) stored in the Holy of Holies was to remind YHWH of his irrevocable commitment to Israel.

For their part, the Israelites verbally bound themselves to God, promising to listen to his voice and keep his covenant (Exod 19:5–6) by declaring three times, "All that YHWH has spoken we will do" (Exod 19:8; 24:3, 7), and ritually accepting the blood of the covenant sprinkled on themselves (24:7). The formal ratification procedures

---

39. That revelation is preserved in three easily identifiable documents embedded in the narrative of the Pentateuch: the Decalogue (עֲשֶׂרֶת הַדְּבָרִים, Exod 20:1–21), the Covenant Document (סֵפֶר הַבְּרִית, Exod 20:22—23:19); the Instructions on Holiness (Lev 17–27). See Fig. 4.6.

40. For full discussion, see chapter 10, "O Day of Rest and Gladness": Rediscovering the Gift of Sabbath, below, pp. 198–224.

reached their climax with elders of Israel feasting on the mountain in the presence of God (24:9–11). For the ritual establishment of the covenant all that remained was for God to provide his people with two copies of the covenant in summary form (the two tablets, Exod 24:12; 31:18), which would eventually be placed in "the ark of the covenant of YHWH" (אֲרוֹן בְּרִית יְהוָה, Exod 40:20; Deut 10:1–10). If one of these tablets reminded YHWH of his commitment to Israel, the other representing Israel's commitment was stored in the Holy of Holies because YHWH was the divine witness to their commitments and guarantor of their fidelity.

The people remained at Sinai for fifteen months, during which time they flagrantly broke the covenant by worshiping the golden calf. The significance of the act was demonstrated symbolically by Moses smashing the tablets of the covenant. However, in response to his intercession, YHWH graciously renewed the covenant with them, symbolized by the production of a new set of tablets, identical to the first. (Exod 34:1–28; Deut 9:6–10:11). Thereafter, with Moses acting as mediator of the revelation, he declared in even greater detail his personal commitment to Israel and their obligations to him (Leviticus). This revelation culminated in the covenant blessings and curses (Lev 26:1–39), and the promise that if, in the future, God should suspend the blessings and visit his people with the curse, the curse would not be the last chapter in Israel's history. In the end, he would remember his covenant and restore the triangular covenantal relationship that had been suspended because of their rebellion (Lev 26:40–46; Deut 4:25–31).

More than a year later the Israelites left Sinai as God's covenant people on a mission—to claim the land of Canaan, and thereby complete the covenantal triangle, which would enable them to enjoy the prosperity God had promised them and provide a context from which to fulfill the mission to which God had called them (Exod 6:2–8; 19:4–6). Ideally their experience in the land should serve not only as a microcosm of Eden where God, his creatures including humans, and the environment lived in perfect covenantal harmony, but also as a model to the world of what the grace of God can yield in a fallen world. Unfortunately, the generation that signed on to the covenant at Sinai would never witness the completion of the covenantal triangle, for when the land lay before them they rebelled against YHWH and refused to accept the future he had designed for them (Num 14:1–45). As punishment for their unbelief and rebellion, God sent them back into the desert, sentencing them to thirty-eight years of aimless wandering until that entire generation had died.

Phase 3: The Renewal of the Covenant with Abraham's Descendants on the Plains of Moab

The book of Deuteronomy represents the third chapter in the history of the Israelite covenant. Camped on the Plains of Moab on the east side of the Jordan, under Moses' supervision, the new generation of Israelites engaged in an elaborate covenant renewal ritual through which God bound himself anew to his people, and the people bound themselves anew to him (Deut 26:16–19). While Deuteronomy does not actually describe the covenant renewal ritual, the significance of the events that underlie the book is summarized in 27:10: "Today you have become the people of YHWH your God" (הַיּוֹם הַזֶּה נִהְיֵיתָ לְעָם לַיהוָה אֱלֹהֶיךָ).

The book of Deuteronomy (Hebrew אֵלֶּה הַדְּבָרִים, "These are the Words") consists largely of Moses' farewell pastoral addresses to his people, with "covenant" functioning as his overarching theme, and seeing the Israelites faithfully live out the covenant righteousness it called for in the promised land as his goal. Although many treat the covenant involved in Deuteronomy as a separate covenant (referred to either as the Moab Covenant or the Palestinian Covenant),[41] the fact that Moses opened his second address by reciting the Decalogue demonstrates that the covenant to which this generation of Israelites committed themselves was not a new covenant, distinct from the one made at Sinai.[42] On the contrary, because the people who were about to cross the Jordan and claim the promised land had not participated in the Sinai ceremonies, it was necessary for them to renew and ratify the covenant, so that they could enter the land as the covenant people of God. Moses' present objective was not only official, but especially pastoral, to prepare them for life in the land by instructing them on the fundamental principles of covenant relationship, applying previously revealed laws to new circumstances within the land, and concluding with a reiteration of the covenantal blessings and curses. In Deut 28 he spelled out the consequences of their performance within this covenant relationship for them, depending on their future fidelity or infidelity to their Suzerain. When Moses had finished his covenantal addresses he produced a written copy ("the Torah," הַתּוֹרָה) and charged the Levites to read it in its entirety every seven years when all the people gather at the central sanctuary for the Festival of Booths (Sukkoth), presumably as part of regular covenant renewal ceremonies (Deut 31:9–13).

However, like the ceremonies at Sinai (Exod 24), the covenant procedures underlying the book of Deuteronomy involved only God and his people. They lacked involvement of the third member of the covenantal triad—the land. For this reason, in Deut 27, to complete the covenantal triangle Moses prescribed a ceremony that was to be performed in the heart of the promised land, at Mounts Gerizim and Ebal, as soon as the people had crossed the Jordan. Josh 8:30–35 recounts how the Israelites, under Joshua's leadership, fulfilled this charge.[43]

Although through his covenant with Israel YHWH had set his people high above all the nations "for praise, praise and in fame and in honor" (לִתְהִלָּה וּלְשֵׁם וּלְתִפְאָרֶת, 26:10), in Deuteronomy both Moses and God express a realistic view of the Israelites,

---

41. For bibliography, see Barrick, "The Mosaic Covenant," 214, n. 8.

42. The clause, מִלְּבַד [דִּבְרֵי־]הַבְּרִית אֲשֶׁר־כָּרַת אִתָּם בְּחֹרֵב, in 28:69b[29:1b] is elliptical. The broader context requires interpreting this verse as the colophonic conclusion to the preceding address (as in the Hebrew Bible), alluding specifically to 26:16–19, rather than as the introduction to chapters 29–30. This colophonic conclusion following the blessings and curses is analogous to the conclusion to the stipulations of the covenant at Sinai, as preserved in Lev 26:46: "These are the ordinances and judgments and instructions [of the covenant] that YHWH instituted between himself and the people of Israel on Mount Sinai through Moses." Accordingly, we should interpret verse 69b[29:1b] something like, "besides the [words of the] covenant he had made with them at Horeb." See further, Block, *Deuteronomy*, 646–47, 662–63.

43. For full discussion of the literary and theological significance of Deut 27, see chapter 8, "What Do These Stones Mean?" below, pp. 152–76.

anticipating future apostasy and defection that would call for the curses (Deut 4:25–29; 29:14–27[15–28]; 31:16–18, 27–29; 32:1–18). However, reinforcing the hope of Lev 26:40–45, Moses declared that the divine judgment would not mean the end of the covenant. On the contrary, since the curses constituted integral parts of it, when the judgment came, it happened precisely as predicted, proving that the covenant was still in force. Nevertheless, the covenant also promised that when the curses had achieved their purpose God would be gracious, remember his commitment to the ancestors (the patriarchs and the exodus and conquest generations inclusively), respond to their prayers and their repentance, perform in them a heart transplant, and renew his covenant relationship with them (Deut 4:30–31; 30:1–10). The covenantal hope would never die. Moses anticipated the day in the distant future when the ideals of the covenant initiated with Abraham, established with his descendants at Sinai, and renewed on the Plains of Moab would be fully realized.[44]

Phase 4: The Fulfillment of Covenant Ideals in the New Israelite Covenant (Jer 31:27–40)

With our review of these three stages of the growth of the Israelite covenant, we have established the context for the final stage—at least as outlined in the Hebrew Bible—the new Israelite covenant. As anticipated, especially in Deut 29 and 31, the history of Israel in the promised land proved to be a history of failure—not of the covenant, but of the people. Finally, after centuries of rebellion, in 722 BCE Samaria and the Northern Kingdom of Israel fell to the Assyrians (2 Kgs 17), and in 586 BCE Judah and Jerusalem fell to the Babylonians (2 Kgs 24–25). Having had enough, YHWH brought on his people the full fury of the covenant curses as predicted in Lev 26 and Deut 28. Contrary to common opinion, the devastation of the land and the exile of its population did not mean the end of God's covenant with his people. Indeed, the prophetic warnings of judgment (especially Jeremiah and Ezekiel) were rooted in the covenant curses, which were essential elements of the covenant itself. In Daniel's remarkable prayer of confession, the exiled Judaean recognized that the judgment had transpired precisely as spelled out in the covenant (Dan 9:1–19, esp. vv. 7–14). As already noted, within the covenant itself YHWH declared that Israel's history would not terminate in judgment and exile. In the end he would remember his covenant and mercifully regather the people, renew the covenant, and restore their relationship with the land, thereby restoring in full the triangular covenant relationship. The prophets spoke variously of this new relationship as a "covenant of peace" (בְּרִית שָׁלוֹם, Isa 54:9–10; Ezek 34:25; 37:26), an "irrevocable (i.e., eternal) covenant" (בְּרִית עוֹלָם, Isa 55:3; 61:8; Jer 32:40; 50:5; Ezek 16:60; 37:26), and a "new covenant" (בְּרִית חֲדָשָׁה, Jer 31:31).

This perspective is particularly firm in the determinative text, Jer 31:23–40. From the broader context (30:1—33:26) it is obvious that in this "new covenant" text Jeremiah was concerned primarily—if not exclusively—with his own people Israel, and their

---

44. For fuller discussion of Israel's hopeful future in Deuteronomy, see below, "All Israel Will Be Saved: An Examination of Moses' Eschatological Vision in Deuteronomy," below, pp. 312–34.

relationship to God and the land they once occupied. Addressing the exilic situation (cf. 29:1–32), this segment opens with a thesis statement, announcing the reversal of the exile in 30:3: "Look, days are coming—the declaration of YHWH—when I will restore the fortunes of my people, Israel and Judah, says YHWH, and I will bring them back to the land that I gave to their fathers, and they shall take possession of it." As was true of God's cosmic covenant (33:20, 25), God had bound himself irrevocably to the nation and the Davidic house (33:14–26). Jeremiah anticipated the day when the covenantal triangle would be completely restored, a reality demonstrated concretely by the land being fruitful once more (33:1–13). Whereas the book of Isaiah—especially in its closing chapters—tends to universalize the scope of the covenant, here Jeremiah's focus was on his own people and his own land. The nations enter the picture only as agents of God's judgment (32:26–35) or as the objects of YHWH's destructive power (30:8–11), and not as participants in his salvation.

Jeremiah identified two problems that plagued the nation of Israel throughout their history and that the "new covenant" would correct. First, instead of internalizing the Torah and writing it on the tablets of their hearts, Israelites/Jews took pride in possessing the symbol of the covenant, the ten principles of covenant relationship inscribed on tablets of stone. Second, instead of "keeping" (שָׁמַר) the covenant, they broke it (הֵפֵרוּ אֶת־בְּרִיתִי, 31:32). We must note that the problems involving the covenant had always been exclusively Israel's problem. They did not lie with YHWH, who was fully and irrevocably committed to his people (cf. Lev 26:44; Judg 2:1), and for whom fidelity to the covenant was fundamental to his character (Exod 34:6–7; Deut 7:9; 32:4; Dan 9:4; etc.). Neither was there any problem with the covenant itself. YHWH's decisions are never flawed and he never creates a defective institution (Deut 32:4). The problems involving the covenant had always been Israel's issue. Jeremiah's covenantal vision of the relationships among YHWH, his people, and the land is perfectly continuous with the covenant that God had made with Abraham (Gen 17:7, 13, 19; 1 Chr 16:15–18 = Ps 105:8–11), confirmed with Israel at Sinai (Lev 24:8), and renewed with the new generation on the Plains of Moab (Deut 4:29–31). Through the new/eternal/peace covenant, Israel would be transformed from the inside out and finally realize the ideals of the covenant made long ago and anticipated by Moses in Deut 30.[45]

As envisioned in Jer 31:27–34, the "new" covenant involved four essential benefactions for Israel: (1) the internalization of the Torah (31:33b); (2) the renewal of the covenant, expressed in the formula, "I will be their God and they shall be my people" (31:33c); (3) the knowledge of God (31:34a); and (4) the forgiveness of sin (31:34b). Israel's faithlessness at Sinai (the golden calf incident; Exod 32) and at Kadesh-barnea (Num 13–14) demonstrated that none of these features characterized the generation as a whole that YHWH had rescued from Egypt. Despite having heard the Decalogue from YHWH's own mouth and having heard Moses recite it again as well as the "judgments" (מִשְׁפָּטִים) of the "Covenant Document" (סֵפֶר הַבְּרִית, Exod 34:3–4, 7), and despite having thrice declared their willingness to do "all that YHWH has spoken" (19:8; 24: 3, 7), obviously the Torah was not written on the nation's hearts. Despite having participated in the covenant ratification

---

45. Cf. Beckwith ("The Unity and Diversity of God's Covenants," 117), who notes that "the New Covenant does not abrogate the former covenants, but rather embraces and completes them."

ceremony and bound themselves on oath to YHWH (Exod 24:7–8), it is obvious that for Israel the words of the covenant formula (an adaptation of the marriage formula; cf. Jer 31:2) had not taken root in their minds. Despite having observed and benefitted from YHWH's "signs and wonders," whose goal was to declare to Israel (Exod 6:6–7; 10:2; etc.) and the Egyptians (Exod 7:5, 17; 8:18[22]; 14:4, 18; etc.) that their Savior was YHWH, it is obvious they did not know him. Despite YHWH's promise in Exod 34:6–7, that he forgives every kind of sin, and despite his provision of rituals to effect forgiveness, that generation's persistent rebellion in the desert and faithless refusal to receive YHWH's promise of land (Numbers 13–14) proved that they had forfeited the privilege of forgiveness.

But none of these features of the New Covenant was absolutely new.[46] There had always been new covenant Israelites who had the Torah of God in their hearts/minds (Gen 26:5; Num 14:24; Deut 6:6; Ps 119:11); who delighted in covenant relationship with God (Exod 29:45; Lev 26:12); who knew God (Exod 33:13; cf. Judg 2:10); and who rejoiced in the knowledge of sins forgiven (Lev 4:20, 26, 31, 35; 5:10, 13, 16, 18, 26[6:7]; 19:22). Examples include not only Abraham and faithful descendants like Moses, Boaz, David, and Josiah, but also gentile converts like Caleb, Rahab, and Ruth. Caleb presents an especially significant case, whom YHWH characterized as "my servant Caleb" (עַבְדִּי כָלֵב), "with him is a different spirit" (הָיְתָה רוּחַ אַחֶרֶת עִמּוֹ), and "he is full after me" (וַיְמַלֵּא אַחֲרָי).[47]

Then what was new? Obviously it was not the essence of the covenant, since everything promised in the New Covenant had already been promised in the Old. This suggests that rather than involving an absolutely new covenant Jeremiah envisions the renewal of the Old, except that this time YHWH guarantees that the ideals of the Old would be finally and fully realized. The newness of the New Covenant was found in the new divine initiative with respect to the entire people and in the nature of the covenant community itself, as captured in the word "all" (כֹּל, 31:34): "They will *all* know me, from the least to the greatest." Whereas in the past true covenant relationship had been experienced by only a few, the righteous remnant, for the masses the covenant remained an external reality, written on tablets of stone, but not on their hearts. It would not be so in the future that Jeremiah envisioned.

As in Jer 31:21–22, with this promise of the "new" covenant God looked forward to a new day when all Israel would embrace Him. At that time, the boundaries of spiritual Israel and physical Israel would finally be coterminous (Fig. 4.7), and the bond of commitment from both sides would be indissoluble. But this would not be a *new* covenant in an absolute sense.[48] Jeremiah anticipated no deliverance from the law as if, like Pharaoh,

---

46. Cf. Lehne (*The New Covenant in Hebrews*, 34), who rightly observes that the new covenant does not envision a new Torah, and that it involves the traditional covenant formula, and the promise of complete forgiveness, which is often encountered in the Hebrew Bible. However, she mistakenly identifies the internalization of the Torah and the knowledge of YHWH as new elements (cf. pp. 32–34).

47. On Caleb and the indwelling Spirit of God in the First Testament, see Block, "The View from the Top," 191–207.

48. Contra Pettegrew, "The New Covenant," 251–70, especially 53–54. Certain segments of the Qumran Community viewed Jeremiah's בְּרִית חֲדָשָׁה as "renewed covenant." See Talmon, "The Community of the Renewed Covenant," 12–13. Talmon writes, "He [Jeremiah] invokes God's promise to renew in the future the ancient covenant which he had established with the exodus generation (Jer

the law held the people in bondage. Nor would it signal any adjustment in God's standards of righteousness. Rather, it signaled a day when the Israelites would finally enjoy the freedom envisioned by the original Israelite covenant, a freedom that celebrates both the knowledge and the application of the Torah because it will be internalized in the hearts of all Israel. For all these reasons, read in context we should look upon Jeremiah's new covenant as a renewal and ultimate realization of the covenant that God had made long ago with Abraham, had established with the exodus generation of his descendants at Sinai, and had renewed with the Conquest generation on the Plains of Moab.

Figure 4.7
The Relationship between Physical Israel and Spiritual Israel
As Perceived by Moses and Jeremiah

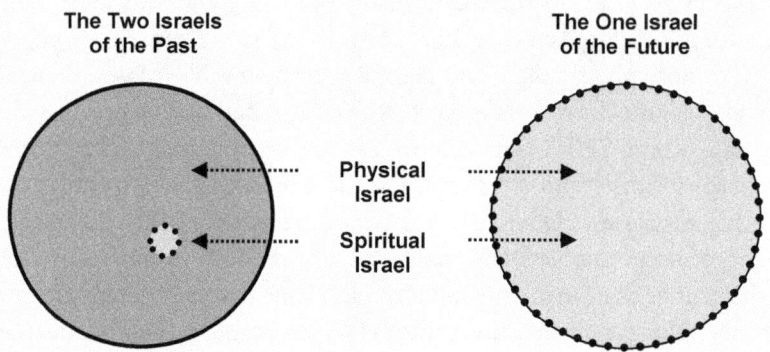

But what shall we make of the New Testament's disposition toward this renewed Israelite covenant? On this matter New Testament texts go in several directions. Sometimes they spiritualize the notion of Israel, which in the aftermath of the incarnation consists of all who believe in Jesus and are indwelt and sealed by the Spirit. It is well known that the Gospels present Jesus both as the Davidic Messiah and as the incarnation of YHWH, the God of Israel. In Matthew the renewed Israel consists of those whom Jesus has "saved" from the bondage of sin.[49] In the tradition of Isaiah, Matthew anticipates the universalizing of the body of the "saved" (Matt 28:19–20), while the book of Acts traces the process by which the covenant community expanded, each advance being signaled by a fresh outpouring of the Spirit of God (Fig. 4.8). The new covenant community began with Jews from all over the world who believed in Jesus (Acts 2:4, 33, 38), but successively incorporated Samaritans (half-Jews ethnically and spiritually) who believed in Jesus (Acts 8:14–17), Gentile proselytes ("God-fearers") in the land of Israel who believed in Jesus

---

31:32), and which had been suspended in the wake of the destruction of Jerusalem and the ensuing exile (Jer 31:15–22)." While Talmon's view of a "suspended" covenant is problematic (the blessings of the covenant had indeed been suspended, but the imposition of the curses demonstrated it was actually in force), his interpretation of the phrase, בְּרִית חֲדָשָׁה, is correct.

49. In using exodus language (σῴζω) and in naming Mary's child "Jesus" (= Hebrew *Jehoshua*) in Matt 1:21 God does not portray him as a second Joshua—Joshua was not involved in the exodus from Egypt and the conquest of Canaan is not presented as saving action—but as YHWH, whose salvation Moses memorialized by renaming Hoshea ("He saves") as Jehoshua ("YHWH has saved"; Num 13:16).

(Acts 10:44–48; cf. 11:16), and finally anyone in the world (represented by the Ephesian Christians) who believed in Jesus (Acts 19:6). Paul continued this spiritualizing tendency, applying the ancient covenant formula to the church: "We are the temple of the living God; as God said, 'I will live in them and walk among them, and I will be their God, and they shall be my people'" (2 Cor 6:16; cf. Gen 17:7; Exod 6:7; Deut 26:17; Jer 30:22; Ezek 36:28).[50]

Figure 4.8

The Expansion of the Covenant Community in the New Testament

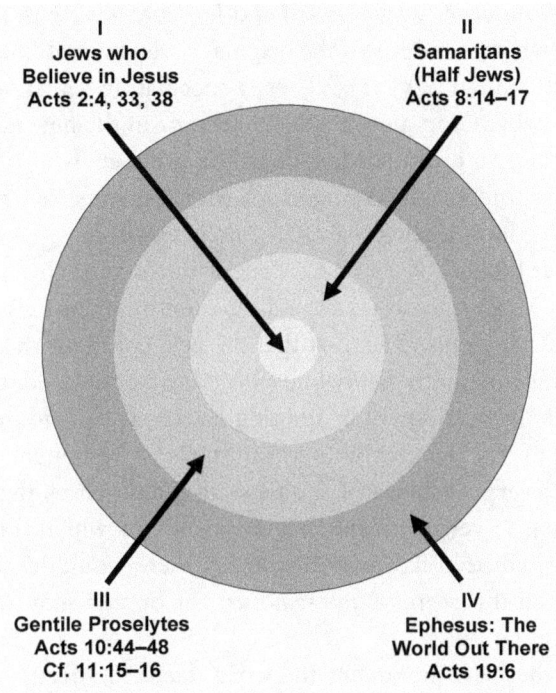

I
Jews who
Believe in Jesus
Acts 2:4, 33, 38

II
Samaritans
(Half Jews)
Acts 8:14–17

III
Gentile Proselytes
Acts 10:44–48
Cf. 11:15–16

IV
Ephesus: The
World Out There
Acts 19:6

However, we should not interpret this spiritualizing and universalizing move to mean that the ethnic/national nature of the covenant was either forgotten or superseded—as if the church replaced Israel in an absolute sense. On the contrary, in Rom 9–11 Paul emphatically declared that while Gentile believers have been grafted into the covenant community, a future for physical Israel remains. In these chapters Paul answers those who imagine that the spiritualization of Israel meant that from this point on physical descent from Abraham would lose its significance in the divine scheme; the church universal had supplanted and superseded the Israelite covenant community. However,

---

50. Paul's distinctive expression, "the Israel of God" (τὸν Ἰσραὴλ τοῦ θεοῦ) in Gal 6:16 is commonly interpreted as a reference to the church, the elect called out of all the nations. With Eastman ("Israel and the Mercy of God," 367–395), I interpret the phrase to refer, not to Christians as the new covenant community, but to the people of Israel (Paul's physical kin) for whom the apostle pleads for divine mercy. Similarly, Barclay, *Paul and the Gift*, 420–21, 445. Cf. Sanders, *Paul, the Law, and the Jewish People*, 176.

in these chapters he declares his passion "for my brothers, my physical relatives" (ὑπὲρ τῶν ἀδελφῶν μου τῶν συγγενῶν μου κατὰ σάρκα). Lest readers miss his identification, he adds, "They are Israelites" (οἵτινές εἰσιν Ἰσραηλῖται), and then lists their distinctive privileges in the divine soteriological agenda:

> To them belong the adoption (ἡ υἱοθεσία), the glory (ἡ δόξα), the covenants (αἱ διαθῆκαι),[51] the giving of the Torah (ἡ νομοθεσία), the worship (ἡ λατρεία), and the promises (αἱ ἐπαγγελίαι); to them belong the patriarchs (οἱ πατέρες), and from their race, according to the flesh, is the Christ (ὁ Χριστὸς) who is God over all, blessed forever. Amen (Rom 9:4–5).

Indeed in fulfillment of Deut 30:1–10 and Jer 31:31–37, with great excitement he anticipates the day when the ideals of the original covenant will finally be realized—all Israel will be saved (Rom 11:25–32).[52] I resist speculating under what circumstances this will transpire—whether in a millennial context or in the new heavens and the new earth, but it is difficult to imagine Moses and the prophets who followed in his train (like Isaiah, Jeremiah, and Ezekiel) being happy with contemporary supersessionists, for whom God's eternal commitments evaporate into irrelevance.

Whatever other biblical writers have done with the new covenant, in Heb 8:6–13 the author of Hebrews appears to take the discussion in an entirely new direction. On the surface this passage seems to suggest that the new covenant was necessary because the old covenant was inherently faulty and needed to be replaced; the author presents the superiority of the new covenant by quoting Jer 31:31–34, and in so doing provides the longest citation of any Hebrew Bible text in the New Testament. With strange logic he declares that the very existence of the new covenant proves that the old covenant was faulty. According to verse 7, if the first covenant—by which the author meant the Israelite covenant—had been flawless (ἄμεμπτος), there would have been no need for the new covenant. But this seems a *non sequitur*. The existence of something new need not mean the old was faulty.

Elsewhere in the New Testament the word ἄμεμπτος occurs four times, always with a high moral sense.[53] In the LXX the word translates תָּמִים, "perfect," a quality that

---

51. Despite the plural, Lehne misinterprets these statements (*New Covenant in Hebrews*, 72):
[W]e can surmise that Paul had primarily the *Abrahamic covenant* in view in Romans 9–11). Indeed throughout this section the Sinai covenant as such is never mentioned despite the discussion of the Law (in 9:30—10:13). Paul's focus is on God's election and call through his inscrutable mercy, for which Abraham serves as a paradigm." [emphasis hers].
The adoption, the glory, the covenants, the Torah, and the service of which Paul speaks are all tied to the covenant YHWH made with Israel at Sinai.

52. While the echoes of Isa 27:9 and 59:12 in Rom 9:26–27 are widely recognized, the echoes of Jeremiah's new covenant utterance are often overlooked: "all Israel" alludes to "they will all know me" (Jer 31:32); "this is my covenant with them" alludes to "this is the covenant that I will make with the house of Israel after those days" (31:33); and "when I take away their sins" alludes to "I will forgive their iniquity, and I will remember their sin no more" (Jer 31:34). Contra Beale (*A New Testament Biblical Theology*, 710) and many others (further bibliography is provided), Lehne rightly notes that "Paul is *here* referring to the *future* redemption of Israel, which would be closer to the original thrust of the prophecy on the NC" (*New Covenant in Hebrews*, 72 [emphasis hers]).

53. Luke 1:6 (of Zechariah and Elizabeth, who "were both righteous before God, walking

YHWH demanded of Abraham (Gen 17:1). Whatever ἄμεμπτος means elsewhere, it cannot mean that the first covenant was a mistake or that it was imperfect in its design, for as we have already noted, YHWH is perfect in character, in all his actions, and in his revelation. In context it probably means that YHWH intentionally built into the old covenant—which as we have seen is characterized as irrevocable and eternal—some aspect that was intended to become obsolete. That element cannot have been the heart of the covenant, for the foundational features of the new covenant as described in Jer 31:31–40 were also fundamental to the old covenant.

The book of Hebrews is clear on what that displaced element is: the cultic system represented by the high priest, the tabernacle, and the sacrifices, which for Israel represented YHWH's graciously revealed gift whereby imperfect but believing Israelites could maintain their covenant relationship with him. While the specific forms were distinctive for the Israelite covenant established at Sinai, the divine provision for fellowship with God through shadow sacrificial and priestly institutions antedates this covenant by millennia. Indeed, ever since our ancestors left the Garden of Eden the faithful have been relating to God through these rituals in special sacred spaces. The tabernacle and its cult represented a fully revealed and divinely legitimated replica and shadow of the true heavenly temple for Israel. Now that Christ has been revealed as the real and eternal sacrifice, there is no more need for tabernacle, priest, or sacrifices for the covenant people to experience forgiveness of sins, internalization of the Torah, knowledge of God, and the presence of their covenant Lord.

Rather than elaborating on the flaws of the old covenant, the author of Hebrews is quick to declare that the problem lay with Israel (Heb 8:8). Had they [or humanity in general] been faultless, there would have been no need either for the shadow institutions or even for the work of Jesus Christ himself. Both of these represented God's gracious provision for fellowship with himself in a post-fall world. Indeed, the author of Hebrews is clear, that the sacrifice of Christ is the key to our covenant relationship with God. However, Hebrews also views Christ's work as the key to ancient Israel's well-being, as well as the well-being of all the redeemed from the beginning of time: "For this reason he is the mediator of a new covenant, so that those who are called may receive the promised eternal inheritance, because a death has occurred that redeems them from the transgressions under the first covenant" (9:15; NRSV).

At this point one also wonders about the traditional interpretation of another statement in Heb 12:22–24:

> But you have come to Mount Zion and to the city of the living God, the heavenly Jerusalem, and to innumerable angels in festal gathering, and to the assembly of the firstborn who are enrolled in heaven, and to God, the judge of all, and to the spirits of the righteous made perfect, and to Jesus, the mediator

---

blamelessly [ἄμεμπτοι] in all the commands and ordinances of the Lord"; Phil 2:15 (of believers, who are to be blameless [ἄμεμπτοι] and innocent, children of God without blemish in the midst of a crooked and twisted generation, among whom you shine as lights in the world"; Phil 3:6 (of Paul, who claims to have been blameless [ἄμεμπτοι] with respect to the righteousness called for by the Torah); 1 Thess 3:13 (of believers, whose hearts are to be blameless [ἄμεμπτοι] in holiness before our God and Father, at the coming of our Lord Jesus with all his saints.

of a new covenant, and to the sprinkled blood that speaks a better word than [the blood of] Abel" (ESV).

Assuming "the blood of" is an appropriate insertion (it is lacking in the Greek), what is the significance of this "blood of Abel"? Most commentators understand it to be the blood that cries out for vengeance for his murder (Christ's blood is better because it offers forgiveness). Admittedly elsewhere "the blood of Abel" refers to his death (Matt 23:35; Luke 11:51), but it is doubtful that reading is intended here.[54] Rather, this text should be read in the light of the general argument of the book and in particular the previous reference to Abel in Heb 11:4: "By faith Abel offered to God a more acceptable sacrifice than Cain's. Through this act he [Abel] received approval as righteous, God himself giving approval to his gifts; he died, but through his faith he still speaks" (NRSV). Abel's offering was better than Cain's, but Jesus' blood is superior to the blood of Abel's sacrifice, because the latter too was part of the shadow system. Christ's blood provided the grounds for even Abel's acceptance with God—along with all other believers since the beginning of time who participated in shadow rituals.

Herein lies the significance of Jesus' immortal words at his institution of the Lord's Supper (Eucharist): "This cup is the new covenant in my blood. Do this, as often as you drink it, in remembrance of me" (1 Cor 11:25; cf. Luke 22:20). The sacrifice of Jesus Christ provides the basis for God's establishment of any relationship with him, pre-Abraham, under the Israelite covenant, and in our own time after of the incarnation. When First Testament believers presented their offerings in faith and with pure hearts, like we, they too experienced the atoning work of Christ (planned before the foundation of the world.[55]

The Administrative [Royal] Covenant

In Gen 1–2 humanity's relationship with God derived naturally from their respective roles as Creator and created. Initially Adam and Eve accepted their status as vassals and vice-regents of God. These texts highlight humanity's privileged and honorific role. First, human beings were created last, as God's climactic act in creation. Second, among all living creatures (נֶפֶשׁ חַיָּה), God created humankind (Hebrew אָדָם) specially to function as his image, that is, to serve as his viceroy, his representative and authorized deputy in governing the world (Gen 1:26–28; Psalm 8). Third, Gen 2 casts Adam as a king delighting in the garden in which he had been placed, with Eve as his queen.[56] Fourth, later interpretation of the genealogy in chapter 5 identifies Adam as "the son of God" (Luke 4:38). In the ancient world, "son" functioned as a title for a vassal, opposite "father," the designation for the suzerain (2 Kgs 16:7).

---

54. While he goes a different direction than I suggest, Allen (*Hebrews*, 593–94) offers a helpful critique of the traditional interpretation.

55. Cf. Matt 25:34; Eph 1:4; Heb 4:3; 1 Pet 1:20; Rev 13:8; 17:8.

56. On Adam's status/role as king in a royal garden, *rather than* as priest in a temple, see Block, "Eden: A Temple?" 3–32.

Along with noting humankind's honorific status, Gen 1–2 highlights the obligations laid on humankind as vassals of God. In relation to God, they were to submit to him, accepting the divinely established boundaries of moral and economic behavior (2:16–17), and generally governing the world on his behalf, as he would were physically present (1:26–28). In relation to the world Adam was charged to "serve" (עָבַד) and "guard" (שָׁמַר) the garden (2:15).[57] With this choice of expressions the narrator declares that the world was not created for us, but that we were created for it. Humankind's function within the cosmic administrative order was to maintain the triadic triangle binding Creator, realm, and the living occupants of that realm in a vibrant and harmonious relationship (Fig. 4.9). In the preliterate world of Gen 2, the two special trees in the garden symbolized the blessings and curses that became regular features of ancient treaties.

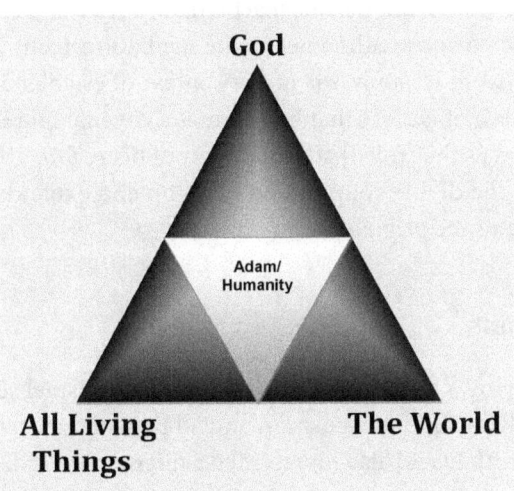

Figure 4.9
The Role of Adam/Humanity
in the Cosmic Administrative Order

Since Adam's role arose naturally from his having been created by God, since the pre-fall world functioned perfectly according to the divine plan, and since the term בְּרִית is missing from the accounts, there is no need to seek a covenant in this environment. However, it did not take long for matters to change, specifically for the vassal to betray his Suzerain and his charge. As a consequence of the "king's" rebellion the *shalom* of the kingdom disintegrated, and to this day "all creation" groans under the weight of human sin and awaits the day of humanity's redemption, for that will also be the day of the cosmos' liberation as well (Rom 8:19–23).

---

57. For further discussion, see Block, "To Serve and to Keep," 116–42.

The Noachian [Second Adam] Covenant

Even though Adam and Eve (and all their descendants) were banished from Eden as a consequence of their rebellion against the divine Suzerain, the narratives of Gen 4–9 suggest that individuals were still able to relate positively to God.[58] Whether or not this was made possible by a covenant that God instituted with humanity in the context of their expulsion from the garden, the great deluge was God's response to pervasive human and cosmic rebellion (Gen 6:1–8) and fulfilled the curse represented by the Tree of the Knowledge of Good and Evil: all land life perished. Obviously, even in the midst of the judgment humankind's status as vassal of God and caretaker of the earth was maintained. Unlike Adam, Noah was a faithful steward of the world in his charge. Complying with the "absurd" orders of his Suzerain, he provided for the rescue of a remnant of all land creatures from the divine fury. God's promise to "establish" (הֲקִים) his covenant with Noah (Gen 6:18) and the attention paid to Noah in Gen 9 reflect his administrative role within the context of the triadic cosmic covenantal arrangement. However, as noted earlier, Gen 6:18 is ambiguous. Does אִתָּךְ, "with you," mean the covenant that YHWH establishes would be with Noah, hence Noachian, or does it mean that he will establish his covenant with the cosmos with Noah as the mediating agent (like Moses at Sinai)? Both interpretations seem to apply, for in the context of establishing his covenant with the cosmos in Genesis 9, it is clear that he assumes a covenantal relationship with Noah as a second Adam and as the [royal] administrator of his realm. This status is clear from Gen 9:1–7, in which the divine commission picks up and expands on many features of God's original charge to the original Adam in Gen 1–2.

The Davidic Covenant

If the covenant involving YHWH, the land of Canaan, and Israel served as a microcosm of the covenant involving God, the cosmos, and all living creatures, then it makes sense that God's covenant with David also represented a microcosm of his covenantal relationship with Noah, a second Adam (Fig. 4.10). While the monarchy was anticipated from the beginning of Israel's history (Gen 17:6, 16; 35:11; 49:10; Num 24:17; Deut 17:14–20; 1 Sam 2:10), the covenant with their king was formalized with David (2 Sam 7; 2 Chr 17; Ps 89; 132). Based on the frequency of occurrences of his name, the man after God's own heart—that is, the person he had in mind from the beginning (1 Sam 13:14; cf. Deut 17:15)—was the most significant human character in Israel's history. Key benefactions attending this covenant include the honorific title of "son of God" (2 Sam 7:14; Pss 2:7; 89:27–28[26–27]) and the promise of eternal title to the throne of Israel (2 Sam 7:11–16; 23:5). However, several significant obligations accompanied these privileges: demonstrating an exemplary life of Torah righteousness and humility (Deut 17:14–20;

---

58. Note YHWH's acceptance of Abel's offering (Gen 4:4), people calling upon the name of YHWH in the days of Enosh (4:26); Enoch walking with God (5:22–24); Noah finding grace in YHWH's eyes (6:8) and being recognized as righteous (אִישׁ צַדִּיק), blameless (תָּמִים), walking with God (6:9), and being commissioned in advance on YHWH's behalf to preserve remnants of humanity and the animals during the Great Deluge (6:13–22).

Ps 1:1–3), and governing Israel justly as God's viceroy (Ps 72; Isa 32:1–8). Although David himself acknowledged the special significance of his kingship for Israel (2 Sam 7:23–27), he also recognized its universal significance: וְזֹאת תּוֹרַת הָאָדָם ("This is a revelation concerning humanity" (2 Sam 7:19). The cosmic implications of the election of David to the throne of Israel are celebrated by psalmists (Ps 2; 72; 110) and prophets alike (Isa 11:1–9; Mic 5:1–4[2–5]). The Davidic king's role was not only microcosmic of Adam's role; he would actually become a second Adam.

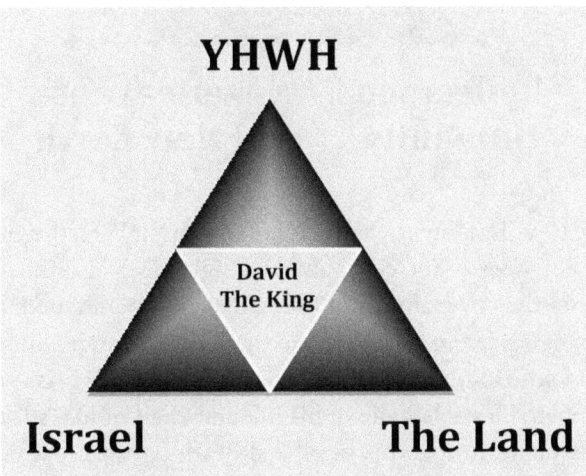

Figure 4.10
The Role of the King
in Israel's Administrative Order

The New Testament paints a complex picture of Jesus. On the one hand he is God, the cosmic Lord and Creator of heaven and earth (John 1:1–2; Col 1:16–17), incarnate in human form, and on the other he is a second Adam. Luke traces Jesus' ancestry back to creation, viewing him as the heir of the original Adam, whom he gives the honorific title of "son of God" (Luke 3:38). As a new Adam Jesus is the fountainhead of a new and righteous race (Rom 5:14–19; 1 Cor 1:15, 45) and embodies all humanity. And as the perfect image of God (Rom 8:28–29; Col 1:15; Heb 1:2–4), he reconciles the cosmos to God, exercises authority over the whole cosmos (Matt 28:18–19), and administers all things perfectly (Col 1:18–20). Indeed, throughout the book of Revelation Jesus, portrayed as "The Lamb," is the focal point of the new heavens and the new earth (Rev 19–21).

Despite this cosmic vision of the role of Jesus Christ, the New Testament devotes more time to his royal role as heir to and fulfillment of the Davidic covenant. Although he performs functions normally associated with priests and prophets, "Christ" is a fundamentally royal title. He is the Messiah, the son of David (Matt 1:1; 21:9; Mark 10:47; Luke 18:39; Rom 1:3; 2 Tim 2:8; Rev 5:5; 22:16), "the Lion of the tribe of Judah" (Rev 5:5), and "the son/root of Jesse" (Luke 3:32; Acts 13:22; Rom 15:12). The frequent allusions to Isaiah 53 in the New Testament cast him in the role of the servant of YHWH, a self-sacrificing, but fundamentally Davidic figure (Fig. 4.11).

Figure 4.11
The Role of Jesus Christ in the Eschatological Cosmic Administrative Order

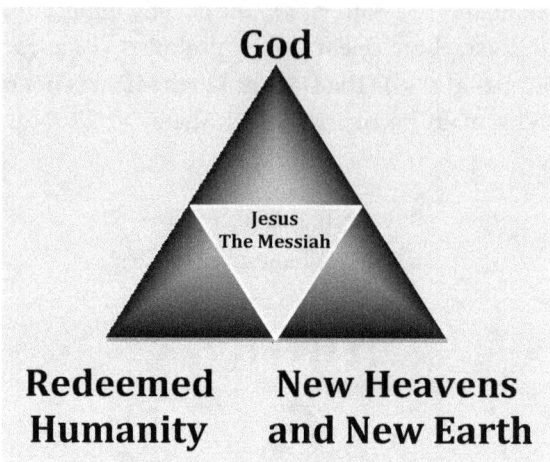

Although the New Testament identifies Jesus with YHWH, the God of Israel, which locates him at the top apex of the covenantal triangle, he is also the divinely appointed ruler through whom the covenant is put into effect and maintained, which puts him at the heart of the triangle. Herein lies the key to the New Testament understanding of covenant relationship with God. As the Davidic Servant of YHWH (Isa 52:13—53:12), and as "the Good Shepherd" Jesus laid down his life on behalf of his "sheep" (John 10:11).[59] By Jesus' own statement, through his sacrificial death on the cross he effected the new covenant (Luke 22:20; 1 Cor 11:25), reconciling humanity and the cosmos to God (Col 1:20), liberating us and the cosmos from the bondage of sin (Rom 8:18–25), and making us new creations, so we may function as true and righteous images of God (2 Cor 5:17). With the longest citation of any Hebrew Bible text in the New Testament, Heb 8:8–13 links Jesus' priestly and sacrificial work explicitly to the new covenant envisioned by Jeremiah (31:31–34). Whereas the prophet's original vision did not extend beyond ethnic Israel, the sacrificial work of Christ provides the basis for all restored relationships with God and for our salvation. Under the old version of the Israelite covenant, the temple worship involved replica ritual acts by which, if offered in faith by righteous worshipers, the sacrifice of Christ, slain before the foundation of the world (1 Pet 1:19–20) was applied to Israelite saints. Now that the true and eternal sacrifice has come, the rituals by which God's covenant with Israel was maintained are obsolete.[60] Indeed, the effectiveness of all the covenants—cosmic, Israelite, and royal—is grounded in the work of Christ. As cosmic Lord, he is the source and end of all things (Col 1:16–17); as YHWH he is the redeemer of his people—ethnic and spiritual Israel (Rom 10:13); and as the son of God and son of David he guarantees the administration of all the covenants to the praise and the glory of God.

---

59. For further discussion of Jesus as the Messianic Servant, see Block, "My Servant David," 49–46.

60. For fuller discussion of how the Israelites experienced forgiveness and enjoyed fellowship with God through the sacrificial rituals he provided, see Block, *For the Glory of God*, 247–59.

5

Deuteronomic Law[1]

WITHIN THE NARRATIVE WORLD of the Hebrew Bible, the laws contained in the book of Deuteronomy represent the fourth major collection of ethical ordinances in the Pentateuch—after the Decalogue (Exod 20:2–17), the Book of the Covenant (Exod 20:22—23:19; cf. סֵפֶר הַבְּרִית, in Exod 24:7), and the Holiness Code (Lev 17–26). I refer to these texts as Israel's constitutional documents because they define the boundaries of Israel's conduct before the deity (YHWH), each other, and the outside world.

The Nature and Function of Deuteronomic Law

Scholars do not agree on what constitutes Deuteronomic Law. Most limit it to Deut 12–26—often called the Deuteronomic Code (DC). However, some add chapter 28, while others limit the DC to explicitly legal prescriptions within these chapters. Indeed, many scholars believe that the first task of students of this material is to peel away layers of later additions, especially the theological commentary, in order to isolate the original legal core, which presumably constituted the original Deuteronomic law book.

While some scholars think that some form of Deuteronomy inspired Hezekiah's reforms at the end of the eighth century BCE, more consider the earliest version of Deuteronomy to be the product of Josiah's reform—a view often linked with Martin Noth's proposal for a Deuteronomistic History (DH).[2] This is the scroll that Josiah's workers reportedly "found" in the Temple (2 Kgs 23:8–20), and which the young king used to support his centralization of the cult, along with economic and judicial power in court-appointed officials in the late seventh century BCE. Around the time of the destruction of Jerusalem and the exile of the Judeans to Babylon editors transformed the legal document into a profoundly theological treatise. This edition highlighted the judgment of YHWH as the inevitable consequence of the nation's rebellion against him. A second Deuteronomistic edition of the book of Deuteronomy was produced in the postexilic

---

1. This is a stylistically modified version of an article previously published in *The Oxford Encyclopedia of the Bible and Law*, ed. Brent Strawn; 2 vols. (Oxford: Oxford University Press, 2015) 1:182–95. I am grateful to the editor and the publisher for their kind permission to republish it here.

2. Noth, *The Deuteronomistic History*.

period (after 539 BCE), the most notable additions being chapters 4 and 29–30.³ While freely allowing for later editing, Eckart Otto has recently proposed a four-stage process: (1) the late pre-exilic law book, associated with Josiah's reform (chapters 12–26, 28), revising and expanding the Book of the Covenant; (2) an exilic "Horeb redaction," adding chapters 5–11; (3) a late exilic "Moab redaction," adding chapters 1–4, 29–30; (4) a final postexilic edition, associated with the production of the Pentateuch/Hexateuch.⁴

The relationship of chapters 27–28 to chapters 12–26 is unclear. In genre and content chapter 27 diverges significantly from chapter 26: a monologue by Moses (chapters 5–26) gives way to successive speeches by Moses and the elders (27:1–8), Moses and the Levitical priests (27:9–10), and finally Moses alone (27:11–26). Although the move was anticipated in 11:26–32, apart from 27:9–10, chapter 27 directs the gaze across the Jordan to a future ritual on Mounts Ebal and Gerizim. Since the opening of chapter 28 is linked thematically and stylistically with 26:16–19, it appears that chapter 27 was secondarily inserted in its present location. Even so, chapter 28 is distinct generically from chapters 12–26, consisting not of laws, but of blessings (28:1–14) and curses (28:15–68). Blessings are less common, but curses are more often associated with ancient Near Eastern treaties than with laws. Nevertheless, having blessings and curses follow the laws brings Deuteronomy into remarkable conformity with Hammurapi's laws, which ended similarly.⁵

Even so it is not clear that the Deuteronomic Law should be limited to chapters 12–26 and 28, and isolated from the surrounding materials. Admittedly the heading in 12:1, "These are the statutes and judgments . . . ," seems to signal a section break, and together with 26:16, which echoes the vocabulary of 12:1, creates a literary frame around 12:2—26:15. However, by this reasoning, chapters 5–11 should also be included in the Deuteronomic Law, since this section is framed by similar statements (5:1; 11:32). Furthermore, unlike the Book of the Covenant, the Holiness Code, and Deut 12–26, chapters 5–11 begin with a recitation of the Decalogue, the basic constitutional document (5:6–21). The editors of the book have reinforced the impression that chapters 5–11 belong to Deuteronomic Law by providing an otherwise unprecedented double heading before 5–11: "Now this is the Torah (הַתּוֹרָה) that Moses set before the Israelites. These are the stipulations (הָעֵדֹת), decrees (הַחֻקִּים) and the judgments (הַמִּשְׁפָּטִים) that Moses spoke to the Israelites" (4:44–45).

The expressions in verse 45 all have a legal flavor: (1) הָעֵדֹת is cognate to Akkadian *adê* and Aramaic *ʿdy*, both of which are used in treaty contexts, hence "covenant stipulations."⁶ (2) חֻקִּים speaks of decrees prescribed and inscribed in writing by a person with power.⁷ (3) While מִשְׁפָּטִים ("judgments") may refer narrowly to casuistic laws (cf. Exod 21:1)—with the form deriving from precedent-setting legal judgments—

---

3. For discussion, see Crüsemann, *The Torah*, 204–212; Preuss, *Deuteronomium*, 164; on the editing of the DH, McKenzie, "Deuteronomistic History," 2:160–168.

4. Otto, *Deuteronomium 1,1–4,43*, 231–57.

5. Kitchen, and Lawrence. *Treaty, Law and Covenant in the Ancient Near East*. 1:179–185; Roth, *Law Collections from Mesopotamia and Asia Minor*, 135–40.

6. *HALOT*, 791.

7. Cf. *HALOT*, 346–347.

in Deuteronomy and elsewhere the expression refers to divine judgments regarding appropriate behavior of God's vassal, Israel. This impression is reinforced by suffixed forms of the expression (מִשְׁפָּטַי/מִשְׁפָּטָיו, "my/his judgments") and specific statements that punctuate chapters 5–11 (5:31; 6:1, 20; 7:11; 8:11; 11:1). Remarkably, while these terms had been introduced in 4:1 and 5, apart from the frame (12:1; 26:16) similar statements are missing in 12–26. Given these textual signals, to limit the Deuteronomic Law to 12–26 seems unwarranted.

Form-critical considerations support this conclusion. The book of Deuteronomy is dominated by three speeches attributed to Moses (1:6—4:40; 5:1b—26:19 and 28:1–68; 29:1[2]—30:20). Whatever the origins of these addresses, the structure of chapters 5–26 and 28 parallels ancient Near Eastern treaties: historical prologue (5:1–5), stipulations (5:6—26:19), blessings and curses (28:1–68). Assuming chapters 5–11 belong to the Deuteronomic Law, the covenantal nature of Deuteronomic Law is reinforced by frequent appearances of the word בְּרִית ("covenant") in this second address (eleven times), and an additional sixteen times in the materials that frame this address (4:13, 23, 31; 28:69[29:1]; 29:8[9]; etc.). However, unlike other ancient Near Eastern legal collections, Deuteronomy does not involve laws established by a king, but calls for loyalty to the divine king demonstrated through conduct involving all of life (a point that holds true for the Israelite king as well; see Deut 17:14–20). And unlike ancient Near Eastern treaties, Deuteronomy does not call for loyalty to a foreign ruler and/or his successors. Although בְּרִית occurs only once in chapters 12–26 (17:2), treating this material as a separate document disconnected from its literary environment weakens its theological and covenantal force.

While chapters 5–26 contain many laws, retaining the link between 5–11 and 12–26 raises the question whether "law" is an appropriate designation for either. Several considerations argue against this. First, the term תּוֹרָה, rendered *nomos* in the Septuagint and generally "law" in English, does not mean primarily "legislation," but "instruction, teaching," which may occur in many forms (including historical reminiscences in chapters 1–4 and the Song in chapter 32). In Deuteronomy this word exhibits the same semantic range as Greek διδαχή or διδασκαλία ("teaching"). Second, although Moses is frequently portrayed as "commanding" (√צוה) the people (1:18; 3:18; 12:21), the narrator's locutionary expression for his verbal action is represented by √דבר, "to speak" (1:1, 3; 4:45; 31:1), or √אמר, "to say" (1:5), while his illocutionary goal is represented as "teaching" (√למד, 4:1, 5, 14; 6:1; 31:19, 22) or "setting [the Torah] before" (√נתן or שִׂים לִפְנֵי) the people (4:8, 44; 30:1, 15, 19).[8]

Third, despite the new introduction in 12:1, neither the style nor tone of the address changes appreciably after chapter 11. Law-like commands are sprinkled throughout chapters 12–18, but the style of most of this material is scarcely more legal than chapters 6–11. Concentrations of laws do not occur until chapters 19–25, but even here motive clauses and God-talk contribute to a profoundly theological and parenetic flavor. Furthermore, chapters 12–26 contain the rhetorical features found in chapters 5–11: (1) the "I-you" form of direct address, along with the less personal third-person casuistic

---

8. On locutionary and illocutionary speech action, see Vanhoozer, *Is There a Meaning in This Text?*, 207–259.

forms; (2) *Numeruswechsel*, the alternation of singular and plural forms, presumably for rhetorical effect; (3) appeals to Israel to keep alive the memory of their past and YHWH's past grace (15:15; 16:3, 12; 24:9, 18, 22; 25:17–19); (4) references to past divine commands (e.g., 20:17: "as YHWH your God commanded you"), promises ("as YHWH your God promised you"; see, e.g., 12:20; 15:6; 18:2; 26:18–19), and oaths ("as he swore to you/your ancestors"; see, e.g., 13:18[17]; 19:8; also 28:9); (5) exhortations to self-watch and diligence in obedience (12:1, 13, 19, 28, 30; 13:1[12:32], 19[18]; etc.); (6) appeals to love (13:4[3]) and fear YHWH (13:5, 12[4, 11]; 14:23; 17:13, 19) and for wholehearted (13:4[3]; 15:7, 9–10; 17:17, 20; etc.) and full-bodied (13:4[3]; 26:16) devotion; and (7) a vast array of positive (Deut 12:25, 28; 13:18[17]; etc.) and negative (15:9; 17:17; 19:10; etc.) motive clauses. Other rhetorical—as opposed to legal—features continue as well: appeals to and quotation of divine speech (17:16; cf. 5:28b–31; 9:12–14; 10:1–2, 11), recollections of past events (23:4–5[3–4]; 25:17–18; 26:5–9), and the introduction of interlocutors and prescribed responses (12:20; 15:9; 17:14; 18:21; 20:3; 26:3, 5–10, 13–15).

The didactic and parenetic tone of chapters 12–26 is reinforced by sensitivity to the people's personal desires with respect to the consumption of meat away from the central sanctuary (12:15, 20–22) and the desire for a king (17:14–20). In sum, treating Deut 12–26 primarily as "law" and limiting "law" to this section obscures its theological agenda and invites readers to expect legislation like that passed in our own modern legislatures. The entire book is "Torah"—which is best understood as instruction in righteous living as defined by the spokesman (Moses) for the divine suzerain (YHWH). Chapters 12–26 cannot be rightly understood independently of Deuteronomy as a whole and separated from chapters 5–11; nor can the individual laws in 12–26 be rightly understood apart from the hortatory and theological comments within which they are embedded.

The Interpretation of Deuteronomic Law

Through the years, critical interpretation of the Deuteronomic Law has taken several different forms. The following are neither mutually exclusive nor necessarily sequential, but four different approaches may be highlighted. First, some have focused on the forms of the laws. Albrecht Alt distinguished between casuistic and apodictic law, the former being generally cast in the third person and in the "If . . . then" form, while the latter were cast as imperatives in the second person ("you shall/shall not . . . ").[9] Less helpfully, Alt argued that casuistic laws were rooted in the Canaanite legal milieu, while the apodictic laws were authentically Israelite.[10] However, comparison with ancient law collections and treaty texts demonstrates that both forms were widely used from the early second millennium and often occurred within the same documents.[11]

Second, for a time many scholars focused on searching for the origins of the laws. Three major responses emerged. (1) Deuteronomy and its laws originated in Levitical

---

9. Alt, "The Origins of Israelite Law."

10. Ibid., 278–332.

11. Kitchen and Lawrence, *Treaty, Law and Covenant*, 3:267–276; cf. Weinfeld, "The Origin of Apodictic Law," 63–75.

priestly circles. In the spirit of Moses and cognizant of long-standing traditions they tried to revive a fidelity to YHWH demonstrated by abhorring all things pagan.[12] (2) Deuteronomic Law originated in prophetic circles. The portrayal of Moses as a prophet and Deuteronomy's passion for social justice, critique of kingship, and passionate stance against apostasy have much in common with prophets like Elijah and the writing prophets of the eighth–sixth centuries BCE.[13] (3) Deuteronomic Law derives from courtly scribal circles. The emphasis on the fear of YHWH and wisdom, opposing themes of life and death and deed and reward/retribution, the disposition toward the natural order, and the portrayal of Moses as teacher recall the wisdom literature.[14] Given Moses's traditional roots in the tribe of Levi (Exod 6:16–26), Deuteronomy's explicit portrayal of him as a prophet (Deut 18:15, 18; 34:10), and his didactic method, none of these proposals should surprise us.

Third, some have focused on the relationship between the Deuteronomic Law and nonbiblical texts, particularly second millennium BCE law collections like the Laws of Lipit-Ishtar, the Laws of Eshnunna, the Laws of Hammurapi, the Hittite Laws, and the Middle Assyrian Laws. Since a fragment of an eighteenth–seventeenth century BCE legal text in Akkadian that resembles the Laws of Hammurapi has surfaced in Hazor,[15] we should in principle entertain the idea of a widespread Mesopotamian legal tradition that could have found its way to Israel. But how directly elements from that tradition influenced the Deuteronomic Law is debated.[16] If the Book of the Covenant has directly borrowed and transformed the Laws of Hammurapi,[17] then the possibility certainly exists for contact with Deuteronomy. However, demonstrating influence is not a simple matter, and the links may simply reflect long-standing and widespread legal traditions.[18]

More recently the focus has shifted away from non-biblical law codes to non-biblical treaty traditions, especially from the Neo-Assyrian period. The discussions tend to focus on the covenant curses of Deut 28, but the influence is thought to extend to the laws, especially Deut 13. Some have argued that the authors of Deuteronomy had access to a written record of loyalty oaths (*adê*) imposed by Neo-Assyrian emperors on their vassal states, and that the authors of Deuteronomy inverted such oaths by using their language to inspire unqualified and total loyalty to YHWH.[19] Appealing to the tablet containing Esarhaddon's loyalty oath in the temple at Tayinat,[20] some suggest a copy of Esarhaddon's loyalty oath was on display in the temple in Jerusalem.[21]

---

12. Von Rad, *Deuteronomy*, 23–27; *Studies in Deuteronomy*, 66–67.

13. On locutionary and illocutionary speech action, see Vanhoozer, *Is There a Meaning in This Text?*, 207–259.

14. Alt, "The Origins of Israelite Law."

15. Ibid., 278–332.

16. Kitchen and Lawrence, *Treaty, Law and Covenant*, 3:267–276; cf. Weinfeld, "The Origin of Apodictic Law," 63–75.

17. Von Rad, *Deuteronomy*, 23–27; *Studies in Deuteronomy*, 66–67.

18. Nicholson, *Deuteronomy and Tradition*, 68–70.

19. Weinfeld, *Deuteronomy and the Deuteronomic School*.

20. See Ebeling, "Tel Hazor Excavations."

21. Otto, "Rechtsformen in Deuteronomium xii–xxvi und im Mittelassyyrischen Kodex der Tafel

But this interpretation seems unlikely. First, the lexical and conceptual links are too tenuous to argue for the Deuteronomic Law's certain dependence on the Neo-Assyrian treaties.[22] Second, since Neo-Assyrian emperors were heirs of a long treaty tradition extending back to the third millennium BCE,[23] it is unwise to associate the Deuteronomic Law exclusively with Neo-Assyrian treaties. In fact, many features of Pentateuchal covenantal texts exhibit a closer affinity with late second millennium Hittite treaties than with later Neo-Assyrian counterparts.[24] However, given the geographic and cultural distance between the Hittites and ancient Israel, direct borrowing seems unlikely. Although no suzerain-vassal treaties have been discovered in Egypt, recent investigations recognize strong evidence for the conceptual, covenantal world of Deuteronomy in Egyptian texts from the later second millennium BCE.[25] Geographically situated next door to Israel, Egypt could have mediated covenantal concepts that we recognize more clearly in Hittite texts.

Fourth, seeking to explain the evolution of the text, with keen redaction-critical eyes European scholars particularly have tried to identify layers of text within the Deuteronomic Law, peeling them off like an onion, until they arrive at an original core. Martin Rose identifies four strata in these materials: Stratum I (the legal core) derives from the time of Hezekiah (715–696 BCE or slightly later). Stratum II modifies the laws slightly and is dated to the time of Josiah (639–609 BCE or slightly later); Stratum III represents the older Deuteronomistic edition from the time of the destruction of Jerusalem (587 BCE) and Judah's exile. This "preacher" addresses the reader/hearer with plural pronouns, fixes the law in a historical situation (prior to crossing the Jordan), and emphasizes obedience to God. Stratum IV represents the younger Deuteronomistic edition from the end of the Babylonian exile (539 BCE) to the early postexilic period. This editor concretizes the prohibitions on local cult sites and emphasizes the need for their destruction in the sharpest tones.[26] While comprehensive and tidy, such atomization of the text often depends upon modern Western definitions of literary propriety and style, and obscures the rhetorical nature and force of the final canonized form of the second address.

A fifth approach currently gaining momentum explores how the Deuteronomic Law relates to other constitutional texts, especially of the Covenant and the Holiness Codes. Scholars generally agree that the Deuteronomic Law builds upon the Book of the Covenant,[27] but the nature of that relationship is disputed. Some identify the Book of the Covenant as a *traditum* (source text) that has been updated as the *traditio* (derived text) in the Deuteronomic Law to suit a new historical situation.[28] Indeed some

---

A (KAV 1)."

22. David Wright, *Inventing God's Law*.
23. Wells, "The Covenant Code and Near Eastern Legal Traditions."
24. See Dion, "Deuteronomy 13"; Otto, "Treueid und Gesetz."
25. Lauinger, "Some Preliminary Thoughts on the Tablet Collection in Building XVI from Tell Tayinat."
26. Stackert, "The Treaty of/and Deuteronomy Once Again."
27. Zehnder, "Building on Stone? Deuteronomy and Esarhaddon's Loyalty Oaths (Part 1)."
28. See Kitchen and Lawrence, *Treaty, Law and Covenant* 1:1–16; 2:5–9.

argue that just as the author of the Book of the Covenant intentionally borrowed from and subverted Laws of Hammurapi,[29] so the authors of the Deuteronomic Law used the language and concepts of the Book of the Covenant, not to confirm or reaffirm the latter, but to subvert, marginalize, replace, and deny its legitimacy.[30] While many consider the Priestly law and the Holiness Code as antedating the Deuteronomic Law,[31] recently some have argued that what the authors of the Book of the Covenant did to the Laws of Hammurapi, and what the Deuteronomic Law did to the Book of the Covenant, the authors of the Holiness Code have done to the Deuteronomic Law—that is, intentionally superseded, subverted, and supplanted the prior text even while using its language.[32] However, it seems far more likely that successive constitutional documents would build on, supplement, and reinforce antecedent texts rather than replace them. Differences in detail often relate to changes in envisioned circumstances, rather than to fundamental and conceptual disagreements.[33] Furthermore, this approach involves an anachronistic view of the nature of textual authority.[34] Even if the Book of the Covenant intentionally refuted the Laws of Hammurapi, a foreign text with alien views of deity and justice, or if the Deuteronomic Law intentionally subverts the Neo-Assyrian treaty tradition, it seems unlikely that one Pentateuchal source would deliberately repudiate the legitimacy of another—especially when both claimed divine authority.

Although most critical scholars associate the Deuteronomic Law either with the reforms of Josiah or Neo-Assyrian treaty forms, some have recently argued that the laws of Deuteronomy derive from the Persian period. Among the factors that supposedly point to a Persian era provenance for the Deuteronomic Law are the following:[35] (1) The monarch plays no role in *Urdeuteronomium* (17:14–20 is deemed a later addition). (2) Assuming no state infrastructure or state administration, texts like 12:14 (בְּאַחַד שְׁבָטֶיךָ, "in one of your tribes"; cf. also 12:5) presuppose tribal structures. (3) It lacks specific references to Judah, Jerusalem, and the temple (בֵּית יהוה in 23:19[18] is vague). (4) It projects a vision of the future, rather than the present—YHWH "will choose" (יִבְחַר) the place to establish his name (12:5, 11, 14; etc.). (5) The so-called name theology suggests a time when the temple no longer existed. (6) The Elephantine papyri (fifth century BCE) seem oblivious to any cult centralization program, as envisioned in Deut 12.

However, given the emphases in other postexilic writings on right worship in Jerusalem, the state of the Davidic house, and Judah (1–2 Chronicles, Haggai, Zechariah,

---

29. See Berman, "CTH 133 and the Hittite Provenance of Deuteronomy 13"; Zehnder, "Building on Stone? Deuteronomy and Esarhaddon's Loyalty Oaths (Part 2)."

30. Morschauser, "'Do Not Look to Egypt?'"

31. Rose, *5. Mose: 12–25. Einführung und Gesetze*.

32. Levinson, *Deuteronomy and the Hermeneutics of Legal Innovation*; Lohfink, "Fortschreibung? Zur Technik von Rechtsrevisionen im deuteronomischen Bereich"; Otto, "Aspects of Legal Reforms and Reformulations in Ancient Cuneiform and Israelite Law," 160–196, esp. 192–196; Otto, *Deuteronomium 1,1–4,43*, 231–238.

33. Fishbane, *Biblical Interpretation in Ancient Israel*, 5–19.

34. David Wright, *Inventing God's Law*.

35. Levinson, *Deuteronomy and the Hermeneutics of Legal Innovation*, 149–153; Stackert, *Rewriting the Torah*, passim; idem, "The Holiness Legislation and Its Pentateuchal Sources"; but see LeFebvre, *Collections, Codes, and Torah*, 71, n. 54; Otto, *Deuteronomium 1,1–4,43*, 234.

Malachi), it seems unlikely that a postexilic author as profoundly theological as the author of Deuteronomy would have been silent on all these matters. By presupposing a date as late as the Josianic or Persian period, we have eliminated an equally plausible explanation for these features, namely, that the Deuteronomic Law antedates the monarchy, and to the extent that it speaks of them, they are perceived as future realities. However, only a minority of scholars accepts this interpretation.

Some Postulates of Deuteronomic Law.

If we reject Deuteronomy's own statements regarding its origin,[36] we may freely speculate how or under what circumstances the Deuteronomic laws were produced, but our conclusions remain just that—speculations. In the end the best clues to the laws' significance reside in the ordinances and the contexts in which they occur. If we interpret the Deuteronomic laws as we have them, that is, embedded within a profoundly theological and hortatory composition that includes chapters 5–11, and is cast as Moses' second oration, we may identify a series of postulates that undergird them. Some of these are unique to Deuteronomy; others reflect perspectives expressed either in earlier legal collections or in the Sinai narratives.

First, Deuteronomy views the law as a divine gift. Not only does Moses speak according to all that YHWH commanded him (1:3; 4:5, 14; 6:1), but also the revelation of the covenant stipulations, ordinances, and judgments (מִשְׁפָּטִים, חֻקִּים, עֵדֹת) is presented as a gracious divine act—along with the rescue from Egypt and the gift of the land promised to the ancestors—for Israel's good, their survival, and their assurance of divine approval (6:20–25). Indeed, their receipt of the law at Horeb is presented as a unique event in human history (4:9–14, 32–36), and their possession of the Torah makes them the envy of the nations, because it symbolizes the deity's nearness and because of its uniquely righteous character (4:5–8).

Second, Deuteronomy envisions a community based upon covenant rather than on law.[37] Because the Deuteronomic Law ties law to covenant it differs significantly from ancient Near Eastern legal collections, but carries forward and strengthens the Book of the Covenant. As noted earlier, the notion of covenant underlies the structure of the book, but the covenantal foundation of Deuteronomic Law is also highlighted by the elevenfold use of the word בְּרִית in the second address, the identification of the Decalogue as "the tablets of the covenant" (לֻחוֹת הַבְּרִית, 9:11, 15), and the reference to the sacred container as "the ark of the covenant of YHWH" (אֲרוֹן בְּרִית יהוה, 10:1–8; 31:9, 25–26). Even more significantly, Deuteronomy is laced with covenantal vocabulary in its description of YHWH's relationship to Israel and of the Israelites' relationship to each other:[38] (1) adaptations of the covenant formula, "I will be your God and you will be my people" (26:17–18); (2) ubiquitous references to YHWH as "your God" and "our God";

---

36. Haran, "Holiness Code."

37. Stackert, *Rewriting the Torah*; idem, "The Holiness Legislation and Its Pentateuchal Sources"; also Levinson and Stackert, "Between the Covenant Code and Esarhaddon's Succession Treaty."

38. McConville, "Deuteronomy's Unification of Passover and Maṣṣôt: Vogt, *Deuteronomic Theology and the Significance of Torah*, 171–191 et passim.

(3) special designations for Israel: "a holy people belonging to YHWH" (7:6; 14:2, 21; 28:9); "his treasured people" (עַם סְגֻלָּה, 7:6; 14:2; 26:18); YHWH's "very own possession" (עַם נַחֲלָה, 4:20; cf. "YHWH's portion," חֵלֶק יהוה, 32:9); YHWH's "sons" (בָּנִים אַתֶּם לַיהוה, 14:1; cf. 8:5); (4) special verbs expressing suzerain-vassal relationship: "to serve YHWH" as his vassal (√עבד, 6:13; 10:12, 20; 11:13; 28:47); "to fear YHWH" (√ירא, 6:2, 24; 10:12, 20; 14:23; 17:19); "to demonstrate love for YHWH" (√אהב, 5:10; 6:5; 7:9; 10:12; 11:1, 13, 22; 13:4[3]; 19:9; cf. 30:6, 16, 20) as YHWH has demonstrated love for Israel (4:37; 7:13; 10:15, 18; 23:6[5]); "walking in YHWH's ways" (הלך + בִּדְרָכָיו, 5:33; 8:6; 10:12; 11:22; 19:9; 26:17; 28:9; cf. 30:16), or "walking after YHWH" (√הלך + אַחֲרֵי יהוה) as opposed to walking after other gods (6:14; 8:19; 11:28; 13:3[2]; 28:14); "to act with/keep covenant faithfulness" (עָשָׂה + חֶסֶד, 5:10; √אֶת־הַחֶסֶד שמר [of YHWH]); "to keep the covenant" (שמר + הַבְּרִית√, 7:9, 12 [of YHWH]), as opposed to "breaking" YHWH's covenant (הֵפִיר הַבְּרִית, 31:16, 20 [of Israel]), or "abandoning it" (√עזב, 29:24[25]); "holding fast to YHWH" (דָּבַק בַּיהוה, 4:4; 10:20; 11:22; 13:5[4]; cf. 30:20), as opposed to "abandoning him" (√עזב, 28:20; cf. 31:16); and, of course, "keeping and doing" his commands (√שמר + √עשה) or "keeping his commands by doing them" (שָׁמַר לַעֲשׂוֹת, 4:6; 5:1; etc.). Unlike the treaties imposed by Hittite and Assyrian emperors on lesser vassals, either through conquest, or by cowing them into submission, YHWH redeemed his people from the brutality of Egypt and invited them to a covenant relationship that has as its goal their good, their life, and their well-being.

Third, the primary objective of Deuteronomic Law is the creation of a righteous society. This goal is declared in slogan form in 16:20: "Righteousness, righteousness you shall pursue." Since this statement follows immediately after the charges to appoint judges and the warning not to distort justice (מִשְׁפָּט, vv. 18–19), most translations and commentators render צֶדֶק צֶדֶק in 16:20 as "Justice only justice." However, this interpretation overlooks the shift in vocabulary and the variegated nature of Deuteronomic Law. The word צֶדֶק refers to behavior in accord with an established standard, in this instance the covenant stipulations as defined by YHWH.[39] Elsewhere Deuteronomy applies the root √צדק to YHWH—who always acts perfectly, justly, faithfully, and uprightly (32:4)—and to the ordinances and judgments, whose righteous character is acknowledged by the nations (4:8). According to 6:25, YHWH acknowledges full obedience as righteousness (צַדִּיקִים), while 24:13 identifies returning a debtor's cloak at nightfall as a specific act of righteousness (צְדָקָה). Although social justice is rightly viewed as a dimension of righteousness, the types of actions cited immediately after 16:20 involve religious behavior (16:21—17:7). Within chapters 12–28 צֶדֶק applies to fidelity to the divine judgments (הַמִּשְׁפָּטִים) regarding right behavior in relationship to YHWH (e.g., 16:21—17:7), one's family (e.g., 24:1–5), the community (e.g., 24:17–22; 25:13–16), and even to the environment (22:6–7).

Fourth, Deuteronomic Law is especially concerned to protect those who are economically and socially vulnerable from abuse at the hands of those with economic and social power. This is evident in the Deuteronomic version of the Decalogue. Addressed primarily to the heads of households, the Decalogue seeks to rein in their propensity to exercise authority in self-interest rather than the interests of the household. This is reflected

---

39. Najman, *Seconding Sinai*.

especially in the Deuteronomic version of the Sabbath command, which grounds the ordinance, not in the divine pattern of creative work and rest (Exod 20:11), but in the need for rest by all—including animals—who work in the domestic unit, and reminding the heads of households of Israel's own experience of abuse in Egypt (Deut 5:12–15). Deuteronomy's modification of the commands on coveting represents part of the same trajectory.[40] The same concern is reflected in frequent appeals to care for widows, the fatherless, aliens, and Levites (10:18–19; 14:29; 16:11, 14; 24:17–22; 26:12–13), as well as particular instructions for charitable treatment of indentured servants (15:1–18), a foreign wife taken in battle (21:10–14), the son of the unloved wife in a bigamous household (21:15–17), domestic animals (22:1–4), a wife who is wrongfully divorced (24:1–5), and the widow of a man who has died without an heir (25:5–10), to name just a few.

The instructions on kingship (17:14–20) are part of this picture. In the ancient world kings were thought to have three primary roles: (1) to ensure the administration of justice within the kingdom; (2) to secure the nation's well-being in the face of foreign threats; and (3) to patronize the national cult in order to promote the goodwill of the gods of the land by building temples for them. However, this paradigm often degenerated to exploitation of royal power over citizens in self-interest. Deuteronomy's law of the king is not critical of kingship in principle, but seeks to curb royal excess. These instructions declare that the primary responsibility of Israel's kings was to embody covenant righteousness by submitting to the Torah, fearing YHWH, walking in his ways, and remembering that they are brothers within the Israelite population. Like heads of households and other leaders, kings exist for the well-being of those they lead, rather than the reverse.

The remarkable notion of king as brother of his subjects suggests to some that egalitarian ideals distinguished ancient Israel from the nations around.[41] Significantly, the Deuteronomic Law does not restrict this notion to royal authorities. Although the term אָח often refers to actual brothers (13:7[6]; 25:5–9), the expression usually applies to fellow Israelites, as opposed to non-Israelites (15:3; 23:20–21[19–20]; 24:7, 14). According to the Deuteronomic Law all leaders must treat the rest of the Israelites as "brothers": kings (17:15, 20), Levitical priests (10:9; 18:2, 7), prophets (18:15, 18), judges (1:16); and those with economic power are "brothers" to their servants (15:2–3, 7, 9, 11–12; 23:20–21[19–20]; 24:7, 14). From a sociological perspective, this egalitarian impulse may derive from the simple origins of the people or the peripheral contexts in which the Israelites lived—constantly threatened by outside powers[42]—which makes it even more remarkable that simple people living in such peripheral contexts should have produced such profound literature in general and such sophisticated laws in particular.

Within the narrative world of Deuteronomy, this egalitarian notion derives from several sources. First, as suggested by the extensive use of the word אָח, "brother" (40+ times), Deuteronomy perceives Israelites in the main as ethnically cohesive, sharing descent in a common ancestor, Jacob/Israel. This conviction is reflected also in references to Israel as בְּנֵי יִשְׂרָאֵל ("sons of Israel") in 23:18[17] and 24:7, and in references to "your

---

40. See Pakkala, "The Date of the Oldest Edition of Deuteronomy."
41. Cf. Sonnet, *The Book within the Book*.
42. Cf. Mendenhall, "The Conflict between Value Systems and Social Control."

fathers, Abraham, Isaac, and Jacob" (6:10; 9:5, 27; cf. 1:8; 29:12[13]; 30:20; 34:4) in allusions to the patriarchal traditions, especially to YHWH's covenant with the fathers (5:3; 7:12; 8:18; cf. 4:31; 29:24[25]; 31:16, 20; 34:4), his promise/oath of land to the fathers (12:1; 19:8; 26:3, 15; etc.), and the "creedal" recognition of the ancestral narratives (10:22; 26:5–10). However, this sense of "brotherhood" extended beyond Israel. The ordinance of 23:8[7] forbids abhorring an Edomite, because he is Israel's brother, alluding to the portrayal of Esau, the eponymous ancestor of the Edomites, as Jacob's brother in the patriarchal narratives (cf. 2:8; Gen 25:19–34).

Second, the Deuteronomic Law grounds this egalitarian vision in the Israelites' shared experience of slavery in Egypt (5:6, 15; 6:12, 21; 7:8; 8:14; 13:6, 11[5, 10]; 15:15; 16:12; 24:18, 22; etc.), redemption/rescue by YHWH (4:32–40; 11:2–4; 13:6, 11[5, 10]; 15:15; 16:1; 20:1; 21:8; 24:18; 26:8), survival of divine judgment at Horeb (9:7–26), and testing in the desert (8:2–16; 11:5–6; cf. 4:3–4; cf. 29:4–5[5–6]).

Third, although the Deuteronomic Law does not use the language of *imitatio dei*, 10:17–19 calls on the Israelites to extend egalitarian compassion to resident aliens (גֵּר); like YHWH they are to demonstrate covenant commitment (√אהב) to them with concrete acts of love, remembering that once they too were aliens in Egypt (v. 19; cf. 23:8b[7b]; 24:22). Indeed, the Deuteronomic Law extends the prescribed compassion for marginalized natives (widows, fatherless, Levites) to resident aliens (10:18; 14:29; 16:11, 14; 24:19–21; 26:12–13), as well as the prohibition on oppressing Israelite hired servants (24:14). Elsewhere the Deuteronomic Law calls on Israelites to offer asylum to fugitives fleeing slavery under a foreign master (23:16–17[15–16]).

A fifth postulate is that *Deuteronomic Law reflects a profoundly democratic impulse*. The egalitarian impulse acknowledged above should not be confused with modern egalitarianism, which understands the concept in profoundly sociopolitical terms, that is, people enjoy equal status and equally free access to positions of power. Nor should we anachronistically impose our notion of democracy (one person, one vote), as opposed to autocracy, on this postulate. The social world of ancient Israel was pervasively patricentric, which meant that male heads of households governed domestic affairs, and elders, a collection of male heads of households, governed the affairs of the community. Accordingly, the Decalogue in Deut 5, and most of the charges in 6–11 and ordinances in 12–26 are addressed to the heads of households, whom the Deuteronomic Law holds primarily responsible for the pursuit of "righteousness, only righteousness" (צֶדֶק צֶדֶק, 16:20).

Many understand 16:18—18:22 as a sort of *politeia*, a utopian constitution with a strong centralized government able to enforce conformity to the Deuteronomic Law.[43] This section is also significant for those who suggest Deuteronomy was composed to bolster royal agendas of centralization and secularization of Israelite society.[44] It deals successively with judges and legal administration (16:18—17:13), the king (17:14–20), Levitical priests (18:1–8), and prophets (18:9–22)—institutions perceived as instruments supporting centralized power. Most scholars believe that 17:14–20 actually curbs royal behavior, but the king's position as head of state is taken for granted. In 16:18

---

43. Weinfeld, *Deuteronomy and the Deuteronomic School*, 74–110.

44. Levinson, *Deuteronomy and the Hermeneutics of Legal Innovation*, 98–143; Weinfeld, *Deuteronomy and the Deuteronomic School*, 233–236, 168–171.

judges are viewed as professionals who would replace priests at local sanctuaries, with the tribunal at the central sanctuary assigned the task of resolving insoluble cases.[45] The law concerning priests in 18:1–8 supposedly reflects the elimination of local sanctuaries, conceding to those who served there a role at the central sanctuary.

On closer inspection it is difficult to see how this *politeia* bolsters royal power or supports a revolutionary agenda of centralization. None of these sections is actually addressed to the office holders, as if they are now the focus of attention. Concerning judges, not only are the people charged to appoint them (16:18a), but also the instructions on the administration of justice that follow (vv. 18b–19) are addressed to the people—that is, heads of households, who are ultimately responsible for each community's well-being. Furthermore, the central tribunal in 17:8–13 is not portrayed as a group of magistrates who reinvestigate difficult cases (a sort of Supreme Court of appeal), but as a continuation of the tradition of Moses, who submitted the most difficult cases to YHWH for an oracular decision (Exod 18:13–23). As for the royal ordinance, it authorizes the people to install a king whom YHWH chooses, and then describes for the people's benefit how the king is to conduct himself (17:14–20). Similarly, the ordinance concerning the priests (18:1–8) is not addressed to priests—they are spoken of in the third person—the addressees ("you") continue to be the heads of households, if not the Israelite population in general. This ordinance has less to do with new status for Levitical priests than challenging the population to ensure their well-being. How the instructions regarding prophets (18:9–22) support either a centralizing or secularizing agenda is not obvious. Admittedly prophets like Samuel and Nathan supported the kings, particularly David and Solomon, but they had no real political power, and unlike other ancient Near Eastern prophets, in Israel they are often depicted as functioning in opposition to kings. Furthermore, the intent of this ordinance is to guide *the people* in their disposition toward prophets and to reassure them that YHWH would provide persons who would carry on the prophetic work of Moses. This focus on heads of households as the locus of government and guardians of orthodoxy (12:29—13:19[18]) and right ethical conduct continues through chapter 26, and extends to the blessings and curses in chapter 28. Rather than interpreting the alternation of singular and plural forms (*Numeruswechsel*) as evidence of divergent sources, this literary phenomenon serves a rhetorical function. The use of the singular in the Decalogue suggests this form involves individual Israelites, while the plural addresses Israelites as whole.[46]

Sixth, Deuteronomic Law demands exclusive and unqualified allegiance to YHWH. This perspective contrasts starkly with the religious situation outside Israel, where patron deities willingly tolerated their devotees' simultaneous worship of other gods. In this respect chapters 12–26 carry forward the principal agenda of chapters 5–11, which had repeatedly called for love and service of YHWH with all one's heart/mind (לֵב), being (נֶפֶשׁ), and resources (מְאֹד, 6:4–5; 10:12–13; 11:13; cf. 13:4–5[3–4]), and which had identified "the evil" (הָרַע) as violating the covenant and going after other gods (4:25; 9:18; cf. 17:2–7). The notion is expressed most emphatically in the severe warnings against apostasy in chapter 13. Whether they be a prophet, a close relative, or anyone else in the community, anyone who encourages defection from YHWH to another god is to

---

45. Block, "'You shall not covet your neighbor's wife.'"
46. Sparks, "The Egalitarian Spirit in Biblical Law."

be executed to purge the evil from their midst (v. 6[5]), and in the last case, the offender's entire village is to be utterly destroyed (√חרם, verses 16–19[15–18]).

The Deuteronomic Law's program of centralization of worship is fundamental to this commitment. Introduced in chapter 12, the concept keeps recurring, being alluded to by references to "the place that YHWH will choose for his name," a formula that occurs six times in this chapter and fifteen times hereafter (14:23–25; 15:20; 16:2, 6–7, 11, 15–16; 17:8, 10; 18:6; 26:2; cf. 31:11). The policy demands destruction of all Canaanite shrines and the obliteration of the names of the gods of the land from their installations (12:2–3; cf. 7:1–5). Instead of worshiping YHWH in a multiplicity of places, the Israelites are invited to make pilgrimages to the place he will choose to establish his name. Some view this call for centralized worship as a theological revolution, replacing notions of real divine presence, symbolized by the כָּבוֹד ("glory"), with a more abstract view of God, symbolized by "the name of YHWH" (שֵׁם יהוה).[47] However, this interpretation has recently been challenged from several directions. Not only are worshipers invited "to the [very] presence of YHWH" (לִפְנֵי יהוה, 12:7, 12, 18; etc.),[48] but also YHWH's choice of a place "to put his name" is best interpreted more concretely, alluding to the practice of officials imprinting their names on land they claimed and deities imprinting them on the places they had chosen for their residence, that is, the temple.[49] The idiom has less to do with the nature of divine presence manifested than with YHWH's claim to ownership of the land and his desire to meet with Israelites in worship. Here Israelites could come to see the face of YHWH (31:11; cf. 16:16); hear the Torah read (31:11); learn to fear YHWH (14:23; 31:9–13); rejoice before YHWH (12:12, 18; 14:26; 16:11–12, 14; 26:11); eat before YHWH (12:7, 18; 14:23, 26, 29; 15:20; 18:6–8); present their offerings/sacrifices (12:11, 26–27) and tithes (14:22–27); consecrate the firstborn of the herd or flock (15:19–23); celebrate the three annual pilgrimage festivals of Passover (16:1–8), the Festival of Weeks (Pentecost, 16:9–12), and the Festival of Booths (16:13–17; 31:9–13); receive the divine verdict on insoluble legal cases (17:8–13); recall YHWH's saving and providential grace (26:1–11); share gifts of charity with those marginalized (26:12; cf. 10:12–22); and demonstrate communal solidarity in worship (12:12; 14:27–29; 16:11). This was also the place where Levites served in the name of YHWH (18:6–8).

It is commonly thought that the Deuteronomic Law's vision of centralization was absolute; supposedly abrogating and replacing the altar law in Exod 20:24, which seems to authorize simultaneous worship in more than one place.[50] When the Israelites have destroyed every Canaanite shrine in the land (12:1–3), YHWH will choose a place to which he will invite his people to eat and celebrate in his presence—a place, in short, for ongoing fellowship with him (12:5–12). The impression that after that ritual activity elsewhere will be strictly forbidden seems to be strengthened by 12:13–14: Israelites are not to offer burnt offerings in every place they see, that is, wherever they like.

47. Ibid., 118.

48. Wilson, *Out of the Midst of the Fire*, 66–73.

49. Halpern, *The Constitution of the Monarchy in Israel*, 226–233; McBride, "The Polity of the Covenant People"; Nelson, *Deuteronomy*, 213.

50. Levinson, *Deuteronomy and the Hermeneutics of Legal Innovation*, 98–143; Weinfeld, *Deuteronomy and the Deuteronomic School*, 233–236, 168–171.

However, the vision of a centralized cult may not have been as absolute as we have thought. First, although some interpret "burnt offerings" [עֹלֹת] in 12:13 as representative of all types of offerings,[51] it is possible the word is intended more narrowly. Not all offerings were totally consumed on the altar. Furthermore, the lists of offerings relating to the central sanctuary in Deuteronomy all omit שְׁלָמִים, offerings of well-being.

Second, the instructions that follow seem to open the door to sacred observances in the towns where the people live (vv. 15–27). The verb √זבח, which in Deuteronomy always and elsewhere usually refers to sacral slaughter, suggests that the Deuteronomic Law views any consumption of meat as a sacrifice of sorts.[52] This interpretation is reinforced by 14:1–21, which identifies the Israelites as "sons" (בָּנִים) of YHWH their God, a holy people (עַם קָדֹשׁ לַיהוה), chosen from all the nations to be God's treasured people (עַם סְגֻלָּה), and then authorizes for human consumption the flesh of the kinds of creatures that YHWH accepts as sacrifices. This provision may be rooted in the people's status as a holy people (עַם קָדֹשׁ לַיהוה, 14:2), which recalls the inscription on the High Priest's medallion (Exod 28:36).

Third, Deut 16:21 anticipates people building an altar of YHWH for themselves. Strictly speaking the text prohibits a sacred pole (אֲשֵׁרָה) next to the altar. The expression, "for yourself" (לְךָ), seems to assume the legitimacy of private altars, in contrast to the altar at the central sanctuary. The statement also contrasts with Exod 20:24–25, which consistently speaks of the altar as built for YHWH.

Fourth, although Deut 27:5–7 involves a pre-settlement context, it calls for the erection of an altar on Mount Ebal for whole burnt offerings to YHWH and well-being offerings, which the people are invited to eat as they celebrate before YHWH (לִפְנֵי יהוה). Several factors suggest that this place was not intended as the permanent "place that YHWH would choose to set his name": (1) YHWH will not identify that place until the people are secure in the land (12:10); (2) the instructions for constructing the altar and the ceremonies at the site recall Exod 20:24–26, on the one hand, and 24:5, on the other, rather than the altars associated with the tabernacle or the temple; and (3) the tabernacle, which represented the central sanctuary in premonarchic times (Josh 22:19, 29), is nowhere in view.

Fifth, the Deuteronomic Law frequently speaks of the Levites "in your gates" (12:12, 18; 14:27, 29; 16:11, 14; 26:12) or "from any of your gates out of all Israel" (18:6). Since "your gates" represents metonymically the towns of ordinary Israelites, apparently Levitical priests were not restricted to Levitical towns (cf. Num 35:1–8; Josh 21:1–42; 1 Chr 6:39–66[54–81]; 13:2). Inasmuch as 18:1–8 assumes that Levitical priests who go to the central sanctuary have access to the priestly perquisites there, we may reasonably suppose that in the outlying communities Levites were also serving "in the name of YHWH," tending to the spiritual needs of the people. This would involve a host of religious and ritual exercises, including instructing the people in the Torah (Deut 33:10), ministering at critical moments in villagers' lives (marriage, births, deaths), and officiating at local religious observances. It is doubtful the people's

---

51. Weinfeld, ibid., 233–236.

52. Römer, "Deuteronomy in Search of Origins," 118–119; Tigay, *Deuteronomy*, 62. McConville ("Singular Address") reverses the significance of the singular and plural forms.

religious fidelity could be maintained with only three mandated annual festivals at the central sanctuary, and difficult to imagine them routinely going to the central sanctuary to worship from the farthest corners of the land—since for many people this would have been a three or more days' walk.[53]

Sixth, while biblical narratives do not speak explicitly of Levitical priests' involvement at local cult centers, anecdotal evidence in the DH suggests that altars dotted the landscape. Many of these were legitimate. Samuel began priestly service at Shiloh, the central sanctuary (1 Sam 2:18—3:21), but he also built an altar to YHWH at Ramah (7:17), pleaded with Israel to repent of their sin (7:3–4), prayed for them (vv. 5, 8), led the people in water rituals and fasting before YHWH (v. 6), presented whole burnt offerings to YHWH (vv. 9–10), and led the people in commemorative rituals of thanksgiving (v. 12). Later he performed sacrificial rituals at the high place in Zuph (9:11–14), and hosted a sacrificial occasion with Jesse and his family in Bethlehem (16:1–5).

Without criticism, elsewhere we read of altars at Ophrah (Judg 6:24, 26), the threshing floor of Araunah (2 Sam 24:18–25), Gibeon (1 Kgs 3:4), and on Mount Carmel (1 Kgs 18:30–35; cf. Elijah's references to YHWH's altars [pl], 1 Kgs 19:10, 14). These installations contrast with illegitimate altars at Bethel and Dan (1 Kgs 12:32–33; 13:1–5), in the cities of Samaria (1 Kgs 13:32), and those associated with Ahaz (2 Kgs 16:4) and Manasseh (2 Kgs 21:3–5), etc. In light of these texts, it seems that within the Deuteronomic framework acceptable worship to YHWH could be conducted away from the central sanctuary.

In sum, while scholars have interpreted the Deuteronomic vision of centralized worship and Josiah's reforms as absolute, this image should probably be modified. Centralized worship by the entire nation would have united Israel in their memory of YHWH's saving actions and bolstered a faith that claims that "YHWH alone is our God" (Deut 6:4–5). However, life happened in homes and communities. Among other functions, it seems the Levitical priesthood was instituted to promote faith and ethical living throughout the land of Israel. Although the Deuteronomic historian holds the kings largely responsible for the nation's demise, particularly for their introduction of pagan practices to the central sanctuary, the book of Judges suggests that spiritual recidivism did not always happen from the top (Judg 3:7; 6:25–27; 17–18). Indeed, the case of Micah and Jonathan, the grandson of Moses (Judg 18:30), proves that in outlying regions the temptation to apostasy and compromise on matters of faith and ethics was strong. Ultimately the nation's abandonment of YHWH resulted in their exile, in fulfillment of the curses of Deut 28:15–68.

The Afterlife of Deuteronomic Law.

The influence of the Deuteronomic Law on the rest of the Hebrew Bible and on the New Testament is well documented. In the first instance, the generic designation for this part of Deuteronomy ("the Torah Document" [סֵפֶר הַתּוֹרָה], 28:61; 29:20[21]; 30:10; 31:26; known outside the book as "the Torah of Moses" [תּוֹרַת מֹשֶׁה], Josh 8:31–32; 23:6; 2 Kgs

---

53. Weinfeld, *Deuteronomy and the Deuteronomic School*, 218.

14:6; 23:25; Neh 8:1; Dan 9:11, 13; Mal 3:22[4:4]), was extended to the entire book of Deuteronomy and ultimately to the Pentateuch as a whole (Matt 5:17; Luke 24:44; Acts 28:23; Rom 3:21; etc.). While scholars debate the direction of influence, literary and conceptual links with the Deuteronomic Law pervade the Psalter and the prophets, and extend to the New Testament. It is widely recognized that in the Gospels Jesus cites the book of Deuteronomy more than any other book in the Hebrew Bible, and that allusions to Deuteronomy occur throughout the epistles, both Pauline and General. Indeed, it could be argued that with Jesus' dyadic adaptation of the Shema and Lev 19:18 in "the Great Commandment" he captured the heart and covenantal essence of the Deuteronomic Law: "You shall love the LORD your God with all your heart and with all your soul and with all your mind . . . and you shall love your neighbor as yourself" (Matt 22:37, 39; Mark 12:29–31; cf. Luke 10:27).

6

In the Tradition of Moses

The Conceptual and Stylistic Imprint of Deuteronomy
on the Patriarchal Narratives[1]

A Survey of Approaches to the Relationship between Deuteronomy and the Patriarchal Narratives Interpretation

AFTER TWO CENTURIES OF critical investigation, scholarly opinion on the relationship between Deuteronomy and the rest of the Pentateuch has reached no consensus. The options available today include the following:

1. Moses was the author of the entire Pentateuch. The Talmud represents this position,[2] and Christians generally accepted it until the Enlightenment. It is widespread among laypeople and still occasionally defended by conservative scholars,[3] though the latter often allow for updating of geographical and historical matters.[4]

2. The authority of the Pentateuch derives from an historical Moses, and it contains substantial materials he may have written (e.g., the speeches in Deuteronomy; cf. 31:9–13), but the books that make up this corpus were composed later.[5]

3. The so-called "deuteronomic" elements in the Pentateuch reflect the antiquity of deuteronomistic style and theology ("proto-Deuteronomy"), which may be identifiable in the Decalogue and which came to full bloom in the book of Deuteronomy.[6]

---

1. Weinfeld, *Deuteronomy and the Deuteronomy School*, 190–209.

2. According to *Baba Bathra* 14b, "Moses wrote his own book and the portion of Balaam and Job."

3. See Allis, *The Five Books of Moses*; Archer, *A Survey of Old Testament Introduction*, rev. ed., 89–26; Young, *An Introduction to the Old Testament*, rev. ed., 42–46; Merrill, *Deuteronomy*, 22–23 (though technically Merrill comments only on the authorship of Deuteronomy).

4. Grisanti, "Deuteronomy," 459–61; idem, "Josiah and the Composition of Deuteronomy," 110–38.

5. For a pre-monarchic date for Deuteronomy, see Vogt, "'These Are the Words Moses Spoke,'" 61–80. For a date in the time of the United Monarchy, see Block, "Recovering the Voice of Moses," *JETS* 44 (2001): 385–408; reprinted in idem, *Gospel according to Moses*, 21–51. Wenham suggests that Genesis was not written much later than 950 BCE. Wenham, *Genesis 1–15*, xliv-xlv.

6. The foremost proponents of this view are Brekelmans, "Die sogenannten deuteronomischen

4. The production of the Pentateuch involved the combination of several sources (JEDP) that were produced separately, but that were combined serially by redactors.[7] Prior to the addition of the P material, a Deuteronomic/deuteronomistic redactor inserted statements, phrases, and words into the patriarchal narratives that aligned with the vocabulary and theology of Deuteronomy. The most obvious and widely recognized Deuteronomic segments are Gen 18:17–19; 22:16–18; 26:4–5 (traditionally credited to E).[8] According to Joseph Blenkinsopp,

> This kind of language is indistinguishable from the homiletic and hortatory style of the Deuteronomists. Similar language occurs at intervals throughout the ancestral history (e.g., 16:10; 26:24; 28:15; 35:1–4), allowing for the possibility that a D writer has edited narrative source material in a manner analogous to the presentation of prophetic narratives in Dtr, e.g., the stories about Elijah and Elisha.[9]

5. The author of Deuteronomy is the author of the Pentateuch. Rejecting the notion of a separate and coherent P narrative, Rolf Rendtorff observes that the first comprehensive Pentateuch bears a marked "Deuteronomistic stamp," and that the deuteronomic theological school produced it.[10] While not arguing for a single author, H. H. Schmid suggests the Pentateuch was the result of an "[inner] jahwistischen Redaktion- und Interpretationsprozess." However, as a whole, Genesis–Numbers presents a highly developed Deuteronomic theology.[11] R. N. Whybray has proposed

---

Elemente in Gen.-Num, 90–96; Lohfink, "Die These vom 'deuteronomischen' Dekalog-anfang," 99–109. For a helpful survey of the antecedents and successors to Brekelmans' and Lohfink's theories, see Ausloos, "The 'Proto-Deuteronomist': Fifty Years Later," 531–58.

7. Many have admitted the difficulty of distinguishing JE from D. See, e.g., Wellhausen, *Die Komposition*, 74, 86; indeed, Wellhausen grants the spiritual affinity between JE and Deuteronomy (*Die Komposition*, 94, n. 2).

8. According to Baden none of the expressions in 26:5 is Deuteronomic; the verse belongs to J. He suggests that J "typically uses clusters of legal terminology to signify general obedience to the will of Yahweh (since J has no law code to which it might refer). Indeed, there is no logical reason that a deuteronomic editor would insert references to obedience to actual laws, since in both Genesis 26:5 and Exodus 15:26 no laws have yet been given." (*Composition of the Pentateuch*, 139).

9. Blenkinsopp, *The Pentateuch*, 122. Already in the nineteenth century John W. Colenso asserted that the D-elements derive from the author who composed the book of Deuteronomy (*The Pentateuch and the Book of Joshua Critically Examined*, 145). Although Erhard Blum departs significantly from classical forms of the Documentary Hypothesis represented by JEDP, he provides the most detailed presentation of this approach in his opus *Die Komposition der Vätergeschichte*. Dispensing with J and E, he argues that independent "Abrahamgeschichte" and "Jakobusgeschichte" were combined to create "die Vätergeschichte," and linked to narratives in the preceding chapters to create the first "Deuteronomic" Pentateuch, to which the P materials were later added. For reviews of Blum's work, see Whybray, *The Making of the Pentateuch*, 210–13; O'Brien, "The Story of Abraham and the Debate over the Source Hypothesis," 1–17. A. D. H. Mayes argues that Genesis–Numbers never existed independently, but was composed as an introduction to an existent deuteronomistic history (*The Story of Israel between Settlement and Exile*, 141).

10. Rendtorff, *The Old Testament*, 162; and more fully, idem, *The Problem of the Process of Transmission in the Pentateuch*.

11. See Schmid, *Der sogenannte Jahwist*.

a single author for the entire Pentateuch, which was produced as part of a comprehensive national history, analogous to Herodotus' *Histories*.[12] Like the Greek work, the Pentateuch contains a mass of traditional and fictional material yielding a sixth century BCE "literary masterpiece."[13]

In recent decades, the results of computer-assisted research have also challenged source- and redaction-critical findings. Thirty years ago Yehuda T. Radday and Haim Shore demonstrated on linguistic grounds that in Genesis the separation of J from E is groundless, and that evidence for P as a separate source should be attributed to differences in genre rather than to separate authors. They observed that the style and vocabulary suggest three sorts of discourse, but they bear no relationship to the traditional sources J, E, and P.[14] In Genesis three distinct registers of discourse are on display, linked specifically to words attributed to the narrator (N), human speakers (H), and the Deity (D), respectively.[15] Although many today recognize E as a phantom,[16] some resist this move,[17] and P's place as a source in the narratives of Genesis is largely unchallenged.[18] Radday and Shore's pessimism regarding a scholarly hearing of their evidence has largely proved true.[19]

Perhaps the new work by Israeli scholars under the rubric of "The Tiberias Project" will move the computer assisted source analysis forward.[20] However, if the first publication by scholars working on the project is any indication,[21] its participants are subject to the same temptation to negation, bisection, and suppression of evidence that characterizes 200 years of source and redaction critical work.[22] The pressure from the academic guild is overwhelming.

12. Herodotus, *Hist.* 4.117–120 (Godley, LCL).

13. Whybray, *Making of the Pentateuch*, 242.

14. For a summary of their conclusions, see Radday and Shore, *Genesis: An Authorship Study*, 189–90. For more particular questions concerning a P narrative source as purportedly represented by Gen 1, 17, and 23, see pp. 209–10.

15. For an analysis of these registers, see Rabin, "Linguistic Aspects," 218–24.

16. See Levin, "Righteousness in the Joseph Story," 227–29.

17. See most recently Stackert's chapter "The Elohist Source," 70–125.

18. Blum attributes the fragments 23, 27:46–28:9; 35:9–15; 48:3–7, as well as the larger block, chapter 17 to P (*Komposition der Vätergeschichte*, 420–58). He is less certain about chapter 23, which may represent an independent tradition (*Komposition der Vätergeschichte*, 443–46). According to Baden, in the patriarchal narratives P is restricted to chapters 17 and 23 (*Composition of the Pentateuch*, 178).

19. They wrote, "The conclusion that the two [J and E] [. . .] were one will predictably be repudiated. Such dysfunction is not unique in scholarship. Even scientists tend to shut their eyes to data liable to collide with an existing cherished theory." They cite the supposed discovery of Uranus by Sir William Herschel; although astronomers had seen this planet at least twenty times before, its existence had been suppressed as fact (Radday and Shore, *Genesis*, 217). Cf. Joshua Berman's recent note that critical scholars regularly try to secure dates for specific biblical texts by negating, bisecting, and suppressing contrary evidence. Berman, "Historicism and Its Limits," 297–309.

20. For an introduction to the project, see https://www.youtube.com/watch?v=MDjx99KTMto.

21. See Dershowitz, Akiva, Koppel, and Dershowitz, "Computerized Source Criticism of Biblical Bexts," 253–71.

22. According to Dershowitz et al., the computer analysis of Gen 1:1–2:4a "places the section

The Evidence for a Relationship between Deuteronomy and the Patriarchal Narratives

Although Pentateuchal scholars have recognized links between Deuteronomy and the Tetrateuch, for more than 150 years they have also recognized the special lexical, linguistic, and stylistic characteristics of Deuteronomy.[23] In this essay my interest is not the distinctive features of deuteronomic style or vocabulary, but the opposite—Deuteronomy's links with the Abraham, Isaac, and Jacob narratives, spanning Gen 11:27–35:29, and identified internally as the Terah (11:27–25:11), and Isaac (25:19–35:29) תּוֹלְדוֹת ("generations").[24] This is not to say that the links with Deuteronomy are limited to the patriarchal narratives, but that this study is limited to this segment of the Tetrateuch. As I observe occasionally below, many of the shared features also occur in other parts of the Hexateuch.

When I began this project I did not expect to find many links between D and PN, beyond those snippets of patriarchal text that scholars had already identified as "Deuteronomic/deuteronomistic (cf. above). However, having marinated in Deuteronomy for the past fifteen years, my eyes and ears have been sensitized not only to Deuteronomy's diction, but also to the book's conceptual world. When I returned to the biblical accounts of Abraham, Isaac, and Jacob with these "Deuteronomic lenses," what I discovered caught me by surprise.

I have divided the links between D and PN into eight categories, moving from the most explicit (specific lexemes) to the vaguest (conceptual) connections: (1) morphological links; (2) individual lexemes; (3) idioms involving more than one lexeme; (4) toponyms; (5) ethnics; (6) verbal formulas involved in the promises to/covenant with the ancestors; (7) the human responses of faith and obedience; and (8) other theological motifs. These categories are not exhaustive. For example, one should also identify the syntactical and other literary features of the respective texts. But that presupposes a detailed discourse linguistic analysis of both texts, which time and space preclude. The boundaries separating the categories identified are rarely crisp, but for heuristic purposes this will serve as an organizing taxonomy. The first few categories are listed more or less in alphabetic order. Obviously each entry in the list deserves further discussion, but limitations of space mean we must concentrate on cataloguing the data. The purpose of this paper is to invite readers to assess the evidence cited and to begin the discussion.

---

in the predominantly non-P cluster, despite Bible scholars' nearly unanimous agreement that it is Priestly in origin." Their explanation is awkward: it may have been thrust into the non-P cluster by the dominance of the words אלהים ("God") and ויאמר ("and he said") and the particle כי (*kî*), which are typical of non-P materials. They conclude, "It may therefore be worth considering our method's results in the light of the questions surrounding the literary history of Gen 1:1–2:4a." ("Computerized Source Criticism," 269). Should they not rather have said, "It may therefore be worth considering the questions surrounding our understanding of the literary history of Gen 1:1–2:4a in the light of the method's results"?

23. For catalogues of distinctively Deuteronomic/deuteronomistic elements, see Weinfeld, *Deuteronomy and the Deuteronomic School*, 320–65; Driver, *Deuteronomy*, lxxvii–xcv; Colenso, *Pentateuch and the Book of Joshua*, 391–406. Colenso discusses not only expressions that never occur in the Tetrateuch and are therefore unique to and/or typical of D, but also expressions that are common in the Tetrateuch, but absent from D (cf. also Driver, *Deuteronomy*, lxxxiv).

24. Curiously in neither case are the תּוֹלְדוֹת ("generations") named after the dominant character.

Morphological Links

1. הָאֵל in place of הָאֵלֶּה, "these" (Gen 19:8, 25; 26:3, 4; Deut 4:42; 7:22; 19:11).[25]

2. הוּא for הִיא, 3rd fem. sing. pronoun.[26] Whereas in the rest of the Hebrew Bible this pronoun is always הִיא, in the Pentateuch this form occurs only eighteen times (never in D).[27] By contrast, the otherwise unusual form הוּא appears almost 200 times, being distributed among all five books (with Genesis having more than fifty and D thirty-five). That it occurs in all of the purported JEDP sources, but never outside the Pentateuch seriously undermines longstanding critical theories for the growth of the Pentateuch.[28]

Shared Lexemes[29]

3. אָהַב, "to love." The lexeme אָהַב occurs fourteen times in Genesis, but is never used of God's love for human beings.[30] By contrast, in D two-thirds of the ca. two dozen occurrences involve either YHWH's love for people (the ancestors, 4:37; 10:15; Israel, 7:8, 13; 23:6[5]; sojourners, 10:18) or Israel's love for YHWH (5:10; 6:5; 7:9; 10:12; 11:1, 13, 22; 13:4[3]; 19:9; 30:6, 16, 20). Horizontally, it is used of the Israelites' love for sojourners (10:19), a servant for his master (15:16, cf. Exod 21:5), and a husband for his wife (21:15–16). The last reference is especially significant, providing guidance in bigamous cases where the husband loves one wife more than the other, as was the case in Jacob's relationship with Leah and Rachel (Gen 29:30–32). The scarcity of אָהַב in Exodus–Numbers (only Exod 20:6 [= Deut 5:10]; 21:5; Lev 19:18, 34) reinforces the sense of linkage between D and PN.

4. הָפַךְ, "to overthrow" (Gen 19:21, 25, 29; Deut 29:22[23]).

5. חָשַׁק, "to love" [heartfelt impassioned love] (Gen 34:8; Deut 21:11; used theologically of YHWH's love for Israel in Deut 7:7; 10:15).[31]

---

25. The long form occurs 80 times in the Pentateuch; the short form occurs once in the rest of the Pentateuch (Lev 18:27), but is not found elsewhere in the Hebrew Bible.

26. For a full, if dated study of this phenomenon, see Rendsburg, "A New Look at Pentateuchal HWʾ," 351–69.

27. Gen 14:2; 19:20; 20:5; 26:7; 38:25; 40:10; Exod 1:16; Lev 5:11; 11:39; 13:6, 10, 21; 16:31; 20:17, 18; 21:9; Num 5:13, 14. Rendsburg overlooks Gen 19:20; 26:7; 40:10; Exod 1:16; Lev 5:11; 13:6; 20:18. הַהִיא never occurs ("A New Look," 351, n. 1).

28. According to Rendsburg, this represents an early form of the language before the adoption of a distinctive third feminine singular pronoun, הִיא, which he sets in the Davidic or Solomonic period ("A New Look," 365).

29. In addition to the examples given here from PN, see also from the Joseph story, תּוֹעֵבָה, "abomination," in Gen 43:32; 46:34; cf. Deut 7:25, 26 +15x (also in Exod 8:22[26]; Lev 18:22–30; 20:13).

30. Of a parent's love for a child (Abraham/Isaac, 22:2; Isaac/Esau and Rebekah/Jacob, 25:28; Jacob/Joseph, 37:3, 4; 44:20); of a husband's love for his wife (Isaac/Rebekah, 24:67; Jacob/Rachel, 29:18, 30; and Leah's hope that Jacob will love her, 29:32); an unmarried man for an unmarried woman (Shechem/Dinah, 34:3); a man's love of food (Isaac, 27:4, 9, 14).

31. The word is rare, appearing elsewhere as a verb only in 1 Kgs 9:19 = 2 Chr 8:6; Ps 91:14; Isa 21:4; 38:17, and as a noun חֵשֶׁק only in 1 Kgs 9:1, 19; 2 Chr 8:6). For discussion of this word, see

6. מַעֲשֵׂר, "tithe" (Gen 14:20; 28:20–22; Deut 14:22; 26:12; cf. 12:6, 11, 17; 14:23, 28). Tithes are mentioned in Leviticus (27:30–32) and Numbers (18:21–28), but by linking the tithe with the creed-like declaration naming the Aramean ancestor (Deut 26:12), D forges a link with Genesis.

7. נָבִיא, "prophet" (Gen 20:7; Deut 13:2–6[1–5]; 18:15–22; 34:10).[32]

8. עֵד, an object as "a witness" to a covenant (Gen 31:44, 48, 52; Deut 31:21, 26).

9. עֲקָרָה, "to be barren" (Gen 11:30; Deut 7:14).[33]

10. פָּלָא, "to be difficult, beyond one's ability" (Gen 18:14; Deut 17:8; 30:11).[34]

11. הִשְׁחִית, "to destroy" (Gen 18:28; 19:13–14).[35]

12. שמד, meaning "to be destroyed, to destroy," of populations (Gen 34:30; Deut 1:27).[36]

Shared Phrases/Idioms[37]

13. אֱלֹהֵי [הַ]נֵּכָר, "foreign gods" (Gen 35:2, 4; Deut 31:16; 32:12).[38]

14. בֵּרֵךְ וְהִרְבָּה, "to bless and multiply" (Gen 17:20; 22:17; 26:4, 24; 28:3; Deut 7:13; 30:16).[39]

15. דָּגָן וְתִירֹשׁ, "grain and wine" (Gen 27:28, 37; Deut 7:13; 11:14; 12:17; 14:23; 18:4; 28:51; 33:28).[40]

Levenson, *The Love of God*, 40–42, 167–68, 176–77.

32. The word also occurs in Exod 7:1; Num 11:29; 12:6, but Abraham's intercessory responsibility was embodied most dramatically by Moses after the golden calf debacle (Deut 9:8–21, 25–29).

33. Elsewhere only in Exod 23:26.

34. The root occurs elsewhere in the Pentateuch (Exod 3:20; 34:10; Lev 22:21; 27:2; Num 6:2; 15:3, 8; Deut 28:59), but never with this sense.

35. In Exodus–Numbers the form, מַשְׁחִית ("destroyer") occurs twice (Exod 12:13, 23), where it concerns YHWH's judgment of Egypt at the time of Israel's first Passover.

36. Cf. Deut 1:27; 2:12, 21, 22, 23; 4:3, 26; 6:15; 7:4, 23, 24; 9:3, 8, 14, 19, 20, 25; 12:30; 28:20, 24, 45, 48, 51, 61, 63; 31:3, 4; 33:27. Elsewhere in the Tetrateuch only in Lev 26:30 and Num 33:52, but of pagan cult installations.

37. In addition to the examples given below from PN, from the Joseph story, note also (1) עֵינְכֶם אַל־תָּחֹס, "your eye shall not pity," Gen 45:20 (toward inanimate objects); cf. לֹא־תָחוֹס עֵינְךָ, Deut 7:16; 13:9[8]; 19:13, 21; 25:12 (toward humans); (2) לֹא יוּכַל, "to be unable," Gen 43:32; cf. Deut 21:16; 22:19, 29; 24:4.

38. אֱלֹהֵי הַנֵּכָר, "foreign gods," occurs outside Genesis only in Josh 24:23; Judg 10:16; 1 Sam 7:3; 2 Chr 33:15. The expression, אֱלֹהִים אֲחֵרִים, "other gods," is much more common, occurring eighteen times in D (Deut 5:7; 6:14; 7:4; 8:19; 11:16, 28; 13:3, 7, 14 [2, 6, 13]; 17:3; 18:20; 28:14, 36, 64; 29:25[26]; 30:17; 31:18), and frequently in the Deuteronomistic History. While rooted in the Decalogue (Exod 20:3; Deut 5:7), it occurs only once more in Exodus–Numbers (Exod 23:13); cf. the abbreviated version, אֵל אַחֵר, "another God," in Exod 34:14.

39. The combination "bless and multiply" never occurs in Exodus–Numbers.

40. Except for the poetic occurrence (Deut 33:28), in D this pair always occurs with יִצְהָר, "olive oil," and they always occur in this order: grain, wine, oil. None of these is the common word for the commodity. Whether or not the expressions imply a special quality of the product, D's usage in place of לֶחֶם, יַיִן, and שֶׁמֶן involves a subtle anti-idolatry polemic. See Block, "Other Religions in Old

16. טַל הַשָּׁמַיִם, "dew of heaven" (Gen 27:28, 39; Deut 33:13, 28).[41]

17. יֵיטַב לְ, "to go well for/with [you]" (Gen 12:13; cf. also 40:14; Deut 4:40).[42]

18. יָרַד מִצְרַיְמָה לָגוּר שָׁם, "To go down to Egypt to sojourn there" (Gen 12:10; Deut 26:5).

19. עָשָׂה חֶסֶד, "to demonstrate steadfast love" (Gen 19:19; 20:13; 21:23; 24:12, 14, 49 [divine חֶסֶד]; 32:11[10]; cf. 40:14; 47:29; Deut 5:10 = Exod 20:6 [divine חֶסֶד]).[43]

20. הִרְחִיב אֶת־גְּבֻלְךָ, "to extend your borders" (Gen 26:22; Deut 12:20; 19:8). Here the verb, הִרְחִיב, "to extend, expand [space]," provides the only lexical connection between PN and D. Despite the addition of "as he promised you" (כַּאֲשֶׁר דִּבֶּר־לָךְ) in Deut 12:20 and "as he swore to your ancestors" (כַּאֲשֶׁר נִשְׁבַּע לַאֲבֹתֶיךָ) in 19:8, PN never speak about the ancestors' or their descendants' future גְּבוּל. The closest we get is Gen 23:17–18, which declares that the Hittites deeded the entire area (גְּבוּל) around the cave at Machpelah over to Abraham. Nevertheless, the expansion of Isaac's *Lebensraum*, memorialized in the new toponym, Rehoboth (רְחֹבוֹת), presents a microcosm of the territorial expansion defined in Gen 15:18 and anticipated elsewhere (12:7; 13:14–17; 15:7–21; 26:4; 28:13; 35:12). However, the first explicit promise to expand Israel's גְּבוּל ("territory") occurs in Exod 34:24.

21. שָׁמַע אֶל־עֳנִי, "to hear/listen to [someone's] afflictions" (Gen 16:11; Deut 26:7).[44]

Toponymic Links[45]

22. אֵלוֹן[י] מוֹרֶה, "the oak[s] of Moreh" (Gen 12:6; Deut 11:30). Given the importance of the ancestors in D,[46] remarkably D never names the sites most important in PN (Shechem, Hebron, Beersheba, Bethel). The location of Mounts Gerizim and Ebal אֵצֶל אֵלוֹנֵי מֹרֶה, "beside the oaks of Moreh," is as close as we get. The expression, אֵלוֹן[י] מוֹרֶה, "the oak[s] of Moreh," occurs in the Hebrew Bible only in these two texts.[47] The geographic note in Deut 11:30 suggests that by entering Canaan from

---

Testament Theology," 208–209. The combination of דָּגָן and תִּירוֹשׁ occurs elsewhere in the Tetrateuch only in Num 18:12, albeit in reverse order.

41. D casts the idiom in different form, clarifying טַל הַשָּׁמַיִם, but Moses' benediction of the tribes is linked with Isaac's blessing of Jacob (and virtual curse of Esau). These words do not appear together elsewhere in the Tetrateuch.

42. Cf. Deut 1:23; 4:40; 5:16, 29; 6:3, 18; 8:16; 12:25, 28; 22:7; 28:63. The idiom occurs in Deut 5:16, but is missing in the Exodus version of the Decalogue (Exod 20:12).

43. The idiom is otherwise missing in the Tetrateuch. Elsewhere D speaks of "keeping the covenant and the steadfast love" (שָׁמַר הַבְּרִית וְהַחֶסֶד, 7:9, 12).

44. The envoy's statement in Gen 16:11 appears to be poetic shorthand for "YHWH has heard your cry and seen your affliction." Cf. also Exod 3:7.

45. The terms differ, but in this context note also Edom's possession (אֲחֻזָּה) of land (Seir, Gen 36:43); Deut 2:12 uses יְרֻשָּׁה ("possession") and characterizes the land as granted (נָתַן) to them by YHWH.

46. On this subject, see Hwang, *The Rhetoric of Remembrance*.

47. גִּבְעַת הַמּוֹרֶה, "Teacher's Hill," in Judg 7:1 refers to a different site.

across the Jordan the Israelites could quickly reach the site where both Abraham (12:6) and Jacob (33:18–20) had celebrated YHWH's fulfillment of his promises and staked their divinely based claim to this land by building altars.[48] That the Israelites as the people of YHWH would cement their claim to this land there is especially significant,[49] since Jacob had renamed the place אֵל אֱלֹהֵי יִשְׂרָאֵל, "El, the God of Israel" (Gen 33:20).[50]

23. אֶרֶץ הַכְּנַעֲנִי, "land of the Canaanite" (Gen 12:6; cf. 50:11; Deut 11:30). Although Genesis lacks the construct phrase, the collocation of the gentilic כְּנַעֲנִי, "Canaanite," with אֶרֶץ, "land," links these texts. Note also references to the Canaanite in the land in 13:7; 24:3; and 34:30. Remarkably, in contrast to D, PN never hints at a Canaanite moral or religious problem.[51] If anything, the narrator casts them as more righteous than the ancestors. First, Melchizedek ("Malki is righteous" or "My king is Zedek[Zaddik]"),[52] the king of Salem, was priest of El Elyon (אֵל עֶלְיוֹן), whom Abraham acknowledged as his political and priestly superior. Second, in 20:1–18 God characterizes Abimelek, king of Gerar, as a man of internal piety (תָּם לֵבָב, "blameless of heart")[53] and external ethical morality (נִקְיוֹן כַּף, "clean of hand," vv. 5–6),[54] in contrast to the self-serving patriarch (vv. 2, 11–13). Third, the narrator casts the Hittites of Kiriath-Arba (Hebron), located "in the land of Canaan" (אֶרֶץ כְּנָעַן; cf. 33:18), as profusely generous to Abraham (23:3–9). Fourth, Shechem's rape of Dinah was reprehensible (34:2), but in the rest of the chapter the Hivites of Shechem behave more honorably than Jacob's family, who are "odious (הִבְאִישׁ) among the inhabitants of the land, the Canaanites and Perizzites" (v. 30). Fifth, after his own duplicitous actions, Judah acknowledged that the Canaanite Tamar was more righteous (צְדָקָה) than he (38:26). These characterizations give credence to the divine statement in 15:16 and betray the narrator's own context which contrasts with Abraham's time when the iniquity of the Amorites was not yet full.[55]

24. צֹעַר, "Zoar" (Gen 13:10; 14:2, 8; 19:22, 23, 30; Deut 34:1b–3).[56]

---

48. Both texts locate Shechem "in the land of Canaan" (12:5; 34:18).

49. On the significance of the ceremony at Gerizim and Ebal, see chapter 8, "What do These Stones Mean?" below, pp. 152–76.

50. Jacob had departed the land as Jacob ("trickster"), but he returned with a new name and a new relationship with the patron Deity.

51. Abraham's warning to his servant not to allow Isaac to marry a woman "from the daughters of the Canaanites" (Gen 24:3, 37) appears contradictory to our point, but the prohibition is not grounded in ethical or theological considerations. As a first-generation immigrant, Abraham may have been concerned about maintaining contact with his roots (מוֹלֶדֶת). Cf. Gen 11:28; 12:1; 24:4, 7; 31:3, 13; 32:10[9].

52. "מַלְכִּי־צֶדֶק," HALOT, 1:593.

53. El Shadday's charge to Abram to be "blameless" in 17:1 involves the etymologically related term תָּמִים.

54. This expression occurs elsewhere only in Pss 26:6 and 73:13.

55. It seems he intentionally associated Amorites, rather than Canaanites, with the evil (עָוֹן).

56. Zoar is never named in Exodus–Numbers and appears elsewhere only in Isa 15:5 and Jer 48:34.

25. סְדֹם וַעֲמֹרָה, "Sodom and Gomorrah" (Gen 13:10; Deut 29:22[23]; 32:32).[57]

26. שַׁעַר הָעִיר, "gate of the/his/their town" (Gen 23:10, cf. v. 18; 34:20;[58] Deut 22:24; cf. 21:19; 22:15).[59]

27. The maximalist definition of the promised land (Gen 15:18; Deut 1:17; 11:24).[60]

Ethnicons

28. [הָ]אֲרַמִּי, "[the] Aramean" (Gen 25:20; 28:5; 31:20, 24; Deut 26:5).[61]

29. הָאֵמִים, "the Emmites" (Gen 14:5; Deut 2:10–11).

30. הַחֹתִי[ם] בְּשֵׂעִיר/בְּהַרְרָם שֵׂעִיר, "the Horite[s] in Seir/the mountains of Seir" (Gen 14:6; 36:20, 21, 29, 30; Deut 2:12, 2:22).

31. הַזּוּזִים/זַמְזֻמִּים, "the Zumites/Zamzummites" (Gen 14:5; Deut 2:20–21). The identification of the Zumim of Genesis with the Zamzummim of D is not in doubt.[62]

32. רְפָאִים, "Rephaim" (Gen 14:5; 15:19–21; Deut 2:11, 20; 3:11, 13).[63]

33. The lists of peoples occupying the promised land (Gen 15:19–21; Deut 7:1; 20:17). Whereas Deut 20:17 follows the stereotypical listing by naming six Canaanite nations,[64] Deut 7:1 (also Josh 3:10; 24:11) completes the quota of seven by adding the Girgashites, and links this text directly to God's promise to Abraham in Gen 15:1–21.

---

57. Neither Sodom nor Gomorrah is mentioned in Exodus–Numbers.

58. Cf. Gen 19:2, which refers to "the gate of Sodom" (שַׁעַר־סְדֹם). On the use of שַׁעַר ("gate") in the Pentateuch, see van Wolde, *Reframing Biblical Studies*, 81–86.

59. Deuteronomy 21:19 speaks of "the elders of his town" at "the gate of his place" (זִקְנֵי עִירוֹ וְאֶל־שַׁעַר מְקֹמוֹ), and 22:25 of taking the accused "to the elders of the town at the gate" (אֶל־זִקְנֵי הָעִיר הַשַּׁעְרָה). "Gate" and "town" are never conjoined elsewhere in the Tetrateuch.

60. While the specification of the great Euphrates River (הַנָּהָר הַגָּדֹל נְהַר־פְּרָת) as the northern boundary, and assumption of the "River of Egypt" (נְהַר מִצְרַיִם) as the southern border, are absent in Exodus–Numbers, the maximalist definition appears in slightly modified form in Exod 23:31 and Josh 1:4.

61. Elsewhere the Tetrateuch never mentions Arameans.

62. So already Symmachus and the Genesis Apocryphon 21:29. Greek reads ἔθνη ἰσχυρά, "a strong people."

63. Remarkably none of these three ethnicons (Rephaim, Emmim, Zamzummim) appears in Exodus–Numbers, while Genesis is silent on עֲנָק/עֲנָקִים/בְּנֵי עֲנָקִים (Anak/Anakim/sons of Anakim), another common ethnicon for the aboriginal population of Canaan.

64. So also Exod 3:8, 17; 23:23; 33:2; 34:11; Josh 9:1; 11:3; 12:8; Judg 3:5. Exodus 13:5 omits Perizzites. Numbers 13:29 heads a list of four with Amalekites (a non-autochthonous Edomite group (Gen 36:12, 16), located in the Negeb, followed by Hittites, Jebusites, and Amorites, who occupy the hill country, and concluding with Canaanites ("lowlanders"), who occupy the coastal region and the Jordan valley. For discussion of these lists, see Ishida, "The "Implications of the Lists of Pre-Israelite Nations," 461–90. Assuming that the list has grown gradually, because the Genesis list is the longest, Westermann concludes that this is the oldest list (*Genesis 12–36*, 230). On the fallacy of this sort of reasoning, see Kilchör, *Mosetora und Jahwetora*, 39–40; 90–92, 101–102, 201–202, 292.

34. רְאוּבֵן, "Reuben" (Gen 35:22; Deut 33:6). "Reuben" serves as a personal name in Gen 35:22 but as a tribal name in Deut 33:6. However, while the first part of the latter is a benediction of sorts, the second half functions as a not-so-subtly veiled curse, alluding to Reuben's immoral act with his father's concubine, Bilhah.[65] Jacob's "blessing" for Simeon and Levi in Gen 49:5–7 is actually a "curse," expressly linked to their violence against the people of Shechem in Gen 34. This contrasts with how the "Blessing of Moses" treats these tribes. Whereas Levi's defense of YHWH at Massah eclipses his involvement at Shechem, Simeon is forgotten.

Formulas Relating to the Ancestral Promises/Covenant[66]

35. אֲנִי יְהוָה אֲשֶׁר הוֹצֵאתִיךָ מִן, "I am YHWH who brought you out of. . ." (Gen 15:7; Deut 5:6; 13:6[5]). While the statements in D follow post-exodus convention,[67] the adaptation of the formula to Abraham's migration from Ur is extraordinary. The narrator (and the character YHWH) hereby casts Abraham as a devotee of the God of the exodus.

36. וְהָיִיתִי לְךָ/לָהֶם לֵאלֹהִים, "I will be your/their God" (Gen 17:7, 8; Deut 26:17–19). This is the first half of the two-part "covenant formula": "I will be your God, and you shall be my people" (Exod 6:7; Lev 26:12). Even though the pure form of the first part of the formula never occurs in D, the 300+ occurrences of suffixed forms "your God," and "our God" assume it, and rituals underlying the book of Deuteronomy celebrate the fulfillment of YHWH's promise in Gen 17:7–8 to be the God of Abraham's descendants. The significance of the ceremonies suggested by Deut 26:17–19 is reinforced in 27:9b–10:

> "Keep silence and hear, O Israel: **This day you have become the people of YHWH your God.** You shall therefore listen to the voice of YHWH your God, keeping his commands and his statutes, which I command you today."

37. אָבִיךָ/אֲבֹתֶיךָ/אֲבֹתֵיכֶם/[אָנֹכִי אֱלֹהֵי יְהוָה אֲנִי], "[I am] YHWH the God of your father[s]" (Gen 26:24; 28:13; Deut 10:22; 26:7).[68]

38. כָּרַת בְּרִית, "to cut [make] a covenant" (Gen 15:18;[69] Deut 4:23; 5:2, 3; 9:9; 28:69[29:1]; 29:11, 24 [12, 25]; 31:16.).[70]

---

65. Compare the explicit link in Jacob's "blessing" for Reuben in Gen 49:3–4.

66. Here I have arranged the items logically, rather than alphabetically.

67. Exod 6:7; 20:2; 29:46; Lev 19:36; 22:33; 25:38, 42, 55; 26:13, 45; Num 15:41. An alternative form of the divine introduction/deliverance formula uses the verb עָלָה (hiphil), "to bring up" (Deut 20:1; Lev 11:45; note also the perverse adaptation of the formula to the golden calf, Exod 32:4).

68. Cf. also Deut 4:1; 6:3; 12:1; 27:3; 29:24[25]. Note especially Exod 3:6, "I am the God of your father, the God of Abraham, the God of Isaac, and the God of Jacob." Also Exod 3:13, 15–16; 4:5; 15:2 (sing.); 18:4 (sing.).

69. The idiom is used elsewhere of human covenants (21:27, 32; 26:28; 31:44).

70. However, this covenant is never specified as the covenant made with Abraham. The idiom is used of YHWH's covenant with Israel elsewhere in the Tetrateuch (Exod 24:8; 34:10, 27). Exodus 23:32 and 34:12, 15 respectively forbid making covenants with other gods and with the Canaanites.

39. הָקִים בְּרִית, "to establish/confirm a covenant" (Gen 17:7, 19, 21; Deut 8:18).[71]

40. God's promise to multiply (הִרְבָּה) the descendants (זֶרַע) "like the stars of the sky" (כְּכוֹכְבֵי הַשָּׁמַיִם; Gen 22:17; 26:4; Deut 1:10; 10:22; 28:62).[72] Note also the references to the numerable nature of Jacob's descendants who went to Egypt in Gen 46:6–7 and Deut 26:5.

41. God's promise to make a great nation (גּוֹי גָּדוֹל) of Abraham and his descendants (Gen 12:2; 18:18; cf. 46:3;[73] Deut 4:7–8; 26:5).

42. God's sworn promise (נִשְׁבַּע) to give land to Abraham's offspring (Gen 24:7; 26:3;[74] Deut 1:8; 11:9; 34:4; cf. also 31:21). In the following, the lexical links are less precise, but the conceptual connections are apparent.

43. God's election of Abraham and his descendants (Gen 18:19, with יָדַע, "to know"); Deut 4:37; 7:6–7; 10:15; 14:2, all with בָּחַר, "to choose").

44. God's promise to make Abraham and his descendants a blessing to the nations (Gen 12:3; 18:18; 22:18; 26:4; 28:14; Deut 4:6–8; cf. 26:19).

45. Outsiders recognizing YHWH or being blessed because of Israel's blessed status (Gen 21:22; 26:28–29; 30:30; Deut 28:10).

46. The promise of divine protection (Gen 15:1; 26:24; Deut 7:21; 20:3–4; 31:6; 31:8).

47. Israel's dominance over outsiders (Gen 22:17; 24:60; 27:29, 37; Deut 26:19; 28:1, 10, 13).

48. Claiming the land (Gen 13:17;[75] Deut 11:24).

49. Israel's sojourn (גּוּר) in the foreign land of Egypt (Gen 15:13; Deut 10:19).[76]

---

71. The formula also occurs in Exod 6:4 and Lev 26:9. Related conceptually to Deut 4:31, the latter speaks of YHWH's fidelity to his covenant in the distant future. However, instead of confirming the covenant, in Deut 4:31 Moses declares that YHWH will "not forget" (לֹא יִשְׁכַּח) the covenant with Israel's ancestors. לֹא יִשְׁכַּח אֶת־הַבְּרִית ("He will not forget the covenant") is equivalent to זָכַר אֶת־הַבְּרִית ("He remembered the covenant") in Gen 9:15, 16; Exod 2:24, 6:5; Lev 26:42, 45, casting doubt on Weinfeld's claim that the latter is a mark of P (*Deuteronomy and the Deuteronomic School*, 230).

72. Cf. also Exod 32:13. Remarkably, only Genesis uses the comparative idioms, "like the sand of the sea[shore]" (Gen 22:17; 32:12[11]) and "like the dust of the earth" (13:16; 28:14).

73. Cf. also 35:11. God gave the same promise to Ishmael in Gen 17:20; 21:8. Twice in Exodus–Numbers YHWH threatened to transfer the promise from Abraham's descendants to Moses (Exod 32:10; Num 14:12).

74. Cf. Gen 50:24. References to the sworn grant of land also occur in Deut 4:31; 6:10, 18, 23; 7:8, 12, 13; 8:1, 18; 9:5; 11:9, 21; 26:3; 28:11; 30:20; 31:7, as well as in Exod 13:5; 32:13; 33:1; Num 14:16. The forms of the promises of land vary. Gen 12:2 and 28:13 omit references to an oath. The remainder alternate between variations of the collocation, נִשְׁבַּע . . . נָתַן, "he swore [. . .] to give," and elliptical statements without נָתַן, "to give."

75. בְּתוֹךְ הִתְהַלֵּךְ ("to walk back and forth in the midst of") carries overtones of "staking one's claim," or "acting as one who already held title [to the land]." Thus Wiseman, "Abraham in History and Tradition, 147 and 155, n. 31.

76. According to Deut 23:8[7], the memory of Israel's sojourn in Egypt was to temper their treatment of the Egyptians; they had served as their hosts at a critical time in their history. This motif is memorialized in the name of Moses' son Gershom (Exod 2:22; 18:3) and surfaces elsewhere as

50. Divine terror/dread striking those who encounter the ancestors and their descendants (Gen 35:5;[77] Deut 2:25; 11:25).[78]

51. The brotherhood of Jacob/Israel and Esau/Edom (Gen 25:23–34; 32:4[3]; Deut 23:7[6]).

Dispositional and Ethical Responses to God/YHWH

52. Generic fear of God (יִרְאַת אֱלֹהִים/יְרֵא אֱלֹהִים) with ethical implications[79] (Gen 20:11, cf. 42:18; Deut 25:18).[80]

53. The fear (יָרֵא, trusting awe) of YHWH (Gen 22:12; Deut 4:10; 31:12–13).[81]

54. Trust in YHWH (הֶאֱמִין בַּיהוה) (Gen 15:6; Deut 1:32; 9:23).[82]

55. "To listen to the voice, obey" (שָׁמַע לְקוֹל/שָׁמַע בְּקוֹל) (Gen 22:18; 26:5; Deut 4:30; 26:17; 28:1–2).[83]

56. To swear by YHWH, or by his name (נִשְׁבַּע בִּשְׁמוֹ) (Gen 24:3;[84] Deut 6:13; 10:20).

57. To walk/stand before YHWH (הִתְהַלֵּךְ/עָמַד לִפְנֵי יהוה) (Gen 17:1; 18:22;[85] 24:40; Deut 10:8; 18:5). D does not use the verb, הִתְהַלֵּךְ, but the idiom עָמַד לִפְנֵי יְהוָה, "to stand before YHWH," presupposes the person has been invited to the presence of God. Whereas הִתְהַלֵּךְ אֶת־הָאֱלֹהִים, "to walk with God," speaks of intimate communion, "to walk before YHWH" implies access to the divine court and service as YHWH's commissioned agent. This notion is on display in Gen 18, where Abraham intercedes for Sodom and Gomorrah.[86] The idea of appearing before YHWH is explicit

---

motivation for ethical living (Exod 22:20[21]; 23:9; Lev 19:4).

77. In Gen 31:42 פַּחַד ("Fear") functions as an epithet of the God of Isaac (before Laban the Aramean).

78. The motif of divine terror going before the Israelites surfaces in Exod 15:16 (אֵימָתָה וָפַחַד, "terror and dread") and 23:27 (אֵימָה). The root פחד occurs three times in Deut 28:66–67, denoting Israel's fear of the nations.

79. Although the divinity is specifically identified as YHWH, the notion also appears in Lev 19:14, 32; 25:15, 36, 43.

80. Cf. Exod 1:17, 21.

81. This use of יָרֵא is frequent in D: Deut 4:10; 5:29; 6:2, 13, 24; 8:6; 10:12, 17, 20; 13:5[4]; 14:23; 17:19; 25:18; 28:58; 31:12, 13.

82. On הֶאֱמִין, "to believe, demonstrate trust," in the Tetrateuch, see also Exod 4:1, 5, 8, 9, 31; 19:9; Num 14:11; 20:12.

83. Cf. Deut 8:20; 9:23; 13:5[4], 19[18]; 15:5; 21:18, 20 (of a son to parents); 26:14; 27:10; 28:15, 45, 62; 30:2, 8, 10, 20.

84. Cf. Gen 21:23–24, where Abraham swears before Abimelech by God (בֵּאלֹהִים). The notion of swearing specifically by YHWH's name appears elsewhere in the Tetrateuch only in Lev 19:12.

85. The idiom also involves lesser persons standing before human superiors. See Gen 41:46; 43:15; 47:7.

86. Verse 22 is text-critically problematic. While MT and all the versions have Abraham standing before YHWH, this is one of the eighteen alleged *tiqqune sopherim*. The Masorah in *BHS* claims the original reading had YHWH standing before Abraham. Cf. *Gen. Rab.* 49.7: "R. Simon said: 'This is a

in the D texts, which speak of YHWH choosing the Levitical priests "to serve him and bless [the people] in his name."

58. Prostration before (הִשְׁתַּחֲוָה לְ) deity (Gen 22:5; 24:48; Deut 5:9; 26:10). The verb הִשְׁתַּחֲוָה denotes a physical gesture of prostration in submission and homage before a superior.[87] Although Genesis frequently reports mundane prostration before a human superior,[88] D only employs the word theologically, and except for 26:10, in keeping with the demand for exclusive devotion to YHWH, it always occurs in prohibitions of prostrations before other deities (8:19; 11:16; 17:3; 29:25[26]; 30:17).

59. שָׁמַר דֶּרֶךְ יהוה/הָלַךְ בְּדֶרֶךְ יהוה, "to keep/walk in the way of YHWH" (Gen 18:19; Deut 5:33; 8:6; 10:12; 11:22; 13:6[5]; 19:9; 26:17; 28:9; 30:16). "To keep/walk in the way/ways of YHWH" is ambiguous, meaning either "to walk" (i.e., conduct one's life) as YHWH does (cf. 10:18–19), or "to walk" as YHWH commanded one to walk. Texts that speak of keeping the commands/ordinances "by walking in the way of YHWH" (5:33; 8:6; 11:22; 13:6[5]) render the latter sense explicit. Since "keeping the commands" is frequently linked with "walking in the way of YHWH," the charge to "keep the way of YHWH" in Gen 18:19 may represent intentional shorthand conflation of the Deuteronomic expressions. In any case, this text clarifies the idiom with לַעֲשׂוֹת צְדָקָה וּמִשְׁפָּט, "by practising righteousness and justice," which involves thoroughly Deuteronomic vocabulary.[89] However, the characterization of "the Judge of all the earth" as one who "executes justice" (יַעֲשֶׂה מִשְׁפָּט) in Gen 18:25 blurs the boundary between keeping God's commands and imitating him.

60. Righteousness/a righteous person/to be righteous/to demonstrate righteousness/to declare someone righteous (צֶדֶק/צְדָקָה/צָדַק/צַדִּיק/הִצְדִּיק) (Gen 15:6; 18:19, 25; cf. 38:26; Deut 6:25; 16:20; 25:1). Of the links between Genesis and D, this may be the most remarkable of all. The root צדק occurs 46 times in the Pentateuch, only nine of which occur in Exodus–Numbers. These are limited to three contexts,[90] and each recalls corresponding texts in PN or D.[91] Genesis and D employ the root צדק with a similar range of meaning,[92] and both use the root as a verb and in at least two forms of the noun.[93]

---

correction of the Scribes for the *Shekinah* was waiting for Abraham." However, Emanuel Tov deems it unlikely that the original would have had YHWH standing before Abraham (*Textual Criticism of the Hebrew Bible*, 60–61).

87. For fuller discussion, see Block, *For the Glory of God*, 12–17.

88. Gen 18:2; 19:1; 23:7, 12; 27:29; 33:3, 6, 7; 37:7, 9, 10; 42:6; 43:26, 28; 47:31; 48:12; 49:8.

89. Cf. Deut 6:25; 33:21; 2 Sam 8:15; 1 Kgs 10:19.

90. Exod 9:27 (צַדִּיק); 23:7–8 צֶדֶק [2x], הַצַּדִּיק); Lev 19 (צֶדֶק, v. 15, 4x in v. 36).

91. Compare Exod 9:27 with Gen 38:26; Exod 23:7–8 with Deut 25:1; Lev 19:15 with Deut 1:16 and 16:18; and Lev 19:36 with Deut 25:15.

92. Compare Gen 15:6 and Deut 6:25; 24:13 (צְדָקָה); the juxtaposing of צַדִּיק with רָשָׁע, Gen 18:23 and Deut 9:4–5; 25:1; exercising justice (עָשָׂה מִשְׁפָּט/שָׁפַט) with righteousness (Gen 18:25; Deut 1:16; 16:18; cf. 25:1); righteousness in economic assessments (Gen 30:33; Deut 25:15); divine righteousness/administration of righteousness (Gen 15:6; Deut 6:25; 9:4–6; 24:16; 32:4; 33:21).

93. Verb: צְדָקָה, Gen 38:26 (qal); נִצְטַדָּק, 44:16 (hithpael); וְהִצְדִּיקוּ, Deut 25:1 (hiphil); Nouns: צֶדֶק, Deut 1:16; 16:18, 20; 25:15; 33:19; צְדָקָה, Gen 15:6; 18:10; 30:33; Deut 6:25; 9:4–6; 24:13; 33:21; צַדִּיק,

61. The prohibition on intermarriage with Canaanites (Gen 24:3; 28:1; 34:9–10, 16–17, 21; Deut 7:2–4, 16). As noted earlier, the positive picture of Canaanites the author of PN paints is striking, and raises questions concerning the rationale behind Abraham's demand that Isaac's wife be from the Arameans in Haran, Isaac and Rebekah's problems with Esau's Hittite wives (26:34–35), and Rebekah's rejection of a potential Hittite wife for Jacob (27:46). Would this have been an issue had YHWH later not prohibited such intermarriage? The case of Shechem is especially significant, because Jacob's sons speak expressly of becoming one people with the Shechemites through intermarriage (וְהָיִינוּ לְעַם אֶחָד, Gen 34:16). The entire chapter seems to be narrated in the light of the later prohibition.[94]

62. The motif of testing (נִסָּה) (Gen 22:1; Deut 8:2, 16; 13:4[3]). This motif is not unique to PN and D (cf. Exod 15:25; 16:4; 20:20), but it is more fully developed in D than elsewhere, including the prohibition against Israel testing YHWH (6:16; 33:8; cf. Exod 17:2, 7; Num 14:22).

63. שָׁמַר בְּרִית, "to keep a covenant" (Gen 17:9–10; Deut 7:9; 29:8[9]; 33:9).[95]

64. הֵפִיר הַבְּרִית, "to break a covenant" (Gen 17:14; Deut 31:16, 20).[96]

65. שָׁמַר מִשְׁמֶרֶת, "to keep [God's] charge" (Gen 26:5; Deut 11:1).[97]

66. שָׁמַר מִצְוֹתַי/מִצְוֹתָיו, "to keep God's commands" (Gen 26:5; Deut 13:5[4]).[98]

67. שָׁמַר חֻקּוֹתַי/חֻקּוֹתָיו, "to keep [God's] ordinances" (Gen 26:5; Deut 6:2).[99]

68. הִשָּׁמֶר לְךָ/לָכֶם פֶּן, "guard yourself/yourselves lest…" (Gen 24:6; 31:24; Deut 4:9, 23; 6:12; 8:11; 11:16; 12:13, 19, 30; 15:9).[100]

69. שָׁמַר תּוֹרֹתַי/הַתּוֹרָה, "to keep my instructions/the Instruction" (Gen 26:5; Deut 17:19). While Gen 26:5 shares תּוֹרָה with D, Exod 16:28 provides the closest analogue to this text (the plural refers to divine instructions generically). Although this usage

---

Gen 18:23–28 (6x); 20:4 (cf. also 6:9; 7:1).

94. This concern is not unique to Deut 7:2–4, but rooted in Exod 34:15–16.

95. Precisely, Deut 29:9[10] speaks of "keeping the words of this covenant and doing them" (וּשְׁמַרְתֶּם אֶת־דִּבְרֵי הַבְּרִית הַזֹּאת וַעֲשִׂיתֶם אֹתָם). According to Weinfeld (*Deuteronomy and the Deuteronomic School*, 330), P's equivalent to שָׁמַר הַבְּרִית is זָכַר הַבְּרִית, "to remember the covenant" (cf. Gen 9:15), in which case vv. 9–10 should be deleted from chapter 17 as a non-P insertion in a pericope that is universally applied to P. See, e.g., Blum, *Komposition der Vätergeschichte*, 420–32; Westermann, *Genesis 12–36*, 251–71. Against this interpretation, the computer analysis of Dershowitz et al. ("Computerized Source Criticism," 266) identified Gen 16:2—19:22 all as non-P.

96. The idiom also occurs in Lev 26:15, 44; Judg 2:1.

97. The expression links D and PN, but it occurs only here in both books. The phrase occurs frequently in Leviticus–Numbers: Lev 8:35; 18:30; 22:9; Num 1:53; 3:7, 8, 28, 32, 38; 8:26; 9:19, 23; 18:3, 4, 5; 31:30, 47.

98. Cf. also Deut 11:22; 13:19[18]; 19:9; 26:17, 18; 27:1; 28:9, 45; 30:10, 16.

99. See also Deut 8:11; 10:13; 11:1; 28:15, 45; 30:10, 16. However, the phrase also occurs in Exodus–Numbers: Exod 13:10; Lev 18:4, 5, 26; 19:19, 37; 20:8, 22. Remarkably שָׁמַר מִשְׁפָּטִים, "keep the judgments" never occurs in Genesis.

100. The idiom occurs nowhere else in the Tetrateuch.

is missing in D, the articular form, הַתּוֹרָה, occurs twenty times. Except for 32:46, it always functions as a formal title to the body of Moses' instruction.[101]

Shared Theological Motifs

While many lexical and idiomatic links are relatively easy to establish, exploration of the relationship between PN and D needs to include questions of ideology and theology. Some evidence we have tracked above borders on this, such as the relationship between Shechem in PN and Ebal and Gilgal in Deut 11 and 27. However, the phrase, [יּ]אֵלוֹן מוֹרֶה, "the oak[s] of Moreh," links these texts. Here I shall consider two additional issues: the portrayal of Egypt and the characterization of Abraham.

70. The Portrayal of Egypt

Both PN and D present an ambivalent picture of Egypt, namely, as a house of slavery for Israel and as a gracious host of the ancestors. Not surprisingly, the proportion of strokes devoted to each is reversed. While Egypt's role as the "house of slavery" (בֵּית עֲבָדִים) dominates D,[102] it receives only passing and veiled attention in Gen 15:13–14, which anticipates both Israel's enslavement and their exodus from Egypt. The reference to four hundred years makes little historical sense apart from the narratives in Exodus,[103] and limited theological sense without reference to D.

On the other hand, Genesis highlights Egypt's role as gracious host to the patriarchs in times of crisis (Gen 12:10–20; 37–50) and as the context in which the family of seventy individuals (Gen 46:27) became an innumerable population (cf. Exod 1:7).[104] This positive role receives scant attention in D. We may hear an allusion in Deut 10:19, "You shall love the alien (גֵּר), for you were foreigners (גֵּרִים) in Egypt." Most interpret the statement negatively—"Don't treat the alien the way you were treated in Egypt"—, but the statement is ambiguous and may be understood positively—"Love the alien, remembering how the Egyptians treated you." Verse 22 strengthens this possibility, noting the outcome of Israel's sojourn in Egypt, namely the mushrooming of Israel's population in fulfillment of YHWH's repeated promise to the ancestors (Gen 13:16; 22:16–17; 26:4; 28:14; 32:12[11]).[105] The only explicit deuteronomic reference to Egypt's positive role

---

101. Deut 1:5; 4:8, 44; 17:11, 18, 19; 27:3, 8, 26; 28:58, 61; 29:20, 28[21, 29]; 30:10; 31:9, 11, 12, 24, 26; 32:46. The poetic statement in 33:4 lacks the article on תּוֹרָה (tôrâ) but it obviously identifies a body of instruction, rather than individual teachings. In 33:10 the suffixed form, תּוֹרָתְךָ, "your Torah" is definite. הַתּוֹרָה represents a body of teaching elsewhere only in Exod 24:12, where it refers to the Decalogue, which is expressly described as something to be taught (לְהוֹרֹתָם), rather than legislated.

102. בֵּית עֲבָדִים, "house of slavery," occurs in Deut 5:6; 6:12; 7:8; 8:14; 13:6, 11[5, 10]. See also 5:15; 6:21; 15:15; 16:12; 24:11, 18, 22.

103. Note the incomplete sentence in Exod 2:28: וַיַּרְא אֱלֹהִים אֶת־בְּנֵי יִשְׂרָאֵל וַיֵּדַע אֱלֹהִים, "God saw the people of Israel—and God knew. [. . .]" Knew what? Presumably that the time to carry out what was promised in Gen 15:13–14 had come.

104. The roles are reversed. Whereas Gen 12:10–20 portrays Pharaoh as more righteous than the patriarch, 21:10–13 portrays Abraham and Sarah as exploitative owners of Hagar the Egyptian.

105. Gen 15:14 only hints at this dimension of the Egyptian experience; YHWH declares they will emerge with great wealth (יֵצְאוּ בִּרְכֻשׁ גָּדוֹל).

in Israel's history occurs in 23:8b[7b]: "You shall not treat an Egyptian as contemptible, because you were an alien in his land." In contrast to the harsh treatment prescribed against Ammonites and Moabites in vv. 4–7[3–6], once the Israelites have settled in the land, they are to welcome third-generation Egyptians even to the assembly of YHWH (קְהַל יְהוָה, vv. 8–9 [7–8]). This awareness probably accounts both for the detail in the narrator's description of Jacob and his family's descent into Egypt (Gen 37–50) and the inclusion of the otherwise unflattering story of Abraham's descent (Gen 12:10–20). Abraham's moral compromises in the face of the Egyptians reinforce the impression of faithlessness in response to the famine in Canaan. Nevertheless, his journey with Sarah anticipates Jacob's later divinely sanctioned descent (Gen 46:1–7).

71. *The Characterization of Abraham*

Because many of the comments relating to the patriarch's character in PN are cast with a Deuteronomic flavor, critical scholars see these as secondary interpolations. However, their ubiquity calls for another look. The following "baker's dozen" represent a few significant literary brushstrokes of Abraham:

a. Abraham was chosen (יָדַע) by YHWH (18:19; cf. the election [בָּחַר] of Israel in Deut 4:37; 7:6–7; 10:15; 14:2).

b. Abraham was a paragonic "God-fearer" (יְרֵא אֱלֹהִים אַתָּה, 22:12; cf. Deut 4:10; 31:12–13).[106]

c. Abraham trusted in YHWH (וְהֶאֱמִן בַּיהוָה, 15:6; cf. Deut 1:32; 9:23).

d. Abraham listened to the voice of God (עֵקֶב אֲשֶׁר־שָׁמַע, 22:18; עֵקֶב אֲשֶׁר שָׁמַעְתָּ בְּקֹלִי, אַבְרָהָם בְּקֹלִי, 26:5; cf. Deut 4:30; 26:17; 28:1–2).

e. Abraham swore by YHWH's name (אַשְׁבִּיעֲךָ בַּיהוָה אֱלֹהֵי הַשָּׁמַיִם וֵאלֹהֵי הָאָרֶץ, 24:3; cf. Deut 6:13; 10:20).

f. Abraham walked before YHWH (הִתְהַלֵּךְ לְפָנָי, 17:1; יְהוָה אֲשֶׁר־הִתְהַלַּכְתִּי לְפָנָיו, 24:20; cf. Deut 10:8; 18:5).

g. Abraham did physical obeisance before YHWH (וְנִשְׁתַּחֲוֶה וְנָשׁוּבָה אֲלֵיכֶם, 22:5 [cf. 24:48; cf. Deut 5:9; 26:10).

h. Abraham kept/walked in the way of YHWH (יְדַעְתִּיו לְמַעַן אֲשֶׁר יְצַוֶּה אֶת־בָּנָיו וְאֶת־בֵּיתוֹ אַחֲרָיו וְשָׁמְרוּ דֶּרֶךְ יְהוָה, 18:19; cf. Deut 5:33; 8:6; etc.).

i. Abraham demonstrated that he was a righteous man (וַיַּחְשְׁבֶהָ לּוֹ צְדָקָה, 15:6; cf. Deut 6:25; 16:20; 25:1).

j. Abraham refused to let his son Isaac marry a Canaanite (לֹא־תִקַּח אִשָּׁה לִבְנִי מִבְּנוֹת הַכְּנַעֲנִי, Gen 24:3;[107] cf. Deut 7:2–4).

k. Abraham passed the test of his faith (Gen 22:1, וְהָאֱלֹהִים נִסָּה אֶת־אַבְרָהָם; cf. Deut 8:2, 16; 13:3[2]).

---

106. For detailed discussion of the semantic range of the root ירא, see chapter 14, "The Fear of YHWH: The Theological Tie that Binds Deuteronomy and Proverbs," below, pp. 283–311.

107. Similarly, Isaac (Gen 28:1, but cf. 34:9–10).

l. Like his offspring Abraham was charged to keep the covenant (Gen 17:9, וְאַתָּה אֶת־בְּרִיתִי תִשְׁמֹר אַתָּה וְזַרְעֲךָ אַחֲרֶיךָ לְדֹרֹתָם; cf. Deut 29:8[9]; 33:9; cf. Deut 17:19 and Exod 16:28).

m. Abraham kept YHWH's charge, commands, ordinances, and the *torahs* (Gen 26:5; וַיִּשְׁמֹר מִשְׁמַרְתִּי מִצְוֹתַי חֻקּוֹתַי וְתוֹרֹתָי; cf. Deut 6:2; 11:1; 13:5[4]). This correlation is most remarkable of all. Although the patriarchal narratives never attribute love for YHWH to the three ancestors,[108] Deut 11:1 glosses love for YHWH with keeping his charge, his commands, his *torahs*, and his judgments. To be sure, the lexemes appear in a different order, but strikingly three of the four match. The only exception is "my instructions," which Deuteronomy replaces with מִשְׁפָּטָיו, "his judgments.[109]

Some have tried to drive a spiritual and ethical wedge between Abraham and Moses. Interpreting Exodus–Deuteronomy generically as a biography of Moses *sub lege* ("under the law") in contrast to the Genesis biography of Abraham, who lived *ante legem* ("before the law"), John Sailhamer has argued that Abraham embodied the divinely approved pattern of a life of faith, while Moses demonstrated the inevitable failure of a life driven by law.[110] The data cited above expose the flaws in this approach. To the narrator of Genesis Abraham was the paragon of faith and righteousness as defined by YHWH's covenant with Israel generally and laid out in detail in D.

The watchword of the Torah of Moses is צֶדֶק צֶדֶק תִּרְדֹּף, "Righteousness, only righteousness you shall pursue" (Deut 16:20). As elsewhere in D, here צֶדֶק/צְדָקָה, "righteousness," denotes the vassals' loyalty before their Suzerain, demonstrated in response acceptable to the Suzerain.[111] In Gen 15:6 Abraham exhibited "righteousness" (צְדָקָה) by trusting (הֶאֱמִן) in YHWH, and in 22:12 he demonstrated awed trust in YHWH (יְרֵא אֱלֹהִים) by radical obedience in the face of a preposterous divine demand.[112] Abraham's conversation with YHWH over the fate of Sodom and Gomorrah in Gen 18:16–33 demonstrated that for him "righteousness" was neither theoretical nor hypothetical, but profoundly ethical, in keeping with YHWH's expressed goal of his election: "I have singled him out, that he may instruct his children and his posterity to keep the way of YHWH by doing what is righteous (צְדָקָה) and just (מִשְׁפָּט), in order that YHWH may fulfill for Abraham what he has promised him" (18:19). Except for the single ordinance of circumcision (Gen 17:10–14),[113] and the general charges to "walk before me, and be blameless" (הִתְהַלֵּךְ לְפָנַי וֶהְיֵה תָמִים, Gen 17:1),[114] we have no record of YHWH revealing

---

108. Cf. Isa 41:8 and 2 Chr 20:7, which identify Abraham as "my/your beloved" (אֹהֲבִי/אֹהַבְךָ, respectively). While most translations treat the suffix as a subjective genitive (Abraham was the object of YHWH's love; cf. Isa 48:14), morphologically the Hebrew construction could also be interpreted objectively, "who loves me/you."

109. For further discussion, see Levenson, *Inheriting Abraham*, 142–44.

110. Sailhamer, "Compositional Strategies in the Pentateuch," 272–89.

111. On the meaning of צדק/צְדָקָה in Deuteronomy and extra-biblical inscriptions, see Block, "The Grace of Torah," 15–17.

112. Sirach 44:20 interprets Abraham's "fear" in this instance as "faith" (πιστός).

113. The act of circumcision is here cast within divine speech (וַיֹּאמֶר אֱלֹהִים אֶל־אַבְרָהָם), rather than legislation. Cf. 17:23, which describes Abraham's obedience in non-legal terms: "as God has spoken with him" (כַּאֲשֶׁר דִּבֶּר אִתּוֹ אֱלֹהִים).

114. Also cast as divine speech (וַיֹּאמֶר אֵלָיו, "and he said to him"), rather than legislation.

to him what "righteousness" and "justice" might entail. Even so, in Gen 26:5 YHWH explicitly credited Abraham with precisely the response demanded of Israel by YHWH himself at Sinai, and that Moses had called for on the Plains of Moab: "He has listened to my voice and kept my charge (מִשְׁמַרְתִּי), my commands (מִצְוֹתַי), my ordinances (חֻקּוֹתַי), and my instructions (תּוֹרֹתָי)." This is the righteousness of which Moses spoke in Deut 6:25, and this is the wisdom of which Ben Sirach wrote in the second century BCE:

> Abraham was the great father of a multitude of nations, and no one has been found like him in glory. He kept the Torah of the Most High (νόμον ὑψίστου), and entered into a covenant with him; he certified the covenant in his flesh, and when he was tested he proved faithful (Sir 44:19–20; NRSV modified).[115]

Deuteronomistic Features in the Patriarchal Narratives and the Composition of the Pentateuch

I follow scholarly consensus in acknowledging that the form, style, and intent of D differ dramatically from both the Pentateuchal narratives and the other constitutional documents (Decalogue, Book of the Covenant, Instructions on Holiness, and regulations governing worship and the priesthood).[116] My goal in this essay has been to demonstrate that despite D's distinctive features, the book exhibits a plethora of tight lexical, stylistic, and conceptual links with PN. However, as our occasional forays into the narratives of Joseph, the exodus, and the desert wanderings, and our references to Israel's other constitutional documents have shown, Deuteronomic features are scattered throughout the Pentateuch. How do we best account for these interconnections?

If we follow prevailing scholarly reconstruction of the Pentateuch's composition, we will probably treat these common elements as proto-deuteronomic features that later inspired the author of D or as editorial amendments to earlier documents post-dating the composition of D. Benjamin Kilchör has recently argued in convincing detail in *Mosetora und Jahwetora* that the order of the constitutional documents in the Pentateuch reflects the order of the composition of these respective documents.[117] The internal biblical evidence suggests that the Decalogue (Exod 20:2–17; Exod 31:18; 34:28–29; Deut 4:13; 5:6–22; 10:1–5), the Book of the Covenant (Exod 20:22–23:19; cf. 24:4), the speeches of Moses in D (31:9–13), and the concluding song (31:19, 22) were committed

---

115. Although Jacob's removal of foreign gods (Gen 35:2–4) recalls Deut 7:3–5, as men of faith/righteousness, both Isaac and Jacob appear as flatter figures than Abraham. Both the Deuteronomistic historian and the Chronicler pick up the collocation הַגֵּכָר אֶת־אֱלֹהִים הָסִיר, "put away the foreign gods" (Josh 24:14, 23; Judg 10:16; 1 Sam 7:3; 2 Chr 33:15). However, there is no need here to follow Second Temple Jewish literature that claims that Abraham actually had access to the laws of the Torah centuries before Moses (cf. Baruch 3:36b–4:4). For full discussion of this matter, see Levenson, *Inheriting Abraham*, 113–75.

116. With Radday and Shore these differences are best attributed to distinctions in genre rather than to different authors (*Genesis*, 189–90). What I identify as "constitutional documents" most refer to as the legal material. I find the latter characterization misleading generically.

117. See note 63 above.

to writing almost immediately after their promulgation. Proof of the separate textual existence of the Instructions on Holiness is less clear. The seventeen occurrences of the narrative heading, וַיְדַבֵּר יְהוָה אֶל־מֹשֶׁה לֵּאמֹר, "And YHWH spoke to Moses saying," suggest that Lev 17–27 consists of at least seventeen (or eighteen) discreet pronouncements.[118] Leviticus 26:46 suggests that at one stage this may have been a colophon for a written collection of divine "ordinances, judgments, and instructions" (הַחֻקִּים וְהַמִּשְׁפָּטִים וְהַתּוֹרֹת), perhaps commencing with Lev 17:1.[119] But the author of the Pentateuch has intentionally embedded these documents in narratives recounting the divine hand on the ancestors, their descent into and exodus from Egypt, the covenant making events at Sinai, the desert wanderings, and in Deuteronomy their imminent entry into Canaan, in fulfillment of the covenant promises to the ancestors and reiterated to the exodus generation (Gen 15:13–21; Exod 2:24; 3:9; 6:6–8; 23:20–31).

Concerning what kinds of sources underlie the ancestral and exodus narratives, we may only speculate. With reference to the latter, Exod 17:14 and Num 33:2 suggest that while the Israelites journeyed from Egypt to the promised land they kept a written diary of their experiences. While the literacy assumed here need not apply to the time of the patriarchs, at least four centuries earlier,[120] it is unlikely that memories of YHWH's call of Abraham and oversight of the lives of the ancestors would not have been treasured and at least passed on orally from generation to generation, perhaps until the time of the exodus. The formula, אֵלֶּה תּוֹלְדֹת, "These are the generations," followed by the personal name of the line whose history follows, either in the form of a genealogy or a narrative,[121] hints at records of some sort. The reference to a "document" (סֵפֶר) in Gen 5:1 (זֶה סֵפֶר תּוֹלְדֹת אָדָם) suggests that written sources may underlie these narratives.[122] It is plausible that, along with their more explicitly sacerdotal responsibilities, after their installation to priestly service, at an early stage some Levites assumed the role of custodians of Israel's patriarchal traditions, that these traditions were passed on orally for centuries, and were finally committed to writing on separate documents, some of which are identifiable by this תּוֹלְדֹת formula.[123] Having committed these memories to writing, the Levites will have had these documents in hand when the Israelites crossed the Jordan into the promised land. These records represent the sources of the PN as we now have them in Genesis.

If this hypothetical reconstruction is correct, then the documents the Israelites carried across the Jordan would have included sacred narratives, legal constitutional material from Sinai, Moses' hortatory valedictory addresses, as well as commemorative songs and hymns. Whether or not the people treasured these separate documents as

---

118. Lev 17:1; 18:1; 19:1; 20:1; 21:16; 22:1, 17, 26; 23:1, 9, 23, 26, 33; 24:1, 13; 25:1; 27:1. To these we should probably add וַיֹּאמֶר יְהוָה אֶל־מֹשֶׁה ("and YHWH said to Moses") in 21:1, which introduces a speech for the priests (vv. 1–15).

119. Note the colophon-like ending to chapter 16.

120. But see the essay by Hess, "Second Millennium BC Cuneiform from the Southern Levant and the Literature of the Pentateuch," forthcoming in *Exploring the Composition of the Pentateuch*.

121. Gen 2:4; 5:1; 6:9; 10:1; 11:10, 27; 25:12, 19; 36:1, 9; 37:2; Num 3:1.

122. Many scholars assign these *tôlĕdōt* formulas to the Priestly layer, some viewing them as the skeleton for the original Priestly narrative. See Blum, *Komposition der Vätergeschichte*, 432–446.

123. Cf. Garrett, *Rethinking Genesis*.

scripture and used them in worship we cannot know. However, we know this was true of Moses' Torah—which he charged the Levites to read before the entire assembly at the festival of Sukkoth every seven years (Deut 31:10–12, 24–26)—and of the "Song of YHWH"—which was to function as a sort of national anthem.[124] We do not know what use Israelites made of the other Pentateuchal documents in early worship, though tradition has it that the Israelites recited the Decalogue at Shavuoth in commemoration of YHWH's establishment of his covenant with Israel at Sinai.[125]

But when were these disparate documents collected, arranged, and integrated into the composition we know as the Pentateuch? Whybray has made a strong case for interpreting the entire Pentateuch as a coherent document, composed by a single author, à la the Greek historian Herodotus. While his extremely late dating of the Pentateuch is dubious, his impression that the author was a profoundly gifted historian is sound. Indeed, Martin Noth's assessment of the Deuteronomistic History applies here as well: this composition is the product of an author, not an editor, who "brought together material from highly varied traditions and arranged it according to a carefully conceived plan."[126] Based on anticipatory statements in earlier texts (e.g., Gen 17:7–8; Exod 3:12), the proportion of text devoted to getting Jacob's family into Egypt (Gen 37–50), and from there to Sinai (Exod 1–18), and especially the amount of text space involving Israel's experiences at Sinai,[127] obviously the heart of this plan is YHWH's establishment of his covenant with Israel at Sinai (Exod 19–Lev 26; cf. Fig. 6.1, below, page 125).[128]

Making the most of the sources available to him, the author has created an impressive narrative, equal if not superior in literary quality to anything the Greek historians Herodotus and Thucydides produced in the fifth century BCE. The pervasive links between PN and D suggest the author was thoroughly schooled in the Torah of Moses, and that he wrote from the perspective of the promises to the ancestors having been fulfilled. The composer of Israel's first comprehensive Scripture perceived the covenant ratification rituals at Sinai as the establishment (הָקִים בְּרִית) of the covenant made with

---

124. On which, see Block, "The Power of Song," 162–88.

125. See Weinfeld, "The Decalogue," 12–15.

126. Noth, *The Deuteronomistic History*, 1–110.

127. Assuming ca. 280 years for the patriarch's lives (Abraham was 100 when Isaac was born [Gen 17:1]; Isaac was ca. 50 when Jacob was born [25:20–21]; Jacob was 130 years old when he went to Egypt [47:9–28]), a 430-year sojourn in Egypt (Exod 12:41), and 40 years from the time of the exodus to Moses' death (Deut 1:3; the "biography of Moses" [Exod 1:1—Deut 34:12] spans 120 years [Deut 34:7]), 16% of historical time (120/750 years) takes up 78% of narrated time (Exodus–Deuteronomy = 59369 words/Gen 12:27—Deut 34:12 = 76276 words). Even more dramatic, 0.13% of historical time (less than one year at Sinai; cf. Exod 19:1; Num 10:11) takes up 28% of narrated time (Exod 19:1—Lev 27:34 = 21393 words/Gen 12:27—Deut 34:12 = 76276). The figures are even more impressive when we consider that a segment of Moses' first address in Deuteronomy (4:9–31), and the entire second (4:44—11:32) and third (12:1—26:19; 28:1–69[29:1]) addresses represent commentary on Israel's Sinai experience. Therefore, we must add 9522 words to the 21393 above, yielding 30915 words: 41% of the text is devoted to 0.13% of the historical time. These figures are based in part on the statistics provided in the "Statistical Appendix" to *Theological Lexicon of the Old Testament*, 3:1444–45.

128. Note the concluding colophons at Lev 26:46 and 27:34. Compare Jacob Milgrom's diagram of "The Theological-Literary Structure of the Hexateuch," in *Numbers*, xviii.

Abraham (Gen 17:7, 19; Exod 6:4–7), and the incorporation of his descendants into the mission announced at the outset (Gen 12:1–3; cf. Exod 19:5–6).

Figure 6.1
The Place of Sinai/Horeb in the Plot of the Pentateuch

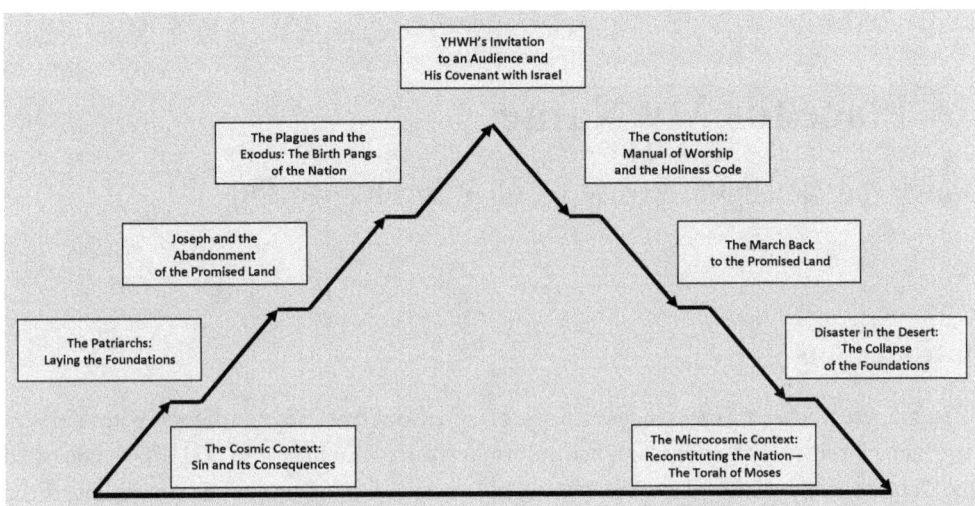

Whenever the entire Pentateuchal project was completed, the compiled valedictory addresses of Moses (D) apparently constituted the תּוֹרַת מֹשֶׁה (Torah of Moses) that provided the basis of David's charge to Solomon in 1 Kgs 2:2–4, that Josiah's men discovered in the Temple in 621 (2 Kgs 23:3–16), and that Ezra read before the assembled gathering of returned exiles in Jerusalem (Neh 8:1–18). The person responsible for the narrative stitching in D may well have been the author of the entire Pentateuch. While Hosea's use of D suggests the early eighth century BCE as the *terminus ad quem* for the entire project,[129] it may have been completed centuries earlier.[130] Eventually, in recognition of the literary unity of Genesis–Deuteronomy, the title given to the book of Deuteronomy (תּוֹרַת מֹשֶׁה) was applied to the entire Pentateuch, so that by New Testament times Jesus could summarize the contents of the Hebrew Bible as ὁ νόμος Μωσέως καὶ οἱ προφῆται καὶ οἱ ψαλμοί (Luke 24:44).

---

129. For convincing defense of the chronological priority of D vis à vis Hosea, see Carsten Vang, "When a Prophet Quotes Moses," 277–303.

130. Except for Juha Pakkala's last argument (for which there is a better explanation than he proposes), his nine arguments for a Persian date for D all fit much more naturally in the premonarchic period ("The Date of the Oldest Edition of Deuteronomy," 394–95). This impression is reinforced by the virtual absence of theophores involving *Yah* or *Yeho* in the Pentateuch. יוֹכֶבֶד (Jochebed, Moses and Aaron's mother, Exod 6:20), יְהוֹשֻׁעַ (Joshua, Num 13:16), and יוֹאָשׁ (Joash, Judg 6:11–12) are the only exceptions. However, Num 13:16 credits Moses with changing Joshua's name from הוֹשֵׁעַ to יְהוֹשֻׁעַ (in the wake of the revelatory events associated with the exodus and the Sinai experience). Per Carsten Vang (in private communication, February 26, 2016), the paucity of YHWH names in the Pentateuch suggests the patriarchal stories incorporated in the Pentateuch were fairly fixed written traditions prior to the tenth century.

7

"A Place for My Name"

Horeb and Zion in the Mosaic Vision of Israelite Worship[1]

Introduction

THE RELATIONSHIP BETWEEN ISRAEL's protracted but one-time audience with YHWH at Sinai/Horeb and the regular encounters between Israelites and YHWH envisioned by Deuteronomy at the place YHWH would choose for his name has not received the attention it deserves. In an earlier publication I suggested that

> the place that YHWH chooses for his name ensures a means of communion with all Israel in perpetuity, analogous to his communion with them at Horeb, except that here Moses democratizes the experience. At Horeb only a privileged few ate in YHWH's presence; here Moses opens fellowship with him to everyone.[2]

Upon further reflection and study, this proposal seems unwarranted; inasmuch as the contrasts between the Israelites' worship at Horeb[3] and their future worship at the central sanctuary as envisioned in Deuteronomy are much more dramatic than their shared features, the former actually provides a foil for the latter. My strategy in this paper is first to investigate Deuteronomy's disposition toward Horeb and the events that happened there, and then to explore Deuteronomy's vision for the kind of experiences that Moses anticipated would transpire in the future at the place that YHWH would choose

---

1. This is a stylistically modified version of an article that was previously published in the *Journal of the Evangelical Theological Society* 58 (2015): 221–47, and is a version of a paper presented to the Evangelical Theological Society in San Diego, November, 2014. I am grateful to Andreas Köstenberger, editor of the Journal, for his kind permission to republish it here. The study was inspired by Michael Kibbe, whose Wheaton College Ph.D. dissertation, now published as *Godly Fear or Ungodly Failure? Hebrews 12:18–29 and the Sinai Theophanies*," explored the inner biblical story of Israel's encounter with YHWH at Sinai, beginning with Exod 19–24 and ending with Hebrews 12. I am grateful to Michael and to Franklin Wang for reading earlier drafts of this paper, and for their helpful suggestions in improving it.

2. Block, *Deuteronomy*, 308.

3. In keeping with Deuteronomy's preferred designation, I shall refer to the mountain where YHWH established his covenant with Israel as Horeb, rather than Sinai.

to establish his name. My method is largely inductive and constructive, sifting through the text of Deuteronomy to determine which features of the Israelites' encounters with YHWH at these two places were shared and which features were unique.

Sinai/Horeb in the Book of Deuteronomy

The toponym, Sinai (סִינַי) occurs only once in Deuteronomy, in the exordium to Moses' farewell blessing of the tribes of Israel:

> YHWH came from Sinai
>   and dawned upon them from Seir;
> He shone forth from Mount Paran;
>   accompanied by myriads of holy ones,
> and fire emanating from his right (33:2, author translation).

In its details the entire exordium (vv. 2–5) is extremely difficult to interpret, but the gist seems clear. YHWH is portrayed in glorious theophanic form as coming from the mountains in the desert, presumably to deliver his people, and to be acknowledged as king over all the tribes of Israel. The place from which he came is identified by three names: Sinai, Seir, and Mount Paran. To Moses and the Israelites camped on the plains of Moab east of the Jordan almost forty years later (2:7), these three names identified generally the mountainous region in the southern Sinai Peninsula. There YHWH had confirmed Israel as his covenant people in fulfillment of his promise to their ancestor Abraham in Gen 17:7. But now from a distance, both in time and space, in Deut 33:2–5 the Horeb theophany takes on a different significance. Here YHWH appeared as the divine warrior who rose in defense of his people Israel. This text perceives Horeb not primarily as a place where the law was given or where YHWH's covenant with Israel was formalized, but as the place where YHWH had appeared in his cosmic and transcendent glory, accompanied by a myriad of holy ones and sending out fire from his right side.

In Deuteronomy Moses' preferred designation for the mountain of revelation is Horeb (חֹרֵב). The name occurs nine times in the book, twice in the narrative frames to the first two addresses (1:2; 28:69[29:1]),[4] four times in the first address (1:6, 19; 4:10, 15), and three times in the second address (5:2; 9:8; 18:16).[5] Whereas "Sinai" is often preceded by "Mount,"[6] "Horeb" never is. While the narrator's preference for Horeb suggests he has been caught up by the spirit of Moses, it is unclear why this name should have been favored over Sinai. Since the name is related etymologically to חָרְבָּה, "wasteland, ruin," it may reflect Moses' disposition toward the mountain as a nondescript and empty piece of land in contrast to the "good land" (אֶרֶץ טוֹבָה) of Canaan (8:7–10; 9:6;

---

4. Like Moses in 33:2, in 1:2 the narrator associates Horeb with Seir, though he notes that Seir lay between Horeb and Israel's destination Kadesh-barnea. Seir/Horeb is traditionally identified with Jebel Musa ("Mount of Moses"), which rises 7486 feet above the southern Sinai desert.

5. Deuteronomy accounts for more than one half of the occurrences of the name. Cf. Exod 3:1; 17:6; 33:6; 1 Kgs 8:9; 19:8; 2 Chr 5:10; Ps 106:19; Mal 3:22[4:4].

6. Exod 19:11, 18, 20, 23; 24:16; 31:18; 34:2, 4, 29, 32; Lev 7:38; 25:1; 26:46; 27:34; Num 3:1; 28:6; Neh 9:13; cf. Acts 7:30, 38; Gal 4:24–25 in the New Testament.

11:10–12).⁷ A more ideological explanation is also possible.⁸ Contrary to the intention reflected in Exod 19–24, after four decades of putting up with this miserable generation (cf. Deut 1:9–12), for Moses Sinai represented a spiritual "wasteland."⁹ This should have been the place where Israel's history as the officially recognized people of YHWH began. Not only had YHWH entered into covenant relationship with them there, but there he had also revealed himself and his will in a manner previously unimaginable (Deut 4:9–15, 36). But Moses associates Horeb with Israel's rebellion (9:7–21). For him Horeb represented a false start (cf. 5:1–5), since there the previous generation had apostatized and ignited YHWH's fury (9:8). With his preference for "Horeb," Moses may also have intentionally sought to detract attention away from the physical site, which served as only a temporary "mountain of God," and to prepare his audience for "the [permanent] place that YHWH will choose" in the land of Canaan (cf. 12:5, 11, 14, 18, 26, etc.).

Like the narrator in 1:2, in his recollections Moses recognized that Horeb was the place from which the Israelites had set out for the promised land as YHWH's covenant people. Their journey had indeed begun in Egypt (9:7), but instead of heading directly to Canaan YHWH had led them here for a special appointment with himself. Although he had entered into covenant relationship with his people here (5:2), they had broken that covenant within forty days by worshiping the golden calf (9:7–21). After Moses' intercession for the people, YHWH had renewed the covenant (9:25—10:5), and eventually they set out from there for their final destination in Canaan (1:6, 19).

Moses' recollections of Israel's encounters with YHWH at Horeb are concentrated in three primary texts (4:9–15; 5:1–33; 9:8—10:11) and alluded to in several others (4:33, 36; 18:16). His descriptions in the first two suggest that what transpired between YHWH and Israel on Mount Horeb was an extremely formal event, involving an audience with YHWH in the fullest sense of the expression. Because Moses' primary concern in Deut 9 was the people's rebellion against YHWH at Horeb, he mentioned the actual audience with YHWH only in passing (v. 10), but long enough to characterize that event as "the day of the assembly" (יוֹם הַקָּהָל; cf. 10:4; 18:16), to identify the primary feature of that event as "all the words that YHWH spoke with you" (כָּל־הַדְּבָרִים אֲשֶׁר דִּבֶּר יְהוָה עִמָּכֶם), and to set the context "at the mountain from the midst of the fire" (בָּהָר מִתּוֹךְ הָאֵשׁ).

Moses did not name the mountain in Deut 4:33 and 36, but twice he remembered that the people heard God's/YHWH's voice (קוֹל), noting first that he was speaking (מְדַבֵּר, v. 33) and second that they heard YHWH's words (דְּבָרָיו) from the midst of the fire (מִתּוֹךְ הָאֵשׁ). Moses' rhetorical question ("Has any people heard the voice of God speaking from the midst of the fire as the Israelites have heard it, and survived?") hints at the extraordinary nature of the event and the potentially life threatening force of the word of God (v. 33). Moses would recount in greater detail this dimension of Israel's experience at Horeb in 5:1–33, and later in 18:16 recall the problem by quoting the people's verbal response to YHWH's speech: "Do not let me hear the voice of YHWH my God or see

---

7. The expression, "good land" (אֶרֶץ טוֹבָה) occurs ten times in Deuteronomy: 1:25, 35; 3:25; 4:21–22; 6:18; 8:7, 10; 9:6; 11:17.

8. Similar to Ezekiel's avoidance of "Zion," because his syncretistic generation had claimed the sacred place as a [false] basis for security.

9. For further discussion on the issue, see Perlitt, "Sinai und Horeb," 303–22.

this great fire any more, or I will die." By referring to "people" (עַם) in 4:33, he highlighted the corporate nature of the experience at Horeb.

In 4:36 Moses noted that the purpose of the divine speech was to discipline (יִסַּר) Israel. YHWH had not appeared simply to add an eighth item to the wonders of the world. In 8:5 the word יִסַּר will be used of YHWH training Israel as a man trains his son, presumably to walk in his ways. In this context the discipline obviously does not refer to punishment, but to education. He does not declare the goal of the instruction here, but 4:10 suggests "to fear YHWH" as a possibility. However, the theological conclusion drawn in 4:35 and 39 suggest that the intent was that Israel might "know that YHWH alone is God"; the God of Israel is *sui generis*—in a class all his own.

In remembering that YHWH had let his voice be heard from heaven but that it had been heard on earth from the midst of the fire, Moses drew attention to a fundamental conviction in Israelite theology: YHWH is *both* in heaven, his true residence, *and* on earth, in the very midst of the fire. Indeed, as in Exod 3, the fire functions as the visible symbol of his presence, a fact reinforced syllogistically by the last clause of verse 36:

> On earth YHWH reveals his fire;
> YHWH speaks from the midst of the fire;
> Therefore YHWH is present in the fire.[10]

Hundley rightly notes that YHWH's presence is much more than "a disembodied voice." Although veiled, his presence in the fire is real. If other ancient Near Easterners could conceive of their gods as being simultaneously in heaven and within their statues, surely YHWH could be present in heaven and on earth at the same time.[11] Indeed, with the fire YHWH brings his radiant and lethal splendor to earth without deserting heaven.

The fullest descriptions of Israel's Horeb experience are found in 4:9–15 and 5:1–33. On first sight Moses appears to set the stage for the former by highlighting its significance in 4:7–8: For which other great nation has a god so near to it as YHWH our God is whenever we call to him? And what other great nation has statutes and judgments as righteous (צַדִּיקִים) as this entire *Torah* that I am setting before you today?

To be sure, Horeb was the place where YHWH revealed his statutes and judgments (חֻקִּים וּמִשְׁפָּטִים; cf. Exod 21:1—23:19),[12] but the references to calling on YHWH and this *Torah* that Moses is presenting to the people "today" point in a different direction. The emphatically redundant opening to verse 9 (רַק הִשָּׁמֶר לְךָ וּשְׁמֹר נַפְשְׁךָ מְאֹד, "Only guard yourself and watch yourself diligently") and the focus in verses 9–10 on "events" (הַדְּבָרִים) the people witnessed" (רָאוּ עֵינֶיךָ) and "a day" (יוֹם) when all Israel stood before YHWH at Horeb distinguish that event from what is currently transpiring on the Plains of Moab (Fig. 7.1).

---

10. For full discussion of the real presence of YHWH in Deuteronomy, see Wilson, *Out of the Midst of the Fire,* especially pp. 66–73.

11. Hundley, "To Be or Not to Be," 538–40.

12. If חֻקִּים refers to divine decrees (from a root meaning "to engrave" [a text]), then מִשְׁפָּטִים refers to divine "judgments" concerning the righteous conduct of YHWH's vassals.

THE TRIUMPH OF GRACE

Figure 7.1
The Syntactical and Discourse Structure of Deuteronomy 4:9–10

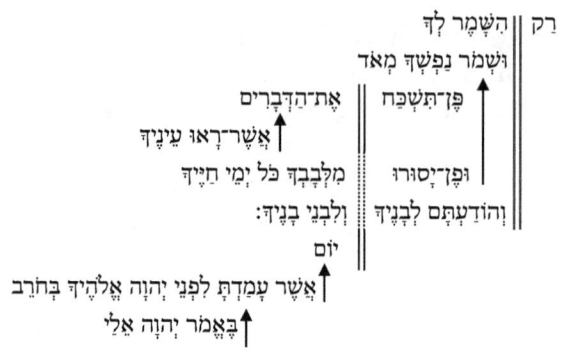

The "events" that transpired on that "day" (vv. 10b–14) may be summarized as follows:

1. At Horeb YHWH charged Moses to assemble the people for an audience with him (v. 10b).

2. The people assembled at the foot of the mountain, which blazed with fire and whose top was shrouded in deep darkness (v. 11).

3. YHWH spoke audibly from the mountain declaring his covenant, that is, the ten basic principles of covenant relationship (v. 13).[13]

4. YHWH charged Moses to teach the "statutes and judgments" (חֻקִּים וּמִשְׁפָּטִים) to Israel (v. 14).

Moses' recollection is cryptic, awaiting a fuller recounting in chapter 5. However, several features highlight the formality of Israel's encounter with YHWH at Horeb. First, Horeb was the place where Israel stood before YHWH (עָמַדְתָּ לִפְנֵי יְהוָה אֱלֹהֶיךָ בְּחֹרֵב, v. 10).[14]

---

13. Whereas NIV treats "the Ten Commands" [sic, read "Ten Words"] as appositional to "covenant," verse 13 consists of two clauses, the first declaring the principal idea and the second clarifying it: "Then he declared to you his covenant, that is, he commanded you to do the Ten Words." The first clause refers to the entire process of covenant making through YHWH's speech at Horeb, which obviously includes the announcement of the Decalogue, but it includes much more. The second clause concretizes the image by drawing attention to the Decalogue as the official covenant document by which the Israelites are to live. "The Ten Words" should be treated as object of the infinitive, "to do" (לַעֲשׂוֹת), which YHWH commanded the people. For discussion, see most recently Hwang, *The Rhetoric of Remembrance*, 192–96. Hwang builds on the work of Lohfink and Braulik, "Deuteronomium 4,13 und der Horebbund," 29–33.

14. The idiom, "to stand before" a human superior, may involve either courtiers before the king (1 Kgs 12:8//2 Chr 10:8, Rehoboam's counsellors) or individuals in a formal hearing (1 Kgs 3:16, prostitutes before Solomon; 2 Kgs 4:12, Shunamite woman before Elisha; 5:15, Naaman before Elisha; 8:9, Hazael before Elisha). As a theological idiom the expression is used generally of having God's approval (1 Sam 6:20; Ezra 9:15; Jer 15:19; cf. Ps 15:1; 24:3), but usually more specifically of (1) officials in YHWH's court: a spirit (1 Kgs 22:21//2 Chr 18:20); Levitical priests (Lev 9:5; Deut 10:8; 18:7; Ezek 44:15; cf. Zech 3:1); prophets (Elijah, 1 Kgs 17:1; 18:15; 19:11; Elisha, 2 Kgs 3:14; 5:16; Rechabites [Jonadab], Jer 35:19); an advocate (to stand in the breach, Gen 18:22; 19:27 [Abraham]; Ps 106:23

Second, technically in essence this event was not primarily theophanic, but auditory—an audience with YHWH. Regarding the first, the people saw no form (תְּמוּנָה) of God (4:12, 15); indeed, the mountain was shrouded in "darkness, cloud, and deep gloom" (חֹשֶׁךְ עָנָן וַעֲרָפֶל).[15] Metaphorically the intense darkness and cloud expressed the perceptible though invisible presence of God, but practically they protected the Israelites from the lethal dose of divine glory.

Regarding the second, the choice of הַדְּבָרִים (literally, "the words") in the clause, הַדְּבָרִים אֲשֶׁר־רָאוּ עֵינֶיךָ ("the events that your eyes saw") hints at the focus of the revelation, that is, the "words" (הַדְּבָרִים, vv. 9, 12) and the "voice/sound" (קוֹל, v. 12a, b) of YHWH. The preponderance of verbs for speech reinforces this impression: YHWH caused the people to hear (הִשְׁמִיעַ, v. 10) his words, he spoke (דִּבֶּר, v. 12) to them, he declared (הִגִּיד) to them his covenant, and he commanded the Ten Words (v. 13). Moses identifies the sound the people heard as "the Ten Words" (עֲשֶׂרֶת הַדְּבָרִים),[16] which functioned as shorthand for the covenant YHWH made with Israel at Horeb. Significantly, although the Israelites standing before Moses possessed no visual image of the Horeb experience, the "sound" of YHWH's voice had been inscribed on stone tablets (v. 13; cf. 10:4), elsewhere referred to as "the tablets of the covenant" (לוּחֹת הַבְּרִית, 9:9, 11, 15).

Third, on that occasion (בָּעֵת הַהִוא) YHWH charged Moses to teach Israel the statutes and judgments, a shorthand expression for the regulations and laws revealed at Horeb (4:14). Here Moses does not even hint at the reasons behind the transition from YHWH's direct address of the people (4:10–13) to Moses' mediation of the revelation to follow. Chapter 5 will provide those details.

Moses begins his second address by recounting in considerable detail what the Israelites had experienced at Horeb. Inasmuch as the core of that text is devoted to repeating with some slight modifications the words that had previously come from YHWH's lips (5:6–21), in Moses' mind the heart of that event involved YHWH's verbal communication with his people. Verses 2–5 and 22–33 provide a narrative frame for these words.

The narrative preamble and the opening call to attention (5:1) create anticipation for instruction on the statutes and judgments YHWH had revealed at Horeb. Instead we hear Moses' interpretation of what happened at the mountain. Significantly, to Moses Horeb was not merely the location of divine verbal revelation; it was also the place where God made a covenant with the present generation of Israelites (v. 3).[17] His transfer of the present generation to Horeb is just one element in a series of events in which they supposedly had participated: (a) YHWH made a covenant (כָּרַת בְּרִית) with them

---

[Moses]; Jer 15:1 [Moses, Samuel]; Ezek 22:30); two witnesses (Rev 11:4); (2) people before God for judgment (Dan 7:10) or a formal convocation (Deut 4:10; 29:9[10], 14[15]; 2 Chr 20:13).

15. The choice of words intentionally echoes Exod 19:16 and 20:21. Ezekiel 34:12 speaks of "a day of cloud and deep gloom" (יוֹם עָנָן וַעֲרָפֶל), suggesting this combination represented a stock phrase. Cf. also Ps 97:2.

16. On the Decalogue as "ten words," see Block, "The Decalogue in the Hebrew Scriptures," 4–5; idem, "Reading the Decalogue Right to Left," 24–25.

17. The heaping up of expressions focuses attention on this people here and now: "with us" (עִמָּנוּ, v. 2); "indeed with us, we, these, here, today, all of us, living" (כִּי אִתָּנוּ אֲנַחְנוּ אֵלֶּה פֹה הַיּוֹם כֻּלָּנוּ חַיִּים, v. 3).

(vv. 2–3); (b) YHWH spoke (דִּבֶּר) directly[18] to this generation from the midst of the fire (v. 4); (c) through Moses YHWH declared his word (הִגִּיד אֶת־דְּבַר יְהוָה) to them; and (d) YHWH's "saying" (לֵאמֹר) the Decalogue (v. 5) made this generation the recipient of his communication. By specifying "this covenant" (הַבְּרִית הַזֹּאת, v. 3) and reciting the Decalogue Moses superimposes the present covenant ratifying procedure on the Plains of Moab over the events at Horeb and superimposes his current addresses on the "statutes and judgments" (v. 1) over the "Book of the Covenant" and the remainder of the Horeb revelation. Furthermore, although the boundaries between the discreet elements of the people's experience at Horeb are blurred, he casts his own role in the present context as the fulfillment of that requested by the people at Horeb and assigned to him by YHWH (v. 5).

The boundaries among the elements of the Horeb experience may be blurred in verses 1–5, but this is definitely not the case in verses 5:22–30, as Moses focuses on a singular element: the people's response to YHWH's speech from the midst of the fire. He has been broaching this subject carefully, teasing his present audience with his reference to the "darkness, cloud, and deep gloom" (4:11), asking whether anyone could survive the voice of deity speaking from the midst of the fire (4:33), alluding to the purpose of this element (יָסַר, "to discipline," 4:36), and specifically attributing their stopping short of ascending the mountain to fear before the fire (5:5). After Moses had recited YHWH's words from the fire he could focus on the people's reaction to those words.[19] His recollections divide into four parts: a narrative summary of what has transpired (v. 22), followed by three roughly equal parts, each involving a different voice: the people (vv. 23–27), YHWH (vv. 28–32), and Moses (5:32—6:3). Inasmuch as the last section involves Moses fulfilling his newly assigned role, for our purposes, we need to examine only verses 22–31.

The Transcriptional Epilogue (5:22)

Although usually considered the introduction to the next literary section extending from 5:22 to 6:3,[20] on form-critical grounds and based on ancient treaty form, this verse represents a colophonic conclusion to Moses' recitation of the Decalogue, summarizing what the narrator described in greater detail in Exod 24:12–18 and 31:18.

Echoing expressions that he had used in 4:11–14, Moses reminds the people once more of several key facts.

1. The words of the covenant were declared by YHWH himself (cf. 4:10, 13).
2. The words were declared publicly to the entire assembly (קָהָל; cf. 4:10).
3. YHWH spoke from the midst of the fire (cf. 4:12, 15, 36; also 5:4).

---

18. Since the Israelites saw no form of YHWH (4:12, 15), here "face to face" (פָּנִים בְּפָנִים) cannot be interpreted literally, but functions idiomatically for "directly, one on one."

19. Although 5:5 suggests the people's fear preceded hearing the word, in 4:33 he had hinted at the potentially lethal force of the words.

20. Thus Craigie, *Deuteronomy*, 164; Weinfeld, *Deuteronomy 1–11*, 319–27; Tigay, *Deuteronomy*, 72; Merrill, *Deuteronomy*, 157–58; C. J. H. Wright, *Deuteronomy*, 90. Not so Ridderbos, *Deuteronomy*, 99–100; Labuschagne, *Deuteronomium*, 1:56–57.

4. The mountain was wrapped in cloud and deep darkness (cf. 4:11).
5. YHWH spoke with a (loud) voice (cf. 4:12).
6. YHWH's direct communication with Israel was limited to the Decalogue (cf. 4:13–14).[21]
7. YHWH's transcription of the Decalogue on two tablets of stone and his delivery of the documents to Moses confirmed the permanent validity of the Decalogue for the Israelites.

Moses observes that YHWH's revelation at Horeb was visual (fire and thick cloud), oral (YHWH spoke words with a strong voice), and textual (written on two tablets of stone). But he also notes the continuity between the oral and the textual revelation: what YHWH said, that he wrote, and no more. And there can be no mistaking the authority of the document: YHWH, the covenant Suzerain, both spoke it and wrote it. He spoke the words to the whole assembly, but he placed the document into the hands of Moses, his authorized interpreter of the text.

The People's Response to the Theophany at Horeb (5:23–27)

Moses describes the response of the assembly (קָהָל, v. 22) in rather official terms. Upon hearing the thunder of YHWH's voice (קוֹל גָּדוֹל, literally "big voice/sound," v. 22), a delegation of tribal leaders (רָאשֵׁי שְׁבָטִים) and elders (זְקֵנִים)[22] approached Moses on behalf of the people with a specific request. Sounding like an utterance crafted by a speechwriter, the request consists of three parts, each opening with a rhetorical marker: (1) "Look" (הֵן), followed by a description of the visual experience at Horeb (v. 24); (2) "And now" (וְעַתָּה), followed by an expression of the *Angst* the theophany had created in the people (vv. 25–26); (3) "You approach [YHWH] and listen..." (קְרַב אַתָּה וּשֲׁמָע), followed by a proposal to resolve the crisis (v. 27). Here Moses has expanded what the narrator had reported in ten words in Exod 20:19 into a carefully constructed seventy-five-word address.

Moses' report of the leaders' speech notes three dimensions of the Horeb experience: (1) They acknowledged the sight as a revelation of divine glory and majesty[23]—as if YHWH had permitted a glimpse inside his heavenly palace. (2) They recognized the sound from inside the fire as YHWH's voice. (3) They expressed amazement that they had survived a direct encounter with divinity (v. 24; cf. 4:33). However, the rhetorical questions that follow (vv. 25–26) suggest the people were unsure they had escaped; the great fire from which they heard the sound of YHWH's voice could still consume them

---

21. With the clause, "and he added nothing more" (וְלֹא יָסָף), Moses formally declares the end of YHWH's direct speech to the assembly.

22. These leaders appear elsewhere: "the heads of your tribes," 1:15; 29:9[10]; elders, 27:1; 29:9[10]; 31:9, 28.

23. Note the assonance/rhyme in the combination of words, כְּבֹדוֹ and גָּדְלוֹ, "his glory" and "his greatness," which may function as a hendiadys, "his majestic glory." NJPSV translates, "his majestic presence."

(v. 25);[24] under normal circumstances for any mortal to be addressed by divinity from the midst of the fire would have been deadly (v. 26).[25] The people's questions reflect their confusion. In the same breath they recognize the deadly threat of God's voice and that this God who speaks is "the living God." While their confession may not have risen to the sort of monotheism suggested in 4:35 and 39, it seems to acknowledge that despite YHWH's invisibility behind the darkness and deep gloom, he presented a stark contrast to visible but lifeless gods of wood and stone (cf. 4:28).

The people's questions also recall the narrator's comment after reporting the Israelites' eating and drinking on the mountain as guests of God (cf. Ps 23:4–6), "Yet he did not stretch out his hand against them" (Exod 24:9–11). If they were unsure of their place at YHWH's table after the covenant had been ratified, we should not be surprised that prior to the ratification—the scene described in 5:22–33—the people were still unsure about their safety in the presence of God. To ward off the danger resulting from further exposure to the lethal voice and fire of God, they requested that Moses serve as a buffer, a sort of lightning rod between them and God (v. 27).[26] In so doing they formally acknowledged Moses' authority to represent them before YHWH and YHWH before them. Indeed, from now on they will treat the voice of Moses as if it were the very voice of God.[27]

YHWH's Response to the People's Proposal (5:28–31)

After recounting YHWH's positive response to the leaders' request (v. 28a),[28] Moses reproduces his speech, which consists of four parts. First, YHWH declares in the first person what Moses had reported in the third person regarding his (YHWH's) response. Unlike the gods of wood and stone worshiped by the nations, which have ears but do not hear (4:28), YHWH, who has no literal ears, has heard his people—even though they have not addressed him. He overheard what they said to Moses.

Second, YHWH affirms the correctness of the people's response explicitly (by commending them for their request to Moses) and implicitly (by acknowledging that their words reflect a proper mental and spiritual disposition, v. 28b). Whereas in Exod 20:20 Moses had asserted that YHWH had come (בָּא) to the Israelites to test (נִסָּה) whether or not they feared him, God hereby declares both that they had passed that test and that

---

24. Their choice of words, "for this great fire will consume us," reinforces the epithet, אֵשׁ אֹכְלָה, "consuming fire," that Moses had used of YHWH in 4:24.

25. Hebrew כָּל־בָּשָׂר may refer to all living creatures (Gen 6:17, 19; Num 18:15), but usually refers more particularly to humankind (Gen 6:12, 13; Isa 40:5, 6; etc.).

26. The construction, קְרַב אַתָּה וּשֲׁמָע וְשָׁמַעְנוּ וְעָשִׂינוּ . . . וְאַתְּ תְּדַבֵּר אֵלֵינוּ . . . ("You approach and listen . . . and you speak to us . . . and we will listen and do . . .") is both official and emphatic.

27. See further, Michael Kibbe, *Godly Fear or Ungodly Failure?* 52–59.

28. In contrast to Moses' expansionistic recollection of the people's speech people in verses 24–27 (cf. Exod 20:19), YHWH's speech in response is missing in the earlier narrative. In Exod 20:19–21 Moses' interpretation of God's intent with the foregoing revelation follows immediately after the people's request.

the divine intent declared in 4:10 had been accomplished[29]—in some measure.[30] And having passed the test, the Israelites declared their readiness to hear further revelation from God, albeit indirectly through a mediator.[31]

Third, YHWH declares his longing that the impulse reflected in the Israelites' response to his visual and verbal speech would be internalized, and demonstrated by keeping all his commands (כָּל־מִצְוֹתַי, not only the Decalogue), all the time (כָּל־הַיָּמִים, literally "all the days," v. 29). This longing is expressed with an awkward optative question: מִי־יִתֵּן וְהָיָה לְבָבָם זֶה לָהֶם לְיִרְאָה אֹתִי וְלִשְׁמֹר אֶת־כָּל־מִצְוֹתַי כָּל־הַיָּמִים. The question may be interpreted idiomatically as, "If only they had this kind of heart, so they would fear me and observe all my commands all the days."[32] Exodus 20:20 provides the needed background for this comment; responding to the people's fright in the wake of the Horeb revelation, Moses had explained that its purpose was to "instill the fear of God *on their faces* so they would not sin" (וּבַעֲבוּר תִּהְיֶה יִרְאָתוֹ עַל־פְּנֵיכֶם לְבִלְתִּי תֶחֱטָאוּ). Both texts assess the "fear" of the Israelites positively, but after four decades of history with this people YHWH and Moses recognize how superficial their response had been.[33] Their lips and faces expressed the right disposition, but within forty days they would prove how shallow their commitments were. What was needed is described elsewhere as a divine heart implant,[34]—or, to use Moses' preferred metaphor, a circumcised heart, which is demonstrated in whole-hearted and full-bodied love for YHWH (10:16; 30:6). In this context that disposition would be demonstrated by

---

29. Despite contextual differences, this testing event recalls Gen 22, which begins with the narrator's note that God tested (נִסָּה) Abraham by asking him to sacrifice his son (v. 1). And then after Abraham's remarkable act of obedience, the narrator quotes the envoy of YHWH declaring (on behalf of YHWH), "Now I know that you fear (יְרֵא) God, for you have not withheld your son, your only son, from me." For a recent study of the motif of testing in these and other texts, see G. Smith, *The Testing of God's Sons*.

30. Kibbe (*Godly Fear or Ungodly Failure?*) argues that YHWH's goal was actually not achieved; the divine longing for a continuation of the present disposition (v. 29) suggests a flaw in their disposition (pp. 97–100), which the golden calf incident confirmed (pp. 64–67). Moses' claim that Israel has been rebellious since the day he knew her (9:7, 24), and his appeal to stop misbehavior today (12:8) suggest the problem persists with the present generation.

31. So also Merrill, *Deuteronomy*, 159. Moses' positive interpretation of the people's response to the divine revelation at Sinai contrasts with that of John H. Sailhamer, who speaks of "a growing distance between God and the people—one that was not intended at the outset of the Sinai narrative" (*Introduction to Old Testament Theology*, 286, n. 47). For expressions of his negative interpretations of the Horeb experience, see also Sailhamer, *The Meaning of the Pentateuch*, 374-415; Sailhamer, *The Pentateuch as Narrative*, 46–57, 281–88, 435–38. The way the covenant is ratified in Exod 24:1–11 suggests the opposite. For fuller response to Sailhamer, see Kibbe, *Godly Fear or Ungodly Failure?* 24, 26–27, 33–35, 49–51.

32. The first part, מִי־יִתֵּן וְהָיָה לְבָבָם זֶה לָהֶם, formally rendered, "Who will grant and they will have this their heart," is idiomatic for, "O that they had such a heart as this!" The idiom recurs in 28:67, and in varied forms in Exod 16:3; Num 11:29 ("O that all the people of YHWH were prophets"); Job 6:8; 11:5; 13:5; 14:4; 19:23; 23:3.

33. In Exod 20:20 the word "fear" (יִרְאָה) is used in two different senses. In the wake of the terrifying revelation at Horeb, Moses says, אַל־תִּירָאוּ, "Do not be terrified." However, contra Weinfeld (*Deuteronomy 1–11*, 325), YHWH's aim in the theophany had not been to terrorize the people, but to instill in them reverence and awe (יִרְאָה) that would motivate righteous living (cf. Deut 10:12–13).

34. Moses will hint at this in 29:3[4] (cf. 1 Kgs 3:9, 12; Jer 24:7; 32:39; Ezek 11:19; 36:26), though in Deut 28:65 he threatens the people with the opposite: YHWH will give them an anxious heart.

full observance of the divine Suzerain's commands, which would result in permanent well-being for this generation and their descendants (לְמַעַן יִיטַב לָהֶם וְלִבְנֵיהֶם לְעֹלָם).³⁵ However, despite YHWH's affirmation of the people and his desire for their well-being, the tone of Moses' report is ominous. Within weeks YHWH's doubts would be realized.

Fourth, after instructing Moses to dismiss the people, in fulfillment of the leaders' request YHWH inducts Moses into the office of mediator. Using the language of the court, in verse 31 the divine King invites him to enter his presence: "But you, here, stand with me that I may speak to you" (וְאַתָּה פֹּה עֲמֹד עִמָּדִי וַאֲדַבְּרָה אֵלֶיךָ). But this conversation will be anything but casual; YHWH will declare to Moses "the entire command,³⁶ that is, the statutes and judgments" (כָּל־הַמִּצְוָה וְהַחֻקִּים וְהַמִּשְׁפָּטִים), which Moses would then "teach" (לָמַד) the people to govern their conduct in the promised land.

In Deut 9:8—10:11 Moses recounts one more Horeb experience. But this event is chronologically separated and generically different from the "day of the assembly" described in chapters 4–5. To be sure it involves Israel at worship, but this is not the sort of worship YHWH expected from his newly established covenant people. Forgetting their earlier commitments and blatantly violating the first principle of covenant relationship (4:15–24; 5:6–10), within forty days they manufactured and worshiped substitute gods. Had Moses not intervened for them, YHWH would have destroyed them. However, in response to his intercession YHWH withdrew his threat and renewed the covenant—a fact symbolized by the production of new tablets, inscribed with the identical text of the original (10:1–5).

In his recollection of these events Moses does not portray the gracious character of YHWH with the explicit strokes of the narrator of Exod 32–34 (cf. 33:19; 34:6–7). Despite YHWH's gracious acceptance of Israel as his covenant people and his gracious renewal of the covenant after this rebellion, forty years later in Moses' mind Horeb was not the sort of place to which one would want to return for renewed encounters with YHWH. On the one hand, the place was too closely associated with Israel's rebellion and near annihilation (cf. 9:7, 24). On the other hand, while we should not underestimate YHWH's extraordinary grace in inviting Israel to an assembly before him, the Israelites shrank back from close encounters of this kind, because they had had little or no previous experience with YHWH. In their minds Horeb was a scary place.

Zion in the Book of Deuteronomy

Having explored Deuteronomy's portrayal of Horeb, we may now turn our attention to the book's disposition toward Zion. By using the term "Zion" I do not concede to

---

35. For the first time in the book Moses links fear toward YHWH and well-being. In 4:40 he had linked obedience with well-being, but without reference to fear as the motivating disposition. On the links between fear, obedience and life/well-being, see also 6:2, 24; 17:19–20; 28:1–4. The book of Malachi offers a prophetic study on the relationship between fear/reverent awe and life.

36. The singular form is intentional (cf. 6:1, 25; 7:11; 8:1; 11:8, 22; 30:11, also 15:5; 17:20; 19:9; 27:1; 30:1; 31:5), referring to the basic covenantal demand: absolute and unreserved loyalty to YHWH as declared in the first principle of the Decalogue and as Moses will expound in chapters 6–11. So also Weinfeld, *Deuteronomy 1–11*, 326; Lohfink, *Das Hauptgebot*, 55–56.

critical orthodoxy that the book of Deuteronomy is the product of late scribes eager to centralize political power in the Davidic king (whether Hezekiah or Josiah) by imposing on the people exclusively centralized worship,[37] or even worse, to use the central sanctuary and Levitical towns as taxation centers to finance royal ambition.[38] Assuming Deuteronomy antedated the deuteronomistic history and the Psalms and Prophets, it would be wrongheaded to read later highly developed Zion theology into Moses' vague reference to the place that YHWH would choose. However, the one who inspired him in this address ultimately had Jerusalem in mind, even as he would have David in mind in 17:15.[39] After David had brought to Jerusalem "the ark of God, which is called by the Name, the name of YHWH Ṣebaʾoth" (2 Sam 6:2), and after "YHWH had given him rest from all his enemies around him" (7:1), David concluded it was time to build a temple for YHWH. The use of הֵנִיחַ, "to give rest," suggests the narrator viewed the construction of the temple as the fulfillment of Deut 12:5–10.[40]

I acknowledge that I am using the toponym "Zion" anachronistically. The name appears often in the Prophets and the Psalms, but is used by the Deuteronomistic historian only twice (2 Sam 5:7; 1 Kgs 8:1).[41] "Zion" occurs twice more, but both times within a speech by the prophet Isaiah (2 Kgs 19:21, 31 = Isa 37:22, 32).[42] Many have noted the absence of references to Zion or Jerusalem or the temple in Deuteronomy,[43] and some have used this as evidence for a Persian date for *das Urdeuteronomium*.[44] Following the lead of the psalmist, I use the name because Zion represented the fulfillment of what Deuteronomy envisions as "the place YHWH chooses to establish for his name":

כִּי־בָחַר יְהוָה בְּצִיּוֹן	YHWH has chosen Zion;
אִוָּהּ לְמוֹשָׁב לוֹ׃	He has desired it for his residence.
זֹאת־מְנוּחָתִי עֲדֵי־עַד	"This is my permanent resting place;
פֹּה־אֵשֵׁב כִּי אִוִּתִיהָ׃	Here I will reside, for I have desired it." (Ps 132:13–14)

---

37. I have argued against absolute centralization in two essays, "Deuteronomic Law," above, pp. 89–104; "'The Meeting Places of God in the Land,'" below, pp. 177–97.

38. On which see chapter 9, "The Meeting Places of God in the Land," below p. 197.

39. Ps 78:69–71 links the election of Mount Zion within the tribal territory of Judah (as opposed to Joseph/Ephraim) as YHWH's eternal dwelling place with the election of David as king.

40. Psalm 132 links YHWH's election of and covenant with David with the election of Zion as his dwelling place.

41. Both occurrences are repeated by the Chronicler. In 2 Sam 5:7 (= 1 Chr 11:5) the name is glossed with "it is the city of David" (צִיּוֹן הִיא עִיר דָּוִד), and in 1 Kgs 8:1 (= 2 Chr 5:2), the name glosses "the city of David" (עִיר דָּוִד הִיא צִיּוֹן).

42. On Zion and the Zion traditions in the historiographic writings, see Groves, "Zion Traditions," 1019–25.

43. The expression, בֵּית יְהוָה occurs only in 23:19[18], but as in Exod 23:19 and 34:26, the phrase is a generic designation for the sanctuary as the divine residence, and could just as well apply to the tabernacle.

44. Thus Pakkala, "The Date of the Oldest Edition of Deuteronomy," 394–95. However, evidence like this argues more naturally for an ante-monarchic provenance for *das Urdeuteronium*.

The Place of the Place in Deuteronomy's Vision of Worship

Although the place is never named, the notion of a place where "YHWH would choose to establish his name" is part of a larger map of Deuteronomic historical and theological geography.[45] However, in his addresses Moses' gaze is cast largely on Israel's future place in the land promised to the ancestors,[46] and to YHWH residing at his chosen place (מָקוֹם). This is the place that concerns us, for this was Israel's destination. There they would worship him when their journeys were over and they were living in the land allotted to them and living out the ideals of which their ancestors could only dream.

In this book Moses refers to the place that YHWH would choose to establish his name twenty-one times.[47] The "place formula" occurs in a variety of forms, ranging from the most elemental, "the place that he will choose" (16:16; 31:11), to the most complex, "the place that YHWH your God will choose out of all your tribes to put his name and to establish it" (12:5). This most complex form—which happens to be the first in the book—makes four fundamental assertions concerning "the place." (1) YHWH, the God of Israel, will choose the place.[48] (2) It will be chosen from within the tribal territorial allotments.[49] (3) It will bear YHWH's name. The expression speaks of divine ownership: just as a person who bears the name of YHWH is recognized as belonging to YHWH,[50]

---

45. In Moses' recollection, Egypt was the place of YHWH's multiplication of the population in fulfillment of the promises to the ancestors, but also the place of oppression and ultimate redemption and revelation through YHWH's mighty acts (1:30; 4:34; 6:21; 10:22; 11:3; 16:12; 24:18; 26:5—8); Sinai/Horeb was the place of covenant and revelation of the divine will for Israel (4:9–15; 5:2; 18:16; 28:69[29:1]), but also of Israel's failure (9:7–21) and YHWH's gracious covenant renewal (9:25—10:5); the desert was a place of providential care (1:31; 8:15–16), but also of testing (8:2–6) and failure (1:19–46; 6:16; 9:22–24); the Plains of Moab was a place of covenant renewal (11:26–28; 26:16–19; 28:69–29:20[29:1–21]; 30:11–20) and Moses' farewell (31:1—34:12). On the importance of time and place in Deuteronomy, see McConville and Millar, *Time and Place in Deuteronomy*.

46. Deut 1:8; 1:21; 1:35; 4:1; 6:3; 6:10; 6:18; 6:23; 7:13; 8:1; 9:5; 10:11; 11:9; 11:21; 12:1; 19:8; 26:3; 26:15; 27:3; 28:11; 30:5; 30:20; 31:7; 31:16; 31:20.

47. Deut 12:5, 11, 14, 18, 21, 26; 14:23, 24, 25; 15:20; 16:2, 6, 7, 11, 15, 16; 17:8, 10; 18:6; 26:2; 31:11. For variations/echoes of the formula in later writings, see Josh 9:27; 2 Kgs 21:7; 23:27; Jer 7:12; Ezra 6:12; Neh 1:9.

48. Moses does not say how that choice would be made or communicated, but the location was revealed to David through Gad the prophet (2 Sam 24:18–25; 1 Chr 21:18). On the initiative of deities in ancient Near Eastern accounts of temple construction, see Hurowitz, *"I Have Built You an Exalted House,"* 135–67.

49. Predicted in Numbers 34 and fulfilled by Joshua in Josh 14–19. The history of Israel's worship at a single sanctuary involved three distinct phases: (1) at the center of the camp during their desert wanderings; (2) at a series of locations in the land of Canaan during the nation's transition from tribal government to a monarchy: Mount Ebal/Shechem (Deut 27; Josh 8:30–35; 24), Bethel (Judg 20:26–27), Shiloh (Judg 21:19–21; 1 Samuel 1–3; Jer 7:12–14; Ps 78:60); and (3) at a permanent location after the transition was complete. For a successive interpretation of "the place that YHWH will choose" see Wenham, "Deuteronomy and the Central Sanctuary," 103–18; McConville, "Time, Place, and the Deuteronomic Altar-Law," 89–139; McConville, *Law and Theology in Deuteronomy*, 98–35.

50. On which, see Block, "Bearing the Name of YHWH with Honor," 61–72. Cf. Exod 20:7; Deut 5:11; Isa 44:5. Isaiah 18:7 speaks of the temple as the place of YHWH's name. Note also the references to "building a house for the name of YHWH" (2 Sam 7:13; 1 Kgs 3:2; 5:17–19[3–5]; 8:17–20, 44, 48).

so the place bearing the imprint of his name is recognized as his possession.[51] The idiom "to put his name there" (לָשׂוּם/לְשַׁכֵּן אֶת־שְׁמוֹ שָׁם) alludes to the practice of inscribing the name of the founder of a building on the foundation stone. By putting his name on a place YHWH validates the location as the place of legitimate worship.[52] (4) The place will be the goal of Israel's pilgrimages.[53]

Given the frequency of the place formula in Deuteronomy, readers may be fixated on geography and forget that the place represents something much greater. In the ancient world temples were not merely monuments for people to visit; they were viewed as residences for deities. The frequent association of "the place that YHWH would choose" with phrases like לִפְנֵי יְהוָה, "before YHWH,"[54] and אֶת־יְהוָה, "with YHWH" (16:16; 17:12; 31:11), reinforces this interpretation. The emphasis on "the place" highlights the presence and accessibility of the One who actually dwells in heaven (4:39),[55] but who condescends also to reside on earth for the purpose of communing with his people.[56]

---

51. For equivalent expressions in Akkadian texts, see EA 287:60–63 (*ANET* 488; cf. EA 288:5, *ANET* 488); in an Egyptian text, Rameses III builds a temple for Amon "as the vested property of your name" (*ANET* 261). Here the expression is equivalent to "the place where YHWH causes [people] to remember his name" in Exod 20:24, or "the place on which my name is called/read," which later always refers specifically to the city of Jerusalem (Jer 25:29) or the temple/house of YHWH (1 Kgs 8:43; Jer 7:10, 11, 14, 30; 32:34; 34:15). The same expression (קָרָא שֵׁם עַל) is used of Israel as the elect people of YHWH in Deut 28:10 and 2 Chr 7:14, and is applied to a prophet in Jer 15:16, and the elect nations in Amos 9:12; Isa 63:19 notes the nations are not called by God's name.

52. On the inscription of a name on the foundation stone of a temple for its validation, see S. Dean McBride, *The Deuteronomic Name Theology*, 93–94. The translation of לְשַׁכֵּן שְׁמוֹ, "to establish his name," assumes virtual synonymity for שׂוּם, "to set, place," and שַׁכֵּן, "to establish," and that שַׁכֵּן is a shaphel form of כּוּן, "to establish," rather than a piel infinitive of שָׁכַן, "to dwell." Thus Brockelmann, *Grundriss der vergleichenden Grammatik der semitischen Sprachen*, 1:522. Much of the evidence for this position derives from Akkadian counterparts to the Hebrew expression. See McBride, *Deuteronomic Name Theology*, 204–10; Richter, *The Deuteronomistic History and the Name Theology*; Richter, "The Place of the Name in Deuteronomy," 342–366. LXX translates, ἐπονομάσαι τὸ ὄνομα αὐτοῦ ἐκεῖ ἐπικληθῆναι, "to call for his name to be invoked there." Recognizing the oddity of the consonantal text, the Masoretes pointed the word as if from שָׁכַן, "to dwell," and attached it to the following verb, "you shall seek his dwelling place." The Targums read "to make his Shekinah dwell there." For discussion of the textual and grammatical issues involved, see Tov, *Textual Criticism of the Hebrew Bible*, 42; McCarthy, *Deuteronomy*, 85*–86.*

53. Whereas elsewhere the verb דָּרַשׁ, "to seek," usually speaks of looking for something, or enquiring, or even caring for, that is, to seek someone else's welfare (11:12), here the idiom, דָּרַשׁ אֶל־הַמָּקוֹם, literally, "to seek to the place," means "to make a pilgrimage to the place," or "to visit the place with spiritual intent." Cf. Tigay, *Deuteronomy*, 120. See also Amos 5:5, and Isa 11:10, "you may make a pilgrimage to the place" (דָּרַשׁ אֶל).

54. 10:8; 12:7, 12, 18; 14:23, 26; 15:20; 16:11; 18:7; 19:17; 24:4, 13; 26:5, 10, 13; 27:7; 29:9, 14[10, 15]; cf. earlier references to events "before YHWH": 1:45 (at Kadesh-barnea the people wept before YHWH); 4:10 (at Horeb the people stood before YHWH); 6:25 (people are recognized as righteous before YHWH because of their obedience); 9:18, 25 (Moses fell down [הִתְנַפֵּל] before YHWH to intercede for the people). For a thorough discussion of the significance of לִפְנֵי יְהוָה, "before YHWH," in Deuteronomy, see Wilson, *Out of the Midst of the Fire*, 142–97.

55. As Solomon recognized repeatedly in his prayer of dedication for the place that is stamped with the name of YHWH: 1 Kgs 8:23, 30, 32, 34, 36, 39, 43, 45, 49.

56. A deeply entrenched scholarly tradition interprets the temple as the residence for the name of YHWH (שֵׁם יְהוָה) as a late theological abstraction of earlier perceptions of real presence. See Weinfeld,

The Function of the Place in Israel's Worship

Examining specifically what YHWH invited the Israelites to do "before his face" magnifies the significance of this conclusion. Limiting ourselves initially to contexts in which the place formula occurs, we observe that the Israelites were invited to come there to "see the face of YHWH" (31:11; cf. 16:16), to hear the Torah read (31:11) and thereby learn to fear YHWH (14:23; 31:9–13), to celebrate the three great annual pilgrimage festivals,[57] to present their offerings and recall YHWH's saving and providential grace (26:1–11), to demonstrate their covenant commitment to YHWH horizontally by gifts of charity to the marginalized (26:12; cf. 10:12–22), to demonstrate communal solidarity by celebrating with their children, servants, the Levites, and aliens (12:12; 14:27–29; 16:11), to settle legal disputes before the Levitical priest/judge (17:8–13). This was also the place where Levites would serve in the name of YHWH, standing before him, and blessing the people in his name (10:8; 18:6–8).

Many today view Israel's worship as involving obligatory cultic actions demanded by YHWH to satisfy his need for honor, which the people would perform dutifully in response to divine commands. Supposedly all males were compelled to go to the central shrine three times a year to observe the national festivals of Passover/Unleavened Bread, Weeks, and Booths (16:1–17), and if they could drag the females in their families and their neighbors with them so much the better. However, the picture painted by Deuteronomy is very different.

Deuteronomy 12:2–14 lays the attitudinal foundations.[58] Although most translations render this unit as a series of legal prescriptions, its genre is established by the hortatory sermonic injunctions that punctuate it (vv. 4, 8–9, 13–14) and the festive nature of the activities to transpire at the site. Indeed, if we render many of the verbs in verses 5–7 modally rather than as imperatives we will recognize that this represents an invitation to celebrate in the presence of YHWH rather than a deontological command to worship him:

> But you *may* make pilgrimages (lit. "seek") to the place YHWH your God will choose from among all your tribes to put his Name there to establish it. To that place you *may come*; there you *may bring* your burnt offerings and sacrifices, your tithes and special gifts, what you have vowed to give and your freewill offerings, and the firstborn of your herds and flocks. There, in the presence of YHWH your God, you and your families *may* eat and you

---

"Deuteronomy, Book of," 175–78. In recent years, this interpretation has come under increasing scrutiny. See especially Richter, *The Deuteronomistic History and the Name Theology*; Vogt, *Deuteronomic Theology and the Significance of Torah*; Wilson, *Out of the Midst of the Fire*; Wilson, "Central Sanctuary or Local Settlements?" 323–40.

57. Passover (16:1–8), Festival of Weeks (Pentecost, 16:9–12), Festival of Booths (16:13–17; 31:9–13).

58. For fuller discussion of this text, see Block, "The Joy of Worship," 98–117. On worship as joyful celebration, see also Weinfeld, *Deuteronomy and the Deuteronomic School*, 210–24); Braulik, "The Joy of the Feast," 27–65; idem, "Commemoration of Passion and Feast of Joy," 67–85; Willis, "'Eat and Rejoice Before YHWH,'" 276–94.

may celebrate in everything you have put your hand to, because YHWH your God has blessed you (vv. 5–7).

Translating the text this way yields a profoundly positive picture of Israelite worship at the central sanctuary (Zion).

First, the Israelites are invited "to come to/enter" the place where YHWH resides. To render the verb בּוֹא as "go," as many translations do, obscures the intent. Speaking on behalf of YHWH, Moses says, "There you may come/enter."[59] The verb perceives the Israelites' movement from the perspective of the person at the destination, rather than a person sending them off.[60]

Second, in agreement with the previous verb, the Israelites are invited to bring (הֵבִיא) all their offerings to YHWH (vv. 6, 11). Again, as authorized spokesman for YHWH, Moses envisions the action from the vantage of the divine host at the worshipers' destination rather than their homes scattered throughout Israel.[61] His catalogue of seven types of offerings reflects his enthusiasm: "whole burnt offerings," "animal sacrifices," "tithes," "specially dedicated donations," "votive offerings," "freewill offerings," and "the firstborn of herds and flocks." The list is obviously not exhaustive, but represents Israel's entire cultic provision for fellowship with YHWH.

Third, the Israelites are invited to eat there in the presence of YHWH.[62] As elsewhere in ancient Near Eastern and biblical contexts, eating together was a ritual act of communion, often symbolizing a covenantal relationship.[63] However, unlike pagan offerings that were presented as food for the gods, the present instructions focus on the offerings as food for the worshipers. The Israelites' God will host his vassals at this banquet table, but he will not eat with them.[64]

Fourth, the Israelites are invited to celebrate the blessing of YHWH on their work. Whereas verbs for joy and celebration occur in the Horeb regulations only in Lev 23:40, the second address in Deuteronomy sets the mood of worship with the verb שָׂמַח, "to rejoice, to celebrate," various forms of which occur eight times in connection with appearing before YHWH.[65]

---

59. "To go" would have been expressed with הָלַךְ.

60. The opposite of בּוֹא, "to come, enter," is יָצָא, "to go out" (cf. 28:6, 19). The former is the Hebrew Bible's equivalent to Jesus' invitations, "Come to me all you that labor and are loaded down" (Matt 11:28), and "If any are thirsty, let them come to me and drink" (John 7:37).

61. So also v. 11. In v. 26, "to take" the offering to a place is expressed with נָשָׂא, "to carry."

62. On "eating before YHWH," see Wilson, *Out of the Midst of the Fire*, 161–65.

63. Gen 31:54; Exod 24:5–11.

64. In Exod 18:12 a select group involving Moses, Aaron, and the elders of Israel ate with Jethro "before God." Compare Uriah's eating before David (2 Sam 11:13), Adonijah's supporters eating before him (1 Kgs 1:25), and Jehoiachin's eating "before" his overlord, the king of Babylon (2 Kgs 25:29// Jer 52:33). In Ezek 44:3, the prince (נָשִׂיא) eats "before YHWH." At Sinai/Horeb the elders had observed the glorious presence of YHWH as they ate and drank (Exod 24:10–11), but there is no hint of YHWH dining with them. This pattern recalls the banquet that Joseph prepared for his brothers (Gen 43:26–34). Not only did the brothers sit in rank according to age, but they sat "before" (לִפְנֵי) Joseph, rather than "with" him (v. 33).

65. Deut 12:7, 12, 18; 14:26; 16:11, 14–15; 26:11; but cf. also 27:7, which envisions a special ritual event celebrating the completion of the covenant triangle involving YHWH, Israel, and the land at

Fifth, Moses extends the privilege of access to all. Whereas at Horeb access to the table had been granted only to Moses, Aaron, Joshua, and the elders (Exod 24:9–11), in Zion all will be welcome—heads of households, sons and daughters, male and female servants, as well as landless Levites, aliens, widows, and the fatherless within their towns (Deut 12:12, 18; 16:11, 14; 26:11; 31:10–12). In Zion Israelites will celebrate both the vertical relationship graciously established by YHWH and their common membership in the covenant community.

This freedom of access to the presence of YHWH and confidence in his acceptance characterizes not only other "Zion" texts in Deuteronomy, but life away from the sanctuary as well. In the sequel to 12:1–13, Moses emphasizes that offerings presented to YHWH must be eaten at the central sanctuary (vv. 14–19). However, if Israelites desire to eat meat where they live, they may do so freely, provided the animals are ritually clean (of the type acceptable as sacrifices to YHWH) and the sanctity of the animal's life is respected by draining the blood (vv. 20–28). In a sense, every slaughter is a sacrifice and every meal is worship, suggesting that the so-called food laws in 14:1–21 invite the Israelites to imagine themselves dining at YHWH's table whenever they sit down for a meal. The emphasis in this text is not on foods prohibited, but on the full range of foods available to YHWH's covenant people, identified at the outset as his "sons" (בָּנִים), "a holy people belonging to YHWH" (עַם קָדוֹשׁ לַיהוָה), chosen (בָּחַר) to be his "special treasure" (עַם סְגֻלָּה). The Israelites may enjoy precisely those foods that YHWH accepted as offerings.

Rather than considering the annual tithe of 14:22–29 to be a burdensome duty, we should recognize in YHWH's blessing of the fields and herds another occasion for him to invite them to come and eat in his presence. Indeed, YHWH finds such delight in fellowship with his people that he expressly removes hindrances to participation. When distance from the central sanctuary renders it impractical for worshipers to carry the tithe physically, they may come to the sanctuary with silver and purchase all the food they want at the destination (v. 26). Meanwhile those with means are to ensure that the privilege and satisfaction of eating in YHWH's presence is open to all: Levites, aliens, the fatherless, widows (vv. 27–29).

Similar considerations characterize the offering of the firstborn in 15:19–23, where, as in 12:5–14 and 14:22–29, the key verbs may be interpreted modally:

> Each year you and your family *may* eat them in the presence of YHWH your God at the place he will choose. If an animal has a defect, is lame or blind, or has any serious flaw, you must not sacrifice it to YHWH your God. You *may* eat it in your own towns. Both the ceremonially unclean and the clean *may* eat it, as if it were gazelle or deer (vv. 20–23).

Mount Ebal (on which, see chapter 8, "What Do These Stones Mean?" below, pp. 152–76). The root שמח also occurs in 24:5 and 33:18, where it speaks of rejoicing in other circumstances. It seems that Moses has generalized the tone of the legislation concerning the Festival of Booths in Lev 23:40 to all worship before YHWH: when the tithe is presented (14:21–27), at the Festivals of Weeks (16:9–12) and Booths (16:13–17), the presentation of first fruits (26:1–11), and the Israelites celebration of arrival in the promised land (27:1–8).

As is the case with the annual tithe (14:22–29), we should not interpret the divine demand for the firstborn of flocks and herds as an intrusive and burdensome duty. Rather, the consecration of the animal symbolized Israel's privileged status as YHWH's firstborn among the nations, and the arrival of the first offspring to each ewe or heifer reminded the people of YHWH's delight in their company. Each new birth represented an invitation to come and eat in his presence.

This positive understanding of the sacrifices climaxes in 26:1–15, where, for the first time, Moses offers some ritual detail, in this case involving the presentation of first fruits of the field. Although we may imagine similar rituals being performed by devotees of the fertility gods of Baal and Asherah, Moses will not allow Israel's cult to degenerate to mere fertility religion. This annual event offers another occasion for the people to celebrate YHWH's grace in their history as well. Indeed, the creed they are to recite during the ritual touches on the offering presented only at the very end. After handing the offering to the priest and affirming, "I declare today to YHWH your God that I have come to the land YHWH swore to our forefathers to give us" (v. 3), they are to say:

> My father was a wandering Aramean; he went down into Egypt with a few people and lived there and became a great nation, powerful and numerous. But the Egyptians mistreated us and made us suffer, putting us to hard labor. Then we cried out to YHWH, the God of our fathers, and YHWH heard our voice and saw our misery, toil and oppression. So YHWH brought us out of Egypt with a mighty hand and an outstretched arm, with great terror and with miraculous signs and wonders. He brought us to this place and gave us this land, a land flowing with milk and honey; and now I bring the firstfruits of the soil that you, O YHWH, have given me. (vv. 5–10; author's translation)

The center of gravity in this "Little Creed" is not celebration of the present harvest, but grateful commemoration of YHWH's gracious establishment of Israel as his covenant people and his provision of this good land in fulfillment of the promises to the ancestors.

The Relationship between Horeb and Zion as Places of Worship

Having explored Deuteronomy's disposition toward Horeb and Zion we may now stand back and reflect on the relationship between these two places. In the past I have imagined a fairly close relationship between the two, with Zion making permanent the presence of YHWH among his people and giving them ongoing access to him, as they had at Horeb. This was indeed true of the tabernacle, which functioned as a portable temple (identified as a מִשְׁכָּן, "dwelling" and מִקְדָּשׁ, "sanctuary," Exod 25:8–9), eventually to be replaced by the permanent temple in Jerusalem. However, the Tabernacle was less a provision for worship at Horeb, than for future worship away from this place. More significantly, Israel's encounters with YHWH at Horeb differed fundamentally from the encounters envisioned at the central sanctuary in Deuteronomy. This becomes clear if we summarize the data on each in synoptic tabular form (Table 7.1, pages 144–45).

Table 7.1
Horeb and Zion: A Comparison
(Unless otherwise indicated, all references are to Deuteronomy)

Feature	Horeb	Zion
Event	"Day of the assembly" (יוֹם הַקָּהָל, Deut 4:10; 10:4; 18:18)	Annual pilgrimage festivals (חַג), three times a year (Passover, Shabuoth, Sukkoth 16:16). Time of firstfruits (רֵאשִׁית, 18:4–6; 26:2), bringing the firstborn (12:6, 17; 14:23; 15:19–20), and the tithe (14:23–24)
Name of the Place	Sinai (33:2); Horeb	Unnamed ("the place," הַמָּקוֹם)
Location	Vicinity of Seir, Paran (33:2). Eleven days' journey from Kadesh-barnea (1:1–2)	In the land (26:3). In one of the tribal territories (12:5, 14)
Topography	On the mountain (הָהָר, 5:4, 5, 22; 9:10; 10:4)	Never specified
Characterization of the Place	Holy (Exod 3:5). Sanctified by YHWH's glorious presence (Exod 19)	Nondescript. Where name is imprinted (לְשַׁכֵּן שְׁמוֹ שָׁם, 12:5; שׁוּם שְׁמוֹ שָׁם, 12:11; 14:23; 16:2, 6, 11). Cf. "your holy abode" (מְעוֹן קָדְשְׁךָ, Exod 15:13). Cf. "look down from your holy dwelling place, from heaven" (הַשְׁקִיפָה מִמְּעוֹן קָדְשְׁךָ מִן הַשָּׁמַיִם, Deut 26:15)
Atmosphere	Terror (Deut 4:33; 5:5, 23–27; 18:16). Fear (יָרֵא, in the sense of "fright")	Joy and celebration (שָׂמַח, 12:7,12, 18; 14:26; 16:11, 14; 26:11). Trusting awe (יָרֵא, in the sense of "reverence and awe")
Officials	Only Moses was officially involved, but his role was prophetic, rather than priestly (18:15–18). Moses, Aaron, Joshua, Nadab and Abihu, 70 elders (Exod 24:1, 9). The nobles of the sons of Israel (אֲצִילֵי בְּנֵי יִשְׂרָאֵל, 24:11). Passing references to priests (19:22, 24) and Aaron (19:24), but they do not participate in the ritual. Young men (נַעֲרֵי בְּנֵי יִשְׂרָאֵל), who offer the whole burnt and fellowship offerings, 24:5	Elders and Levitical priests receive the Torah (31:9). Levitical priests (1) carry the Ark; (2) stand before YHWH; (3) serve YHWH's name (10:8; 18:5–8); (4) bless in YHWH's name (10:8; 18:5–8); (5) pronounce oracular judgments in insoluble cases (17:8–13); (6) receive the firstfruit offerings of worshipers (26:3–4).
Identity of the Worshipers	The people (הָעָם, Deut 4:10, 33). "Your people" (עַמְּךָ, 9:12)). "Your whole assembly" (כָּל־קְהָלְךָ, 5:22)	All Israel (32:11). "The assembly of YHWH" (קְהַל יהוה, 23:2–4, 9[1–3, 8]). Heads of households, sons and daughters, male and female servants, Levites (12:12, 18; 16:11, 14). Men and women, children, aliens (31:12). Widows, fatherless, aliens (14:27–29; 16:11, 14; 26:12–13)

Status of Worshipers and their Relationship to YHWH	Status/role as "treasured possession" (סְגֻלָּה), kingdom of priests (מַמְלֶכֶת כֹּהֲנִים), holy nation" (גּוֹי קָדוֹשׁ) a future prospect (19:4-6). Separated from YHWH: (1) three days' preparation required (Exod 19:10-16) (2) at the top of the mountain (3) which was fenced off (Exod 19:12-13, 21-24) (4) shielded from YHWH by "darkness, cloud, and gloom" (הַחֹשֶׁךְ הֶעָנָן וְהָעֲרָפֶל, 4:11) Near at the foot of the mountain (4:11) Only Moses goes higher up the mountain (Exodus 19);	Status as "sons of YHWH" (בָּנִים לַיהוָה), chosen to be "holy people belonging to YHWH" (עַם קָדוֹשׁ לַיהוָה), "treasured people" (עַם סְגֻלָּה) out of all the peoples on earth, is a present reality (7:6; 14:1-2; 26:18-19; cf. Exod 28:36). Direct and immediate access to YHWH without barriers or an intermediary, to eat and celebrate before YHWH (לִפְנֵי יְהוָה אֱלֹהֶיךָ, 12:7, 12; 16, 18, 14:23, 26; 15:20; 16:11, 16; but cf. 27:7).
Divine Activities on the Occasion[s]	Focus is on YHWH's actions: YHWH cut the covenant with Israel (כָּרַת בְּרִית עִמָּנוּ, 5:2-3) YHWH spoke to the people "face to face," but from the midst of the fire (4:10, 13-14, 33, 36; 5:5, 6-27) YHWH wrote the words of the covenant on two tablets of stone (4:13; 5:22; cf. 10:4)	Focus is on human actions: YHWH receives the offerings of the people (12:6, 11; 15:19) YHWH hosts celebrations and fellowship meals eaten in his presence (12:7, 12; 16, 18, 14:23, 26; 15:20; 16:10-11, 15-16) YHWH receives the ministry of the priests (10:8; 18:6-7; 26:2-3) YHWH reveals solutions to insoluble judicial problems (17:8-13) YHWH speaks through the reading of the Torah (31:9-13)
Human Activities on the Occasion	Stood before YHWH (see below) Shrank back in fear before YHWH (5:5, 22-31; 18:16) Participated in covenant ratification rituals and were amazed that they survived (Exod 24:1-11)	Making pilgrimages to the place (וְשָׁכַן . . . שְׁמוֹ שָׁם/אֶל־הַמָּקוֹם כִּי, 12:5; 16:1-8 [Passover], 16:9-12 [Weeks/Shebuoth/Pentecost], 16:13-17; 31:9-13 [Sukkoth/Booths]). Entering there (וּבָאתָ שָׁמָּה, 12:5; cf. 23:21; 31:16, of entering the land) Bringing offerings there (וַהֲבֵאתֶם שָׁמָּה, 12:6, 11; 26:2) Eating and celebrating YHWH's blessing of their work in his presence (12:7, 12; 16, 18, 14:23, 26; 15:20; 16:11, 16; but cf. 27:7) Seeing the face of YHWH" (31:11; cf. 16:16) Hearing the Torah read (31:11), and thereby learn to fear YHWH (14:23; 31:9-13) Recalling YHWH's saving and providential grace (26:1-11) Demonstrating covenant commitment to YHWH horizontally by gifts of charity to the marginalized (26:12; cf. 10:12-22) Demonstrating communal solidarity by celebrating with their children, servants, the Levites, and the alien (12:12; 14:27-29; 16:11) Settling legal disputes before the Levitical priest/judge (17:8-13) Observing Levites serving in the name of YHWH, standing before him, and blessing the people in his name (10:8; 18:6-8).

Remarkably, the most significant—if not the only—common denominator between Horeb and Zion is that here God's people encounter him; otherwise the contrasts are stark.

1. The Horeb event was a "one-off" "day of assembly" (יוֹם הַקָּהָל, 9:10; 10:4; 18:16); Zion is not only the location of the three annual national festivals, but also envisioned as hosting people continuously as they bring their firstfruts and the firstborn of their herds and flocks.

2. Horeb has two names; "the place" in Deuteronomy is not named at all; the divine host and the events that transpire there are more important than the location.

3. The Horeb encounter was a bilateral event involving only YHWH and his people in a faraway location; Zion is located within the promised land, the third element in the trilateral covenant relationship, and chosen specially by YHWH.[66]

4. Whereas the Horeb encounter happened on a mountain, and time will demonstrate "the place" also to be on a mountain,[67] Deuteronomy has no interest in its elevation. A cultic event will happen "before YHWH your God" (לִפְנֵי יְהוָה אֱלֹהֶיךָ) on Mounts Gerizim and Ebal (chapter 27), but like the Horeb encounter, this was envisioned as a "one-off" event and exhibited more links with the rituals at Horeb than those envisioned for Zion.[68]

5. Whereas Horeb was declared to be a "holy place" by virtue of YHWH's presence there (Exod 3:5; cf. 19:10-24), the only place that Deuteronomy modifies with the adjective "holy" is heaven, YHWH's "holy dwelling place" (מִמְּעוֹן קָדְשֶׁךָ, 26:15). Otherwise Zion is characterized as "the place where YHWH's name is imprinted" (לְשַׁכֵּן שְׁמוֹ שָׁם, 12:5, 11; 14:23; 16:2, 6, 11).

6. Whereas the encounter with YHWH at Horeb produced terror among the Israelites, Zion is envisioned as awe-inspiring, but not at all terrifying; it will be a place of close fellowship, confidence, and celebration (שָׂמַח, 12:7, 12, 18; 14:26; 16:11, 14; 26:11).

7. Whereas Deuteronomy speaks only of Moses' official role at Horeb—though it is characterized as prophetic (18:15-18), rather than cultic—[69] in Zion Levitical priests will (a) carry the Ark; (b) stand before YHWH; (c) serve YHWH; (d) bless in YHWH's name (10:8; 18:5-8); (e) pronounce oracular judgments in insoluble cases (17:8-13); and (f) receive the firstfruit offerings of worshipers (26:3-4).

---

66. On which see Block, *The Gods of the Nations*, 93-112.

67. Zion is referred to as Mount Zion or otherwise associated with a mountain more than thirty times in the First Testament.

68. See chapter 8, "What Do These Stones Mean?" below, pp. 152-76.

69. Aaron's only role in Deuteronomy involved his heterodox manufacture of the golden calf (9:20). The Sinai narrative in Exodus has Moses playing a leading role in the event, though Moses, Aaron, Nadab and Abihu, seventy elders, and some young men were involved in the ratification rituals (24:1-11). Exodus 19:22-24 makes passing references to priests, but they apparently were not involved in the ritual.

8. Deuteronomy refers to the worshipers at Horeb only generically and collectively as "the people" (4:10, 33), "your [i.e., Moses'] people" (9:12), and "your whole assembly" (כָּל־קְהַלְכֶם, 5:22). In 23:2–4[1–3] and 9[8] the worshipers at "the house of YHWH" (בֵּית יְהוָה, cf. v. 19) are identified collectively as "the assembly of YHWH" (קְהַל יְהוָה). In general the second person masculine verbs in texts like 12:1–14 assume the involvement of heads of households in worship at Zion, but Moses' democratization of worship at "the place" is striking.

9. Whereas Exod 24:1–11 restricts the climactic phase of worship at Horeb—ascent up the mountain and eating in the presence of YHWH—to Moses, Aaron, Joshua, Nadab and Abihu, and seventy elders, Deuteronomy invites entire households and communities, specifying men and women, sons and daughters, male and female servants, widows, the fatherless, aliens, and economically marginalized Levites into the presence of YHWH.[70]

10. Regarding the status of the worshipers, Deut 4:11 locates the worshipers near the foot of the Mount Horeb, but no one except Moses is authorized to come any closer than that to YHWH. This image matches that of Exod 19, which highlighted YHWH's separation from the people. On the one hand, they needed three days to prepare for the meeting with YHWH (Exod 19:10–16); on the other hand, YHWH alone was at the top of the mountain, which was fenced off (19:12–13, 21–24), and the people were shielded from his lethal radiance by the "darkness, cloud, and gloom" (חֹשֶׁךְ עָנָן וַעֲרָפֶל, Deut 4:11). Deuteronomy envisions the people in Zion in the very presence of God, "seeing his face."

11. Insofar as Exodus speaks of the status of the worshipers, their standing/role as "treasured possession (סְגֻלָּה), kingdom of priests (מַמְלֶכֶת כֹּהֲנִים), and holy nation" (גּוֹי קָדוֹשׁ) is cast as a future prospect (19:4–6). By contrast, Deuteronomy envisions these as a present reality; indeed it is as YHWH's "sons" (בָּנִים אַתֶּם לַיהוָה, 14:1), "his holy people" (עַם קָדוֹשׁ אַתָּה לַיהוָה), his "treasured people," (עַם סְגֻלָּה), specially chosen from all the peoples on earth (בָּחַר . . . מִכֹּל הָעַמִּים אֲשֶׁר עַל־פְּנֵי הָאֲדָמָה) that they are invited to eat at his table and celebrate in his presence (14:1–21).

12. Like Exod 19–24, Moses' radically theocentric characterization of the events of Horeb focused on YHWH's actions: YHWH spoke to the people face to face (5:4), but he spoke from heaven and out of the midst of the fire (4:10, 13–14, 33, 36; 5:5, 6–27); YHWH cut the covenant with Israel (יְהוָה אֱלֹהֵינוּ כָּרַת עִמָּנוּ בְּרִית בְּחֹרֵב, 5:2–3); and YHWH wrote the words of the covenant on two tablets of stone (4:13; 5:22; cf. 10:4). As we will see below, Moses' portrayal of worship on Zion focuses on human actions, with YHWH's involvement being assumed rather than described: YHWH receives the offerings of the people (12:6, 11; 15:19); YHWH hosts celebrations and fellowship meals eaten in his presence (12:7, 12, 16, 18, 14:23, 26; 15:20; 16:10–11, 15–16); YHWH receives the ministry of the priests (10:8; 18:6–7; 26:2–3); YHWH reveals solutions to insoluble judicial problems (17:8–13); YHWH speaks through the reading of the Torah (31:9–13).

---

70. Deut 12:12, 18; 14:27–29; 16:11, 14; 26:12–13; 31:12.

13. As for the human activities, at Horeb the people initially stood before YHWH (4:20, 11), but at the sound of his voice from the midst of the fire they shrank back in fear before him (5:5, 22–31; 18:16).[71] Here the contrast with Zion may be greatest. While one of the goals of the appointments with YHWH at the central sanctuary was to learn to fear (יָרֵא) YHWH,[72] that fear has a fundamentally different character. In Zion there is no hint of terror in his presence. On the contrary, the encounter reflects total confidence, trust, security, and delight at coming before him. Twice Moses speaks explicitly of coming to the sanctuary "to see the face of YHWH your God" (16:16; 31:11). Apparently Moses assumed this direct encounter would happen when the Torah was heard.[73] The references to worshipers' activities at the central sanctuary reinforce the impression of intimacy and comfort in the presence of YHWH.

Concluding Reflections

How shall we account for these fundamental differences between Israel's encounter with YHWH at Horeb and her future encounters at the place that he would choose for his name? Several possibilities exist. The Horeb experience was never intended to be normative or regular; this was a one-time event, whose function differed fundamentally from the anticipated regular worship of YHWH in the central sanctuary. One goal of this encounter was to introduce the Israelites more fully to YHWH, the God of the exodus, and in so doing clarify the meaning of the divine name, YHWH (cf. Exod 3:12–15).[74] To this point they had witnessed his awesome deeds against the Egyptians and in Israel's favor; deeds that had demonstrated that YHWH was God in heaven above and on earth below (Deut 4:32–39). However, the Horeb encounter declared his transcendent glory and ultimately his grace with unprecedented brilliance. Even though the Israelites became the covenant people, they should never take his grace for granted.

---

71. Exodus 24 has the people involved in the covenant ratification rituals, assenting to the will of the divine Suzerain as revealed in "all the words of YHWH" (כָּל־דִּבְרֵי יְהוָה, presumably "the [Ten] Words" [cf. Deut 4:13; 10:4]) and "all the judgments" (כָּל־הַמִּשְׁפָּטִים, Exod 24:3) recorded in "the Covenant Document" (סֵפֶר הַבְּרִית, 24:7), and passively receiving the blood of the covenant (דַּם־הַבְּרִית) sprinkled on them (24:8). And when it came to eating in the presence of YHWH, the elders were amazed to survive the experience (24:10–11).

72. Cf. Deut 14:23, וְלָמְדוּ לְיִרְאָה אֶת־יְהוָה אֱלֹהֵיכֶם 31:13, לְמַעַן תִּלְמַד לְיִרְאָה אֶת־יְהוָה אֱלֹהֶיךָ כָּל־הַיָּמִים; כָּל־הַיָּמִים אֲשֶׁר אַתֶּם חַיִּים עַל־הָאֲדָמָה.

73. As with the finite verb יֵרָאֶה in 16:16, in 31:11 the Masoretes vocalized the present infinitive לֵרָאוֹת as a niphal form, i.e., "to appear," a reading that is followed by LXX, SamP, and most modern translations. However, not only is בּוֹא לֵרָאוֹת אֶת־פְּנֵי, "to come to appear before," unnecessarily redundant, but also the natural preposition following this reading would be אֶל־פְּנֵי, literally, "to the face of," (Exod 23:17), or לִפְנֵי, "before." Treating אֶת as the direct object marker, the verb is better rendered transitively, "to see." The sense "appear" is communicated more conventionally by לִפְנֵי בּוֹא, "to come before" (Exod 28:30, 35; etc.). On the Masoretic vocalization as a secondary development to prevent people from imagining that YHWH's face could actually be seen, see Tigay, *Deuteronomy*, 159; *HALOT*, 1160; D. Vetter, "ראה *rʾh* to see," 1179–80.

74. For a detailed analysis of this subject, see Surls, *Making Sense of the Divine Name in the Book of Exodus*.

Second, Horeb had a particular axial significance in the unfolding of God's plan of redemption through his chosen people. If the exodus from Egypt marked the beginning of Israel's history as an independent people (Exod 12:2), Horeb was the place where YHWH formally declared Israel to be his covenant people. Through the ritual at Horeb those who had been the slaves (עֲבָדִים) of Pharaoh and the Egyptians (Deut 5:6; 6:12, 21; 7:8; 8:14; 13:6, 11[5, 10]) were inducted as privileged vassals (עֲבָדִים) of YHWH.[75] Here YHWH established with Abraham's descendants the covenant he had first made with the ancestor and transferred Abraham's commission to them (cf. Gen 12:1–3), in fulfillment of his promise in Gen 17:7: "I will establish my covenant (וַהֲקִמֹתִי אֶת־בְּרִיתִי) between me and you and your descendants after you throughout their generations as an everlasting covenant, to be your God and the God of your offspring after you" (Gen 17:7).[76] This was that moment.

Third, as heirs of the ancestors, through the rituals at Horeb Israel was formally commissioned as YHWH's agent of blessing to the world. While this ritual is perceived both as a marriage[77] and as an adoption ceremony,[78] Israel's vassaldom was to be missional; Horeb marked the place of Israel's ordination for priestly service. The exodus narrative will ground the key concepts of "treasured possession" (סְגֻלָּה), "kingdom of priests" (מַמְלֶכֶת כֹּהֲנִים), and "holy nation" (גּוֹי קָדוֹשׁ) in YHWH's claim to the whole earth (כִּי־לִי כָּל־הָאָרֶץ, Exod 19:4-6). In Deuteronomy Moses says little explicitly of Israel's mission, but picks up some of this vocabulary (סְגֻלָּה, Deut 7:6; 14:2; 26:18), adapts the rest—Israel is a "holy people belonging to YHWH your God" (עַם קָדוֹשׁ אַתָּה לַיהוָה אֱלֹהֶיךָ; 7:6; 14:2, 21; 26:19)—and then casts that mission in his own words: "And he will set you high above all nations that he has made, in praise and in fame and in honor (לִתְהִלָּה וּלְשֵׁם וּלְתִפְאָרֶת); and for you to be a people holy to YHWH your God, as he had [previously] declared" (26:19).

The experience at Horeb did indeed involve an audience with YHWH and included ritual acts of worship. However, because Israel was not formally covenantally related to him when these proceedings began and because their experience of YHWH to this point was limited, they rightly shrank back in fright at YHWH's arrival on the mountain. While they had observed a microcosm of his glory in the pillar of cloud/ fire (Exod 13:21, 22; 14:19, 24), what happened at Horeb was unlike anything they had

---

75. In the exodus narrative, the choice of verb in YHWH's appeal to Pharaoh, "Let my people go that they may serve (עָבַד) me" (Exod 4:23; 7:16; 7:27[8:1]; 8:16[20]; 9:1, 13; 10:3, 7) is deliberate, signaling something more specific than "worship," as the word is usually translated. This word anticipates the moment when Israel will become YHWH's vassals (עֲבָדִים).

76. While scholars and theologians generally draw sharp distinctions between the Abrahamic covenant and the covenant made with Israel at Horeb, this is unwarranted; they are one and the same. For fuller discussion of the relationship between the Abrahamic and Israelite covenants, see chapter 4, "Covenance: A Whole Bible Perspective," above, pp. 60–88.

77. This perspective is implied in the Decalogic reference to inciting YHWH's passion (קִנְאָה) through the worship of other deities him (Exod 20:2–6; Deut 5:6–10), but explicitly expressed by later prophets (Hosea 1–3; Ezek 16:1–14).

78. Hence the references to Israel as YHWH's sons in Deut 14:1; etc. On "sonship" as a metaphor for vassaldom, see Jer 3:19–20. For discussion, see Block, "The Privilege of Calling, 151–52; Sohn, *The Divine Election of Israel*, 62–73; Sohn, "'I Will Be Your God and You Will Be My People,'" 355–72; B. Kim, "Enlarge the Place of Your Tent," 31–34.

ever experienced, and as it turns out, the nation would never experience again. This was an inaugural moment.

By contrast, from the outset the experiences envisioned for the place that YHWH would choose to brand with his name were intended as ongoing means of celebrating YHWH's saving and covenantal grace, and in maintaining the health of Israel's relationship to their Redeemer. In that respect, Zion would be a fixed and permanent successor to the tabernacle, the symbol of YHWH's presence among his people and the key to his dispensing of grace. In the grand divine scheme, the land of Canaan was to serve as a new Eden, and the Israelites as a new microcosmic humanity, creating an island of *shalom* in a fallen world and declaring to the nations what divine grace can accomplish. Within that agenda Horeb had no function, but Zion would be the link between heaven and earth. From here YHWH's grace should have flowed out to the entire world. While Israel as a nation failed in this vision, the eighth-century prophets looked forward to the day when Zion would be the spiritual capital of the earth:

> 1 In the last days the mountain of YHWH's temple will be established
> as the highest of the mountains;
> it will be exalted above the hills,
> and peoples will stream to it.
> 2 Many nations will come and say,
> > "Come, let us go up to the mountain of YHWH,
> > to the temple of the God of Jacob.
> > He will teach us his ways,
> > so that we may walk in his paths."
> The Torah will go out from Zion,
> the word of YHWH from Jerusalem.
> 3 He will judge between many peoples
> and will settle disputes for strong nations far and wide.
> They will beat their swords into plowshares
> and their spears into pruning hooks.
> Nation will not take up sword against nation,
> nor will they train for war anymore.
> 4 Everyone will sit under their own vine
> and under their own fig tree,
> and no one will make them afraid,
> for YHWH Almighty has spoken.
> 5 All the nations may walk in the name of their gods,
> but we will walk in the name of YHWH our God for ever and ever.
> 6 "In that day," declares YHWH, "I will gather the lame;
> > I will assemble the exiles and those I have brought to grief.
> 7 I will make the lame my remnant,
> > those driven away a strong nation.
> > YHWH will rule over them in Mount Zion
> > from that day and forever.

> ⁸ As for you, watchtower of the flock,
>   stronghold of Daughter Zion,
>   the former dominion will be restored to you;
>   kingship will come to Daughter Jerusalem."
> (Mic 4:1–8, NIV, adapted; cf. Isa 2:1–4)

Epilogue

Having established the distinctions between Horeb and Zion, we may have discovered a vital clue to the context of the only occurrence of the name Zion in the book of Hebrews.[79] Since through the work of Christ the new covenant is established and the ideals of God's covenant with Israel are realized (Jer 31:27–40; Heb 8:10–13), there is no need for God's people to go back to Horeb and start all over again. On the contrary, the Hebrew Christians

> have come to Mount Zion and to the city of the living God, the heavenly Jerusalem, and to innumerable angels in festal gathering, and to the assembly of the firstborn who are enrolled in heaven, and to God the judge of all, and to the spirits of the righteous made perfect, and to Jesus, the mediator of a new covenant, and to the sprinkled blood that speaks a better word than [the sacrifices] of Abel. (Heb 12:22–24, NRSV)[80]

In Christ the shadow institutions have been replaced by the real, and the inaugural observances of Horeb are rendered passé. Nevertheless, much of what is said here of New Testament believers could have been said of ancient Israelites, as in the following paraphrase:

> You have come to Mount Zion, to the city of the living God, the earthly Jerusalem, and to an innumerable host in festal gathering, and to the assembly of the firstborn who are enrolled in heaven,[81] and to God the judge of all, and to the spirits of the righteous made perfect, and to YHWH, the one who has established you as his covenant people, and to the sprinkled blood [of Christ] through which your forgiveness is assured.

---

79. For full discussion of the relationship between Sinai and Mount Zion, that is, the heavenly Jerusalem, in Hebrews 12, see Kibbe, *Godly Fear or Ungodly Failure?* Kibbe has not considered adequately the data concerning "Zion" in Deuteronomy.

80. On this interpretation of κρεῖττον λαλοῦντι παρὰ τὸν Ἄβελ, see chapter 4, "Covenance: A Whole Bible Perspective," above, pp. 60–88.

81. Cf. Exod 32:32–33; Ps 69:29[28]; Dan 12:1. The links between the Hebrews text and Ps 69:29[28] are especially striking: "Let them be blotted out of the book of the living; let them not be enrolled among the righteous" (NRSV).

8

"What Do These Stones Mean?"

The Riddle of Deuteronomy 27[1]

Introduction

DEUTERONOMY 27 IS A riddle at many levels. First, it is a cultic riddle: Why this curious combination of prescribed rituals, and why this ritual inscription of the Torah on plastered stones? Second, it is a theological riddle: What is the significance of this ritual within the theology of Deuteronomy and the First Testament as a whole? Third, it is a literary riddle: What is this chapter doing here within the overall flow of the book? I shall address the last issue first.

Deuteronomy 27 in Its Present Literary Context

The chapter consists of three speeches, successively attributed to Moses and the elders of Israel (vv. 1b–8), Moses and the Levitical priests (vv. 9b–10), and Moses alone (vv. 11–26). The threefold reference to Moses by name (vv. 1, 9, 11)[2] and the involvement of the elders and the Levitical priests in the addresses contrast with the lengthy first-person discourse of chapters 5–26. In style and content this chapter is intrusive, interrupting what would otherwise have been a smooth transition from chapter 26 to chapter 28.[3] It seems that in the oral delivery and in the transcription of Moses' second address

---

1. This is a stylistically modified version of an article that was previously published in the *Journal of the Evangelical Theological Society* 56 (2013): 17–41. It expands on my brief comments on Deut 27:1–8 in *Deuteronomy*, 623–29, and is an adaptation of a paper read at the annual meeting of the Evangelical Theological Society in Milwaukee, WI, November, 2012. I am grateful to Andreas Köstenberger, editor of the *Journal*, for his kind permission to republish it here, and to my assistants Carmen Imes and Jordan Brown, who read earlier versions of this paper and offered many helpful suggestions for its improvement.

2. We have read Moses' name only eight times prior to this: Deut 1:1, 3, 5; 4:41, 44, 45, 46; 5:1.

3. Note the following links between Deut 26 and 28: (1) The vocabulary and motifs of 28:1 echo 26:16–19. In both, adherence to the revealed will of God as expressed in the laws and in Moses' exposition thereof is characterized as "obeying his voice/the voice of YHWH your God" (שְׁמַע בְּקוֹל). The idiom derives from Exod 19:5, where listening to YHWH's voice is explicitly paired with keeping his covenant, but it appears often in Deuteronomy: 4:30; 8:20; 9:23; 13:4, 19[3, 18]; 15:5; 26:14, 17;

(31:9) Deut 28 followed immediately after chapter 26. Indeed several factors suggest the speeches in chapter 27 fit best after 31:29:[4] (1) The elders will be involved later in formal proceedings relating to the ratification of the covenant (29:9–10[10–11]);[5] (2) Together with the Levitical priests they will functions as custodians of the Torah of Moses (31:9); (3) Along with scribal officials (שֹׁטְרִים) they will later appear before Moses to hear the words of the Torah—with the heavens and the earth as witnesses (31:28); (4) The charge in 27:3 and 8 to transcribe "all the words of this Torah" (כֹּל דִּבְרֵי הַתּוֹרָה הַזֹּאת) assumes a written copy of Moses' speeches on the Plains of Moab, suggesting the speeches of this chapter were given after the speeches in chapter 31.

I grant that my reconstruction is speculative, but it seems the events behind the text might have transpired something like this. Having delivered his final pastoral addresses to his congregation on the Plains of Moab, Moses committed "this Torah" to writing. He handed the documents to the Levitical priests and elders and charged the former to read this entire Torah to the people every seventh year at the festival of booths (31:9–13). In the meantime, stored beside the Ark of the Covenant (31:24–26), this canonical Torah would be a permanent witness to the pact to which both YHWH and the people had committed themselves (31:24–26).[6] Mindful of the people's fickleness (31:27–29), before the elders Moses expressed his anxiety over their spiritual state once the restraining influence of his physical presence would be removed (31:27–29). Thereafter, Moses and the elders returned to the people and instructed them in the final phase of the covenant renewal ceremonies, which would transpire inside the promised land. By involving the elders in these instructions Moses ensured continuity between the present proceedings and those that would subsequently take place at Mount Ebal.[7]

27:10; 28:1, 2, 15, 45, 62; 30:2, 8, 10, 20. (2) These are the only two instances in the book where Israel's privileged status is characterized as being set high above all the nations (נְתָנְךָ עַל כָּל הַגּוֹיִם). (3) Echoes and allusions to 26:16–19 continue in the blessings outlined in 28:1–14. Deuteronomy 26:19 and 28:9 both speak of Israel as a holy people (עַם קָדֹשׁ) belonging to YHWH; both link this status expressly with "keeping his commands" (שָׁמַר מִצְוֹתָיו) and "walking in his ways" (הָלַךְ בִּדְרָכָיו); and both declare the effects this will have on the nations/peoples of the earth.

4. Eduard Nielsen suggests the cultic background for the present ceremony is to be found in Deut 31:9–13, that is, the seventh-year Feast of Tabernacles, when all Israel would hear the leaders recite the Torah. See "A Note on Zechariah 14,4–5," 37.

5. The elders appear second in a list of participants that includes the heads of the tribes (רָאשֵׁי שְׁבָטִים), elders (זְקֵנִים), scribal officials (שֹׁטְרִים), all the men of Israel (כָּל אַנְשֵׁי יִשְׂרָאֵל), the children (טַף), women (נָשִׁים), and the alien (גֵּר). In this and other respects as we shall see the event parallels the covenant making event at Horeb (5:23).

6. On which see Sonnet, *The Book within the Book*, 139.

7. Although the narrator does not mention Joshua here, several factors suggest that he would have been included among the elders: (1) he had previously served as Moses' right hand general in military conflicts (Exod 17:8–14); (2) he had served as Moses' assistant (מְשָׁרֵת) on Mount Horeb (Exod 24:13; 32:17; 33:11; cf. Num 11:28); (3) he had represented the tribe of Ephraim when the twelve men were sent to scout out the land of Canaan (Num 13:16; 14:6, 30, 38); (4) Moses had already ordained him as his successor (Num 27:18–23; Deut 31:1–8); (5) Joshua certainly qualified to be an elder, for he was one of the three oldest men present (in addition to Moses and Caleb); (6) although Josh 8:33 notes that elders, scribal officers, and Levitical priests were involved in the ritual at Ebal and Gerizim—as called for in Deut 31:24–29—Joshua was the "elder" who actually presided over the rituals prescribed in Deut 27:1–8. Based on these considerations, Joshua was surely included among the elders. This

But why would the editor insert a speech here that belongs after 31:29? Some[8] suggest that because chapter 27 is located before the covenant blessings and curses (chapter 28), it corresponds to the provision in second millennium BCE Hittite treaties for the production of written copies of the covenant.[9] But this interpretation is unlikely. Whereas official Hittite versions were written on portable materials and deposited in the presence of the deity, here the text is copied from the official document to mundane rocks unrelated to a sanctuary and needing first to be plastered with lime (27:4). Furthermore, whereas the Hittite documents were retrieved and read aloud before the subordinate at stated intervals (like the "scrolled" Torah in 31:9–13), the present chapter anticipates a one-time event—at Ebal, shortly after the Israelites have crossed the Jordan.[10] The text is silent on future repetition of this ritual.[11] Others suggest that the inscribed pillar called for in verses 2–8 functions as witnesses to a solemn treaty ceremony—in addition to the heavens and the earth (30:19) and the Song (32:1–42; cf. 31:19).[12]

The best clue to the reason for insertion of chapter 27 between 26:16–19 and chapter 28 is found in Deut 11:26–32. There Moses had anticipated this moment and had identified Mounts Gerizim and Ebal [in the vicinity of the oak of Moreh] by name as Israel's destination beyond the Jordan. Indeed, the large block of material preserved in 26:16—28:69[29:1] exhibits a resumptive expository relationship to 11:26–32, though presenting the main issues in reverse order (Table 8.1, page 155).[13]

These two segments may be interpreted either as a frame around Moses' exposition of the terms of the covenant, its decrees, judgments, and stipulations (12:1—26:15), or as the respective conclusions to the two major components of Moses' second address (5:1b—11:32; 12:1—28:69[29:1]). The involvement of the elders here also creates an artful *inclusio* with 5:22–33, where Moses had last referred to the elders of his own generation.[14] Their appearance with Moses in his final addresses not only adds weight

---

interpretation is reinforced by the genre of the speeches in this chapter. For the first time in the book the Mosaic speech act is introduced with וַיְצַו, from צִוָּה, "to command, charge."

8. See Thompson, *Deuteronomy: An Introduction and Commentary*, 19.

9. For examples see the treaty between Suppililiuma I of Hatti and Shattiwaza of Mitanni and the treaty between Muwatalli II of Hatti and Alaksandu of Wilusa, texts 6A §13 and 13 §16, respectively in Beckman, *Hittite Diplomatic Texts*, 46–47 and 91. Remarkably first millennium BCE Neo-Assyrian treaty texts make no such provisions.

10. According to Josephus, Deut 27 required that the sacrifices were to be offered on the altar only once (*Ant* 4.308). For a full discussion of Josephus' treatment of Deut 27 and Josh 8:30–35, see Begg, "The Cisjordanian Altar(s) and their Associated Rites According to Josephus," 192–211.

11. Neither does Josh 8:30–35, which narrates Joshua's fulfillment of the present charge, anticipate future repetition of the ritual.

12. Thus Kitchen and Lawrence, *Treaty, Law and Covenant in the Ancient Near East*, Part 3, 120. Note also his later comment (p. 123), "[In] chapter 27, we find the command later to enact a *solemn ceremony*, verses 11–26 . . . including future *deposition of the text* on a stela . . . (27:4–8), which is also a form of *witness* . . . ; all three items feature in or with treaties . . ." (emphasis original).

13. Similarly, McConville, *Deuteronomy*, 387.

14. There Moses describes the moment at Mount Horeb when the elders had approached him, pleading that YHWH stop talking directly with them or they would die. They requested that Moses alone appear before YHWH to receive his revelation and that he relay to the people all that God would say. YHWH agreed, declaring that from then on he would speak to Moses and Moses would teach the

to his exhortations, but attests to Moses' fidelity in carrying out the earlier request of the people (5:27) and the charge of YHWH (5:31).

Table 8.1
The Relationship between Deut 11:26–32 and 26:16—28:69[29:1]

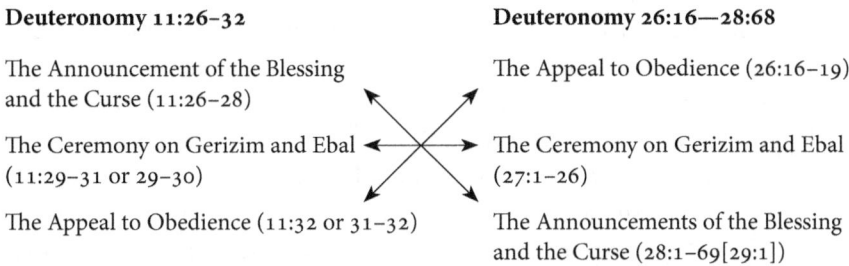

Deuteronomy 11:26–32	Deuteronomy 26:16—28:68
The Announcement of the Blessing and the Curse (11:26–28)	The Appeal to Obedience (26:16–19)
The Ceremony on Gerizim and Ebal (11:29–31 or 29–30)	The Ceremony on Gerizim and Ebal (27:1–26)
The Appeal to Obedience (11:32 or 31–32)	The Announcements of the Blessing and the Curse (28:1–69[29:1])

The Literary Integrity of Deuteronomy 27

Critical scholars tend to interpret Deut 27 as a collage of several ritual traditions. First, since Josh 4:19—5:12 reports that after the Israelites had crossed the Jordan they performed their first rituals at Gilgal, some suggest this text involves a Gilgal tradition. The erection of twelve stone pillars in Josh 4:20 supposedly represents an alternative version of the present command to set up large stones on which to inscribe the Torah (Deut 27:2–3).[15] Second, the location of the present ceremony at Ebal and Gerizim (vv. 4–7) and the blessing and curse ritual (vv. 11–13) point to a Shechem tradition, linked to the renewal of the covenant under the leadership of Joshua (Josh 24).[16] Third, the association of Levi with Simeon, Judah, Issachar, Joseph, and Benjamin on Gerizim in Deut 27:12 suggests an ancient tradition when Levi was still considered a "secular" tribe.[17] Fourth, verses 14–26 complicate the matter further. Here the Levites are involved in a liturgical role reading only curses to the people, though verses 12–13 had called for both blessings and curses.[18]

---

people and exhort them to obedience that they might prosper in the land.

15. Cf. Mayes, *Deuteronomy*, 340–41; Nelson, *Deuteronomy*, 316.

16. Cooper and Goldstein ("The Cult of the Dead and the Theme of Entry into the Land," 292), confuse Gilgal and Shechem when they write, "The stones are to be conveyed from the place of the Jordan crossing to Mount Ebal (Shechem), where they are to be installed."

17. Cf. Eissfeldt, "Gilgal or Shechem," 90–101; Seebass, "Garazim und Ebal als Symbole von Segen und Fluch," 22–31. For brief recent representation of this approach see Biddle, *Deuteronomy*, 395.

18. Critical scholars tend to begin their analysis of this unit by reconstructing its literary evolution. For example, Merendino ("Dt 27:1–8: Eine literarkritische und überlieferungsgeschichtliche Untersuchung," 194–207) identifies three stages in the history of the text: (1) the original text, written in the time of Hezekiah, consisted of verses 1, 3b, 5a, 7; (2) verses 5b–6 represent a later addition; (3) verses 2b–3a and 8 derive from a Josianic rewriting; (4) verse 4 was added in a fourth stage; (5) the "deuteronomists" completed the present text by adding verse 1b and making a few minor additions elsewhere. For an equally complex reconstruction of the history of the text see Nielsen, *Deuteronomium*, 244–46. Naʿaman argues that the entire chapter is exilic: "Shechem and Jerusalem in the Exilic and Restoration

Despite seemingly disparate features, the editor of Moses' speeches intentionally combined and juxtaposed them to create a single account. Arguing for a unified text, Andrew E. Hill suggests this chapter is constructed after the model of a royal land grant ceremony symbolized and described on Babylonian boundary stone (*kudurru*) inscriptions.[19] Hill's impulse is sound, though recent advances in the interpretation of these stones call for refinement of his thesis. This chapter actually involves several elements typically found in Babylonian Entitlement *narû* inscriptions, whose function was to "commemorate the acquisition or affirmation of an entitlement" to an on-going benefit within a "feudal system."[20] Cast as a series of authoritative addresses by a representative of the divine landowner, like *narû* inscriptions Deuteronomy 27 commemorates Israel's entitlement to the land promised to the ancestors, calling for (1) erection of inscribed stones (vv. 2–4, 8); (2) construction of an altar and cultic activity before the deity (vv. 5–7);[21] (3) inscription of the text of the entitlement, in this case granted by the divine owner (vv. 3, 8);[22] (4) listing of witnesses (the twelve tribes, vv. 12–13);[23] and (5) a culmination in imprecations for those who violate the inscription (vv. 15–26).[24] These features all make sense within the broader Near Eastern context of the events. However, as we shall see, as a unit the chapter presents a theology far greater than the sum of these conventional parts, and far greater than the Babylonian Entitlement *narû* inscriptions.[25]

The cohesion of Deut 27 is communicated literarily as well. The three unequal parts[26] reflect an ABA pattern, the two larger outside parts (vv. 1–8; 11–26) sandwiching a short hortatory challenge in the middle (vv. 9–10; Table 8.2).

Table 8.2
The Structure of Deuteronomy 27

The Future Performative Ritual (vv. 1–8)	The Present Challenge (vv. 9–10)	The Future Verbal Ritual (vv. 11–26)

Period," 7–32 (Hebrew); Naʿaman, "The Law of the Altar in Deuteronomy and the Cultic Site Near Shechem," 141–61.

19. Hill, "The Ebal Ceremony as Hebrew Land Grant," 399–406.

20. Slanski, *The Babylonian Entitlement narûs (kudurrus)*, 151.

21. Verses 4–7. Compare the images of cultic scenes carved on the *narû* stones. Ibid., 141–43, 165–66. On the significance of the present altar see below.

22. On the text of Babylonian Entitlement *narûs*, see ibid., 169–74.

23. In the Babylonian Entitlement *narû* inscriptions, gods are listed, but not as witnesses; the witnesses are human, drawn from the upper ranks of Babylonian governmental tones authorities. Ibid., 175–76.

24. On the imprecations in Babylonian Entitlement *narûs*, see ibid., 176–79.

25. Cf. the theological interpretation of the chapter as a whole by Barker, "The Theology of Deuteronomy 27," 277–303.

26. Verses 1–8 (123 words); verses 9–10 (30 words); verses 11–26 (173 words).

While the outer rituals diverge, the accounts are linked in several ways. (1) As already noted, for the first time in the book the Mosaic speech act is characterized as "a command, charge" (צִוָּה, vv. 1, 11) suggesting a common genre.[27] (2) In contrast to covenant renewal rituals transpiring on the Plains of Moab alluded to elsewhere in the book (11:26–28; 26:16–19; 29:1[2]—30:20; 31:24–29), the rituals prescribed in verses 1–8 and 11–26 are described as future actions to be performed in the promised land without Moses as presiding officer (vv. 2, 4, and 12). (3) Both rituals are to take place on Mount Ebal (vv. 4, 13), though the latter rituals also involve Mount Gerizim, located opposite Ebal (v. 12).[28] It seems best, therefore, to interpret this chapter as a literary unit. Our challenge is trying to understand the function of the parts in relation to each other and to the rest of the book. Time and space constraints demand that the remainder of this paper focus on verses 1–8.

---

27. See note 7 above. This phenomenon occurs elsewhere in the book only in chapter 31, where the form appears three times (31:10, 23, 25). Although Moses appears as the subject of the verb צִוָּה more than thirty times, these are the only places where the narrator prepares the reader for a speech from Moses with this verb. The nearest analogues within Moses' own speeches occur in 3:18, 21 and 15:11, where the first-person form of the verb is followed by a speech cast as a direct quotation, and 2:4, where YHWH's command to Moses to "charge" the people is followed by a verbatim quotation of the charge.

28. The Samaritan Pentateuch locates the prescribed altar of Deut 27:4–5 on Gerizim, rather than Ebal. On the sectarian tendencies of the Samaritan Pentateuch, see Tov, *Textual Criticism of the Hebrew Bible*, 74–90, esp. 77–78 and 87–88.

Commemorating the Basis of Israel's Claim to the Land (Deuteronomy 27:1–8)

Figure 8.1
A Hebrew-English Synopsis of Deuteronomy 27:1–8

וַיְצַו מֹשֶׁה וְזִקְנֵי יִשְׂרָאֵל אֶת־הָעָם לֵאמֹר שָׁמֹר אֶת־כָּל־הַמִּצְוָה אֲשֶׁר אָנֹכִי מְצַוֶּה אֶתְכֶם הַיּוֹם׃	1	Moses and the elders of Israel charged the people: "Observe the entire charge that I am charging you today.
וְהָיָה בַּיּוֹם אֲשֶׁר תַּעַבְרוּ אֶת־הַיַּרְדֵּן אֶל־הָאָרֶץ אֲשֶׁר־יְהוָה אֱלֹהֶיךָ נֹתֵן לָךְ וַהֲקֵמֹתָ לְךָ אֲבָנִים גְּדֹלוֹת וְשַׂדְתָּ אֹתָם בַּשִּׂיד׃	2	On the day you cross the Jordan into the land that YHWH your God is giving you, you shall erect large stones and plaster them with plaster.
וְכָתַבְתָּ עֲלֵיהֶן אֶת־כָּל־דִּבְרֵי הַתּוֹרָה הַזֹּאת בְּעָבְרֶךָ לְמַעַן אֲשֶׁר תָּבֹא אֶל־הָאָרֶץ אֲשֶׁר־יְהוָה אֱלֹהֶיךָ נֹתֵן לְךָ אֶרֶץ זָבַת חָלָב וּדְבַשׁ כַּאֲשֶׁר דִּבֶּר יְהוָה אֱלֹהֵי־אֲבֹתֶיךָ לָךְ׃	3	And you shall write on them all the words of this Torah when you cross over to enter the land that YHWH your God is giving you, a land flowing with milk and honey, just as YHWH, the God of your fathers promised you.
וְהָיָה בְּעָבְרְכֶם אֶת־הַיַּרְדֵּן תָּקִימוּ אֶת־הָאֲבָנִים הָאֵלֶּה אֲשֶׁר אָנֹכִי מְצַוֶּה אֶתְכֶם הַיּוֹם בְּהַר עֵיבָל וְשַׂדְתָּ אוֹתָם בַּשִּׂיד׃	4	When you cross the Jordan, you shall set up these stones, concerning which I have charged you today, on Mount Ebal, and you shall plaster them with plaster.
וּבָנִיתָ שָּׁם מִזְבֵּחַ לַיהוָה אֱלֹהֶיךָ מִזְבַּח אֲבָנִים לֹא־תָנִיף עֲלֵיהֶם בַּרְזֶל׃	5	There you shall construct an altar to YHWH your God, an altar of stones. You may not use any iron tool upon them.
אֲבָנִים שְׁלֵמוֹת תִּבְנֶה אֶת־מִזְבַּח יְהוָה אֱלֹהֶיךָ וְהַעֲלִיתָ עָלָיו עוֹלֹת לַיהוָה אֱלֹהֶיךָ׃	6	With natural stones you must construct the altar of YHWH your God, and on it offer burnt offerings to YHWH your God.
וְזָבַחְתָּ שְׁלָמִים וְאָכַלְתָּ שָּׁם וְשָׂמַחְתָּ לִפְנֵי יְהוָה אֱלֹהֶיךָ׃	7	There you shall sacrifice fellowship offerings, and you may eat [them] there, and you may celebrate in the presence of YHWH your God.
וְכָתַבְתָּ עַל־הָאֲבָנִים אֶת־כָּל־דִּבְרֵי הַתּוֹרָה הַזֹּאת בַּאֵר הֵיטֵב׃	8	And you shall write on the stones all the words of this Torah to formalize it [the covenant].

The speech that makes up most of verses 1–8 divides into three parts: (1) a brief opening appeal to scrupulous adherence to the present prescriptions (v. 1b); (2) summary instructions regarding the prescribed ritual (vv. 2–3); and (3) a more detailed description of the prescribed ritual (vv. 4–8; see Table 8.1). I am especially concerned about the rituals described in parts 2 and 3, which function as two panels of a diptych. Although they exhibit distinctive flavors and emphases, the repetition of key phrases and expressions points to a deliberately constructed and coherent whole. Figure 8.2 highlights the parallels and differences by juxtaposing the texts synoptically:

"WHAT DO THESE STONES MEAN?"

Figure 8.2
A Synopsis of Deuteronomy 27:2–3 and 27:4–8

27:2-3	27:4-8

וְהָיָה בַּיּוֹם אֲשֶׁר תַּעַבְרוּ אֶת־הַיַּרְדֵּן .... 27:4— וְהָיָה בְּעָבְרְכֶם אֶת־הַיַּרְדֵּן
אֶל־הָאָרֶץ אֲשֶׁר־יְהוָה אֱלֹהֶיךָ נֹתֵן לָךְ
תָּקִימוּ אֶת־הָאֲבָנִים הָאֵלֶּה .... וַהֲקֵמֹתָ לְךָ אֲבָנִים גְּדֹלוֹת
אֲשֶׁר אָנֹכִי מְצַוֶּה אֶתְכֶם הַיּוֹם בְּהַר עֵיבָל
וְשַׂדְתָּ אֹתָם בַּשִּׂיד: .... וְשַׂדְתָּ אֹתָם בַּשִּׂיד:
וּבָנִיתָ שָּׁם מִזְבֵּחַ לַיהוָה אֱלֹהֶיךָ מִזְבַּח אֲבָנִים
לֹא־תָנִיף עֲלֵיהֶם בַּרְזֶל:
אֲבָנִים שְׁלֵמוֹת תִּבְנֶה אֶת־מִזְבַּח יְהוָה אֱלֹהֶיךָ
וְהַעֲלִיתָ עָלָיו עוֹלֹת לַיהוָה אֱלֹהֶיךָ:
וְזָבַחְתָּ שְׁלָמִים
וְאָכַלְתָּ שָּׁם
וְשָׂמַחְתָּ לִפְנֵי יְהוָה אֱלֹהֶיךָ:
וְכָתַבְתָּ עַל־הָאֲבָנִים .... וְכָתַבְתָּ עֲלֵיהֶן
אֶת־כָּל־דִּבְרֵי הַתּוֹרָה הַזֹּאת .... אֶת־כָּל־דִּבְרֵי הַתּוֹרָה הַזֹּאת
בַּאֵר הֵיטֵב:
בְּעָבְרֶךָ לְמַעַן אֲשֶׁר תָּבֹא
אֶל־הָאָרֶץ אֲשֶׁר־יְהוָה אֱלֹהֶיךָ נֹתֵן לָךְ
אֶרֶץ זָבַת חָלָב וּדְבָשׁ
כַּאֲשֶׁר דִּבֶּר יְהוָה אֱלֹהֵי־אֲבֹתֶיךָ לָךְ:

And it shall be [that] -----------	And it shall be [that]
on the day you cross over the Jordan --------	when you cross over the Jordan,
to the land that YHWH your God is giving you,	
you shall set up **large** *stones,*	you shall set up these stones,
	concerning which I command you today,
	on Mount Ebal,
and you shall plaster them with plaster, ------	**and you shall plaster them with plaster,**
	and there
	you shall build an altar to YHWH your God,
	an altar of stones.
	You shall wield no iron tool on them;
	you shall build an altar to YHWH your God
	of uncut stones.
	And you shall offer burnt offerings on it
	to YHWH your God,
	and you shall sacrifice peace offerings
	and you shall eat there,
	and you shall rejoice before YHWH your God,
and you shall write on them -------------	and you shall write on the stones
all the words of this Torah, -------------	all the words of this Torah
	to formalize it [the covenant].
when you cross over to enter	
the land that YHWH your God is giving you,	
a land flowing with milk and honey,	
as YHWH, the God of your fathers, has	
promised you.	

159

Each segment commences with וְהָיָה, "and it shall be," followed by a temporal marker of the context when and where the ritual is to be performed:[29] when the Israelites have crossed the Jordan. Thereafter these panels share a common skeleton, consisting of three basic commands:

> You shall set up [large] stones,
>
> And you shall plaster them with plaster,
>
> And you shall write on them all the words of this Torah.

Each panel contains significant internal repetition. Emphasizing the context of the ritual, the first twice specifies the destination as "the land that YHWH your God is giving you." Emphasizing the ritual itself, the second twice adds a fourth element to the triad of commands: "And you shall build an altar to YHWH your God."

Panel A (vv. 2–3)

The three ritual commands in verses 2b–3a represent the heart of the first panel. Complex subordinate clauses at the beginning (v. 2a) and at the end (v. 3a) establish the context for the proceedings and frame the central core. Chronologically, they are to be performed "on the day" the Israelites cross the Jordan into the land that YHWH promised them. Obviously "day" does not mean within twenty-four hours of crossing the Jordan. It would have taken much longer than a day for all the Israelites and their possessions to cross the river and travel thirty miles to Mount Ebal. Just as הַיּוֹם in 4:10 and 15 had focused attention on the *events* associated with YHWH's revelation and covenant with Israel at Horeb, so here הַיּוֹם means "in association with the event of crossing the Jordan River." That future day is distinct from "this day," in verses 1 and 9–10, that is, the events associated with the convocation of the Israelites on the Plains of Moab.

Moses' attention to the land sends an early clue concerning the significance of this ritual. First, with two identical clauses he declares that Israel is crossing over "to the land that YHWH is giving to them" (vv. 2–3). Second, he describes the land as desirable and spontaneously providing food for its inhabitants, employing an idiom repeated many times in the book: it "flows with milk and honey" (v. 3b).[30] Third, he adds, "just as YHWH the God of your ancestors promised you" (v. 3b). Together these three expressions highlight the conviction that the events that are imminent represent the completion of the mission on which Moses had embarked forty years earlier and YHWH's fulfillment of his promises to the patriarchs.[31] Because the previous generation had

---

29. On the discourse function of וְהָיָה, see van der Merwe, Naudé, and Kroeze, *A Biblical Hebrew Reference Grammar*, 331.

30. Cf. Deut 6:3; 11:9; 26:9, 15; 27:3; 31:20.

31. At the time of Moses' call and commission YHWH had promised to give the Israelites the land he had sworn to Abraham, Isaac, and Jacob (Exod 6:8; cf. Gen 17:8). Indeed, the characterization of the land as "a land flowing with milk and honey" derives from YHWH himself, who had used this idiom in his initial encounter with Moses (Exod 3:8) and reiterated it repeatedly on the journey (Exod 3:17; 13:5; 33:3; Lev 20:24). On the ancestors in Deuteronomy, see Hwang, *The Rhetoric of Remembrance*.

refused to receive the grant of land thirty-eight years earlier,[32] they had perished in the desert. However, YHWH had not forgotten his promise. These rituals celebrate YHWH's fidelity to his word, and when the Israelites leave this place these stones will remain as reminders of his covenant faithfulness to the patriarchs and to the Israelites.

Verses 2b–3a reduce the rituals to the barest details: erect large stones, plaster them with lime, and write on them all the words of this Torah. But what do these actions mean? Each element deserves separate comment.

The Stone Monuments.

The verb הֵקִים, "to erect, set up," suggests that the stones in question were to be set up as vertical pillars. Ancient Near Easterners erected commemorative monuments for a variety of reasons: as memorials to military conquests,[33] political accomplishments,[34] treaties,[35] judicial achievements,[36] and religious devotion.[37] While pillars function similarly in the First Testament,[38] their most commonly attested use involved מַצֵּבוֹת, phallic symbols of Baal. Moses' earlier denunciations of such pillars (7:5; 22–26) and the elaboration in 27:4–8 obviously exclude this significance here.

Although the plural אֲבָנִים גְּדֹלוֹת, "large stones," in Deut 27:2 suggests the erection of more than one pillar, the text does not state how many were required. Based on the number of tribes involved in the liturgical imprecations in verses 12–13, twelve would seem appropriate, in which case the present ritual would echo part of the covenant ratification ceremony celebrated at Horeb forty years earlier (Exod 24:4). Although the function of the stones differed, remarkably after the Israelites had crossed the Jordan they set up a memorial consisting of twelve stones, "according to the number of the tribes of the sons of Israel" (Josh 4:1–9).[39] Based on the convention of later Greek colonizers

32. See Num 13:27; 14:8; 16:13, 14.

33. E.g., the *Victory Stela* of Naram-Sin (2254–2218 BC), on which see Winter, "Trees on the Mountain: Landscape and Territory on the Victory Stela of Naram Sin of Agade," 63–72. See also the Merneptah Stela celebrating his Asian conquests (1215 BCE); *ANET*, 376–78; for bibliography see Sparks, *Ancient Texts for the Study of the Hebrew Bible*, 389–90.

34. E.g., the Black Obelisk of Shalmaneser of Assyria. For the image see *ANEP*2, figs. 351–55; for a translation of the text see *ANET*, 278–81.

35. E.g., the eighth-century BCE treaty between Bar-Gaʾyah and Matiʿel from Sefire. For the image see *ANEP*2, figs. 659–61; for the text see *COS* 2.82.

36. E.g., Hammurapi's Law Code; for the image see *ANEP*, Fig. 246; for the text see *ANET*, 163–80; *COS* 2.131.

37. E.g., the thirteenth-century BCE stelae from Hazor, including one inscribed with hands upraised to the crescent moon. For illustration and brief discussion see Mazar, *Archaeology of the Land of the Bible 10,000–586 B.C.E.*, 254. The excavations at Gezer have unearthed ten pillars, some three-meters high, aligned in a north to south direction. See Avi-Yonah, "Gezer," 429–43, esp. 437.

38. Memorials to (1) conquest: Ebenezer, "stone of help," commemorating Israel's victory over the Philistines, 1 Sam 7:12; David's memorial on the River Euphrates, 1 Chr 18:3; (2) political achievements: Saul, 1 Sam 15:12; cf. Absalom, who erected a monument because he had no son to keep the memory of his name alive, 2 Sam 18:18; (3) treaties: between Jacob and Laban, Gen 31:45; (4) religious devotion: pillar (מַצֵּבָה) at Bethel (Gen 28:18, 22; 35:14); Joshua's pillar at Shechem (Josh 24:26–27).

39. Cf. also Elijah's altar on Mount Carmel, which consisted of twelve stones "according to the

erecting monuments to commemorate arrival at a destination, and Moses' charge to perform these rituals "on the day you cross the Jordan," Moshe Weinfeld suggested these memorialize the conclusion of a journey.[40] By this interpretation, if the ritual involved twelve stones it signaled the end of the journey for all the tribes of Israel, including those who claimed land east of the Jordan.

The Plaster on the Stone Monuments.

The action involves plastering stones[41] with a white alkaline compound consisting of water and calcium oxide derived from limestone that was readily available in the vicinity of Ebal and Gerizim. This plaster hardens as the water evaporates, leaving a smooth coating over the object.[42] Plastering rough surfaces for artistic and literary purposes is well attested as early as the Chalcolithic paintings at Ghassul, but it is not clear how the Torah was to be written on these pillars. Had Moses called for inscribing the text with chisels the inscription would certainly have been more durable, but it would also have involved arduous work and required much more space than a smooth surface to contain the entire text. If it was etched with a sharp object the dark color of the rock beneath the plaster would constitute the text. However, it seems most likely that the Torah was written with ink or paint, something like the eighth-century BCE "Balaam Text" at Deir ʿAlla in Jordan. However, unlike the latter, where the text was written on an inside wall, exposed to the elements, a legible text would not have survived long. But even without the text, the pillars could have stood for generations as lasting memorials to the present event. Conceivably, when Joshua assembled the tribes of Israel at Shechem for his last address and to renew the covenant (Josh 24), they met at this very spot. Joshua had earlier erected the pillars himself (Josh 8:30–35), and they were probably still standing at the time of his last convocation of the tribes. Nevertheless, although the pillars may have been reused later as a rallying point, apparently Moses expected the texts inscribed thereon to be usable only this one time.

The Text of the Torah on the Stones.

Although Moses had earlier charged the people to write his words on their hearts, the doorposts of their houses, and the gates of their towns (6:9; 11:20), and instructed the future king to write for himself a copy of this Torah on a scroll (17:18), these antecedents

---

number of the sons of Jacob" (1 Kgs 18:31).

40. Weinfeld, "The Pattern of the Israelite Settlement in Canaan," 280.

41. The text represents a typical Hebrew construction, involving a verb and a noun from the same root: וְשַׂדְתָּ אֹתָם בַּשִּׂיד, literally, "and you shall plaster them with the plaster." שִׂיד is a denominative verb from the homonymous noun, which denotes "lime." While the verb occurs only here (vv. 2, 4), the noun occurs elsewhere only in Isa 33:12 and Amos 2:1. Both contexts speak of the atrocious practice of burning human bones to produce lime.

42. While plaster is attested in the region from Neolithic times, in the Iron Age it was commonly used to waterproof cisterns, and occasionally used by wealthier people to plaster the walls and floors of their houses. See further, Herr, "Plaster," *ISBE* (rev. ed.) 3.883.

offer little aid in solving the riddle of this aspect of the ritual on Mount Ebal. The former inscriptions may have involved short texts, perhaps the Shema or the Decalogue,[43] but having the king copy "this Torah" in the presence of the Levitical priests apparently required the precise copying and reading of all of Moses' present addresses. If the general population was forbidden from adding to or deleting from the Torah (4:2), how much less the king, who was to embody it.

If the speeches in chapter 27 were delivered in the context of the proceedings at the end of chapter 31, then "all the words of this Torah" involved the entirety of Moses' farewell pastoral addresses preserved in Deuteronomy. This would have posed no logistical problem. By word count of English translations of the respective documents, Moses' three speeches total are approximately twice as long as Hammurapi's law code,[44] which takes up less than three-fourths of the surface area of the ca. seven-foot stela of Hammurapi. The entire text of Moses' speeches could easily have been transcribed on two six-foot stelae. But if the present rituals involved twelve pillars, as I have suggested, then the average number of words on each pillar would have been fewer than 2,000 and the pillars themselves would have needed to be no taller than three feet.[45] Even so, for the moment the purpose of the inscription remains unspecified.

Panel B (vv. 4–8)

The second panel of this address is slightly longer than the first.[46] Whereas the first panel described the location of the prescribed ritual in general terms,[47] now Moses specifies בְּהַר עֵיבָל, "on Mount Ebal." The choice of Ebal for this ceremony is logical on several counts. First, Mounts Ebal and Gerizim appear at the precise midpoint of a straight line plotted "from Dan to Beersheba," the common stereotypical idiom for referring to the entire land of Israel from the northern to the southern border.[48]

---

43. Though "these words" that Moses charged the people to put on their hearts/minds and recite constantly to their children probably involved the entire Torah, that is, his speeches in the book of Deuteronomy. On the possibility of memorizing such a large text, see Carr, *Writing on the Tablet of the Heart*, 8–14.

44. Ideally one should compare the lengths of these documents in their original form, the Babylonian version of the Law Code and the Hebrew version of Deuteronomy. However, since the Law Code is written in syllabic script and Deuteronomy was originally written only with a consonantal alphabet, it is difficult to establish a precise comparison. According to L. W. King's translation (*The Code of Hammurabi*, reprint of 1910 edition), the Code has slightly more than 11,000 words. According to the ESV, the word count for the three speeches of Moses is slightly more than 23,000.

45. Barker ("The Theology of Deuteronomy 27," 286) suggests plausibly that the use of the verb בָּאֵר in v. 8 creates an inclusio with 1:5, reinforcing the view that the texts written on the stones included all of Deut 1–26.

46. Panel A has 48 words; panel B has 59. The framework (vv. 4, 8) repeats much of the essential information already presented in the first panel, though in greatly abbreviated form. Indeed, in verse 4 the characterization of the stones as הָאֲבָנִים הָאֵלֶּה, "these stones," and אֲשֶׁר אָנֹכִי מְצַוֶּה אֶתְכֶם הַיּוֹם, "[about] which I am commanding you this day," assumes the preceding.

47. "When you cross over to enter the land that YHWH your God is giving you, a land flowing with milk and honey, as YHWH, the God of your fathers, has promised you."

48. Judg 20:1; 1 Sam 3:20; 2 Sam 3:10; 17:11; 24:2, 15. Alternatively we could draw a line from Ijon,

Figure 8.3
The Location of Mounts Gerizim and Ebal

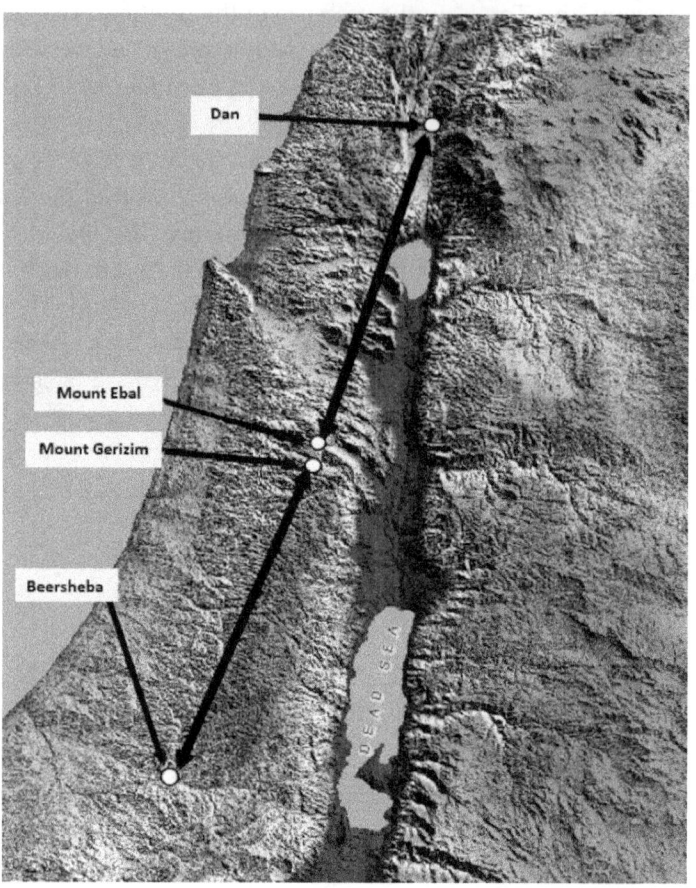

Second, rising more than 3,000 feet above sea level and 1,200 feet above the surrounding terrain Mount Ebal is one of the highest mountains in the region; from its peak most of the promised land was visible, from Mount Hermon in the north to the Jerusalem highlands in the south, and from the Mediterranean Sea in the west to the hills of Gilead and Bashan across the Jordan River. Third, this was an extremely important site in Israel's ancestral traditions. Although Genesis mentions neither Ebal nor Gerizim, Shechem, located between these mountains, was Abraham's first recorded stopping point in the land to which YHWH had guided him. Here YHWH had appeared and declared explicitly that this was the land he was giving to him, to which Abraham responded by building an altar (Gen 12:6–7).[49] Decades later, when Jacob returned from Haran with his family, at Shechem he bought a piece of land, built an altar, and named it אֵל אֱלֹהֵי יִשְׂרָאֵל, "El, the God of Israel." In so doing he acknowledged the providential conjoining

---

at the northernmost end of the Huleh valley (cf. 1 Kgs 15:20; 2 Kgs 15:29; 2 Chr 16:4), to Tamar and Ezem (exact locations unknown), but apparently southeast of Beersheba (Josh 15:29; 19:3; 1 Chr 4:29).

49. In 11:30 Moses alluded to this event with his reference to the "oaks of Moreh." Apart from this tradition, as an outsider he would probably not have been aware of the name Moreh, or of the distinctive association of this place with oaks.

of deity, subject, and land (Gen 33:18–20; cf. 35:4). By locating this ceremony at Ebal and Gerizim, Moses invites the nation to acknowledge God's faithfulness in finally fulfilling the promise to the ancestors.

The bulk of this panel is taken up with a new subject: instructions for constructing an altar (vv. 5–6a) and for celebrating rituals at the altar (vv. 6b–7).

Instructions for Constructing an Altar at Ebal (vv. 5–6a).

Moses begins by calling for the construction of the altar "there" (שָׁם), that is, at Mount Ebal, and then he adds that this altar must be built of natural stones, rather than of stones chiseled to shape[50] with an iron tool.[51] Although this altar will serve a one-time event, quite distinct from the altar involved in regular worship at the tabernacle or temple, the proscription adapts Exod 20:25, "If you make an altar of stones for me, do not build it with dressed stones, for you will defile it if you wield (הֵנִיף) a tool against it."[52] The present call for natural stones suits the ceremonial context. Just as animals to be sacrificed were to be "perfect" (תָּמִים, e.g., Lev 1:3) and "without blemish" (מוּם, Deut 15:21), so the stones to be used in the altar for sacrifices were to be "whole, complete" (שְׁלֵמָה). Apparently attempting to improve them with human effort and man-made tools would actually defile them.[53]

According to verses 6b–7 the rituals to be performed at the altar included whole burnt offerings (עוֹלֹת) to YHWH, fellowship/peace offerings (זֶבַח שְׁלָמִים), eating "there" (שָׁם), and celebrating (שָׂמַח) in YHWH's presence. This prescription recalls instructions for worship at the central sanctuary in 12:7 and 18, where Moses had invited Israelites to make regular pilgrimages to the place that YHWH would choose to establish his name, and there to present their whole burnt offerings (עוֹלֹת) along with other offerings to

---

50. The verb הֵנִיף, from נוּף, "to raise," in the hiphil stem means "to wield, to swing."

51. The expression אֲבָנִים שְׁלֵמוֹת, literally "complete, healthy stones," occurs elsewhere only in Josh 8:31, which is based on this text," and in 1 Kgs 6:7, where the singular form, אֶבֶן שְׁלֵמָה, "natural stone," applies to stones that were apparently pre-prepared at a quarry (מַסָּע), to prevent the sound of hammer, chisel, or any other iron tool from being heard at the site of the temple as it was being built.

52. It is not clear how the involvement of human hands in shaping stones would defile (חָלַל) them. Per a speculative rabbinic tradition, "Iron was created to shorten man's days, and the altar was created to lengthen man's days; it is not proper that what shortens should be lifted against what lengthens" (*m. Mid.* 3:4).

53. So also Olyan, "Why an Altar of Unfinished Stones?" 161–71. Olyan applies to these stones Mary Douglas' paradigmatic notion that "wholeness" and "completeness" which were to characterize priests and the bodies of sacrificial animals, are characteristic of holiness. See further, Douglas, *Purity and Danger*, 51–52.

Adam Zertal has discovered the remains of a large stone structure on the northern slope of Mount Ebal. Although its function is disputed, it is dated to the early Iron Age, and its framework was made of uncut stones and filled with soil, as prescribed here and in Exod 20:24–25. For preliminary discussion of the site, see Zertal, "Ebal, Mount," 255–58; Zertal, "An Early Iron Age Cultic Site on Mount Ebal," 105–65; Zertal, "Has Joshua's Altar Been Found on Mount Ebal?" 26–44. For a detailed study of this site and this structure, see Hawkins, *The Iron Age Structure on Mount Ebal*. For summary assessment of the evidence, see Kitchen, *On the Reliability of the Old Testament*, 232–34.

YHWH (12:5, 11, 13–14, 21).⁵⁴ Verse 7 contains the only reference to שְׁלָמִים in the book. Since it is missing in the catalogue of gifts to be presented to YHWH in chapter 12, זָבַח שְׁלָמִים, "to sacrifice fellowship offerings," is an umbrella expression for all offerings (זְבָחִים, cf. 12:6, 11, 27).⁵⁵ The combination of whole burnt offerings and fellowship offerings presents a holistic view of sacrifice: sacrificial victims presented to God and consumed entirely by fire, and sacrifices that provided nourishment for the worshiper respectively.⁵⁶ Moses' invitation to eat the שְׁלָמִים with joy and celebration in the presence of YHWH is remarkable, since elsewhere in Deuteronomy לִפְנֵי יהוה ("in the presence of YHWH"), is usually associated with the central sanctuary where YHWH has chosen to establish his name. Apparently he conceived of Mount Ebal as a temporary residence of YHWH, a sequel to Horeb where the Israelites had ratified YHWH's covenant with them decades earlier.

In addition to linking our text to the altar law in Exod 20:24–26,⁵⁷ the combination of whole burnt and fellowship offerings also binds this ceremony even more tightly to the covenant ratification rituals in Exod 24:1–11. As in our text, there (1) an altar was constructed at the foot of a mountain; (2) it was associated with whole burnt and fellowship offerings; (3) which symbolized YHWH's presence. However, the involvement of pillars in the rituals at both sites provides a concrete link between these two texts. Although in Exod 24:4 the narrator had noted that the Horeb ceremony had involved twelve pillars representing the twelve tribes of Israel, he did not explain their role in the ritual. Unlike our text, he expressly distinguished the pillars from the written documents involved in the covenant ratification procedure. Although the permanent copy to be deposited in the Ark of the Covenant had not yet been produced (Exod 24:12), apparently Moses had transcribed the "words" (דְּבָרִים) of that covenant, that is the Decalogue, and the stipulations (מִשְׁפָּטִים), that is "the covenant document" (סֵפֶר

---

54. Except for 27:7 and 13:17[16], which treats booty from a city that turns away from YHWH and is burned as an עוֹלָה to him, elsewhere in Deuteronomy whole burnt offerings are always prescribed for YHWH at the central sanctuary.

55. The derivation of שְׁלָמִים, from a root שלם, "to be whole, complete," suggests these sacrifices were a divinely granted provision for celebrating the well-being worshipers experienced in relationship to the deity. Leviticus 7:11–18 applies the expression שְׁלָמִים to different types of joyful offerings: thanksgiving sacrifices (תּוֹדָה), vowed sacrifices (נֶדֶר), freewill offerings (נְדָבָה).

56. On the šĕlāmîm, see Averbeck, "שלם," 130–43; Milgrom, *Leviticus 1–16*, 217–25; G. Anderson, "Sacrifices and Sacrificial Offerings: Old Testament," 878–79. B. Levine (*In the Presence of YHWH*, 3–54) interprets this as "an efficacious gift of greeting, offered in the presence of YHWH." Others have viewed the שְׁלָמִים variously as "communion offerings" (De Vaux, *Ancient Israel*, 427), "restitution payments" (G. B. Gray, *Sacrifice in the Old Testament*, 7), "peace offerings" (Cooke, *A Critical and Exegetical Commentary on Ezekiel*, 473), or "final offering" (Rendtorff, *Studien zur Geschichte des Opfers im alten Israel*, 81–83). The high proportion (10 percent) of fallow deer remains among the sample of diagnostic bones discovered at the Mount Ebal cult site is intriguing (Hawkins, *Iron Age Structure*, 64, 179–82). Whether or not this site derives from a time when Israelites were not yet completely settled but somewhat dependent on wild game for their own diet, it reinforces my view that Israelite dietary boundaries (Deut 14:1–21) were linked to the sacrifices—the types of animal meats that YHWH accepted as offerings were approved for Israelite consumption—which strengthened the covenant bond between deity and people (hence the designation שְׁלָמִים).

57. These two expressions are frequently combined: Exod 20:24; 24:5; 32:6; Num 10:10; 15:8; Josh 8:31; 22:23, 27; Judg 20:26; 21:4; 2 Sam 24:25; 1 Kgs 9:25; 1 Chr 16:1; 21:26; Ezek 43:27.

הַבְּרִית) on scrolls. Inasmuch as סֵפֶר [usually translated "book"], means simply "written document," irrespective of the materials on which or with which the text was written,[58] Moses could conceivably have written the covenant stipulations on the twelve pillars. However, it is unlikely that the object Moses "took" (לָקַח) in his hands and read before the people (Exod 24:7) was one or more of these pillars. For the narrator the pillars simply represented the twelve tribes of Israel, memorializing the inclusion of all of Jacob's descendants in the covenant that YHWH had originally made with Abraham and promised to his descendants (Gen 15:13–21; 17:4–8).

Instructions for Transcribing "This Torah" on the Pillars (v. 8)

In verse 8 Moses returns to the matter of the text on the pillars, though he still does not explain directly why "all the words of this Torah" were to be written on them. Were they to be read aloud off the rocks to the assembly? This seems superfluous since the Levites already had the scroll that Moses had produced (31:9–13). Were they to be transcribed so future visitors to the site could be reminded of the principles of the covenant relationship outlined in the Torah? Or were they to be transcribed in anticipation of covenant renewal events like the event led by Joshua at Shechem. This is unlikely, since Josh 24 mentions neither the pillars nor the Torah inscribed thereon. To the contrary, Joshua wrote his own words[59] in the document of the Torah of God (בְּסֵפֶר תּוֹרַת אֱלֹהִים) and he erected his own "great stone" (אֶבֶן גְּדוֹלָה) under the oak next to YHWH's sanctuary (מִקְדַּשׁ יהוה). The narrator offers no hint of recollection of the earlier event described in Josh 8:30–35.

The last two words of the second panel, בַּאֵר הֵיטֵב (v. 8), provide the best clue to the significance of the transcription of the Torah. Most translations and commentators read verse 8 as an appeal for meticulous copying of all the words of Torah on the erected stones.[60] By this interpretation this statement reinforces Moses' earlier warning against adding to or subtracting from the Torah (4:2). Establishing the meaning of the phrase is frustrated by the fact that it occurs only here, though we have encountered the first word in the concluding clause of the preamble to the book: (1:5).[61] Most translations render הוֹאִיל בֵּאֵר here as "he began to expound" (NIV) or "he undertook to expound" (NRSV, NJPSV) or "he undertook to explain" (ESV) the Torah, as if the phrase speaks of clarification and explanation.[62] Moses' addresses obviously expound on previous revelation, particularly the implications of the Israelite covenant for a people about to

---

58. Since books as we know them would not be invented until almost a millennium later, it is anachronistic and misleading to call this document "the Book of the Covenant."

59. Presumably the speech of 24:2–15, and perhaps the dialogue that transpired between him and the people in 24:16–24.

60. Cf. "very plainly" (ESV), or "very clearly" (NIV, NRSV), or "very distinctly" (NAS; cf. NJPSV).

61. The verb בֵּאֵר occurs outside Deuteronomy only in Hab 2:2, where it refers to engraving words on a writing surface.

62. In post-biblical Hebrew, the word means "to expound, provide exposition." See Jastrow, *Dictionary of the Targumim*, 135. Similarly, Palestinian Aramaic, "to explain, write." See Sokoloff, *A Dictionary of Jewish Palestinian Aramaic*, 83.

enter the land promised under the Abrahamic covenant (cf. Gen 15:7–21; 26:3; Exod 6:2–8). However, this understanding neither exhausts the meaning of הוֹאִיל בֵּאֵר, nor reflects its primary meaning. Recent scholarship suggests the expression speaks more to the *purpose* of Moses address in 1:5 and the *purpose* of the inscription in 27:8 than to their content or their nature.

The Hebrew form בֵּאֵר (D-stem) is related to Akkadian *burru*, "to confirm," that is "put a legal document in force."[63] From the perspective of speech-act theory, according to Deut 1:5 Moses' locutionary oral act of proclaiming the Torah, along with the covenant renewal rituals alluded to in the book (e.g., 26:16–19; 29:8–17[9–18]), were driven by the illocutionary goal of legally binding this generation of Israelites to the covenant to which their parents had signed on at Horeb, and to which Abraham had signed on by accepting circumcision as the mark of the covenant. Correspondingly, in 27:2–8 the goal of the transcriptional locutionary act was not merely to transform the Torah on pillars of stone of Moses into a monument.[64] Rather, the written verbal action served the illocutionary goal of binding the land to YHWH and his people, thereby completing the tripartite covenant relationship, a subject that I shall now consider in greater detail. Perhaps these illocutionary goals are also reflected in the form of the transcription. Coming rains would wash the words off the pillars and they would be absorbed by the soil, thereby binding the land itself to the covenant reflected in the Torah, as well as to the people and the God who whose relationship is expressed in the Torah.

The Theological and Literary Significance of Deuteronomy 27

Whereas the ritual in Exod 24:1–11 had sealed the covenantal bond between Israel and YHWH, that event had not fulfilled the divine agenda declared to Moses at the time of his call (Exod 3:8) and reiterated many times thereafter (e.g., Exod 6:2–8). Indeed, Moses has repeatedly declared in his addresses to the people on the Plains of Moab that YHWH's purpose in rescuing Israel from Egypt was that he might give his people the land he had sworn to the ancestors.[65] The Horeb event had sealed the covenant between two parties in what would ultimately be a tri-partite relationship. According to plan the third member (the land) should have been incorporated into the scheme within a matter of months if not weeks after leaving Horeb. However, because of the people's rebellion at Kadesh-barnea the plan to complete the triangle had been on hold for thirty-eight years. By linking this ritual with the ceremony at Horeb Moses anticipates the long awaited moment. The purpose of this ritual is to incorporate the land into this complex of covenantal relationships and to secure Israel's title to that which YHWH had promised long ago and was now delivering into their hands.[66] This ritual commemorates the basis of

---

63. Cf. *CAD* 2 (1965), 127. For fuller discussion, see Schaper, "The 'Publication' of Legal Texts in Ancient Judah," 230; Braulik and Lohfink, "Deuteronomium 1,5 באר את־התורה הזאת: 'er verlieh dieser Tora Rechstkraft,'" 49.

64. Thus Assmann, "Altorientalische Fluchinschriften und das Problem performativer Schriftlichkeit," 233–256.

65. Deut 1:8, 35; 6:10, 18, 23; 7:13; 8:1; 10:11; 11:9, 21; 19:8; 26:3, 15; 28:11; 30:20; 31:7, 20, 21, 23.

66. See further below.

Israel's claim to the land: it is YHWH's free gift to them as their grant (נַחֲלָה). Within this context the transcription of the Torah onto the pillars would be a performative act whereby the land is formally incorporated into the covenant triangle (see Fig. 8.4).

If this interpretation of Deut 27:1–8 is correct, how are we to understand the cultural, theological, and literary significance of the event prescribed here? Biblical scholars generally and evangelical scholars in particular are extremely grateful to Sandra Richter, who has clarified the significance of "the place for YHWH's name."[67] Against those who argue that Deuteronomy's "Name theology" represents a revolution in religious thinking, according to which YHWH is no longer perceived to be actually present in his temple, but is represented there in some hypostatic way by his Name, Richter argues convincingly that the phrases שַׁכֵּן שֵׁם and שִׂים שֵׁם, "to set the name," reflect a borrowed idiom represented in Akkadian as *šuma sakānu*, meaning "to inscribe/erect a monument bearing the name and proclaiming ownership and hegemony."[68]

Figure 8.4
The Completion of the Israelite Covenantal Triangle

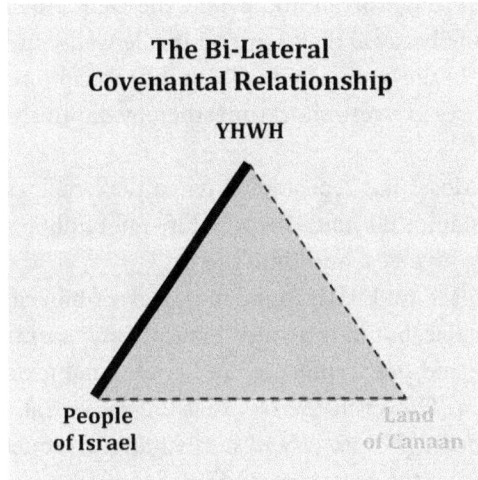
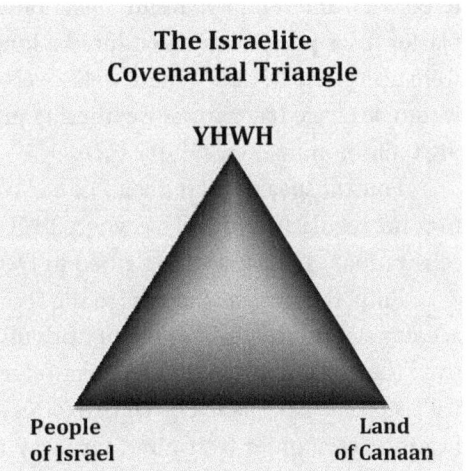

Accordingly, the place that he chooses to establish his name is ultimately viewed as stamped with his name; this is the place he claims for himself and at which he has chosen to reside.[69] So far Richter's work is very helpful. However, I am not so sure about her secondary proposal. It may be that for those responsible for compiling Deut 5–27, Mount Ebal was "the first locale where Yahweh had 'placed his name,'"[70] but her specific

---

67. Richter, *The Deuteronomistic History and the Name Theology*; Richter, "The Place of the Name in Deuteronomy," 342–66.

68. Accordingly, the first word in שַׁכֵּן שְׁמוֹ is not a factitive D verb form (from שָׁכַן, to dwell"), meaning, "to cause his name to dwell," as it is often understood.

69. See further, Block, "No Other Gods," 247–56.

70. Richter, *Deuteronomistic History and the Name Theology*, 366.

claim that the pillars in 27:4–5 function as triumphal monuments[71] inscribed with the words and "heroic acts of Yahweh"[72] is problematic on several grounds.[73]

First, although the present ritual is to be performed "before YHWH" (27:7), neither 11:29–32, which anticipates, nor chapter 27, which prescribes the Mount Ebal ritual, mentions YHWH's name (שֵׁם) or speaks of YHWH choosing (בָּחַר) this place as a permanent dwelling place.

Second, Richter's reading of the stelae of 27:4–5 as triumphal monuments inscribed with the words and "heroic acts of Yahweh" does not match the contours of the text. Deuteronomy 27 suggests this was to be one of the Israelites' first cultic observances after they crossed the Jordan, *preceding* the conquest of the land, rather than a commemoration of conquests already achieved. Furthermore, chapter 27 is devoid of any military features. Rather than reciting YHWH's heroic acts, this inscription involves "all the words of this Torah" (כָּל־דִּבְרֵי הַתּוֹרָה הַזֹּאת), that is, some version of Moses' exposition of covenant relationship as presented in chapters 5–26, if not including chapters 1–4.

Third, whereas victory monuments were typically made of stone with inscriptions chiseled into the rock so they would endure, these stelae consisted of natural stones plastered over, and then apparently inscribed with some sort of ink. Unlike the Deir ʿAllah plaster inscriptions, which endured a long time because they were on inside walls, and were ultimately buried,[74] these stelae were out in the open, which meant the inscriptions would be effaced by natural weathering processes in a very short time, thereby diminishing their monumental significance.

Fourth, speaking on behalf of YHWH, Moses has repeatedly invited the Israelites to come regularly to the place where YHWH stamps his name for worship—not military celebrations. The rituals prescribed in Deut 27 involve a one-time event.

Fifth, the closest analogue to the ritual on Mount Ebal is found, not in extra-biblical accounts of the erection of victory or votive stelae, but in the inner-biblical Sinai narrative. The association of whole burnt offerings and peace offerings and covenantal texts with stelae links this event with Exod 24:1–11. However, the fact that the earlier ratification ceremonies transpired far away from the promised land necessitated a sequel involving the land. By eating the covenant meal in the presence of YHWH *in the land he has given them* (27:7), the Israelites will celebrate the completion of the triangle.

As noted above, the function of this ritual is suggested by the expression, בַּאֵר הֵיטֵב. Moses does not require the Levites to read the Torah before the people in this ritual, as they would regularly at Sukkoth (Festival of Booths; 31:9–13), or even as he had done with the "Covenant Document" at Horeb (Exod 24:1–11). As a literary rather than oral speech act this event formalizes the covenant relationship binding YHWH, Israel, and the land. Whereas Moses' oral proclamation of the Torah (1:5) had bound this generation of Israelites to the covenant ratified at Horeb, apparently this part of the ritual

---

71. Ibid., 361.

72. Ibid., 347.

73. For a helpful critique of Richter, see Hundley, "To Be or Not to Be," 533–55.

74. On the Deir ʿAllah inscriptions, see Hoftijzer and van der Kooij, *Aramaic Texts from Deir ʿAllah*; Hoftijzer and van der Kooij, *The Balaam Text from Deir ʿAllah Re-evaluated*; Hackett, *The Balaam Text from Deir ʿAllah*.

would proceed silently. Plastering the rock and writing the text, rather than chiseling the inscription coheres with the erection of the altar of uncut stones, and with Moses' call for silence (הַסְכֵּת) in verse 9.

But why was it necessary to inscribe the Torah on the pillars, if the text was not to be read to the people? It is clear from 27:11–26 that the ritual at Ebal and Gerizim would include loud oral proclamation, but that proclamation would not include reading the Torah. For whose benefit then would these ritual actions be performed? To be sure, the people will have been moved when Joshua fulfilled these prescriptions in Josh 8, because this ceremony concretized their claim to the land on which the soles of their feet now stood (cf. 11:24–25; Josh 1:3; 14:9). However, this ceremony seems to have been also for the land's benefit. In Deuteronomy the land is often portrayed as animate, a vital and responsive partner in this covenant relationship.[75] Through the transcription of the Torah on the pillars the land is stamped not only with the name of YHWH, but also with his covenant. From now on the land will be held accountable for how it responds to its covenantal mandate and how it treats Israel. Furthermore, it now becomes a witness to the covenantal privileges and responsibilities to which YHWH and the Israelites have committed themselves.

This interpretation may explain the verbal acts that follow in the remainder of chapter 27. In verses 9–10 Moses reiterates his challenge to the people before him to demonstrate fidelity to YHWH by living according to the covenant stipulations, but with the imprecations of verses 11–26 he casts his gaze to the land beyond the Jordan and to Israel's future there. As noted above, the liturgy prescribed in verses 11–26 is entirely verbal and oral. The text divides stylistically and substantively into two parts. In verses 11–13 the Levites participate as a group alongside the rest of the tribes; in verses 14–26 they are at the center of the action pronouncing the curses. The first part anticipates the proclamation of blessings and curses, while the second reports only the latter. Apparently these two segments represent two phases of a complex ritual involving the recitation of both blessings and curses as part of a covenant renewal ceremony (some version of chapter 28?). Like the imprecations inscribed on Babylonian Entitlement *narûs*, the speech act involving the curses in verses 14–26 seems to have had an entirely different illocutionary goal. The movement from verses 12–13 to 14 suggests the ritual of verses 15–26 is intended as a response to the blessings and curses recited—presumably by leading Levites as liturgical leaders. The size of the assembly and the role of the mountains as witnesses require the Levites to declare the curses loudly.[76] Hearing the declarations reinforces the incorporation of the mountains (as metonymy for the

---

75. The land is often portrayed as personal. In Deuteronomy, the land yields (נָתַן) fruit (11:17), flows with milk and honey (6:3; 11:9; 26:9, 15), and is blessed (33:13). Indeed, Israel's allotted territory is a land for which YHWH cares (11:12; דָּרַשׁ, "to seek," is shorthand for "whose welfare [שָׁלוֹם] he seeks"). But this portrayal is common elsewhere: the land faints (Gen 47:13); disgorges its inhabitants (Lev 18:25, 28; 20:22); devours them (Lev 26:38; Num 13:32); mourns (Isa 33:9; Jer 12:4, 11; etc.); languishes (Isa 33:9); acts as a prostitute (Lev 19:29; Hos 1:2); sins (Ezek 14:13); feels shame (Jer 51:47); hears (Jer 22:29); enjoys its sabbaths (Lev 26:34, 43); opens its mouth (Gen 4:11; Num 16:30); swallows (Num 16:30); fears (Joel 2:21); is dismayed (Jer 14:4); and gives strength (Gen 4:12).

76. The expression קוֹל רָם, "high voice," occurs only here. Elsewhere קוֹל גָּדוֹל, "big voice," is preferred: Gen 39:14; Deut 5:22; 1 Sam 7:10; 28:12; etc.

land) in the deity-nation-land covenantal triangle, and their role as witnesses to the oath under which the Israelites place themselves. In so doing they recognize that should the people prove unfaithful, Moses is not the one who curses them; they have invoked the curse on themselves.

Conclusion

I return to the question I raised at the beginning: why did the narrator break up Moses' second address and insert chapter 27 here? Since the narrator provides no rationale for what he has done, we are free to speculate. Here are a few preliminary thoughts.

First, given the special interest of 26:16–19 and 28:1–14 in Israel's place in the world, the narrator may have been concerned to bring the image of Israel back to earth. YHWH did not only set Israel high above the nations (26:16; 28:1) and stamp this people with his name (28:1, 9–10), but he also stamped the land with his name.[77] YHWH's claim to ownership of the land antedates the Israelites' arrival (Lev 25:23), but this ritual sends a signal that that claim will now take effect, inasmuch as the people bearing his name have arrived, and the land itself has received the imprint of the covenant.

Second, psychologically, analogous to the intermission in a dramatic performance, this chapter offers readers and hearers a chance to pause and catch their breath, before they encounter head-on the blessings and curses that end the second address, and the horrors of their fulfillment at the beginning of the third address. For twenty-two chapters (two hours if read orally with expository emphasis),[78] we have been listening to Israel's first pastor celebrate the grace of God in salvation, covenant, revelation, and the gift of land. In chapter 28, after verse 14 his tone will change drastically. Not only does chapter 27 give hearers an opportunity to catch their breath; the imprecations at the end set the stage for what is to come. Ultimately, if Israel experiences the curse, they have knowingly brought it on themselves.

Finally, it is interesting to note not only where but also when the rituals prescribed here were to be performed. Repeatedly Moses has placed this ceremony at the top of the agenda after the Israelites cross the Jordan (vv. 2–4, 12), creating the impression that as soon as Joshua has led them across the river, they are to head for Ebal. YHWH hints at the threat Jericho poses to Israel's possession of the land in 32:49, but Moses seems oblivious to the fact that this city represents a significant obstacle to the journey toward Ebal. Nor does he seem aware of the need for certain other ritual performances that Joshua will supervise at Gilgal as soon as the Israelites have crossed the river: erecting memorials to commemorate the crossing (Josh 4:1–24), circumcising all males (5:1–9), and celebrating the Passover (5:10–12). In this chapter his mind is focused on Ebal.

But why can Ebal not wait until after the conquest of the land? Would it not have made more sense to defeat the Canaanites and occupy the land before it was integrated into the covenant? Apparently not. Apparently before Israel commenced the official campaign of conquest, their claim to the land had to be formally legitimized and the

---

77. See further, Block, "No Other Gods," 247–62.
78. On expository reading of Scripture, see chapter 2, "'That They May Hear,'" above, pp. 19–34.

land itself brought into the equation. This was the function of the rituals prescribed in Deut 27.

Addendum: A Note on the Sequence of Events in Joshua

The destruction of Jericho would result in Joshua's fame spreading throughout the land (Josh 6:27). However, the Canaanite kings would not take the Israelite presence seriously until they had completed the rituals prescribed in Deut 27 (Josh 8:30–35). Although most translations fill in the lacuna after the verbal opening of Josh 9:1, וַיְהִי כִשְׁמֹעַ, "When all the kings across the Jordan heard," with something like "of this" (NRSV, NJPSV, ESV) or "of these things" (NIV), the verb actually lacks an object. Some suggest that reports of Israel's defeat at Ai had emboldened the kings to marshal their forces against them (cf. 7:9).[79] However, this interpretation overlooks the fact that the forces of Ai had actually been annihilated and the town had been torched. In fact, the smoke rising to the sky would have been seen for miles around, and the body of the king will have been hanged on a tree for the world to see (8:1–29). The response of the Gibeonites to Ai's demise seems most natural (9:3–21).

Furthermore, the narrator has explicitly separated the defeat of Ai (8:1–29) from the Canaanite kings' reaction in 9:1–2 by locating the account of Israel's convocation at Ebal and Gerizim between these events. Although the first part of the ritual could have proceeded quietly (8:30–32), the second part is entirely aural (vv. 33–35): the tribes stood on Mounts Gerizim and Ebal and heard the blessings and the curses precisely as Moses had prescribed (8:33). Thereafter, apparently introducing a new element, but as prescribed in the Torah itself, Joshua read all the words of the Torah, including the blessings and the curses, presumably from the Torah scrolls themselves, rather than from the inscribed pillars. The narrator fails to report explicitly the imprecations listed in Deut 27:14–26. However, since he emphasizes that the aural part of the ritual was carried out exactly as Moses had prescribed (Josh 8:33, 35), the Levites must have recited the imprecations "with a loud voice" (קֹל רָם, Deut 27:14). After each curse the tribes apparently responded in unison with "Amen!" (vv. 15–26), the sound of which will have reverberated throughout the valley between Ebal and Gerizim and beyond.

Through these rituals the newcomers shamelessly declared their claim to the land and cast themselves on YHWH to deliver it into their hands. This is what seems to have galvanized the Canaanites (9:1–2). But their decision may also have been influenced by what observers would have seen: this was not an assembly of warriors, but a gathering of worshipers, including women, children, and the non-Israelites among them—they should have been an easy target.

The narrator of Joshua notes expressly that Adoni-zedek's appeal to other southern kings was grounded in his intense fear because Gibeon, which was greater than Ai, had joined the enemy (10:1–5). In response to the attack of this alliance on Gibeon and with the blessing of YHWH, Joshua took the initiative and launched the southern campaign of conquest (10:6–43).

---

79. Thus Hess, *Joshua*, 175–76.

THE TRIUMPH OF GRACE

If this campaign was timed to follow the covenantal rituals at Ebal and Gerizim, how do the defeats of Jericho and Ai fit into the picture? The first is easier to answer than the second. Having crossed the Jordan, Jericho represented the gateway to the land. Not only was this one of the strongest cities in Canaan, but it controlled the traffic lanes up and down the Jordan and into the interior of the land. Perhaps this was why the divine strategy for conquering this city differed from the rest. Compared to the other battles, as in the defeat of the Egyptians at the Red Sea, in this event the Israelites were relatively passive. By a supernatural and divine act, after they had obeyed YHWH's ridiculous orders to march around the city in religious (rather than military) procession the walls had come crashing down, after which the Israelites carried out their mopping up operations. The battles of conquest that followed were much more synergistic in nature. To be sure, the Israelites marched out in response to divine orders, but they marched out, and attacked, and YHWH gave them the victory.

But how did Ai fit the strategy of conquest? Ai was not a suburb of Jericho, so this was not an automatic or even natural second step in the conquest of the land. Joshua 7:1 explicitly links the Israelite fiasco at Ai with Achan's violation of the law of *ḥerem*. Although YHWH also emphasized Achan's sin as the cause of the defeat (7:11b–13), remarkably he began his response to Joshua's prayer of confession with a general statement: "Israel has sinned; they have transgressed my covenant, which I commanded them [to keep]" (7:11a). But should this charge be restricted to Achan's offence?

Many have noted Joshua's failure to consult with YHWH the Commander-in-Chief before sending his scouts out to Ai (7:2–3), but no one to my knowledge has noticed the contradiction between Joshua's orders and Moses' instructions in Deut 27. Three times Moses had declared that as soon as the Israelites crossed (עָבַר) the Jordan they were to head for Mount Ebal (27:2, 4, 12). One could get to Ebal via Ai, but Ai is not on the most direct route, and in Josh 7 Ebal does not seem to be on Joshua's mind. More seriously, choosing to go via Ai contradicts Moses' specific instructions in Deut 11:29–32 both chronologically and geographically. Regarding the former Joshua did not head for Ai immediately after crossing the Jordan and opening the gates to the promised land by conquering Jericho. Regarding the latter, Moses gave rather specific directions in 11:30, though on first sight they actually seem quite ambiguous:

הֲלֹא־הֵמָּה בְּעֵבֶר הַיַּרְדֵּן	Are they [Mounts Gerizim and Ebal] not beyond the Jordan,
אַחֲרֵי דֶּרֶךְ מְבוֹא הַשֶּׁמֶשׁ	westward toward the setting sun,
בְּאֶרֶץ הַכְּנַעֲנִי הַיֹּשֵׁב בָּעֲרָבָה	in the territory of the Canaanites who live in the Arabah,
מוּל הַגִּלְגָּל	near Gilgal,
אֵצֶל אֵלוֹנֵי מֹרֶה׃	beside the oak of Moreh?

Moses' rhetorical question[80] offers three significant details about the location of the mountains where the ceremonies were to take place. First, and most obviously it was across the Jordan.[81] Second, it was off to the west. The phrase אַחֲרֵי דֶּרֶךְ מְבוֹא הַשֶּׁמֶשׁ

---

80. The present comment is cast in the same form as the earlier reference to Og's bed in Rabbah (3:11). On "Are they not . . . ?" as idiomatic for "Surely they are . . . ," see Brown, "'Is It Not?' or 'Indeed!'" 201–19.

81. As in 3:20, 25, Moses' perspective in 11:30–31 differs from that of the narrator, for whom

translates literally "beyond the way of the setting of the sun."[82] Since roads are typically named according to the destination to which they lead, this apparently refers to a road that leads west from the Jordan River to Shechem, which lay between Gerizim and Ebal,[83] due north of Ai and north north west of Jericho. Third, it is in the land of the Canaanites, who live in the Arabah in the vicinity of Gilgal, north of Jericho, next to the oaks of Moreh. The Arabah refers to the Jordan Valley gorge that runs from the Sea of Galilee in the north to the Red Sea in the south.

The meaning of the rest of the verse is uncertain. We may assume that Gilgal is the well-known site north of Jericho (cf. Josh 4:19—5:12), and the "oaks/terebinths of Moreh" a prominent grove in the vicinity of Shechem, where YHWH had met with Abraham and Jacob (cf. Gen 12:6). The expression, אַחֲרֵי דֶּרֶךְ מְבוֹא הַשֶּׁמֶשׁ, "behind the way of the coming of the sun," especially distinguishes this route from "the way of the desert" (דֶּרֶךְ הַמִּדְבָּר; Josh 8:15), which Joshua's forces seem to have taken. Moses seems to have in mind a route running north parallel to the Jordan, until it meets up with "Sunset Boulevard"[84] (perhaps up Wadi Farah), which heads west to Gerizim and Ebal. This route would be especially advantageous because there were no major settlements that might interfere with the Israelites' travel. The incongruity between Moses' instructions and Joshua's actions suggest that the conquest of Ai was not on YHWH's agenda for Joshua until after the Ebal ritual had been performed (Fig. 8.5).[85]

It is striking that in the narrative scheme of the book of Joshua, as soon as the Israelites had completed the ceremonies, the Canaanites rose to defend their land. Why did this not happen after the destruction of Jericho? It is possible to interpret this as the work of God, signaling the time to launch the attacks (cf. Josh 10:8), and leading ultimately to the defeat of all the Canaanite kings south of the territory assigned to Benjamin (10:1–43). In 10:42 the narrator summarizes the results: "Joshua captured all these kings and their land at one time, because YHWH, the God of Israel, fought for Israel." This southern campaign was followed by a series of battles against an alliance of northern kings, headed by King Jabin of Hazor (11:1–15). In 11:20 the narrator offers his theological explanation for Israel's successes:

> For YHWH was behind these events, hardening their [the Canaanites'] hearts so they would attack Israel in battle, so that they might be utterly and mercilessly destroyed (הַחֲרִים) and exterminated (הַשְׁמִיד), just as YHWH had commanded Moses.

"beyond the Jordan" is east of the river: 1:1, 5; 4:41, 46–47.

82. On אַחֲרֵי דֶּרֶךְ meaning "beyond," see *DCH* 1.199.

83. Possible routes are suggested by Map 12, in Dorsey, *The Roads and Highways of Ancient Israel*, 172.

84. Thus Tigay, *Deuteronomy*, 116.

85. Since the Gibeonite ruse was a direct response to the defeat of Ai, had Joshua taken the Israelites directly to Ebal this embarrassing episode would also have been avoided.

Figure 8.5
The Right (—) and Wrong (- -) Roads to Ebal[86]

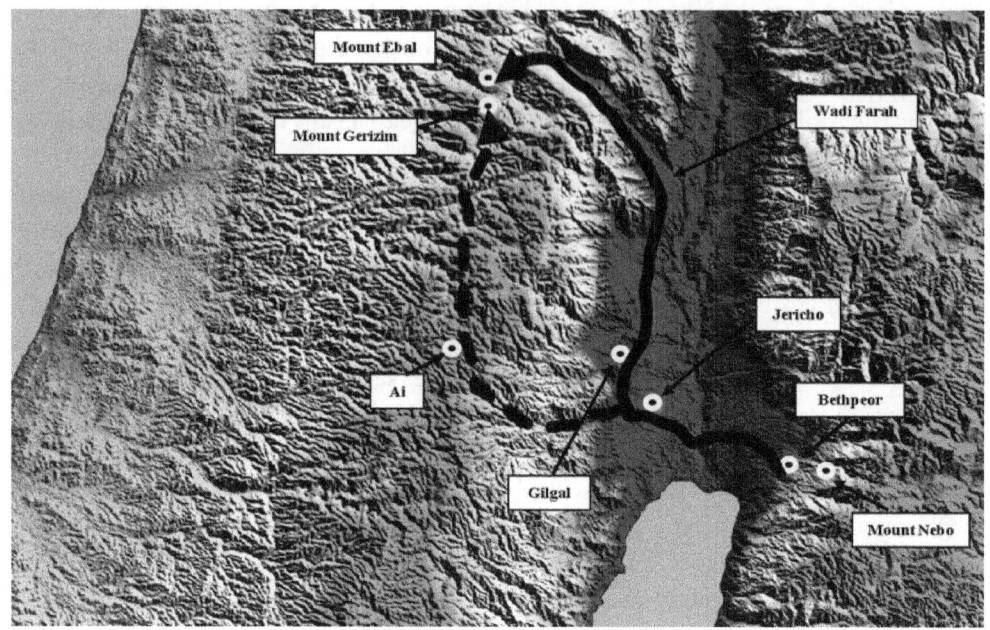

86. Base map adapted with permission from BibleWorks Maps.

9

"The Meeting Places of God in the Land"

Another Look at the Towns of the Levites[1]

Introduction

THE SEARCH FOR THE location, history, and function of the towns of the Levites is a complicated and complex venture.[2] First, while allusions to the status of Levites and their dwelling places occur elsewhere,[3] Levitical towns are the primary subjects of only four texts: Lev 25:32–34; Num 35:1–8; Josh 21:1–42; and 1 Chr 6:39–66[54–81]. Second, the lists of Levitical towns in Josh 21 and 1 Chr 6 contain variant information. Most agree that the Chronicler depended on Joshua, rather than vice versa,[4] though some argue that both are based on a shorter *Urtext*, perhaps similar to the LXX text of Josh 21.[5] Third, the investigation of Levitical towns touches on the status of the Levites and their

---

1. This is a stylistically modified version of an essay that was previously published in *Current Issues in Priestly and Related Literature: The Legacy of Jacob Milgrom and Beyond*, ed. Roy Gane and Ada Taggar-Cohen; Resources for Biblical Study 82 (Atlanta: Society of Biblical Literature, 2015), 93–121. I am grateful to the editors of the volume for their kind permission to republish it here. The title derives from Ps 74:8, כָּל־מוֹעֲדֵי־אֵל בָּאָרֶץ, which the Authorized Version renders "all the synagogues of God in the land." It is an inestimable honor to present this essay in memory and in honor of Jacob Milgrom, a scholarly giant among Lilliputians. I am grateful to Carmen Imes for her careful reading of this essay and for her suggestions for its improvement.

2. We are all indebted to Professor Jacob Milgrom for his contributions to this subject, found particularly in his magnificent commentaries on Leviticus (*Leviticus 23–27*, 2201–4) and Numbers (*Numbers*, 288–90, 502–4), and in a short essay, "The Levitical Town: An Exercise in Realistic Planning," 185–88.

3. Lev 25:32–34; Deut 18:1–8; 1 Chr 9:2; 13:1–3; 26:29–32; 2 Chr 11:13–17; 17:7–9; 19:4–11; 31:17–20; Ezek 45:1–5; 48:8–22.

4. On the text-critical issues involved and the relationship between the lists, see Knoppers, *I Chronicles 1–9*, 430–42; and more briefly, Japhet, *I & II Chronicles*, 145, 159–65. For a dissenting view, see Auld, "The 'Levitical Cities': Texts and History," 194–206.

5. Thus Knoppers, "Projected Age Comparisons of the Levitical Townlists," 21–63. For a helpful survey of discussions of the Levitical town lists, see Hutton, "The Levitical Diaspora (II)," 45–81. Earlier Hutton proposed that the Levites' role in Israel compares with Ahansal tribe in the Atlas Mountains of Morocco. See "The Levitical Diaspora (I)," 223–234.

relationship to Aaronids and Zadokites. Following Wellhausen,[6] many view the lists as late literary creations, reflecting a period when Levites were distinguished from these priestly groups.[7] However, others argue that distinctions between the central sanctuary priesthood and other priests are early and that the tribal expression, "Levites," was often used generally for those responsible for Israel's spiritual welfare.[8] Whatever the historical realities, the narrative world of biblical texts often uses the term "Levites" as a general designation for priestly functionaries.

The purpose of this paper is not to repeat previous attempts to establish the historical contexts in which texts dealing with Levitical towns might have been written, but to explore their socio-religious functions and the implications of our findings for understanding the role of Levitical priests within ancient Israelite society. However, before I discuss scholarly proposals regarding their function it may be helpful to set the geographic context for the discussion.

The three major texts involving the Levitical towns agree that the Israelite tribes were to donate forty-eight towns to the Levites (Num 35:1–5; Josh 21:1–45; 1 Chr 6:39–66[54–81]; Fig. 9.1, next page). Since there were twelve tribes, most tribes contributed four towns. However, Judah allotted nine, though the narrators note that these include Simeon's grants (Josh 21:9; 1 Chr 6:50[65]). The total of forty-eight is achieved by having Naphtali grant the Levites only three towns. These towns were allocated principally to the three main Levitical branches, with the Qohathites, the branch that included Aaron, receiving twenty-three [almost half] the towns, while Gershonites received thirteen, and the Merarite branch received twelve.

Although the locations of some of the towns are uncertain,[9] several features of the lists are noteworthy. First, with several exceptions in each case, most of the Qohathite towns were located in the south, in Judahite and Danite territory, most Gershonite towns were in the north around the Sea of Galilee, and most Merarite towns were east of the Jordan. Second, the Levitical towns included the six asylum towns, three on the west side of the Jordan (Hebron, Shechem, Qadesh) and three in the Transjordan (Bezer, Ramoth, Golan).

---

6. Wellhausen, *Prolegomena to the History of Ancient Israel*, 121–51.

7. See Nelson, *Joshua*, 241. For detailed analyses of the history of the priesthood, see Cody, *A History of the Old Testament Priesthood*; Gunneweg, *Leviten und Priester*; Schaper, *Priester und Leviten im achämenidischen Juda*), esp. chapter 3. Spencer argues that "Aaronites," "Levites," and "Zadokites" are designations for competing factions that vied for control of the Israelite priesthood. In the end, the "P" writer made Levi and his followers secondary priests, ignored the discredited Zadok, and portrayed Aaron as the true priest. See his "Priestly Families (or Factions) in Samuel and Kings," 387–400. Elsewhere ("Levitical Cities," 4.311) Spencer suggests the lists "are creations of the post-exilic period which sought to explain how the Levites fit into the early political, social, and theological structure of ancient Israel." For his full analysis, see *The Levitical Cities: A Study of the Role and Function of the Levites in the History of Israel*.

8. For critiques of the common scholarly reconstructions, see Duke, "Punishment or Restoration," 61–81; McConville, "Priests and Levites," 124–53; Milgrom in conversation with Block, *Ezekiel's Hope*, 141–48.

9. In an exhaustive study forty-five years ago, John L. Peterson devoted almost 700 pages to the archaeological evidence for the Levitical towns (*A Topographical Surface Survey of the Levitical 'Cities' of Joshua 21 and 1 Chronicles 6: Studies on the Levites in Israelite Life and Religion*)

"THE MEETING PLACES OF GOD IN THE LAND"

Figure 9.1
The Locations of the Levitical Towns[10]

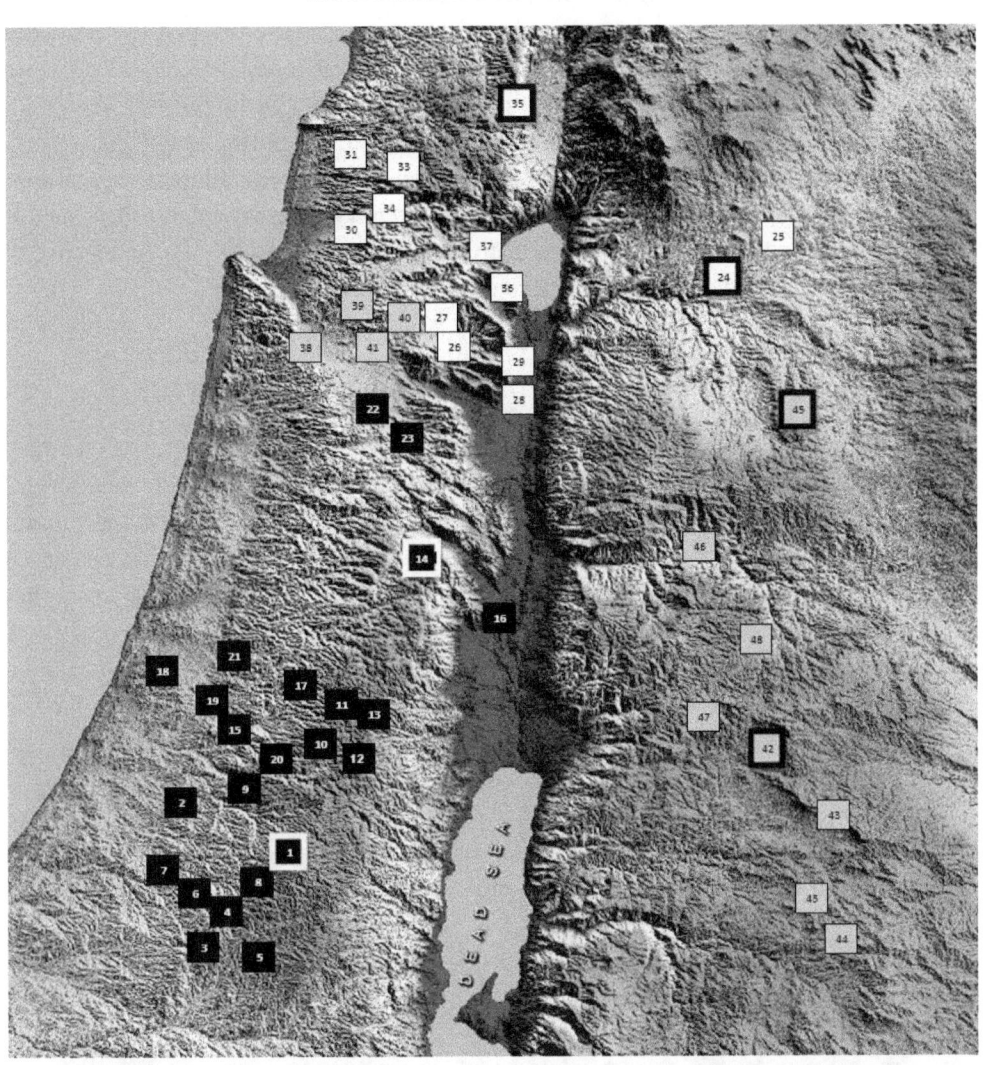

Key	20	Qohathite Levitical Towns	30		Gershonite Levitical Towns
	40	Merarite Levitical Towns	1	35	42	Asylum Towns (underlined below)

1 Hebron	13 Almon	25 Ashtaroth	37 Jokmeam
2 Libnah	14 Shechem	26 Qishion	38 Qartah/Tabor
3 Jattir	15 Gezer	27 Daberath	39 Dimnah
4 Eshtemoa	16 Qibzaim	28 Jarmuth	40 Nahalal
5 Holon	17 Beth-Horon	29 En-gannim	41 Bezer
6 Debir	18 Eltekeh	30 Mishal	42 Jahzah
7 Ain/Ashan	19 Gibbethon	31 Abdon	43 Qedemoth
8 Yuttah	20 Aijalon	32 Helkath	44 Maphaath
9 Beth-shemesh	21 Gath-rimmon	33 Rehob	45 Ramoth
10 Gibeon	22 Taanach	34 Qadesh	46 Mahanaim
11 Geba	23 Ibleam	35 Hammoth-dor	47 Heshbon
12 Anathoth	24 Golan	36 Qiriathaim	48 Jazer

10. Background image copyright © BibleWorks, LLC. Used by permission.

Third, the lists include two prominent sites in the patriarchal traditions, Hebron and Shechem, with awareness that the former had been allotted earlier to Caleb (Josh 21:12). The absence of Jerusalem, Bethel, and Dan suggests the original list antedates the monarchy.[11] Fourth, the list includes several theophoric toponyms involving names of pagan deities: Beth Shemesh (בית שמש, Josh 21:16); Anathoth (ענתות, Josh 21:18), Beth-Horon (בית חורן, Josh 21:22); Be-Eshterah (בעשתרה, a contraction of בית עשתרה, "House of Ashtarah [Astarte?]," Josh 21:27).[12] That Levites were allotted such a high proportion of places with names associated with foreign gods may suggest they were to take the lead in expunging their names from the land (Deut 12:3).[13] The persistence of these names attests to their failure to carry out the mandate.

Levitical Towns as an Economic Base for Levitical Prosperity

The Jubilee ordinance assumes the allocation of towns for the Levites (Lev 25:32–34). However, according to the Pentateuchal narrative, the divine command to do so occurred almost four decades later, when the Israelites were poised to cross the Jordan. Numbers 35:1–8 is sandwiched between prescriptions for allocating tribal territorial grants (33:50—34:29) and the six asylum towns (35:9–34).[14] Verses 6–8 anticipate that these asylum towns would also function as Levitical towns.

These instructions are striking on several counts. First, they appealed to public generosity; the people were to give (נתן) the towns to the Levites, a detail reinforced in Josh 21, which lists the forty-eight Levitical towns they donated. Apportionment of the towns within tribal lands reminded the Israelites that their respective territories were not their own; YHWH was the divine Landlord (cf. Lev 25:23). Since the preceding instructions for partitioning the land of Canaan among the tribes omit the tribe of Levi, one could view these Levitical towns as compensation for tribal territory denied them, in addition to the tithes and firstfruits of Israelite worshipers (Num 18:21–32; Deut 14:27–29; 18:1–8; 26:12–13), though YHWH also offered himself as their allotment (חלק) and special grant (נחלה).[15]

---

11. Whereas Benjamin Mazar, G. Ernest Wright, and William F. Albright had dated the Levitical towns to the eleventh and tenth centuries BCE, Peterson dated the towns he identified as Levitical to the ninth and eighth centuries, based on the archaeological evidence (*Topographical Surface Survey*, 698–705). Even if his conclusions are correct—as seems likely—his evidence has no bearing on the date of the biblical lists. First, none of his evidence distinguished these sites as Levitical, as opposed to hundreds of others he could have surveyed. Second, even if they were Levitical, this would only prove when they functioned that way, rather than when the notion originated. Hezekiah's reforms (2 Chr 29–31) could have represented the first serious attempt at implementing policies that had been in place for centuries. In any case, we must beware of the fallacy of negative proof: absence of evidence is not evidence of absence. For discussion of the fallacy, see Fisher, *Historians' Fallacies*, 47–49.

12. Perhaps also Kibzaim (קבצים, Josh 21:22; ים being the name of the god of the sea, hence "Yamm has gathered"); and Jokneam (יקנעם, Josh 21:34; a corruption of יקמעם, "May 'Am raise up/establish"?; cf. 1 Chr 6:53[68]).

13. Cf. Block, *The Gospel according to Moses*, 268–69.

14. On the asylum towns, see Stackert, "The Urbanization of Asylum," 31–112.

15. Num 18:20 (חלק); Deut 18:1–2; Josh 13:33; Ezek 44:28 (all נחלה).

The towns of the Levites were to serve as dormitory towns in which members of a tribe scattered throughout the country might live (לשבת, Num 32:2, 3). Although the Levites were denied land for producing crops, YHWH provided pastureland around the towns to shepherd their flocks.[16] Jacob Milgrom has plausibly suggested that the allotment, traditionally understood as belts of land around Levitical towns,[17] involved four rectangles extending 1000 cubits from the edge of the town in each direction, allowing the מגרש to grow as the town expanded (Fig. 9.2).[18] While the Levites would be dependent on members of other tribes for grains, vegetables, and fruit, apparently they could raise their own livestock for wool, leather, meat and milk to supplement the donations they received as tithes and offerings.

Figure 9.2
The Expanding Pastureland (מגרש)

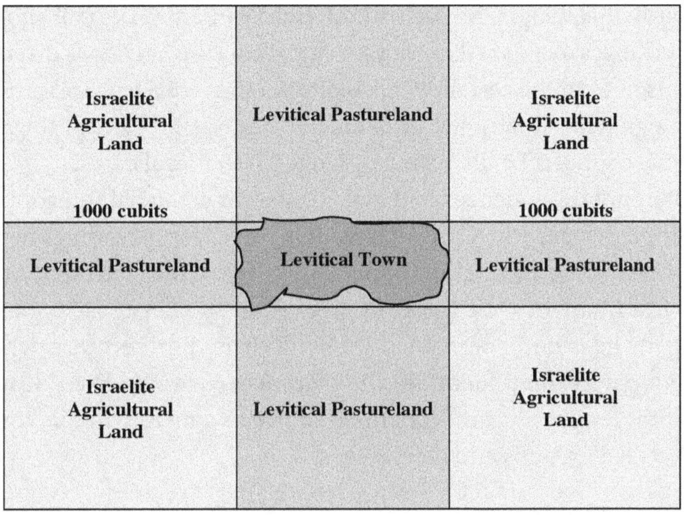

Israelite Agricultural Land	Levitical Pastureland	Israelite Agricultural Land
1000 cubits		1000 cubits
Levitical Pastureland	Levitical Town	Levitical Pastureland
Israelite Agricultural Land	Levitical Pastureland	Israelite Agricultural Land

Although the tribes were to give the Levites these towns, it is doubtful they had exclusive rights to live there. Joshua 21:11 acknowledges that Hebron, which had been granted to Caleb, was also an asylum town. Apparently non-Levites lived in all Levitical towns. However, YHWH's instructions required them to give up tracts within the city's environs to accommodate them. Leviticus 25:32–34 suggests their homes were equivalent to fields of non-Levites; they were subject to laws of jubilee and under normal circumstances would be passed on from generation to generation.[19] This provision

---

16. Hebrew מגרש apparently derives from גרש, "to drive, drive out." Although not attested with animals as the object, in everyday speech the verb may have been used of driving herds of sheep or cattle. It is used of driving the Amorites out of their land (Exod 34:11), and in the Mesha Inscription of Chemosh driving the king of Israel away from Mesha ("The Inscription of King Mesha," translated by Smelik [COS 2.23: 138]). Milgrom (*Leviticus 23–27*, 2204) rightly suggests that מגרש refers to "a place into which animals are driven [i.e., pens]."

17. Cf. *HALOT*, 546.

18. Milgrom, "The Levitical Town," 185–88; idem, *Numbers*, 502–4.

19. For fuller discussion of this text, see Milgrom, *Leviticus 23–27*, 2201–4.

prevented non-Levites from claiming their homes, thereby impoverishing them and preventing them from performing their religious duties in the community (see below). This policy did not apply to the pastureland around the towns, which was not to be parceled into private holdings nor sold. As property of all the Levites, it served as a community pasture for their flocks. Ezekiel's vision reinforces the notion of the inviolability of Levitical property (Ezek 48:14). In short, the institution of Levitical towns was an economic arrangement intended in part to secure the well-being of Levites.

Levitical Towns as Judicial Centers

It is commonly assumed that the Levites functioned as judges who adjudicated legal cases in the courts,[20] which would suggest that Levitical towns functioned as bases for the national judicial system.[21] Samuel, a Qohathite (1 Chr 6:18[33]), had a regular circuit, judging at Bethel, Gilgal, Mizpah, and Ramah (1 Sam 7:15-17), and he appointed his own sons as judges over Israel (1 Sam 8:1-5). While the narrator's disposition toward the last action is unclear, he certainly discredits his sons (cf. Deut 16:19; 24:17). For our purposes it is significant that none of Samuel's sites was a Levitical town, and that no biblical narrative depicts a Levite sitting as judge to hear legal cases.

The Deuteronomic evidence cited by Leuchter for a judicial role for priests is dubious.[22] First, although Deut 16:18 and 17:8 envision judicial proceedings being conducted in the gates of towns, no judicial function is implied by the statement in 18:6 that the Levite comes from "any of your gates" (שעריך). That the Levite is "sojourning" (גר) in the town suggests he is not a permanent resident there. Furthermore, while in Deuteronomy "in your gates" often identifies the place where people live,[23] it never refers to the location of the "court." "Gates" functions simply as a metonym for "towns," that is, a settlement protected by walls and gateways.

---

20. See especially Leuchter, "'The Levite in Your Gates,'" 417-36.

21. If this assumption is granted it is a small step to proposing that under the Josianic reforms the Levites' role shifted "from a cultic position to one that is strictly juridical and administrative" (ibid., 425) and that their agenda became political, viz., to administer the centralizing reforms of Josiah. Some go so far as to suggest that the institution of the tithe, particularly the acceptance of silver instead of produce (Deut 14:22-29), ultimately functioned as a tax to support Josiah's centralized political and military administration (see, e.g., Schaper, *Priester und Leviten*, 95-112). Benjamin Mazar suggested that Solomon built Levitical towns at strategic locations in newly occupied territories and installed Levites as civil servants, who supervised royal estates and collected taxes ("The Cities of the Priests and Levites," 193-205). Milgrom (*Numbers*, 507) notes that "the clearly archival note of 1 Chronicles 26:29-32 . . . pointedly demonstrates that the Levites were assigned administrative functions in Transjordan at the end of David's reign." For full discussion of this text, see Japhet, *I & II Chronicles*, 453-55, 463-66.

22. Leuchter, "'The Levite in Your Gates,'" 421-25.

23. The Levite alone (14:27; 18:6); with children, servants, and livestock (5:14 [cf. Exod 20:10]; 12:12; 12:18; 16:11, 14); with the fatherless and widows (14:29; 16:11, 14; 26:11-13); with fellow Israelites (24:14; 31:12). Significantly all of these cases that involve Levites identify the person only with respect to tribe, "the Levite" (הלוי), and without reference to priestly role (cf. הכהנים הלוים, "the Levitical priests").

Second, in Deuteronomy Levitical priests never actually function as judges who hear cases and weigh evidence to render judicial decisions. As custodians of Torah they were to supervise the king as he wrote a copy of the Torah for himself (17:18), presumably to ensure that he neither added to it nor subtracted from it (cf. 4:2; 13:1[12:32]), and they were to read it at the central sanctuary before the assembled worshipers every seven years on Sukkoth (31:9–13). Deuteronomy 18:1–8 envisions Levitical priests sharing in the offerings Israelites present to YHWH and traveling to the central sanctuary to serve YHWH there. In Deut 20:1–4 the priest functions as chaplain, preparing troops for battle by encouraging them not to be afraid because YHWH their God goes before them to secure victory. In the ritual involving the red heifer in 21:1–9 the priest does not adjudicate the case of an unsolved murder[24] but supervises a ritual designed to absolve Israel of bloodguilt. Deuteronomy 24:8 casts Levitical priests as teachers of the people and guardians of the people's purity, overseeing the treatment of defiling skin diseases. Deuteronomy 27:9–26 involves Levitical priests in the anticipated covenant-renewal ritual at Mounts Ebal and Gerizim immediately after the Israelites enter the land. None of these texts has the priest functioning as a judge administering justice in a court of law.[25]

Deuteronomy 17:8–13 may be the exception that proves the rule. The people are to bring insoluble cases involving homicide or assault to the central sanctuary for resolution. Although Levitical priests and a judge have the final word (v. 9), the primary addressees are ordinary citizens. Like 16:18–20 and 17:2–7 these instructions involve the people in maintaining righteousness in judicial matters. Deuteronomy 17:8–13 presents the actions of the priests/judge in one short statement (vv. 9c), while focusing on the people's responsibilities: to present the case to the priest/judge (vv. 8b–9) and to execute the decision (vv. 10–12b). Rather than offering the accused another chance to have the case reviewed, the process provides a resource for local adjudicators,[26] identified as "the Levitical priests and the judge" (v. 9)[27] Most scholars view "the judge who is in office

---

24. ועל פיהם יהיה כל ריב וכל־נגע translates literally, "and every dispute and every assault shall be according to their declaration." English translations generally interpret this as settling disputes and violent cases. However, this passage portrays the priest ministering (שרת) to YHWH and blessing (ברך, piel; object: the people) in his name, and specifies the goal of the ritual as securing atonement for YHWH's people (לעמך כפר), to atone for bloodguilt (ונכפר להם הדם), and to purge the guilt of innocent blood from their midst (תבער הדם הנקי מקרבך; 21:8–9). Therefore, the clause in v. 5 should be translated, "and their declaration in every dispute and every assault shall stand." Presumably the ritual would end with the priest's announcement on YHWH's behalf that the bloodguilt had been lifted and the curse replaced with the blessing. Cf. Block, *Deuteronomy*, 491–92.

25. Contra van der Toorn, who comments, "In the perspective of Deuteronomy, the Levitical priests have the monopoly on Torah and legal expertise; the focus on instruction and jurisdiction throws other sacerdotal prerogatives into the shadows." (*Scribal Culture and the Making of the Hebrew Bible*, 168). They do indeed have the monopoly on the Torah, but the remainder of this statement is incorrect.

26. So also Nelson, *Deuteronomy*, 221.

27. The expression הכהנים הלוים, "Levitical priests" appears in Deuteronomy for the first time in 17:9 (cf. v. 18; 18:1; 24:8; 27:9). Elsewhere this group is identified simply as הכהנים, "the priests" (19:17; 20:2 [sing.]), or הַכֹּהֲנִים בְּנֵי לֵוִי, "the priests, the descendants of Levi" (21:5; 31:9), or לוי[ה] שבט, "the tribe of Levi" (10:8; 18:1) On their duties, see 10:8; 18:1, 3; 26:4; 27:9–10; 31:9–11, 24–26). See further McConville, "Priests and Levites," 124–53; Rehm, "Levites and Priests," 4:303–5. The priestly writings never explicitly ascribe a judicial role to priests. Although Num 5:11–31 involves a legal/moral case,

at that time" as a layperson who joins a group of priests (note the plural) to hear the case (cf. 19:15–21).²⁸ However, the references to the sanctuary (vv. 8, 10) and the location of the procedure "before YHWH" (19:17)²⁹ suggest that in 17:9 "the judge" (השפט) functions appositionally to "the Levitical priests," specifying an individual selected from among them to preside over and to announce the decision.³⁰

In Deut 17:9 the LXX and the Samaritan Pentateuch read MT's ודרשת as a plural ודרשו, "and they shall inquire," suggesting the tribunal would repeat the lower court's investigation (cf. 13:15[14]; 17:4).³¹ However, here דרש means "to make inquiry," rather than "to investigate," and the verb refers to seeking oracular guidance from YHWH.³² The use of משפט in the last clause of verse 9 reinforces this interpretation.³³ As priestly "judge," the designated official is heir, not to the "judges" of Exod 18:22 and 25 (or Deut 1:13–16c), but to Moses, to whom the people came to "inquire" (דרש) of God (Exod 18:15, 19; Deut 1:17d).³⁴ However, unlike Moses, the priestly "judge" at the central sanctuary could use the Urim and Thummim to determine the mind of God.³⁵

The charge to execute the divine judgment represents the center of gravity in this panel (Deut 17:10–12b). Since verse 10 demands action, "the word of judgment" (דבר המשפט) in 17:9 would include both a declaration of guilt or innocence and the actions

---

the priest does not adjudicate the legal process but subjects the accused to a "trial by ordeal," and YHWH himself declares the verdict.

28. Moshe Weinfeld suggests two independent judicial traditions have been combined (*Deuteronomy and the Deuteronomic School*, 235).

29. Exodus 21:6 and 22:7–8[8–9] also speak of judicial cases being resolved "before God."

30. On the conjunction "and" as an explicative *waw*, see GKC §154 n. (b). The clause, "who is [in office] in those days," leaves open whether these persons served for life like high priests, or rotated off when their term expired. The use of the plural in 19:17 (הכהנים והשפטים) suggests a panel of judges drawn from the priests.

31. Thus Driver, *Deuteronomy*, 208.

32. Thus *DCH*, 2:474. On לדרש דבר, "to seek a word," as an idiom for oracular inquiry, see 1 Kgs 14:5; 22:5 (= 2 Chr 18:4); Ezra 10:16.

33. The noun is used elsewhere of a divine pronouncement in response to inquiry (Judg 13:12; 1 Sam 2:12–13; 8:10–11) or a cry for rescue (Judg 4:5).

34. While Exod 18:19 envisions Moses bringing most difficult cases to YHWH, as in Deut 17:9, the use of דרש in search of a משפט in Exod 18:15 involves an oracular consultation. Similarly, Jackson, "Law in the Ninth Century," 387, n. 105.

35. On the oracular use of the Urim and Thummim in the priest's "breastpiece of the judgment" (חשן המשפט), see Exod 28:30; Lev 8:8. If we abandon the common political interpretation of the broader context (Deut 16:18—18:22; cf. Block, *Deuteronomy*, 399), several features of this text are clarified: (1) the characterization of difficult cases with the verb, נפלא; elsewhere the root refers to miraculous or "wonderful" divine actions, as opposed to ordinary events (Deut 1:17; Exod 18:26); (2) the location of the inquiry at the sanctuary, rather than "in your gates" (Deut 17:8, 10); (3) the absence of any reference to an investigation by priests or judge; this tribunal simply declares the outcome; (4) the phrase דבר המשפט, "the word of decision," which suits an oracular context perfectly (cf. v. 11); (5) the twofold occurrence of the idiom, על פי, lit. "according to the mouth" (vv. 10, 11), which suggests the officials do not establish but only declare the verdict (vv. 9, 10, 11); (6) the later reference to "the priest who stands there to serve YHWH your God" (v. 12). These elements do not belong in a judicial inquiry conducted by a lay official. The procedure presents YHWH as Judge in the ultimate court, and the priest at the sanctuary who declares the verdicts is his representative.

against a person declared guilty. If the "word" the priest declares represents the divine judgment in a case that normal procedures had failed to resolve, the immediate context might suggest the Torah to be taught by the priestly tribunal (v. 11) involves specific instructions related to the case at hand.[36] However, the usage of the expression in Deuteronomy and the Levites' role as instructors of Torah (33:10), argues in favor of the Torah as taught in these addresses. By executing the divine decision as prescribed, Israelites pursue righteousness as determined in this case and as taught in the Torah. Demanding the same rigorous compliance with a specific revelation from God as he does with the Torah (5:32; 17:20; 28:14), in this context deviation "to the right or to the left" refers to punishing more severely or leniently than the ruling prescribed, or substituting the prescribed sentence with a different action. Therefore the present instructions conclude with a stern warning: failure by the defendant or those charged to execute the judgment to comply with the divine decision is presumptuous and constitutes defiance against God (17:12a–b). Refusal to hear the priestly judge who represents YHWH and declares his verdict, is as reprehensible as idolatry itself (cf. 17:5–7a), and deserving of the death penalty.

If Josianic scribes who "envisioned Levites as suitable candidates for the position of official regional jurists"[37] produced these texts they have thoroughly camouflaged their intentions. Levites might have been included among the "judges" (שפטים) and "officials" (שטרים, 1:15–17; 16:18–19), but to characterize local Levitical priests as the default juridical agents[38] is unwarranted. Texts such as 17:8–13 and 19:15–21 involve Levitical priests in judicial proceedings, but only to present cases to YHWH for divine adjudication. The expressions, "before YHWH" (לפני יהוה) and "who are [in office] in those days" (אשר יהיו בימים ההם) link these passages, while the plurals, "priests and judges," in 19:17 suggest local settings. However, as in 17:8–9, in 19:17 the priests probably do not serve as judges, but as YHWH's representatives overseeing the procedures, ensuring the pursuit of "righteousness, only righteousness" (צדק צדק, 16:20) as specified in the Torah, and securing purgation of the evil from Israel. In any case, the burden of justice rests on the shoulders of the people (16:18–19; 19:15–21), who select the judges—presumably from the elders of their communities.[39] This is not to deny that Levitical priests ever served in a judicial capacity. However, since in the administration of justice the Levitical priests' role primarily involved representing YHWH and guarding Torah, to view Levitical towns chiefly as judicial centers seems unwarranted.[40]

---

36. Thus Mayes, *Deuteronomy*, 269.

37. Thus Leuchter, "'The Levite in Your Gates,'" 426.

38. Ibid., 423.

39. On the role of elders in the administration of justice, see Deut 19:8–13; 21:1–9, 18–21; 22:13–21; 25:5–10. For full discussion of these texts, see Willis, *The Elders of the City*. Significantly the instructions concerning asylum towns—which were included among the Levitical towns—assign responsibility for the adjudication of homicide refugee cases to the "assembly" (Num 35:9–15). Whether the עדה is a national political body representing all Israelites, adult males or chieftains (thus Milgrom, *Numbers*, 335) or a local assembly of elders (on the possibility see Levy and Milgrom, "עֵדָה ʿēdâ," 477), the absence of Levitical priests is significant.

40. In the Chronicler's report of Jehoshaphat's reform (2 Chr 19:4–11) the regulations concerning judges in the towns throughout the land ("town by town"; vv. 4–7) apparently involved neither Levites nor Levitical towns. Whether or not the appointment of priests and Levites (vv. 8–11) was localized

Levitical Towns as Centers of Pastoral Ministry

The silence of scholars on the religious function of Levitical towns is extraordinary.[41] Studies of ancient Israelite religion/religions give scant attention to the subject,[42] and when they do they are preoccupied with whether the lists in Josh 21 and 1 Chr 6 are utopian or realistic.[43] Since these discussions are largely hypothetical, perhaps the time has come to explore the biblical evidence to see how the Levitical towns might have functioned socio-religiously. I shall address this subject under two headings: (1) explicit statements concerning Levites in the constitutional materials, especially Deuteronomy; and (2) narrative accounts involving Levites.

The Activities of Levitical Priests in the Constitutional Materials

As noted earlier, the book of Deuteronomy offers some insight into the religious functions of Levitical priests:[44] carrying the ark of the covenant in processions (10:8; 31:9);

---

in Jerusalem, the program emphasizes their role in maintaining the relationship between the people and YHWH, rather than priestly adjudication of cases. On this text, see Jackson, "Law in the Ninth Century," 376–89.

41. Peterson's unpublished dissertation, *Topographical Surface Survey,* is a notable exception. His concluding twenty-five pages focus on the significance of these towns in Israel's religious life.

42. In *A History of Israelite Religion in the Old Testament Period,* Albertz never mentions Num 35:1–5 and disposes of Josh 21 and 1 Chr 6 with a single dismissive comment, "I regard the tradition of the forty-eight Levitical cities (cf. Josh 21; 1 Chr 6) as a later artificial systematization" (p. 263, n. 94). The subject is never addressed by Ringgren *Israelite Religion*; van der Toorn, *Family Religion in Babylonia, Syria and Israel*; Miller, *The Religion of Ancient Israel*; Hess, *Israelite Religions*; or any of the essayists in *Ancient Israelite Religion,* ed. Miller, Hanson, and McBride, or *Religious Diversity in Ancient Israel and Judah,* ed. Stavrakopoulou and Barton. Ziony Zevit (*The Religions of Ancient Israel*) does slightly better, offering a helpful map (610), and devoting a couple of pages to the subject (656–58). He acknowledges that "Levites were the recognized bearers of common—though not necessarily uniform—tradition," but ill-advisedly interprets the Levitical guild-caste as "part of the royal bureaucracy/public works and services sector, assigned or allotted the right to reside in various cities and villages in tribal territories" (656–57). Vaux (*Ancient Israel,* vol. 2, *Religious Institutions,* 366–67) devotes two pages to Levitical towns, but is preoccupied with the origins of the lists and has nothing to say about their religious function.

43. Those who argue for a realistic interpretation tend to find the origin of these lists in the time of the United Monarchy, usually from the reign of David. Chris Hauer Jr., opined that David allotted these towns to the Levites in the interests of the "national royal ecclesiastical cult dedicated to Yahweh, the God who had guided his own royal destiny. The settlement of Levites, a tribe of sacerdotal specialists notorious for their Yahwistic zeal, at points of particular concern about the country, would certainly serve this policy" ("David and the Levites," 33–54). For antecedents of this view, see Albright, "The List of Levitical Cities," 49–73; Mazar, "The Cities of the Priests and Levites," 193–205. Proponents of the utopian interpretation of the lists disagree on their antiquity. Kaufmann (*The Biblical Account of the Conquest of Canaan,* 40–46), argues for a pre-monarchic date; Haran suggests that while the tradition may have historical roots, the lists reflect the utopian vision of pre-exilic Priestly authors ("Studies in the Account of the Levitical Cities," Part I: "Preliminary Considerations," 45–54; Part II: "Utopia and Historical Reality," 156–65). Ben Zvi ("The List of the Levitical Cities," 77–106) argues for a post-monarchic date for Josh 21.

44. Deuteronomy does not distinguish between priests and Levites, but uses a variety of expressions to refer to those charged with responsibility for the spiritual well-being of the people: הכהנים

standing before YHWH and serving him (10:8; 17:12; 18:5, 7); representing YHWH in blessing the people in his name (10:8; 21:5); declaring the divine judgment in otherwise insoluble cases (17:9); supervising the king as he copied the Torah (17:18); serving as witnesses on YHWH's behalf in legal proceedings (19:17); guarding the Torah (31:9); instructing the people on the distinctions between clean and unclean and supervising purification rituals (24:8); presiding over covenant-renewal rituals (27:9, 14); performing cultic rituals before YHWH (33:10); and teaching YHWH's judgments (משפטים) and his Torah in Israel (33:10).[45]

While the last function is commonly recognized, how Levitical priests would fulfill this role deserves further comment. Deuteronomy 31:9–13 requires them to read the entire Torah orally to the nation at the central sanctuary every seven years at the Sukkoth festival. However, it is unlikely this was the only time the people heard the Torah. Since Deut 6:6–9 calls on parents to take "these words" (presumably the Torah) to heart, that is memorize them, and recite them diligently to their children,[46] presumably Levitical priests bore responsibility for teaching it to the people, just as Moses had taught (למד) the Song of YHWH to the Israelites by "putting it in their mouths" (שימה בפיהם; 31:19–22; cf. 32:44–46). In the absence of written copies, having memorized the Torah themselves, the Levitical priests' could teach the Torah by reciting it in the towns and villages where they lived and assisting the people in memorizing it.[47] The historian's observation that the generation that succeeded Joshua "did not know YHWH nor the great deeds he had done for Israel" (Judg 2:10) reflects the massive failure of the heads of Israel's households and the Levitical priests to keep alive the memory of YHWH's redemption and his covenant stipulations.[48] Some have suggested that the eighth-century BCE prophet Hosea represented a faithful remnant of these Levitical priests. Thinking and speaking like one, he denounced the people for their covenantal infidelity and their liturgical recidivism.[49]

Many have studied Israel's national cult and the nature of personal and family religion, but the practice of religion and spiritual leadership at the clan or community level deserves more attention. In any society people look to a spiritual leader, not only for instructing them in the traditions and mores of the past, but also for comfort when grieving and blessing at significant moments (e.g., the birth of a child). Israel's priestly writings call for the involvement of priests as spiritual physicians in women's purification

---

הלוים, "Levitical priests" (17:9, 18; 18:1; 24:8; 27:9); הכהנים, "the priests" (19:17; 20:2 [sing.]), or הכהנים בני לוי, "the priests, the descendants of Levi" (21:5; 31:9), or שבט לוי[ה], "the tribe of Levi" (10:8; 18:1).

45. On priestly duties and responsibilities in general, see Nelson, *Raising Up a Faithful Priest*, 83–110; Miller, *The Religion of Ancient Israel*, 162–74.

46. Hebrew וְשִׁנַּנְתָּם involves the verb שנן, "to repeat." The speech act does not entail speaking "about these words," but reciting them to the children at every opportunity. The statement need not assume general literacy. If ancient Greeks could memorize Homer's *Iliad* and *Odyssey* in their entirety, and would recite these epics to inspire the ancient values of "love of glory, virtue of cunning, and the importance of the preservation of honor" (thus Carr, *Writing on the Tablet of the Heart*, 99–104), ancient Israelites could have memorized the entire Torah (i.e., the speeches in Deuteronomy).

47. Cf. Carr, *Writing on the Tablet of the Heart*, 132–34.

48. Cf. the "Deuteronomic" recollection of YHWH's past favors attributed to the divine envoy (מלאך יהוה) in Judg 2:1–5, a prophet (נביא) in Judg 6:7–10, and YHWH himself in 10:11–14.

49. See Cook, *The Social Roots of Biblical Yahwism*, 231–66.

rituals after childbirth (Lev 12), in cases of defiling skin diseases (Lev 13–14), in cleansing a house infected with mold (Lev 14:33–57), and in personal purification rituals (Lev 15). These texts envision a people gathered around the central sanctuary ("tent of meeting," 12:6; 14:11, 23; 15:14, 29), and Milgrom rightly noted that they do not involve Levites (Deuteronomy's Levitical priests), but only the priests.[50] However, if the principles underlying these purity/impurity ordinances had any force for the nation settled in the promised land, it would be unreasonable for those who were ritually unclean to run to the central sanctuary every time they became impure through childbirth, skin diseases, bodily discharges, or contact with a moldy house or with cadavers. If Levites could be authorized to take care of the Tabernacle, it is reasonable to suppose that they could also be commissioned to oversee purification rituals and pronounce those who had been defiled as clean in the far reaches of the land. Presumably they would also have officiated at community religious observances and supervised the practice of Sabbath-keeping.

Indeed, Israel's constitutional literature provides several hints that Israel's theocratic structures had room for local liturgical expression. Regulations for constructing altars in Exod 20:24–26 are open to altars at various sites.[51] The absence of the article on "altar of earth" (מזבח אדמה, v. 24) and "altar of stones" (מזבח אבנים, v. 25) suggests these are generic instructions, rather than prescriptions for the altar at the central sanctuary. The clause, "in every place where I cause my name to be remembered" (בכל המקום אשר אזכיר את שמי) presupposes simultaneous worship at more than one place. Whereas the tabernacle altar (Exod 27:1–8; 38:1–7), later temple altar (2 Chr 4:1), and Ezekiel's altar (Ezek 43:13–17) bore no resemblance to the altar prescribed here, the Iron Age I structure on Mount Ebal appears to have been constructed according to these specifications.[52] However, unlike Bethel and Shiloh, biblical texts never associate the Ebal site with the tabernacle. Anticipating worship at every place that YHWH caused his name to be remembered, he promised to meet and bless the people there. Indeed Milgrom has argued forcefully that P's doctrine of religious centralization was limited, and that it recognized the legitimacy of other regional sanctuaries.[53] Furthermore, following Yehezkel Kaufmann and reversing his earlier position, Milgrom has demonstrated that H also assumes the ongoing validity of multiple sanctuaries. Especially critical here is Lev 26:31: "I will lay your cities waste, and will make *your sanctuaries* desolate, and I will not smell your pleasing odors" (*NRSV*; emphasis mine). In contrast to the previous verse, here מקדשיכם refers to legitimate cult centers where sacrifices were presented.[54]

All this supposedly changed with Josiah's reforms in the late seventh century BCE. Interpreting Deuteronomy as a seventh-century document produced to support the king's centralization of religion and political power in the crown, most assume the

---

50. Milgrom, *Leviticus 1–16*, 1.

51. So also, Levinson, *Deuteronomy and the Hermeneutics of Legal Innovation*, 28–34.

52. See Zertal, "An Early Iron Age Cultic Site on Mount Ebal," 105–65. For the definitive study of this site, see now Hawkins, *The Iron Age Structure on Mt. Ebal*.

53. Milgrom, *Leviticus 1–16*, 28–42, and more briefly in Milgrom, *Leviticus 17–22*, 1503–4.

54. So also, Milgrom, *Leviticus 23–27*, 2320. For fuller discussion of multiple sanctuaries in H, see idem, *Leviticus 17–22*, 1503–14.

book's call for worship at "the place that YHWH would choose to establish his name"[55] excluded legitimate worship of YHWH at any other location. Milgrom writes,

> There is agreement that D's major innovation is its abolition of the local sanctuaries. Thus it is not surprising when D prescribes a sanctuary ritual it invariably states explicitly, emphatically, and repetitively that henceforth it must be observed only at one chosen sanctuary.[56]

However, this interpretation seems unlikely on several counts. First, it is unrealistic. Although the three annual pilgrimage festivals should have united Israel in a common tradition, theology, and faith (Exod 23:14–19; Deut 16:1–17), the latter cannot be maintained by legislating participation in national observances while outlawing local expressions, either at the community level or within the family. Deuteronomy does indeed require minimally three annual pilgrimages to the central sanctuary (16:1–17), but true religion is personal and local, lived out in everyday activities of work and play, and celebrated in domestic and communal spiritual rituals.

Second, even Deuteronomy, which provides the strongest mandate for centralization of worship, seems to open the door to worship away from the central sanctuary. The use of the verb, זבח, "to sacrifice, slaughter" (12:15, 21), the link between Israel's kosher food and acceptable offerings to YHWH (12:15, 22; cf. 14:1–21),[57] the care required in following divine prescriptions in slaughtering animals, especially with reference to blood (12:16, 23–25), the explicit link with well-being (12:25), and the recognition that these are acceptable acts "in the eyes of YHWH" (הישר בעיני יהוה, v. 25; cf. v. 28), suggest that every meal involving meat is a sacred act of worship.[58] Furthermore, the reference to "the altar of YHWH your God that you make for yourself" (אשר תעשה לך) in 16:21 involves compromising a legitimate act (building an altar to YHWH) with an illegitimate one (erecting an Asherah pole beside the altar of YHWH). While Deuteronomy emphasizes worship at the central sanctuary, and forbids the worship of any other gods anywhere, it does not proscribe legitimate worship of YHWH elsewhere.

Priestly writings elsewhere distinguish the ritual service of Aaronic and Zadokite priests from the rest of the Levites, who maintained the sanctuary but did not have access to the inner sanctum (Num 18:1–32; cf. Ezek 44:1–27).[59] This coheres with the vision of centralized worship at the tabernacle while "the hosts of YHWH," marched to the land promised the ancestors, and with Ezekiel's idealized/utopian view of the nation's

---

55. Variations of the formula occur twenty-one times in the book (12:5, 11, 21; 14:23–25; etc.). On the "place name formula" in Deuteronomy, see Richter, *The Deuteronomistic History and the Name Theology*; idem, "The Place of the Name in Deuteronomy," 342–66.

56. Milgrom, *Numbers*, 505; cf. idem, *Leviticus 1–16*, 187.

57. Cf. Block, *Deuteronomy*, 341–52.

58. Similarly, Vogt, *Deuteronomic Theology and the Significance of Torah*, 181–83; contra Levinson, *Deuteronomy and the Hermeneutics,* 35–38. There is no need to relegate this to the category of "profane [i.e., nonsacrificial] slaughter" as Milgrom does, or to attribute D's preference for זבח (which Milgrom acknowledges denotes sacred slaughter) over שחט (which Milgrom says denotes common slaughter) to "ignorance of its [שחט] technical meaning as developed by P." Milgrom, *Leviticus 1–16*, 716–17.

59. For Milgrom's discussion of this issue, see "Excursus 1: Ezekiel and the Levites," in *Ezekiel's Hope*, 141–48.

ancestral homeland, dominated by the sanctuary, the reserve of the נָשִׂיא ("prince"; Ezek 45–46, 48) and the city named "YHWH Shammah" (Ezek 48:35).

Because Deuteronomy envisions a realistic world, with the Israelites settled in their allotted tribal territories, it does not distinguish priests from Levites and recognizes the logistical difficulties of centralized worship for the scattered people (cf. 12:20–28; 14:24–27). Deuteronomy highlights the worship of the nation and individuals at "the place YHWH has chosen to establish his name," but it also anticipates Levitical priests living throughout the land. The references to Levites "in your gates" (12:12, 18; 14:27, 29; 16:11, 14; 26:12) or coming "from your gates" (18:6) do not concern Levitical towns, but towns where ordinary Israelites live. The book does not envision Levites living in monastic isolation in towns reserved exclusively for them; rather they will be regular fixtures wherever Israelites reside. If resident aliens (גר) commonly sought employment among the Israelites, we may reasonably suppose that Levites were welcome in these communities not merely as freeloaders, but presumably to minister to the people. Although they were permitted to own homes, because Levites were denied tribal territory, like aliens, widows, and the fatherless, they were dependent upon the Israelites' charity. The people's treatment of Levites "in their gates" would thus serve as a barometer of their spiritual condition.

The Activities of Levitical Priests in Hebrew Narratives

Apart from Josh 14:4 and chapter 21, and 1 Chr 6, explicit references to Levitical towns in biblical narratives are rare. The Chronicler reports that David gathered all the priests and Levites who lived "in towns that have pasturelands" (בערי מגרשיהם) to celebrate the return of the ark from Kiriath-jearim (1 Chr 13:2). Second Chronicles 11:13–14 reinforces the image of Levites away from the central sanctuary, noting that when Jeroboam established his cult centers at Bethel and Dan the priests and Levites in all Israel came "from all their districts" (מכל גבולם) and stood with Rehoboam. When Jeroboam barred Levites from ministering as priests for YHWH (מכהן ליהוה) they abandoned "their pasturelands and their property" (מגרשיהם ואחזתם), apparently referring to Levites' holdings in other towns, and moved to Judah and Jerusalem (2 Chr 11:14). Later Jehoiada the priest assembled the Levites from all the towns of Judah to Jerusalem for the installation of Josiah as king (2 Chr 23:1–11, esp. v. 2). According to 2 Chr 31:19, in Hezekiah's time priestly descendants of Aaron also lived in "the fields of the pasturelands of their towns" (בשדי מגרש עריהם).[60]

In reconstructing the place of Levitical priests outside the environs of the central sanctuary, 2 Kgs 23:8–9 is a crux. Having purged the Temple of pagan objects and personnel (vv. 1–7), Josiah extended his campaign to the city of Jerusalem and its environs (vv. 10–14), Judah (vv. 8–9) and the Neo-Assyrian province of Samaria (vv. 15–20). Given his severe treatment of syncretistic priests in Jerusalem (v. 5) and the high places in Samaria (v. 20), his response to the priests at the high places of Judah is modest, if not generous. I interpret "priests of the high places" (כהני הבמות, 2 Kgs 23:9) as legitimate

---

60. The reference to "fields" may suggest some of the pastureland was under cultivation.

priests of YHWH ministering in high places outside Jerusalem, in contrast to the "idolatrous priests" (כמרים, v. 5).[61] After destroying the cult centers he brought all the former to Jerusalem. Although they were denied direct access to the altar, they were welcomed to the fellowship of priestly colleagues. We may also speculate that, because away from Jerusalem these high places were subject to local syncretistic pressures, Josiah may have brought these Levitical priests to Jerusalem to participate in his religious agenda and renew their commitments to orthodox Yahwism. McConville argues rightly that this did not signal the failure of the centralizing agenda of Deut 18:1–8.[62] Since the altar rituals in Jerusalem were the preserve of the Zadokite priests, to exclude them from the inner sanctuary was not a punitive policy.

While they do not all mention Levitical towns, other texts suggest Levitical priests were scattered throughout the land, performing rituals at community cult centers and serving as spiritual leaders for the people. The narratives offer numerous illustrations of the latter. In contrast to the Aaronid Eli, Samuel was a Qohathite, the grandfather of Heman the musician (1 Chr 6:18–23[33–38]). His father Elkanah resided in Ramathaim of the Zophites, in the hill country of Ephraim (1 Sam 1:1).[63] Judg 17–20 demonstrates that Levites were identified both by tribe of origin and by their geographic location. Although non-Aaronids were barred from the high priesthood, Deut 18:6–8 explains how Samuel, an Ephraimite, could minister to YHWH in the sanctuary at Shiloh. However, Samuel's destiny was neither tied to Shiloh nor limited to the role of a priest. Whereas the nation recognized him as prophet (1 Sam 3:19–21), he also functioned as "governor"[64] of a small region in the nation's heartland (7:15–16). His home was in Ramah, but he also governed from Bethel, Gilgal, and Mizpah. As priest he built an altar to YHWH at Ramah (7:17), but as pastor to the nation he pleaded with Israel to repent of their sin (7:3–4), prayed for them (vv. 5, 8), performed water rituals before YHWH (v. 6a), led the people in fasting (v. 6b), presented burnt offerings to YHWH (vv. 9–11), and presided over commemorative rituals of thanksgiving (v. 12). Later he presented sacrifices at the high place in Zuph (9:11–14, 22–24), and hosted a sacrificial occasion with Jesse and his

---

61. כמרים is a loanword from Akkadian *kimru*, "priest," via Aramaic. Cf. *DNWSI* 1.515–16; Tawil, *An Akkadian Lexical Companion for Biblical Hebrew*, 166. Legitimate high places are also acknowledged elsewhere (1 Sam 9:12–14; 10:5, 13; 1 Kgs 3:4).

62. McConville, "Priests and Levites," 132–35.

63. Since 1 Sam 1:19 locates Elkanah and Hannah's house in Ramah, this could be a variant name of Ramathaim. However, given Ramah's location in Benjamin and the transience of Levites (see Judg 17–20), in 1 Sam 1:1 the narrator seems to have distinguished Elkanah's origins from his residence. Susan Ackerman considers associating Ramathaim-zophim with New Testament Aramatea (modern Rentis) or with Khirbet Raddana ("Who is Sacrificing at Shiloh? The Priesthoods of Ancient Israel's Regional Sanctuaries," 38). Ramathaim ("twin peaks") could also be linked with Shechem, a Levitical town in Ephraim (Josh 21:21), located between the "twin peaks" of Mounts Gerizim and Ebal. Many question the originality of the Chronicler's genealogy of Samuel. According to Japhet, "a genealogy of the prophet Samuel has been transplanted into the line of the Kohathites, in an attempt to Provide Samuel with a legitimate Levitical pedigree" (*I & II Chronicles*, 153), but ultimately the concern is to legitimize the musician, Heman, a grandson of Samuel (156).

64. Hebrew שפט should not be restricted to arbitration of civil disputes, but be understood more broadly as "govern" (cf. Block, *Judges, Ruth*, 21–25).

family in Bethlehem (16:1–5). The narrator never suggests that these priestly services away from the central sanctuary were illegitimate.⁶⁵

If Samuel represents legitimate Levitical priestly service, Judg 17–21 recounts the adventures of Levitical priests who lost their spiritual and professional way. After presenting the origins of Micah's apostate household cult (Judg 17:1–5), the narrator's focus turns to a Levite who stumbles upon Micah. By withholding his name until the end of this story (18:30) readers are invited to generalize this person's characteristics to Levites as a group. Identified by status (נער), geography (from Bethlehem), clan (ממשפחת יהודה), tribe (a Levite), and vocation (גר; 17:7), the Levite is characterized as a shiftless man, "going to sojourn wherever he might find" (17:8; cf. 17:9). While most translations fill the gap with something like "a place" (NRSV, NJPSV), the text does not specify the object of the Levite's search, inviting the reader to contemplate other possibilities: a treasure, home, job, place to minister, wife, someone who will take him in.

Micah's conscience apparently troubled him for having ordained his son as priest of his private installation. Capitalizing on the arrival of the Levite, he tried to legitimize his cult and secure YHWH's favor by installing the newcomer as his priest (17:10–13). The Levite happily accepted the offer, but his professional infidelity did not stop there. When Danite scouts arrived they recognized the Levite's voice—apparently he had previously spent some time with the Danites—and asked him what he was doing there, to which he shamelessly answered that Micah had hired him and he had become his priest (18:3–4). In response to the Danites' request for an oracular word from YHWH regarding the prospects for their scouting venture, he replied, "Go in peace; the road on which you are traveling is before YHWH" (18:5–6). Although the expression, נכח יהוה דרככם, is ambiguous, the Danites interpreted it in their favor. Later, when the entire Danite tribe appeared, the Levite abandoned his patron and sold his services to the highest bidder (18:19), in effect blessing the Danite thugs who stole Micah's cultic objects and his priest, and sanctioning their establishment of a new shrine at Laish/Dan (18:27–31). We do not learn the Levite's identity until the end of the story; he was Jonathan, the grandson of Moses.⁶⁶ This account illustrates how quickly and deeply the spiritual recidivism affected pre-monarchic Israel (cf. 2:10–12), suggesting that the absence of faithful Levitical priests contributed to the problem.

---

65. The narrators locate other altars away from the central sanctuary without criticism: Ophrah (Judg 6:24, 26); the threshing floor of Araunah (2 Sam 24:18–25); Gibeon (1 Kgs 3:4); Mount Carmel (1 Kgs 18:30–35—note Elijah's reference to YHWH's altars [pl]; 1 Kgs 19:10, 14). These altars contrast with illegitimate installations at Ophrah (Judg 6:25–32), Bethel and Dan (1 Kgs 12:32–33; 13:1–5), the towns of Samaria (1 Kgs 13:32), on the high places and hills and under every green tree (2 Kgs 16:4) and alternate altars in Jerusalem (2 Kgs 16:10–16; 2 Kgs 21:3–5); etc.

Archaeologists have recently discovered evidence for early monarchic cultic shrines at Khirbet Qeiyafa and Tel Motza. For the former, see Garfinkel, "Three Shrines from Khirbet Qeiyafa" (paper presented at the Society of Biblical Literature Annual Meeting, Chicago, 18 November 2012); for the latter see the report of discoveries by Anna Eirikh, Hamoudi Khalaily and Shua Kisilevitz, at http://www.mfa.gov.il/mfa/israelexperience/history/pages/temple_vessels_biblical_tel_motza_26-dec-2012.aspx.

66. On the superscripted *nun* in מנשה to read "Manasseh," rather than "Moses," see Tov, *Textual Criticism of the Hebrew Bible*, 52–53; Block, *Judges, Ruth*, 511–12.

The narrator's portrait of the Levite in Judg 19–20 is not quite as round as that of Jonathan ben Mosheh, but it is equally troubling, inasmuch as his domestic dispute precipitated a national crisis that brought the nation to the brink of disaster. Judges closes with the Benjaminite tribe all but eliminated for their defense of evil and the women of Israel helpless victims of male monstrosity (21:6–23). The narrator portrays the nameless Levite (who figures only at the beginning of this series of events; 19:1—20:7) as self-interested and heartless, so that in the end readers wonder who killed his concubine (cf. 19:27—20:6). In contrast to Samuel, these Levites lacked a moral compass and awareness of the place of their tribe in the divine agenda. In this world no one, not even YHWH was king (17:6; 18:1; 19:1; 21:25).

The Role of Levitical Towns in Israelite Life

The place of Levitical towns in these narratives is unclear, since narratives involving Levites rarely involve Levitical towns. Apart from the theophoric names that associate sites with cult installations before the Israelites arrived (see above), texts involving Levitical towns rarely mention cult centers used by Israelites. The asylum towns may be exceptions. Since persons seeking refuge from an avenger would cling to an altar (Exod 21:14; 1 Kgs 1:51; 2:28–29), asylum towns (which also functioned as Levitical towns[67]) probably contained shrines, though Haran suggests this did not apply to other Levitical towns.[68] Distinguishing between "shrines" (houses of God involving an altar and other cult installations at which priests ministered) and "high places" (במות, represented simply by open air altars[69]), Haran observes that while the former were rare, the latter were scattered throughout the land.[70] Later texts note that Anathoth, a Levitical town (Josh 21:18), was home to the priestly figures Abiathar (1 Kgs 2:26) and Jeremiah (Jer 1:1; 32:7–9), though evidence for a shrine is lacking.[71] However, the case of Micah in Judg 17 suggests these distinctions may be too absolute. The manufacture of a household idol (17:4) could easily escalate into the construction of a household shrine (בית אלהים, v. 5), complete with image, ephod, תְּרָפִים (těrāpîm), and ordained priest. If cultic activities happened in other places, Levitical priests would probably have performed such rituals in Levitical towns.[72] Indeed, it seems the institution of Levitical towns was intended

---

67. Josh 20:7–8 identifies the following: Kadesh in Galilee [Naphtali] (21:32); Shechem in Ephraim (21:21); Kiriath-Arba [Hebron] in Judah (21:11); Bezer in Reuben (21:36); Ramoth in Gilead [Gad] (21:38); Golan in Bashan [Manasseh] (21:27). The bracketed references identify them as Levitical towns.

68. Haran, "Preliminary Considerations," 53.

69. According to these distinctions the tenth–ninth century installation in Arad must be classified as a "shrine," but its legitimacy is cast in doubt two standing pillars signifying devotion to more than one God (perhaps YHWH and his Asherah), and a seventh-century ostracon inscribed "the house of YHWH" (בית יהוה), which may refer to the Jerusalem temple, or suggest this installation competed with the central sanctuary. On this site, see Aharoni, "Arad: The Israelite Citadels," 82–87.

70. Haran, "Preliminary Considerations," 53, n. 14; "Utopia and Historical Reality," 160.

71. Abiathar ministered at Nob (1 Sam 22:19–20) and Jerusalem (2 Sam 15:29), and his forbears ministered at Shiloh (1 Sam 1–4; 14:3).

72. Contra McConville, *Law and Theology*, 134–35, and Haran, "Preliminary Considerations," 51–53.

to serve a critical purpose in the maintenance of religious fidelity and pastoral care of the Israelite population (Fig. 9.3). Rather than serving as instruments of Josianic social, political, and economic centralization, together Levitical towns and Levitical priesthood reflected a deliberately centrifugal religious strategy.

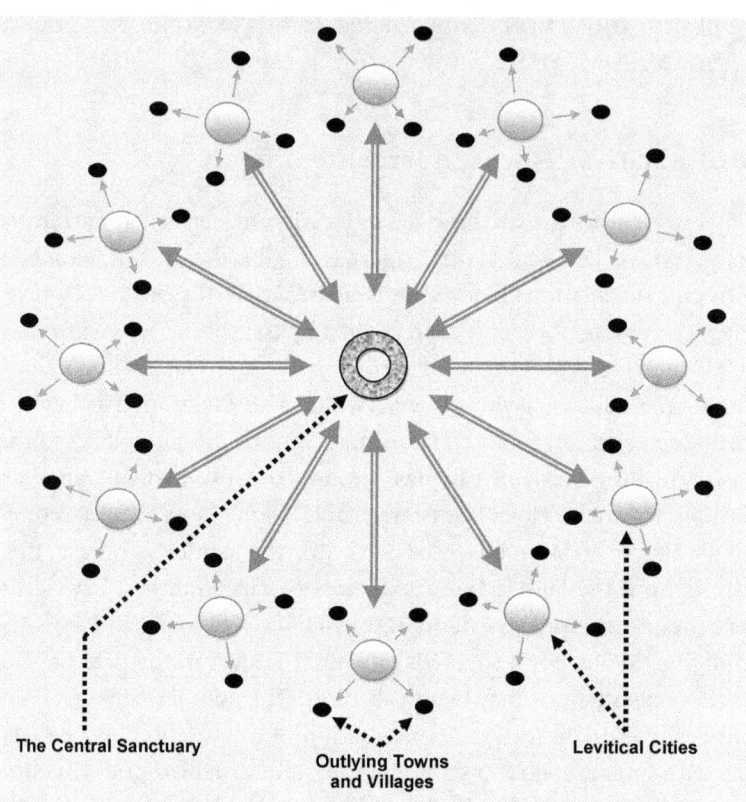

Figure 9.3
A Schematic Portrayal of the Location and
Function of the Levitical Towns

The Central Sanctuary   Outlying Towns and Villages   Levitical Cities

Priestly texts and deuteronomic writings alike envision a religious world dominated by a central sanctuary, where national festivals would be celebrated and rites of penitence observed (Yom Kippur). All males were required to attend the festivals of Pesach/Matsot (Passover/ Unleavened Bread), Shavuoth (Weeks), and Sukkoth (Booths; Exod 23:14–27; 34:23; Deut 16:16–17), but Deuteronomy encourages heads of households to bring along wives and children, aliens and Levites (12:12; 16:11). In addition to these scheduled observances, YHWH invited his people to his presence when they brought tithes (14:22–29), consecrated the firstborn of the flock (15:19–23); and presented the firstfruits of the harvest (26:1–11). The high priest and his Aaronid/Zadokite clan presided over the ritual at the central sanctuary, while other branches of Levites served as supporting cast.

This spiritual fervor needed to be maintained between the festivals, in the everyday life of family and community. Moshe Weinfeld recognized the absurdity of people from the farthest corners of the land routinely worshiping at the central sanctuary.[73] It seems that Levitical towns and Levitical priests were appointed to promote faith and facilitate worship throughout the year and in every region. Despite scholars' neglect of John L. Peterson's work, his conclusion that Levitical priests were "the theological educators of ancient Israel," and that their towns were "outposts for the Mosaic teaching,"[74] demands reconsideration, if not expansion. These institutions provided means for meeting Israel's pastoral needs, for communal and clan expressions of faith, and for instruction on righteousness in everyday life.

There were only forty-eight Levitical towns. What about communities not serviced by Levitical priests stationed there? Remarkably, of sites mentioned as places of sanctioned worship led by Levites at altars outside Jerusalem, only Gibeon was a Levitical town (1 Kgs 3:4; cf. Josh 21:17). Presumably the Levites' ministry radiated from Levitical towns to outlying settlements. Susan Ackerman reasonably proposes that regional במות ("high places") scattered throughout the land provided places of worship for people living within a twenty-five- to thirty-kilometer radius.[75] Individuals, families, clans, and entire village communities came to these altars to renew their relationship with YHWH, to be instructed in his saving acts, to encounter him personally, or to receive a blessing from him. The role of Levitical priests in the rituals at these sites is largely unknown, but under normal circumstances such worship was legitimately Yahwistic. References to Levites "in your gates" in Deuteronomy[76] are not addressed to Levites, but to heads of lay households, charged to care for Levites living in their midst, presumably serving as spiritual leaders in the community.[77]

The boundaries separating priestly activity in outlying towns, Levitical towns, and the central sanctuary were not absolute. Deuteronomy 18:6–8 suggests priests were free to move back and forth from Levitical town to central sanctuary and vice versa[78] (which also opened the door to Levitical priests losing their spiritual and professional way).[79] Although verses 1–8 excluded Levitical priests from the country from officiating at the central altar, this provision guaranteed them access to priestly portions of the people's offerings when they were in Jerusalem, table fellowship with priests at the central sanctuary, and opportunities for spiritual enrichment. Within this centrifugal system communication between axle and rims should have promoted the orthodoxy of Levitical priests as they returned to their places of service in the outlying regions, where temptations to compromise with pagan rites associated with those sites were strong. Having

---

73. Weinfeld, *Deuteronomy and the Deuteronomistic School*, 218.

74. Peterson, *Topographical Surface Survey*, 724, following D. Wright, "The Levites in Deuteronomy," 325–30. See also Boling, "Levitical Cities: Archaeology and Texts," 31.

75. Cf. Ackerman, "Who is Sacrificing at Shiloh?" 33, n. 26.

76. Deut 12:12, 18; 14:27, 29; 16:11, 14; 18:6; 26:12.

77. The economic vulnerability of Levitical priests dependent on the charity of laypeople is reflected in the frequency with which Deuteronomy mentions them alongside other groups of vulnerable people (12:12, 18, 19; 14:29; 16:11, 14; 26:11–13).

78. Contra Taggar-Cohen, who comments, "It seems likely that priestly families belonged to a certain temple and remained in their own towns of origin" ("Covenant Priesthood, 21).

79. Cf. Judg 17–20. Mal 2:1–9 suggests the problem persisted into post-exilic times.

begun his reforms at the axle (2 Kgs 23:1–7), Josiah extended them to outlying regions, demolishing cult installations throughout the land because they had been compromised as badly as the central sanctuary. Since Josiah appears not to have purged any legitimate priests in Jerusalem,[80] it should not be a surprise that he let country Levites retain their status. Second Kings 23:8–9 does not declare his motive for bringing them to Jerusalem. However, rather than challenging the central sanctuary priesthood (23:8–9), he probably intended to reorient the Levitical priests to the Deuteronomic vision of Yahwistic orthodoxy, and presumably in time to send them back to the towns and villages to carry on their priestly service.[81]

Although the origins of the synagogue in Judaism largely remain a mystery,[82] with this interpretation we may have stumbled upon a generally overlooked possibility. In Psalm 74 the psalmist laments the loss of the basic institutions that served the spiritual needs of the nation: the destruction of the temple, the silencing of the prophetic voice, and the burning of "all the meeting places of God in the land" (כל מועדי אל בארץ, 74:8).[83] In keeping with Exod 20:24–25, this comment assumes legitimate places throughout the land where the people would come for communal religious gatherings, presumably supervised by Levites, and God would keep appointments with people. Although the hub of this centrifugal structure could never be transferred to another location, the Levitical towns and outlying centers of worship served as ready precedents for the establishment of institutions, such as the synagogue, for the maintenance of faith wherever remnants of the nation might be found.

Conclusion

Scholars will continue to debate whether the biblical vision of the Levitical priesthood and the Levitical towns represents utopian ideals or historical realities, and what the role of the Levitical priests and the function of the Levitical towns were within that vision. The reconstruction provided here differs radically from the prevailing orthodoxy among critical scholars, which often relies upon speculative readings of specific texts and is sometimes driven as much by presuppositions brought to the reading as the evidence of the texts themselves. Obviously I have my own presuppositions, and I grant that some of my interpretations are speculative, but sometimes a look at the data from a different perspective can be helpful.

---

80. Hilkiah the high priest (הכהן הגדול) and his descendant retained the position until the exile and beyond (1 Chr 6:39–41[13–15]; Ezra 7:1–5).

81. McConville rightly sees the transfer of the priests to Jerusalem as "a measure taken against cultic corruption" (*Law and Theology*, 133). This was probably not conceived as a permanent arrangement, for it would have left outlying populations without regular pastoral care, instruction in the Torah, and oversight in community cultic observances.

82. For brief comment, see Morton Smith, "Jewish Religious Life in the Persian Period," 258–59. For fuller discussion of the options, see Lee I. Levine, *The Synagogue*, 19–41. Levine proposes that its precursor might be found in the city gate, which functioned as the focal point of communal activity (26–31).

83. In 74:4 the same expression (מועד) is used of the temple.

Based on the foregoing analysis of the role of Levitical towns in the religious life of ancient Israel the following observations arise. First, the Levitical towns represent an ancient idealistic arrangement designed not primarily to serve economic and political ends, but to promote the religious well-being of the people. Second, the distribution of the Levitical towns throughout the land recognizes that deep faith is demonstrated not primarily in annual pilgrimages to the central sanctuary but in everyday life, and it is in their daily experiences that people need spiritual mentoring and care. Third, in the ideal world, this spiritual care should have been provided by the Levitical priests, who used the Levitical towns as bases of ministry but went out from there to the villages to instruct the people in their faith, to supervise the maintenance of purity regulations, to lead in local religious observances, and to provide general pastoral care to the citizens. Fourth, although the boundaries between the service of Levitical priests and the Aaronic/Zadokite priests of the central sanctuary were clearly drawn, under ideal circumstances these two groups would not have been rivals who struggled for hegemony in the realm of the cult. Rather, their ministries were intended to be complementary, promoting exclusive devotion to YHWH at the central sanctuary and throughout the land, on the one hand, and giving all access to the presence and blessing of YHWH, on the other. This was the ideal. Unfortunately, the reality on the ground rarely matched the ideal. The historical narratives speak of quick, rampant, and persistent recidivism on all fronts. The trauma of 586 BCE testifies, not to the failure of the Levitical towns as an institution, but to the failure of those in whose hands YHWH had placed the care of his people—both political and spiritual.

I offer this study in honor of Professor Milgrom, who has contributed so much to our understanding of all things religious and spiritual in ancient Israel, in the hope that it will stimulate further dialogue on an intriguing but underresearched topic.

10

"O Day of Rest and Gladness"

Rediscovering the Gift of Sabbath[1]

Introduction

I GREW UP IN another millennium and in what seems like another planet—the rural world of northern Saskatchewan. I retain many images of my childhood in my mind, but one I will never lose is the sight and sound of my mother and the rest of the small Mennonite Brethren congregation singing with incredible enthusiasm:

1. O day of rest and gladness,	2. On Thee, at the creation,
O day of joy and light,	The light first had its birth;
O balm of care and sadness,	On Thee, for our salvation,
Most beautiful, most bright:	Christ rose from depths of earth;
On Thee, the high and lowly,	On Thee, our Lord, victorious,
Through ages joined in tune,	The Spirit sent from heav'n,
Sing holy, holy, holy,	And thus on Thee, most glorious,
To the great God Triune.	A triple light was giv'n.
3. Thou art a port protected	4. Today on weary nations
From storms that round us rise;	The heav'nly manna falls;
A garden intersected	To holy convocations
With streams of paradise;	The silver trumpet calls,
Thou art a cooling fountain	Where gospel light is glowing
In life's dry dreary sand;	With pure and radiant beams,
From Thee, like Pisgah's mountain,	And living water flowing,
We view our promised land.	With soul-refreshing streams.

---

1. This is an expanded version of a lecture presented at a conference on "A Theology of Rest and Recreation," hosted by Liberty University, Lynchburg, VA, on March 2, 2017. I am grateful to Carmen Imes and Rebekah Josberger, who read earlier versions of this paper and offered significant counsel for its improvement.

5. New graces ever gaining
From this, our day of rest,
We reach the rest remaining
To spirits of the blessed.
To Holy Ghost be praises,
To Father, and to Son;
The church her voice upraises
To Thee, blessed Three in One.

While some may protest that this ode to the Sabbath borders on the deification of the day,[2] I must admit that the vision painted here by Christopher Wordsworth (1807–1885), Bishop of Lincoln and nephew of William Wordsworth, seems quite foreign today. Some have tried to recapture the joy of Sabbath rest that is celebrated in this song,[3] and that practising Jews treasure.[4] However, in evangelical circles today, there is a strong push to get rid of the Sabbath as an unwelcome and quite unnecessary vestige of Old Covenant and Puritanical (or in my context, Anabaptist/Mennonite) legalism.[5]

I grant that with hindsight some of the regulations governing our Sunday observance when I was growing up seem like arbitrary fencing of boundaries: no public swimming, no playing ball on public property, and no hunting crows or gophers on Sunday. However, there was something wistfully grand about slowing down on a Saturday afternoon; milking cows half an hour early, preparing our Sunday School lessons after supper; and then on Sunday not having to go out to the field, or hoe in the garden, to have our cousins over for the afternoon, to go for a long walk, to read (we had no television).

2. Thus Burton, "Denouncing Sabbath Worship." However, this criticism is overly literalistic and fails to recognize how poetry works. Hymn writers have treated other subjects similarly, addressing treasures of the faith in second person, as in:

Holy Bible, Book divine,
Precious treasure, thou art mine:
Mine to tell me whence I came;
Mine to teach me what I am.

Or in third person, as in:

In the cross of Christ I glory,
towering o'er the wrecks of time;
all the light of sacred story
gathers round its head sublime.

3. Several authors have recently tried to recapture the vision reflected here: Allender, *Sabbath*; Wirzba, *Living the Sabbath*; Baab, *Sabbath Keeping*; Dawn, *Keeping the Sabbath Wholly*.

4. For the classic statement, see Heschel, *The Sabbath: Its Meaning for Modern Man*; contemporary electronic statements are readily accessible on the internet: see Senator Joe Lieberman, *The Gift of Rest*, summarized at https://www.ou.org/jewish_action/05/2011/the_gift_of_rest/; Rich, "Shabbat."

5. Blomberg, "The Sabbath as Fulfilled in Christ," 305–58: Schreiner, "Good-bye and Hello: The Sabbath Command for New Covenant Believers," 159–88. For a helpful collection of essays on the biblical and historical issues involved in discussions of the Sabbath, see Carson, ed., *From Sabbath Day to Lord's*. Unfortunately, except for Harold P. Dressler's chapter 2, "The Sabbath in the Old Testament" (pp. 21–42), First Testament scholars' voices are missing in the volume. The same is true of Donato, ed., *Perspectives on the Sabbath: 4 Views*.

But these days we are so distracted, we find quiet and calm intolerable; we are addicted to noise and frenetic activity. If it is not work, it is our iPhones and the internet. The closest we come to keeping the Sabbath is watching football all afternoon. When the games are over we feel guilty, and if our team loses, in frustration we throw up our hands and scream, "I'll never get those six hours of my life back."

But how can we think more deeply about the Sabbath and Sabbath-keeping? We all know that rest is necessary to refresh our bodies; many published studies confirm the deleterious effects of workaholism and simply refusing to stop and take a break.[6] But if we would think theologically about rest and Sabbath we must move beyond pragmatics. And if the Scriptures are our sole ultimate source of truth regarding faith and practice, then we must finally—or should we say first—ask some important questions: What does the Bible have to say about rest and Sabbath keeping? What does the Bible say we may or may not do on the Sabbath? If we adhere to those guidelines, have we kept the Sabbath?

Actually, we need to ask deeper questions, like, "What is the theological significance of rest and Sabbath-keeping?" To answer that question, we often need to read between the lines and explore the fundamental theological convictions underlying what the Scriptures have to say on the topic. Regarding the Scriptural teaching on "a theology of Sabbath rest," this essay will proceed in stages, beginning with a consideration of the words used to describe that rest, and then to an exploration of how the Bible talks about that rest.

First Testament Perspectives on the Seventh-Day Sabbath

In searching for biblical evidence for the seventh-day Sabbath in the First Testament we are largely limited to the Pentateuch. The subject surfaces occasionally in later books, especially in contexts involving the failure to observe the day appropriately (Neh 13; Jer 17:19–27; Amos 8:5). Isaiah had a very positive view of the observance, linking delight in the Sabbath tightly with delight in YHWH himself (58:13–14), issuing a special benediction for those who observe the day (Isa 56:2), and envisaging the day when foreigners will celebrate their participation in the covenant with YHWH by keeping the Sabbath (56:3–8).[7]

In this paper I shall organize the First Testament teaching on the Sabbath under five principle theses, several of which come with attendant corollaries.

---

6. For a survey of some of the literature from a psychological perspective, see Fisher, "Sabbath for Those Who Serve, 1–2.

7. Ezekiel's three references to the Sabbath all pertain to Temple practices (Ezek 46:1, 4, 12). Some of the texts cited above will resurface in the discussion below. In this paper, I reserve the upper case form of the word for the seventh-day Sabbath, referring to all other sabbaths with the lower case.

1. *The vocabulary associated with the seventh-day Sabbath highlights its primary significance as a cessation of the daily creative work (מְלָאכָה) involved in administering the world as God's vice regents and in maintaining the life of the family and community.*

Any discussion of Sabbath rest must begin with the Hebrew word, שַׁבָּת, which occurs 111 times in the First Testament. Although Moses never uses the word in Deuteronomy, except when he quotes the Decalogue, which is cast as divine speech, as we will see, the spirit underlying the Deuteronomic grounding of the command pervades the entire book. Here and elsewhere, the word usually refers to the seventh-day Sabbath (Exod 20:11; Deut 5:15), but it also applies to sabbatical years (one year in seven, Lev 25:2–6; 26:34–35, 43), and to monthly and annual holy days.[8] The noun derives from a root used in everyday life for simply stopping an activity, or of something coming to an end, or of bringing something to an end, that is to exterminate.[9] By itself the root is not particularly sacred/cultic. The demand for absolute stoppage of work is represented by the expression, שַׁבַּת שַׁבָּתוֹן, "sabbath of sabbaths." Although this phrase is constructed slightly differently, it functions superlatively, like מֶלֶךְ מְלָכִים, "king of kings," שִׁיר הַשִּׁירִים, "song of songs," and קֹדֶשׁ הַקֳּדָשִׁים, "most holy place."[10] Observances in this category included the seventh-day Sabbath (Exod 16:23; 31:15; 35:1),[11] the sabbatical year (Lev 25:4), and Yom Kippur ("Day of Atonement," Lev 16:31; 23:32).

The nuance of rest in relation to the Sabbath depends upon the context and association with specific words for "rest." Remarkably the primary word for rest in the Hebrew Bible, נוּחַ, "to rest, enjoy repose, relax,"[12] occurs only three times in contexts involving the seventh-day Sabbath: Exod 20:11 = Deut 5:12–14; Exod 23:12.[13] The Decalogue acknowledges for the first time that the Sabbath that YHWH enjoyed in Gen 1–3 involved

---

8. This is usually the case when שַׁבָּת is associated with חֹדֶשׁ, "new moon" (2 Kgs 4:23; 1 Chr 23:31; 2 Chr 2:3; 8:13; 31:3; Neh 10:34; Isa 1:13; 66:23; Ezek 45:17; 46:1, 3; Hos 2:13; Amos 8:5), when the word is plural (שַׁבָּתוֹת, Lev 19:30; 26:2; here the sabbaths are associated with the sanctuary [מִקְדָּשׁ], which is never true of the seventh-day Sabbath), when it is associated with other expressions for cultic activities (appointed festivals: מוֹעֲדִים/מוֹעֲדוֹת, Lev 23:37–38; 1 Chr 8:13; 2 Chr 31:13; Lam 2:6; Ezek 44:24; 45:17; Hos 2:11; "her celebrations": מְשׂוֹשָׂהּ, Hos 2:11), and sometimes when associated with the cognate noun, שַׁבַּת שַׁבָּתוֹן, Lev 16:31; 23:32, cf. v. 39).

9. Of people ceasing to exist/disappearing (Lam 5:14; Isa 14:4 [oppressor]; 33:8); of work (מְלָאכָה, Neh 6:3); of distress or defeat (Isa 14:4); of strife (Prov 22:10); of agricultural seasons (Gen 8:22); of sacrifices/offerings (Dan 9:27), etc.

10. Milgrom (*Leviticus 23–27*, 1959) suggests the וֹן ending changes the noun שַׁבָּת into an adjective.

11. In this paper, I reserve the upper-case form of the word for the seventh-day Sabbath, referring to all other sabbaths with the lower case.

12. From which we get נֹחַ, "Noah."

13. The root also occurs in Exod 16:23–24, though in the hiphil stem, with the sense, "to set aside," instructing people on gathering manna for six days and noting that YHWH will withhold it on the Sabbath. Neither of the cognate nouns, מְנוּחָה and מָנוֹחַ, "place of quiet, tranquility," ever appears in Sabbath contexts. For "place of quiet," see Gen 49:15; Ps 23:2; Jer 51:59; Isa 28:12; Ruth 1:9. The word is used of Canaan as home for Israel (1 Kgs 8:5); the temple as God's dwelling place (Isa 66:1), and the "house of rest" for the ark 1 Chr 28:2. For "tranquility," see Gen 8:9; Deut 28:65; Ruth 3:1; Isa 34:14; Lam 1:3.

repose (יָנוּחַ), in addition to refraining from work. The third command extends the divine pattern of resting at the end of the week to the entire Israelite household, including children, aliens, servants, and draft animals.

Exodus 23:12 is explicit in securing the well-being of animals and humans who serve the domestic economy; the Sabbath provides oxen, donkeys, and servants opportunity for rest (יָנוּחַ) catching their breath (וְיִנָּפֵשׁ). The latter expression occurs elsewhere only twice. Recounting the course of David's flight from his son Absalom, in 2 Sam 16:13–14 the narrator notes, "The king and all the people who were with him arrived at the Jordan exhausted (עֲיֵפִים); and there he caught his breath (וַיִּנָּפֵשׁ; vv. 13–14)."[14]

Exodus 31:17 is more problematic. This verse concludes the last of seven divine speeches instructing the Israelites how to construct the tabernacle and its furnishings and how to dress the priests who would serve there:[15]

> It [the seventh-day Sabbath] is an eternal (irrevocable) sign (אוֹת לְעֹלָם) between me and the Israelites, for in six days YHWH made the heavens and the earth, but on the seventh day he ceased (שָׁבַת) [work] and caught his breath (וַיִּנָּפַשׁ).

We understand clearly what it means for humans to recover from exhaustion, but how can this be true of God, who never wearies (Isa 40:28–29)? We could resolve the problem in one of two ways: either we dismiss this statement as merely anthropological and metaphorical speech or we interpret יִנָּפֵשׁ in a more nuanced way. While the word often involves refreshment by ingesting food and water, or lying down to sleep (cf. 2 Sam 17:27–29; Jer 31:25; Ps 23:1–2), it could also mean "to be emotionally charged, to be inspired," perhaps by celebrating what has transpired. This suits Gen 2:1–2 perfectly, since God had just declared everything that he had made to be superlatively good (טוֹב מְאֹד, Gen 1:31).[16] While the significance of this possibility will surface later,[17] from this

---

14. עֲיֵפִים denotes exhaustion either because of hunger (Gen 25:29) or physical exertion as in this incident. Cf. Jer 31:25,

15. The seven speeches (25:1–30:10; 30:11–16; 30:17–21; 30:22–33; 30:34–38; 31:1–11; 31:12–17) correspond to the seven days of creation in Gen 1, with the seventh Sabbatical day representing the climax of the week.

16. This divine delight is reflected in poetic creation odes like Ps 104 and Job 40–41.

17. Hebrew uses one more "restful" word in connection with the Sabbath, specifically the sabbatical years, namely רָצָה (Lev 26:34, 43; 2 Chr 36:21). This term may either mean "to enjoy, delight in" (ESV, NLT, NRSV, NIV) or function as its homonym, "to make amends/compensate for, to restore." Although the root שבת is missing, that Joel 2:25 should use the term, שָׁלַם, "to pay back," in place of רָצָה in a related context argues for the latter meaning. Joel 2:25: "I will compensate you (וְשִׁלַּמְתִּי) for the years that the swarming locust has eaten, the hopper, the destroyer, and the cutter—my great army, which I sent against you." Similarly, Milgrom (*Leviticus 23–27*, 2333), who suggests that in this context the word functions as a synonym for כִּפֶּר, "to atone for." CSV is inconsistent in its renderings, translating רָצָה אֶת־שַׁבְּתֹתֶיהָ as "make up for its Sabbaths" in Lev 26:34, 43, but as "enjoy its Sabbath rest" in 2 Chr 36:21. Biblical Hebrew uses many other words that connote "rest, calmness, being at peace," (שָׁקַט, בֶּטַח, רָבַץ), though none is explicitly linked with the Sabbath. But note the linkage of the roots בטח and שבת in Ezek 34:25: "I will make a covenant of peace with them and eliminate (הִשְׁבִּית) dangerous animals in the land, so that they may live securely (לְבֶטַח) in the wilderness and sleep in the forest."

point forward, I shall focus primarily on the seventh-day (weekly) Sabbath; touching on other "sabbaths" only as they relate to the seventh-day Sabbath.

2. *Israel's seventh-day Sabbath was a sacred institution.*

The Scriptures highlight the Sabbath not only as a day when work stops, but also as especially holy in several ways. First, the Sabbath was sacred because it was instituted by God. This is obviously true of God's own seventh-day Sabbath (Gen 2:1–3), but it also applies to the Sabbath that humans are to observe. Every Pentateuchal text concerning the Sabbath involves divine speech (Exod 20:9–11 [= Deut 5:13–15]; 31:12–17; Lev 23:3, 11–16; 24:8; Num 28:9–10), including the instructions for gathering manna in Exod 16:22–30. On the surface, Moses appears to have initiated the conversation about the special Sabbath day provisions, but when YHWH responded to the violation of his instructions, he began with the question, "How long will you refuse to keep *my* commands and *my* instructions?" (Exod 16:28). In the closing statement, he emphasizes that the Sabbath itself and the provisions for the Sabbath are gifts from YHWH (v. 29).

The divine origin of the Sabbath has significant implications for interpreting Jesus' debates with the Pharisees over the institution. Deliberately performing many miracles on the Sabbath, his comments infuriated them. His response in Matt 12:5–8 is particularly telling:

> ⁵ Have you not read in the Torah that even though the priests on Sabbath duty in the temple profane (βεβηλοῦσιν) the Sabbath they are innocent? ⁶ I tell you that something greater than the temple is involved here. ⁷ If you had known what these words mean, "I desire mercy, not sacrifice," you would not have condemned the innocent. ⁸ For the Son of Man is Lord of the Sabbath.

Instead of saying, "One greater than the priests is here," as we might expect, after his opening question he places himself over both the temple personnel and the temple itself. The last comment trumps it all (κύριος γάρ ἐστιν τοῦ σαββάτου ὁ υἱὸς τοῦ ἀνθρώπου). For all their efforts to fence the Sabbath with their halakhic regulations,[18] the Sabbath the Pharisees had overstepped divine authority, which Jesus hereby restored! The Jewish leaders deemed this blasphemy, demanding the death penalty (cf. Matt 12:14; Luke 6:1–11).

Second, the Sabbath is sacred because God granted the day special status and function. The narrator first recalls this in Gen 2:3, but YHWH reiterates it with a verbatim quotation in the Decalogue in Exod 20:11:

Genesis 2:3	וַיְבָרֶךְ אֱלֹהִים אֶת־יוֹם הַשְּׁבִיעִי וַיְקַדֵּשׁ אֹתוֹ	And God blessed the seventh day and sanctified it.
Exodus 20:11	עַל־כֵּן בֵּרַךְ יְהוָה אֶת־יוֹם הַשַּׁבָּת וַיְקַדְּשֵׁהוּ	Therefore, YHWH blessed the Sabbath day and sanctified it.

---

18. On which, see Rowland, "A Summary of Sabbath Observance in Judaism, 43–56.

By blessing the Sabbath, YHWH invoked his good will upon it and endued it with power to fulfill his purpose. By sanctifying it, he set it apart for special sacred function. The latter does not mean that prior to God's declaring the seventh day to be holy, it was not holy. In a sense, everything that comes from God's hand is holy. This was certainly true of the "superlatively good" pre-fall world (טוֹב מְאֹד, 1:31), though, the narrator's perspective may have been colored by post-fall realities. In the images in Figure 10.1 below, the third image reflects intertestamental synagogue realities, when the Sabbath was marked by corporate worship—a practice that Christians continued when they moved from a seventh-day Sabbath to a first day Lord's Day. Since true worship involves reverential acts of submission and homage before God in all of life,[19] and God's people are to demonstrate love for him with all their inner being (לֵב), their entire bodies (נֶפֶשׁ), and all their resources (מְאֹד, Deut 6:4–5; 10:12—11:1; Rom 12:1–2),[20] all of life is holy. By designating one day in seven as particularly sacred, God in effect declared that time itself was sacred. The day set apart served as a constant reminder of that fact.

Figure 10.1
Concentric Gradations of Holiness

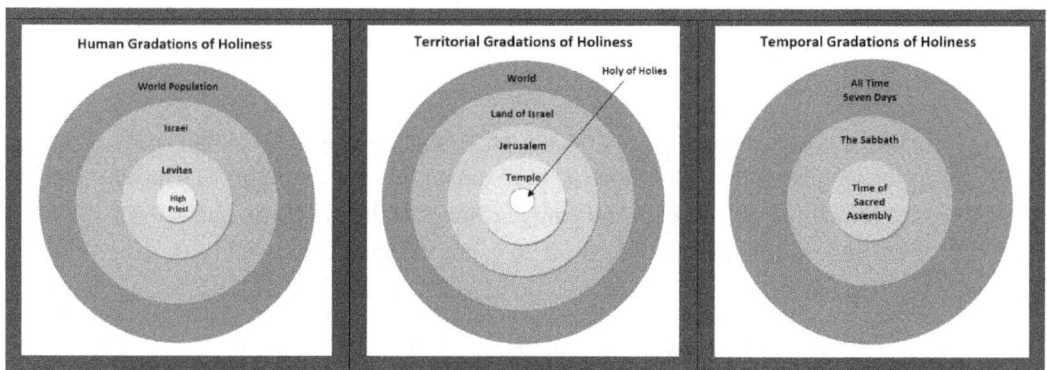

It is not difficult to imagine a particular space (the tabernacle/temple) to be uniquely holy because God's presence is localized there in some sense,[21] or a particular person (the high priest) to be uniquely holy by virtue of his role in the tabernacle/temple ritual (Fig. 10.1).[22] But just as divine holiness extended beyond the sanctuary to the whole

---

19. For a development of this thesis, see Block, *For the Glory of God*, 55–140.

20. On which see Block, "How Many is God," 193–212; reprinted in *How I Love Your Torah, O LORD*, 61–72.

21. Cf. Exod 3:1–6; 19:9–24; Deut 23:15[14]. The expression "holy city" is used of Jerusalem/Zion a half dozen times (עִיר הַקֹּדֶשׁ, Neh 11:1, 18; Isa 48:2; 52:1; Dan 9:24).

22. The high priest's status was reflected in the medallion he wore on his forehead inscribed with קֹדֶשׁ לַיהוה, "Holy to YHWH" (Exod 28:36; 39:30) and by his special ordination/consecration to serve in the inner sanctuary (Exod 29; Lev 8). While less concentrated, this holiness extended to Levitical priests who assisted in worship and taught Torah in Israel (Deut 33:10), and were installed in their sacred offices by special consecration in their thirtieth year (Num 4:30).

land,²³ and beyond the high priest to the people of Israel generally,²⁴ so the sanctity of time extended beyond the Sabbath to the other six days of the week. Although we may construe the entire week of creation as a sacred event, God "inhabits" the Sabbath in a particular sense. In Abraham Heschel's words, "The Sabbath is the presence of God in the world, open to the soul of man. It is possible for the soul to respond in affection, to enter into fellowship with the consecrated day."²⁵ Heschel may have gone too far in personifying the day itself, but he was on to something. By alerting Israel to the divine origin of the universe, the Exodus version of the Sabbath command (Exod 20:8–11) challenged the Israelites to resist materialistic commitments and invited them to share in the eternal, to bask in the awareness of the presence of God in all things and in all time.

3. Israel's Sabbath was a humanitarian, rather than a cultic institution.

Many perceive ancient Israel's Sabbath as a cultic observance, alongside their sacred festivals and the sacrifices, by which the faithful celebrated and maintained their privileged relationship with YHWH, and by which Israelites distinguished themselves from other peoples. Like circumcision and kosher dietary regulations, the Sabbath supposedly functioned as an external marker of identity and membership in the covenant community. Based on Second Temple writings and rabbinic sources, on the one hand, and Paul's epistolary responses to Judaizers on the other, this conclusion seems logical. However, we must emphasize that these are not our only or even the primary sources for ancient Israel's understanding of the Sabbath. To a large extent, the Sabbath regulations that Jews observed in New Testament times had developed during the Second temple period. Although the halachic rules governing the people's activities on the Sabbath were well intentioned—to aid them in keeping the Sabbath command—they stifled the people's freedom and smothered the spirit of the Torah. Apparently, the function of Paul's retreat to Arabia after his conversion and commissioning to serve the risen Christ was to wean him of Jewish tradition and the oral Torah as the base of his beliefs and to drive him back to written Scriptures, particularly the Torah of Moses.²⁶ If we go back to the Pentateuch for our information on Sabbath ideals, we discover a very different picture.²⁷

---

23. Isa 64:9 speaks of "your holy cities" [עָרֵי קָדְשֶׁךָ], and "holy mountain" occurs more than two dozen times (e.g., Ps 2:6; Isa 11:9; Jer 31:23; Ezek 20:40; Dan 9:16, 20; Joel 2:1; Obad 1:16; Zech 8:3). The expression "holy land" occurs only twice in the First Testament: Ps 78:54 (גְּבוּל קָדְשׁוֹ, lit. "his holy territory"); Zech 2:12 (אַדְמַת הַקֹּדֶשׁ, "holy land").

24. In Deuteronomy, the phrase, "a holy people belonging to YHWH" (עַם קָדוֹשׁ לַיהוה, 7:6; 14:2, 21; 26:19) applies the inscription on the High Priest's medallion to the people as a whole. Exodus 19–24 recounts their national consecration service, when they are commissioned as YHWH's "kingdom of priests" (מַמְלֶכֶת כֹּהֲנִים) and "a holy nation" (גּוֹי קָדוֹשׁ; 19:6). Elsewhere their calling as YHWH's "the holy people" (עַם הַקֹּדֶשׁ, Isa 62:12; 63:18; Dan 12:7) is to carry out Abraham's mission of being a light to the world. Note also the charges to the people to be holy, as YHWH is holy (Lev 19:2; cf. 1 Pet 1:16).

25. Heschel, *The Sabbath*, 60.

26. On which see chapter 18, "Hearing Galatians with Moses," below, pp. 374–404.

27. Jesus captured the contrast between the normative perspectives of the Torah and the perspectives of Judaism with his pronouncements of woe upon the scribes and Pharisees in Matt 23:13–39 and Luke 11:37–52).

First, contrary to the prevailing view among Christians, Israel's constitutional writings never prescribe any religious ritual for the Sabbath. Indeed, from the biblical records it is impossible to determine what sorts of religious rites the Israelites might have observed on the Sabbath. To be sure, Num 28:9–10 calls for special libations and whole burnt offerings at the central sanctuary on the Sabbath, and 2 Chr 9:32 notes that the Kohathites prepared the Bread of the Presence on the Sabbath, but the people's observance of the day had nothing to do with the sanctuary. To the contrary, they were to observe the Sabbath in the villages where they lived and worked. The closest we get to a ritual observance is the use of the trumpet to announce the onset of the Sabbath. In Lev 23:3, YHWH declares, "There are six days when you may work, but the seventh day is a day of Sabbath rest, a day of sacred assembly. You are not to do any work; wherever you live, it is a Sabbath to the LORD" (NIV). This statement is significant for three reasons: it recognizes the Sabbath as a divine ordinance; the day belongs to YHWH;[28] it reinforces the observation above that the Sabbath was a domestic institution, a gift to be received and celebrated "wherever you live" (בְּכֹל מוֹשְׁבֹתֵיכֶם); and it involves an officially proclaimed observance; it is "a day of sacred assembly." Or is it?

The nature of the Sabbath observance envisioned here is unclear. It revolves around the expression, מִקְרָא־קֹדֶשׁ, which is usually translated as "sacred assembly" (NIV, CSB) or "holy convocation" (ESV, NRSV, NAS; cf. "sacred occasion," NJPSV). However, in English "sacred assembly" and "holy convocation" both reflect dubious interpretations, as if the function of the Sabbath was primarily to provide a time for the community to gather for ritual worship.

The phrase מִקְרָא־קֹדֶשׁ is found exclusively in the Pentateuch, and that eighteen times.[29] The meaning of קֹדֶשׁ is clear—something is "holy, sacred"—but the referent is not. Does the phrase mean the "proclamation" itself is holy?[30] Or is this elliptical speech, proclaiming something else to be holy, either an assembly,[31] or the actual day. The word מִקְרָא itself is problematic. Deriving from a root, קָרָא, "to call out," and in a derived sense, "to read" (all reading was oral), most English translations appear to assume that this was a summons to corporate worship.[32] However, rather than referring to the people or the assembly that gathered, מִקְרָא identifies either the day whose arrival the summons announced or the act of summoning itself.

In ancient Israel, such summonses were typically made by blowing the trumpet. Numbers 10:2–3 calls for the manufacture of two silver trumpets (צוֹצְרֹת), to be used

---

28. The declaration, הוּא לַיהוָה, "It belongs to YHWH," recalls the characterization of Israel as "sons belonging to YHWH" (בָּנִים אַתֶּם לַיהוָה, Deut 14:1), or "a holy people belonging to YHWH" (עַם קָדוֹשׁ לַיהוָה, Deut 26:19; cf. 7:6; 14:2, 21).

29. Exod 12:16; Lev 23:2–4, 7–8, 21, 24, 27, 35–37; Num 28:18, 25–26; 29:1, 7, 12.

30. Analogous to "holy ground" (אַדְמַת קֹדֶשׁ, Exod 3:5), "holy mountain" (הַר קֹדֶשׁ, Ezek 28:14), "holy day" (יוֹם קֹדֶשׁ, Neh 10:21), etc.

31. The common interpretation assumes something like "holy assembly" (קְהַל קֹדֶשׁ), though the abstract expression never occurs in the Hebrew Bible. The closest we get is "assembly of the holy ones" (קְהַל קְדֹשִׁים), in Ps 89:6[5], and Num 16:3 which speaks of the whole congregations as holy (כָּל־הָעֵדָה כֻּלָּם קְדֹשִׁים) and then identifies them as "the assembly of YHWH" (קְהַל יהוה). Cf. Lev 19:2.

32. Cf. Deut 31:11–13: the Levites are to read (קָרָא) the Torah in the hearing of all the people at Sukkoth every seven years. In Neh 8:8 מִקְרָא denotes the act of reading.

"to summon the community and [to signal] the breaking of camp" (הָיוּ לְךָ לְמִקְרָא הָעֵדָה וּלְמַסַּע אֶת־הַמַּחֲנוֹת). This instrument was needed to send a signal to the entire camp of Israel in one "blow." Numbers 31:6 illustrates its use: "Moses sent out 1,000 from each tribe to war, accompanied by Phinehas son of Eleazar the priest, the custodian of the sacred utensils and the trumpets for sounding the charge" (וּכְלֵי הַקֹּדֶשׁ וַחֲצֹצְרוֹת הַתְּרוּעָה בְּיָדוֹ).[33] The association of trumpets with תְּרוּעָה (literally "trumpets of the blast") is important for interpreting the word in other contexts. Although the blast of the trumpet in Num 10:3 summons (נוֹעֲדוּ) the whole community (כָּל הָעֵדָה) to the tent of meeting (אֹהֶל מוֹעֵד), the intent was not ritual worship; the context clearly involves signaling the community to break camp and move on. The trumpet blast serves a different purpose in verse 9, rousing YHWH to action and rescue his people from an outside enemy. Verse 10 envisages the use of trumpets to signal the beginning of the annual festivals and the beginning of the months.[34]

Some mistakenly interpret תְּרוּעָה ("trumpet blast") in Lev 23:24 as ritual shouting (cf. CSB); others get this word right, even when they get the following מִקְרָא קֹדֶשׁ wrong.[35] The last sentence is best rendered something like, "You shall observe it [the first day of the seventh month, the Festival of Trumpets] as a day of total cessation of labor, a reminder, a trumpet blast, a holy proclamation, (יִהְיֶה לָכֶם שַׁבָּתוֹן זִכְרוֹן תְּרוּעָה מִקְרָא־קֹדֶשׁ). Like a herald announcing the arrival of a king, the blast of the trumpet signaled the arrival of a holy day. This was not a call to corporate worship at the central sanctuary, but a summons to all to put down their tools. The blast also reminded (זִכְרוֹן) the people that the Day of Atonement was just around the corner (on the tenth day of the month, v. 27) and that it was time to prepare.

Since trumpet blasts throughout the land signaled the highest holy day (Lev 25:9), the same probably applied to the first of the seventh month (23:24), and to the arrival of the Sabbath as prescribed in Lev 23:3.[36] This מִקְרָא־קֹדֶשׁ was not "a holy assembly," but "a holy proclamation," presumably at sundown, calling all the people to come in from the fields or the markets and receive the gift of the Sabbath.[37]

---

33. Other texts identify the instrument used to signal an event or to call people to action as a שׁוֹפָר: Lev 25:9; Josh 6:5, 20; 2 Sam 6:15; 1 Chr 15:28; 2 Chr 15:14; Job 39:25; Ps 47:6; Jer 4:19; Amos 2:2; Zeph 1:16.

34. For additional contexts for the blowing of the trumpet, see 1 Chr 15:28; 2 Chr 13:132; 15:14.

35. See ESV, NLT, NRSV, NJPSV, NAS.

36. A stone bearing the inscription, לבית התקיעה, "to the place of trumpeting / blasting," discovered at Haram esh-Sharif in Jerusalem in 1969, illustrates the practice in Jerusalem in the Second Temple period. Presumably the rock was located at the pinnacle of the temple and marked the place where the priest stood to signal the beginning of the Sabbath with a loud trumpet blast. For full discussion, see Demsky, "When the Priests Trumpeted the Onset of the Sabbath," 50–52. For a photo of the inscription, see http://www.bibarch.com/Images/instrument6.jpg. Josephus explains the trumpet's function: From the Pastophoria, where one of the priests stood "to give notice, by sound of trumpet, in the afternoon of the approach, and on the following evening of the close, of every seventh day, announcing to the people the respective hours for ceasing work and for resuming their labours." (Josephus, *Jewish Wars*, 4.9.12, p. 329).

37. Although most villages probably had a central place where they gathered for religious rituals, this was not a call to assemble for worship. See further, chapter 9, "'The Meeting Places of God in the Land,'" above, pp. 177–97.

Remarkably, apart from a passing reference to the Sabbath in 2 Kgs 4:23, a brief note of Jehoiada's provisions for guard duty for the Temple on the Sabbath in 2 Kgs 11:5–9 (cf. 2 Chr 23:4–8), and a curious reference to a Sabbath canopy on the Temple (2 Kgs 16:28), the pre-exilic narratives of the Hebrew Bible never mention the Sabbath, let alone associate it with ritual corporate worship.

Second, in its origin Israel's seventh-day Sabbath institution was unconnected to their cultic calendar and the regular rituals at the central sanctuary. The Genesis narratives are silent on whether the patriarchs celebrated the gift of the Sabbath. Since YHWH characterized Abraham as a model of the righteousness called for by the Torah (Gen 26:2–5; cf. Deut 6:24–25), it seems more likely that he observed the seventh-day Sabbath than that he did not. In any case, it is striking that the first reference to the institution appears long before the Israelites reached Sinai/Horeb, where they were officially confirmed as YHWH's covenant people. The narrative account in Exod 16 is remarkable in several respects.

a. Since the gift of manna began at the exact midpoint of the journey from Egypt to Sinai (16:1; cf. 19:1), the Israelites were observing the Sabbath at least six weeks before they had arrived at the mountain, and even longer than that before the regulations concerning the tabernacle ritual and the festivals were revealed.

b. While the Israelites were obviously puzzled by the manna (v. 15),[38] they expressed no curiosity about the Sabbath itself. Moses' statement, "Tomorrow is a day of total rest, a holy Sabbath to YHWH," and the following explanation (vv. 23–29) apparently does not announce a new institution. Rather Moses hereby began to explain generally how the divine gift of manna fits into an existing convention and specifically why people could gather double their daily quota of manna on the sixth day (v. 29). Indeed, Moses speaks of the Sabbath as having been instituted in the past.

c. Whereas the formal Sabbath ordinances prohibited the kind of work that people did every day in their stewardship over their environment and in maintaining their own lives (מְלָאכָה, Exod 20:9–10; 31:15; Lev 23:3; Deut 5:13–14; cf. Gen 2:2–3), this command prohibits gathering food for which they did not work. The proscription would apply so long as the Israelites are journeying from Egypt to the promised land, but once they reached the land the manna would stop, and with it the relevance of this dimension of the Sabbath observance (Josh 5:12).[39]

d. Like the manna itself, the Sabbath was a divine gift (כִּי־יְהוָה נָתַן לָכֶם הַשַּׁבָּת, v. 29) to be received and observed with gratitude, rather than as a burdensome constraint. The notion seems to have underlain Jesus' comment in Mark 2:27, that "The Sabbath was designed for humans, and not humans for the Sabbath" (τὸ σάββατον διὰ τὸν ἄνθρωπον ἐγένετο καὶ οὐχ ὁ ἄνθρωπος διὰ τὸ σάββατον).

---

38. Hence its name מָן (v. 31), which plays on the question the people asked in v. 15: מָן הוּא, "What is that?"

39. Once in the land, the Sabbath ordinance would govern harvesting the produce of the land, though the narratives are silent on this matter.

The narratives of the exodus, the convocation at Sinai, and the desert journeys paint a picture of a people prone to unbelief, ingratitude, and infidelity. Nevertheless, somehow a memory of the institution, apparently revealed long ago and in the Exodus version of the Decalogue declared an ordinance rooted in creation (Exod 20:11), had survived the Israelites' 400-year exile in Egypt.

Third, the humanitarian intent of the Decalogue is reinforced by the constitutional and literary context where it is embedded. Depending on how one numbers the "Ten Words,"[40] the Sabbath command is either the third or fourth principle of Israel's foundational constitutional document.[41] Many, especially in the tradition of Luther, isolate the Decalogue from the rest of the constitutional documents[42] in the Pentateuch, and treat it as a distillation of Natural Law, and therefore universally and permanently normative, in contrast to the other documents, which involve distinctly Israelite regulations, whose obsolescence is announced by the New Covenant.[43] In contrast to those who maintain the Decalogue's authority for Christians because nine of the ten commands are reaffirmed in the New Testament (the Sabbath ordinance is the only exception), proponents of the "natural law" view salvage the Sabbath ordinance by [mistakenly] focusing on what they perceive to be its primary significance: a day of corporate worship.[44]

Apart from the silence of the Pentateuch on the Sabbath as a day of corporate worship, this approach is untenable on several grounds. First, although the Decalogue was special in some senses, it is misleading to view it simply as Natural Law—as if through reason alone humans could deduce its commands—and therefore uniquely universal in its force—or to view it as distinctly Natural Law, in contrast to the other constitutional documents. Regarding its origin, like all the other covenant documents, the Decalogue was divinely revealed (Exod 20:1), intended for a particular people, whom YHWH had redeemed from slavery in Egypt (20:2), to be put into practice in the land of Canaan (20:12). As cast in the Scripture, the document is neither universal nor Natural Law. Regarding its special status, to be sure, only the Decalogue was (a) communicated to the people directly by YHWH himself; (b) preserved on tablets of stone; (c) written by God's own finger (Exod 31:18; Deut 9:10; 10:4); and (d) housed in its own special

---

40. The Greek expression, δέκα λόγοι, "ten words" (Exod 34:28; Deut 10:4; cf. δέκα ῥήματα in Deut 4:13) captures Hebrew עֲשֶׂרֶת הַדְּבָרִים perfectly.

41. Calvinist Protestants treat the Sabbath ordinance as the fourth command, while Eastern Orthodox, Roman Catholic, and Lutheran commentators combine the prohibitions against worshiping any God but YHWH and the prohibition of images, so that the Sabbath command is the third of ten. Discourse linguistic analysis of the Decalogue clearly favors the latter interpretation. For discussion, see Block, "Reading the Decalogue Right to Left," 21–55; for fuller discussion, see DeRouchie, "Counting the Ten," 93–126.

42. Israel's constitutional documents include (1) the Decalogue (Exod 20:1–21); (2) the "Covenant Document" (סֵפֶר הַבְּרִת, Exod 24:7), usually referred to by scholars as "the covenant code" (Exod 20:22–23:19); (3) the Instructions on Holiness, usually identified as "The Holiness Code" (Lev 17–26); the deuteronomic Torah (Deut 5–26, 28), though usually restricted to 12–16 and called the Deuteronomic Law Code." Cf. chapter 5, "Deuteronomic Law," above, pp. 89–104.

43. See Bauckham, "Sabbath and Sunday in the Protestant Tradition," 313–15. This view is represented by Arand, "Luther's Radical Reading of the Sabbath Commandment," 216–61.

44. They do so by arguing more strongly for guarding the Sabbath's sanctity as a day of worship than as a day of rest. This is a small step since it is the Word [of God] that sanctifies. Cf. Arand, 256–61.

repository, called the Ark of the covenant of YHWH" (אֲרוֹן בְּרִית יהוה, Deut 10:8; 31:9, 25, 26); and (d) stored in the Holy of Holies (Exod 26:33–34; Lev 16:2), never to be seen by human eyes.[45] However, there is no evidence whatsoever, either in the First or in the New Testament that among the constitutional documents it had unique force or authority either for Israel or for Christians, or that it embodied the moral will of God more perfectly than the rest of the Sinai revelation or Moses exposition thereof in the Deuteronomic Torah. Although Moses cited the Decalogue in full in his farewell addresses to Israel (Deut 5:6–21), we need an extremely fine microphone to hear any echoes of it in the First Testament.[46]

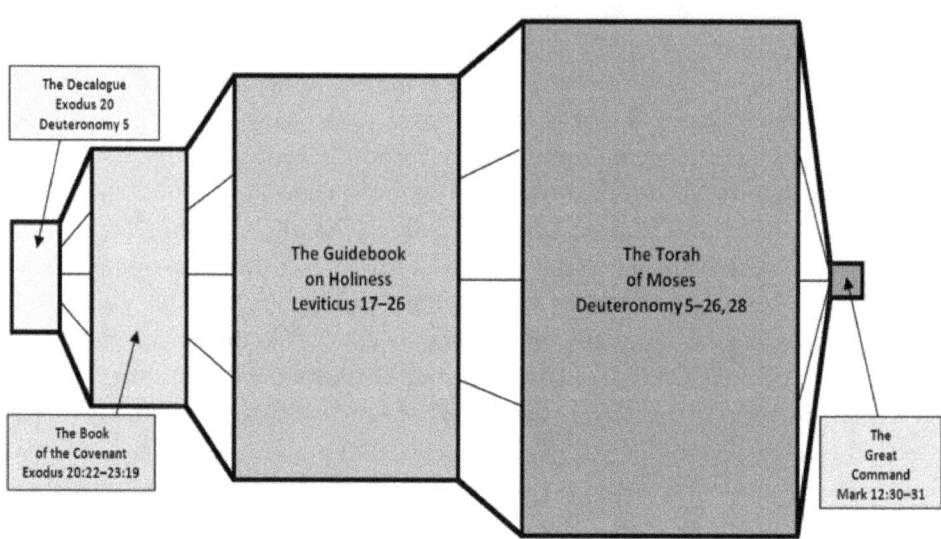

Figure 10.2
The Growth of Israel's Constitutional Tradition

Second, this approach misunderstands fundamentally the relationship between the Decalogue and the other constitutional documents (Fig. 10.2). This document is the foundation stone of a covenant whose terms will be spelled out in greater detail with subsequent revelation.[47] With ten firm declarations the document sketches a world view and covenantal ethic to be embodied by those whom YHWH has graced with redemption. This ethic is not different from that called for in the Covenant Document, the Instructions on Holiness, or the Torah of Deuteronomy. Indeed, the same epithet, "words of the covenant" (דִּבְרֵי הַבְּרִית) is used of both the Decalogue (Exod 34:28), and

---

45. In keeping with ancient custom, two identical tablets were stored in the Holy of Holies, one for remind YHWH of his covenant commitment to Israel, and the other to remind him of Israel's commitment to him, in keeping with his role as divine guarantor.

46. Some cite Hos 4:2; Jer 7:9; Ps 50:7; 81:11[10]. For discussion, see Block, "Reading the Decalogue Right to Left," 21–55; idem, "The Decalogue in the Hebrew Scriptures," 21–25.

47. A point well made by Lincoln, "From Sabbath to Lord's Day," 355–58. For fuller discussion, see Block, "Reading the Decalogue Left to Right," 42–46; "The Decalogue in the Hebrew Scriptures," 17–21.

the Torah of Moses (Deut 28:68[29:1]). Jesus summarized this ethic brilliantly by declaring: "You shall demonstrate love to YHWH your God with your whole heart/mind, your whole being, and all your resources, and you shall demonstrate love to your neighbor as yourself" (Luke 10:27; Fig. 10.3).

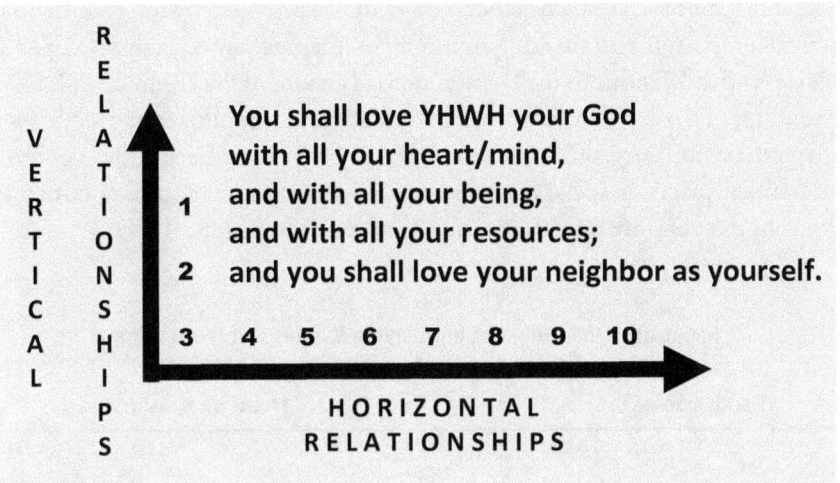

Figure 10.3
The Dimensions of the Decalogue

Craig Blomberg and Tom Schreiner rightly acknowledge that the First Testament never commands seventh-day Sabbath worship [assuming by "worship" they mean corporate ritual events], but they reject the notion that the Israelite institution has any bearing on Christians. Blomberg argues that because only the Sabbath ordinance of all the Decalogue commands is never endorsed in the New Testament, it is not part of "the law of Christ."[48] Schreiner agrees that it is not a part of the "law of Christ," but then adds that the Sabbath is part of the shadow institutions that point to a future reality fulfilled in Christ, which, like the food laws and circumcision, are rendered obsolete because in Christ the new covenant declares the end of the old covenant.[49]

The first of these arguments is flawed on two accounts. On the one hand, it is based on silence: absence of evidence is not evidence of absence. In fact, one may argue the reverse; we should limit that which is passé to what the New Testament declares to be so (like the food laws and circumcision for Gentile believers, Acts 10:9–16; 15:1–20). If the New Testament does not reiterate the Sabbath ordinance, we should assume it continues. On the other hand, and more seriously, it reflects a fundamental misunderstanding of the Sabbath command and the context in which it is embedded. The Supreme command in its two dimensions captures the essence of the ethical world view of the Decalogue (Fig. 10.3). Addressed principally to heads of households, the Decalogue seeks to ensure that they always act in the interest of others. The first two commands obviously seek the interest of YHWH, who had rescued his people from slavery in Egypt and stamped them

---

48. Blomberg, "The Sabbath as Fulfilled in Christ," in *Perspectives on the Sabbath: 4 Views*, 322–28.
49. Schreiner, 170, 174–80.

with his name. The last seven seek the interest of the members of their households and their neighbors.⁵⁰ When we recognize that the Hebrew word אָהֵב and its Greek equivalent ἀγαπάω, mean "covenant commitment demonstrated in action in the interest of the other person,"⁵¹ we understand Jesus' comment that the entire Torah and the Prophets "hang" (κρεμάννυμι) on the two commands: they summarize the ethical response to YHWH's grace in calling Israel to covenant relationship with himself.

This may seem obviously true of the first two and last seven commands, but what about the third, the Sabbath command? The evidence provided by the command is clear, but ambivalent, pointing in two different but complementary directions, depending on whether we read the Exodus or the Deuteronomy versions of the command [Table 10.1].⁵² The grounding of the Sabbath in the divine paradigm in Exodus suggests that a fundamentally vertical concern, that is, love for YHWH is at issue here. However, extending the requirement/privilege of Sabbath rest beyond the male head of the household to all who invest in its economy introduces the horizontal dimension.

Table 10.1
A Synopsis of the Sabbath Command in Exodus and Deuteronomy

Exodus 20:8–11	Deuteronomy 5:12–15
זָכוֹר אֶת־יוֹם הַשַּׁבָּת לְקַדְּשׁוֹ׃	שָׁמוֹר אֶת־יוֹם הַשַּׁבָּת לְקַדְּשׁוֹ
	כַּאֲשֶׁר צִוְּךָ יְהוָה אֱלֹהֶיךָ׃
שֵׁשֶׁת יָמִים תַּעֲבֹד	שֵׁשֶׁת יָמִים תַּעֲבֹד
וְעָשִׂיתָ כָּל־מְלַאכְתֶּךָ׃	וְעָשִׂיתָ כָּל־מְלַאכְתֶּךָ׃
וְיוֹם הַשְּׁבִיעִי שַׁבָּת לַיהוָה אֱלֹהֶיךָ	וְיוֹם הַשְּׁבִיעִי שַׁבָּת לַיהוָה אֱלֹהֶיךָ
לֹא־תַעֲשֶׂה כָל־מְלָאכָה	לֹא תַעֲשֶׂה כָל־מְלָאכָה
אַתָּה וּבִנְךָ־וּבִתֶּךָ עַבְדְּךָ וַאֲמָתְךָ	אַתָּה וּבִנְךָ־וּבִתֶּךָ וְעַבְדְּךָ־וַאֲמָתֶךָ
וּבְהֶמְתֶּךָ	וְשׁוֹרְךָ וַחֲמֹרְךָ וְכָל־בְּהֶמְתֶּךָ
וְגֵרְךָ אֲשֶׁר בִּשְׁעָרֶיךָ׃	וְגֵרְךָ אֲשֶׁר בִּשְׁעָרֶיךָ
	לְמַעַן יָנוּחַ עַבְדְּךָ וַאֲמָתְךָ כָּמוֹךָ׃
כִּי שֵׁשֶׁת־יָמִים עָשָׂה יְהוָה אֶת־הַשָּׁמַיִם וְאֶת־הָאָרֶץ	וְזָכַרְתָּ כִּי־עֶבֶד הָיִיתָ בְּאֶרֶץ מִצְרַיִם
אֶת־הַיָּם וְאֶת־כָּל־אֲשֶׁר־בָּם	וַיֹּצִאֲךָ יְהוָה אֱלֹהֶיךָ מִשָּׁם בְּיָד חֲזָקָה וּבִזְרֹעַ נְטוּיָה
וַיָּנַח בַּיּוֹם הַשְּׁבִיעִי	
עַל־כֵּן בֵּרַךְ יְהוָה אֶת־יוֹם הַשַּׁבָּת	עַל־כֵּן צִוְּךָ יְהוָה אֱלֹהֶיךָ
וַיְקַדְּשֵׁהוּ׃	לַעֲשׂוֹת אֶת־יוֹם הַשַּׁבָּת׃

50. See Block, "The Decalogue in the Hebrew Scriptures," 9–17; "Reading the Decalogue Right to Left," 30–40.

51. For a convincing discussion of אָהֵב, "love," as active and concrete demonstration of commitment to the well-being of the next person, rather than abstract, expression, see Malamat, "'You Shall Love Your Neighbor as Yourself,'" 111–15; cf. also Levenson, *The Love of God*, 1–36.

52. Hence the location of #3 in Fig. 10.3.

Exodus 20:8–11	Deuteronomy 5:12–15
Take note of the Sabbath day by sanctifying it.	Keep the Sabbath day by sanctifying it, as YHWH your God has commanded you.
For six days you may labor and do all your work, but the seventh day is a sabbath to YHWH your God.	For six days you may labor and do all your work, but the seventh day is a sabbath to YHWH your God.
[On it] you may not do any work— you, your son or daughter, your male or female slave, your livestock, or the foreigner who is within your gates.	[On it] you may not do any work— you, your son or daughter, your male or female slave, your ox or donkey, or any of your livestock, or the foreigner who is within your gates, so that your male and female slaves may rest as you do.
For in six days YHWH made the heavens and the earth, the sea, and everything in them; and he rested on the seventh day. Therefore, YHWH blessed the Sabbath day and sanctified it.	Remember that you were a slave in the land of Egypt, and YHWH your God brought you out of there with a strong hand and an outstretched arm. Therefore, YHWH your God has commanded you to observe the Sabbath day.

Whereas the Exodus version offers a profoundly theological and vertical basis for Israel's observance of the Sabbath, Deuteronomy strengthens the institution's horizontal ethical significance by specifying the draft livestock as donkeys and oxen and inserting a motive clause: "so they may rest (יָנוּחַ) as you [the head of the household] do." Instead of appealing to YHWH's creation of the world in six days and his resting on the seventh as the paradigm for Israel's week, the Deuteronomic Decalogue appeals to Israel's memory of their experience in Egypt—working without the benefit of a Sabbath—and YHWH's gracious rescue from this oppression to strengthen the compassionate ethical stance of the command. This is not a cultic ordinance foreshadowing a future reality, but reflects the heart of the Supreme command: the head of the household is to demonstrate "love" by ensuring the well-being of all the members of the domestic unit, children, servants, and draft animals. As is the case with all Israel's "laws"—with the exceptions that the New Testament explicitly identifies as shadow cultic institutions, of which the Sabbath is not one—instead of asking, "As a Christian, do I need to keep this law?" we should ask, "How does God expect me to keep this law?" The Sabbath ordinance is first and foremost a humanitarian, rather than cultic or ritual ordinance.

4. *Israel's seventh-day Sabbath was a fundamentally covenantal observance.*

This is suggested by embedding the command in the Decalogue, whose terms are identified elsewhere as "his [i.e., YHWH's] covenant" (בְּרִיתוֹ), written on tablets of stone (Deut 4:13), which are themselves called "the tablets of the covenant" (לֻחֹת הַבְּרִית, Deut 9:9, 11, 15; Heb 4:4 [αἱ πλάκες τῆς διαθήκης]), and "the tablets of the covenant stipulations" (לֻחֹת הָעֵדָת, Exod 31:18; 32:15, 34:29), or simply "the covenant stipulations" (הָעֵדָת, Exod

25:16),⁵³ and by storing them in the sacred box, identified as "the ark of the covenant [of YHWH your God]" (אֲרוֹן בְּרִית־יְהוָה אֱלֹהֵיכֶם).⁵⁴

While the Decalogue is clearly a covenant document, Exod 31:13–17 highlights the covenantal significance of the Sabbath command in particular:

Exodus 31:13–17

אַךְ אֶת־שַׁבְּתֹתַי תִּשְׁמֹרוּ	You must keep my Sabbaths,
כִּי אוֹת הִוא בֵּינִי וּבֵינֵיכֶם לְדֹרֹתֵיכֶם	for it is a sign between me and you throughout your generations,
לָדַעַת כִּי אֲנִי יְהוָה מְקַדִּשְׁכֶם׃	that you may know that I am YHWH who sets you apart.
וּשְׁמַרְתֶּם אֶת־הַשַּׁבָּת	So you shall observe the Sabbath,
כִּי קֹדֶשׁ הִוא לָכֶם	for it is holy to you.
מְחַלְלֶיהָ מוֹת יוּמָת	Whoever profanes it must be put to death.
כִּי כָּל־הָעֹשֶׂה בָהּ מְלָאכָה	If anyone does work on it,
וְנִכְרְתָה הַנֶּפֶשׁ הַהִוא מִקֶּרֶב עַמֶּיהָ׃	that person will be cut off from his people.
שֵׁשֶׁת יָמִים יֵעָשֶׂה מְלָאכָה	For six days you may do your work,
וּבַיּוֹם הַשְּׁבִיעִי שַׁבַּת שַׁבָּתוֹן	but on the seventh day, there must be a Sabbath of complete rest,
קֹדֶשׁ לַיהוָה	dedicated to YHWH.
כָּל־הָעֹשֶׂה מְלָאכָה בְּיוֹם הַשַּׁבָּת	Anyone who does work on the Sabbath day
מוֹת יוּמָת׃	must surely be put to death.
וְשָׁמְרוּ בְנֵי־יִשְׂרָאֵל אֶת־הַשַּׁבָּת	The Israelites must keep the Sabbath,
לַעֲשׂוֹת אֶת־הַשַּׁבָּת לְדֹרֹתָם	by observing it throughout their generations
בְּרִית עוֹלָם׃	as an eternal [irrevocable] covenant.
בֵּינִי וּבֵין בְּנֵי יִשְׂרָאֵל אוֹת הִוא לְעֹלָם	It is an eternal sign between me and the Israelites,
כִּי־שֵׁשֶׁת יָמִים עָשָׂה יְהוָה	for in six days YHWH made
אֶת־הַשָּׁמַיִם וְאֶת־הָאָרֶץ	the heavens and the earth,
וּבַיּוֹם הַשְּׁבִיעִי שָׁבַת וַיִּנָּפַשׁ׃	but on the seventh day he rested and was refreshed.

Many have rightly noted how tightly the Sabbath is tied to YHWH's covenant with Israel.⁵⁵ However, their dismissal of the Sabbath as a shadow feature of a defunct covenant glosses over significant contrary evidence.

First, the First Testament applies the same vocabulary of permanence and irrevocability to the covenant YHWH made with Israel at Sinai that it uses of other covenants, which are generally acknowledged to be eternal. Like the covenants made with the cosmos (Gen 9:16; cf. Isa 24:5), Abraham (1 Chr 16:15–18; Ps 105:8–11; cf. Gen 17:7, 13, 19; cf. 9:16), and David (2 Sam 23:5), the Israelite covenant⁵⁶ is characterized as a בְּרִית עוֹלָם, "eternal/irrevocable covenant" (Exod 31:16; Lev 24:8; Ezek 16:60). Other texts

---

53. On this interpretation of הָעֵדֻת, see Block, "Reading the Decalogue Right to Left," 27–28.

54. Deut 31:26; Josh 3:3–14; 6:6; Judg 20:27; 1 Sam 4:4–5; 2 Sam 15:24; 1 Chr 15:24–29; 2 Chr 5:2; 16:6; Heb 9:4 (τὴν κιβωτὸν τῆς διαθήκης).

55. "Good-bye and Hello," 164–70.

56. Because we identify other covenants by the name of the earthly covenant partner (i.e., cosmic, Abrahamic, Davidic), what others call the Mosaic or Sinai covenant I call the Israelite covenant.

speak of YHWH never breaking his covenant (Judg 2:1), taking his covenant into account forever (יִזְכֹּר לְעוֹלָם בְּרִיתוֹ, Ps 111:5), commanding his covenant forever (Ps 111:9), his eternal covenant faithfulness to Israel (חֶסֶד עוֹלָם, Isa 54:8), and they apply the constancy of the universe to YHWH's covenant with Israel (Isa 54:9–10; Jer 31:35–37). While access to the benefits of all covenants was conditioned on faith demonstrated in obedience, a covenant declared to be eternal (עַד עוֹלָם) cannot be revoked or terminated (cf. Judg 2:1; see Fig. 10.4).[57]

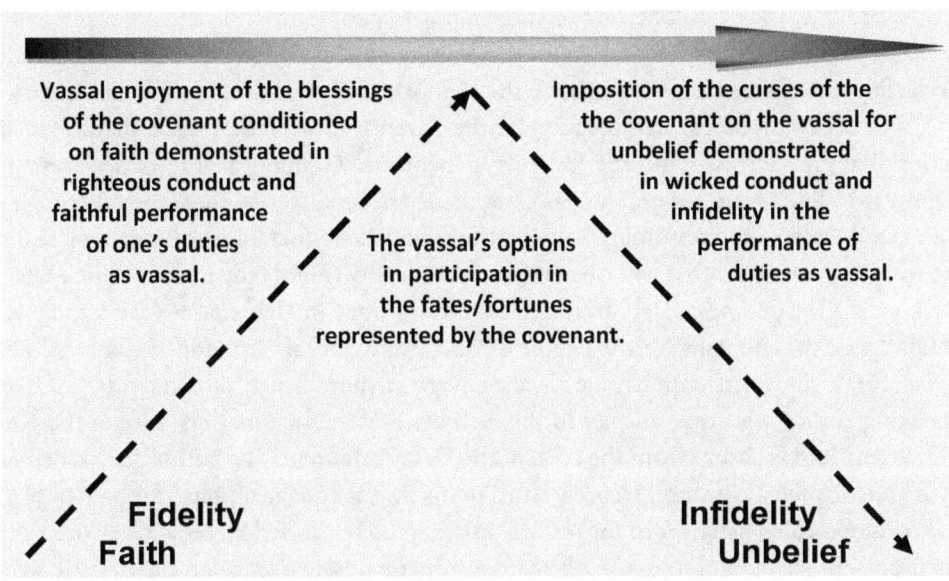

Figure 10.4
God's Irrevocable Covenant Commitment

Second, this interpretation wrongfully drives a wedge between the covenant made with Abraham and the covenant established with Israel at Sinai/Horeb. The covenant ceremony at Sinai (Exod 19–24) involved not the replacement but the establishment (הֵקִים, Exod 19:5–6) of the Abrahamic covenant in fulfillment of YHWH's promise in Gen 17:6–8; (cf. 18:19). Indeed, not only does the book of Deuteronomy merge the Abrahamic and Israelite covenants,[58] but the author of the patriarchal narratives also casts Abraham as faithful to the covenant made at Sinai (cf. Gen 22:12; 26:4–5),[59] and as the embodiment of covenant righteousness as called for in Moses' final addresses to his people in Deuteronomy (cf. Deut 6:25; 10:12–11:1; 16:20).

Third, in appealing to the citation of Jer 31:27–34 in Heb 8:7–12 to contrast the new covenant established by Jesus Christ with the "first [covenant]" and to declare the absolute end of the Israelite covenant, they fail to distinguish between the shadow institutions granted by YHWH to Israel as means of maintaining the covenant relationship with him and the essence of the covenant itself, for which the new covenant offers

---

57. Contra Schreiner, ibid., 167.
58. Hwang, *The Rhetoric of Remembrance*, 232.
59. On which see chapter 6, "In the Tradition of Moses," above, pp. 120–22.

nothing new. Many Israelites "under" the Israelite covenant were *de facto* new covenant believers as described by Jeremiah: the Torah was written on their hearts;[60] they enjoyed the relationship promised by the covenant formula, "I will be their God and they will be my people";[61] they knew YHWH,[62] and they delighted in the forgiveness of sins.[63] These features are not new either in Jeremiah 31 or in the New Testament. The only new element that Jeremiah envisioned was that "all of them" (כֻּלָּם) would experience these graces (Jer 31:34; Heb 8:11). But Jeremiah's vision was quite parochial. Like Moses in Deut 30:1–10 and Paul in Rom 11:26–27, the prophet anticipated the day when "all Israel will be saved"; that is, the boundaries of physical and spiritual Israel will be virtually coterminous. In citing this text, the author of Hebrews declares that the work of Christ provides the basis for God's relationship with people anytime and anywhere; both retrospectively and prospectively. With the coming of Christ, that which had been made accessible to Israelite believers through the shadow institutions was fulfilled in Christ.

Fourth, Schreiner's identification of the seventh-day Sabbath as a shadow institution like the sacrifices and the festivals is incorrect. Granted, Hebrews declares that believers in Jesus have entered his rest, but using the language of metaphor theory, just because a First Testament image (vehicle) functions as a metaphor of a greater reality (tenor) does not mean that with the arrival of the reality (tenor) the image (vehicle) itself disappears. The author of Hebrews declares the contrary in Heb 4:9, "So then, there is a Sabbath rest that remains for the people of God" (ἄρα ἀπολείπεται σαββατισμὸς τῷ λαῷ τοῦ θεοῦ).[64] The word σαββατισμὸς is a neologism [new word] fabricated by a Greek speaking author who was steeped in the Hebrew Bible. It occurs only here in the New Testament, and is absent from the LXX of the First Testament. The author has transliterated and adapted a common Hebrew word to his own language and used it here in place of κατάπαυσις, his usual word for rest. In so doing he reminded Hebrew Christians that their present participation in the ultimate rest made possible through the priestly work of Christ does not mean they are denied the gift of the weekly Sabbath.[65] If (and this is

---

60. Implied in Gen 26:5 (Abraham); Num 14:24 (Caleb). It is also suggested by the reference to the circumcision of the heart as a metaphor for the internalization of faith in Lev 26:41; Deut 10:16; 30:6; Jer 4:4. For other expressions of this see Deut 6:6; Ps 19:7–13[6–12]; 37:31; 40:8[7]; 119:11; cf. 51:12[10]; Prov 3:1–3; 7:3; Isa 51:7.

61. The purpose of the new covenant is identical to the Israelite covenant: to establish relationship (cf. Lev 26:12; Exod 29:45; Jer 24:7; 2 Cor 6:16; Rev 21:3).

62. Exod 33:13; cf. Judg 2:10; 1 Sam 2:12; 3:7; Isa 19:21; Isa 45:5; Jer 2:8; 4:22; 9:2[3], 6[5], 24[23]; 10:25; 24:7; Ezek 38:16; Hos 2:22[20]; 5:4; 8:2; 13:4; Ps 36:11[10]; 79:6; 87:4; Job 18:21; 24:1; Prov 3:6; Dan 11:32, 38; 1 Chr 28:98.

63. The present verb is used of forgiveness experienced long before this dozens of times. God is always the subject. Absolute: Num 14:20; 1 Kgs 8:30, 39; 2 Kgs 24:4; Isa 55:7; Amos 7:2; Lam 3:42; Dan 9:19; 2 Chr 6:21, 30. With *lamedh* of person: Num 30:6, 9, 13; Deut 29:19[20]; 1 Kgs 8:50; 2 Kgs 5:18; Jer 5:1, 7; 50:20; 2 Chr 6:39. With *lamedh* of thing: Exod 34:9; Num 14:19; 1 Kgs 8:34, 36; Jer 31:34; 33:8; 36:3; Ps 25:11; 103:3; 2 Chr 6:25, 27; 7:14. With *lamedh* of person and *beth* of thing: 2 Kgs 5:18. Niphal "to be forgiven" with *lamedh*: Lev 4:20, 26, 31, 35; 5:10, 13, 16, 18, 26[6:7]; 19:22; Num 15:22, 23, 28.

64. The verb, ἀπολείπω, "to remain [in place]," should be interpreted in its most natural sense and in keeping with its usage in 4:6 and 10:26.

65. For more detailed defense of this interpretation, see McCarty, "The Seventh Day Sabbath," 24–28; contra Schreiner, "Good-bye and Hello," 181; Blomberg, "The Sabbath as Fulfilled in Christ,"

a significant "if") in Galatians Paul appears to speak of the seventh-day Sabbath as an external marker of Jewish identity that is irrelevant for Gentile believers in Jesus, he probably does not mean the Sabbath in principle, but the burdensome regulations that Pharisaic and Halachic tradition had imposed on Jews in their overly scrupulous efforts to "fence" the Sabbath law.[66]

Returning to Exod 31:12–17, the tight linkage of the Sabbath to the covenant explains the severity of the punishment for those who violate the Sabbath. Because this was the sign (אוֹת) of the covenant, to go out and engage in normal workaday activities was to reject the covenant, and to repudiate one's own standing in covenant relationship with YHWH. Those who profane (חִלֵּל) the holy day (קֹדֶשׁ), that is, treat it as ordinary, have renounced the grace of YHWH demonstrated in their salvation from bondage in Egypt and in their status as the sanctified covenant people of YHWH. For this reason, the violation of the Sabbath was as serious an offense as idolatry, and tantamount to "hating" (שָׂנֵא) YHWH (Exod 31:14–15; cf. 20:4–6; Deut 5:8–10). Jeremiah 17:19–27 offers a striking application of this principle. The prophet uses carrying a load (מַשָּׂא, presumably produce from the field or merchandise to be sold or traded) out of one's house and through the gates of Jerusalem as shorthand for all the work (מְלָאכָה, v. 24) involved in everyday labors. He invokes the blessings of the covenant on those who "sanctify the Sabbath day" (לְקַדֵּשׁ אֶת־יוֹם הַשַּׁבָּת), not by participating in worship, but by refusing to do this work on "the Sabbath day" (vv. 24–26). He invokes the covenant curses on those who perform this sort of economic work on the holy day, and in so doing refuse to "sanctify the Sabbath day."

Isaiah 56:1–8 celebrates the covenantal significance of keeping the Sabbath:

כֹּה אָמַר יְהוָה	1	Here is what YHWH has said,
שִׁמְרוּ מִשְׁפָּט וַעֲשׂוּ צְדָקָה		Preserve justice and execute righteousness,
כִּי־קְרוֹבָה יְשׁוּעָתִי לָבוֹא		for my salvation is coming soon,
וְצִדְקָתִי לְהִגָּלוֹת׃		and my righteousness will be revealed.
אַשְׁרֵי אֱנוֹשׁ יַעֲשֶׂה־זֹּאת	2	How privileged is the one who does this,
וּבֶן־אָדָם יַחֲזִיק בָּהּ		and any human being who holds fast to it,
שֹׁמֵר שַׁבָּת מֵחַלְּלוֹ		who keeps the Sabbath without profaning it,
וְשֹׁמֵר יָדוֹ מֵעֲשׂוֹת כָּל־רָע׃		and refuses to do any evil!
וְאַל־יֹאמַר בֶּן־הַנֵּכָר	3	Do not let a foreigner
הַנִּלְוָה אֶל־יְהוָה לֵאמֹר		who has joined himself to YHWH say,
הַבְדֵּל יַבְדִּילַנִי יְהוָה מֵעַל עַמּוֹ		"YHWH will surely exclude me from His people";
וְאַל־יֹאמַר הַסָּרִיס		and do not let the eunuch say,
הֵן אֲנִי עֵץ יָבֵשׁ׃		"Look, I am a dried-up tree."

350, as well as his response to McCarty, pp. 85–86

66. Analogous to Paul's use of τὰ ἔργα νόμου, "the works of the law" (Rom 3:20, 28; Gal 2:16; 3:2, 5, 10). On "works of the law" as external Jewish identity markers, see Dunn, "Works of the Law and the Curse of the Law (Galatians 3,10–14)," 528; idem, *Jesus, Paul, and the Law*, 196; N. T. Wright, *The New Testament and the People of God*, 237–38. For rabbinic treatment of the Sabbath regulations, see *Mishnah Shabbat*, 7.

כִּי־כֹה אָמַר יְהוָה	4	For here is what YHWH has said,
לַסָּרִיסִים אֲשֶׁר יִשְׁמְרוּ אֶת־שַׁבְּתוֹתַי		"For the eunuchs who keep my Sabbaths,
וּבָחֲרוּ בַּאֲשֶׁר חָפָצְתִּי		and choose what pleases me,
וּמַחֲזִיקִים בִּבְרִיתִי:		and hold firmly to my covenant,
וְנָתַתִּי לָהֶם בְּבֵיתִי וּבְחוֹמֹתַי	5	I will give them, within my house and within my walls,
יָד וָשֵׁם טוֹב מִבָּנִים וּמִבָּנוֹת		a memorial and a name better than sons and daughters.
שֵׁם עוֹלָם אֶתֶּן־לוֹ		I will give each of them an everlasting name
אֲשֶׁר לֹא יִכָּרֵת:		that will never be cut off.
וּבְנֵי הַנֵּכָר הַנִּלְוִים עַל־יְהוָה	6	And the foreigners, who join themselves to YHWH
לְשָׁרְתוֹ וּלְאַהֲבָה אֶת־שֵׁם יְהוָה		to minister to him and to love the name of YHWH,
לִהְיוֹת לוֹ לַעֲבָדִים		to become his servants—
כָּל־שֹׁמֵר שַׁבָּת מֵחַלְּלוֹ		all who keep the Sabbath without profaning it,
וּמַחֲזִיקִים בִּבְרִיתִי:		and who hold firmly to my covenant—
וַהֲבִיאוֹתִים אֶל־הַר קָדְשִׁי	7	I will bring them to my holy mountain
וְשִׂמַּחְתִּים בְּבֵית תְּפִלָּתִי		giving them reason to celebrate in my house of prayer.
עוֹלֹתֵיהֶם וְזִבְחֵיהֶם לְרָצוֹן עַל־מִזְבְּחִי		Their burnt offerings and sacrifices will be accepted on my altar,
כִּי בֵיתִי בֵּית־תְּפִלָּה יִקָּרֵא לְכָל־הָעַמִּים:		for my house will be called a house of prayer for all nations—
נְאֻם אֲדֹנָי יְהוִה	8	the declaration of the Lord YHWH,
מְקַבֵּץ נִדְחֵי יִשְׂרָאֵל		who gathers the dispersed of Israel—
עוֹד אֲקַבֵּץ עָלָיו לְנִקְבָּצָיו:		"I will gather others, besides those already gathered."

5. Israel's seventh-day Sabbath was to be received as a gift that made Israel the envy of the world.

We find no parallels to the Israelite seventh-day Sabbath in the literary records of the ancient world. But this was but one of the many gifts that the Israelites received from their divine redeemer and that symbolized their status as YHWH's covenant people, elevated high above the nations "for praise, fame, and glory" (לִתְהִלָּה וּלְשֵׁם וּלְתִפְאָרֶת, Deut 26:19). On the one hand, this privilege involved Israel's own "praise, fame, and glory," but on the other, this was a derived glory, reflecting the "praise, fame, and glory" of the One whose name they bore. Indeed, the book of Deuteronomy twice anticipates the amazement the nations would express when they observed the Israelites:

> [5] See, I have taught ordinances and judgments just as YHWH has charged me, that you might observe them in the land that you are about to enter and occupy. [6] So keep them and do them, for this is [a mark of] your wisdom and discernment in the plain view of the peoples, who, when they hear all these ordinances, will say, "What a wise and discerning people is this great nation!" [7] Indeed, what [other] great nation has a god so near to it as YHWH our God is whenever we call to him? [8] And what [other] great nation has ordinances and judgments as righteous as this entire Torah that I am setting before you today? (Deut 4:5–8).

⁸ YHWH will command the blessing upon you in your storehouses, and in all that you undertake; he will bless you in the land that YHWH your God is giving you. ⁹ YHWH will establish you as his holy people, as he has sworn to you, if you keep the commands of YHWH your God and walk in his ways. ¹⁰ Then all the peoples of the earth will see that you are branded with the name of YHWH [lit. "YHWH's name is read/called over you"] and they will be in awe of you. (Deut 28:8–10).[67]

Theological and Practical Reflections

The Sabbath was but one of the graciously bestowed benefits that came with being the people of YHWH. It was to be accepted with gratitude, joy, humility, modesty, and love—that is, covenant commitment demonstrated in life that honored the divine Suzerain, whose name they bore. If we assume that the Sabbath was essentially a domestic observance, rather than a communal ritual event, what significance did it have and how would it have been observed?

First, at the most earthly level, the seventh-day Sabbath served a humanitarian agenda, offering Israelite workers an opportunity to catch their breath and be refreshed for the work required in the week to follow. To be human is to work; this is not a consequence of the fall. However, the exhaustion that comes from work is a penalty we pay for our rebellion. This happens not only because the body itself is subject to fatigue and pain in a post-fall world, but also because the environment we are charged to guard and serve (Gen 2:15) resists and fights against our lordship (3:17–18). In our day, we are like rats in an overcrowded cage, competing for space and for resources. The Sabbath invites us to slow down and live!

The shape of Christian observance of the Sabbath may vary, depending on context and the nature of one's work. For ministers and other church workers, Sunday is the heaviest day of the week. Obviously, these folks will need to look upon a different day of the week as the Lord's gift to them. For those of us whose work consists of reading and research, or sitting at the computer most of the week, reading heavy theological treatises on the Sabbath is no break. I am ethnically Dutch, so for me the most therapeutic activity is gardening, digging in the dirt, pulling weeds, dead-heading wilted flowers, even mowing the lawn. But I refuse to do the last of these on the Sabbath, because the noise of my mower might disturb my neighbor, for whom the Sabbath means an afternoon nap.

In keeping with the humanitarian nature of Israel's Sabbath this institution invites to give ourselves to compassionate action. For heads of households, this means ensuring the members of the family participate fully in the Sabbath. For those who are heads over others in other social contexts, this means ensuring the well-being of all in our employ. As followers of Christ, we exhibit his righteousness when we call those who labor and are burdened with the work and cares of this world to find rest in him (Matt 11:28). And as Jesus himself demonstrated through his healing miracles on the Sabbath, there is no

---

67. On Israel "bearing the name of YHWH," see now Imes, *Bearing YHWH's Name at Sinai*.

better context in which to proclaim the Lord's deliverance through acts of mercy and in so doing invite them to participate in the life to come.

Second, by rooting the Sabbath in the God's own actions in the week of creation, the Exodus version of the Decalogue presents the Sabbath as an opportunity for Israelites to declare their fundamentally theological perspective on life. To be sure, in contrast to modern western materialists, all ancient peoples assumed the involvement of the gods in all of life, but by observing the Sabbath Israelites declared publicly their conviction that the universe has its origin in their God, YHWH. Indeed, although covenantal signs like the rainbow (Gen 9:17) and circumcision (Gen 17:11) served primarily as reminders of the relationship for the parties to the covenant, the Sabbath invited the world to observe the benefits of covenant relationship; it symbolized both Israel's status as a city on a hill (Deut 26:19) and her mission of demonstrating to the watching world—still languishing under the curse—the shalom that divine grace achieves.

Psalm 92, identified as "A Psalm, a song for the Sabbath day" (מִזְמוֹר שִׁיר לְיוֹם הַשַּׁבָּת, v. 1), captures the mood and the substance of Sabbath observance. The first person singular pronouns that dominate the psalm reflect the domestic if not individual nature of Sabbath observance, though appropriately, when the psalmist's attention turns to the central sanctuary, he shifts into the plural collective mode (v. 13[12]). The Sabbath presents Israelites a chance without distraction to bless YHWH for his covenant faithfulness (v. 3[2]),[68] for the magnificence of his handiwork,[69] his sovereignty over his enemies (vv. 8–10[7–9]), his actions on the psalmist's behalf (vv. 11–12[10–11]). The psalm concludes by declaring his optimism regarding the future because his security is in his "rock," who is uncompromisingly upright (יָשָׁר, v. 16[15]). By sanctifying one day in seven faithful Israelites reminded themselves that time itself is sacred. For three or four days after the Sabbath they lived in the afterglow of the moment, and then come mid-week they would find new energy in living in anticipation of the sacred day.

Third, apart from declaring a theological perspective on life generally, keeping the Sabbath was an act of faith. Indeed, in the first reference to human beings observing the Sabbath it is presented as a test (נִסָּה) whether or not the Israelites would trust YHWH to provide for them on the Sabbath and whether or not they would faithfully obey his commands (Exod 16:4). Faithful Israelites received the rest it offered as a gift, and trusted YHWH so to bless their work the other six days that their needs on the Sabbath would be more than satisfied by YHWH. The Sabbath afforded the Israelites an opportunity every seven days to enjoy the fruits of their labor, and to bless YHWH as the source of their well-being. Deuteronomy 8:11–29 highlights the importance of crediting YHWH for any successes one enjoys and presents a severe warning to all who forget to credit him

---

68. Whereas חֶסֶד and אֱמוּנָה occur together only in the Psalms (36:6[5]; 40:11[10]; 88:12[11]; 89:2, 3, 25, 34, 50[89:1, 2, 24, 33, 49]; 92:3[2]; 98:3; 100:5), both in the Psalms and elsewhere חֶסֶד is more commonly linked with אֱמֶת (e.g., Gen 24:27, 49; Exod 34:6; 2 Sam 2:6; Ps. 25:10; etc.).

69. It is unclear whether מַעֲשֵׂי יָדֶיךָ, "the works of your hands (v. 92:5[4]) and מַעֲשֶׂיךָ, "your works" (v. 6[5]) refer to creation (cf. Ps 8:7[6]; 19:2[1]; 102:26[25]; 143:5;) or to YHWH's specific actions on behalf of the psalmist (cf. Ps 28:5; 111:7; Isa 5:12; 64:8), though the plural form may support the former.

for their success. Indeed, in his farewell addresses Moses repeatedly spoke of YHWH blessing the work of human hands: (Deut 2:7; 14:29; 15:10; 16:15; 24:19; 28:12).

But this raises the question: What is meant by the "work of one's hands"? The expression, מַעֲשֵׂה יְדֵי [הָ]אָדָם, the work of human hands," often refers to idols that people manufacture.[70] This sort of work is forbidden on other grounds at any time (Deut 4:15–24; 5:6–10). Based on the divine paradigm in Gen 2:1–3, where God's work is identified as מְלָאכָה and consists of the things he makes, this would certainly involve exercising human dominion over the earth by manufacturing things,[71] but the expression is used much more broadly of commercial activity/travels (Ps 107:23; Prov 18:9; 22:29), and the daily work performed in food production, tending animals, building houses, transporting goods (Jer 17:19–27); in short, the workaday efforts needed to maintain and sustain life. The Sabbath is profaned, not so much by failing to attend religious assemblies, or wrongly performing religious rituals, but by imposing on it workaday actions.

Jeremiah expressly declares that when people heed YHWH's voice by not transporting goods or tools (מַשָּׂא) on the Sabbath day they have "sanctified" (קָדַשׁ) it (17:24), and when they refuse to heed his voice on the Sabbath they have not "sanctified" it (v. 27). Although the Jewish tradition "fenced" this command with all sorts of absurd regulations,[72] Isaiah 56:1–8 is more general, linking "profaning (חִלֵּל) the Sabbath" with "doing any evil" (עָשָׂה כָל־רָע, v. 2), whereas "keeping my Sabbaths" (שָׁמַר אֶת־שַׁבְּתוֹתַי) involves "choosing [to do] whatever pleases me [i.e., YHWH]" (בָּחַר בַּאֲשֶׁר חָפָצְתִּי) and "holding fast to my covenant" (הֶחֱזִיק בִּבְרִיתִי, v. 4). Verse 6 casts the issue negatively: those who are joined (הַנִּלְוִים) to YHWH, minister (שֵׁרֵת) to him, love (אָהַב) the name of YHWH, function as his vassals (עָבַד), and hold firmly (הֶחֱזִיק) to his covenant do not "profane" (חִלֵּל) the Sabbath. It is not that the forbidden activities are evil in themselves; on the contrary, performed on the other six days they represent sacred acts of true worship.[73] In effect, by functioning as divine viceroys (images of God) people sanctify (קָדַשׁ) "profane time." However, if performed in a context that YHWH has declared particularly holy, they profane (חִלֵּל) "sacred time" (cf. Fig. 10.5, below, page 222).

This does not mean that no work is allowed on the Sabbath. The priests at the sanctuary presented special Sabbath day offerings (Num 28:9–10); Ezek 46:1 requires opening the eastern gate of the inner court of the temple on the Sabbath day—a gate that was closed on the other six days; and Exod 12:16 allows for work involved in preparing the Passover meal, which happened on one of the highest and holiest sabbaths of the year. Even when food was prepared on the day before the Sabbath, it would still require some work to spread it out on the table, and to remove dishes after the meal. But eating of the fruits of human labor while strolling on a path that happened to run through a

---

70. Deut 4:28; 2 Kgs 19:18; 2 Chr 32:19; Ps 115:4; 135:15; Isa 37:19; Ho 14:4; Mic 5:12; Jer 1:16; cf. Isa 2:8. Note also מַעֲשֵׂה יְדֵי חָרָשׁ, "the work of the hands of a craftsman": Deut 27:15; Jer 10:3, 9; Hos 13:2.

71. I.e., craftsmanship: Exod 31:1–5; 35:31; 38:24; 39:43; Neh 4:9, 16; 5:16; 6:3,9; 13:30; 1 Chr 22:15; 28:21; 29:1.

72. *Mishnah Shabbat*, 7.

73. Elsewhere I have explained true worship as "reverential acts of submission and homage before the divine Suzerain in response to his gracious revelation of himself and in accord with his will." Block, *For the Glory of God*, 23. In this volume I develop this thesis in detail.

field of grain (cf. Matt 12:1–8) differs fundamentally from preparing the field for planting or harvesting the crop, or transporting the produce to market (Jer 17:27).

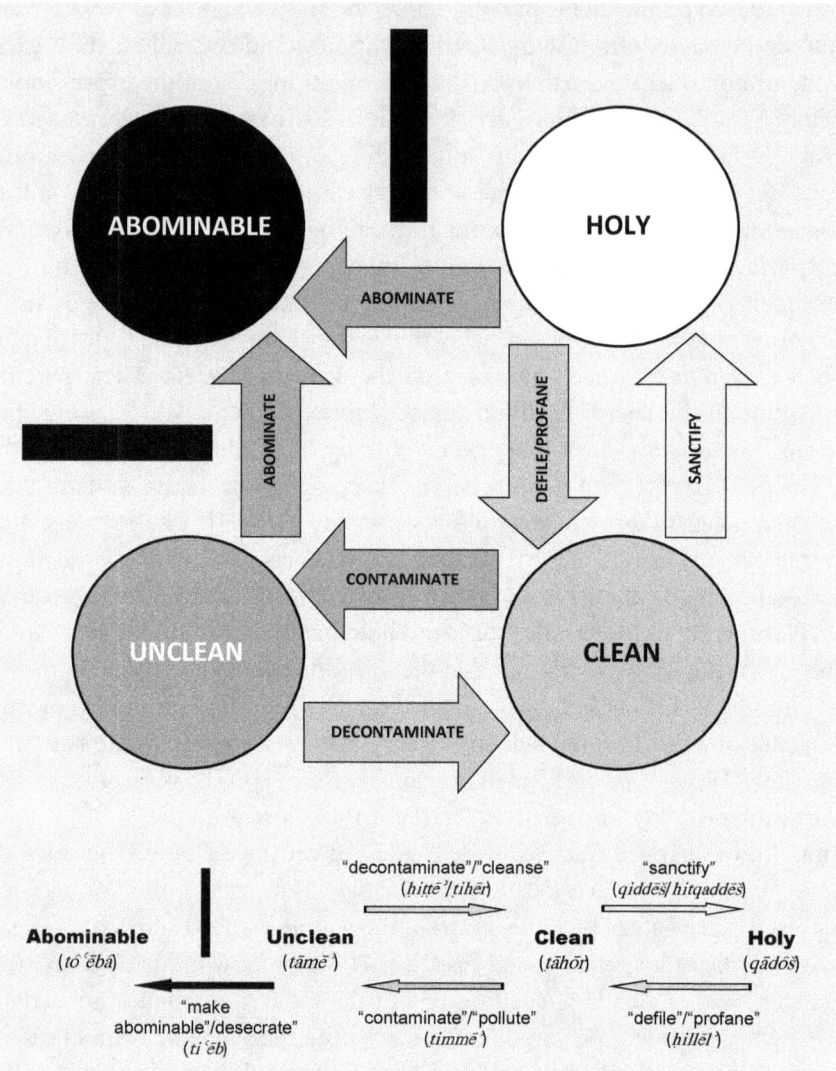

Figure 10.5
The Sacred-Clean-Unclean-Abominable Continuum

While Jewish tradition fenced the command not to light a fire on the Sabbath (Exod 35:3) in many strange ways,[74] presumably because prior to the invention of matches lighting a fire involved arduous work, the ordinance was probably never intended to prevent people from using oil lamps on the Sabbath. Jesus caught the spirit of the Sabbath perfectly, when he declared that the Sabbath was made for people and not the reverse (Mark 2:27), and when refused to rebuke his disciples for removing grain from the heads

---

74. Such as installing "Sabbath elevators" in hotels that stop on every floor on the Sabbath to prevent turning on the light on the button that identifies the floor one desires.

of wheat while on a stroll on the Sabbath (Mark 2:23–26). In emergencies, like when a child or ox falls in a well, it is not a violation of the Sabbath to rescue them (Luke 14:5). Indeed, Jesus not only used this illustration to explain his healing of the critically ill man on the Sabbath (vv. 1–4), but he seemed to go out of his way to provoke the Jewish leaders by performing such acts of mercy on the Sabbath.

Psalm 90:17 acknowledges that every success in human labor depends upon YHWH's blessing/establishment of the work of our hands. The institution of the Sabbath afforded a chance every seven days to reflect on YHWH's blessing during the past week and to pray for his continue favor on the work of the coming week. But this was to be more than an exercise in fertility religion. As at the time of the presentation of the first fruits offerings (Deut 16:1–5), with its roots in the Israel's experience of redemption from slavery (5:15), the weekly Sabbath invited the observer to look all the way back to the beginning of their history.

Fourth, if Israel's seventh-day Sabbath was a fundamentally covenantal observance, it was the sign to YHWH and the world that those in this quiet and tranquil household belonged to YHWH, and they were celebrating that relationship by demonstrating their trust in him to take care of them not only the seventh day, but throughout the year. By observing one day in seven as holy to YHWH Christians may declare to YHWH our trust in him, and we declare to the world around us that our primary identity is defined spiritually, rather than materially. The more secular and atheistic the world around us becomes, the greater the opportunity for witness. We would be in a different space if we allowed ourselves one day in seven to reflect theologically on the origins of the universe in God's creative act (Exodus), and in his recreation of a new people through his magnificent acts of redemption (Deuteronomy).

Finally, the Sabbath both reminded Israelites of the shalom of Eden past and symbolized the Edenic future that awaits the cosmos as a whole. In the beginning, God installed humankind as vice-regents in a perfect environment, inviting them to enjoy all the delights of the garden. The triangular relationship involving YHWH, Israel, and the land of Canaan as their special grant (נַחֲלָה) was a microcosm of the original ideal world (Fig. 10.6). By celebrating the Sabbath Israelites looked back to the world from which all humanity came and looked forward to the time when all humanity would share in the perpetual Sabbath rest. The Sabbath symbolizes the blessed privilege we enjoy in this life, it also reminds us of the eschatological Sabbath that awaits the cosmos at the end of the ages.

Figure 10.6
The Relationship between the Cosmic and Israelite Covenants

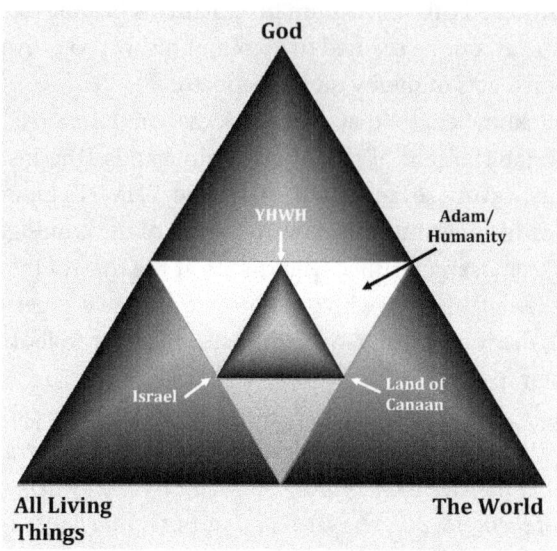

Conclusion

Having laid out the significance of the Sabbath for truly faithful Israelites of the First Testament, we begin to see how off base we are when we ask, "Do Christians need to keep the Sabbath?" To many the Sabbath is another burden that we dump when we trust in Jesus. How sad! Why would we protest our heavenly Father giving us this blessed gift? Why would we not want to keep it? This is an awesome gift! The Lord invites us to put aside the cares of this world one day in every seven, and he promises to take care of the seventh. The Lord invites us to celebrate his day to day grace and goodness in our lives, but also to remember how our privileged story begins. If Israel's seventh-day Sabbath was to be received as a gift that made Israel the envy of the world, the celebration of this day by Christians offers a glorious opportunity to witness to the grace of God not only in the gift of the Sabbath, but the Sabbath becomes a symbol of the broader privilege we enjoy in knowing the will of God clearly and unequivocally. Of course, modern Western materialists and humanists are not concerned about knowing the will of God, but we need to be aware that in this regard they are out of step with the majority the human population through the centuries.

The time has come to recover a biblical theology of Sabbath rest, which means on the one hand, putting an end to legalistic fencing of the day with all sorts of do's and don'ts *a la* the Pharisees of Jesus and Paul's day, and on the other hand to putting an end to the stubborn anti-Sabbatarianism that we observe in some circles. The Lord invites us to celebrate the covenant that he has established with us in Jesus Christ. Through the 6 +1 rhythm of our lives he invites us to proclaim to a frantic, hurting, and lost world the peace that is available through Jesus Christ. He invites us to enjoy the day, to make the most of the fruits of our labors, and to rest in him.

11

The Patricentric Vision of Family Order in Deuteronomy[1]

Introduction

IT IS MORE THAN a quarter of a century since David Clines declared Gen 1–3 "irredeemably androcentric" and in so doing rejected the authority of the Bible for modern readers.[2] Troubled by the tone of Clines' expression and especially by his rejection of the Bible's authority, fifteen years ago I made my first focused foray into biblical perspectives related to family roles and ethics.[3] At that time I suggested that if we would understand the normative view of the family in both the First and the New Testaments, we need to replace the words "patriarchy" and "patriarchal" with "patricentricity" and "patricentric." While this proposal has received encouraging support from some,[4] others continue to argue for retaining the word *patriarchy* in evangelical discourse on the family.[5] However, given the detrimental effects rigid patriarchalism has had on our families on the one hand, and the ideal domestic portrait painted by the First Testament on the other, the issue certainly deserves another look.

Here I shall explore further the patricentric ideals of family relationships, especially the roles fathers were to play within the household in the everyday life of Israelites once they had crossed into the promised land, as portrayed in Moses' speeches in Deuteronomy. Deuteronomy is clear that Israel's mission before a watching world was to demonstrate the transformative effects of divine grace in shaping the culture. Once

---

1. This is a stylistically modified version of an essay originally presented at the Quadrennial Conference of the Tyndale Fellowship in July, 2016, in Hoddeston, UK, and prepared for publication in *Marriage, Family and Relationship: Biblical, Doctrinal and Contemporary Perspectives*, edited by Philip Johnston, Thomas A, Noble, and Sarah Whittle (London: InterVarsity, 2017), 11–29. I am grateful to the editors of the volume for their helpful suggestions for its improvement and for their kind permission to republish it here.

2. Clines, "What Does Eve Do to Help?" 25–48.

3. See Block, "Marriage and Family in Ancient Israel," 33–102. See also Block, "'You shall not covet your neighbor's wife,'" 449–74.

4. See Andreas Köstenberger with David W. Jones, *God, Marriage and Family*, 93–107, *et passim*; Andreas and Margaret E. Köstenberger, *God's Design for Man and Woman*, 60–61 *et passim*.

5. Moore, "After Patriarchy, What?," 569–76.

in Canaan, the Israelites were to function as a restored humanity in microcosm. At the end of his third address, Moses declared YHWH's determination to set this nation "high above all the nations that he has made for [his] fame and renown and glory," and that they would be "a holy people to YHWH your God as he promised" (Deut 26:19).[6] If and when they would fulfil their commission as "lights of the world" (Matt 5:14–16), then the peoples around would recognize Israel's unique privileges in having a God who was near and who heard them when they cried out to him, and who had graciously revealed his will to them (Deut 4:6–8).

Definitions

Before we explore the Deuteronomic vision of patricentrism, we need to define our terms. Sociologists and anthropologists identify several different paradigms of domestic and communal administration.

> *Patriarchy*: "the system of male dominance by which men as a group acquire and maintain power over women as a group."[7] Some Christians object that we cannot let secular writers define 'the grammar of our faith,'[8] but the fact remains that their definitions determine how many people think. This is true both in the broader culture and among those who are theologically and biblically illiterate. Within evangelical contexts we may insist on our idealized and nuanced definitions, but then we lose all prospects of addressing the world out there.

> *Matriarchy*: "a system in which women rule."[9] Significantly some feminists do not view matriarchy as the female variety of patriarchy, but idealize it as an egalitarian world in harmony with nature.[10] However, it seems these are the only terms under which it is possible to identify any matriarchal culture at all.[11]

> *Diarchy*: a system in which rule is shared by two persons, usually with clearly delineated areas of responsibility. In domestic contexts, this would involve roles divided by gender, for example the husband/father leading in the procurement of food and heavy work (hunting, tilling) and wife/mother leading in the processing and preparing of food (tending garden plants, cooking).

---

6. Unless otherwise indicated all biblical translations in this chapter are the author's.

7. As defined by Ferguson, "Patriarchy," 265. See further Pavla Miller, "Patriarchy," 419–24.

8. Moore, "After Patriarchy, What?" 574.

9. As defined in unsigned article, "Matriarchy," in B. Smith (ed.), *Oxford Encyclopedia of Women*, 226.

10. Ibid., p. 227.

11. Using very specific criteria, anthropologists have identified several societies as led by females: the Mosuo in China, the Minangkabau in Indonesia (the largest known matrilineal society), the Akan of Ghana, the Bribri in Costa Rica, the Tibeto-Burman Garos and the Nagovisi in New Guinea. However, while some of these societies are matrilineal, they are not actually matriarchal in administration and government. For further discussion of matriarchy, see Sanday, *Women at the Center*; idem, "Matriarchy," 192–95.

Egalitarian government: a system in which all members of a household are equal and have equal access to positions of authority and rule. In a truly egalitarian household roles are not defined either by gender or age.

Anarchy: a system that is uncontrolled by convention or regulation, and in which no member of the household has authority to exert power over anyone else, or to try to ensure order. Usually this results in a chaotic and turbulent environment.

Having identified the possibilities, we shall now explore which of them fits the ideal biblical pattern. Of course, at the outset we must distinguish between the realities in ancient Israel as reflected in the narrative texts, and the ideals as promulgated in the constitutional documents. As is well known, the narratives often paint troubling pictures of male abuse in household situations. I have addressed elsewhere the problem in the book of Judges,[12] but such abuse was not limited to this troubled period in Israel's history. From the patriarchal narratives we note the abuses by Abraham and Isaac, both of whom in flagrant self-interest were willing to sacrifice their wives to save their own skins (Gen 12:10–20; 20:1–18; 26:7–11). David's offences involving women are also well-documented: his polygyny (involving his wives Ahinoam, Abigail, Maacah, Haggith, Abital, Eglah, Bathsheba and concubines; 2 Sam 3:2–5; 1 Chr 3:1–9) and his adultery with Bathsheba (2 Sam 11—12). But these images contrast sharply with the portrayal of righteous ideals in Deuteronomy (cf. Deut 16:20), to which we now turn.

The Androcentricity of Deuteronomy

Given the pervasively androcentric character of both the Hebrew Bible and the New Testament,[13] we should not be surprised by the androcentricity of Deuteronomy. Cast as a collection of Moses' final pastoral addresses to his congregation, a major concern of this book is to govern the behavior of men. The tone is established by the recitation of the Decalogue at the beginning of the second address (5:6–21). The second person of direct address in the book ("you") is always masculine. While the masculine in Hebrew is often used generically for everyone without specific reference to gender, never are women addressed directly as women. Indeed, when women's well-being and women's conduct are at issue, the style adopted is telling. These regulations are concerned primarily with men's treatment of women, rather than the conduct of the women themselves. The second person is reiterated in the motive clause following the prescribed response to an offense, "Thus *you* shall purge the evil from your midst" (21:21; 22:21, 22, 24).

The captive bride (21:10–14). This text is expressly addressed to males, and deals with the woman in the third person ("she").

---

12. Block, "Unspeakable Crimes, 46–55."
13. Carol Meyers notes that, of the 1,426 personal names in the Hebrew Bible, 1,315 (89%) identify men and only 111 (9%) identify women. See "Every Day Life," 245. For alternative but similar statistics, see Bohmbach, "Names and Naming in the Biblical World," 33–39.

The second ranked wife (21:15–17). This text is cast in the third person ("If a man ...") and focuses on the man's responsibility to the second-ranked wife, rather than on her rights or her behavior.

The mother of a rebellious son (21:18–21). After opening in the third person masculine like the previous text ("If a man ... "), the text quickly expands the focus to the son's "father and mother" and thereafter uses third person plural verbs and pronouns, which are masculine by default.

The wife falsely accused of lying about her virginity (22:13–21). This ordinance also begins in the third person "(If a man ...). While ostensibly dealing with a woman whom the husband accuses of deceit at their wedding, the focus is actually on a man whose accusations are proved false. As a brief addendum, it prescribes how the wife is to be treated should the accusations be true, with instructions for the (male) elders of the town (vv. 20–21).

Accomplices in adultery and victims of rape (22:22–29). This ordinance is complex, involving at least four different scenarios. The series begins with a hypothetical case involving a man's action, "If a man is found ..." (v. 22), and the focus continues to be on the male (vv. 23–27). None of these cases is addressed to the female involved.

The divorced woman (24:1–4). This case also begins with a hypothetical situation involving a man "(If a man ... "). Although the man finds something problematic in his wife, the emphasis throughout is on his conduct.

Levirate marriage (25:5–10). The ordinance opens with a note on a domestic scene from the male perspective, "When brothers live together and one of them dies ... ". Its concern is the maintenance of the dead man's name and estate, but the focus then shifts to his widow's response in the face of her brother-in-law's refusal to marry her.

The disrespectful woman (25:11–12). This is the most enigmatic text of the series. Here the issue is a woman's attempt to rescue her husband from an attacker, specifically her inappropriate grabbing of his genitals. Unlike the preceding ordinances, this one actually concerns primarily the actions of a woman. It could have been cast as a second person feminine command: "If your husband is fighting ... you (fem.) may not ... ". In the end, though, the ordinance is addressed to those responsible for maintaining order: 'Then *you* (masc.) shall cut off her hand' (v. 12).

These cases reinforce the androcentric character of the book of Deuteronomy. But does an androcentric culture require domestic patriarchalism? If we accept the definition of patriarchy given above, the answer is not necessarily "yes." However, just because texts—even constitutional texts that present social ideals—are androcentric, this does not mean the social structures will be patriarchal. Indeed, Deuteronomy especially raises the question whether or not patriarchy characterizes the ideals presented in the Mosaic Torah, especially as the term is generally understood and as defined above. As I argued previously, if we would accurately represent the ideals of the Torah, we need to replace the word *patriarchy* with *patricentrism*, for several reasons.

First, the domestic counterpart to androcentrism (as envisioned by Moses in Deuteronomy) is not patriarchy but patricentrism. Androcentrism need not by definition be preoccupied with structures of power and control; rather it may be concerned primarily with loci of responsibility and care. The patricentric Israelite disposition concerning the household is reflected transparently in the designation of a family unit (whether nuclear or extended) as a "father's house" (בֵּית אָב). As in most ancient Near Eastern cultures, Israelite families were patrilineal (descent traced through the father's line),[14] patrilocal (married women joined their husband's household), and patriarchal in some sense (the father governed the household).[15] However, the term "patricentric" says more about the genealogical relationships than about power. A household could be nuclear (father, mother, children), but it could also extend to three or four generations (cf. Deut 5:9) and include elderly parents and even grandparents,[16] and it often contained other members (male and female servants). However, the core involved the blood relatives, the descendants of the household head, along with the wives of male members. This accounts for the book's oft-expressed concern for "the alien, the fatherless, and the widow," who were economically vulnerable because they lacked an adult male (usually the father, but possibly an older brother) who would take care of them.[17]

Second, the term *patriarchy*, literally "the rule of the father," places inordinate emphasis on the power a father exercised over his household.[18] In recent years feminist interpreters have helpfully pointed out the dark side of patriarchy reflected in many biblical narratives.[19] However, such approaches tend to interpret abusive male behavior as natural expressions of patriarchy, despite the fact that the authors often deliberately cite such conduct to demonstrate the degeneracy of the times and the persons involved.[20] By definition, heads of households exercised authority over their families. But with the Canaanization of the Israelites, their normatively compassionate patriarchy rapidly degenerated to cancerous, corrupt, irresponsible, self-centered and exploitative exercise of

---

14. See the genealogies in Genesis 5, 10, 36, etc.

15. For discussion see Patai, *Family, Love and the Bible*, 17–18.

16. Cf. van der Toorn, *Family Religion*, 194–205; Schloen, *The House of the Father*, 147–50. Schloen argues that in Iron Age Israel only one third of the households would have consisted of joint families with more than one conjugal couple and their immature children.

17. Deut 10:18; 14:29; 16:11, 14; 24:19–21; 26:12–13; 27:19.

18. See, for example, Patai's discussion of "The Powers of the Patriarch," in *Family, Love and the Bible*, 114–24.

19. These interpreters are correct in characterizing as abusive: Abraham's passing off his wife Sarah as his sister (Gen 12:10–20), Lot's offer of his two daughters to the thugs of Sodom (Gen 19:8), Jephthah's sacrifice of his daughter (Judg 11:34–40), the Israelite men's authorization of Benjaminite warriors to kidnap girls for wives (Judg 21:19–24), David's adultery with Bathsheba and murder of her husband (2 Sam 11:1–27), Amnon's rape of his half-sister Tamar (2 Sam 13:1–19), to name just a few horrendous episodes. For a keen analysis of some of these troubling texts, see Trible, *Texts of Terror*.

20. Nowhere is this more evident than in the book of Judges, the central thrust of which is to expose the Canaanization of Israelite society. The horrendous abuse of women in the book represents but one of the symptoms of a culture gone horribly wrong. See Block, "Unspeakable Crimes," 46–55.

power. The energies of the household were invested in maintaining the status and power of its head rather than the well-being of its members (Fig. 11.1). But this was a far cry from the normative ideal of patriarchy.[21] Because many associate this term *a priori* with this kind of abuse, the expression is best avoided.[22]

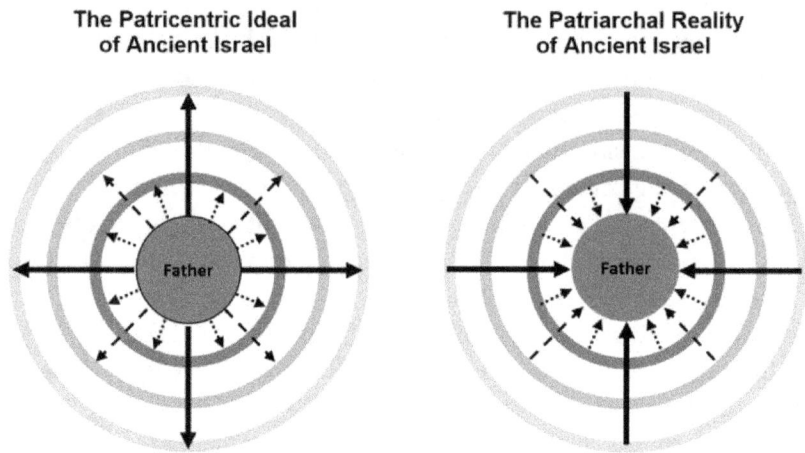

Figure 11.1
The Patricentric Ideal and the Reality in Ancient Israel

Third, *patricentrism* reflects the normative biblical disposition toward the role of the head of a household in Israel more accurately than *patriarchy*. It is clear that, just as the father's house (בֵּית אָב) was the nucleus of the clan (מִשְׁפָּחָה), so the father was the nucleus of the father's house. And just as in a physical sense the house inhabited by the head of the extended family represented the nucleus of the compound, so the head of the family functioned as its center. Like the spokes of a wheel, family life ideally radiated outward from him. In fact, as Johannes Pedersen noted long ago, "wherever a man goes he takes 'his house' with him."[23] Biblical genealogies trace descent through the male line;[24] a married couple resided within the household of the groom; in references to a man and his wife or a man and his children the man is generally named first (Gen 7:7); children were born to the father (Gen 21:1–7); fathers negotiated family disputes (Gen 13:1–13; 31:1–55); God generally addressed heads of the household (Gen 3:9; 12:1; 35:1);[25] when

---

21. Remarkably, the verb מָשַׁל "to rule, govern," characterizes the relationship of the father (אָב) to his household only once in the Hebrew Bible, viz., Gen 3:16, where it expresses a symptom of the world gone wrong after the entrance of sin.

22. So also Carol Meyers, who prefers to characterize Israelite society in general as *androcentric* rather than *patriarchal*; see "The Family in Early Israel," 34–35. But as the expression "father's house" suggests, families in particular were *patricentric*.

23. Pedersen, *Israel: Its Life and Culture*, 1.51. See for example, the deliverance of Noah and his house, which included his wife and his sons' wives (Gen 7:1, 13).

24. The exceptional inclusion of four women in the genealogy of Jesus in Matthew 1 is driven by the rhetorical aims of the evangelist.

25. This normal pattern throws into even sharper relief the exceptional character of Judg 13:1–23,

families worshipped, the head of the household took the initiative (Gen 8:13–22; 12:7–8; 35:2–15; cf. Job 1:4–5); when a man died without descendants his "name" died (Deut 25:5–6; Ruth 4:5, 10; 1 Sam 24:18–22). In short, the ideal domestic community was built around the father; if in every respect it bore his stamp, it also looked to him as the one primarily responsible for its well-being.[26]

Patricentrism in the Book of Deuteronomy

But how does this picture play out in the ideal Israelite world that Moses laid out in the book of Deuteronomy? Despite Deuteronomy's pervasive concern for the well-being of the family, especially in chapters 12–26, remarkably the expression "father's house" occurs only twice, and that in one sentence in 22:21. Regarding a woman who proved not to have been a virgin at marriage, Moses prescribed:

> Then the men of her town shall bring the young woman (הַנַּעֲרָה) out to the door of her father's house (בֵּית־אָב), and they shall kill her by stoning, because she has committed this outrage (נְבָלָה) in Israel by prostituting her father's house (לִזְנוֹת בֵּית אָבִיהָ).

Patricentrism in the Decalogue (5:6–22)

Although most evangelical readers today assume the Decalogue is authoritative for all Christians, few are aware that strictly speaking this foundational document of YHWH's covenant with Israel is addressed primarily to the male head of an Israelite household.[27] The "you" (masculine singular throughout) is an adult male, who is responsible for the practice of religion in the "household" (5:8–10) and thereby the welfare of the family, who in a particular sense bears the name of YHWH (v. 11), who is in charge of the work of the household (vv. 13–14), whose "household" includes sons and daughters, male and female servants, resident aliens, draft animals and other livestock (v. 14), and who is tempted to take his neighbor's wife, as well as his home and fields, servants, animals and any other property (v. 21).[28] We must note, however, that this identification of the

---

where the divine envoy prefers to address an otherwise unnamed woman concerning the birth of a child to her husband, Manoah, who is named.

26. For full discussion, see Josberger, "Between Rule and Responsibility," 33–102.

27. My arguments for this interpretation are developed more fully in Block, "The Decalogue in the Hebrew Scriptures," 9–11; "Reading the Decalogue Right to Left," 30–34.

28. If the significance of the "you" is to be extended, it might include the father's wife, whose honorific status within the household the fourth command explicitly guards. Although the male head's adultery with the neighbor's wife would inevitably have implications for his own marriage, remarkably the document says nothing about his treatment of his own wife. Undoubtedly the mother was to promote and be as exercised about the well-being of the entire household as the father. On her status within the household, see further below. Based on the discourse grammar of the Decalogue, with Roman Catholics and Lutherans (as opposed to Reformed Protestants), I identify the command to honor father and mother as the fourth (rather than fifth) command. For brief discussion, see Block, "Excursus A: How Shall We Number the Ten Commands?" following "Reading the Decalogue Right

male head of the household as the primary addressee does not absolve others of its the Decalogue's authority over them. But they represent secondary audiences. In keeping with a fundamental tenet of biblical leadership, the primary function of leaders is not defined in terms of the tasks they are expected to perform but in terms of the kind of persons they are to be. If the primary function of the head of the nation was to embody the ethical and spiritual values of the community (Deut 17:14–20), the same was true for heads of households. The household's members should be able to observe the head and know what kinds of persons they were to be. Therefore, if idolatry or adultery were wrong for the household heads, they were also wrong for the rest of the family.

Contrary to the views of many, the Decalogue is not a gentlemen's agreement protecting the status of men or guaranteeing them a certain economic standard or enabling them to live in peace, while the rest of the household are overlooked.[29] Rather, this document recognizes and reins in the temptation of heads of households to act like little Pharaohs (cf. the reference to Egypt, v. 6), exploiting those in their charge and running roughshod over them in the way that the Egyptians had treated their forbears (v. 15). Indeed the document itself may be viewed as a bill of rights, protecting the well-being of the household *against* the abuse of fathers who are concerned only about themselves and care little for those who live under their roof, as illustrated in Table 11.1.[30]

Table 11.1
The Decalogue as the World's Oldest Bill of Rights (Deut 5:6–21)

	Command	Rights Involved
	I am YHWH your God, who brought you out of the land of Egypt, out of the house of slavery.	The basis of the Bill of Rights in redemption (cf. Deut 6:20–25)
1	You shall have no other gods before me; you shall not make for yourself a carved image . . . to bow down to them or serve them.	YHWH has the right to his people's exclusive allegiance.
2	You shall not bear the name of YHWH your God in vain.	YHWH has the right to proper representation and loyal service.
3	Remember the Sabbath day, to keep it holy.	A man's household has the right to days of rest (i.e., humane treatment).
4	Honour your father and your mother.	A man's parents have the right to his respect and care.

---

to Left," 56–60. For more detailed defence of this interpretation, see DeRouchie, "Counting the Ten," 93–126.

29. See most recently the blog post by Cheryl Anderson, "Audience of the Ten Commandments," at <http://www.bibleodyssey.org/tools/video-gallery/a/audience-of-the-ten-commandments-anderson.aspx>. Accessed July 2, 2016.

30. This approach differs fundamentally from that of David Clines, who argues that the document was drafted to secure the interests of elites and those who wield power. See Clines, "The Ten Commandments, Reading from Left to Right," 97–112.

	Command	Rights Involved
5	You shall not murder.	Others have the right to life.
6	You shall not commit adultery.	Others have the right to sexual purity and secure marriages.
7	You shall not steal.	Others have the right to property.
8	You shall not bear false witness against your neighbor.	A man's neighbor has the right to an honest representation and reputation, especially in court.
9	You shall not covet your neighbor's wife.	A man's neighbor has the right to freedom from fear that he desires his wife.
10	You shall not covet your neighbor's house, field, human resources, animal resources, or anything else.	A man's neighbors have the right to freedom from fear that he desires their household resources.

Recognizing that the male head wields the power in the household, the Decalogue seeks to limit the wrongful exercise of that power. Like other leadership institutions, it assumes that people in leadership occupy these positions for the sake of those whom they lead, in contrast to prevailing perspectives and the constant temptation to view others as props for the leader's status and well-being.[31] However, the modifications in Deuteronomy to the Exodus version of the commands regarding coveting (Deut 5:21a; cf. Exod 20:17a) caution against treating women as mere chattel. The inclusion of "your mother" in the charge to honour parents (Deut 5:16) suggests the Israelite ideal moves in the direction of complementarianism (parents may play different roles, but they were worthy of equal honor).[32] That Lev 19:3 places "mother" before "father" in its call for respect from children, and that a home could also be identified as a "mother's house" (בֵּית אֵם), especially in accounts involving daughters (Gen 24:28; Ruth 1:8; Song 3:4; 8:2), may not reflect an egalitarian diarchy, but certainly assume a complementarian relationship and equal ontological status.[33]

Patricentrism in the Specific Instructions in Deuteronomy 12–26

When we read Deuteronomy as a whole we notice its pervasively patricentric—as opposed to patriarchal—perspective. It is all about the heads of households seeking the

---

31. For further discussion, see Block, "Leader, Leadership, Old Testament," 620–26.

32. This image pervades the book of Proverbs, which not only portrays a noble woman as creatively and energetically engaged in economic activity for her household (31:10–31), but also twice characterizes her instruction as teaching (*tôrāh*), and frequently identifies her as worthy of honor equal to that of a child's father (10:1; 15:20; 19:26; 20:20; 23:22, 25; 28:24; 29:15).

33. Hence the command to honor father and mother (5:16; cf. Lev 19:3), and the involvement of mothers in cases involving children (Deut 21:18–21).

well-being of those in their charge, rather than protecting their status and power. In particular, it pays special attention to women's rights, as long recognized by scholars.[34]

1. *The concern for widows (10:17–18, et passim)*

We begin with Deuteronomy's remarkable concern for the members of the community marginalized and economically vulnerable because they lack the security provided by a male figure, either a father or husband. Beginning in 10:18 and on nine further occasions, the book declares the responsibility of Israelites, particularly of household heads, for the well-being of the widow, the fatherless and the alien.[35]

2. *Invitations to participate in worship (12:12, et passim)*

Like the "Book of the Covenant" in Exod 21–23, the Deuteronomic Torah requires all males to gather at the central sanctuary three times a year for the Festivals of Passover and Unleavened Bread, Weeks, and Booths (16:16; cf. Exod 23:14–17; 34:23). However, in contrast to the segregation that would characterize worship centuries later in Herodian times, Deuteronomy invites women, both free and slave, to worship freely in the presence of YHWH at the central sanctuary (12:12, 18; 16:11, 14; 31:12).

3. *The manumission of female slaves (15:12)*

Whereas the regulations concerning the manumission of indentured slaves in the Book of the Covenant had spoken only of male slaves (Exod 21:2–11), the corresponding instructions in Deut 15 expressly stipulate that the law applies to both male and female slaves (v. 12).

4. *Military exemption for new husbands (20:7)*

Like the instructions involving a newly constructed house (v. 5) and a newly planted vineyard (v. 6), the one-year exemption of a newly betrothed man from military service appears to be interested primarily in his enjoyment of his new commitment. However, this ordinance also has the interests of his bride in mind. She would hope to have conceived a child before he leaves for his tour of duty "lest he die and another man take her." Further, 24:5 speaks expressly of the man tending to his new wife's happiness for the year.

---

34. Thus Weinfeld, *Deuteronomy 1–11*, 318; idem, *Deuteronomy and the Deuteronomic School*, 282–92.

35. See footnote 15 above.

5. The captive bride (21:10–14)

For women, few circumstances are more fearful than conquest by a foreign army. It is clear from the concluding motive clause, "because you have degraded her" (21:14),[36] that the goal here is to prevent male abuse of women in warfare. This paragraph assumes a soldier's right to marry a woman in circumstances where contractual arrangements with the bride's family are impossible,[37] and then to divorce her. But it appeals to Israelite men to be both humane and charitable in their treatment of foreign women, who are forced to become a part of the Israelite community through no decision or fault of their own.

6. The second-ranked wife (21:15–17)

Bigamous and polygamous marriages provide fertile soil for the mistreatment of women. This text assumes that one of the wives will be favored by the man, which could lead to favored treatment of her son when his property is divided. The present provision secures the status and well-being of the son of a rejected wife who happened to be the first-born. Since children were responsible for the care of their parents in old age, it also protects the interests and rights of the second-ranked wife.

7. The mother of a rebellious son (21:18–21)

While the opening clause, "If a *man* . . . ," reflects the patricentrism of ancient Israel, the instructions on dealing with the "stubborn and rebellious son" modify this by explicitly including the child's mother *with* his father as the aggrieved party, and by involving her in every phase of the legal process: *they* chastise him; *they* seize him; *they* bring him out; *they* tell the elders of the child's insubordination to *them*. These instructions prevent the male head of the household from operating only in self-interest, and force him also to protect his wife from abuse by a son.

8. The wife falsely accused of lying about her virginity (22:13–21)

This paragraph divides into two parts, a primary case involving a false accusation (vv. 13–19) and a counter-case in which the charges prove to be true (vv. 20–21). Whereas the latter makes no attempt to defend a woman who is actually guilty of lying, the former goes to great lengths to protect a woman from false accusations by her husband. The text (a) invites the woman's parents (both father and mother) to come to her defence—a remarkable provision in a patrilocal society; (b) calls for a public hearing of the case before the elders—commensurate with the public nature of the slander; (c) invites the

---

36. Contrary to common understanding (e.g., Nelson, *Deuteronomy*, 254; McConville, *Deuteronomy*, 330) the verb here (עָנָה, piel) does not refer to "rape" or "sexual abuse." Wolde has demonstrated that in juridical contexts the word serves an evaluative function, expressing downward social movement and should be translated "debased": "Does ʿinnâ Denote Rape?" 528–44.

37. *Contra* Pressler, *The View of Women*, 11.

presentation of objective evidence to counter the false accusations; (d) provides for the turning of the tables between the accused and the plaintiff; (e) calls for the public disciplining of the man; (f) secures the honor of the woman's parents by forcing the man to pay compensation for his charge of "damaged goods"; and (g) prohibits the man from divorcing the woman, thus ensuring her economic well-being for life.

Many modern readers will find the last prescription unpalatable. Surely divorce is better than living with a man who has publicly defamed his wife. However, ancient texts should be read in the light of their own intention rather than modern conventions. From the perspective of the husband, this order assumes that punishment will have a rehabilitative effect; having been publicly shamed he will return to his wife and assume his responsible role in caring for her. From the perspective of the woman, this order guarantees her security; she will be cared for all her days. From the perspective of her parents, they may keep the bride price (plus the fine); but more importantly, they can relax because their daughter is restored to a socially protective environment.[38] From the perspective of the community, the elders who witnessed the proceedings become guarantors of the man's good behavior.

9. *The victims of rape (22:23–29)*

Here Moses provides instructions for two scenarios involving rape of a virgin, distinguished by whether or not the victim is engaged. The first case is interesting for the distinction it draws between rape in a town (vv. 23–24) and out in the country (vv. 25–27).[39] It assumes that if the act occurs in town an innocent woman will cry for help and either her fiancé or her townspeople will rescue her. However, since there is no one in the countryside to hear her protests, it gives her the benefit of the doubt and assumes her innocence. Meanwhile the man must be executed.[40]

The second case involves a virgin who is not engaged. Whereas Exod 22:15[16] considers the man's actions to be seductive, here Moses speaks of the man seizing the woman and "lying" with her. The prescribed response focuses entirely on the man. Because he has deflowered and degraded the woman, he must pay her father fifty shekels. This payment is not a fine (as in v. 19) but the bride price, since she then becomes a wife

---

38. This is difficult for modern westerners to understand, given the high value we place on individual physical, psychological, and emotional well-being, as opposed to the well-being of the community.

39. This compares with ancient Hittite laws that distinguish rape cases occurring in the mountains and those in a woman's house, the latter being deemed a capital offence. See HL ¶¶197–198 (Roth, *Law Collections*, 237).

40. Texts like this answer accusations of double standards, as in the unsigned article on "Adultery" in Tierney (ed.), *Women's Studies Encyclopedia*: "The double standard, that only the woman's infidelity deserves serious punishment, has permeated thinking in all patriarchal societies. It rests in large part on the idea of a woman as property" (14). According to Gerda Lerner, "Hebrew men enjoyed complete sexual freedom within and outside marriage." Lerner, *The Creation of Patriarchy*, 170. Comments like this are wrong, not only because they disregard the evidence of this text in Deuteronomy, but also because they ignore the fact that the Decalogue is addressed to men and does not even consider female adultery.

whom he can never divorce. On the surface, it looks like Deuteronomy has tightened the law recorded in Exodus and eliminated all other options for the poor woman but to become the wife of her violator.[41] However, the issue is probably not that simple. The point here is that, if the man pays the bride price and the father agrees to accept him as a son-in-law, the man must fulfil all the marital duties that come with sexual intercourse, and in so doing guarantee the woman's social security.

10. The divorced woman (24:1–4)

This text has been the subject of more attention than most of the above. Interpretations vary, but the key is found in properly identifying where the unit shifts from "if" (the protasis) to "then" (the apodosis). The syntax is admittedly ambiguous, but the following table represents the most likely flow and structure of the text:

The problem	When a man takes a woman, and marries her, if she finds no favor in his eyes because he has found some defect in her,
The prevailing practice	and he writes her a certificate of divorce, and he puts it in her hand, and sends her out of his house,
The complication	if she departs from his house, and goes and becomes another man's wife, and if the latter man hates her, and he writes her a certificate of divorce, and puts it in her hand, and he sends her out of his house, if the latter man dies, who took her to be his wife,
The proscription	then her former husband, who sent her away, may not take her again to be his wife, after she has been declared defiled,
The rationale	for that is an abomination before YHWH, and you shall not bring sin upon the land that YHWH your God is giving you as a grant.

Contrary to common opinion, this text does not authorize or even regulate divorce *per se*—the practice is assumed—but seeks to prevent further abuse by a husband after he has divorced his wife (cf. 21:10–14). Technically the primary issue is not divorce but palingamy, i.e., remarriage to a former spouse.[42] Moses protects the woman from

---

41. According to Lerner, "Implicitly, this forces a woman into an indissoluble marriage with her rapist (Deut 22:28–29)"; *Creation of Patriarchy*, 170.

42. Cf. Westbrook, "Prohibition on Restoration of Marriage in Deuteronomy 24:1–4," 388; Pressler, "*The View of Women*, 46–47. For the traditional interpretation, see Hugenberger, *Marriage*

abuse by her first husband, by reiterating the existent procedures for releasing wives from marriage. Further, he insists that when a husband divorces his wife he relinquishes his authority over her. Having humiliated her by insisting she declare herself unclean, he may not reclaim her if she has remarried and then loses her later husband through divorce or death. The legislation protects the woman by requiring the husband to produce a severance document as legal proof for the dissolution of the marriage. Without this document, the husband could demand to have her back at any time; and if she were to remarry, he could accuse her of adultery.[43]

11. Levirate Marriage (25:5–10)

The primary purpose of this institution was to secure the integrity of families and inherited estates, which was threatened when a married man died without having fathered an heir. This could be achieved by the widow marrying the deceased's brother, i.e., his nearest unmarried male relative. The first child born of this union would be legally considered the child of the deceased, bearing his name and retaining his property. Verses 7–10 contemplate the case in which the nearest relative refuses to perform this duty on behalf of his dead brother. The legal process affords the widow remarkable freedom of movement and influence in prosecuting the case. She appears before the elders and presents her complaint (v. 7b). The elders of the town summon the brother-in-law and speak to him (v. 8a). If he refuses publicly to do his duty (v. 8b), the widow then performs a ritual of public humiliation—removing her brother-in-law's sandal and, in a gesture of rudeness and humiliation,[44] spitting in his face (v. 9). By announcing, "This is what shall be done to the man who will not build his brother's house," the widow shows that her response is neither impulsive nor idiosyncratic, but accords with established legal procedure. Although the woman expressly acts in the interests of her deceased husband, she also defends her own honour. This text therefore discourages a man with levirate responsibility from simply disregarding it and abandoning his widowed sister-in-law. The elders of the city are to stand by the woman against a potentially callous male.

Conclusion

In the past three decades, feminist scholars have rightly alerted readers of the Scriptures to misogynistic elements in the biblical texts. It is clear that the documents were all written from an androcentric perspective. It is also clear that household heads were just as prone as other community leaders to twist positions of responsibility into positions of power, and to exercise that power in brutal self-interest. It is tempting to assume that the narratives of such abuse reflect the Israelite norm and demonstrate that the system itself is fundamentally flawed. The stories do indeed prove the fulfilment of the prediction made by God at the fountainhead of human history: "I will greatly increase your pangs

---

as a Covenant, 76–81.

43. So also, Christopher Wright, *God's People in God's Land*, 217.
44. Cf. Num 12:14; Job 17:6; 30:10; Matt 26:67; 27:30; Mark 10:34; 14:65; Luke 18:32.

in childbearing; in pain you shall bring forth children; you shall crave the power of your husband, but he will *rule* over you" (Gen 3:16).

Because of humanity's sin, a woman's role became not only painful but also frustrating. And because of the ongoing sins of men, women are all too often treated as subjects rather than as co-regents in the exercise of dominion over the earth. It is easy to forget that this represents neither the biblical ideal nor the covenantal norm. According to the standards signalled by the Decalogue and developed in greater detail in the Deuteronomic Torah, the role of the "father" in the "father's house" involved primarily care and protection of all those under his charge. However, this care and protection often degenerates to exploitation and abuse of women as if they are nothing more than household property, as disposable as sheep or oxen. Contemporary efforts to determine and re-establish biblical ethical norms must pay attention not only to accounts of the way it was, but especially to texts that outline the way it should have been. In this and many other respects the book of Deuteronomy offers a glorious gospel, setting a trajectory of male-female relations that leads ultimately to Paul's statements in Eph 5:25–33:

> Husbands, love your wives, as Christ loved the church and gave himself up for her, that he might sanctify her, having cleansed her by the washing of water with the word, so that he might present the church to himself in splendor, without spot or wrinkle or any such thing, that she might be holy and without blemish. In the same way husbands should love their wives as their own bodies. He who loves his wife loves himself. For no one ever hated his own flesh, but nourishes and cherishes it, just as Christ does the church, because we are members of his body. "Therefore a man shall leave his father and mother and hold fast to his wife, and the two shall become one flesh." This mystery is profound, and I am saying that it refers to Christ and the church. However, let each one of you love his wife as himself. (ESV)

The seeds of this perspective were planted long ago in God's covenant with Israel. May they sprout and may this plant flourish anew among God's people today.

12

Wrestling with God

A Study on Prayer in Deuteronomy[1]

Introduction

UNTIL RECENTLY HUMAN BEINGS generally have had an intense sense of alienation from the divine. Many modern Westerners dismiss the notion of divinity itself as fiction; this is a mythical construction of unenlightened minds. However, the desperate need for contact with the gods in the ancient Near East is expressed poignantly in prayers, as in King Mursili II's desperate plea for divine rescue from a plague that had struck the Hittites (1321–1295 B.C),[2] and in the "Prayer to Every God," recovered from Ashurbanipal's library.[3] The latter is a pathetic plea to get relief from suffering, which the supplicant is convinced he has experienced because he has violated some divine law. However, it is also an implicit protest that he should not to be singled out for divine wrath because he does not know which god he has offended, what the crime is that he has committed, and what it will take to appease the god's fury.[4]

The book of Deuteronomy asserts that on all three counts the ancient Israelites were an extremely privileged people, the objects of remarkable divine grace. First, their God had introduced himself to them by name: "I am YHWH your God who brought you out of the land of Egypt" (Deut 5:6). Second, he had clearly revealed himself and his will to his people (4:9–13; 6:20–25; 30:11–14). Third, he actually heard them when they prayed (4:7–8). The Israelite hope/confidence is expressed in the name Jaazaniah (יְאַזַנְיָהוּ/יְזַנְיָה), "YHWH [h]ears," which appears to have become especially popular in Judah's waning years.[5]

---

1. This as an expanded version of a paper presented at the annual meeting of the Institute of Biblical Research in Atlanta, Georgia, on November 20, 2015. I am grateful to Franklin Wang for his careful reading of an earlier version of this paper and his helpful suggestions for its improvement.

2. For translation, see Singer, in *Hittite Prayers*, 58–59.

3. For the text in translation, see Stevens, in *ANET*, 391–92; Foster, *Before the Muses*, 763–65.

4. For further discussion of the prayer, see Block, "Other Religions in Old Testament Theology," 232–36. This essay was originally published in *Biblical Faith and Other Religions: An Evangelical Assessment*, 43–78.

5. But see YHWH's declared refusal to hear in Ezek 8:18. The name was so common that biblical

Moses highlighted the problem posed by pagan deities in 4:28: these gods of wood and stone are "the work of human hands; they neither see, nor hear, nor eat, nor smell." A later psalmist was more specific:

> ² Why should the nations say, "Where is their God?"
> ³ Our God is in the heavens; he does whatever he pleases.
> ⁴ Their idols are silver and gold, the work of human hands.
> ⁵ They have mouths, but do not speak; eyes, but do not see.
> ⁶ They have ears, but do not hear; noses, but do not smell.
> ⁷ They have hands, but do not feel; feet, but do not walk;
> they make no sound in their throats.
> ⁸ Those who make them are like them;
> so are all who out their trust in them (Ps 115:2–8).[6]

Moses captures Israel's unique privilege in having a God who actually hears human supplicants in Deut 4:6–8: "Surely, that great nation is a wise and discerning people." *For what great nation is there that has a god so close at hand as is YHWH our God whenever we call upon Him?"*[7] Israel's God had no literal ears, but he heard his people!

Twice in his addresses Moses concretized the idiom declared generally in 4:7. Both texts involve the response of a poor person to tightfistedness by an economic superior:

הִשָּׁ֣מֶר לְךָ֡	15:9	Take care,
פֶּן־יִהְיֶ֣ה דָבָר֩ עִם־לְבָבְךָ֨ בְלִיַּ֜עַל		lest a nasty thought enter your mind,
לֵאמֹ֗ר		and you say,
קָֽרְבָ֣ה שְׁנַֽת־הַשֶּׁ֣בַע שְׁנַ֣ת הַשְּׁמִטָּה֒		"The seventh year, the year of release is near,"
וְרָעָ֣ה עֵֽינְךָ֗ בְּאָחִ֙יךָ֙ הָֽאֶבְי֔וֹן		and your eye be evil against your poor brother,
וְלֹ֥א תִתֵּ֖ן ל֑וֹ		and you refuse to give him [his due],
וְקָרָ֤א עָלֶ֙יךָ֙ אֶל־יְהוָ֔ה		and *he cry to YHWH* against you,
וְהָיָ֥ה בְךָ֖ חֵֽטְא׃		and you be guilty of sin.

---

writers often identified persons who bore it by patronymic: "son of Jeremiah" (2 Kgs 25:23; Jer 35:3); "son of the Maacathite" (Jer 40:8); "son of Hoshaiah" (Jer 42:1); "son of Shaphan" (Ezek 8:11); "son of Azzur" (Ezek 11:1). For citations in Hebrew and Aramaic seals, bullae, and correspondence from this period, see Block, *Ezekiel Chapters 1–24*, 290, n. 41; Dobbs-Alsopp, Roberts, Seow, and Whitaker, *Hebrew Inscriptions*, 599–600. The name has also surfaced as Izin-Yāma (ᵐi-zi-ni-a-ma) in the corpus of texts from Babylon recently published by Pearce and Wunsch, *Documents of Judean Exiles and West Semites*, No. 51:14.

6. Cf. also Ps 135:13–18; Isa 44:12–20.

7. Unless otherwise indicated, all translations in this essay are my own.

בְּיוֹמוֹ תִתֵּן שְׂכָרוֹ	24:1	On the same day you shall give him his wages,
וְלֹא־תָבוֹא עָלָיו הַשֶּׁמֶשׁ		before the sun sets
כִּי עָנִי הוּא וְאֵלָיו הוּא נֹשֵׂא אֶת־נַפְשׁוֹ		(for he is poor and he is counting on it),
וְלֹא־יִקְרָא עָלֶיךָ אֶל־יְהוָה		so *he does not cry to YHWH* against you,
וְהָיָה בְךָ חֵטְא׃		and you be guilty of sin.

Moses observes that YHWH not only hears the prayers of priests, and kings, and other social elites; even the socially marginalized have access to his ears.

Moses: The Prophetic Man of Prayer

Although Moses was involved in priestly, judicial, administrative, and legislative activities, neither the narrator nor Moses himself ever applies to him epithets like "priest" (כֹּהֵן), "judge" (שֹׁפֵט), or "lawgiver/legislator" (חֹקֵק). Judging by the speech act verbs used of him, in Deuteronomy Moses is primarily the mediator and teacher of divine revelation.[8] In his first address Moses spoke as YHWH commanded him (1:3, 6–8, 2:1; 4:5), and the dominance of verbs for "teaching" and "learning" (למד, 4:1, 5, 14; cf. also v. 9, נָתַן לִפְנֵי, "to set before") demonstrate that his role was primarily pedagogical; he was to teach Israel "the [covenant] stipulations, ordinances, and judgments" [הָעֵדֹת וְהַחֻקִּים וְהַמִּשְׁפָּטִים, 4:45]). This parenetic tone and style continue in the second address.[9]

Remarkably the only professional title that Deuteronomy applies to Moses is נָבִיא, "prophet" (18:15–22, esp. 15; 34:10). However, this epithet is appropriate because fundamentally prophets were officials who had access to the divine presence[10] and were authorized to speak for God to the latter's intended audience.[11] While Exod 3–4 is commonly understood as Moses' call to divine service, unlike the calls of Isaiah (Isa 6) and Jeremiah (Jer 1), this was not primarily a call to declare the will of God to the people, but

---

8. For detailed discussion of Moses' role in Deuteronomy and the pedagogical/parenetic genre of his addresses, see Block, "Will the Real Moses Please Rise?" 68–103.

9. Ibid, 88–101.

10. See Jer 23:18, 21–22:

> But which of them (false prophets) has stood in the council of YHWH to see or to hear his word?
> Who has listened and heard his word?
> ....
> I did not send these prophets, yet they have run with their message;
> I did not speak to them, yet they have prophesied.
> But if they had stood in my council, they would have proclaimed my words to my people
> and would have turned them from their evil ways and from their evil deeds.

On the relationship between prophetic membership in the divine council and intercessory responsibilities, see Gordon, "Where Have All the Prophets Gone?" 78–85.

11. This distinguishes true prophets from charlatans, who claim to speak for God but have never been sent out by him. For biblical portrayals of the differences, see Deut 18:9–22; Jer 23:9–40; 28:1–17; 29:1–23). For scholarly discussion of the subject, see Brenneman, "True and False Prophecy," 781–88. Further bibliography is provided.

to be YHWH's agent of divine deliverance for enslaved Israel. In Num 12:6–8 YHWH described his relationship to Moses in prophetic terms, but the event presupposes what had happened at Sinai/Horeb (see below); earlier narratives had applied the noun נָבִיא explicitly only to Aaron (Exod 7:1).

Although Exod 19–20 is not structured as a prophetic call narrative, it is apparent from Moses' second address in Deuteronomy that he interpreted this as the moment of his prophetic call. Indeed, once the Israelites arrived at Horeb YHWH would use him primarily as a prophet: "Moses went up to God and YHWH called out to him from the mountain, 'Thus you shall say to the house of Jacob and declare to the descendants of Israel'" (19:3). On the mountain YHWH dictated to Moses the message he was to relay to the people, ending with, "These are the words that you shall declare to the descendants of Israel" (v. 6), which Moses dutifully did (v. 7). YHWH provided a clue to his impending status in verse 9: "Look, I am coming to you in a thick cloud, so that the people may hear when I speak with you, and may also place their confidence in you forever." The interchanges in this chapter involving YHWH, Moses, and the people clearly reflect his prophetic status. The people's response and Moses' actions in Exod 20:19–21 demonstrate that YHWH had fulfilled his prediction in 19:9. Nevertheless, while the narrator portrays him entering the presence of YHWH, he avoids the term נָבִיא.[12]

Moses also avoided the expression when he recounted the event four decades later. However, his citation of the people's request at Horeb in Deut 5:22–33 describes the activity of a prophet: "Go near yourself and listen to all that YHWH our God says. Then you tell us everything he tells you, and we will listen and act [accordingly]" (v. 27). In responding YHWH affirmed both the people's reaction to their encounter with him (v. 28) and the role they envisioned for Moses, emphasizing his teaching [rather than legislative] function (v. 31).[13] Having granted Moses open access to his presence and commissioned him to speak for him to the people, apparently YHWH had formally inducted Moses into the prophetic office. Moses reinforced this impression in Deut 18:9–22. In their preoccupation with the identity of "the prophet like Moses,"[14] historically interpreters have missed the primary foci of the passage: the response of the people to future authorized messengers (vv. 9–19),[15] and the integrity of the prophetic office (vv. 20–22).[16]

---

12. "The people stood at a distance, while Moses approached the thick darkness where God was." For detailed discussion of this portrayal of Moses, see Kibbe, *Godly Fear or Ungodly Failure?* 24–32.

13. Hebrew, וְאַתָּה פֹּה עֲמֹד עִמָּדִי וַאֲדַבְּרָה אֵלֶיךָ אֵת כָּל־הַמִּצְוָה וְהַחֻקִּים וְהַמִּשְׁפָּטִים אֲשֶׁר תְּלַמְּדֵם וְעָשׂוּ בָאָרֶץ אֲשֶׁר אָנֹכִי נֹתֵן לָהֶם לְרִשְׁתָּהּ׃

14. For brief discussion of whether this concerns an individual eschatological messianic figure or more generally prophets who followed in Moses' train, see Block, *Deuteronomy*, 434–47. For discussion of the perception of Jesus as the eschatological messianic prophet in New Testament times, see chapter 17, "A Prophet Like Moses: Another Look at Deuteronomy 18:9–22" below, pp. 349–73; and Block, "My Servant David," 26–32.

15. People who reject the divine provision and consult diviners instead are condemned as "abominable to YHWH" (תּוֹעֲבַת יְהוָה, 9–14), and those who reject future prophets' messages are held as accountable as the present generation was to the words of Moses (vv. 15–19).

16. Authorized spokespersons speak only in the name of YHWH and in accord with the message they receive from YHWH (vv. 20–22).

To this point, the discussion of Moses as prophet has focused on his role as conduit and authorized interpreter of divine revelation. However, once YHWH had admitted a prophet to his throne room to be privy *to* divine communication, he also opened the door to influence *from* the prophet. Prophets were more than transmitters of revelation from the deity to the people; they could also relay messages from and concerning the people to the deity (cf. Exod 19:3–25),[17] or present their own private issues before him.

The former happens in the context where the word נָבִיא ("prophet") appears for the first time in the Hebrew Bible (Gen 20:1–18). After the Patriarch had shamefully passed off Sarah as his sister for the second time (cf. Gen 12:10–20), YHWH declared to Abimelech, king of Gerar, "Now then, return the man's wife; for he is a prophet (נָבִיא), and he will pray for you and you shall live. But if you do not restore her, know that you shall surely die, you and all that belong to you" (v. 7).[18] Functioning as "prophet," Abraham prayed for Abimelech, and YHWH healed him and the women in his household.

Although this marked the first occurrence of the word נָבִיא, this was not the moment of Abraham's first "prophetic" service. Having invited him "to walk before me" in Gen 17:1,[19] in 18:16–33, YHWH asked a rhetorical question: "Shall I hide from Abraham what I am about to do [to Sodom]?" (v. 17). After reflecting on the Patriarch's future and his present honorific standing with him (vv. 18–19), and noticing the sound coming from Sodom, YHWH investigated the problem and contemplated the appropriate response (vv. 20–21). This opened the door for Abraham's intervention, and the Patriarch respectfully[20] accepted the challenge.[21] Against the backdrop of YHWH's charge to "keep the way of YHWH by doing righteousness and justice" (וְשָׁמְרוּ דֶּרֶךְ יְהוָה לַעֲשׂוֹת צְדָקָה וּמִשְׁפָּט, v. 19), the narrator notes that Abraham addressed YHWH's justice (v. 25). The patriarch's response at the end of this conversation suggests that his perspective on the situation in Sodom had come to align with YHWH's.

---

17. Note especially the last clauses of Exod 19:8 (וַיָּשֶׁב מֹשֶׁה אֶת־דִּבְרֵי הָעָם אֶל־יְהוָה, "And Moses brought the words of the people back to YHWH ") and v. 9 (וַיַּגֵּד מֹשֶׁה אֶת־דִּבְרֵי הָעָם אֶל־יְהוָה, "And Moses reported the words of the people to YHWH").

18. Hebrew, וְעַתָּה הָשֵׁב אֵשֶׁת־הָאִישׁ כִּי־נָבִיא הוּא וְיִתְפַּלֵּל בַּעַדְךָ וֶחְיֵה וְאִם־אֵינְךָ מֵשִׁיב דַּע כִּי־מוֹת תָּמוּת אַתָּה וְכָל־אֲשֶׁר־לָךְ:

19. Unlike "to walk with God" (הָלַךְ/הִתְהַלֵּךְ אֶת־הָאֱלֹהִים), which speaks of fellowship and communion (Gen 5:22, 24; 6:9; Mic 6:8; Mal 2:6; Rev 3:4), like עָמַד לִפְנֵי, "to stand before [a superior]," the Hebrew idiom, הִתְהַלֵּךְ לִפְנֵי, "to walk before [a superior]," derives from the royal court. A person who stood or walked "before the king" served as his confidant and courtier (Dan 1:4). Persons in the First Testament so designated who served as agents of God include the patriarchs (Gen 17:1; 24:40; 48:15), priests (1 Sam 2:30), and kings: David (1 Kgs 3:6; 8:25; 9:4; presumably also Ps 56:14[13]; 116:9), Solomon (1 Kgs 9:4), and Hezekiah (2 Kgs 20:3 = Isa 38:3).

20. Abraham addressed YHWH as אֲדֹנָי, "Lord," five times (vv. 3, 27, 30, 31, 32). Although he had begun boldly (vv. 23–25), modest verbal expressions of the patriarch's subordination to YHWH always follow the epithet.

21. In *BHS*, the Masoretic note claims the original reading had YHWH standing before Abraham. Cf. *Gen. Rab.* 49.7, "R. Simon said: 'This is a correction of the Scribes for the *Shekinah* was waiting for Abraham." However, Tov (*Textual Criticism of the Hebrew Bible,* 60–61) deems it unlikely that the original would have had YHWH standing before Abraham. For further discussion of these "intentional corrections of the scribes," see Arzi, "Tikkun Sopherim," 723. On this text, see McCarthy, *The Tiqqune Sopherim and Other Theological Corrections,* 70–76.

Although YHWH had condescendingly entered Abraham's world, Abraham had functioned faithfully as a prophetic intercessor.

Moses' Intercessory Prayer (9:18–19, 25–29)

Moses embedded two remarkable prayers in his speeches before the assembly of Israel on the Plains of Moab: a personal prayer in the first address (3:23–29), and an intercessory prayer in the second address (9:18–19, 25–29).[22] Although the personal prayer precedes the intercessory prayer literarily (within Deuteronomy), according to the narrative sequence of Exodus–Numbers Moses' prayer on behalf of his people occurred almost forty years prior to his private prayer (cf. 2:7; 8:2, 4; 29:4[5]). The former was uttered at Horeb shortly after the Israelites had left Egypt, which meant that at the time of this recollection the events that precipitated it were a distant memory. By contrast, the circumstances surrounding the personal prayer will have been fresh in his mind, the event having transpired near the place where he delivered the address in which it is embedded. Indeed, since it had probably happened within weeks, if not days, of the present convocation of this generation of Israelites on the Plains of Moab, the effects of YHWH's response still hang over the book like a cloud (cf. 32:48–52; 34:1–12).[23]

Like the portrayal of Abraham in Gen 18 and 20, the psalmist recognized the critical intercessory role played by Moses in 106:19–23:

> [19] They made a calf at Horeb and worshiped a cast image.
> [20] They exchanged the glory of God for the image of an ox that eats grass.
> [21] They forgot God, their Savior, who had done great things in Egypt,
> [22] wondrous works in the land of Ham, and awesome deeds by the Red Sea.
> [23] Therefore he said he would destroy them—
> had not Moses, his chosen one,[24] stood in the breach before him,
> to turn away his wrath from destroying them (NRSV).[25]

---

22. Remarkably neither of these texts receives any sustained treatment in the standard studies on prayer in the Hebrew Bible: Greenberg, *Biblical Prose Prayer*; Clements, *In Spirit and in Truth*; Balentine, *Prayer in the Hebrew Bible*; Miller, *They Cried to the Lord*; Brueggemann, *Great Prayers of the Old Testament*; Matlock, *Discovering the Traditions of Prose Prayers*. In the most recent work, Gary Millar devotes one page to Moses' private prayer (*Calling on the Name of the Lord*, 41–42) and one footnote (n. 48) to his intercessory prayer.

23. It is unclear why Moses did not embed a second intercessory prayer in his report of events at Kadesh-barnea in 1:19–46. Preserved in Num 14:12–19, that prayer rivals in eloquence, content, and effect both the biographer's rendering of his original prayer at Sinai (Exod 32:10–14) and Moses' own recollection of it in Deut 9:18–19, 25–29. See below.

24. Although the verb changes, the psalmist's characterization of Moses as YHWH's chosen (בָּחַר), recalls Gen 18:19, where YHWH referred to Abraham as the object of his choice, albeit with a different verb, יָדַע.

25. The influence of Deuteronomy is reflected in the designation of the mountain as Horeb, the only occurrence of this name in the Psalter.

The Context of Moses' Intercessory Prayer (Deut 9:18–19)

Before considering the prayer of Moses itself, it is instructive to observe how YHWH invited his intervention. Whereas in Gen 18:17 YHWH had opened the door to Abraham with a rhetorical question ("Shall I hide from Abraham what I am about to do?"), in response to the apostasy involving the golden calf YHWH had issued a virtual command to Moses not to intervene: הֶרֶף מִמֶּנִּי, "Release from me [your hand]" (Deut 9:14).[26] Ostensibly an order, the statement, "Let me go,"[27] reflects the extraordinary bond between YHWH and Moses. In "begging" Moses to leave him alone that he might give full vent to his fury (Exod 32:10) and destroy Israel, paradoxically YHWH actually opened the door for his intervention.[28]

Moses' response to the people's sin, YHWH's threat, and his charge to leave him alone involved four elements: (1) a symbolic gesture of smashing the tablets (vv. 15–17); (2) a symbolic gesture of intercession before YHWH (vv. 18–19); (3) an intercessory gesture on behalf of his brother Aaron (v. 17); and (4) a symbolic gesture of disposing of the calf (v. 21). The brief reference to his prayer for Aaron contributes to the present discussion, but I shall focus on Moses intercession for the people, which is the focus of verses 18–19 and 25–29:

> [18] Then I threw myself down before YHWH as [I had done] before, forty days and forty nights. I neither ate bread nor drank water, because of all the sin that you had committed, by doing the evil in the sight of YHWH, thereby provoking him to anger. [19] For I was afraid of the anger and fury that YHWH bore against you, so that he intended to destroy you. But YHWH listened to me that time also.
>
> . . . .
>
> [25] So I threw myself down before YHWH for these forty days and forty nights, because YHWH had said he would destroy you. [26] And I prayed to YHWH,

---

26. הֶרֶף is a hiphil form of רָפָה, "to relax, let go," in the qal stem. The present expression is elliptical for הֶרֶף יָדְיךָ מִמֶּנִּי, "let your hands go from me," i.e., "release me." Cf. Josh 10:6. While the change from הַנִּיחָה לִּי, "Let me rest," in Exod 32:10, seems merely stylistic, the present idiom is more concrete, in keeping with Moses' heightening of YHWH's fury in his recollection of the event. YHWH's determination to "blot out Israel's name from under heaven" intensifies the image of divine fury.

27. Cf. Houtman, who translates the idiom, "Do not stop me" (*Exodus*, vol. 3, *Chapters 20–40*, 645). Targums Pseudo-Jonathan and Onqelos read אנח בעותך מן קדמי, "Desist from your prayer to me" (*Targum Pseudo-Jonathan: Deuteronomy*, 32). Targum Neophiti is even more explicit and expansive: מגע גרמך מן קדמיי מן למבעי, "Refrain yourself before me from begging mercy for them" (*Targum Neofiti 1: Deuteronomy*, 61). For the Aramaic texts, see *Targum Palaestinense in Pentateuchum*, vol. 5, *Deuteronomium*, 94–95. These readings accord with rabbinic exegesis, which seemed to assume that if Moses would pray for the Israelites, YHWH would not destroy them. Cf. *b. Ber* 32a, *ExR* XLII.9.

28. Cf. Moberly, *At the Mountain of God*, 50. According to Balentine (*Prayer in the Hebrew Bible*, 136), this is "a form of invitation by prohibition." Keil goes farther, suggesting that YHWH hereby placed the fate of Israel in Moses' hands and coaxed him to carry out his mediatorial role (*Genesis und Exodus*, 595).

'O Lord YHWH, do not destroy your people and your possession, whom you have redeemed through your greatness, whom you have brought out of Egypt with a mighty hand. ²⁷ Remember your servants, Abraham, Isaac, and Jacob. Disregard the stubbornness of this people, or their wickedness or their sin,

²⁸ . . . lest the country from which you brought us will say, "Because YHWH was unable to bring them into the land that he promised them, and because he hated them, he has brought them out to slaughter them in the desert." ²⁹ After all, they are your people and your possession, whom you brought out by your great power and by your outstretched arm.

In verses 18–19 Moses describes his symbolic gesture of intercession before YHWH. With our preoccupation with Moses and those who followed in his train as conduits of divine revelation, the intercessory obligations and privileges that came with the prophetic office are easily overlooked.²⁹ Moses' non-verbal response to the divine threat consisted of prostration before YHWH and fasting. The former, represented by הִתְנַפֵּל, refers to the act of a supplicant hurling himself/herself down to the ground before a superior (in this case YHWH) as a gesture of submission and urgent entreaty.³⁰ Moses' forty-day-and-night fast reinforced his urgency. Whereas previously he had fasted to concentrate on his official role as recipient of communication *from* YHWH for the people (v. 9), now this action highlighted his concentration on his intercessory role *before* YHWH on behalf of the people.³¹

Moses' explanation of the intensity of his intercession involved two motive clauses (v. 18b). He summarized the grievous nature of the people's crime, speaking of "the sin that you have sinned³² by doing the evil in the sight of YHWH," and thereby provoking him to anger (הִכְעִיס). This statement recalls 4:25, where Moses anticipated a similar future crisis in the land, precipitated by the manufacture of images (פֶּסֶל), which he interpreted as "doing the evil in the sight of YHWH," and resulting in his vexation/

---

29. Later prophets also followed in the intercessory train of Abraham: Samuel (1 Sam 12:23), Amos (Amos 7:1–9), and Jeremiah (Jer 18:20). A notable exception was Ezekiel, whom YHWH expressly forbade from functioning as an אִישׁ מוֹכִיחַ (Ezek 3:26).

30. The hithpael form נָפַל, "to fall," is rare, occurring elsewhere only in Gen 43:18 (where it means "to attack," that is, "to throw oneself upon someone"), verse 25 of our text, and Ezra 10:1. In the last reference this gesture is accompanied by prayer, confession, and crying before the temple in a communal ritual of mourning. The use of the hithpael is matched by other hithpael verbal expressions involved in prayer: הִתְפַּלֵּל, "to pray," (cf. Deut 9:26; Ezra 10:1); הִתְחַנֵּן, "to implore the mercy of" (Deut 3:23); הִתְוַדָּה, "to confess" (Ezra 10:1; Neh 9:3; Dan 9:4). On the symbolic significance of the act, see Gruber, *Aspects of Nonverbal Communication in the Ancient Near East*, 131–33.

31. That his intercession involved a forty-day struggle with YHWH is additional information, not found in Exod 32:11–13. It is unclear to which event Moses referred when he added כָּרִאשֹׁנָה, "as at first," in Deut 9:18. In this context, he refers to three forty day-night periods (9:9, 18; 10:10), two of which involved fasting (9:9, 18), but a comparable reference to previous prostration is missing. Since the exodus narrative reports two additional intercessory prayers by Moses in 33:30–35 and 34:9, the sequence of events was complex. In any case, here Moses' intent was not to recount the events with chronological precision, but to highlight theologically significant elements involved in the crisis.

32. Hebrew עַל כָּל־חַטַּאתְכֶם אֲשֶׁר חֲטָאתֶם, lit. "on account of all your sin that you had sinned," involves a verb and object from the same root, a common practice in Hebrew.

provocation (הִכְעִיס).³³ Moses reinforced the intensity of his response to the prospect of YHWH destroying Israel in verse 19 by using the rare word יָגֹר, "to be terrified," to express his own emotion,³⁴ followed by his three-fold reference to YHWH's fury: אַף, "anger," חֵמָה, "heat," and קָצַף, "to provoke."

Moses' present report of YHWH's response lacks the drama of "and YHWH relented (נָחַם) concerning the harm with which he had threatened his people," in Exod 32:14. Nevertheless, "And YHWH listened to me at that time as well," expresses his relief even as he reported this event thirty-eight years later.³⁵ The note reflects YHWH's extraordinary relationship with his representative, and declares that the prayer of this righteous man was indeed powerful and effective (James 5:16).

The Content of Moses' Intercessory Prayer (Deut 9:25–29)

Hearers recognize that the recollection of Moses' actual prayer in verses 25–29 belongs immediately after his report of his physical gestures of intercession in verses 18–19. However, between the framework represented by verses 7–8 and 22–24 Moses' singular rhetorical goal has been to demonstrate that, far from being morally worthy to receive the land of Canaan from YHWH, the Israelites had actually disqualified themselves. Naming additional places associated with rebellion in rapid-fire succession in verses 22–24, Moses spoke directly about YHWH's fury in response to the peoples' sin and the punishment they deserved. Even in recalling his own frightful reaction, he knew that YHWH's pronouncement of death on his people was just. Inserting the prayer in its natural location would have disrupted the flow and shifted attention away from the sinful people to God himself.

Displaying significant stylistic and substantive connections with the narrator's reports of Moses' prayers in Exod 32:11–13 and Num 14:13–19, Moses' recollection of his intercession involved a masterful combination of pathos and argumentation, undergirded by a profound covenantal theology. We may highlight the distinctive argumentation of the prayer as recalled here by juxtaposing it with the argumentation found in the earlier narratives (Table 12.1):

---

33. As in this text, the definite form הָרַע, "the evil," suggests a specific crime, that is, violation of the Supreme Command by worshiping divine rivals.

34. The word occurs elsewhere in Deuteronomy only in 28:60, speaking of intense dread at the thought of being afflicted with the diseases of Egypt.

35. It seems most logical to link the added particle גַם, "also, as well," to כָּרִאשֹׁנָה, "as at first, previously," in verse 18. This invites comparison of YHWH's response to this intercessory gesture with his answer to the prayer in Exod 32:11–14. However, recalled almost four decades later, Moses may have had in mind other crises during the desert wanderings in which his intercession resulted in sparing the people. Cf. Exod 14:15; 15:25; Num 11:2; 12:13–14; 14:13–20; 21:7–9.

Table 12.1
A Synopsis of Moses' Argumentation in His Intercessory Prayers

	Exodus 32:11–14	Numbers 14:13–19	Deuteronomy 9:26–29
1	Israel is YHWH's people, not his (v. 11a).		Israel is YHWH's people, not his (v. 26a).
2	YHWH has invested great effort in saving the Israelites from the bondage of Egypt: by implication, to destroy them would mean this was effort was wasted (v. 11b).	YHWH has invested great effort in saving the Israelites from the bondage of Egypt; by implication, to destroy them would mean this was effort was wasted (v. 13).	YHWH has invested great effort in saving the Israelites from the bondage of Egypt; by implication, to destroy them would mean this was effort was wasted (v. 26b).
3	YHWH's reputation among the nations will be damaged if he destroys Israel; they will think his intent was malicious from the beginning—to destroy Israel in the desert (v. 12).	YHWH has been uniquely close to his people: he is in their midst and has been personally leading them; by implication, it makes no sense to destroy them (v. 14).	Hold back for the sake of the patriarchs; overlook the sin of their descendants (v. 27).
4	Hold back for the sake of the patriarchs; to them he promised to multiply their seed and give them the land of Canaan as their possession forever (v. 13).	YHWH's reputation among the nations will be damaged if he destroys Israel; they will think that he slaughtered them in the desert because he was unable to carry through on his promise to give them the land (vv. 15–16).	YHWH's reputation among the nations will be damaged if he destroys Israel; they will think that he brought them out to destroy them in the desert because he was unable to carry through on his promise to give them the land, and because he hated them (v. 28).
5		YHWH's gracious character is in question; he has proved himself merciful in the past—may he be gracious again and forgive his people (vv. 17–19).	Israel is YHWH's people, not his (v. 29a).
6			YHWH has invested great effort in saving the Israelites from the bondage of Egypt; by implication, to destroy them would mean this was effort was wasted (v. 29b).

Moses' argumentation is most complex in the Deuteronomic version of his intercessory prayer. Before examining his specific contentions, we should note the structure of the passage and the rhetorical devices Moses employed to move God.

Structurally, verses 25–29 consist of a prose preamble (vv. 25–26a), followed by an extended quotation of Moses' prayer (vv. 26–29).[36] Unlike the narrative of his response in Exod 32:11–14 and Num 14:13–19, here Moses did not follow up the report of his prayer with a notice of YHWH's answer. In Exod 32:14 the narrator announces explicitly, "Then YHWH relented (נִחַם) and did not bring on his people the disaster he had threatened" (v. 14). In Num 14:19 the narrator quotes YHWH's response: "Then YHWH said, 'I have forgiven (סָלַח), according to your word'" (Num 14:20; cf. Moses' use of סְלַח in 14:19). In the present self-effacing autobiographical account, instead of announcing his effectiveness as an intercessor Moses moved immediately to reporting the replacement of the tablets of the covenant that he had smashed (Deut 10:1–5).

The preamble to the prayer (vv. 25–26a) involves several expressions encountered earlier in this context. Moses reminded his audience of his prostration (הִתְנַפֵּל) before YHWH (cf. v. 18a), his forty-day-and-night fast (cf. v. 18b), and his motivation: YHWH had said he would destroy (הִשְׁמִיד) Israel (cf. v. 19). This recapitulation was necessitated by the literary distance between Moses' first reference to his intercession in the face of YHWH's threat (vv. 18–19) and the actual words of the prayer (vv. 26b–29). The generic designation of his verbal response to God (v. 26) is the same as it had been with reference to his intercession for Aaron (v. 20); he "prayed to YHWH." The hithpael form, הִתְפַּלֵּל, denotes intercession to gain a favorable decision from a superior.[37] While it often involves intercession on behalf of someone else (Gen 20:7; Num 21:7; 1 Sam 7:5; Job 42:8), this is not always the case.[38]

As for the prayer itself, Moses began formally with the vocative, אֲדֹנָי יְהוִה, "O Lord YHWH," whereby he both acknowledged his own vassal status and addressed God by his personal name, "YHWH."[39] Unlike many other biblical prayers, which follow the address with doxological descriptors concerning God, acknowledging either his recent action or his personal qualities,[40] Moses immediately launched into his demands. The prayer is dominated by three imperatives: (1) "Do not destroy your people" (v. 26); (2) "Remember your servants, the patriarchs" (v. 27a); and (3) "Do not look on the sin of your people" (v. 27b). We might compare Moses' present wrestling with YHWH with a comparable earlier event. Whereas at the time of Moses' call YHWH was determined to get Moses' will in line with his own (Exod 3–4), this time Moses was determined to bend YHWH's will. Refusing to take "No" for an answer, he interceded urgently for his people, appealing to God's mercy, reputation, and fidelity to his promise. Each demand deserves brief comment.

---

36. Cf. the form and structure recognized by Miller, *They Cried to the Lord*, 342–43.

37. The etymology of הִתְפַּלֵּל remains uncertain (cf. *HALOT*, 933). On the word, see Verhoef, "Prayer," 1060–61; Schultz, "פלל," 627–28. Its relationship to the piel form, פִּלֵּל, "to pronounce judgment," is not clear, though the latter is used in 1 Sam 2:25 in the sense of "to be the arbiter, intercessor" (cf. Ezek. 16:52). Based on usage, הִתְפַּלֵּל is obviously related to the most common noun for "praise prayer," תְּפִלָּה. For a helpful study on prayer in the historiographic books, see Boda, "Prayer," 806–11.

38. 1 Sam 1:10; Dan 9:4; 2 Sam 7:27; 1 Kgs 8:30, 35, 42, 44, 48; 2 Chr 7:14.

39. This contrasts with Exod 32:11, where Moses begins with "Why?" and then adds, "O YHWH," and Num 14:13, where he dispenses with all such formalities and launches immediately into his argument.

40. See Gen 32:10–13[9–12]; 1 Chr 29:10–29; 2 Kgs 19:15b–19; Dan 9:1–27.

1. "Do not destroy your people" (v. 26).

The language of Moses' first demand is striking on several counts. First, the verb הִשְׁחִית, "to destroy, exterminate," is the same word he had used earlier to reassure the Israelites that YHWH is a compassionate God; he will not fail his people, nor "destroy" them, nor forget his covenant with the ancestors (4:31).[41]

Second, Moses personalized the object of the verb by adding the suffix, and then qualifying עַמְּךָ, "your people," with נַחֲלָתְךָ, "your special possession." With the former, he not only threw back into YHWH's court the ball he had been tossed in verse 12, but he also highlighted Israel's status as YHWH's covenant people. Forty days earlier on Horeb, YHWH had established his covenant with them, taking Israel as his people and becoming their God, in fulfillment of his own declared aims in Gen 17:7 and Exod 6:7. If YHWH would destroy Israel he would eliminate his partner in covenant. Moses reinforced his appeal to YHWH's personal relationship with Israel by characterizing them as "your special possession."[42] Although נַחֲלָה is usually translated with inheritance language, this is a feudal metaphor whereby YHWH claims Israel out of all the nations for his own direct prized possession (cf. 32:8–9).[43]

Moses' argumentation was deliberate, responding directly to YHWH's own statement in verse 12. On the one hand, his choice of verb in אַל־תַּשְׁחֵת, "Do not destroy," played on the root YHWH had used when he spoke of Israel becoming "corrupt" (שִׁחֵת). On the other hand, he also reacted directly to YHWH's disowning the Israelites by speaking of them as "your people, whom you brought out of Egypt." In appealing to YHWH's self-interest—surely he would not destroy his prized possession—Moses also served notice, "Don't put this lot on me! They are your people, not mine."

Third, Moses reminded YHWH that Israel was the product of his own extraordinary saving efforts. The man would accept neither the credit (cf. the people's statement in Exod 32:1) nor the blame (cf. YHWH's statement in v. 12) for the people who had gathered at Horeb. On the contrary, YHWH had "redeemed" (פָּדָה) them himself "with his greatness," and brought them out of Egypt "with a strong hand." Moses probably had in mind YHWH's speech in Exodus 6:2–7, where he had expressly declared that the purpose of the deliverance was to rescue the Israelites from their enslavement to Pharaoh, and to claim them for himself as his own covenant people.[44] Again appealing to divine self-interest, Moses suggested that if YHWH would destroy this people now, all this effort would have been wasted.

---

41. הִשְׁחִית often functions as technical military language for devastating conquered land and exterminating the population. For analysis of the root שחת in Hebrew, see Conrad, "שָׁחַת, šaḥat," 583–95. Although Israel and other nations are often the object, the word עַם, "people," occurs in this position only in 2 Sam 24:16.

42. This is one of only four places in Deuteronomy where Israel is called YHWH's נַחֲלָה (cf. 4:20; 9:20; 32:9).

43. This usage of נַחֲלָה places it within the same semantic field as חֵלֶק, "portion," and סְגֻלָּה, "treasured possession" (7:6; 14:2; 26:18).

44. See also Lev 25:55, "For the descendants of Israel belong to me as vassals (עֲבָדִים); they are my vassals (עֲבָדַי), whom I brought out of the land of Egypt: I am YHWH your God."

2. "Remember your servants, the patriarchs" (v. 27a).

Moses' second demand was cryptic: "Remember (זְכֹר)[45] your servants, Abraham, Isaac, and Jacob." Presumably because he had already frequently alluded to the patriarchs, further details were not needed. A comparison of this statement with its counterpart in Exod 32:13 confirms that he had in mind specifically YHWH's covenant commitments to the ancestors. There he had added, "to whom you swore by yourself, and to whom you promised, 'I will multiply your descendants like the stars of the sky, and this entire land of which I have spoken I will give to you as an eternal grant (נַחֲלַת עוֹלָם).'" By raising this issue Moses reminded YHWH that if he would break the covenant he had ratified with Israel at Horeb, he would violate his irrevocable covenant with the ancestors. His characterization of Abraham, Isaac, and Jacob as "your servants/vassals" (עֲבָדֶיךָ) appealed to YHWH's deep attachment to the ancestors. Moses had recognized this special relationship in 4:37, where he had declared that YHWH chose Israel as the object of his deliverance and beneficiary of his kindness because of his "love" (אָהַב) for the ancestors.

3. "Do not look on the sin of this people" (v. 27b).

Moses' expressed his third demand most fully and most daringly, calling upon YHWH to turn away (אַל־תֵּפֶן אֶל, lit., "Do not turn to") from the "stubbornness" (קְשִׁי הָעָם, cf. קְשֵׁה עֹרֶף, "stiff of neck," in vv. 9, 13), "wickedness" (רֶשַׁע, a stylistic variation of רִשְׁעָה in vv. 4–5), and "sin" (חַטָּאת) of "this people" (הָעָם הַזֶּה). Moses' use of three words to describe the Israelites' spiritual and moral state expresses the superlative degree (i.e., "utter sinfulness"), and by charactering them as "stiff-necked" and referring to them as "this people," he assented to YHWH's contempt for them. Moses neither excused his people nor minimized their sin. He could only plead for mercy, that YHWH would turn the other way and overlook their fundamentally sinful condition.[46] Within the overall argument of chapter 9, this is extremely significant, undercutting again any Israelite claims to the land based on moral superiority over the Canaanites.

Moses' rationale for this demand is daring. First as a warning to YHWH,[47] he declared that if he would destroy this people his reputation among the nations would be damaged (v. 28b).[48] As Moses had noted in 4:6–8 and 32–40, YHWH had chosen and rescued Israel to showcase to the world that he alone is God and that all his ways are righteous. As he frequently did in his valedictory addresses, Moses highlighted the public reaction by placing it on the lips of interlocutors, in this case the Egyptians, identified

---

45. As elsewhere זָכַר is not an antidote to amnesia, as if YHWH would forget anything, any more than שָׁכַח signifies an actual loss of memory. Rather זָכַר signifies, "to take into account, to act on the basis of."

46. See further Miller, *They Cried to the Lord*, 270–71.

47. The construction of the negative motive clause, with an introductory פֶּן, "lest," followed by imperfect verbs, is identical to the forms of his warnings to his own people in previous contexts: 4:9, 16, 19, 23; 6:12, 15; 7:22, 25; 8:11–12.

48. This argument occurs also in the Exodus version of the prayer (Exod 32:12) and in Moses' prayer at Kadesh-barnea (Num 14:14–16). See further Miller, ibid., 272–73.

as "the country out of which you brought us" (הָאָרֶץ אֲשֶׁר הוֹצֵאתָנוּ מִשָּׁם).[49] Egypt was an appropriate representative of hypothetical observers, since they had suffered the greatest loss when YHWH had "robbed" them of a significant portion of their population. Furthermore, Moses had told Pharaoh that the reason for the Israelites' journey into the desert was to serve YHWH[50] and to celebrate a feast in his honor.[51]

The first part of the Egyptians' quotation expresses two hypotheses, both of which should have been intolerable to YHWH. First, having succeeded in freeing this people from the Egyptians, YHWH would realize that this mission was impossible. Unable to see the Israelites through to the promised and, as he had promised (cf. Exod 3:8; 6:6–8), he simply slaughtered them in the desert. The second hypothesis is even more sinister. Rather than being driven by love (אָהַב) for the ancestors (Deut 4:37) and their descendants after them (7:6–9), as Moses had declared to the people, YHWH's removal of the Israelites from Egypt was driven by hatred (שִׂנְאָה from שָׂנֵא). Before the eyes of both Israelites (cf. Exod 14:11–12) and Egyptians the scheme of Israel's salvation would be exposed as a cynical and diabolical plot. The Egyptians would scarcely have distinguished between immediate divine causation and ultimate human responsibility for the people's fate. Moses hereby argued that for the sake of his own reputation YHWH had to overlook the people's sin and resume his mission.

Concluding where he had begun, Moses reminded YHWH again that Israel was his people, his treasured possession, in whose rescue he had invested a great deal of energy (v. 29; cf. v. 26). He should therefore overlook their rebellion and carry on with his project.

YHWH's Response to Moses' Prayer (10:1–5)

In Deut 9:19 Moses had noted in passing that YHWH listened to his prayer (v. 19), but unlike the narrator of these events in Exod 32:14, he did not describe YHWH's response. Having left the issue hanging, in Deut 10:1–5 he resumed the unfinished business. If Moses' smashing of the original divinely inscribed tablets demonstrated symbolically that the worship of the golden calf had terminated YHWH's covenant with them, then the manufacture of new identical tablets demonstrated symbolically that YHWH had taken them back. Moses reinforced this conclusion by noting YHWH's appointment of the Levitical priests as guarantors and guardians of the covenant (10:8–9), and his order to move on from Horeb to claim the land that he had promised on oath to the ancestors (v. 11). By declaring again that YHWH listened to him (v. 10), Moses suggested that these actions proved that YHWH had retracted his intention to destroy his people.

Moses' reticence to speak of having moved YHWH to change his heart (נָחַם) reflects not only his modesty, but also his determination to keep the focus on YHWH

---

49. Later interpreters' discomfort with this metonymic statement is reflected in the Samaritan Pentateuch and all the versions (LXX, Syriac, Targums, Vulgate), which read, עַם הָאָרֶץ, "people of the land." For other examples of geographic entities functioning metonymically for their inhabitants, see Gen 41:57; 1 Sam 17:46; 2 Sam 15:23; etc.

50. Exod 3:12; 4:23; 7:16; 7:26[8:1]; 20[8:28]; 9:1, 13; 10:3, 7–8, 11, 24, 26; 12:31.

51. Exod 3:18; 5:1, 3, 17; 8:4, 23–24[8, 27–28].

and his grace. The narrator may praise the man (Deut 34:5–12), but the man would not praise himself. This episode was not about him; it was about God and his grace toward his people. If and when they would cross the Jordan, this would not happen because of their superior numbers (cf. 7:6–10), or strength (8:17–18), and certainly not because of their superior righteousness (9:1–23). Nor would it happen because of their leader, however fearless he had been in interceding on their behalf. It would be due entirely to the grace of God.

Moses' Personal Prayer (3:23–29)

In contrast to Moses' downplaying of his own role in his intercessory prayer, his report of his personal prayer is candidly self-interested. Whether or not his original audience was aware of the events described in 3:23–29 prior to his telling, lacking a counterpart in the narratives of Numbers this account catches hearers by surprise. Although Num 20:1–12 provides the historical background to this prayer, and Num 27:12–14 probably reflects the occasion, neither text alludes to Moses' impassioned personal plea. Because the latter involved a private encounter with YHWH on Mount Abarim, had Moses not divulged this information no one would have known of Moses' embarrassingly ineffectual conversation with YHWH.

In verse 23 Moses declares the genre and context of his prayer. The expression אֶתְחַנַּן, from a root, חָנַן, "to be gracious, to favor someone," followed by the preposition אֶל, "to," means "to implore the mercy/grace of," and signals a specific and pointed request.[52] If the cognate noun, חֵן, speaks of undeserved action by a superior toward an inferior,[53] then הִתְחַנֵּן involves seeking such a response from the superior. By definition the superior is not obligated to respond as requested.[54]

The only clue Moses provides regarding the occasion of the prayer is vague; "at that time," apparently refers to events following the defeat of the two Amorite kings. Excited by those conquests, the 120-year-old man was desperate to see his dream of entering the promised land fulfilled; his sights were on "home" just across the Jordan. The prayer itself is short, consisting of twenty-nine words (not counting deictic אֶת) and taking up only verses 24 and 25, but it contains several typical features of biblical prose prayers.

The Invocative Address: אֲדֹנָי יְהוִה ("O Adonay YHWH)"

As in 9:26, the only other occurrence in Deuteronomy of this double invocation, with this invocation Moses sought to establish contact with the invisible deity. In the address Moses made two significant points. First, by opening with אֲדֹנָי, which means "lord, master," he acknowledges his own inferior status; YHWH is his Suzerain. Moses

---

52. Cf. Merrill, *Deuteronomy*, 111. For studies of this important root/word, see Freedman and Lundbom, "חָנַן," 22–36; Stoebe, "חנן ḥnn to be gracious," 1.439–47.

53. See Snaith, *The Distinctive Ideas of the Old Testament*, 127–30.

54. The expression is also used of prayers to God in 1 Kgs 8:33, 47, 59; 9:3; Ps 30:9[8]. Cf. the use of the word in human relationships Gen 42:21.

acknowledges his role in this relationship explicitly with his reference to himself as עֶבֶד, "your servant/vassal," in the following statement.[55] Although he often characterized the Israelites' status as slaves in Egypt with the same word (e.g., 6:21; 28:68), it actually word bore a wide range of meanings from servile slave to royal government officials. In courtly circles the title עֶבֶד הַמֶּלֶךְ, "servant of the king," identified a person with a high position (2 Sam 18:29; 2 Kgs 22:12 = 2 Chr 34:20; 25:8).[56] This is confirmed by the plethora of ancient seals and bullae from Israel and its environs bearing epithets like עבד המלך, "servant of the king,"[57] or more specifically, "servant of *RN*," where RN represents a royal name. Only important officials had their own seals; slaves did not.[58] Moses' self-identification as YHWH's servant declares both his subordinate status and his official role in the administration of YHWH's people.

Second, by adding the personal name "YHWH," Moses acknowledged the theological foundation for this prayer—YHWH's accessibility and his own personal relationship with God (cf. 4:7).[59] Whatever the etymology of the name, its significance was revealed through YHWH's election of Israel and his mighty acts of redemption, his covenant with Israel, and his gift of the promised and (cf. Exod 6:2–8) on one hand, and his gracious forgiveness and propositional utterance on the other (Exod 34:6–7).[60] Moses' plea for grace (cf. Deut 3:23) was based on his personal knowledge of and relationship with Israel's Suzerain.

The Description:

> "You have begun to show to your servant your greatness and your strong hand.
> For what god is there in heaven or on earth who can do the deeds and mighty works you do?"

Many prayers embedded in biblical narratives follow the opening invocation with a description of God, proclaiming his attributes or celebrating his actions.[61] Moses' doxology

---

55. In prayers עַבְדְּךָ, "your servant," functions as more than a courtesy; it expresses humility and subjugation even as it reflects the hope that the עֶבֶד, "servant," will receive a measure of goodwill from his אָדוֹן, "lord." See further Ringgren, "עָבַד *'ābad*; עֶבֶד *'ebed*; עֲבֹדָה," 392.

56. The word עֶבֶד is often found in construct with the names of specific kings: servant of Saul (1 Sam 29:3); of Solomon (1 Kgs 11:26; 2 Chr 13:6); of the king of Babylon (2 Kgs 25:8). Note also the personal name, Ebed-melek (עֶבֶד־מֶלֶךְ) in Jer 38:7–13; 39:15–18.

57. See, for example, the Jaazaniah seal mentioned at the outset, as well as an Edomite seal inscribed, "belonging to Qaws'anal, servant of the king" (לקוסענל עבד המלך) from Tell el-Kheleifeh (Bartlett, *Edom and the Edomites*, 151–57); "belonging to Shema servant of Jeroboam" (לשמע עבד ירבעם) from Megiddo (see Cogan and Tadmor, *II Kings*, 12a); and "belonging to Obadiah servant of the king" (לעבדיהו עבד המלך) an unprovenanced seal (Gibson, *Hebrew and Moabite Inscriptions*, 62, 64).

58. Even more impressive is a recently discovered Anatolian monument erected by a "servant of the king." For translation and discussion of the text, see Pardee, "A New Aramaic Inscription from Zincirli," 51–71.

59. Contrast this with the plight of the author of the "Prayer to Every God," noted above.

60. For detailed discussion, see Surls, *Making Sense of the Divine Name in Exodus*.

61. Cf. Gen 32:10[9]; 2 Sam 7:18–24; 1 Kgs 8:15; 2 Kgs 19:15; Dan 9:4. On the descriptions, see Miller, *They Cried to the Lord*, 63–68. On the form and structure of this prayer, see ibid., 342.

consists of a declarative statement followed by a rhetorical question. The former hints at YHWH's victories over Sihon and Og; in these events Moses had witnessed the beginning demonstrations of YHWH's greatness (גֹּדֶל)[62] and strong hand" (יָדְךָ הַחֲזָקָה). However, the latter expression suggests that Moses was actually looking back to the exodus from Egypt as the beginning/first phase of YHWH's mighty acts.[63] His reference to the beginning of YHWH's revelation (הַחִלּוֹתָ לְהַרְאוֹת) suggests that in his mind and as announced in Exod 3:6–10 and 6:2–9, the exodus was the first of a multi-phased project whose ultimate goal was the delivery of the land of Canaan into the Israelites' hands (cf. Deut 6:20–25; 26:5–9).

The second part of Moses' description of YHWH is cast as a rhetorical question: מִי־אֵל בַּשָּׁמַיִם וּבָאָרֶץ אֲשֶׁר־יַעֲשֶׂה כְמַעֲשֶׂיךָ וְכִגְבוּרֹתֶךָ, in effect, "Who is a god in heaven or earth whose actions can match the mighty acts of YHWH?" The question obviously demands a negative answer: "There is no god like YHWH!" Moses will elaborate fully on this notion at the end of this address (4:32–40).

The Petition:

> "Let me go over and see the good land beyond the Jordan—that fine hill country and the Lebanon."

Moses expressed his petition forthrightly and passionately. His singular desire now was to cross the Jordan and experience (Heb. רָאָה, literally "to see") the good land firsthand.[64] The depth of his grief at being barred entry into the land would be even more apparent later in 8:7–10 and 11:9–12, where in idealized and Edenic detail he described the land. Whereas modern visitors to the land of Palestine perceive the land differently—as a land of rocks and hills—having spent forty years in the desert, to the Israelites any landscape with green would have seemed Edenic. But for Moses Canaan was more than a place on the map; it was a theological idea. The land was good, because YHWH had promised it to the ancestors and reserved it for his people. Moses had never lived there, but he could see "home" across the Jordan; this was the destination toward which he and the people had been headed since they left Egypt (Exod 3:8).

---

62. The word appears only four times in Deuteronomy, always in connection with Israel's exodus from Egypt, YHWH's self-revelation at Sinai, or his victory over the enemies. Deut 5:24 contains a similar confessional statement, acknowledging that YHWH has shown Israel his "glory" and greatness" (כָּבֹד and גֹּדֶל). Cf. also 9:26; 11:2; 32:3.

63. This expression occurs ten times in Deuteronomy: 3:24; 4:34; 5:15; 6:21; 7:8, 19; 11:2; 26:8; 34:12. Each context refers to YHWH's "strong hand" rescuing Israel from the Egyptians. Given the ubiquity in Egyptian iconography of Pharaonic figures with flexed arms wielding a sword or club, this imagery is especially appropriate in statements concerning YHWH's actions toward the Egyptians. On this matter, see Block, *The Book of Ezekiel Chapters 25–48*, 175–76, and more fully, Hoffmeier, "The Arm, of God Versus the Arm of Pharaoh," 378–87.

64. He expressed his pain at the prospect of missing this opportunity by heaping up adjectives to describe the goal (הָאָרֶץ הַטּוֹבָה, "the fertile land"; הָהָר הַטּוֹב הַזֶּה, "this fertile hill country"; הַלְּבָנֹן, "and the Lebanon." "The Lebanon" functioned as a proverbial designation for any lush landscape.

The Divine Response:

> [26] *But YHWH was cross with me because of you and would not listen to me. YHWH said to me, 'Enough from you; do not speak to me anymore of this matter.* [27] *Climb to the top of Pisgah and raise your eyes westward and northward and southward and eastward. You may see it with your eyes, but you will not cross over this Jordan.* [28] *You must charge Joshua, and encourage and strengthen him, because he is the one who will go on ahead of this people, and enable them to receive as their grant the land that you see.*

As recounted here, YHWH's answer to Moses' plea consisted of three parts. First, he declared in no uncertain terms his refusal to grant his request. Apparently angered[65] that Moses had not taken as final his earlier statement that neither he nor Aaron would enter the land (Num 20:12), YHWH cut Moses off;[66] he did not want to hear about the matter again.

Second, YHWH offered Moses a consolation prize. Reversing the order of the requests in verse 25, he invited Moses to climb to the top of Mount Pisgah and look across the Dead Sea and over the Jordan River and take in the sight of the promised land in all directions. While technically, "See (רָאָה) it with your eyes" answers to Moses' second request—that he "see" the land—the level of "seeing" would not satisfy him. While for Moses merely "observing" (rather than "experiencing") the land meant an aborted dream, in YHWH's mind his mission was finished; he had brought the people to the brink of the Jordan.

Third, YHWH charged Moses to prepare Joshua to replace him and lead the people across the Jordan. For Moses, turning over the reins of authority to his apprentice, who would deliver Canaan into Israel's hands, undoubtedly heightened the anguish. But never mind, Moses was to prepare Joshua for the challenges ahead.[67]

Moses' painful epilogic note concluded his recollections of this event with YHWH: they remained in the valley opposite Beth-Peor on the plains of Moab (34:1). His own personal journey was over.

---

65. LXX ὑπερεῖδεν, "to overlook, ignore," mistakenly derives וַיִּתְעַבֵּר from עָבַר, "to pass over." Following Friedman (Commentary on the Torah, s.v.), the translation of הִתְעַבֵּר as "he was cross," preserves the pun in Hebrew. The rare verb הִתְעַבֵּר, appears elsewhere only in Psalms and Proverbs (8x), and is related to a more common substantive עֶבְרָה, "wrath, fury" (34x), though this term is absent in Deuteronomy. In 1:37 and 4:21 Moses used הִתְאַנַּף). For discussion of the word and its cognates, see Schunck, "עֶבְרָה 'ebrâ," 425–30.

66. The construction רַב לְ has been encountered earlier in 1:6 and 2:3. Here the expression is strong, in effect, "Stop it!" or "Shut up!"

67. YHWH's three-fold command to "charge" (צַו), "encourage" (חֲזַק), and "strengthen" (אַמֵּץ) Joshua suggests that the situation in Canaan had not changed since the Israelites had left Kadesh-barnea thirty-eight years earlier.

Reflections on Moses' Inability to Move YHWH

The self-portrait that Moses the man of prayer paints (a literary "selfie") in Deuteronomy sends an ambivalent message. On the one hand, chapter 9 casts him as a bold servant of the people and agent of God, who through prayer moved YHWH to withdraw his threat against his own people and preserve their role in redemptive history. By contrast, in terms of achieving personal goals, his last wrestling match with YHWH was a failure. Even before Moses had finished speaking YHWH ordered him never again to express his desire to enter the promised land.

From our modern Western vantage, we marvel at YHWH's mercy at Horeb, but we question both his justice and his compassion toward Moses at the end of his life. Where was the grace that YHWH had proclaimed so dramatically in Exod 34:6–7 after the golden calf affair? Was the offense that caused him to slam the door to the promised land in Moses' face such an egregious crime? If YHWH could overlook the people's violation of the Supreme Command at Horeb and reinstitute the covenant, could he not forgive Moses and reopen the door for him? Was his request unreasonable? After leading this people for YHWH's sake for forty years, did he not deserve a more sympathetic "Thank you"? Was it not a small thing that he was asking: just to cross the river, breathe the air, touch the land, and taste the fruit on the other side, and then return across the Jordan to die? For Moses the east side of the Jordon obviously did not represent the promised land.

Why was YHWH's answer here so different from what it had been forty years ago? We might begin to address the question by taking a synoptic look at both prayers (Table 12.2).

Table 12.2
A Synopsis of Moses' Prayers in Deuteronomy[68]

Feature	Deuteronomy 3:23–29	Deuteronomy 9:18–19, 25—10:11
Location	Plains of Moab (1:1–5)	Mount Horeb (9:8)
Occasion	YHWH's prohibition of Moses from entering the promised land, in response to his professional and spiritual failure (32:48–52).	YHWH's fury and his threat to destroy Israel for their blatant apostasy (9:8–19).
Petitionary posture	---	Prostration before YHWH (הִתְנַפֵּל, 9:18a, 25a).
Genre of the Prayer	A plea for divine mercy (הִתְחַנֵּן, 3:23).	Intercession for divine change of heart (הִתְפַּקְלֵל, 9:26).
Invocation	O Lord YHWH! (3:24a).	O Lord YHWH! (9:26b).

---

68. See also Appendix A.

Feature	Deuteronomy 3:23–29	Deuteronomy 9:18–19, 25—10:11
Description of Addressee	YHWH has begun to show his incomparable greatness and power in his mighty acts on behalf of Israel (3:24b).	---
The Request	Let me cross over and see the good land (3:25a).	Do not destroy your people. Remember your servants Abraham, Isaac and Jacob. Do not regard the stubbornness and sin of this people (9:27–28).
The Argument	The land is good (3:25b)	Israel is YHWH's people, not Moses' (9:26a, 29a). To destroy Israel would mean YHWH's saving acts were wasted (9:26b, 29b). YHWH's loyalty to the ancestors is at issue (9:27). YHWH's reputation among the nations would be irreparably damaged (9:28).
YHWH's Immediate Response	YHWH was cross with Moses (3:26a). YHWH refused to listen to Moses (3:26a). YHWH ordered Moses to stop and never mention the subject again (3:26b).	YHWH listened to Moses (9:19b; 10:10b), and his will was changed—he was unwilling to destroy Israel (10:10b). YHWH renewed the covenant (10:1–5)
YHWH's Provision for the Future	Moses was to climb Mt. Pisgah and view the land (3:27). Moses was to commission and encourage Joshua to succeed him (3:28).	YHWH commissioned the Levites for divine service (9:26a).
Result	Israel remained camped at Beth-Peor (3:29).	YHWH charged Moses to lead the people on to the promised land (10:11).

The most obvious differences involved the occasions and the goals of the prayers. Whereas Moses' earlier prayer was intended to stave off divine fury against others (his people), the goal of the later prayer was personal and private. Indeed, Moses appears embarrassingly self-absorbed. Whereas at Horeb he was willing to sacrifice ambition[69] and life itself to win the favor of YHWH on the people's behalf with extra-ordinary self-denial (Exod 32:30–34), his account of his personal prayer reveals a man focused on himself and the satisfaction of private wishes. This scarcely looks like the same man. Several factors account for this contrast.

69. YHWH offered to start his project over with him, and in effect make him the patronymic ancestor of his (YHWH's) people (9:14). Had he accepted it we would be talking about Mushites, rather than Israelites.

First, while we may not make too much of arguments from silence, the absence of a reference to physical prostration before YHWH his superior (cf. 9:18, 25) may suggest he took access to the divine presence for granted.

Second, while his invocative address in 3:24 is identical to that in 9:26, and he explicitly acknowledged his status as עֶבֶד (3:24b), the latter could be construed as self-serving, claiming membership in YHWH's court as a ground for a favorable hearing.

Third, although divine descriptions following the invocative address are common in biblical prayers,[70] given the context and nature of Moses' plea one wonders if his characterization of YHWH in 3:24 reflected genuine respect or shallow flattery.

Fourth, whereas his prayer at Horeb consisted of profound theological arguments, the present request involved merely a personal desire. Moses could at least have declared his intention to celebrate YHWH's faithfulness to his promises, perhaps by setting up a memorial altar as Abraham had done at Shechem (Gen 12:7).

Fifth, and most telling of all, without a hint of acknowledgement of his own culpability for an offense that had precipitated YHWH's closing the door to the promised land to him (cf. 32:48–52), when YHWH rejected his request, he blamed the people. Moses' statement in 3:26 deserves a closer look. This is the middle of three variations of this clause in this first address:

גַּם־בִּי הִתְאַנַּף יְהוָה בִּגְלַלְכֶם	1:37	But against me YHWH's fury burned because of you.
וַיִּתְעַבֵּר יְהוָה בִּי לְמַעַנְכֶם	3:26	And YHWH was enraged against me because of you.
וַיהוָה הִתְאַנֶּף־בִּי עַל־דִּבְרֵיכֶם	4:21	And YHWH's fury burned against me because of you.

The first and third statements are awkwardly inserted in their respective contexts, suggesting that as he spoke to the people intense bitterness was boiling just below the surface. Technically Moses was correct. If the Israelites had entered the land from Kadesh-barnea, his offense against YHWH would never have occurred, and by now he would have been enjoying the blessings of the land for almost four decades.[71] However, at another level, the words were patently false; as YHWH would emphasize in 32:49–52 (cf. Num 20:12), Moses had only himself to blame for his failure to enter Canaan. These were not the words of a "suffering servant,"[72] innocently bearing the judgment that rightly belonged to others; they were the laments of a bitter old man, frustrated with God and angry with his people.[73]

---

70. See the prayers of Jacob (Gen 32:9[8]); David (1 Chr 10:11–13); Hezekiah (2 Kgs 19:15b–19), Daniel (Dan 9:4).

71. In his otherwise thorough discussion of Deuteronomy's perspective[s] on the reason for Moses not entering the land, Lim seems oblivious to this fundamental chronological datum ("the Sin of Moses in Deuteronomy," 250–66). Similarly Lee, "The Exclusion of Moses from the Promised Land," 217–39.

72. Contra Miller, "Moses My Servant," 253–54.

73. In his earlier recollections, Moses had been quite transparent about his feelings:

> At that time I said to you, "You are too heavy a burden for me to carry by myself. YHWH your God has multiplied you so that today you are as numerous as the stars in the sky. May YHWH, the God of your ancestors, increase you a thousand times and may he bless you as he has promised! But can I carry your problems, your concerns, and your bickering all by myself? (1:9–12).

Although YHWH's reaction to Moses' personal prayer seems calloused, this episode is just one detail in the literary portrait of a remarkable if complex man. In assessing Moses we need to consider the entire book. After this first address, the only person who spoke of Moses being barred from the land was YHWH himself, and that immediately prior to Moses' decease (32:48–52). In Moses' lengthy second address he never again alluded to this event. Instead he focused on the gospel represented by YHWH's electing and saving actions (4:32–40; 6:20–25; 7:6–11; 10:15; 11:2–4; 26:5–8), YHWH's care in the desert (8:1–5, 15–16), his provision of a homeland in fulfillment of his covenant promises (6:10–11, 23; 7:12–16; 8:7–14; 10:11; 11:9–12; 26:9), and his vision/promise of Israel's well-being (טוֹב) in that land in the future (7:12–16; 8:12–13; 11:13–15; 28:1–14). Occasionally Moses expressed pessimism regarding Israel's spiritual future, but his disposition toward the present generation seems positive. He commended them for their fidelity to YHWH (4:3–4; cf. 5:2–5), and gladly acceded to desires that might surface once they have entered the land: as mundane as eating meat in their home towns (12:15–16, 20–25) and as consequential as the establishment of a human monarchy (17:14–20). Having vented here, he seems to have moved on emotionally.

YHWH had obviously not dismissed him from his service because of his failure to his commission and his Commissioner by not treating YHWH as holy in the midst of the people (לֹא־קִדַּשְׁתֶּם אוֹתִי בְּתוֹךְ בְּנֵי יִשְׂרָאֵל, 32:51). Indeed, after the Meribah-kadesh incident (cf. Num 20:1–13), for thirty-eight years he had faithfully administered and shepherded YHWH's people. In his recollections he acknowledged his privileged role as mediator and interpreter of divine revelation (5:23–33; 18:15–22), warned the people not to add to or subtract from the Torah he proclaimed (4:2; 13:1[12:32]), and pronounced the curse (חֵרֶם) on anyone "who preaches another gospel" (12:28–13:19[18]; 18:20; cf. Gal 1:6–9). Even though the boundaries of Moses' speech are coterminous with the boundaries of YHWH's speech in Deuteronomy, in the end he appeared resigned to his fate.

If hearers of Moses' addresses doubt Moses' disposition toward YHWH, his biographer did not. YHWH's last recorded words reminded him that he would not cross the Jordan: "But you will not cross over there" (וְשָׁמָּה לֹא תַעֲבֹר, 34:4). However, when Moses climbed Mount Pisgah for the last time his standing with YHWH was intact.

First, whereas earlier YHWH had declared that Moses would see the land with his own eyes,[74] the narrator has *YHWH showing him all the land* (וַיַּרְאֵהוּ יְהוָה אֶת־כָּל־הָאָרֶץ, 34:1), and highlighting the totality of the exposition (vv. 1–3). In his final speech YHWH acknowledged his own involvement: הֶרְאִיתִיךָ בְעֵינֶיךָ, lit., "I have caused you to see it with your own eyes."

Second, having identified Moses earlier as "the man of God" (אִישׁ הָאֱלֹהִים, 33:1), the narrator now refers to him by a second honorific title, "servant of YHWH" (עֶבֶד־יְהוָה, 34:5).

Third, he interprets Moses' death in Moab as the fulfillment of the divine word (v. 5).[75]

---

74. 3:27, וְשָׂא עֵינֶיךָ יָמָּה וְצָפֹנָה וְתֵימָנָה וּמִזְרָחָה וּרְאֵה בְעֵינֶיךָ, "Look out to the west and north and south and east. See with your own eyes"; 32:49, וּרְאֵה אֶת־אֶרֶץ כְּנַעַן, "See the land of Canaan"; 32:52, מִנֶּגֶד תִּרְאֶה אֶת־הָאָרֶץ, "From a distance you may see the land."

75. The only comparable narrative account concerns the death of Ahaziah, son of Ahab, who died "according to the word of YHWH" (וַיָּמָת כִּדְבַר יְהוָה), that is, in precise fulfillment of Elijah's prophecy

Fourth, in the burial notice, he describes Moses' unparalleled final privilege; he was buried in a secret place by YHWH himself (v. 6).

Fifth, he highlights Moses' incomparable personal relationship with YHWH; since his death there has been no prophet like him, "whom YHWH knew face to face" (אֲשֶׁר יְדָעוֹ יְהוָה פָּנִים אֶל־פָּנִים, v. 10).

Sixth, contrary to Moses' own statements,[76] and the entire Hebrew Bible, the narrator attributes all the "signs and wonders" (הָאֹתוֹת וְהַמּוֹפְתִים) performed in Egypt to Moses, though he adds that he did so as YHWH's "commissioned" (שָׁלַח) agent.

In the end the narrator has the last word; this idealized view of Moses should determine our reading of the entire book. Nevertheless, it is quite remarkable that in the first address the narrator refused to sanitize Moses' own comments that might have cast his character in a negative light. The biographer's earlier characterization of Moses as "a very humble man, more so than any other man on earth" (עָנָו מְאֹד מִכֹּל הָאָדָם אֲשֶׁר עַל־פְּנֵי הָאֲדָמָה, NRSV) still stood. (Deut 34:10–12).[77]

Whereas through Moses' intercession YHWH was willing to overlook much more serious crimes and take his people back, when Moses demanded this personal favor YHWH refused, "because you did not treat me as holy in the midst of the descendants of Israel" (עַל אֲשֶׁר לֹא־קִדַּשְׁתֶּם אוֹתִי בְּתוֹךְ בְּנֵי יִשְׂרָאֵל, 32:51). Obviously YHWH took Moses' role as leader of the people extremely seriously. Like the king anticipated in 17:14–20, Moses' first responsibility was to embody righteousness as defined by the covenant. Presumably on the principle, "To those to whom much is given, of them much is required, and from those to whom much is entrusted, of them more will be demanded" (cf. Luke 12:48), at this critical moment in the nation's history YHWH could not tolerate leaders publicly violating his trust and misrepresenting his sanctity. Moses had transgressed the fundamental covenant principle: "You shall love YHWH your God," that is, "You shall be covenantally committed to him so that you always act in his interest."[78]

Concluding Reflections on a Deuteronomic Theology of Prayer

Whether we examine these two episodes together or separately, Moses' frank conversations with God illuminate the nature and process of trusting prayer.

First, prayer is an act of worship. If "true worship involves reverential acts of submission and homage to the divine superior in response to his gracious revelation of

---

(2 Kgs 1:16–17). However, Moses' biographer used a different idiom (וַיָּמָת ... עַל־פִּי יְהוָה), which refers not so much to a prediction, but to a divine verdict concerning Moses.

76. Deut 4:34; 6:22; 7:19; 13:2, 3[1, 2]; 26:8; 28:46; 29:1–2[2–3]. Cf. also Exod 7:3; Neh 9:10; Ps 78:43; 135:9; Isa 8:18; 20:3; Jer 32:20, 21. The closest comparable text is Ps 105:27, which speaks of Moses and Aaron performing YHWH's signs and wonders "in the land of Ham."

77. This negative image argues for the authenticity of the first address. A biographer of the seventh century or later, when the image of Moses had been so idealized in the popular imagination, would not have created a speech like this.

78. The essential meaning of "You shall love YHWH your God." On which see Block, *Deuteronomy*, 144, 182–84, 189–90, *et passim*.

himself and in accord with his will,"⁷⁹ then prayer represents the supreme expression of that. When Moses cast himself to the ground (Deut 9:18, 25), addressed God as "Adonay YHWH" (3:24, 9:26), and referred to himself as "your servant" (3:24), he illustrated physical, psychological, and spiritual prerequisites to gaining a hearing with God. YHWH is the divine king; we earthlings are his subjects.

Second, prayer must be grounded in correct theology. In ancient Israel, high theology was demonstrated not so much through the recital of creeds or lofty recitation of divine attributes, as through testimony to and celebration of YHWH's gracious concrete acts on people's behalf. Through YHWH's saving acts at the time of the exodus he had demonstrated his supremacy over all so-called gods. In fact, as Moses declared in 4:32–40, his "signs and wonders" on Israel's behalf were unprecedented in all of human history and demonstrated to all with open eyes of faith that he alone is God. Moses was eager to see the memory of these saving acts kept alive as the Israelites engaged the Canaanites. As they entered the land with its seductive fertility religions and illusory gods, their confidence would need to be in YHWH alone. He may be personally and physically invisible, but the very existence of Israel as a people represents the clearest proof of his existence. Confident prayer is based upon the relationship that God has established with his people.

Third, effectual intercessory prayer requires a "righteous" intercessor (Jas 5:16). As in the rest of the Hebrew Bible, in Deuteronomy the word צֶדֶק/צְדָקָה denotes behavior that conforms to an established standard, the standard in this instance being the covenant stipulations as revealed to the vassal by YHWH, the covenantal Suzerain.⁸⁰ Moses was a righteous man. In interceding for his people at Horeb he demonstrated his "covenant commitment" through actions in their interest. Fully acknowledging their sin, and thereby YHWH's justice in punishing them, when he appealed for YHWH to withdraw his anger he could only plead for mercy. However, his personal prayer reflects a momentary lapse in his righteous conduct. Preoccupied with self-interest he overlooked the sin that had triggered YHWH's closing the door to the promised land for him in the first place. God is not obligated to answer such prayers in the petitioner's favor.

Fourth, even in prayer God remains the Sovereign, and he retains the right to say "Yes" or "No" to a human supplicant's requests. As Moses would assert in 4:6–8, of all the nations, only Israel had a God so near that he heard them whenever they called upon him. But "No" is an answer. When people pray, several different outcomes are possible. (1) As Moses recounted in chapter 9 and the narrator described in Exod 32 and Num 14, through the effectual fervent prayer of a righteous person, God's disposition may be changed (cf. also Jonah 3–4). (2) God may indeed answer fervent prayer affirmatively and effect a change in one's external circumstances (cf. Acts 12:5–17). (3) Through prayer the persons praying may themselves be changed. Rather than bringing God's will into conformity with ours, sometimes through prayer God brings the petitioner's will into conformity with his own will. In such cases this is not a failure of faith, because true faith accepts God's "No." Sometimes that "No" is final.

79. For detailed development of this thesis, see Block, *For the Glory of God*, esp. pp. 23–27.

80. The word means the same with reference to divine Suzerain, whom Deut 32:4 declares to operate justly (כָּל־דְּרָכָיו מִשְׁפָּט) and to be faithful (אֱמוּנָה), righteous (צַדִּיק), upright (יָשָׁר), and lacking in caprice (אֵין עָוֶל). For further discussion, see Block, *How I Love Your Torah, O LORD!* 16–18.

13

How Can We Bless YHWH?

Wrestling with Divine Violence in Deuteronomy[1]

ACCORDING TO THE *WORLD REPORT on Violence and Health*, violence involves "the intentional use of physical force or power, threatened or actual, against oneself, another person, or against a group or community, that either results in or has a high likelihood of resulting in injury, death, psychological harm, maldevelopment, or deprivation."[2] By this definition violence pervades the book of Deuteronomy. What is particularly troubling to many readers today is not so much the violence perpetrated by humans against humans, but the violence perpetrated by and commanded by God. Given modern "enlightened" sensitivities, this violence is difficult to accept. While many have tried to justify divine destructiveness and belligerence in the Hebrew Bible, my purpose in this essay is more modest; I would simply like to understand it as the book of Deuteronomy portrays it.[3] I shall pursue this goal by asking several leading questions: (1) What forms does divine violence take? (2) Who are the objects of divine violence? and (3) What motivates divine violence?

At the outset I recognize that my answers to these questions will be affected by how I read Deuteronomy and the provenance I assign to the book. In critical scholarship, it has become commonplace to stifle the divine voice in Deuteronomy and attribute the book's portrayal of YHWH to misguided "deuteronomists," who, in the Persian period, sought to bolster Jewish identity in the face of external threats, or to mollify the image of God by interpreting divinely prescribed actions against the Canaanites and against their own people as metaphorical and hyperbolic rhetoric intent on preserving a pure

---

1. This is a stylistically modified version of an essay that was previously published in *Wrestling with the Violence of God: Soundings in the Old Testament*, ed. M. Daniel Carroll R., and J. Blair Wilgus; BBRSup 10 (Winona Lake: Eisenbrauns, 2015), 39–50. I am grateful to the editors and to Jim Eisenbraun for their kind permission to republish it here. I am also grateful to Mr. Eisenbraun for his permission to restore several footnotes that were deleted in the previous previous version.

2. This is the definition employed by the Violence Prevention Alliance (VPA), a network of WHO Member States, international agencies, and civil society organizations working to prevent violence. The source of the definition is http://www.who.int/violenceprevention/approach/definition/en/, accessed January 19, 2014.

3. Seitz ("Canon and Conquest," 292) helpfully distinguishes between "*justify*[ing] the ways of God" and "*speaking of God rightly*" (italics his).

religious community. With these approaches, many of the ethical problems raised by the policies prescribed in Deuteronomy evaporate. However, the theological problem remains, inasmuch as Deuteronomy contains a considerable amount of divine speech and even more speech attributed to Moses, who purportedly spoke only as YHWH commanded him to speak (e.g., 1:3; 4:1–2, 45; cf. 30:2). Even if the book represents an "abstract painting" rather than a "photograph" of YHWH, and even if the book presents a late portrait retrojected to an earlier time, if this book was to be deemed canonical—which it was—it creates a troubling image of deity that many reject today. But this raises the question: in what sense can the book of Deuteronomy then be accepted as canonical and sacred Scripture?[4]

If people's ethical conduct is to be inspired by the deities they serve (*imitatio dei*), eventually this image of YHWH would prove ethically problematic for his people, unless they recognized their sacred texts to be fictional.[5] But this seems unlikely. The writers of biblical texts did not think they were writing fiction,[6] and ancient lay readers/hearers would certainly not have thought that was what they were reading/hearing.

The Forms of Divine Violence in Deuteronomy

In tabulating the forms of divine violence in Deuteronomy we note first that Deuteronomy not only attributes violence directly to God, but that he is also ultimately responsible for violent actions he commands others to execute. I shall examine these two categories separately.

The Forms of Direct Divine Violence

A quick survey of statements in which YHWH is the subject of verbs of violence is revealing. Illustrative of the supreme acts of violence are instances in which YHWH kills (9:28 [hypothetical]; 32:39), destroys (2:22; 31:4), exterminates (7:10; 8:20), and strikes (1:4; 28:22, 27–28, 35). With respect to populations specifically, he cuts them off (12:29; 19:1), drives them out (33:27), expels them (6:19; 9:4), leads them off [into exile] (4:27; 28:37), dispossesses them [of their land] (4:38; 9:4), delivers one population/land into the hands of another (1:27; 20:13), scatters them (4:27; 28:64; 30:3), subdues them (9:3), intervenes [to punish] (5:9), and blots out persons' names from under heaven (9:14; 29:19[20]). Given the definition of "violence" above, here we note also Deuteronomy's emphasis on God intimidating and demoralizing people. The book has a remarkably full vocabulary of psychological and emotional violence: YHWH performs "awesome deeds" (4:34; 26:8) and "terror" (32:25), causing "fright" (2:25), "dread" (2:25; 28:67), "trembling" (2:25; 28:65), "confusion" (7:23; 28:20), and "frustration" (28:20). YHWH's determination to operate violently is reflected in 2:30, where Moses observes that just

---

4. Seitz (ibid, 292–308) offers a helpful study of this question in the thinking of the early Church Fathers.

5. Thus C. Anderson, "What about the Canaanites?" 27–72.

6. On this see Lasine, "Fiction, Falsehood, and Reality in Hebrew Scripture," 24–40.

has YHWH had hardened Pharaoh's heart that he might multiply the signs and wonders—all violent actions against Egypt (Exod 4:21; 7:3; 10:1; 14:4)—so "he stiffened Sihon's resolve and hardened his heart." This may be deemed a violent divine act, setting the stage for physical violence as YHWH hands Sihon over to the Israelites and their execution of the principle of ḥērem in verses 33–35. Two texts illustrate YHWH's violence with particular poignancy: the covenant curses in chapter 28, most notably verses 20–29, 35–37, and 59–66, and verses 23–27 of chapter 32, which Deuteronomy casts as a sort of national anthem for the nation.[7]

The Forms of Indirect Divine Violence

Indirect violence involves divinely mandated violent actions performed by a third party. In these instances YHWH hands the instruments of violence into the hands of humans. The actions involved may be grouped into two categories: (1) the forms of violence listed above, that is, violence perpetrated against groups usually in conflict over land or in response to offenses of the population against the divine Suzerain; (2) forms of violence commanded by God but directed against individuals in the administration of justice and righteousness. With respect to the first, YHWH charges Israel "to destroy" the Canaanites (7:24; cf. 33:27), "to exterminate" them (9:3) and their names from under heaven (7:24), "to dispossess" them (7:17; 9:1, 3; 11:23), to execute ḥērem on their population (3:2 [cf. 2:32–35]; 13:16[15]), and "to attack, defeat" (lit. "strike"; 2:33; 3:3; 7:2) with the sword (13:16[15]; 20:13). Israel's required disposition toward Canaanites is declared in 7:16, "Your eye must show no pity toward them." The second category is more extensive and as offensive to some modern readers as the first.[8] In Deuteronomy we find general commands to execute offenders (13:6, 10[5, 9]; 17:6, 7; 21:22; 24:16) and specifically to execute by stoning (13:11[10]; 17:2–7; 21:18–21; 22:20–24), flogging (25:1–3; perhaps also 21:18; 22:18), and mutilation (25:11–12). If a man refuses to honor his deceased brother by marrying his widow, he is to be shamed publicly (25:7–10). Along with these actions, Moses warned Israelites not to be swayed by sentimentality or pity for offenders (19:11–13, 18–21; 25:11–12; cf. 13:9[8]).

The Targets of Divine Violence in Deuteronomy

Non-Israelite Targets of Divine Violence

That the targets of much of YHWH's violence in Deuteronomy are non-Israelites is not surprising. Much of the literature on divine violence in the First Testament has focused on the divine determination to wipe the Canaanites from the land YHWH was handing

---

7. Block, "The Power of Song," 162–88.

8. Seibert (*Disturbing Divine Behavior*, 17–18) lists the following similarly offensive texts from Exodus and Leviticus that demand the death penalty: Exod 21:15 (striking parents); 21:16 (kidnapping); 21:17 (cursing parents); 31:15 (working on the Sabbath); Lev 20:10 (adultery); 20:13a (homosexual acts); 20:15–16 (bestiality); witchcraft (20:27); 24:16 (blaspheming the name of YHWH); 24:17 (murder).

over to Israel. However, this action, anticipated in Deuteronomy, would not represent the first expression of this disposition. In an earlier time south and east of the Dead Sea YHWH had "destroyed" the Emites, Zamzummites, and Horites and delivered their respective lands into the hands of the Moabites, Ammonites, and Edomites.

However, prior to the Israelites' arrival in the region, the primary targets of divine violence were Pharaoh and the Egyptians. YHWH had personally invaded Egypt and terrified the Egyptians with daring acts, signs, wonders, war, a mighty hand, an outstretched arm, and great deeds of terror (4:34).[9] In 11:2–4 Moses describes the climactic destructive act: "Remember . . . what YHWH did to the Egyptian army, their horses and chariots, how he made the water of the Red Sea flow over them as they pursued you."

Closer to home, both in terms of time and location, Moses' audience remembers well the fate of Sihon and Og, the Amorite kings in the Transjordan. After the announcement in 1:4 that YHWH had struck these kings (2:24—3:11), Moses summarizes the event. As Amorites, the peoples they represented were linked to the Canaanite tribes across the Jordan. But Moses paints an ambivalent picture of the Transjordanian Amorites and why they were in the crosshairs of the Israelites and YHWH.

On the one hand, it appears that, in Moses' mind, originally they were not actual targets of divine violence. Reminiscent of the Israelite policy regarding the Edomites, Moabites, and Ammonites (2:1–23), the Israelites seem to have had no interest either in engaging them in battle, nor in claiming their territory. Because they stood between them and their actual destination on the other side of the Jordan, Moses had sent ambassadors to Sihon in Heshbon with overtures of peace, simply requesting permission to pass through their territory and promising not to threaten either the people or their claims to the land.[10]

Moses' account of the event suggests Sihon and Og became targets of Israelite and divine violence only because they rebuffed the overture and marshaled their troops to block Israel's journey to the promised land. This disposition toward the Transjordanian Amorites is understandable, given explicit declarations that the Jordan River represented the eastern boundary of the promised land (Num 34:12) and Moses' own repeated references to crossing the Jordan into the land YHWH is giving Israel as their grant (נַחֲלָה) in fulfillment of the promise to the ancestors.[11]

On the other hand, Moses' report of YHWH's involvement in these events suggests that the latter had Sihon and Og in his crosshairs from the outset. Before Moses offered peace to the Amorite king, YHWH had charged the Israelites to engage Sihon in battle (cf. 2:9) and begin taking possession of the land, declaring that he had given Sihon and his land into their hands (2:24). This impression is reinforced by Moses' attribution of

---

9. See also shorter statements in 6:21–22; 7:18–19; 26:8; 29:1–2[2–3]. The sort of violence involved with the strong hand and outstretched arm is vividly illustrated in Egyptian iconography, which often portrays Pharaoh holding his captive in one hand and with his other hand holding a club raised to strike his captive. For discussion see Hoffmeier, "Egyptian Motifs Related to Warfare and Enemies," 53–70, esp. 57.

10. This request resembles the policy toward distant towns that Moses would later prescribe (20:10–15).

11. Deut 2:29; 3:20; 4:21; 11:31; 12:10; 27:2–3. Joshua 22 highlights the significance of the Jordan as the boundary.

Sihon's rejection of the offer of peace to YHWH, who "had hardened his disposition and stiffened his resolve" for the express purpose of delivering him into the Israelites' power (2:30). In the event, the Israelites executed the ḥērem policy on the population, while keeping the livestock and other booty (2:34–35).

In the defeat of the Transjordanian Amorites we observe in microcosm the upcoming conflict with the dreaded Cisjordanian populations, who are a dominant target for Israelite violence in the remainder of the book. While the previous generation of Israelites had shrunk back in terror before their extraordinary physical size and fortifications (1:28–29), it is apparent that in the intervening forty years their power had not diminished, nor had they become an easier target. Moses still characterizes them as "greater/more numerous and powerful" than Israel (4:38; 7:1; 9:1; 11:23). However, the target of Israel's particularly violent ḥērem policy was strictly circumscribed. In chapter 20, where Moses instructs the Israelites on their conduct of hostilities with outsiders, he establishes distinct policies for "towns that are very far away" and "the towns of these nations nearby" (20:15). While conflicts with the former are to be avoided with overtures of peace, when these are rejected he limits lethal violence to adult males and precludes the slaughter of women and children. By contrast, conflicts with the latter are neither to be avoided nor delayed with offers of peace, but the entire human population is to be annihilated (20:10–17).

Deuteronomy also circumscribes the target ethnographically. In 7:1 Moses identifies seven people groups by name: Hittites, Girgashites, Amorites, Canaanites, Perizzites, Hivites, and Jebusites.[12] Critical scholars' tendency to dismiss this list as fictional and the names as symbolic[13] may resolve the human ethical problem of genocide, but it does not resolve the theological/theodical problem. The image of a deity purportedly commanding the elimination of whole populations remains.[14] Our present concern is the boundary this list places on the extreme form of Israelite aggression. Moses later extends the policy to the Amalekites (25:17–19), but this would be the exception that proved the rule. He does not cast the resolution of the Amalekite problem as a part of the wars of conquest, but projects it into the future when the Canaanites have been defeated and YHWH had given them "rest" from all their enemies. The motivation for the addition of the Amalekites to the policy is quite distinct from the reason for eliminating the Canaanites.

According to 2:2–23, the Israelite stance toward Edomites, Moabites, and Ammonites was to be quite pacific, not only because they posed no hindrance to their occupation of the promised land, but specifically because they were ethnically related to the Israelites.

---

12. Except for the omission of Girgashites, 20:17 repeats the list, though in a different order. For a discussion of these peoples, see Satterthwaite and Baker, "Nations of Canaan," 596–605.

13. MacDonald (*Deuteronomy and the Meaning of Monotheism*, 112) suggests such lists are "stereotypical and ideological" constructions, and do not reflect the ethnic composition of Canaan. Römer (*Dark God,* 88) views the names as representative of "all those who could turn Israel from the exclusive worship of YHWH."

14. So also, Anderson, "What about the Canaanites?" 272.

Furthermore, their title to their respective lands was as inviolable as Israel's would be to the land of Canaan, for YHWH had given it to them as their possession (2:5, 9, 19). As for the peoples to the south and north of Canaan (Egyptians, Arameans, etc.), presumably they would fall under the category of "distant" nations, but they are beyond the purview of Deuteronomy. The exclusion of Philistines from these lists is ethnographically and historically appropriate, because they were technically not Canaanites, but latecomers to the Levant, who originated in the Aegean and did not appear in this region until the twelfth century BCE.

Israelites as Targets of Divine Violence

Given scholars' preoccupation with the genocidal problem involving the Canaanites, many are surprised to learn that these are not the primary targets of divine violence in Deuteronomy. On the contrary, apart from targeting individual Israelites in the administration of justice, the Israelites as a whole appear as the object of YHWH's fury more than twice as often as the Canaanites. These references are concentrated in chapters 9 (in response to the apostasy involving the golden calf at Sinai), 28 (the covenant curses threatened in case of persistent future apostasy), and 32 (vv. 19–22, Israel's national anthem), but they are scattered throughout the book. In 1:27 faithless Israelites wrongly interpreted the exodus from Egypt as an act of divine violence against them motivated by hatred and with the goal of destroying them. In 4:3 Moses recalls YHWH's judgment on idolaters at Baal-Peor. Summary threats of divine judgment for idolatry for which the covenant curses provide graphic explanation are scattered throughout his addresses.[15]

These texts and this emphasis caution against isolating annihilation of the Canaanites as a distinctive ethical problem. Exploration of divine violence in Deuteronomy must take into account all these texts. We cannot understand the genocidal acts against the Canaanites without first considering the divine violence the book threatens against YHWH's own people.[16]

Regarding the internal administration of righteousness and justice, the targets of direct and indirect divine violence vary. The extreme form of punishment, execution, is to be applied to idolaters (5:9; 13:2–19[1–18]; 17:2–7); false prophets who speak in YHWH's name without his authorization or who speak in the name of another god (18:20);[17] Israelites who do not comply with the divine verdict in otherwise insoluble cases (17:12–13); murderers, at the hands of the "blood-avenger" (19:1–13); persistently rebellious children (21:18–21); a woman who proves not to have been a virgin at the time of her marriage (22:20–21); male and female adulterers, if the act occurs in a town

---

15. Deut 4:26–27; 5:9; 6:15; 7:4; 8:19–20; 11:17.

16. For a focused study of divine violence directed at Israel and its implications for modern politics, see Barrett, *Disloyalty and Destruction*.

17. Although no punishment is specified, the death penalty would probably have been applied to practitioners of forbidden forms of divination, sorcery, and necromancy (18:9–14). These practices are condemned as תוֹעֵבָת, "abominations" for which YHWH will drive out the Canaanites (v. 9), and those who practice them are condemned as "the abomination of YHWH" (v. 12).

and the woman is virgin pledged to be married (22:23–24); and male rapists, if the act occurs in the country and the woman is pledged to be married (22:25).

The Motivation for Divine Violence in Deuteronomy

Having identified the targets of divine violence in Deuteronomy, we may now explore YHWH's motivation in these drastic measures. While the ancients viewed all of life with profoundly theological lenses, I shall divide the question into two parts: (1) divine violence in response to domestic and moral conduct and (2) divine violence in response to overtly religious conduct. The former category involves breaches in horizontal relationships, while the latter involves Israelites' vertical relationship with YHWH. These are obviously not mutually exclusive, but this division is heuristically convenient.

The Motivation for Divine Violence in Response to Moral Offenses

Deuteronomy 16:20 declares the goal of all ethical conduct for the Israelites: "Righteousness, righteousness you shall pursue" (צֶדֶק צֶדֶק תִּרְדֹּף). As used in Deuteronomy, צֶדֶק refers to right behavior in accord with an established standard, in this instance the covenant stipulations as defined by YHWH.[18] However, 32:4 includes this expression in the list of YHWH's qualities: "The Rock, his action is perfect (תָּמִים), and all his ways are just (מִשְׁפָּט). A faithful God (אֵל אֱמוּנָה), without deceit (אֵין עָוֶל), righteous (צַדִּיק) and upright (יָשָׁר) is he." The God portrayed in this book is anything but capricious, fickle, impetuous, self-indulgent, and forgetful.[19] Whatever disposition modern readers may have toward YHWH and his violence in Deuteronomy, the book itself understands both within the framework of divine perfection, justice, fidelity, integrity, righteousness, and consistency. These attributes govern both his own conduct and his disposition toward the conduct of human beings—created as his images—but especially toward Israel, whom YHWH claimed as his own,[20] his elect (7:6, 7; 10:15; 14:2), the objects of his redemption/deliverance from slavery[21] and his covenant love,[22] his adopted sons (14:1), his treasured people (7:6; 14:2; 26:18), and his holy people (7:6; 14:2, 21; 26:19; 28:9). Among other expressions of ethical expectation, he calls Israel to "walk in [all] his ways" (8:6; 10:12; 11:22; 19:9; 26:17; 28:9; 30:16). This magnificently ambiguous expression could mean either "to walk in the ways YHWH has commanded" (cf. 5:33; 13:6[5]), or to walk as YHWH walks. This ethical principle of *imitatio dei* is expressly enjoined in 10:17–19, which, after declaring that YHWH demonstrates covenant love toward the

---

18. Deut 4:8 applies the word to the "statutes and judgments" and the entire Torah that Moses declared to the Israelites in Moab.

19. Compare the descriptions of divine behavior by Bottéro, *Religion in Ancient Mesopotamia*, 66–69, and Walton, *Ancient Near Eastern Thought and the Old Testament*, 99–112.

20. Deut 4:34 describes YHWH "taking [Israel] for himself" (cf. also 4:20; 30:4).

21. פָּדָה, 7:8; 9:26; 13:6[5]; 15:15; 21:8; 24:18; הוֹצִיא, 5:6, 15; 6:12, 21, 23; 7:8; 8:14; 13:6, 11[5, 10]; cf. 4:34.

22. אָהֵב, 7:8, 13; 10:15; 23:6[5]; cf. 4:37 [the ancestors]; cf. חָבַב, 33:3; חָשַׁק, 7:7; 15:10.

alien, calls on the Israelites to do the same. If "righteousness" for YHWH meant that he kept the commitments to which he bound himself in his covenant relationship with Israel, this meant that Israel should do the same.

When we examine the types of Israelite behavior that provoked the "righteous" expression of YHWH's violence, we observe two broad categories of offences: those that challenge the integrity of human relationships, especially within the family and the clan, and those that challenge the integrity of God's relationship with his people. Deuteronomy characterizes such breaches of the principle of "righteousness" as תּוֹעֵבָה. The word derives from a root, תָּעַב, "to abhor, to reject as utterly disgusting." This is Moses' favored expression for all things idolatrous (cf. 12:31; 13:15[14]; 17:4; 32:16), but it is also used of taboo food (14:3), defective sacrifices (17:1), transvestite conduct (22:5), prostitution (23:18–19[17–18]), shaming one's wife by divorcing her for some physical issue and then remarrying her (24:4),[23] and cheating in commercial actions (25:16). While the first three jeopardize the divine human-relationship, those that remain undermine the health of the home and the community. But they do more. Deuteronomy presupposes the divine stance toward abominable actions as expressed in Lev 18:19–30: abominable actions defile the land and compromise Israel's status as a "holy people," rendering them absolutely defiled and fundamentally degraded, a degradation that cannot be resolved ritually (see Fig. 13.1, below, page 272). This interpretation is reinforced by Deuteronomy's frequent use of variations of the purgation formula: "and you shall purge the evil from your midst."[24] This formula is applied not only to idolatrous actions (13:6[5]; 17:7) and defiance of the divine determination in an otherwise insoluble legal case (17:12), but also to malicious witnesses (19:19), rebellious sons (21:21), a bride who is discovered not to have been a virgin at the time of her marriage (22:21), adultery by a man or woman (22:22), and kidnapping (24:7). While this purgation assumes the death penalty, the only procedure specified is stoning (17:5–7; 21:18–21; 22:20–21), presumably to avoid contamination of the executioners by direct contact with the criminal.[25]

The purgation formula involves the verb בִּעֵר followed by the preposition מִן, "from," and the object of the preposition. In each occurrence of the formula the object from which contamination is to be purged is the community, identified specifically as "Israel" (17:12; 19:13; 22:22), or more generally as "your midst" (13:6[5]; 17:7; 19:19; 21:9; 21:21; 22:21, 24; 24:7). Significantly the contaminant from which the community is to be purged is neither the criminal himself nor his victim, but the evil deed. This interpretation is reinforced by 19:13 and 21:9, which identify the contaminant as "blood," which functions metonymically for "bloodshed." The characterization of the blood as "innocent" in both cases demonstrates that there is nothing wrong with the blood itself. The issue here is not to wash the people of the blood of the victim, but to absolve them of the guilt of the crime. Until this expiatory action has been taken, culpability for the murder will hang over all the people. Caiaphas had it almost right

---

23. On this interpretation, see Block, *Deuteronomy*, 556–65.

24. The formula "to purge [exterminate] the evil from" appears in 13:6[5]; 17:7, 12; 19:13, 19; 21:9, 21; 22:21, 22, 24; 24:7. Cf. Judg 20:13; 2 Sam 4:11; 1 Kgs 4:10. Except for Deut 19:19, in Deuteronomy all occurrences involve the death penalty.

25. Similarly, Rodd, *Glimpses of a Strange Land*, 12.

when he said, "It is better for you that one man should die ... than that the whole nation should perish" (John 11:50).²⁶

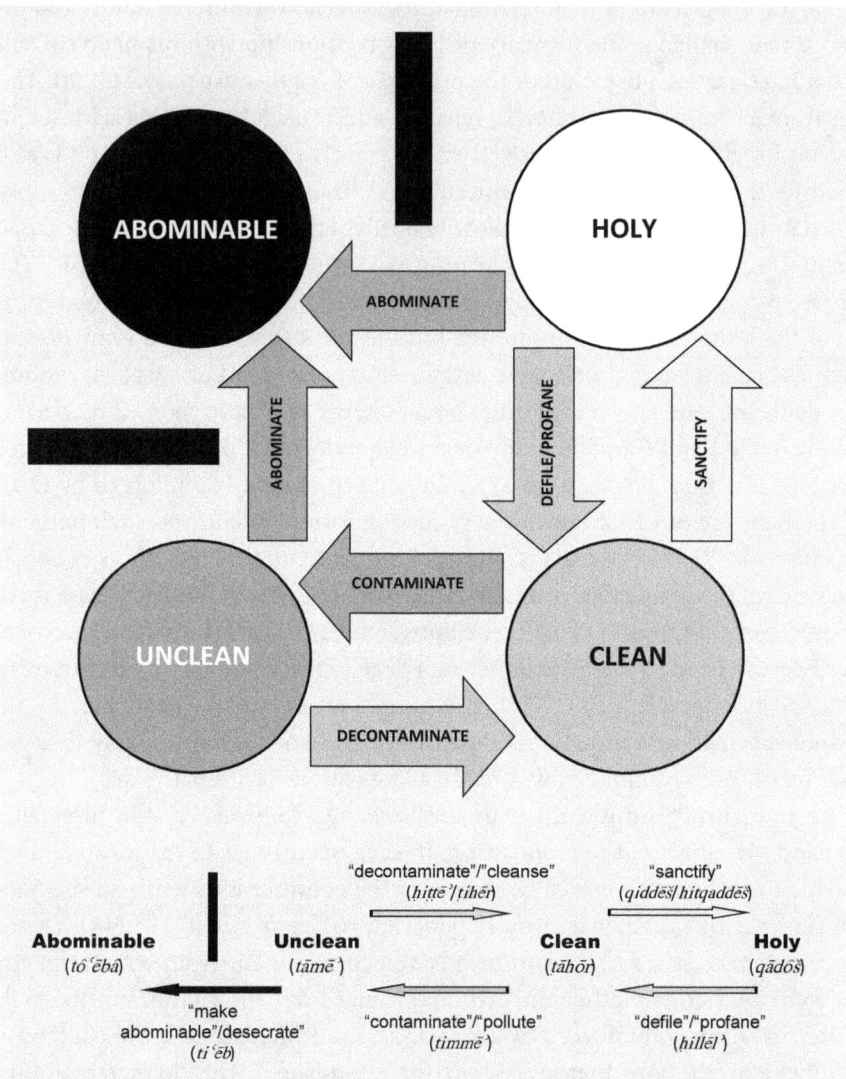

Figure 13.1
The Sacred-Clean-Unclean-Abominable Continuum

While all the purgation texts envision the decontamination of the community, in several the crimes affect the status of the third member of the covenantal triangle, namely, the land. According to 21:22–23, after executing a criminal²⁷ and impaling his body

---

26. Whereas Caiaphas had in mind the substitutionary death of an individual, in these cases the man dies for his own crime, but in the event, he lets the community be spared.

27. The opening clause of v. 22 is extremely dense: "Now if there is in a man a sin [calling for] a judgment of death." Cf. 15:21 and 19:11, the latter of which has the negative variant of this expression. The statement presupposes a process of careful investigation, leading to the conclusion that follows.

on a pole, the body is to be removed and buried before nightfall to avoid desecrating the ground. Although the verb differs, apparently failure to dispose of corpses properly had the same effect on the ground as crimes did on the people. Deuteronomy 24:1–4 is more explicit in declaring the effect of a moral act characterized as "an abomination before YHWH" on the land. If a man defiled his wife by divorcing her for some physical problem,[28] and then remarried her, this would contaminate the land.[29]

These texts all assume the fundamental sanctity of people and land in covenant relationship with YHWH. Unless readers grasp this notion, and the divine grace that underlies it, they will not understand this motivation for divine violence. Through his redemptive and covenantal acts YHWH has transformed an enslaved people into a holy people belonging to himself (7:6; 14:2; 21; 26:18).

However, the motivation behind divine violence in Deuteronomy is more complex than this. Several texts prescribe severe punishments as deterrents for others. It is tempting to link the violent response commanded by YHWH in the face of criminal acts with the link between fear of YHWH and obedience established already at Sinai (cf. 4:10; 5:29).[30] However, following the prescription of a specific punishment, the emphasis shifts from "awed trust" of YHWH to fear of the consequences of one's action. Variations of the formula, "they shall hear and fear and avoid" particular actions occur four times: (1) in response to stoning those who promote idolatry (13:12[11]); (2) in response to the execution of a person who does not heed the divine verdict announced by the priest at the central sanctuary in an otherwise insoluble case (17:13); (3) in response to the punishment of a false witness (19:20); and (4) in response to the stoning of a persistently rebellious son (21:21). Again the concern is a holy community, characterized by willing and grateful obedience to YHWH. Lest Israel relax about this expectation, thrice Deuteronomy warns against letting sentimentality or personal feelings interfere with the administration with the "no pity formula" (13:9[8]; 19:13, 21).[31]

Although we have included divine violence in response to idolatry in passing in the preceding, this subject deserves separate attention, not because its primary concern is the well-being of the community, but because it strikes at the heart of the relationship between Israel and her God and at the heart of monotheistic convictions. Although we usually associate idolatry with worship involving physical images, either man-made of terrestrial materials[32] or the heavenly bodies (4:19; 17:3), and although Deuteronomy

---

28. On this interpretation, see Block, *Deuteronomy*, 556–60.

29. This statement involves the relatively rare hiphil form הֶחֱטִיא, "to contaminate." In the qal stem the verb means "to miss the mark, to sin."

30. Hebrew יָרֵא, "to fear" is used of reverent/trusting awe frequently in Deuteronomy: 6:2, 24; 10:12, 20; 14:23; 17:19; 31:12–13.

31. To these we must add 25:11–12, which commands cutting off the hand of a woman who has grabbed another man's genitals ("appendage of shame"), presumably intending to injure him so he cannot have children, which also strikes at the maintenance of the community's integrity. For a similar interpretation, see McConville, *Deuteronomy*, 371.

32. Designated as "images" (פְּסִלִים, 4:16, 23, 25; 5:8; 7:5, 25; 12:3; 27:15; סֶמֶל, 4:16); "the work of human/a craftsman's hands" (מַעֲשֵׂה יְדֵי אָדָם, 4:28; 27:15); "cast metal image" (מַסֵּכָה, 9:12, 16; 27:15); "other gods of wood and stone" (אֱלֹהִים אֲחֵרִים עֵץ וָאָבֶן, 4:28; 28:36) and "silver and gold" (כֶּסֶף וְזָהָב, 29:16[17]); "loathsome images (שִׁקּוּצֵיהֶם, 29:16[17]); and "feces" (גִּלּוּלִים, 29:16[17]).

prohibits the manufacture of images as objects of worship (4:16, 23, 25; 5:8–9; 27:15), the real issue is the exclusive worship of YHWH, a conviction embodied in the "First Principle of Covenant Relationship" (5:7–10) and the Shema (6:4–5).[33] To worship "other gods"[34] is to "abandon" (28:20; 31:16) and "despise" (31:20) YHWH and to "break" his covenant (31:16, 20).

Israelite Yahwism was unique among ancient religions both in its repudiation of all other gods and in its demand for Israel's exclusive worship.[35] YHWH's claim to Israel's total devotion is rooted not only in the nonexistence of any divine peers but especially in his gracious election, salvation, providential care, covenant, and call to mission. YHWH's past acts on Israel's behalf are celebrated in the climax of Moses' first address (4:32–40), the "domestic catechism" (6:20–25), the "Little Creed" (26:1–11), and the Song of YHWH (32:1–14). For Israel to go after other gods is to trample underfoot the history of divine grace. Israel's mission is embodied in expressions like "a holy people belonging to YHWH" (7:6; 14:2, 21; 26:19), "a treasured people" (7:6; 14:2; 26:18), and summarized in 26:19: "He will place you high above the nations . . . for [his] praise, fame, and glory," a mission that could be fulfilled only if the nation would be faithful to her covenant Lord and YHWH would respond with his blessing (28:1–14; cf. 4:5–8).[36] Because YHWH's agenda for the world depends upon Israel's exclusive devotion, there is no room for compromise on this matter (12:1–4, 29–32), and those who would seek to deflect the people's devotion to other gods must be executed (13:2–19[1–18]; 18:9–22). This is true of individuals who actually choose that course (7:25–26; 17:1–7; 29:13–20[14–21]), as well as the nation as a whole (6:14–15; 11:16–17; 28:15–68; 32:19–25). This violent response will never be understood if we extract it from the narrative of divine grace.

The Motivation for Divine Violence against the Canaanites

Recognizing the motivation for the divine response to idolatry, we may have arrived at the biblical explanation for the violence that Deuteronomy prescribes for Israel's treatment of the Canaanites and the other autochthonous tribes.[37] This is by all accounts the most difficult ethical question in the First Testament, and responses to the issue vary

---

33. On the significance of the Shema, see Block, "How Many Is God?" 193–212. On the broader issue of monotheism in Deuteronomy, see MacDonald, *Deuteronomy and the Meaning of Monotheism*.

34. Deut 5:7; 6:14; 7:4; 8:19; 11:16, 28; 13:3[2], 6–7[5–6], 14[13]; 17:3; 18:20; 28:14, 36, 64; 29:25[26]; 30:17; 31:18, 20.

35. See Block, *the Gods of the Nations*, 61–74; Block, "'No Other Gods,'" 237–71.

36. Although Moberly's metaphorical interpretation of the policy of ḥērem is problematic, his discussion of the relationship between the policy and Israel's election is excellent. See Moberly, *Old Testament Theology*, 41–74.

37. The primary texts addressing the problem occur in 3:18–22; 4:37–38; 6:18–19; 7:1–11, 17–26; 8:20; 9:1–6; 11:23–25; 18:9–12; 31:3. Although technically not part of the conquest of the promised land, the defeat of the Transjordanian Amorite kings in 2:24—3:17 is portrayed as paradigmatic for the Cisjordanian campaign: as commander-in-chief YHWH directs the campaign; YHWH fixes the disposition of the enemy; Israel engages the enemy in battle; Israel applies the policy of ḥērem; Israel allocates the land to their tribes.

greatly. While Jews have rarely applied this policy,[38] regrettably European Christians have misappropriated this policy to justify all sorts of violent behavior, from the expulsion of Muslim Turks from the Holy Land to the annihilation of indigenous populations from the lands they were claiming as new homelands, most notably in the Americas and in Australia.[39] Others have rejected these injunctions outright. The most radical response, represented by the early heretic Marcion, is to repudiate the entire First Testament because the violent God it portrays differs fundamentally from the gracious God of the New Testament, embodied in Christ.[40] More recently Hector Avalos has argued that any depiction of God in the Bible as violent must be rejected as false, and any texts that portray him as such should be deleted.[41] Although Eric Seibert rejects the "Marcionite" label, the effect of his Christocentric hermeneutic is similar: when we encounter texts that portray God differently from Jesus Christ, we must declare, "This is not God," but faulty ancient Israelite representation of the true God.[42] Mainstream First Testament scholars argue that while the policy of *ḥērem* as outlined in Deut 7 and 20 (as well as the conquest narratives in Joshua) appear to describe a ban of the past, they actually represent figurative if not utopian portrayals of a particular present, namely Josiah's efforts to centralize worship in the sixth century.[43] Thomas Römer argues that these texts derive from the Persian era (fifth century BCE), when the loss of identity through contact with "others" threatened the "community in crisis."[44]

Others have tried to salvage the biblical texts by taking a more spiritual or theological approach. Origen allegorized the issue, suggesting that the policy as outlined in Deuteronomy and narrated in Joshua symbolized the conflicts that raged within a person's own soul, and that Christians should root out all vice and sinfulness from within.[45] While few scholars advocate Origen's particular approach, some find the impulse sound, using this as a base to develop a metaphorical interpretation of a policy in defense of monotheism, which is to be realized through the banning of intermarriage with all non-Israelites and the destruction of all pagan religious paraphernalia.[46] More generally Douglas Earl finds the *ḥērem* policy to be a symbol of various notions:

---

38. For a warning to Israeli nationalists against using Scripture to justify violence against Palestinians and defend absolutist rights to the land, see Greenberg, "On the Political Use of the Bible in Modern Israel," 461–71.

39. For examples of Puritan and Calvinist appropriation of these texts, see briefly Collins, "The Zeal of Phinehas: The Bible and the Legitimation of Violence," 3–21, esp. 13–14.

40. On Marcion, see von Harnack, *Marcion*, 15–24.

41. See Avalos, "The Letter Killeth: A Plea for Decanonizing Violent Texts," n.p.

42. See Seibert, *Disturbing Divine Behavior*, 241; Seibert, *The Violence of Scripture*.

43. Creach, *Violence in Scripture*, 104–12; Lohfink, "חָרַם, *ḥāram*," 197.

44. Römer, *Dark God*, 87–91.

45. For representative excerpts of Origen's perspective on the Conquest narratives of Joshua, see Franke, ed., *Joshua, Judges, Ruth, 1–2 Samuel*, 46–50.

46. Thus MacDonald, *Deuteronomy and the Meaning of Monotheism*, 108–23, building on the work of Moberly, "Toward an Interpretation of the Shema," 124–144; Moberly, *Old Testament Theology*, 41–74; Wolterstorff, "Comments on 'What about the Canaanites,'" 283–88.

[S]eparation from idolatry and exclusivist construction of identity (Deut); response to divine action in the world, and rethinking notions of the identity of God's people (Josh); comforting and encouraging oppressed Israel (Isa 34:2; Zech 14:31); and challenging complacent Israel (Josh 7; Jer 25:9).[47]

This interpretation is attractive, because it eliminates the historical and ethical problem of genocide. However, huge problems remain. Not only does it not resolve the offensive image of a violent God, but it also assumes an extremely sophisticated original readership/hearership. With few exceptions, those who heard the words of Deuteronomy read in worship[48] will have imagined a real Moses promulgating a real policy involving real people in a real historical past on behalf of a real God, YHWH the God of Israel. And even if they did not, but accepted its metaphorical quality, the image of God remains: What sort of God inspires such images of himself?

Scholars who follow these approaches assume that God would not and could not command such violence; it is unbecoming not only of humans but especially of deity. This assumption raises serious questions: Have we not thereby cast God in images of our idealized selves? Have we imposed on the biblical texts interpretations that suit our preferred sensitivities? Theologian Stephen N. Williams has argued convincingly, that yes, God could have commanded the slaughter of the Canaanites, but no, he would never have done so glibly, arbitrarily, or capriciously. On the contrary, whether commanding the death of an individual, or the death of entire peoples, he would have done so with a heavy heart.[49] Although the Scriptures portray this violence as an appropriate response to revolt against the Creator, God treasures all that he has created, most of all human beings created especially to function as his images by governing the world on his behalf.[50] The Canaanites were not a subhuman species that could be annihilated without remorse. On the contrary, one of their members, plucked from the first city within the promised land to be destroyed (Rahab; Josh 6:15–25), became an ancestor not only of the Davidic royal line, but also of Jesus Christ, the Savior of humanity (Matt 1:5).

How then shall we interpret the policy of *ḥērem* as outlined in Deuteronomy? I am pessimistic that we will ever find a satisfying answer, but in wrestling with the issue we need to keep in mind a series of considerations. In isolation none satisfies completely, but taken together they may provide a helpful perspective.

First, the Hebrew noun *ḥērem* (חֵרֶם) derives from a verbal root חָרַם/הֶחֱרִים, which means "to devote" something/someone completely to the deity, and thereby exclude it from human/common use.[51] As such the lexeme shares a semantic field with קָדַשׁ/קֹדֶשׁ, "to be holy"/"to consecrate."

Leviticus 27:21–29 uses both expressions of items/people devoted to YHWH, declaring explicitly that "every devoted thing (*ḥērem*; חֵרֶם) is supremely holy (קֹדֶשׁ־קָדָשִׁים)

---

47. Earl, "Holy War and חרם: A Biblical Theology of חרם," 175.

48. Minimally once every seven years at the Festival of Sukkoth (31:9–13).

49. Williams, "Could God Have Commanded the Slaughter of the Canaanites," 161–78; Williams, "Holy War and the New Atheism," 312–31.

50. Gen 1:26–31 (cf. 2:15); Psalm 8.

51. For bibliography on lexical studies of חרם, see Earl, "Holy War and חרם," 154–55, n. 11.

to YHWH" (v. 28). While the links between this text and the charge to "totally destroy" (הַחֲרֵם תַּחֲרִים) the Canaanites in Deut 7:2 are not obvious, that Joshua could declare Jericho and all its contents "devoted to YHWH" (חֵרֶם לַיהָוה) and not to be touched by Israelites (Josh 6:17–20; cf. Mic 4:13), apparently lest they be contaminated by it (cf. Deut 7:25–26),[52] suggests this sacral nuance is retained in the Deuteronomic policy of *ḥērem*—as it is in the Moabite and Sabaean uses of the root.

Second, the Israelite policy of *ḥērem* was not a distinctly First Testament issue. The occurrence of the same word in the ninth century BCE Mesha inscription indicates that similar policies were practiced in the first millennium by the Moabites:

> Then Kemoš said to me: "Go, seize Nebo from Israel!" So I went by night; and I fought against it from the break of dawn until noon; and I took it; and I put all to death: 7000 men and boys, and women and girls, and pregnant women, because I had dedicated (*ḥrm*) it to ʿAštar Kemoš. And I took from there the altar-hearths of YHWH, and I dragged them before the Kemoš."[53]

The word, *ḥrm* also occurs in a seventh-century BCE Old South Arabian text, RÉS 3945:

> And he put its town to *ḥērem* . . . and handed over DHSm and TBNY and DTNT [names of cities] to ʿAlmaqah, and to Sabaʾ.[54]

Lauren Monroe has identified four key elements that this text shares with biblical and Moabite accounts: (1) *ḥērem* involves massive destruction and burning of the town; (2) a significant segment of the population is slaughtered and consecrated to the deity; (3) having been emptied, individual towns in the conquered territory are reoccupied by the victors; (4) to signify occupation of the territory by a new population and its deity, conquerors erect a cult installation.[55]

Third, as prescribed in Deuteronomy, Israel's policy of *ḥērem* was not a human convention, but a divinely ordered policy. Indeed, it is presented as conceived, commanded, executed, and brought to successful fulfillment by YHWH.[56] Even though, for many modern readers, this is precisely the problem, within the conceptual world of the Scriptures, this is a given. As the Creator of all things and all human beings, and as

---

52. Similarly, Kaminsky, "Joshua 7: A Reassessment of the Israelite Conceptions of Corporate Punishment," 331. Earl's rejection of this interpretation requires him to marginalize contrary evidence (Josh 6:19, 24) as "later priestly or post-priestly additions." See Earl, "Holy War and חרם," 157.

53. As translated by Younger, "Some Recent Discussion on the *ḥērem*," 514. For detailed discussion of this text, see Stern, *The Biblical Herem*, 19–56.

54. Text and translation adapted from Monroe, "Israelite, Moabite and Sabaean War-*ḥerem* Traditions and the Forging of National Identity," 334–35.

55. Deut 11:29–32 and 27:1–26 prescribe that the last element should transpire as soon as the Israelites cross over into the land, prior to any battles. According to Josh 8:30–35, this actually happened after the destruction of Jericho and Ai. For brief discussion of this matter, see chapter 8, "What Do These Stones Mean?" above, pp. 152–76. Some have suggested the Hittites had similar policies toward conquered territories. See Del Monte, "The Hittite *Hērem*," 21–45. However, Harry Hoffner cautions against making too much of the cited Hittite texts and against linking Hittite practices with the biblical *ḥērem* (in private communication, 1/21/2014).

56. So also, Merrill, "The Case for Moderate Discontinuity," 80–81.

Sovereign over all, God can do anything he wants with anyone and be right in doing so (Gen 18:25). Although YHWH was Israel's particular commander-in-chief, Deuteronomy presents him operating similarly on behalf of and against other nations as well. Earlier, he had destroyed the Horites in Seir and given their land to Edom (2:5, 12, 22), removed the Emmites from the land east of the Dead Sea and given it to the Moabites (2:9–11), and removed the Zamzummites from their territory east of the Jordan and given it to Ammonites (2:19–21). If YHWH commands Israelites to eliminate Canaanites he is perfectly within his rights to do so. He does not need to justify his actions or his commands (Jer 18:6–10). However, by itself this answer will not satisfy many, and certainly not the "new atheists."[57]

Fourth, Israel's policy of ḥērem directed at Canaanites was neither impulsive nor arbitrary but the culmination of an ancient plan. While this consideration does not remove the sting of the violence against a targeted race of people, readers of the Pentateuch have anticipated this since Gen 15:18–21, where YHWH promised Abraham that after four centuries, he would give their land over to Abraham's descendants. YHWH's fidelity to this promise underlies his call of Moses forty years prior to the delivery of the addresses in Deuteronomy (Exod 3:8; 6:8), and through the defeat of Sihon and Og the Cisjordanian nations were warned of the fate awaiting them. God's elimination of the Canaanites was a necessary step in the history of salvation.[58] In order for Israel to achieve the goals that God had in mind for them—that they might declare to the world his glory and grace—they needed a clean slate. This is a matter of ethical rather than ethnic cleansing. A holy people requires a holy land.

Fifth, the policy of ḥērem functions as a divinely ordained means of dealing with sin. The mandate to eliminate the Canaanites was driven by neither genocidal nor military considerations, but by the eradication of evil and the prevention of evil from spreading to the new population. Although the Canaanites may not have been any more degenerate than other nations, this policy is rooted in the perception of the Canaanites as a wicked people, a characterization anticipated in Gen 15:16 ("the sin of the Amorites has not yet reached its full measure," NIV), and confirmed in Deuteronomy:

> 9:4 It is because of the wickedness of these nations that YHWH is dispossessing them before you.

> 18:12 [B]ecause of these abhorrent practices (הַתּוֹעֵבֹת) YHWH your God is dispossessing them before you.

Idolatry is isolated as a particularly pernicious Canaanite vice:

> When YHWH your God has cut off before you the nations whom you are about to invade to dispossess them, and when you have dispossessed them and are settled in their land, after they have been destroyed before you take care that you are not trapped into imitating them. Do not inquire about their gods, saying, "How did these nations worship their gods? I want to do the

---

57. As represented by Fales, "Comments on 'Canon and Conquest,'" 309–13. For discussion, see Williams, "'Holy War' and the New Atheism," 319–27.

58. Cf. Christopher Wright, *The God I Don't Understand*, 98.

same myself." You must not worship YHWH your God the way they do, because for their gods they have done every abhorrent thing that YHWH hates (כָּל־תּוֹעֲבַת יְהוָה אֲשֶׁר שָׂנֵא). They even burn their sons and their daughters in fire as sacrifices to their gods (12:29–31, my translation).

For Deuteronomy, these practices were worthy of judgment and presented a threat to the spiritual and ethical integrity of Israel, the holy people of YHWH (7:2–5). As Moses emphatically declared in 9:1–24, this did not mean that Israelites would receive the land as a reward for their own moral virtue or spiritual superiority; rather, it represents YHWH's strategy for preserving for himself a holy people.

Sixth, Israel's policy of ḥērem assumes a paradigmatic role both for both Canaanites and Israelites. From a broadly biblical perspective, the Canaanites suffered a fate that ultimately faces all sinners: the judgment of God. The law of ḥērem involves but one of many ways by which YHWH executes judgment upon a sinful people. Later, in poetic verse YHWH will catalogue the resources available to him to accomplish this task when Israel is the targeted people (32:22–25). Within this list of agents, the sword, which serves metonymically for war, is exceptional because it alone involves the active participation of people in carrying out the plan of God.[59] The ḥērem ordinance represents a particular kind of war, but in its objectives, the extermination of the Canaanites is of a piece with God's actions against the human population as a whole in the great deluge (Gen 6–9), his call for the destruction of the Midianites (Num 31), his destruction of Judah (Ezek 4–24), and his eschatological defeat of the forces of evil in Revelation. Insofar as the law of ḥērem was directed against a particular target, it depicts in microcosm the fate that awaits all who reject YHWH as God and Savior. The Scriptures are consistent in their message that evil and rebellion against YHWH yield death. Apart from the grace of God, this is the fate of all. The difference between the Canaanites subject to this law and the ultimate destiny of other sinful inhabitants of the world is that YHWH employed his people Israel as human agents to send them to their fate.

Seventh, Israel's policy of ḥērem was intentionally limited in its scope, both geographically and temporally. It applied only to the seven specific peoples listed in 7:1,[60] and apparently it would be terminated once the conquest of Canaan was complete. Deuteronomy 20:10–18 declares unequivocally that this was not to become the general policy governing Israel's relationships with the nations. When they would wage war against other "distant" nations, the Israelites' primary goal was to seek peace, and even when offers of peace were refused, to deal humanely with the innocent within the population. YHWH retained the right to extend the ḥērem to other peoples (e.g., Midianites, Amalekites), but the Israelites were not free to do so on their own. Philistines, Moabites, Ammonites, and Arameans were outside the scope of this policy.[61] And, contrary to the way Christians have used these texts, this policy provides no warrant for Christian violence against Jews and Muslims during the Crusades, Puritans' campaigns against

---

59. Cf. von Waldow, "The Concept of War in the Old Testament," 34.

60. The number seven does indeed symbolize the totality of Canaanite peoples, but Römer's rejection of this as a list of specific foreigners (*Dark God*, 88) is gratuitous.

61. This may account for David's apparent hesitation to engage the Philistines in 2 Sam 5:17–25.

Catholics in Britain, or Europeans' claim to some sort of "manifest destiny" in their dispossession and slaughter of native North Americans.

Eighth, Israel's policy of *ḥērem* assumed a sense of corporate identity and corporate solidarity that is difficult for modern Westerners to understand. To us each individual is a separate entity and individual liberties and self-fulfillment are the highest ideal. However, according to the ancient Near Eastern ideal, one found one's significance and identity in relation to the community. When one member hurt, they all hurt; when one prospered, they all prospered. For this reason the Decalogue warns fathers against defection to idolatry, lest YHWH "visit the guilt of the fathers" on children "to the third and fourth [generation]."[62] In the ancient world few would have objected on ethical grounds to the fact that children share the fate of their parents. Significantly, this principle applied not only to Canaanite targets of Israel's campaigns, but also to the Israelites themselves (cf. Josh 7:6–26).

Ninth, if Israel's policy of *ḥērem* involves a comprehensive call for the extermination of the Canaanites, it also graciously opens the door for exceptions. Although Deuteronomy consistently portrays Canaanites as enemies of Israel, rather than potential "converts,"[63] the sparing of Rahab and her household demonstrates that Canaanites who would acknowledge YHWH and cast their lot with his people would find grace and deliverance in him. Rahab's confession (Josh 2:8–11) acknowledges that her people had at least forty years of advance warning. So complete was Rahab's incorporation into the community of faith that in the providence of God she became the ancestor of Jesus (Matt 1:5).

Tenth, Israel's policy of *ḥērem* plays no favorites. Although seven specific nations are targeted, Deuteronomy is emphatic that if Israelites will act like Canaanites, abandon YHWH, and serve other gods, they too will be subject to the same law—men, women, and children (7:25–26; 13:12–17[11–16]). Deuteronomy 13:16–17[15–16] prescribes destruction for any Israelite town that defects in terms more severe and encompassing even than chapter 7 and 20:16–18 demand of Canaanite towns. Whereas 7:1–5, 25–26 had called for the utter destruction of the people and their cultic installations and artifacts, and 20:16–18 "any [person] that breathes," 13:16–17[15–16] specifies the inhabitants of that town, and all that is in it, and its livestock. In fact, all its booty (cf. 20:14) shall be gathered in the open square and burnt completely to YHWH.[64] With the

---

62. Deut 5:7–11 (cf. Exod 20:3–6; 34:6–7). Rather than interpreting "to the third and fourth [generation]" linearly, the expression should be read horizontally, referring to the maximum number of generations that would make up a domestic unit. See further, Block, "Marriage and Family in Ancient Israel," 35–40, 44.

63. So also Fretz, "*Ḥērem* in the Old Testament," 15.

64. Accepting Earl's suggestion ("Holy War and חרם," 158) that כָּלִיל be understood according to the common usage, "entirety, entirely, completely" (Exod 28:31; 39:22; Lev 6:15–16[22–23]; Num 4:6; Deut 13:17[16]; Judg 20:40; Isa 2:18; Lam 2:15; Ezek 16:14; 27:3; 28:12). Although the root כלל is used in Punic inscriptions of a specific kind of sacrifice (see *DNWSI* 1:513), an explicitly sacrificial meaning in Hebrew requires an attendant cultic term: Deut 33:10, "They shall offer you incense to savor and whole-offerings (כָּלִיל) on your altar"; 1 Sam 7:9, "Samuel took a nursing lamb and sacrificed it as a whole burnt offering (עוֹלָה כָּלִיל) to YHWH"; Ps 51:21[19], "Then you will delight in righteous sacrifices, in burnt offerings and whole burnt offerings (עוֹלָה וְכָלִיל)." However, contra Earl, the construction, כָּלִיל לַיהוָה, "completely to YHWH," demands a sacral interpretation, even if this is not a sacrifice

privilege of bearing labels like "chosen by YHWH," "holy people belonging to YHWH," YHWH's "treasured people," "sons of YHWH," and being the objects of his affection and redemption (7:6–8; 14:1–2, 21; 26:19), came the weighty responsibility of loving him and representing him well before a watching world. However, because the Israelites lost sight of their mission and went after other gods, in 734–22 BCE the northern kingdom went the way of the Canaanites, and in 586 BCE the kingdom of Judah followed.

Conclusion

None of these answers to divinely mandated violence against the Canaanites will satisfy everyone, and none of them should be taken in isolation. In many ways God's policy of *ḥērem* is inscrutable and incredible, and even distasteful. How could a God of mercy and grace call for the extermination of an entire population? Isaiah 55:8–9 reminds us that the ways of God differ fundamentally from those of human beings; indeed they are often a mystery (Exod 33:13). In the end, modern readers may not like YHWH's policy of *ḥērem*, but the divine will is not determined by human sensitivities or values, and God is not bound by the definition of the World Report on Violence and Health. While for many this is precisely the problem, the challenge for us is not to forget the context in which we find this violence and the violence demanded in Israel's administration of justice.

Apart from faith and gratitude for YHWH's incomparably gracious acts of redemption, covenant, and provision of a homeland, Israel was indeed a nation like any other, and her migration from Egypt to the promised land was no different from the migration of the Philistines from Caphtor and the Arameans from Kir (Amos 9:7), and we could add, the prehistoric migration of Asians across the Bering Strait to the Americas; the relatively recent migration of Europeans to the Americas, southern Africa, and Australia; Russians beyond the Urals into the Far East; and the migration of Chinese throughout southeastern Asia. Sadly, such migrations have often involved the forceful uprooting and slaughter of indigenous of populations.

However, within the context of the Scriptures and the divine program of redemption for humanity, Israel was not a nation like all the rest. YHWH's covenant initiated with Abraham (Gen 15, 17), established with his descendants at Sinai (Exod 19–24), and confirmed with the generation poised to enter Canaan (Deuteronomy), had established her as his covenant people, his adopted sons, his treasured possession, and his holy nation—though not for their own sake. YHWH chose this people specially, redeemed them from slavery, and granted them the land of Canaan for the sake of the world. According to the biblical narrative, in the wake of Adam's sin all of humanity was condemned to the wrath of God. However, unwilling to abandon his creation, God graciously chose Israel to be his agents of mercy to a condemned world, to establish in Canaan a microcosm of the Eden that had been lost, and to display to all the world the divine glory and grace available to them (Deut 26:19).

---

in the sense of a "whole burnt offering" (עוֹלָה).

Inasmuch as YHWH had staked his reputation in the world on this people, the fulfillment of this universal mission depended not only on the continued judgment of evil, but also on displaying an alternative course. The divine focus from the outset was the world, but God's mission demanded an agent grateful for his mercy and pure in its religious devotion and ethic. Like the removal of cancerous growths, threats to Israel's fundamental spiritual health sometimes required radical surgery. However, even more than human surgeons, God does not impose these punishments callously or coldly; he does so with an extremely heavy heart. This does not mean we should be comfortable with divine violence, any more than we should passively accept misfortune and grief in our personal lives. The examples of Abraham (Gen 18), Moses (Exod 32, Num 14, Deut 9), and Amos (Amos 7) invite us to protest divine acts of violence and to question divine actions, but they do not authorize us to protest the divine agenda. Ultimately, their examples challenge us to accept the wisdom and righteousness of God. The challenge for us is that we treasure God's grace in our own lives and pray for him to extend his grace to others. Perhaps when they see what God has done for us, like Rahab outsiders will confess faith in our God.

Postscript

Having wrestled with the theme of divine violence in Deuteronomy it strikes me that such a study should always be preceded by a study of divine grace in the book, not to evade or deny the painful reality, but to provide context for it.[65] Because Israel owed everything she had or was to YHWH's gracious acts on her behalf—apart from which her ultimate fate was the same as the Canaanites—she should have gratefully accepted her role as a trophy of YHWH's mercy, kept herself pure and unspotted from surrounding evils, and evoked the envy and admiration of the world, not because she was so great, but because she bore the name of YHWH (28:9–10). His nearness to his people, his revelation of himself, and the righteousness of his will were without precedent or equal (4:5–8).[66]

---

65. Cf. Seitz' appeal ("Canon and Conquest," 292–308) to read the Deuteronomic prescriptions and narrative accounts against the backdrop of divine grace. For a rejoinder, see Fales, "Comments on 'Canon and Conquest,'" 309–13.

66. I am grateful to Michelle Knight for her helpful responses to an earlier draft of this essay. Of course, any deficiencies in style and content are of my own making.

14

The Fear of YHWH

The Theological Tie that Binds Deuteronomy and Proverbs[1]

Introduction

SCHOLARS HAVE LONG RECOGNIZED the links between the book of Deuteronomy and biblical wisdom writings, especially the book of Proverbs: the hortatory style (e.g., "Hear, O Israel," Deut 6:4; 9:1; "Listen, my son," Prov 2:10; 4:7); the emphasis on teaching and learning (Deut 4:1; Prov 1:2–6; 9:9; etc.); the binary choice between life and death, blessing and curse (Deut 11:26–28; 30:19; Prov 1:29; 3:31; 12:28; 13:14; 14:27; 18:21); specific instructions on moving landmarks (Deut 19:14; Prov 22:28), just weights (Deut 25:13–16; Prov 20:10); wicked behavior as "the abomination of YHWH" (תּוֹעֲבַת יהוה, Deut 5:25; Prov 3:32; etc.);[2] the emphasis on Torah as wisdom (Deut 4:6; Prov 1:7); the need for wise judges (Deut 1:9–18; Prov 8:15–16); and of course, the "fear of YHWH" (Deut 10:12; Prov 1:7; 9:10; etc.).[3] Scholars debate what this says about the relationship between Deuteronomy and Proverbs. Since Moshe Weinfeld's epochal work on the relationship,[4] many agree with him that the impetus for the book of Deuteronomy came from the Israelite court, and that its official sage-like character contributes to its function as a document promoting the centralization of political power in the Davidic monarch.

My aim in this paper is not to critique this hypothesis directly, but to explore more closely the theological tie that binds these books as reflected in the phrase, יִרְאַת יהוה, "the fear of YHWH," and related expressions that occur more than a dozen times in both Deuteronomy and Proverbs.[5] Despite the prominence of this expression/motif in both

---

1. I am very grateful for Will Kynes' kindness in responding to an earlier draft of this essay, for his counsel on improving the presentation, and for alerting me to critical discussions related to my topic. Of course, any deficiencies in argumentation or composition are my own responsibility.

2. The expression תּוֹעֲבַת יְהוָה ("abomination of YHWH") occurs eleven times on Proverbs: 3:32; 11:1, 20; 12:22; 15:8, 9, 26; 16:5; 17:15; 20:10, 23. Cf. also 6:16; 8:7; 13:19; 16:12; 21:27; 24:9; 26:25; 28:9; 29:27.

3. For detailed discussion, see Weinfeld, *Deuteronomy and the Deuteronomic School*, 244–81. For full discussion of the relationship between wisdom and Torah, see O'Dowd, *The Wisdom of Torah*.

4. See previous footnote.

5. For studies of the fear of God in Deuteronomy, see Plath, *Furcht Gottes*, 32–45; Becker, *Gottesfurcht im Alten Testament*, 84–111.

Deuteronomy and the Hebrew wisdom writings, sustained lexical analyses of יָרֵא are rare in discussions of the relationship between Torah and wisdom.[6]

Doing full justice to the use of יָרֵא and other biblical expressions for "fear" in Deuteronomy and the biblical wisdom texts would be a massive undertaking, but we must begin somewhere. In this essay, which is an initial exploratory foray into the subject, I shall limit myself to the notion of "fear" in Deuteronomy and in the book of Proverbs, which offers the most straightforward and fullest presentation of the subject. I shall begin by examining how Deuteronomy understands "the fear of YHWH," and then how this understanding relates to the notion as presented in Proverbs. Although I must explore the full range of the meaning of יָרֵא in these two books, I am particularly interested in the theological usage of the concept, and the expression's role not only in linking these two books, but also in accounting for its significance for biblical theology more generally. Our conclusions will be provisional, pending similar analyses of the use of the notion elsewhere in the canon. Having marinated in the Torah of Moses for the past twenty years makes this a logical place for me to begin.

The Fear of YHWH in Deuteronomy

Not surprisingly, the book of Deuteronomy uses a variety of expressions within the semantic realm of our English word "fear": אֵימָה (32:25); חִיל (2:25); חרד (28:26); חתת (1:21; 31:8); גוּר (1:17; 18:22; 32:27); יגר (9:19; 28:60); חָפַז (20:3); פחד (2:25; 11:25; 28:66, 67); ערץ (1:29; 7:21; 20:3; 31:6); רגז (2:25); שָׂעַר (32:17).[7] However, for theological investigation the primary root is ירא, variations of which occur forty-four times in the book (Table 14.1). Of these, exactly one-half (22) are finite verbs in the qal stem,[8] nine are qal infinitives construct,[9] and in one case the qal participle is used adjectivally in an otherwise verbless clause (7:19). The root appears in other stems only as a niphal, and in each case it involves a participle, employed five times as an adjective (נוֹרָא, 1:19; 7:21; 8:15; 10:17; 28:58), and once as a plural noun (נוֹרָאֹת, 10:21). The book also attests several noun forms based on the root: יִרְאָה (2:25), and מוֹרָא/מוֹרָאִים (4:34; 11:25; 26:8; 34:12).

---

6. McConville ("Wisdom and Torah in Deuteronomy") never mentions "fear"; O'Dowd's comments (*The Wisdom of Torah*, 116–20) are superficial and their link to the notion in Deuteronomy is never contemplated. Although several essays in *Wisdom and Torah* (Schipper and Teeter, eds.) deal with the expression, "fear of YHWH," (יִרְאַת יהוה), ed., discussion and comparison of the semantic range and usage of יָרֵא are missing altogether.

7. For a study of other Hebrew words for within the semantic field of יָרֵא, see Becker, ibid., 6–18.

8. The forms subdivide as follows: qal *qatal* (5:5; 25:18); *weqatal* (31:12; 28:10); *wayyiqtol* (2:4); *yiqtol* appears in simple forms (6:2, 13; 10:20; 13:5, 12[4, 11]; 17:13; 19:20; 21:21); and in admonitory commands, "Do not fear," which occurs with both negative particles אַל (1:21; 3:2; 20:3; 31:6 [* in Table 14.1]) and לֹא (1:29; 3:22; 7:18; 20:1; 31:8 [† in Table 14.1]).

9. Deut 4:10; 5:29; 6:24; 8:6; 10:12; 14:23; 17:19; 31:13; 28:58.

Table 14.1
The Root ירא in the Book of Deuteronomy

	Verb Forms	References
ירא	Qal *qatal*	5:5; 25:18
	Qal *weqatal*	28:10; 31:12
	Qal *yiqtol*	1:21*, 29†; 3:2*, 22†; 6:2, 13; 7:18†; 10:20; 13:5, 12 [4, 11]; 17:13; 19:20; 20:1†, 3*; 21:21; 31:6*, 8†.
	Qal *wayyiqtol*	2:4
יִרְאָה	Qal Infinitive construct	4:10; 5:29; 6:24; 8:6; 10:12; 14:23; 17:19; 28:58; 31:13
יָרֵא	Qal participle	7:19
נוֹרָא	Niphal participle (adjective)	1:19; 7:21; 8:15; 10:17; 28:58
נוֹרָאָה	Niphal participle (noun)	10:21
יָרֵא	Adjective	20:8
יִרְאָה	Noun	2:25
מוֹרָא/מוֹרָאִים	Noun	4:34; 11:25; 26:8; 34:12

While this distribution of forms is interesting, to determine its theological significance we must examine its usage in the book of Deuteronomy. This begins by observing that with its ca. 440 occurrences in the First Testament the root ירא exhibits an extremely wide range of meanings.[10] Recent advances in cognitive linguistics have offered valuable perspective on *how* words like this mean.[11] That a single word may bear different meanings is graphically illustrated by a word like "finch," which identifies small to moderately large seed-eating passerine birds, usually with strong conical beaks (family Fringillidae). Eleven species, all of which have twelve tail feathers and nine primaries, are native to Illinois.[12] However, if we add the modifier "Galapagos" to "finch," the issue becomes much more complicated. Although these are classified as passerine birds, they are not true finches but belong to the same family as tanagers. Fifteen species occupy these islands. They are all dull-colored, but they vary greatly in size and are generally classified in three categories: ground finches, tree finches, and warbler finches.[13]

10. See *HALOT*, 432–34, 560; *DCH* 4:276–82; 5:187–88. For lexical studies on יָרֵא, see Van Pelt and Kaiser, "ירא," 527–33; Fuhs, "יָרֵא *yārē'*; יָרֵא *yārē'*; יִרְאָה *yir'â*; מוֹרָא *môrā'*," 290–315; Stähli, "ירא *yr'* to fear," 568–78; Wanke, "φόβος and φοβέομαι in the Old Testament," 197–205.

11. For a series of essays introducing readers to the broad field of Cognitive Linguistics (CL), see Geeraerts, Dirven, and Taylor, eds., *Cognitive Linguistics: Basic Readings*. For application of CL to biblical studies, see van Wolde, "Cognitive Linguistics and the Hebrew Bible, 247–77.

12. American goldfinch (*Spinus tristis*), common redpoll (*Acanthis flammea*), evening grosbeak (*Hesperiphona vespertina*), gray-crowned rosy-finch (*Leucosticte tephrocotis*), hoary redpoll (*Acanthis hornemanni*), house finch (*Haemorhous mexicanus*), pine grosbeak (*Pinicola enucleator*), pine siskin (*Spinus pinus*), purple finch (*Haemorhous purpureus*), red crossbill (*Loxia curvirostra*), white-winged crossbill (*Loxia leucoptera*).

13. On Galapagos finches, see P. Grant and R. Grant, *40 Years of Evolution: Darwin's Finches on Daphne Major Island*.

What then does the word, "finch," mean? It all depends. Dirk Geeraerts helpfully summarizes the role of Cognitive Linguistics in the search for meaning with four governing principles:[14] (1) "Linguistic meaning is perspectival"; it depends on the vantage from which one construes the world. (2) "Linguistic meaning is dynamic and flexible"; semantic categories are adapted over time and with changing circumstances. (3) "Linguistic meaning is encyclopedic and non-autonomous"; meanings of specific facts/word are related to and integrated with knowledge of other aspects of the world we experience. (4) "Linguistic meaning is based on usage and experience"; dictionaries may define words, but the meanings we experience are determined by how words are used and the cultural and linguistic contexts in which they are embedded. These principles apply not only when we are trying to establish the meaning of "finch," but are especially relevant for trying to establish the meaning of יָרֵא in Deuteronomy and Proverbs.

Fundamentally the root יָרֵא appears to express the dispositional response to persons or forces that potentially or actually exercise authority over one or determine one's well-being. Remarkably those responses may range from sheer terror to confident trust, which on the surface approach opposite concepts.[15] The boundaries separating these various meanings are blurred and in many cases we could argue for a different sense than is usually reflected in our translations (see Fig. 14.1). The usage of ירא in Deuteronomy reflects this entire range.

Figure 14.1
The Semantic Spectrum of ירא Words in Deuteronomy

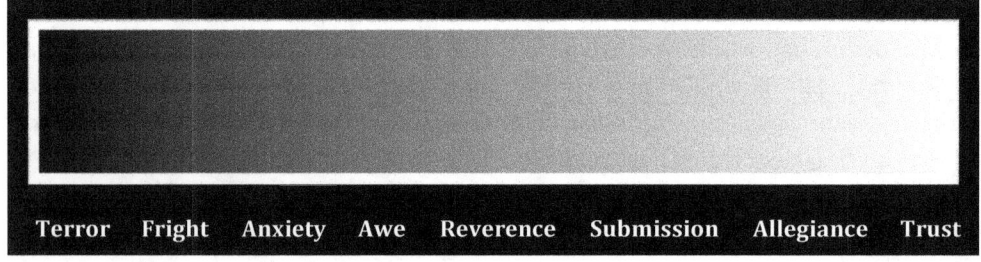

1. Fear as Terror.

In 5:5 Moses summarizes the Israelites' response to the theophany at Horeb with יָרֵא: "You were terrified because of the fire" (יְרֵאתֶם מִפְּנֵי הָאֵשׁ). He graphically describes how they expressed their terror in 5:23–26:

---

14. Geeraerts, "Introduction," 1–28, esp. 3–6.

15. According to Arnold ("The Love-Fear Antinomy in Deuteronomy 5–11, 552–62), "At one end of the spectrum stands a 'pathological anxiety' in the face of the threat, resulting in crippling inactivity. At the other end of the spectrum stands a positive course of action, which when used to characterize one's relationship with YHWH/God is a response of obedience or exclusive worship."

²³ When you heard the sound from the midst of the darkness—while the mountain was ablaze with fire—you, that is all your tribal leaders and your elders, approached me, and you said, ²⁴ "Look! YHWH our God has revealed to us his majestic glory, and we have heard his voice from the fire! Today we have seen God speaking with human beings, yet they live! ²⁵ So now, why should we die? Surely this massive fire will consume us. If we continue to hear the voice of YHWH our God, we shall surely die. ²⁶ For who out of all humankind has ever heard the voice of the living God speaking from the fire as we have, and survived?"[16]

Although Deut 5:26 identifies the fire as the cause of the fear at Horeb, the people knew they had encountered the divine *numen*, which at the same time drew them in to its *mysterium*[17] and repelled them.[18] Amazingly, although they feared for their lives, they survived to tell about it (cf. 4:33).

2. Fear as Fright

Whereas at Horeb Israel had encountered the overwhelming glory of YHWH before which they were defenceless, in encounters with feared human enemies the significance of ירא shifts slightly. Although defeat may well cost the troops their lives, this fate is not inevitable, and except in cases involving the *ḥērem* policy,[19] it does necessarily involve the entire population. ירא as "fright" in this sense is common in Deuteronomy, most notably in contexts involving the encouragement formulas, אַל־תִּירָא and לֹא תִירָא מֵהֶם, both of which translate as "Do not fear [them]."[20] In several occurrences of these formulas Moses strengthens the admonition with emotional correlatives: אַל־תֵּחָת, "Do not be dismayed/emotionally shattered" (1:21; 31:8); אַל־תַּחְפְּזוּ וְאַל־תַּעַרְצוּ מִפְּנֵיהֶם, "Do not panic or be in dread of them" (20:3; cf. 1:29; 31:6). On two occasions YHWH and his spokesman Moses promise that YHWH will turn the tables:

---

16. Cf. Deut 18:16. Compare also the narrator's description of the people's response in Exod 20:18, "When all the people witnessed the thunder and lightning, the sound of the trumpet, and the sight of the smoking mountain, they were terrified and trembled (וַיֵּרְא . . . וַיָּנֻעוּ) and stood at a distance."

17. This accounts for the need for a fence around the mountain to prevent the people from encroaching upon the utterly sacred space and thereby be struck by the divine glory/holiness (Exod 19:12–13, 23).

18. Expressions borrowed from Rudolph Otto's analysis of the *mysterium tremendum*, in *The Idea of the Holy*, 5–73. For discussion of Otto's treatment of the *mysterium tremendum* and its relation to the fear of YHWH in the First Testament, see Becker, *Gottesfurcht*, 60–84; Waltke, "The Fear of the Lord," 17–33. Moshe Weinfeld overstates the difference between Exod 20:20, which has God's fear (i.e., "terror" = Akkadian *pulḫu*) put on the people's faces, and the present text which situates the fear of God in their hearts (*Deuteronomy 1–11*, 325). Both accounts involve the terrifying theophany/ theophony (cf. also Deut 18:16); so also Becker, *Gottesfurcht*, 28–29, 98.

19. On which see chapter 13, "How Can We Bless YHWH? Wrestling with Divine Violence in Deuteronomy," above, pp. 264–82.

20. See Table 14.1 and n. 956 above for references.

Today I will begin to put the dread (פַּחַד) and fear (יִרְאָה) of you on the peoples who are under the whole heaven, who will hear the report about you and will tremble (רָגַז) and shake [in anguish] (חִיל) because of you. (2:25)

No one will be able to stand against you. YHWH your God will lay the dread of you (פַּחְדְּכֶם) and the fear of you (מוֹרַאֲכֶם) on the faces of the entire land (עַל־פְּנֵי כָל־הָאָרֶץ) that you shall tread, as he promised you. (11:25)

Remarkably, and in contrast to Horeb, where the presence of the divine *numen* caused the terror, here the presence of YHWH (20:1; 31:6), the memory of his past actions on their behalf (7:18; 20:1), and the promises of divine action in support of his people (3:2, 22; 7:19) remove the need for the natural response of "fear."

But this sort of fright did not arise only in the face of formidable human foes. Moses also characterizes the terrain through which the Israelites had traveled as "that entire great and terrifying wilderness" (כָּל־הַמִּדְבָּר הַגָּדֹל וְהַנּוֹרָא הַהוּא; 1:19; 8:15). We might place these texts under the next category ("anxiety"), except that 8:15 identifies the *real* cause of the distress: poisonous serpents and scorpions, and the total absence of water.

Equally real and even more frightening are the Deuteronomic prescriptions for the punishment to be imposed upon Israelites for certain crimes: idolatry (13:12[11]); not complying with the oracular judgment of the priest in an otherwise insoluble case (17:8–13); false charges against a fellow Israelite (19:15–21); rebellion and insubordination within the household (21:18–21). In each context, Moses speaks expressly of the purposes of punishment: to purge the evil (בִּעֵר הָרָע) from the community of Israel[21] and to motivate observers not to perpetrate the same crimes for fear of the punitive consequences.

3. Fear as Anxiety

The boundary between "terror" and "anxiety" is indistinct.[22] For our purposes, in part the distinction involves the likely or inevitable reality of the former versus the irreal or hypothetical nature of the latter. We find hints of this in 11:25 [cited above], which locates the dread and fear of Israel "on the faces of the entire land." Those who hear this statement will readily imagine the expressions on the faces of the targets of Israelite aggression at the sight of their forces entering their land.[23] In 2:4 Moses speaks of the descendants of Esau "fearing" Israel, when in fact Israel represents no real cause for fear, since they make no claims to their land. However, one can easily imagine the emotion the appearance of the mass of Israelites camped on the border of Edom might have produced in the hearts/minds of the Edomites. But the fear was groundless. Elsewhere Moses speaks explicitly of the anxiety ("pre-traumatic stress") that anticipation of mili-

---

21. This motivation is not expressed in vv. 7–12[6–11], but we may assume the conclusion to the first scenario (v. 6[5]) carries over to the second and third (vv. 13–19[12–18]) scenarios.

22. Sirach 40:2 speaks of "fear of heart" (φόβον καρδίας).

23. On the psychological and emotional dimension of YHWH's actions on Israel's adversaries, see chapter 13, "How Can We Bless YHWH? Wrestling with Divine Violence in Deuteronomy," above, pp. 264–82.

tary engagement causes in the hearts of new recruits, and the demoralizing effect this may have on the rest of the troops in 20:8:

> And the officers shall also declare to the people, saying, "Is there any man who is fearful (הַיָּרֵא) and timid (רַךְ הַלֵּבָב, lit. "tenderhearted")? Let him return to his house, to prevent him from causing despair in the heart of his fellows like [the despair] in his own heart."[24]

4. Fear as Awe

In contrast to terror and fright, which cause a person to recoil for fear of the consequences, this category of "fear" expresses amazement in the face of an extra-ordinary observation, experience, or event: in common parlance, that which makes us declare, "Wow! That was awesome!" In several texts Moses speaks of the actions that YHWH performed in the people's full view as "awesome":

> Has any god ever dared (נִסָּה) to come and take a nation for himself from the midst of another nation, by daring/challenging acts (מַסֹּת), signs (אֹתֹת), wonders (מוֹפְתִים), war (מִלְחָמָה), a strong hand (יָד חֲזָקָה) and an outstretched arm (זְרוֹעַ נְטוּיָה), and by great (גְּדֹלִים) and *awesome actions* (מוֹרָאִים) like all those [actions] that YHWH your God performed for your benefit in Egypt before your very eyes? (4:34)

> And YHWH brought us out of Egypt with a strong hand and an outstretched arm, with a great and awesome action (מֹרָא גָּדֹל), and with signs and wonders. (26:8)

Moses expresses the same notion in a doxological outburst in 10:21: "He is your praise. He is your God, who, with you, has performed these great and *awesome actions* (אֶת־הַגְּדֹלֹת וְאֶת־הַנּוֹרָאֹת) that your own eyes have seen."[25] In another even more impressive and formal doxology Moses attributes the awesome quality of the divine actions to YHWH himself:

> Indeed YHWH your God is God of gods and Lord of lords, the great, the mighty, and the *awesome El* (הָאֵל הַגָּדֹל הַגִּבֹּר וְהַנּוֹרָא), who is never partial and who never accepts a bribe." (10:17; cf. 7:21).

Although the overwhelming power that YHWH demonstrated in Egypt might have evoked fright in the witnesses, that they were done for Israel's benefit (4:33) rules this out as the primary objective. In 4:34 (and v. 39) Moses declares their revelatory goal:

---

24. Reading the verb in יִמַּס אֶת־לְבַב as a hiphil (יָמֵס) rather than MT's qal. Cf. *HALOT*, 607. According to Deut 1:28, the previous generation of Israelites had experienced the same anguish in response to the scouts' report of giants and gigantic fortifications in the land of Canaan.

25. Reflecting his own awe before the figure of Moses, in an unparalleled move, in 34:12 the narrator attributes these awesome actions to Moses: "the strong hand and the entire awesome and great act (כֹּל הַמּוֹרָא הַגָּדוֹל) that Moses performed in the sight of all Israel."

"To you it was shown, that you might know that YHWH is God; there is no other besides him" (cf. v. 39). YHWH performed the miraculous signs and wonders in Egypt expressly to develop in the Israelites an appropriate awe before him and to give them a lesson in the divine *numen* that they would never forget.[26] For those who received this revelation with submission and faith there was no need for fear in the sense of fright. On the other hand, for those who refused to submit to the awesome God and who persisted in their own ways, this same "great and awesome God" would become a source of extreme fright.

We witness this option in the context of the covenant curses of 28:15–68. Approaching the end of this litany of imprecations to be imposed upon Israel in the event of persistent rebellion against their divine Suzerain, Moses declared,

> If you do not keep all the words of this Torah that are written in this Torah by doing [them and] by fearing this glorious and awesome name—YHWH your God (הַשֵּׁם הַנִּכְבָּד וְהַנּוֹרָא הַזֶּה אֵת יְהוָה אֱלֹהֶיךָ)—then YHWH will bring on you and your offspring extraordinary afflictions, afflictions severe and lasting, and sicknesses grievous and lasting (28:58–59).

He followed this warning up with further details of the consequences of rejecting the God who had graciously rescued Israel from Egypt, called them to be his covenant people, and set them high above the nations for praise, fame, and glory (26:19). To people who respond to the memory of the divine signs and wonders with submission and faith יָרֵא means awe, but those who respond with contempt or a sense of entitlement יָרֵא will ultimately express the frightening result of an encounter with the awesome God.

5. Fear as Reverence

It is possible to be awed by an event or a person, and still exhibit no reverence. We may be awed by the power of our enemies, but still view them cynically or disrespectfully. Reverence usually assumes a positive disposition toward the person or object[27] that one reveres, and is associated with an appropriate level of gravitas. The word יָרֵא is often used in this sense, and as such functions as a virtual synonym for כָּבֵד, "to honor, ascribe worth to."[28] In Deuteronomy we may identify two important texts within this semantic field. The first involves Moses' enigmatic reference to the Amalekites in 25:17–18:

> Remember what Amalek did to you on the way when you came out of Egypt. When you were famished and weary he attacked you on the way when you were faint and weary, and he attacked all the stragglers at the back; he did not fear God (וְלֹא יָרֵא אֱלֹהִים).

---

26. The narrator frequently repeats this revelatory goal in Exodus: 6:7; 7:5, 17; 8:18[22]; 10:2; 14:4, 18; 16:12.

27. Lev 19:30 and 26:3 speak of reverence for the sanctuary.

28. In the Decalogue, the command to honor father and mother uses כָּבֵד (Exod 20:12//Deut 5:16), while the Instructions on Holiness use יָרֵא (Lev 19:3).

This linkage of ירא with אֱלֹהִים is unique in Deuteronomy, but it occurs more than two dozen times in the Hebrew Bible.[29] Whether or not the "fear of God" functions as the First Testament expression for "religion,"[30] it expresses piety that is demonstrated in ethical or cultic behavior.[31] From his observation in Deut 25:18 that Amalek took advantage of defenceless and weak Israelites Moses concluded that the Amalekites lacked reverence for God.

Deuteronomy 28:10 takes the reverential sense of ירא in a different direction: "Then all the peoples of the earth will see that YHWH's name is called/proclaimed over you, and they will show reverence because of you." While most English translations render the last clause, וְיָרְאוּ מִמֶּךָּ, as if Israel is the object of the verb,[32] the preposition מִן should probably be interpreted causally, "on account of you,"[33] which leaves the object of reverence undeclared. Verse 7 speaks of YHWH defending his people against attacks by their enemies, and verse 13 of Israel's international preeminence. However, the nearer context describes Israel's superlative prosperity and fertility (vv. 8, 11–12), YHWH's establishment of Israel as his holy people (הֲקִים לְעַם קָדוֹשׁ), and his name being proclaimed over them. While enigmatic, the immediately preceding clause is significant: וְרָאוּ כָּל־עַמֵּי הָאָרֶץ כִּי שֵׁם יְהוָה נִקְרָא עָלֶיךָ, rendered literally, "Then all the peoples of the earth will see that YHWH's name is proclaimed over/read upon you." This is metaphorical speech, alluding to YHWH's ownership of his people by virtue of his branding them with his name. The branding was obviously not literal, as was the case with ancient Babylonian temple personnel who were physically branded with the symbols of the gods to whom they were devoted,[34] or with Israel's high priest who wore a medallion on his turban, inscribed, קֹדֶשׁ לַיהוָה ("Holy belonging to YHWH; Exod 28:36; 39:30). However, not only had Moses applied this epithet to Israel as a whole (Deut 7:6; 14:2, 21; 26:19), but the peoples will also observe YHWH's blessing and defense of Israel and recognize that they belong to him and have been sanctified for his divine service. This constitutes the fulfillment of 26:19, "He will elevate you high above all the nations that he has made for praise, fame, and glory." They will recognize Israel as glorious, but ultimately the praise will go to YHWH, who has claimed them as his own and deserves all the credit for their well-being—just as the magnificent garb of the high priest reflected the glory of YHWH, the divine occupant of the tabernacle (Exod 28:2, 40).

---

29. (1) The verb יָרֵא + אֱלֹהִים as the direct object ("to fear God"): Gen 42:18; Exod 1:17, 21; Deut 25:18; Neh. 7:2; Job 1:9; Ps 55:20[19]; Eccl 5:6; 8:12; 12:13; Jonah 1:9. Additionally Job 9:35 and 37:24 refer to God with the masculine pronoun. (2) The verbal adjective יְרֵא in construct with אֱלֹהִים ("fearer of God, God fearer"): Gen 22:12; Exod 18:21; Job 1:1, 8; 2:3; Ps 66:16; Eccl 7:18; 8:12. (3) The noun יִרְאָה in construct with אֱלֹהִים ("fear of God"): Gen 20:11; Exod 20:20; 2 Sam 23:3 (2x); Neh 5:9, 15; Prov 2:5.

30. Thus Pfeiffer, "The Fear of God," 41–48.

31. For Pentateuchal texts, see Gen 20:11; 22:12; 42:18; Exod 1:17, 21. See also Job 1:1, 8, 9. In Jonah 1:9 the prophet's professed fear is belied by his behavior.

32. Cf. "They will fear/be afraid of you" (NIV, ESV, NRSV), or "They will stand in awe/fear of you" (HCSB, NLT, NJPSV).

33. On the preposition מִן functioning causally, see GKC §119z; IBHS, 213 (11.2.11d, ##10 and 11).

34. Cf. Dandamaev, Slavery in Babylonia, 488–89. For further discussion of the idiom, see briefly Block, "'In Spirit and in Truth'"), 281, n. 26, and more fully, Imes, Bearing YHWH's Name at Sinai.

While the cause of the nations' praise differs, Moses had provided an analogue to the recognition of Israel's status by virtue of YHWH's action in his first address, when he described the nations' acknowledgement that Israel was uniquely privileged to have a God who heard them whenever they called upon him and who had revealed to them his righteous will concerning their response to his grace (4:6–8). As noted earlier, the object of reverence is not explicitly stated, but if it is Israel, then as is the case with reverence for the sanctuary in Lev 19:30 and 26:3, if outsiders revere Israel ultimately the reverence will be directed to YHWH, whose name they bear.[35] Alternatively the reverence may simply be their response to the way they witness the covenantal triangle involving YHWH, Israel, and the land at work in fulfillment of YHWH's promises and in response to Israel's fidelity.

6. Fear as Submission and Exclusive Allegiance

If true worship involves reverential acts of submission and homage before the divine Suzerain in response to his revelation of himself and in accord with his will,[36] then one of the principal goals of Deuteronomy is to ensure that Israel worships truly by reverentially submitting to YHWH and living in accord with his graciously revealed statutes and ordinances. Israel's unique privilege in knowing the will of their divine patron is reflected in the anticipated international response to Israel's obedience to "the ordinances and judgments" (חֻקִּים וּמִשְׁפָּטִים):

> See, I have taught you ordinances and judgments, as YHWH my God commanded me, that you would do them in the land that you are entering to take possession of it. So keep them and do them, for therein lies your wisdom (חָכְמָה) and understanding in the sight of the peoples. When they hear all these ordinances they will say, "Wow! This great nation is indeed a wise and understanding people."
> Indeed, what great nation is there that has a god as near to it as YHWH our God is to us, whenever we call upon him? And what great nation is there, that has ordinances and judgments as righteous (צַדִּיקִים) as this entire Torah that I am setting before you today? (4:5–8)

The place of "fear" in this agenda is reflected in two ways: (1) by the ethical and spiritual responses identified as correlatives of ירא, and (2) by the repeated explicit association of obedience with this root.[37]

In considering Deuteronomic texts that link ירא with correlative expressions, pride of place must go to Deut 10:12–13. Following the opening rhetorical question, "What

---

35. On the idiom, "bearing the name of YHWH" in the second command of the Decalogue as a mark of divine ownership, see Block, "Bearing the Name of the LORD with Honor,," 61–72; idem, "No other Gods," 237–71, and much more fully, Imes, *Bearing YHWH's Name at Sinai.*

36. For full development of this thesis, see Block, *For the Glory of God.* For a focused discussion of worship in Deuteronomy, see Block, "'In Spirit and in Truth,'" in *Rediscovering Worship,* 1–26, and *The Gospel according to Moses,* 272–98.

37. For a listing of expressions that occur with יָרֵא, see Plath, *Furcht Gottes,* 22.

does YHWH ask of you?" (מָה יְהוָה אֱלֹהֶיךָ שֹׁאֵל מֵעִמָּךְ) in verse 12, Moses prescribes the answer with five infinitives construct:

כִּי אִם־לְיִרְאָה אֶת־יְהוָה אֱלֹהֶיךָ	Only this: to <u>fear</u> YHWH your God,
לָלֶכֶת בְּכָל־דְּרָכָיו	To <u>walk</u> in all his ways,
וּלְאַהֲבָה אֹתוֹ	And to <u>love</u> him,
וְלַעֲבֹד אֶת־יְהוָה אֱלֹהֶיךָ	And to <u>serve</u> YHWH your God
בְּכָל־לְבָבְךָ וּבְכָל־נַפְשֶׁךָ:	with your whole heart and being,
לִשְׁמֹר אֶת־מִצְוֹת יְהוָה וְאֶת־חֻקֹּתָיו	<u>by keeping</u>[38] the command of YHWH and his ordinances.

If the number of stipulations in the Decalogue is governed by the number of digits on our two hands (for heuristic and mnemonic purposes), it seems that the five items listed here represent the digits of one hand [Fig. 14.2].[39] According to this image, the call for fear is primary, not only in terms of sequence, but also in terms of importance; without the opposable thumb a person's hand is almost useless.

Figure 14.2
The Dimensions of Divine Expectation
Deuteronomy 10:12—11:1

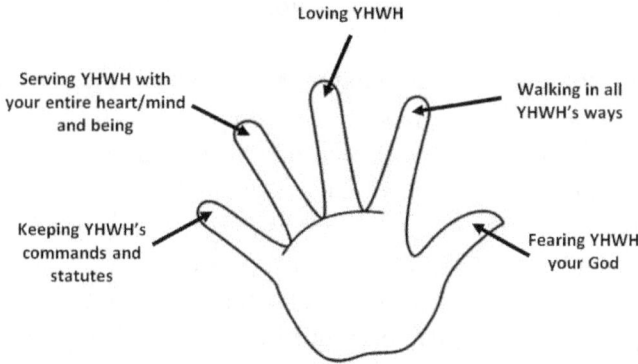

Elsewhere Deuteronomy reinforces this impression by linking fear with active correlatives:

> Now this is the command—the ordinances and judgments—that YHWH your God charged me to teach you, that you may do them in the land to which you are crossing over [the Jordan] to possess it, in order that you may fear (לְמַעַן תִּירָא) YHWH your God, you and your son and your son's son, by keeping (לִשְׁמֹר) all his ordinances and his commands that I charge you [to keep]. (6:1–2)

> So you shall keep the commands of YHWH your God by walking (לָלֶכֶת) in his ways and by fearing him (לְיִרְאָה אֹתוֹ, 8:6).

---

38. On the gerundive use of the *lamedh* + the infinitive construct, see *IBHS* §36.3.3e.
39. For further discussion, see Block, *Deuteronomy*, 268–79.

Indeed, the emphatic construction of Deut 10:20 suggests that active submission has now morphed into total and exclusive allegiance:

[Only] YHWH your God you shall fear (יָרֵא); him you shall serve (עָבַד); to him you shall hold fast (דָּבַק); and by his name you shall swear (10:20) (נִשְׁבַּע).

This injunction builds on 6:13, which is sandwiched between a reminder of YHWH's grace in rescuing Israel from Egypt (v. 12) and a prohibition against "walking after" other gods (v. 14): "[Only] YHWH your God you shall fear (יָרֵא); him you shall serve (עָבַד), and by his name you shall swear (נִשְׁבַּע)." In a context highlighting the severity of the consequences of "going after other gods, 13:5[4] echoes and expands in 10:12:

אַחֲרֵי יְהוָה אֱלֹהֵיכֶם תֵּלֵכוּ	[Only] after YHWH your God you shall walk,
וְאֹתוֹ תִירָאוּ	and [only] him you shall fear,
וְאֶת־מִצְוֹתָיו תִּשְׁמֹרוּ	and [only] his commands you shall keep,
וּבְקֹלוֹ תִשְׁמָעוּ	and [only] to his voice you shall listen,
וְאֹתוֹ תַעֲבֹדוּ	and [only] him you shall serve,
וּבוֹ תִדְבָּקוּן׃	and [only] to him you shall hold fast).

Invitations to go after other gods represent tests of the Israelites' allegiance, whether, in accord with the Shema (6:4–5), they will be wholeheartedly and covenantally committed to YHWH (13:4[3]).[40]

To these we could add Deuteronomic texts in which the verb יָרֵא, "to fear," is followed by the finite verb שָׁמַר, "to keep [the commands]" (e.g., 31:12, on which see further below) or with infinitives construct, either functioning epexegetically[41] or with the *lamedh*, functioning gerundivally.[42] Like the verb, אָהַב, "to love," which Abraham Malamat rightly argues should never be translated with a single English word, but rendered as "demonstrate love,"[43] in these contexts יָרֵא means "exhibit fear by keeping the commands."[44] This is a shorthand expression for demonstrating reverence, submission, and allegiance to the divine Suzerain in response to his gracious revelation of

---

40. On the covenantal significance of the Shema, see Block, "How Many is God?" 61–72.

41. For example, 5:29, לְיִרְאָה אֹתִי וְלִשְׁמֹר אֶת־כָּל־מִצְוֹתַי, "to fear me, that is, to keep all my commands." Cf. 31:12.

42. E.g., 6:2, לְמַעַן תִּירָא אֶת־יְהוָה אֱלֹהֶיךָ לִשְׁמֹר אֶת־כָּל־חֻקֹּתָיו וּמִצְוֹתָיו, "that you might fear YHWH your God *by* keeping all his ordinances and his commands"; 17:19, לְיִרְאָה אֶת־יְהוָה אֱלֹהָיו לִשְׁמֹר אֶת־כָּל־דִּבְרֵי הַתּוֹרָה הַזֹּאת וְאֶת־הַחֻקִּים הָאֵלֶּה לַעֲשֹׂתָם, "to fear YHWH your God *by* keeping all the words of this Torah and these ordinances *by* doing them. Cf. n. 26 above.

43. See Malamat, "'You Shall Love Your Neighbor as Yourself,'" 111–15. For superb discussions of Deuteronomy's use of "love" (אָהַב), see Arnold, "The Love-Fear Antinomy in Deuteronomy 5–11," 552–62; Levenson, *The Love of God*, 1–58. Both authors discuss the nature of "fear" (יָרֵא) and its relationship to "love" (אָהַב). See Arnold, pp. 562–69; Levenson, 29–36.

44. The occasional reversing of the order of the verbs reflects the fluidity of the concepts underlying these expressions, as in Deut 28:58, אִם־לֹא תִשְׁמֹר לַעֲשׂוֹת אֶת־כָּל־דִּבְרֵי הַתּוֹרָה הַזֹּאת הַכְּתוּבִים בַּסֵּפֶר הַזֶּה לְיִרְאָה אֶת־הַשֵּׁם הַנִּכְבָּד וְהַנּוֹרָא הַזֶּה אֵת יְהוָה אֱלֹהֶיךָ, "If you do not keep [the covenant] *by* doing all the words of this Torah that are written in this document by fearing this glorious and awesome name, YHWH your God."

7. Fear as Trust

As was the case with terror and fright, the boundary between "fear as submission/allegiance" and "fear as trust" often blurs. If "fear as submission" involves an enemy, a person's submission may actually demonstrate terror before that person. However, if subordinates love the ones to whom they submit, in their submission they may actually demonstrate trust in that person, in which case יָרֵא may function in place of בָּטַח, "to trust," or הֶאֱמִין, "to believe, to have confidence in."

Although Moses uses both of these words in Deuteronomy, he does so rarely. The former root occurs four times; twice as a noun, בֶּטַח, meaning "security, safety" (12:10; 33:12, 28), and once as a verb, meaning "to trust," albeit with reference to misplaced trust in fortifications (28:52; LXX). הֶאֱמִין occurs twice. In 1:32 Moses complained that in spite of YHWH's promise to fight for Israel (v. 30a), his mighty acts of salvation in Egypt (v. 30b), and his fatherly care in the desert (v. 31) the people "refused to trust" (אֵינְכֶם מַאֲמִינִם) in YHWH their God.[46] Referring to the same event in 9:23, Moses interpreted Israel's refusal to listen to YHWH's voice and enter Canaan from Kadesh-barnea as rebellion and unbelief.[47] This usage of הֶאֱמִין is well-known from Gen 15:6, which speaks of Abraham's remarkable faith when all he had to go on was the promises of God. But these represent the only occurrences of predominantly "faith, trust" words in Deuteronomy.

However, יָרֵא, "to fear," often functions as a substitute for הֶאֱמִין. In his summary of the range of meanings of יָרֵא (above, p. 308 n. 15), Bill Arnold suggests the opposite poles are represented by "'pathological anxiety' in the face of the threat, resulting in crippling inactivity," and "a response of obedience or exclusive worship." This is correct as far as it goes, but given the modern North American context in which "worship" is popularly construed primarily as cultic/liturgical activity before the Deity, this may be misleading. On the surface, Arnold's statement accords with Gen 22:5, where Abraham describes his activities on Mount Moriah with the verb הִשְׁתַּחֲוָה, commonly rendered

---

45. In Jonah's response to the sailors' interrogation he illustrates the link between his identity, the fear of YHWH, and allegiance to him: "I am a Hebrew, and I fear YHWH, the God of heaven, who made the sea and the dry land" (Jonah 1:9). For a recent supportive but revolutionary full discussion of Greek πίστις meaning "allegiance to" in the New Testament, see Bates, *Salvation by Allegiance Alone*. For my interaction with Bates, see Block, "The Fear of YHWH: A Call for Allegiance to YHWH Alone," forthcoming.

46. Instead of rendering הֶאֱמִין as πιστεύω, LXX uses the related but rare word ἐμπιστεύω. The word is common in the Apocrypha, but occurs in the translation of the Hebrew Bible only in Judg 11:20; 2 Chr 20:20[3x]; Jonah 3:5. See further LSJ, 545.

47. וַתַּמְרוּ אֶת־פִּי יְהוָה אֱלֹהֵיכֶם וְלֹא הֶאֱמַנְתֶּם לוֹ וְלֹא שְׁמַעְתֶּם בְּקֹלוֹ. The Greek renders both מָרָה, "to rebel," and הֶאֱמִין, "to believe, trust," with "faith" words: καὶ ἠπειθήσατε τῷ ῥήματι κυρίου τοῦ θεοῦ ὑμῶν καὶ οὐκ ἐπιστεύσατε αὐτῷ καὶ οὐκ εἰσηκούσατε τῆς φωνῆς αὐτοῦ. While ἀπειθέω means primarily "to be disobedient," in the New Testament it occasionally refers to unbelievers: John 3:36; Acts 14:2; Rom 15:31.

"worship," and which the divine envoy recognizes as an expression of יָרֵא (v. 12). However, this interpretation misconstrues both lexemes.

Although הִשְׁתַּחֲוָה is usually translated in English as "worship," literally the word speaks of a physical gesture of genuflection before a superior in submission and homage.[48] In its derived usage, this often involved cultic activity, but it was not limited to this (cf. Ruth 2:10). As for יָרֵא, Gen 22:1 provides the key to the meaning of the divine envoy's response to Abraham's sacrifice of Isaac: "Now I know that you are a God-fearer (כִּי־יְרֵא אֱלֹהִים אַתָּה),[49] seeing you have not withheld your son, your only son, from me" (v. 12). At the beginning of this episode (v. 1) the narrator had formally announced that what follows was intended as a divine test. Despite the absence of הֶאֱמִין in this context, YHWH's demand to sacrifice Isaac (22:2) obviously tested whether Abraham would give YHWH his full allegiance and could trust YHWH to keep his promise to multiply his descendants *through Isaac* (cf. 21:8–12). Here יָרֵא clearly connotes faith, and may be understood as "trusting awe," or "awed trust," which was demonstrated by immediate and unreserved obedience. This interpretation was grasped by Ben Sirach in Sir 44:20: "He kept the Torah of the Most High (νόμον ὑψίστου), and entered into a covenant with him; he certified the covenant in his flesh, and when he was tested he proved faithful (ἐν πειρασμῷ εὑρέθη πιστός)" (NRSV modified).

While the midwives' fear of God in Exod 1:17 and 21 may also be interpreted as trust in God to defend them against the fury of Pharaoh,[50] the sense of "belief" for יָרֵא is nearer the surface in Exod 9:20, where the narrator notes that after Moses' announcement of impending hail, those Egyptian officials who "feared" (i.e., "believed") YHWH's word hastily removed their slaves and livestock to a secure place. Exodus 14:31 conjoins יָרֵא and הֶאֱמִין in a single statement: in the wake of YHWH's annihilation of Pharaoh's army "the people feared (יָרֵא) YHWH; they believed (הֶאֱמִין, LXX ἐπίστευσαν) in him and his servant Moses.[51] This characterization reinforces Walter Moberly's proposal that in the Hebrew Bible "the fear of God" is the primary expression for the appropriate response to him:

> The Old Testament use of "fear of God" is thus more or less equivalent *in function* to the New Testament's use of various forms of "believe/trust" and "have faith" (*pisteuō* and *pistis*) to depict appropriate human response to God; so in

---

48. For fuller discussion see Block, *For the Glory of God*, 12–17.

49. Cf. LXX, ὅτι φοβῇ τὸν θεὸν σύ. Contra LXX and virtually all English translations, which render יָרֵא with a finite verb, this is a verbless clause of classification. Cf. Speiser (*Genesis*, 163), "You are a God-fearing man." As exemplified by Abraham and Job (Job 1:1, 8; 2:3), יָרֵא represents trusting awe demonstrated in righteous living and specific obedience to God's command. Though this text is curiously not cited, for discussion of verbless clauses of classification, see Andersen, *The Hebrew Verbless Clause*, 42–45. The phrase יְרֵא אֱלֹהִים occurs elsewhere in Deut 25:18 (negatively of Amalek) and Eccl 7:18.

50. Weinfeld (*Deuteronomy and the Deuteronomic School*, 274) interprets יָרֵא here (as well as in Gen 20:11; 42:18; Lev 19:14, 32; 25:17, 36, 43; Deut 25:18) as moral restraint. According to Tigay (*Deuteronomy*, 47, and 352, n. 40), the word "is virtually a synonym for ethical behavior and fear of sin (cf. Deut 5:26; 25:18)." Cf. Moberly, *The Old Testament of the Old Testament*, 189. For Gregory S. Smith (*The Testing of God's Sons*, 81–82), יָרֵא involves action in obedience to the will of YHWH, that is, demonstrated loyalty.

51. Interpreting the *waw* on וַיַּאֲמִינוּ explicatively, with NJPSV.

terms of function a Christian way of conveying the tenor of "one who fears God" might be "a believer," "a person of faith" (italics his).[52]

Although Deuteronomy often links יָרֵא with obedience and righteous living,[53] important clues to its meaning are found particularly in the recurring sequence of verbs within the book: reading—hearing—learning—fearing—obeying—living well (Table 14.2).

Table 14.2
The Importance of Hearing the Torah

Reference	Reading	Hearing	Learning	Fearing	Obeying	Living well
1. 4:10		✓	✓	✓		
2. 5:23–29		✓		✓	✓	✓
3. 6:1–3			✓	✓	✓	✓
4. 17:13		✓		✓	✓	
5. 17:19–20	✓	[✓]	✓	✓	✓	✓(?)
6. 19:20		✓		✓	✓	
7. 31:11–13	✓	✓	✓	✓	✓	

For our purposes the fifth and seventh texts, which involve encounters with YHWH through the hearing of the Torah, are especially significant.[54] Whereas Israel's encounter with YHWH at Horeb had terrified the people (4:9–14, 36; 5:5, 23–33; 18:16), Deuteronomy portrays worship at the place where YHWH would establish his name as confident, intimate, and celebrative.[55]

The Torah itself answers how the verb יָרֵא fits this picture. If we understand הַתּוֹרָה (i.e., Moses' addresses in Deuteronomy) primarily as "the law," as many do, then hearing "the law" could evoke fear of negative consequences analogous to the effect hearing verdicts in criminal cases had on the community (13:12[11]; 17:13; 19:20; 21:21). However, if we interpret הַתּוֹרָה as "instruction," whose goal is to promote יָרֵא in the sense of "faith, trust," or even "unqualified/steadfast allegiance" (Paul's πίστις), then its significance for this discussion is obvious. The association of "fear" (יָרֵא) with "love" (אָהַב) in 10:12–13, both of which involve affections demonstrated in action (walking in the ways of YHWH, serving him whole-heartedly, keeping his commands and statutes, and listening to his

---

52. Moberly, *Old Testament Theology*, 245.

53. Deut 5:29; 6:2; 8:6; 10:12–13; 13:5[4]; 17:19; 28:58; 31:12.

54. In the first three the sound of YHWH's voice accompanied by awesome theophanic visual phenomena at Horeb evoked severe fright in the people. The fourth and sixth cases involve warnings against disregarding the divinely rendered decisions in criminal cases (17:13) or repeating the crime (19:20).

55. Signaled by the verb שָׂמַח, in 12:7, 12, 18; 14:26; 16:11, 14–15; 26:11 (cf. Lev 23:40). On the contrast between Israel's frightening one-time encounter with YHWH at Horeb and Israel's intimate regular meetings with him at the central sanctuary, see chapter 7, "A Place for My Name": Horeb and Zion in the Mosaic Vision of Israelite Worship," above, pp. 126–51.

voice), and the fact that this "fear" must and can be learned reinforce this interpretation. Indeed, this was to be the purpose of the Levites' reading the Torah every seven years at the festival of Sukkoth:

> At the end of every seven years, at the set time in the year of release, at the Feast of Booths, when all Israel comes to appear before YHWH your God at the place that he will choose, you shall read this law before all Israel in their hearing. Assemble the people, men, women, and little ones, and the sojourner within your towns, that they may hear and learn (יִלְמְדוּ) to fear YHWH your God, and keep all the words of this law by observing them, and that their children, who have not known it, may hear and learn (וְלָמְדוּ) to fear YHWH your God, as long as you live in the land that you are going over the Jordan to possess (Deut 31:10–13).

The present emphasis accords with the didactic function of YHWH's revelation at Horeb (4:10, though the dimension of terror the Israelites demonstrated there is now obviously missing), the goal of the offering of firstfruits of flocks and herds at the central sanctuary (14:23), the purpose of the king reading the Torah for himself (17:19), and other explicit commands to fear YHWH (6:13, 24; 10:12, 20; 13:5[4]).

But how would hearing the Torah promote faith in YHWH? In this essay I cannot discuss the issue fully, but we may begin by observing how Deuteronomy's characterization of YHWH was intentionally crafted to stimulate Israel's trust in their divine patron.

First, the Torah of Moses portrays YHWH in gloriously transcendent terms, pointing to a trustworthy deity. By itself this image could evoke fright/awe, but in context it is intended to promote confidence (cf. Isa 40:12–31). The concluding "Song of YHWH" opens by ascribing greatness (גֹּדֶל) to him (32:3), a theme that had been declared in earlier doxological descriptions.

כִּי־יְהוָה אֱלֹהֶיךָ בְּקִרְבֶּךָ אֵל גָּדוֹל וְנוֹרָא	7:21	YHWH your God is in your midst, a great and awesome God
יְהוָה אֱלֹהֵיכֶם הוּא אֱלֹהֵי הָאֱלֹהִים וַאֲדֹנֵי הָאֲדֹנִים הָאֵל הַגָּדֹל הַגִּבֹּר וְהַנּוֹרָא	10:17	YHWH your God is God of gods and Lord of lords, the great, the mighty, and the awesome God.
לְיִרְאָה אֶת־הַשֵּׁם הַנִּכְבָּד וְהַנּוֹרָא הַזֶּה אֵת יְהוָה אֱלֹהֶיךָ	28:58	That you may fear this glorious and awesome name, YHWH your God.

YHWH's transcendent power and glory were demonstrated particularly through the "signs and wonders" performed against the Egyptians (4:34; 10:21; 26:8) and for Israel's benefit.[56]

Second, the Torah portrays YHWH in graciously personal terms. Although explicit verbal characterizations of YHWH as gracious in Deuteronomy are rare,[57] Israel's confidence in future restoration after judgment was based on his passionate affection (חָשַׁק)

---

56. Deut 11:2–7 includes YHWH's care for the Israelites in the desert, as well as his punishment of Dathan and Abiram among "all the great acts of YHWH that he executed" (כָּל־מַעֲשֵׂה יְהוָה הַגָּדֹל אֲשֶׁר עָשָׂה). Cf. Exod 15:11.

57. The root חן occurs only in 24:1, which notes its absence in a man with a needy wife.

for the ancestors (10:12) and Israel (7:7),[58] his compassionate character (כִּי אֵל רַחוּם יְהוָה אֱלֹהֶיךָ, 4:31), and his change of heart (וְעַל־עֲבָדָיו יִתְנֶחָם) toward his wayward people (32:36). But Moses laced his valedictory addresses with stories of past experiences of divine grace: YHWH loved the ancestors and elected their descendants for his favor out of all the peoples on earth (4:37; cf. 7:6–7; 10:15; 14:2); he rescued his people from Egypt (4:32–40; cf. 5:6 et passim); he invited Israel to assemble in his presence at Horeb and established his covenant with them there (4:9–31; cf. 5:2–3); he revealed his will to Israel (4:1–8; cf. 5:1–22; 6:20–25; 30:11–20); after their egregious worship of the golden calf he spared Israel and renewed the covenant at Horeb (9:19, 25—10:5); he cared for Israel in the desert (1:31; 8:1–5); he gave them a fruitful homeland (1:7–8; 6:10–11, 23; 8:7–10; 11:9–12; 26:9, 15; 27:3; 32:13–14); he provided leadership in the forms of king (17:14–20), prophets (like Moses; 18:9–20), and Levitical priests (10:8–9; 18:1–8; 21:5; 33:8–11); he confirmed the covenant with the present generation in Moab (26:16–19; 27:9; 28:69[29:1]; 29:11[12]; etc.); he invited Israel to worship and celebrate in his presence (12:1–14; 14:1–21, 26; 16:11–14; 26:1–11); and he desired Israel's well-being (11:18–25; 12:7, 18; 15:10; 23:21[20]; 28:1–14; 30:11–20). Even threats of punishment (e.g., 28:15–68) represent overtures of grace, reminding the people how passionately YHWH treasured his relationship with them and warning them in advance of the consequences of apostasy. Hearing the Torah would remind the people of all these graces, hopefully evoking in them not only fear in the sense awe, but especially the sense of confidence in the one who had chosen them to be his treasured people.

Third, the Torah portrays YHWH as faithful to his word. The exordium to the "Song of YHWH" (chapter 32) begins by proclaiming YHWH's greatness (v. 3), but the next strophe focuses on his faithfulness:

הַצּוּר תָּמִים פָּעֳלוֹ	The Rock, his work is perfect;
כִּי כָל־דְּרָכָיו מִשְׁפָּט	See, all his ways are justice.
אֵל אֱמוּנָה וְאֵין עָוֶל	The faithful God (El), lacking in iniquity,
צַדִּיק וְיָשָׁר הוּא	Righteous and upright is he (32:4).

While אֵל אֱמוּנָה conveys explicitly YHWH's trustworthiness, this quality is also reflected in the last line. In Deuteronomy "righteousness" (צֶדֶק/צְדָקָה) means "conduct in accord with an objective standard," which is established by YHWH within the covenant that he made with his people. Moses celebrated YHWH's perfect embodiment of this trait doxologically in 7:9:[59]

---

58. This rare root appears elsewhere as a verb (חָשַׁק) only in Gen 34:8; Deut 21:22; 1 Kgs 9:19 = 2 Chr 8:6; Ps 91:14; Isa 21:4; 38:17, and as a noun חֵשֶׁק only in 1 Kgs 9:1, 19//2 Chr 8:6). For discussion of this word, see Levenson, *The Love of God*, 40–42, 167–68, 176–77.

59. Cf. Exod 34:6; Ps 86:15.

יְהוָה אֱלֹהֶיךָ הוּא הָאֱלֹהִים	YHWH your God is God,
הָאֵל הַנֶּאֱמָן	the faithful God,
שֹׁמֵר הַבְּרִית וְהַחֶסֶד	who maintains covenant loyalty
לְאֹהֲבָיו וּלְשֹׁמְרֵי מִצְוֹתָיו (Qere)	with those who love him and keep his command,
לְאֶלֶף דּוֹר	to a thousand generations.

While this summary declaration is covenantal from beginning to end, the Torah of Moses proclaims YHWH's faithfulness with repeated reminders of how he has kept the promises associated with his covenant made with the ancestors, established with their descendants at Horeb,[60] and renewed with this generation:[61] (1) YHWH has multiplied the population like the stars of the sky;[62] (2) as predicted in Gen 15:13, after centuries in a foreign land, ending in slavery, YHWH rescued them from their oppressors;[63] (3) now, after the failure of the exodus generation (1:35; 4:25), YHWH is about to deliver the promised land of Canaan into their hands.[64] But YHWH's fidelity to his word is also reflected in his oath that guarantees he will fulfill the imprecations built into the covenant for his people's infidelity. Nevertheless, building on Lev 26:40–45,[65] Moses declares that however horrendous the punishment for rebellion might be (4:26–28; 11:17; 28:15–68; 29:19–27[20–28]), Israel's history would not end with the judgment. With compassionate heart and true to his commitments YHWH would bring his people back from exile and reestablish them in the land promised to the ancestors (4:30–31; 30:1–10; 32:43). Both Moses and YHWH anticipated that the Israelites would soon forget their commitments to YHWH and go after other gods (4:23; 6:12; 8:11, 14, 19; 31:16–18, 26–29), but YHWH would never forget his covenant (4:31). Before the generation about to enter the promised land YHWH guaranteed his people's future with his promise (32:36–43) and his oath.[66]

In addition to stimulating reverent awe (יָרֵא), hearing the reminders of YHWH's compassion toward his people in the past and his declarations of his faithfulness to his words, his covenant, and his people in the future should evoke in hearers the allegiance and faith that Abraham exhibited in Gen 15:6 and 22:1–12. Since this confidence in YHWH represents part of the fuller meaning of יָרֵא in Deuteronomy, hearing the Torah would be critical for maintaining Israel's faith and for their long range well-being in

---

60. Cf. Gen 17:6–8; Exod 6:2–8; 19:4–6; Deut 4:9–31.

61. On "the covenant with the fathers," see Hwang, *The Rhetoric of Remembrance*, 178–232.

62. Deut 1:10; 10:22; 26:5; cf. Gen 15:5; 22:17; 26:4.

63. Deut 4:37; 5:6; 6:12, 21–23; 7:8; 8:14; 13:6, 11[5, 10]; 26:6–8.

64. References to the covenant oath involving the land occur a dozen times in the book: 1:8, 35; 4:21; etc.

65. Assuming Lev 26 antedates Deut 4:25–31; 11:13–28; 28:1–69[29:1]. See now Kilchör, "The Direction of Dependence between the Laws of the Pentateuch," 1–14; idem, *Mosetora und Jahwetora*; contra Stackert, who argues that while using the language of Deuteronomy the authors of the Holiness Code (which includes Leviticus 26) intentionally superseded, subverted, and supplanted the Deuteronomic Law. See his *Rewriting the Torah*; idem, "The Holiness Code," 389–96.

66. Cf. the references to "a covenant . . . with an oath" in 29:11, 13, 20[12, 14, 21].

relation to YHWH (Deut 31:9–13).⁶⁷ We now understand why the five markers of Israel's identity in Deut 10:12–13 begin with "fear/trusting awe," and then move successively through walking in the ways of YHWH, demonstrating love for him, whole-hearted and full-bodied service, and finally to obedience to the commands.

With this understanding we now realize that Renate Egger-Wenzel's description of the God-fearer in Sirach fits Deuteronomy perfectly:

> The God-fearing are a group of people that put their trust in God, listen to his word and his rules, and act accordingly. These people base their behavior on their love of God. And love rooted in trust results in the attempt to please the loved one, by trying to fulfill his wishes (Sir 2:16b: "his law"). Then the recompense (in other words, the reward) will not fail to come: a good outcome, joy, and a blessed end to life, with the support of one's fellows. ⁶⁸

And now we also understand the conclusion to the book of Malachi, and indeed to the First Testament.⁶⁹ Responding to the absence of fear/trust in YHWH in the restored community in Jerusalem in the Persian period, in a series of oracles Malachi prescribes the solution: "Remember the Torah of Moses my servant whom I charged at Horeb [to teach] ordinances and judgments for all Israel" (Mal 3:22[4:4]).⁷⁰ Based on the formulaic sequence reading—hearing—learning—fearing—obeying—living well, I imagine Moses asking, "How shall they live, if they do not obey? How shall they obey if they do not have faith in YHWH? How shall they have faith if they have not learned of him? How shall they learn of him if they do not hear the Torah? How shall they hear the Torah if no one reads it for them?"⁷¹

67. This sequence reinforces Nahum Sarna's contention (*Exodus*, 75) that "faith" in the Hebrew Bible "refers to trust and loyalty that find expression in obedience and commitment."

68. Egger-Wenzel, "'Faith in God' Rather Than 'Fear of God,'" 223.

69. As arranged in LXX and all Christian translations. The Hebrew Bible concludes with 2 Chronicles.

70. Malachi echoes Deut 4:1 and 4:14). Cf. also 6:1.

71. My own adaptation of the words of Paul in Rom 10:14–15. Although the textual links suggest the author was meditating on Ps 105–106, we observe a similar link between reflection on Israel's foundational stories and humbling before God in 4Q185 1–2 I, 13b–15:

> And now please listen my people. Pay attention to me, simpletons. [Become wise?]* by [reflecting on] the great deeds of God [גבורת אלהים], and call to mind the miracles[נפלאות] he performed in Egypt, and his wonders [מופ(ת)ין] in [the land of Ham]. May your hearts tremble [ויערץ] before his awesomeness [פחדו].**

*The word is difficult to read. Allegro, who produced the *editio princeps* (in *Qumrân Cave 4, I [4Q158–4Q186]*, 85), read תמו. Reading ותצמק as "shrivel up," Pajunen ("4QSapiential Admonitions B [4Q185]," 198 and 204) apparently associates the verb with a biblical hapax that occurs only in Hos 9:14, where it refers to dry breasts. But this is speculative and ill-suits the context. Having examined Allegro's photograph, John Strugnell's reading, וחכמו, "Become wise/Gain wisdom," ("Notes en marge du volume V," 270), seems more likely, and suits the context much better. So also, Goff, *Discerning Wisdom*, 140.

**פחדו is rendered variously as "his visitation," (Allegro, 86), "his dread" (Pajunen, 198), "his terror" (Martínez and Tigchelaar, *The Dead Sea Scrolls*, 379), or "his judgment" (Tooman, "Wisdom and Torah at Qumran," 216). However, the context requires something like "his awesomeness" (thus Wise,

With this conclusion, we may also have encountered a critical conceptual link between Paul in Galatians and Moses in Deuteronomy. In Gal 3:2, Paul asks, "Did you receive the Spirit by works of the law or by *hearing* with faith?" (ἐξ ἔργων νόμου τὸ πνεῦμα ἐλάβετε ἢ ἐξ ἀκοῆς πίστεως). Just as Paul's proclamation of the Gospel produced faith, so in an earlier time hearing the Torah of Moses should have produced faith. Although the exodus generation refused to trust YHWH, they did not need this Torah, for they had experienced firsthand YHWH's transcendent power, his gracious deliverance, and his confirmation of his word. Indeed, by signing on to the first two principles of covenant relationship as declared in the Decalogue ("You shall have no other gods besides me" and "You shall not bear the name of YHWH your God in vain," 5:6–11), they had declared their exclusive allegiance to and trust in YHWH. However, while still at Sinai and later at Kadesh-barnea they failed YHWH and the covenant on these very counts. Moses proclaimed the Torah for the present and future generations, to provide constant reminders of YHWH's grace and faithfulness (חֶסֶד וֶאֱמֶת) and to inspire awed trust in him, yielding righteous living (16:20), and securing his favor (6:25).

The Fear of YHWH in Proverbs

In recent decades scholars have rightly paid increasing attention to the relationship between Deuteronomy and the biblical wisdom writings, the core of which is represented by Job, Proverbs, and Ecclesiastes.[72] The vocabulary shared by Deuteronomy with these books is impressive;[73] indeed the ties are strong enough for Moshe Weinfeld to propose that the book of Deuteronomy was the product of sages in the Jerusalem court.[74] Georg Braulik prefers to interpret the wisdom features in the book against the backdrop of Israel's prophetic tradition and the encounter with the intellectual traditions of Mesopotamia forced upon the Judeans through their exile to Babylon.[75] Nevertheless, a given among many is that Deut 4, particularly the reference to wisdom in 4:6–8, derives from the Persian period.[76] The resolution of these issues is far beyond the scope of this paper; my purpose is simply to explore how the motif of the fear of YHWH in Deuteronomy compares with its usage in one wisdom book, the book of Proverbs.[77] This may shed

---

Abegg, and Cook, *The Dead Sea Scrolls*, 274). Although פחד usually refers to the terror an event produces in a human observer, here it is awkwardly attributed to God. The most likely biblical analogue is the epithet פַּחַד יִצְחָק, "Fear of Isaac," in Gen 31:42, 53.

72. For a survey of the issues, see McConville, "Wisdom and Torah in Deuteronomy," 261-76. For fuller discussion from a variety of angles, see Schipper and Teeter, eds., *Wisdom and Torah*.

73. See Sheppard, *Wisdom as a Hermeneutical Construct*, 63–64; Weinfeld, *Deuteronomy and the Deuteronomic School*, 244–47.

74. This would account for what Weinfeld claims to be secularizing and humanistic tendencies in Deuteronomy, as well as its didactic temper. For full discussion, see ibid., 244–306.

75. Braulik, "'Weisheit' im Buch Deuteronomium," 39–69.

76. According to Krüger ("Law and Wisdom according to Deut 4:5–8," 52), "an intellectual group in the province of Yehud cherished the hope that the Mosaic Law (whatever its concrete form) would be accepted by the Achaemenid rulers as a local order of life."

77. Remarkably, in his most recent discussion of the relationship between Deuteronomy and biblical wisdom, McConville ("Wisdom and Torah in Deuteronomy"), pays no attention to the motif

some light on the compositional relationship between the two, but more importantly, it should expand our horizons on a key First Testament theological theme.

The vocabulary of "fear" in Proverbs is more restricted than in Deuteronomy. Of the nine expressions used in Deuteronomy for "fear, fright, terror,"[78] only four are found in Proverbs. Of these two occur only once. In Prov 20:2 אֵימָה refers to the terror an infuriated king creates for his subjects. In 21:15 מְחִתָּה is commonly translated "terror,"[79] but it should probably be rendered "ruin, destruction."[80] The root פחד appears more frequently. As a noun (פַּחַד) it denotes "terror" in 1:26, 27, 33, and 3:25. In 3:24 the qal imperfect verb means "to be anxious, in dread," preventing one from sleeping. The piel form of the verb פָּחַד occurs only twice in the Hebrew Bible. Whereas in Isa 51:13 the verb means "to be anxious, in dread," in the face of the threat of destruction at the hands of an oppressor, in Prov 28:14 it is best interpreted as an elliptical proverb: "How privileged is the person who "fears" (מְפַחֵד) [YHWH], but the one who hardens his heart will fall into calamity."[81] Here the piel form connotes a totally positive disposition, appearing to substitute for יָרֵא, "to fear," in the sense of "to trust."[82] The root חרד appears as a hiphil participle (מַחֲרִיד) in Deut 28:26 (of frightening off birds), but as a noun (חֲרָדָה) referring to "fear" before another human in Prov 29:25.

Variations of the root יָרֵא occur twenty-two times in Proverbs (Table 14.3), exactly one half its occurrences in Deuteronomy, though proportionately its usage exceeds that of earlier book.[83] The root surfaces as a verb five times but only in the qal stem (3:7, 25; 14:16; 24:21; 31:21), and as an adjective three times, always followed by an objective genitive.[84] Remarkably almost two-thirds of the occurrences of the root involve the noun יִרְאָה, always in construct with יהוה, that is, "the fear of YHWH."[85] The absence of this phrase on Deuteronomy heightens its significance for the present discussion.

---

of "fear." See n. 72 above.

78. See page 2 above.

79. Thus ESV, NIV, HCSB, and Waltke, *Proverbs Chapters 15–31*, 162.

80. As in Prov 10:14–15, 29; 13:3; 14:28; 18:7. Cf. NRSV, "dismay"; NJPSV, "ruination."

81. Hebrew: אַשְׁרֵי אָדָם מְפַחֵד תָּמִיד וּמַקְשֶׁה לִבּוֹ יִפּוֹל בְּרָעָה.

82. Waltke comments (*Proverbs Chapter 15–31*, 419), "Trembling here refers to the fear of reverence, not of bondage; of caution, not distrust; of diligence, not despondency." The proverb is conceptually related to Ps 84:6[5], which uses the expression אַשְׁרֵי אָדָם of one whose strength is in YHWH, and especially v. 13[12]: "O YHWH of hosts, blessed is the one who trusts in you!" (יְהוָה צְבָאוֹת אַשְׁרֵי אָדָם בֹּטֵחַ בָּךְ:). Cf. also Ps 33:12 and 144:15, which describe the privileged state of a nation/people (אַשְׁרֵי הַגּוֹי; אַשְׁרֵי הָעָם, respectively).

83. Deuteronomy 44/14,294 words (density of ca. 0.00308); Proverbs 22/6,915 words (density of ca. 0.00318). Lexical statistics from *TLOT* 3.1444–45.

84. Prov 13:13 (אִשָּׁה יִרְאַת־יְהוָה); 14:2 (יְרֵא יְהוָה); 31:30 (יְרֵא מִצְוָה).

85. Prov 1:7, 29; 2:5; 8:13; 9:10; 10:27; 14:26, 27; 15:16, 33; 16:6; 19:23; 22:4; 23:17.

Table 14.3
The Root ירא in the Book of Proverbs

Verb Forms		References
ירא	Qal *qatal*	14:6
	Qal *yiqtol*	3:25 (אַל־תִּירָא); 31:21 (לֹא־תִירָא, indicative)
	Qal imperative	3:7; 24:21
יָרֵא/יְרֵאָה	Adjective	13:13; 14:2; 31:30
יִרְאָה	Noun	1:7, 29; 2:5; 8:13; 9:10; 10:27; 14:26, 27; 15:16, 33; 16:6; 19:23; 22:4; 23:17 (all יִרְאַת יהוה)

My concern here is to compare "the fear of YHWH" in Deuteronomy and Proverbs, to see what implications this might have for our understanding the nature of Israelite wisdom and to assess whether or not the wisdom movement was a humanistic and secularizing development. I shall do so first by exploring the range of meanings of ירא in Proverbs (in relation to Fig. 14.1 above), and then examining the relationship between its usage in Proverbs and the fundamentally covenantal nature of the notion in Deuteronomy.[86] Because the frequency and range of meanings of יָרֵא in Proverbs are both more limited in Proverbs than in Deuteronomy, this phase of the discussion will be briefer than the corresponding discussion for Deuteronomy above.

In Proverbs, the root ירא is never used of terror or paralyzing fright, as we witnessed in Deut 5:5 and 5:23–26. In its place this book always uses פחד (1:26, 27, 33; 3:25; 20:2), though יָרֵא is used of the "anxiety" one feels at the prospect of terror (3:25),[87] or the prospect of snow in winter (31:21). The remaining occurrences of ירא all appear on the right side of the semantic spectrum (Fig. 14.1).[88] The appeal to fear YHWH and the king in 24:21 probably has in mind revering and submitting to both, not because of their power over subjects, but their status as divine and royal patrons respectively. Inasmuch as Prov 13:13 speaks of reward for fearing the "command" (מִצְוָה), as opposed to ruin that results from despising the "word" (דָּבָר), יָרֵא probably suggests reverence for or submission to the command, מִצְוָה presumably functioning as shorthand for the Deuteronomic Torah.[89] This interpretation is reinforced by Prov 16:20, which juxtaposes well-being (טוֹב) that derives from keen attention (מַשְׂכִּיל) to the word (דָּבָר) with the privileged state (אַשְׁרֵי)

---

86. For studies of the fear of God in Proverbs, see Plath, *Furcht Gottes*, 54–76; Becker, *Gottesfurcht*, 210–41.

87. The previous verse (3:24) had also referred to such anxiety with פחד.

88. Compare the assessment of Week's (*Instruction and Imagery in Proverbs 1–9*, 113), that in general the fear of YHWH suggests "a relationship of loyal, obedient respect." I am grateful to Will Kynes for reminding me of Weeks' helpful discussion of wisdom and character in Prov 1–9.

89. Contra Murphy (*Proverbs*, 97), and McKane (*Proverbs*, 454–55), who suggest that דָּבָר and מִצְוָה refer to the instruction of the sage. However, this interpretation arises from a predisposition to divorce wisdom writings from Israel's constitutional texts. The "word" and "command" should be interpreted as shorthand for the Torah of Moses in Deuteronomy (cf. Deut 30:11 and 14, where these two expressions interchangeably refer to the revealed divine word. This is the revelation that Moses charged the Israelites to teach their children in perpetuity (Deut 5:1, 31; 6:1, 6–7; 11:18–19).

of those who trust in YHWH (בּוֹטֵחַ בַּיהוה).⁹⁰ Proverbs 14:16 is even more vague than 13:13: "A wise person fears (יָרֵא) and turns away from evil (רָע), but a fool is reckless and careless." Although the object of "fear" is unspecified, given earlier declarations about the wise ("The fear of YHWH is the first principle of wisdom," 1:7; 9:10), and about the relationship between the fear of YHWH and avoiding evil ("The fear of YHWH is the hatred of evil [רָע]," 8:13; cf. 3:7) those who heard this proverb will automatically have filled in the blank with "fear [YHWH]."⁹¹

Having considered the vague texts, the explicit proverbs linking "fear" with YHWH demand further attention. This occurs in seventeen of the twenty-two passages that speak of יָרֵא. Two of these involve YHWH as the object of the verb in the qal stem (3:7; 24:21), and one uses the genitive construction, יְרֵא יהוה, "fearer of YHWH," that is, "YHWH-fearer" (14:2). The remaining fourteen involve the construct phrase, יִרְאַת יהוה, "the fear of YHWH" (See Table 14.3). For our purposes, we may treat these seventeen together, though we grasp the semantic significance of יָרֵא best by grouping the proverbs logically. They break down into several categories. How far to the right side of the spectrum they fall will be clearer after the discussion below.⁹²

1. The fear of YHWH as the fundamental principle of wisdom.⁹³

יִרְאַת יְהוָה רֵאשִׁית דָּעַת חָכְמָה וּמוּסָר אֱוִילִים בָּזוּ׃	1:7	The fear of YHWH is the first principle of knowledge; fools despise wisdom and instruction.
תְּחִלַּת חָכְמָה יִרְאַת יְהוָה וְדַעַת קְדֹשִׁים בִּינָה׃	9:10	The fear of YHWH is the beginning of wisdom, and the knowledge of the Holy One is insight.

For the view that perceives Israelite wisdom as essentially secular, humanistic, and rooted in extra-Israelite perspectives these reminders of wisdom's Yahwistic and covenantal foundations are problematic.⁹⁴ Here the sages remind hearers of Israel's distinctive epistemology: all knowledge, whether gained from experience and observation, from tradition, or from surrounding cultures must pass through the filter of Israelite faith; to do otherwise is to cast one's lot with fools.

---

90. So also, Waltke, *Proverbs Chapters 1–15*, 564. The poetic nature of these texts accounts for the absence of the article on דָּבָר and מִצְוָה in both proverbs.

91. So also, Waltke, ibid., 595–96; Longman, *Proverbs*, 301–302. Contra Murphy, *Proverbs*, 105.

92. Although Weeks' focus is not on the "fear of YHWH," much of his discussion of "The Function of Wisdom," 105–109, relates directly to that "fear."

93. Variations of these expressions of the notion appear in Job 28:28; Ps 111:10; Eccl 12:13, and repeatedly in Sirach: 1:14, 16, 18, 20, 27; 19:20; 21:11. On the tight relationship between the fear of YHWH and biblical wisdom, see Platt, *Furcht Gottes,* 56–62.

94. For discussion of the rootage of Israelite wisdom in covenant faith, see Schultz, "Unity or Diversity in Wisdom Theology?" 271–306. According to O'Dowd (*The Wisdom of Torah*, 118), in Proverbs "fear" is "a theologically keyword" with Yahwistic theology more broadly and places the one who seeks wisdom in a reflexive position before YHWH.

2. The importance of learning the fear of YHWH.

תַּחַת כִּי־שָׂנְאוּ דָעַת וְיִרְאַת יְהוָה לֹא בָחָרוּ:	1:29	Because they hated knowledge and did not choose the fear of YHWH
אָז תָּבִין יִרְאַת יְהוָה וְדַעַת אֱלֹהִים תִּמְצָא:	2:5	Then you will understand the fear of YHWH and find the knowledge of God.
יִרְאַת יְהוָה מוּסַר חָכְמָה וְלִפְנֵי כָבוֹד עֲנָוָה:	15:33	The fear of YHWH is instruction in wisdom, and humility comes before honor.

Since the fear of YHWH is the first principle of wisdom, it is not surprising that in the sequence of courses on wisdom represented by the book of Proverbs, "the fear of YHWH" is "Wisdom 101."[95] Whereas Job 28:28 expressly equates the "fear of YHWH" with "wisdom" (יִרְאַת אֲדֹנָי הִיא חָכְמָה),[96] Prov 15:33 equates the fear of YHWH with "instruction in wisdom" (מוּסַר חָכְמָה). But achieving this result requires right choices and receiving instruction from the right places. Proverbs 1:29 appears near the end of a lengthy poem in which Dame Wisdom laments fools' rejection of her and her counsel, and in so doing declares explicitly that the fear of YHWH is a choice. Those who hate knowledge reject the fear of YHWH. This principle is reinforced in the lecture to "my son" in chapter 2. If the young man will diligently seek "wisdom" (חָכְמָה), "understanding" (תְּבוּנָה), and "insight" (בִּינָה) like hunters search for treasure, he will understand the fear of YHWH and discover the knowledge of God.

3. The ethical outworking of the fear of YHWH.

אַל־תְּהִי חָכָם בְּעֵינֶיךָ יְרָא אֶת־יְהוָה וְסוּר מֵרָע:	3:7	Do not be wise in your own eyes; fear YHWH, and turn away from evil.
יִרְאַת יְהוָה שְׂנֹאת רָע גֵּאָה וְגָאוֹן וְדֶרֶךְ רָע וּפִי תַהְפֻּכוֹת שָׂנֵאתִי:	8:13	The fear of YHWH is hatred of evil. Pride and arrogance and the way of evil and perverted speech I hate.
הוֹלֵךְ בְּיָשְׁרוֹ יְרֵא יְהוָה וּנְלוֹז דְּרָכָיו בּוֹזֵהוּ:	14:2	Whoever walks uprightly fears YHWH, but the one who is devious in his ways despises him.
בְּחֶסֶד וֶאֱמֶת יְכֻפַּר עָוֹן וּבְיִרְאַת יְהוָה סוּר מֵרָע:	16:6	By steadfast love and faithfulness iniquity is atoned for, and by the fear of YHWH one turns away from evil.

These four proverbs reflect the general teaching of the book of Proverbs: while the fear of YHWH involves one's disposition, it is not merely dispositional, as if God looks on people's hearts but overlooks their actions. On the contrary, those who fear YHWH "hate" (שָׂנֵא) and shun (סוּר) "evil" (רָע).[97] Intellectually the polar opposites of YHWH-

---

95. On the sequential nature of the instructions on wisdom in Proverbs, see Ansberry, *Be Wise, My Son, and Make My Heart Glad*.

96. The syntax conforms to Frances I. Andersen's Rule 2 for Hebrew verbless clauses: In a clause of identification, a pleonastic pronoun precedes the predicate. See Andersen, *The Hebrew Verbless Clause*, 42.

97. The list of offenses in 8:13 recalls Prov 6:16–19, which catalogues seven evils that YHWH hates.

fearers are fools (אֱוִילִים, 1:7), but ethically and morally the latter are also characterized as "the wicked" (רְשָׁעִים, 10:27) and "sinners" (חַטָּאִים, 23:17).

4. The rewards for fearing YHWH.

יִרְאַת יְהוָה תּוֹסִיף יָמִים וּשְׁנוֹת רְשָׁעִים תִּקְצֹרְנָה׃	10:27	The fear of YHWH prolongs life, but the years of the wicked will be short.
בְּיִרְאַת יְהוָה מִבְטַח־עֹז וּלְבָנָיו יִהְיֶה מַחְסֶה׃	14:26	In the fear of YHWH one has strong confidence, and his children will have a refuge
יִרְאַת יְהוָה מְקוֹר חַיִּים לָסוּר מִמֹּקְשֵׁי מָוֶת׃	14:27	The fear of YHWH is a fountain of life, that one may turn away from the snares of death.
טוֹב־מְעַט בְּיִרְאַת יְהוָה מֵאוֹצָר רָב וּמְהוּמָה בוֹ׃	15:16	Better is a little with the fear of YHWH than great treasure and trouble with it.
יִרְאַת יְהוָה לְחַיִּים וְשָׂבֵעַ יָלִין בַּל־יִפָּקֶד רָע׃	19:23	The fear of YHWH yields life; One rests satisfied, without threat of harm.
עֵקֶב עֲנָוָה יִרְאַת יְהוָה עֹשֶׁר וְכָבוֹד וְחַיִּים׃	22:4	The rewards for humility and fear of YHWH are riches and honor and life.
אַל־יְקַנֵּא לִבְּךָ בַּחַטָּאִים כִּי אִם־בְּיִרְאַת־יְהוָה כָּל־הַיּוֹם׃	23:17	Let not your heart envy sinners, but continue in the fear of YHWH all the day.
שֶׁקֶר הַחֵן וְהֶבֶל הַיֹּפִי אִשָּׁה יִרְאַת־יְהוָה הִיא תִתְהַלָּל׃	31:30	Charm is deceitful, and beauty is vain, but a woman who fears YHWH is to be praised.

Texts like these suggest that the primary benefit of fearing YHWH is that it yields "life" (חַיִּים) both quantitatively and qualitatively.[98] With respect to the former, 10:27 declares that those who fear YHWH live longer [than deserved], while the lives of the wicked are cut short. Regarding the latter, 15:16 insists that for those who fear YHWH, life with less is superior to life with more, because turmoil (מְהוּמָה) accompanies the treasures of the godless—hence the encouragement in 23:17 not to envy "sinners." While 22:4 names riches as the reward for fearing YHWH, non-quantifiable benefits include honor and the praise of the community (31:30). According to 14:26, among the benefits enjoyed by YHWH-fearers is confidence in the well-being of children.

Having examined the texts that speak of the fear of YHWH in Proverbs it remains to ask what יָרֵא actually means in this expression. It certainly does not mean terror, or fright, or anxiety, and it probably signifies more than awe and reverence, which pushes its connotations to the far right of the semantic spectrum illustrated in Figure 14.1. Those who fear YHWH obviously submit to him, because they also respect the word and fear the command of YHWH (13:13). However, there is strong evidence that in some of these

---

98. Compare Plath's discussion of the relationship between the fear of God and well-being in *Furcht Gottes*, 64–76.

contexts יָרֵא functions as a virtual synonym for "to believe" (הֶאֱמִין) or to trust (בָּטַח) in YHWH. This is most apparent in 14:26–27:

בְּיִרְאַת יְהוָה מִבְטַח־עֹז וּלְבָנָיו יִהְיֶה מַחְסֶה:	In the fear of YHWH one has strong confidence, and his children will have a refuge.[99]
יִרְאַת יְהוָה מְקוֹר חַיִּים לָסוּר מִמֹּקְשֵׁי מָוֶת:	The fear of YHWH is a fountain of life, that one may turn away from the snares of death.[100]

Since verse 26 understands "the fear of YHWH" as the key to security for parents and their children, it obviously borders on "trust in YHWH." This impression is reinforced by the expression מִבְטָח, "confidence" (a noun derived from בָּטַח, "to trust"), and its correlative in the second line, מַחְסֶה, "refuge."[101] While not as explicit, many other proverbs move in a similar direction. Thus 3:7 counsels the young man not to be wise in his own eyes (i.e., to put his confidence in his own wisdom), but to fear YHWH. While not naming YHWH, 28:14 bears a similar message: "How privileged is the one who fears [YHWH], but those who harden their hearts will fall into calamity." Although often using different vocabulary,[102] the sage repeatedly encourages his young student to place his confidence in YHWH. Note especially the following proverbs, the first of which comes almost immediately before 3:7 cited above:

בְּטַח אֶל־יְהוָה בְּכָל־לִבֶּךָ וְאֶל־בִּינָתְךָ אַל־תִּשָּׁעֵן:	3:5	Trust in YHWH with all your heart,[103] and do not lean on your own understanding.
מַשְׂכִּיל עַל־דָּבָר יִמְצָא־טוֹב וּבוֹטֵחַ בַּיהוָה אַשְׁרָיו:	16:20	Whoever gives thought to the word will discover good, and how privileged is the one who trusts in YHWH.
רְחַב־נֶפֶשׁ יְגָרֶה מָדוֹן וּבוֹטֵחַ עַל־יְהוָה יְדֻשָּׁן:	28:25	A greedy man stirs up strife, but the one who trusts in YHWH will be enriched.
חֶרְדַּת אָדָם יִתֵּן מוֹקֵשׁ וּבוֹטֵחַ בַּיהוָה יְשֻׂגָּב:	29:25	The fear of man lays a snare, but whoever trusts in YHWH is safe.

---

99. With v. 26 we should compare Job 4:6: הֲלֹא יִרְאָתְךָ כִּסְלָתֶךָ תִּקְוָתְךָ וְתֹם דְּרָכֶיךָ, "Is not your fear of God your confidence, and the integrity of your ways your hope?" (NRSV).

100. Prov 14:27 repeats 13:14, except that יִרְאַת יהוה, "the fear of YHWH," substitutes for תּוֹרַת חָכָם, "the teaching of the wise." In 14:27 LXX reads πρόσταγμα κυρίου, suggesting יִרְאַת יהוה was read as תּוֹרַת יהוה. So also Becker, Gottesfurcht, 225.

101. Compare Ps 62:9[8], "Trust in him (בִּטְחוּ בוֹ) at all times, O people; pour out your heart before him; God is a refuge for us." Also, Ps 91:2, "I will say to YHWH, "My refuge (מַחְסִי) and my fortress; my God, in whom I trust (אֶבְטַח בּוֹ)." For מִבְטָח meaning "trust," see also Prov 21:22; 22:19; 25:19. On YHWH as a refuge (מַחְסֶה), see Ps 14:6; 46:2[1]; 61:4[3]; 62:8–9[7–8]; 71:7; 73:28; 91:9; 94:22; 142:6[5].

102. While Proverbs uses הֶאֱמִין of belief/faith in others (14:15; 26:25) it never has YHWH as the object of that faith.

103. To trust in YHWH with one's whole heart means no part of one's affections are left over for any other god—not even the idolatry of self-reliance. The whole-hearted nature of this trust in YHWH is grasped by the psalmist in Ps 86:11: "Teach me your way, O YHWH, that I may walk in your truth; give me an undivided heart to fear your name יַחֵד לְבָבִי לְיִרְאָה שְׁמֶךָ)).

The last proverb is especially interesting, juxtaposing fear and trust, but using חֲרָדָה for יָרֵא and בָּטַח for "trust." In each case the proverb would have made perfect sense had the sage said, "Fear YHWH," using יָרֵא, rather than "Trust in YHWH."

The Fear of YHWH in Deuteronomy and in Proverbs: An Assessment of the Relationship

This exploration into the semantic range of יָרֵא, especially in relation to fearing YHWH, in Deuteronomy and Proverbs reveals a remarkable correspondence, and casts doubt on assessments of Hebrew wisdom as represented by Proverbs as either a secularizing or humanistic development on the one hand, or a movement dependent on outside influence, on the other. Had the latter been the case, we might have expected some version of the phrase "to fear God" (יָרֵא אֶת־אֱלֹהִים), which is occasionally attributed to non-Israelites,[104] but is missing altogether in Proverbs, where true faith is focused on YHWH, the redeemer and covenant God of Israel.

But the connections between the "the fear of YHWH" in Proverbs and the conceptual world of Deuteronomy transcend the association of יָרֵא with YHWH. Indeed, we may identify links for each of the four dimensions of "the fear of YHWH" discussed above.[105] First, although the phrase יִרְאַת יהוה never occurs in Deuteronomy, given the prominence of the motif in this book, the search for the origins of the notion of the primacy of the fear of YHWH might naturally begin here.[106] Having come to fear and believe in YHWH through the events associated with the exodus from Egypt (Exod 14:31), according to Deut 4:10 the declared goal of YHWH's [verbal] self-revelation at Horeb was "that they may learn to fear (יָרֵא) me all the days that they live on the earth, and that they may teach their children [to do so as well]." Israel's disposition toward YHWH begins and ends with fearing him.

Deuteronomy expresses the primacy of the fear of YHWH in other ways as well. In response to the [catechetical] question, "So what then does YHWH your God ask of you?" in Deut 10:12 Moses lists five requirements: fearing YHWH, walking in all his ways, loving him, whole hearted and full-bodied service to him, and observing all his commands and ordinances (10:12–13). While love (אָהַב) of YHWH may be at the center of this pentad of requirements, as noted above, "fear" is named first. This was not only the "first principle of knowledge" (רֵאשִׁית דַּעַת, Prov 1:7) and the "beginning of wisdom (תְּחִלַּת חָכְמָה, 9:10);[107] it was also the first principle of covenant piety.

Second, like the book of Proverbs, Deuteronomy emphasizes the importance of learning the fear of YHWH. The verb לָמַד, "to learn," is followed by the infinitive construct, לְיִרְאָה, "to fear," with YHWH as the direct object four times (4:10; 14:23; 17:19;

---

104. Gen 20:11; Deut 25:18; Job 1:8; 2:3. The expression is often understood generically as "moral restraint." See p. 319, n. 50 above.

105. Schipper offers only limited discussion of the "fear of YHWH," but he argues convincingly for the tight linkage between Torah and wisdom in "When Wisdom is not Enough!" 55–79.

106. Despite critical scholars' tendency to locate the composition of Deuteronomy between the late seventh century BCE and the early part of Persian domination.

107. Cf. רֵאשִׁית חָכְמָה in Ps 111:10.

31:13), and in 31:12 we find forms of these two verbs conjoined: "that they may learn and they may fear YHWH your God" (לְמַעַן יִלְמְדוּ וְיָרְאוּ אֶת־יְהוָה אֱלֹהֵיכֶם). The divine goal in the revelation at Horeb was that the exodus generation might learn to fear YHWH. But this was a one-time event. For future generations, this goal should be achieved through the rituals at the central sanctuary (14:23), but especially through hearing the Torah read by Levites at the Festival of Sukkoth (31:9–13). The Mosaic instructions regarding the king (17:14–20) emphasize that not even the king was exempt from this requirement. The means of his learning to fear YHWH differed slightly, but the source of that fear was identical. Rather than hearing the Levites read the Torah, he was to write a copy of it for himself in the presence of the Levitical priests (as custodians of the Torah), and he was to read it as long as he sat on his throne, "that he might learn to fear YHWH his God" (vv. 18–19), and in so doing represent the people as the paradigmatic Israelite.[108]

Third, the ethical outworking of the fear of YHWH in Proverbs is thoroughly deuteronomic. The latter is highlighted in the catechetical text beginning with Deut 10:12–13, which follows up the call to fear YHWH with demonstrate covenant love for him, walk in his ways, serve him whole heartedly and keep his commands. Furthermore, the ultimate goal of reading/hearing the Torah was not merely to create a disposition toward YHWH, but to provide motivation for ethical living. This was true of the king, whom the fear of YHWH would motivate to observe all the words of the Torah, to remain humble (cf. Prov 15:33), and to prevent him from turning aside left or right from the commands of YHWH (Deut 17:19b–20). The same was true of his subjects, who were to demonstrate their "fearful disposition" with their lives, keeping all the words of the Torah by doing them (31:12).

Fourth, the rewards the sage promises those who fear YHWH read like another page from the deuteronomic note book. In Moses' words, "YHWH charged us to do all these statutes, to fear YHWH our God, for our good, and for our survival (לְהַיֹּתֵנוּ), as is the case today" (6:24). To those who keep all the words of the Torah, Moses promised a long life[109] and well-being,[110] and the declaration of "You are righteous" (cf. v. 25).

These four dimensions of the "the fear of YHWH" highlighted in Proverbs are all found at the beginning of Moses' second address, as Israel's pastor-teacher launches into his valedictory challenge:

> Now this is the command—the ordinances and judgments—that YHWH your God commanded me to teach you, that you may do them in the land to which you are going over, to possess it, ² that you may demonstrate fear of YHWH your God—you and your son and your son's son—by keeping all his ordinances and his commands, which I command you, all the days of your life, and that your days may be long. ³ Therefore, hear, O Israel, and keep [them] by doing [them], that it may go well with you, and that you may multiply greatly,

---

108. Similarly, O'Dowd, *Wisdom of Torah*, 73–78.

109. Deut 4:40; 5:16, 33; 6:2; 11:9; 22:7; 25:15; 30:18; 32:47. For the king, fearing YHWH was the key to sitting long on his throne (17:20).

110. "That it may go will with you" (לְמַעַן יִיטַב לָךְ) and related expressions occur repeatedly: Deut 4:40; 5:16, 29; 6:3, 18; 8:16; 12:25, 28; 22:7; 30:5.

as YHWH, the God of your fathers, has promised you, in a land flowing with
milk and honey (Deut 6:1–2).

This was not only the way of Torah and covenantal righteousness (Deut 16:20); the sage would have us know that this is also the way of wisdom.[111]

Inasmuch as "the fear of YHWH" is fundamental to whatever existed of an Israelite "wisdom tradition," this linkage between Deuteronomy and Proverbs undercuts Weinfeld's theory that Deuteronomy originates in a courtly humanistic and rational wisdom tradition and concerns primarily "the intellectual mental faculty which enables man to distinguish between good and evil in the juridical spheres."[112] It also explains why a text like Ecclesiastes can end with, "When all has been heard, the conclusion of the matter for all humanity is: fear God and keep his commands" (Eccl 12:13);[113] why Baruch 3:36b–4:4 can associate wisdom with the revealed Torah of Moses; and why Ben Sirach (for whom "the fear of YHWH," φόβος κυρίου is an extremely significant notion)[114] can accept the written Torah as the primary (though not exclusive) source of wisdom:

> [23] All this is the book of the covenant of the Most High God
> (βίβλος διαθήκης θεοῦ ὑψίστου),
>   the Torah (νόμον) that Moses commanded us as an inheritance for the
>   congregations of Jacob.
> [25] It overflows, like the Pishon, with wisdom (σοφίαν),
>   and like the Tigris at the time of the first fruits.
> [26] It runs over, like the Euphrates, with understanding (σύνεσιν),
>   and like the Jordan at harvest time.
> [27] It pours forth instruction (παιδείαν) like the Nile,
>   like the Gihon at the time of vintage.
> [28] The first man did not know her (i.e., "wisdom") fully,
>   nor will the last one fathom her.
> [29] For her insight (διανόημα) is more abundant than the sea,
>   and her counsel (ἡ βουλὴ) deeper than the great abyss 25:23–29
> (NRSV, modified).

111. For a brief discussion of "the fear of YHWH" as the link between the theology represented by Hebrew wisdom generally and Deuteronomy, see Clements, "Wisdom and Old Testament Theology," 280–84. Based on an examination of wisdom and the character of instruction in Prov 1–9, Weeks concludes (*Instruction and Imagery,* 104),

> Whatever else it may be, Proverbs 1–9 is religious literature, and even if we acknowledge the possibility that it drew on foreign texts, it is fundamentally still Jewish, Yahwistic religious literature. It consequently operates, to a greater or lesser extent, against an established background of concepts and vocabulary. When, therefore, the work repeatedly advocates adherence to instruction, and when it evokes the Deuteronomic idea of God as instructor, it is hard to believe that the writer would not expect his Jewish readership to see in this a reference to the Torah....

112. *Deuteronomy and the Deuteronomic School,* 246–47. It reinforces Georg Braulik's linkage of wisdom with the Torah in Deuteronomy ("'Weisheit' im Buch Deuteronomium," 39–69.

113. For recent discussion of the ending, see Weeks, in *Wisdom and Torah,* 101–18.

114. The expression φόβος κυρίου occurs nineteen times in Sirach (1:11, 12, 18, 27, 28, 30; 9:16; 10:22; 16:2; 19:20; 21:11; 23:27; 25:6, 11; 27:3; 40:26a, 26b, 27; 45:23). Cf. also "fear of him" (φόβῳ αὐτοῦ) in 2:10.

15

All Israel Will Be Saved

An Examination of Moses' Eschatological Vision in Deuteronomy[1]

Introduction

YHWH, THE GOD OF Israel, planted the seed of humankind's eschatological hope in Gen 3:15, when he predicted the ultimate triumph of the seed of the woman over the serpent who had seduced the first pair to revolt against him. And with their revolt they had subjected not only the human race, but also the entire cosmos to the fury of the Creator. Although some contend that the entire Pentateuch is driven by a vision of an eschatological Messiah,[2] this understanding depends upon a strained reading of some specific texts and unfortunately negative readings of Israel's constitutional documents: the Decalogue (Exod 20:2–17), the Covenant Document (Exod 20:22–23:19), the Instructions on Holiness (Lev 17–26), and the Deuteronomic Torah (Deut 5–26, 28). This is not to deny a significant eschatological thread in the Pentateuch—it is obviously there—but to caution against overlooking the "here-and-nowness" of the first major section of the Hebrew canon.

Since exploring the eschatology of the entire Pentateuch would require an entire volume, it is necessary to restrict our study to a specific segment of the Pentateuch, that is, the book of Deuteronomy. Although this book brings the narrative of Israel's earliest history to a close and concludes the biography of Moses, Deuteronomy consists largely of three embedded farewell pastoral addresses by Moses (1:6—4:40; 5:1—26:19, 28:1–68; 29:1[2]—30:20), a concluding national anthem dictated by YHWH (32:1–43),[3]

---

1. This is a stylistically modified version of an essay originally prepared under the heading, "The Doctrine of the Future in Moses: 'All Israel Shall Be Saved,'" for publication in *Eschatology: Biblical, Historical, and Practical Approaches*, Festschrift in honor of Craig Blaising, ed. D. Jeffrey Bingham and Glenn R. Kreider (Grand Rapids: Kregel, 2016), 107–34. I am grateful to the editors and to Kregel Publishers for their kind permission to republish it here. It is a great honor to devote this essay to my esteemed friend and former colleague, whose life and ministry have been characterized by grace and covenant righteousness. I am grateful to Michelle Knight and Jeffrey Bingham, who read earlier drafts of this paper and made helpful suggestions for its improvement.

2. See Sailhamer, "The Messiah and the Hebrew Bible," 1–22; Sailhamer, *The Meaning of the Pentateuch*, 236–46.

3. On which see Block, "The Power of Song," 162–88.

and Moses' final benedictions for the tribes (33:1–29). In his addresses, Moses offers the most systematic instruction of Yahwistic theology to be found in the Hebrew Scriptures.

Time in Deuteronomy

Among the remarkable features of Moses' speeches in Deuteronomy is the way he addresses the issue of time. On the one hand, his perspective is timeless. Even though most of the people standing before him had not yet been born, he suggests shockingly that they (1) lived in Egypt (29:15–16[16–17]); (2) were enslaved by Pharaoh (6:21; 16:12; 24:18) (3) witnessed YHWH's signs and wonders (1:30; 4:34); (4) came out of Egypt (4:37; 16:1); (5) stood with Moses at Horeb/Sinai when YHWH established his covenant with Israel (4:33; 5:2–5); (6) worshiped the golden calf (9:7–21); and (7) provoked YHWH's wrath with their faithlessness at Massah, Taberah, and Kibroth-hattavah (9:22).[4] But Moses also insists that the covenant renewal rituals on the Plains of Moab that he has been supervising implicate all future generations as well (29:13–14[14–15]).[5] We find a similar blurring of the ancestors. Sometimes the expression אָבוֹת refers specifically to the patriarchs (Abraham, Isaac, and Jacob; 1:8; 6:10; 9:5, 27; 29:12[13]; 30:20), but elsewhere the expression refers to the exodus generation (4:31; 5:3; 6:3;[6] 27:3; 29:24[25]); 31:16), or even the ancestors of future generations who possessed the land (30:5, 9). This blurring of generations spills over into the covenants, so that the covenant YHWH made (כָּרַת) with Abraham (Gen 15, 17), established (הֵקִים) with the exodus generation at Horeb (Gen 17:7; Exod 19:5-6; Deut 8:18), and renewed with the present generation is one and the same.[7]

If Moses' speeches exude a kind of timelessness, this does not mean he is oblivious to present circumstances. On the contrary, his present addresses are largely driven by a very immediate pastoral concern (if not fear). He knows that Israel's next move is to cross the Jordan, but he also knows that since he will die shortly (31:2) he will not be able to cross over with them (1:37; 3:23–29; 4:21–22). Indeed, the narrator reminds readers that YHWH himself announced his imminent death both to him and to Joshua in the "Appointment Tent" (31:14–16) and again after he had taught his people their anthem (32:48–52). The four concluding chapters may be interpreted as a single extended and complex death narrative.[8] This reality lends urgency to everything Moses says, for both

---

4. Cf. Block, *Deuteronomy*, 154-55. In 29:15–16[16–17] Moses speaks of the present generation as having lived in Egypt.

5. In Deuteronomy Michael Fishbane's comment applies: "Sinai is . . . not a one-time event, but for all times; it is not only grounded in the historical past, but hovers in the living present. Sinai stands at the mythic core of religious memory, and the explication of its teachings is a sacred ritual for Judaism" (*Sacred Attunement*, 49).

6. "Land flowing with milk and honey," never occurs in the Patriarchal stories, but first appears in YHWH's conversations with the exodus generation: Exod 3:8, 17; 13:5; 33:3; Lev 20:24; Num 13:27; 14:8; 16:13–14.

7. See further, chapter 4, "Covenance: A Whole Bible Perspective," above, pp. 65–77; Hwang, *The Rhetoric of Remembrance*, 232.

8. Thus Cribb, *Speaking on the Brink of Sheol*, 185–227.

he (31:24–29) and YHWH (31:16–21) fear that as soon as he is gone the Israelites will act corruptly by abandoning YHWH and breaking his covenant. The urgency in Moses' voice is reflected in the expression, הַיּוֹם הַזֶּה, "this day," which he uses sixteen times.[9] Although Moses often deals with past and future events, with this phrase he keeps bringing his hearers back to the present moment of decision on the plains of Moab. Like the other sixty-one occurrences of the word, הַיּוֹם, "today," in the First Testament,[10] in Deuteronomy "this day" highlights the "emphatic contemporaneity" of the entire book.[11] Moses thereby insists that the Israelites are accountable both to the covenant to which they signed on at Horeb and his valedictory appeal, that is, "this Torah" (הַתּוֹרָה הַזֹּאת),[12] that Moses is setting before the people (4:8, 44; cf. 30:1, 10, 15, 19). His primary concern is the fidelity of the present generation.

History in Deuteronomy

None of this should blur our vision for Moses' keen sense of history in Deuteronomy. In contrast to the canonical texts of other ancient peoples, Moses has a clear perception of Israel's past, and a clear sense of where the nation's history is going. We may summarize the key past events as follows:

1. In the beginning "God created humankind on the earth" (בָּרָא אֱלֹהִים אָדָם עַל־הָאָרֶץ, 4:32).[13]

2. YHWH identified the ancestors (Abraham, Isaac, Jacob) as the object of his love (חָשַׁק, אָהַב) and chose (בָּחַר) their descendants after them (4:37; 10:15).

3. YHWH swore to the ancestors that he would give the land of Canaan to them and their descendants.[14]

4. The ancestors lived a precarious existence in the land and ultimately their clan of seventy moved to Egypt (10:22; 26:5).

5. In the indeterminate past YHWH had dislodged the original populations of the regions south and east of the Dead Sea and given them to the Edomites, Moabites, and Ammonites, respectively (2:2–23).

6. Meanwhile in Egypt the clan of Jacob flourished and became a nation (גּוֹי), great, mighty, and innumerable like the stars (10:22; 26:5), but there the Israelites

---

9. Deut 2:22, 25, 30; 3:14; 4:20, 38; 5:24; 6:24; 8:18; 10:8, 15; 11:4; 26:16; 27:9; 29:3, 27[4, 28]. The narrator uses the phrase in 32:48 and 34:6.

10. For a listing of the remainder see Millar, "Living at the Place of Decision, 43, n. 61.

11. Gerhard von Rad, *The Problem of the Hexateuch and Other Studies*, 26.

12. The expression occurs fifteen times in the book: 1:5; 4:8; 17:18–19; 27:3, 8, 26; 28:58, 61; 29:28[29]; 31:9, 11–12, 24; 32:46.

13. The word בָּרָא occurs only here in Deuteronomy.

14. Deut 1:8, 35; 6:10, 18, 23; 7:13; 8:1; 9:5; 10:11; 11:9, 21; 26:3, 15; 28:11; 30:20; 31:20–21, 23; 34:4.

observed the idolatry of the Egyptians (29:16–17[17–18]) and at the end of their stay experienced brutal enslavement by Pharaoh (26:6).[15]

7. By means of signs and wonders YHWH punished the Egyptians, revealed himself to them and Israel, and rescued Israel from the bondage of Egypt (Deut 4:34; 6:22; 7:19; 11:3; 26:8; 29:2[3]; 34:11).

8. YHWH brought Israel to Horeb where he established with them the covenant he had first made with Abraham (4:9–14) and revealed his will in the form of the Decalogue (4:13; 5:1–2) and the "ordinances and judgments" (חֻקִּים וּמִשְׁפָּטִים).[16]

9. No sooner had the Israelites signed on to the covenant than they apostatized and worshiped the golden calf in place of YHWH. However, through the mediation of Moses, YHWH withdrew his threat to destroy them and renewed his covenant with them (9:1–10:11).

10. The Israelites left Sinai and experienced YHWH's remarkable care as they journeyed through the desert to the edge of the promised land (1:19, 30–33; 8:1–6, 15–16; 29:4–5[5–6]; 32:10).

11. At Kadesh-barnea the exodus generation faithlessly refused to enter the promised land, so YHWH sent them back into the desert for forty years, until that generation had died and been replaced by the current generation (1:20–29, 32–46; 2:1–2, 14–15).

12. Most recently, with divine support the Israelites had defeated the Transjordanian kingdoms of Sihon of Heshbon and Og of Bashan, whose land Moses had allotted to the tribes of Reuben, Gad, and a segment of Manasseh (1:4; 2:24—3:17; 4:46; 29:6–7[7–8]).

Moses' historical memory is sharp, but he also has a keen sense of Israel's future, both immediate and long range.

1. Once Moses has died, Joshua will take the reins and lead the people across the Jordan (1:38–39; 3:18–22, 28; 31:3–8, 23).

2. The first event to transpire across the river involves the ritual completion of the covenantal triangle binding the land to deity and nation on Mounts Gerizim and Ebal (11:29–32; 27:1–26; see Fig. 15.1).[17]

---

15. Deut 5:6, 15; 6:12, 21; 7:8; 8:14; 13:6, 11[5, 10]; 15:15; 16:12; 24:18, 22.

16. This pair of expressions, which generally functions as shorthand for the Horeb revelation, occurs fourteen times: Deut 4:1, 5, 8, 14, 45; 5:1, 31; 6:1, 20; 7:11; 11:32; 12:1; 26:16–17. Occasionally it is supplemented by הָעֵדֻת, "the covenant stipulations" (4:45; 6:17, 20). Although חֻקִּים and מִשְׁפָּטִים may be used interchangeably, at root the former refers to divine decrees, while the latter refers to divine judgments concerning righteous covenantal conduct.

17. The bond between YHWH and Israel had been covenantally sealed at Sinai, and was being reinforced by the present rituals—on the Plains of Moab—that underlie the book of Deuteronomy. On the significance of the Gerizim and Ebal ceremony, see chapter 8, "What Do These Stones Mean?" above, pp. 152–76.

Figure 15.1
The Israelite Covenantal Triangle

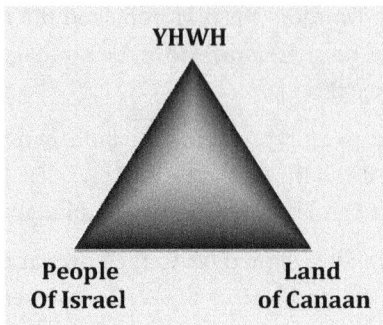

3. Thereafter the Israelites are to engage the Canaanites and occupy their land, which YHWH had sworn to the ancestors (6:10–11; 7:1–26; 8:7–10; 11:8–15, 21–25; 12:1; 17:14; 19:1; 30:20).

4. When the Israelites have rest from all their enemies, YHWH will choose a place to establish his name, to which all Israelites and aliens among them are invited for worship and fellowship with YHWH (12:5, 11, 14, 18, 21, 26; 14:23; 15:20; 16:2, 6–7, 11, 15–16; 17:8, 10; 18:6; 23:17[16]; 26:2; 31:11).

5. If the Israelites demonstrate righteousness and are true to YHWH and his covenant, they will flourish and occupy the land in perpetuity (5:33; 7:12–16; 11:8–17; 22:7; 28:1–14; 31:20).

This is the hope. However, both Moses and YHWH present a more realistic view of the nation, repeatedly expressing doubts about Israel's future fidelity (5:29). Indeed they offer an alternative script, which exhibits strong marks of inevitability.

1. Once the Israelites are in the land, they will abandon YHWH and his covenant. At the end of his first address Moses seems to anticipate this as an event in the distant future (4:25), but by the time he finishes his addresses both he (31:27–29) and YHWH (31:14–20; 32:15–18) expect this to happen immediately upon Moses' decease.

2. YHWH will respond to this rebellion and ingratitude for the grace he had lavished on them through the centuries by withdrawing from them (31:17–18) and pouring on them his fury in the form of the severest of curses (4:25b–28; 11:16, 28; 28:15–68; 29:17–27[18–28]; 30:1; 32:19–25), in effect destroying the covenantal triangle by driving Israel away from himself and from the land.

3. However, the judgment cannot be the last word. Ultimately the Israelites will come to their senses and turn back to YHWH (4:29–30; 30:1–3), and YHWH's compassion (4:31; 30:3; 32:36) will triumph over his fury (32:36–42). He will remember his [irrevocable and eternal] covenant (4:31), regather the people to their land (30:3–5), and circumcise their hearts so that they will love him with whole heart and being and walk in his ways. In effect, the covenantal triangle will be restored.

4. Israel will finally fulfill her mission to the world[18] as YHWH's people, chosen (בָּחַר), treasured (עַם סְגֻלָּה), holy (עַם קָדוֹשׁ), and adopted as his sons (בָּנִים, 7:6; 14:1–2; 26:18–19). The nations will acknowledge not only the righteousness of YHWH's statutes, but also YHWH's nearness to them (4:5–8). Indeed, they will recognize that Israel bears the name of YHWH (28:9–10) and that he has raised them high above all nations for praise (תְּהִלָּה), fame (שֵׁם), and honor (תִּפְאֶרֶת, 26:19). Indeed, along with Israel, the nations and the angels will worship YHWH and celebrate his restoration of the people and their land (32:43).

Deuteronomy's Eschatological Language

With this survey of Deuteronomy's vision of Israel's past and her future we have established the context for considering the Mosaic eschatological vision. After a discussion of Moses' eschatological language, I will consider the features of Moses' eschatological vision, based on specific texts.

Although the Pentateuch as a whole is punctuated with eschatological vocabulary, to argue that "the Pentateuch was written primarily as a presentation of a future messianic hope centered in the tribe of Judah and grounded both in creation and covenant"[19] certainly overstates the case. It overlooks the fact that the books that make up the Pentateuch function as a sort of constitutional document, preserving both a record of divine grace that led to the establishment of Israel as YHWH's covenant people and of the divine revelation intended to guide the people in the fulfillment of his mission for them.[20] Although we find predictions that may legitimately be interpreted messianically, these are not only remarkably scarce,[21] but they are missing entirely from Deuteronomy.[22] The statements that most closely resemble Messianic prediction occur in the Mosaic vision of kingship in Deut 17:14–20, which anticipates the [Davidic] Israelite king as the supreme embodiment of righteousness, as defined by the Torah. With hindsight we recognize that none of Israel's kings fulfilled this vision perfectly,[23] and that only Jesus, David's greatest son, did so (cf. Matt 5:17). However, this perspective is possible only with hindsight; the original text lacks any hint of an eschatological or messianic significance.

---

18. Gen 12:3; 18:18; 22:18; 26:4; Exod 19:4–6; Ps 67.

19. Thus Sailhamer, "The Messiah and the Hebrew Bible," 18.

20. I include Moses' addresses in Deuteronomy as part of that revelation, inasmuch as both the narrator (1:1–5) and Moses (4:5, 14; 6:1) emphasize that his addresses were divinely inspired, and indeed canonical from the outset (4:2),

21. Gen 3:15; 22:17b (Abraham's seed [singular] shall possess the gate of his enemies); 49:8–12; Num 24:9, 17.

22. Contra prevailing opinion, represented, for example by Rydelnik, *The Messianic Hope*, 54–59. I do not interpret Moses' prediction of "a prophet like me" as a prediction of an eschatological prophetic Messiah, but a succession of prophets who would continue like Moses to be God's mouthpieces for Israel. For brief discussion, see Block, "My Servant David," 26–32; for fuller discussion, see chapter 17, "A Prophet Like Moses: Another Look at Deuteronomy 18:9–22," below, pp. 349–73.

23. The historians single out David, Hezekiah, and Josiah as particularly virtuous, but all are flawed to a greater or lesser degree.

When searching for eschatological texts we look for distinctive vocabulary that speaks of "the last days," or "the end of the age."[24] The relevant expressions include קֵץ/קָצֶה, "end, extremity," and אַחֲרִית, "latter, afterward, outcome." קָצֶה occurs nine times in Deuteronomy, but usually with a geographic sense, referring either to the distant horizon, "the end of the heavens/sky" (4:32 [2x]; 30:4), or to "the end of the earth" (13:8[7, 2x]; 28:49 // מֵרָחוֹק, "from far away"; 28:64 [2x]; 30:4). Only in 14:28 does it bear a chronological significance, but the sense is not eschatological: "at the end of [every] three years." The word קֵץ occurs only three times, always with a specifically defined chronological sense: "at the end of forty days and forty nights" (9:11); "at the end of seven years" (15:1; 31:10). Therefore, the קֵץ/קָצֶה vocabulary of Deuteronomy provides no evidence of an eschatological perspective.[25]

Although the word, אַחֲרִית occurs less frequently than קֵץ/קָצֶה it offers slightly stronger evidence for an eschatological significance to Deuteronomy.[26] The word occurs six times,[27] always with a chronological meaning, though only two of these bear a possible eschatological significance.[28] According to 4:30, when Israel is in distress (צַר) because they have experienced YHWH's fury as described in vv. 25–27, "in the latter days" (בְּאַחֲרִית הַיָּמִים) they will return to YHWH their God and listen to his voice.[29]

The eschatological nature of these statements is not as obvious as scholars often assume. Admittedly, the Septuagint translates three of them with some form of ἔσχατος (32:29 uses χρόνος), but in the Greek rendering of Deuteronomy this word is used in a wide variety of contexts,[30] which cautions against premature identification of "the latter days" with "the end of the age" or "the end of time." This caution is reinforced by 31:29, which locates Israel's judgment "in the latter days." From Moses' perspective, the fulfillment of this warning in 722 BCE and 586 BCE might have seemed like "the end of the days," but from our vantage it was not nearly the eschaton. Accordingly, initially we should interpret the expression no more specifically than "in the distant future."

---

24. For discussion, see Klingbeil, "Looking at the End from the Beginning," 174–87.

25. As does the evidence for this word in the rest of the Pentateuch: קֵץ and קָצֶה occur often, but never with an eschatological sense.

26. Cf. Klingbeil, "Eschatological Concepts." 178–83.

27. And four times in the preceding books, three in the context of Balaam's oracles: Gen 49:1 (בְּאַחֲרִית הַיָּמִים, lit. "in the latter days"; Jacob's blessing of his sons concerns the distant future); Num 23:10 (אַחֲרִיתִי, "my end"; the suffix suggests one's personal destiny); Num 24:14 (בְּאַחֲרִית הַיָּמִים, lit. "in the latter days"; as in Gen 49:1, in this narrative introduction to an oracle, Balaam is about to speak of what Israel will do to Moab in the distant future); Num 24:20 וְאַחֲרִיתוֹ, "his end," speaking of Amalek's ultimate destruction (אֹבֵד).

28. Deut 8:16 בְּאַחֲרִיתֶךָ, "in your end), YHWH tested Israel for their "ultimate" good; 11:12 (עַד אַחֲרִית שָׁנָה, "unto the end of the year"), in contrast to the beginning of the year (מֵרֵשִׁית הַשָּׁנָה).

29. Whereas this text locates Israel's restoration after the judgment "in the latter days," 31:29 locates the judgment itself "in the latter days" (בְּאַחֲרִית הַיָּמִים). Deut 32:20 speaks of Israel's destiny in the wake of the judgment as "their end" (אַחֲרִיתָם). In 32:29 a similar expression (לְאַחֲרִיתָם, "with reference to their end") speaks of the destiny of Israel's enemies.

30. Of Israel's destinies (אַחֲרִית + suffix, 8:16; 32:20; in 32:29 the same expression is rendered χρόνος; simply for "afterward" (Heb אַחֲרֹנָה, 13:10[9]; 17:7), "after" Moses' death (אַחֲרֵי מוֹתִי, 31:27, 29); of the "latter" man (הָאַחֲרוֹן, 24:3 [2x]); geographically of "the end of the earth" (קָצֶה, 28:49), and "the western sea" (הָאַחֲרוֹן, 34:2).

Moses actually assumes a four-phased future for Israel: (1) the immediate future following his death (31:27–29); (2) several generations removed from the present after the Israelites have been in the land for some time and become spiritually lethargic (4:25);[31] (3) the distant future (בְּאַחֲרִית הַיָּמִים) when YHWH will have had enough of Israel's infidelity and he pours out his fury on them in the form of the covenant curses (31:29); (4) the period beyond the judgment (also בְּאַחֲרִית הַיָּמִים) when Israel returns to YHWH and listens to his voice (4:29–31). To Moses these last two represented "the distant future";[32] only time would tell whether this would transpire at the end of the age, or even the climactic moment of cosmic history. If we would speak of Moses' "eschatological vision," we should understand that for him Israel's distant future is firmly rooted in both Israel's past and the nation's present.

The Features of Moses' Eschatological Vision

Deuteronomy describes the anticipated first phase of Israel's "distant future" in detail in 28:15–68; 29:[17–27]18–28; and 32:19–25. Since from our perspective this phase has in fact been fulfilled in history, when considering the features of Moses' "eschatological" vision we must focus on those aspects of his vision that have not been realized even in our time: phase 4 of the scheme outlined above. In exploring Moses' (and YHWH's) perspective of Israel's ultimate future we may focus on three specific texts, the first two appearing in prose at the end of Moses' first and third addresses (4:29–31; 30:1–10) and the third in poetic form in the nation's anthem (32:36–43). Each text builds on the preceding.

Deuteronomy 4:29–31

Moses' first "eschatological" statement is brief, and focuses entirely on the restoration of divine human relations—without any reference to the land and its role in the covenantal triangle. The geographic context is established by the words, "there" (שָׁם, v. 28a), that is, in the lands to which YHWH had scattered their few survivors (v. 27) and where they have been serving senseless and insentient humanly manufactured gods of wood and stone (v. 28). Three chronological notes in v. 30 establish the chronological context: (1) "in the distant future" (בְּאַחֲרִית הַיָּמִים, lit., "in the latter days"); (2) "when you experience

---

31. Because the verb נוֹשַׁנְתֶּם is rare in the First Testament, its meaning is unclear. It seems to be derived from a root meaning "old" (ישׁן) but it also sounds like a word meaning "to sleep" (יָשֵׁן), which is occasionally associated with death (Job 3:13; Ps 13:4). In the covenant curses of Lev 26:10, the word describes old and stale grain. In either case, the word suggests a long time in the land, resulting either in lethargy or self-confidence (cf. Deut 8:11–17). Moses seems to anticipate a waning of energy to keep alive the story of divine grace. How quickly this happened is demonstrated in the book of Judges (2:10–13). Moses would probably have been appalled that his own grandson Jonathan would be installed as the first priest of the pagan cult center at Dan (Judg 18:30), on which see Block, *Judges, Ruth*, 512–13.

32. So also, Tigay, *Deuteronomy*, 54; Craigie, *Deuteronomy*, 141.

the distress" (בַּצַּר לְךָ); and (3) "when all these words 'find' (מָצָא) you," that is, the threats of vv. 25b–28 have been fulfilled.

The definite article on "distress" and the expression "these things" indicate that Moses had in mind not "trouble" in general, but a specific set of circumstances. These are summarized in vv. 25b–28, which in style and vocabulary anticipate the detailed recitation of covenant curses in 28:15–68. The essential features are easily identified. The cause of their distress is the fury of YHWH their God, who has been provoked by "the evil" they have perpetrated with their idolatry, which violates the first and Supreme Command of the Decalogue: "you shall have no other gods besides me" (5:7–10).

Moses describes the distress that YHWH threatens to bring on his people in five dimensions. (1) The Israelites will certainly and quickly perish from the land they are about to cross into and possess. (2) Their dream of long life in the land will come to an end,[33] for they will be utterly destroyed.[34] (3) YHWH will scatter them among the peoples, and drive them to another place, like a shepherd drives his flock. (4) A few will survive[35] in the lands where YHWH has driven them. (5) In the lands where the worship of senseless gods is the norm, they will experience the futility of idolatry to the full (v. 4:28). Here Moses fails to mention the element that may have been most distressing of all: being abandoned by YHWH. Later, in 31:17–18 he will summarize the link between idolatry and trouble and the heart of the trouble itself:

> On that day my fury with them will be ignited and I will abandon them; I will hide my face from them, and they will be destroyed. Many disasters (רָעוֹת) and difficulties (צָרוֹת) will "find" (מָצָא) them, and on that day they will ask, "Have these disasters not "found" (מָצָא) us because our God is not with us?" And I will certainly hide my face on that day because of all the wickedness they have perpetrated, for they have turned to other gods.

Obviously, the anticipated judgment would result in the complete disintegration of the covenant triangle: YHWH would abandon his people and his land, the land would be emptied of its people, and the Israelites would be driven off to seek divine aid in a foreign land. However, if the punishment for covenantal infidelity threatened in verses 26–28 was certain, the same would apply to the promise of hope in verses 29–31, which summarize Israel's ultimate destiny. Remarkably this first "eschatological" statement expresses no interest in the role of the land in the covenantal triangle; the focus is entirely on restoring the deity-people relationship. This is expressed from two sides.

---

33. The motif of not prolonging their days occurs often in Deuteronomy (4:40; 5:33; 11:9; 17:20; 22:7; 30:18; 32:47). It negates the desired purpose, "that their days may be lengthened" (5:16 [= Exod 20:12]; 6:2; 25:15).

34. The emphatic constructions, אָבֹד תֹּאבֵדוּן, "you shall certainly perish," and הִשָּׁמֵד תִּשָּׁמֵדוּן, "you shall certainly be destroyed," represent rhetorical hyperbole. As Moses himself will say (v. 27), there will be a few who survive in the lands where they are exiled.

35. Hebrew וְנִשְׁאַרְתֶּם מְתֵי מִסְפָּר, literally "you shall be left men of number," that is, so few one may count them (Gen 34:30; Jer 44:28; Ps 105:12). In Deut 26:5 and 28:62 Moses will use the stylistic variant, מְתֵי מְעָט, "a few men." Both expressions represent the reversal/opposite of what YHWH promises the patriarchs: descendants like the stars of the sky and sands of the seashore (Gen 22:17), and descendants that are innumerable (אֵין מִסְפָּר; Gen 41:49; cf. Deut 10:22; 26:5).

On the one hand, Israel will experience a new disposition toward their God, which is summarized with four verbs arranged in perfectly logical order (vv. 29–30). First, from the land of exile the Israelites will seek YHWH their God. "To seek" (בִּקֵּשׁ) YHWH does not mean to look for him as if he were lost, but to seek him out, approach him humbly, and plead for a return of his favorable attention. Second, they will find (מָצָא) YHWH, if they search for him with all their heart/mind (לֵב) and with their entire being (נֶפֶשׁ).[36] This added condition means the search for YHWH may be neither casual nor occasional, nor one search among many. Moses demands that the people abandon all other searches and seek YHWH alone. Third, they will return to YHWH. The verb means "to turn, to turn around," that is, to walk in the opposite direction, but is regularly rendered "to repent," that is, to turn around spiritually, to abandon one's sinful course and "walk in the ways of YHWH." Fourth, the Israelites will listen to the voice of YHWH, which means not only obeying his commands, but also receiving gladly his reminders of past and present graces, including the words being preached presently by his spokesman Moses. Whereas the covenant curses in chapter 28 conclude with words of distress,[37] without any ray of hope, here Moses patterns his vision of Israel's "eschatological" future on Leviticus 26, which means he cannot let Israel's story end with judgment. And it does not, for Moses will return to this theme in his third address (30:1–10), and expound in considerable detail how this will happen. Here he offers no clues why the Israelites in exile will experience such a dramatic change of heart.

If on one hand Israel will exhibit a new disposition toward YHWH, on the other YHWH will respond by letting himself be found (v. 29) and resuming his communication with them (v. 30). The promise that Israel will find YHWH if they seek him wholeheartedly and that they will hear his voice again suggests that the Deity who had abandoned his people will respond to their search with renewed accessibility and renewed communication. Unlike the gods of wood and stone, he is responsive; indeed, as Moses had declared at the beginning of this chapter, he will be near again to hear their calls to him and he will reveal himself once more (4:7–8).

Moses concludes this summary statement of Israel's "eschatological" hope by announcing three pillars on which this hope rests. First, Israel's hope rests on the compassionate character of God: "For YHWH your God is compassionate El." While the word רַחוּם speaks of warm and tender affection, like the love of a mother toward a child,[38] the phrase אֵל רַחוּם invites hearers/readers to remember Exod 34:6–7, where, this expression heads a list of seven extraordinary divine qualities. YHWH is merciful and gracious, slow to anger, and abounding in steadfast love (חֶסֶד) and fidelity (אֱמֶת), forgiving every kind of sin, while not leaving the guilty unpunished. As Daniel will plead in Dan 9:18, given their history the Israelites have no reason to expect a favorable response from

---

36. Variations of this phrase recur frequently in Deuteronomy: 6:5; 10:12; 11:13; 13:3[2]; 26:16; 30:2, 6, 10. We hear echoes of the present statement in Jer 29:13. In Dan 9 the exiled Daniel models this focused search for YHWH. See also 2 Chr 7:14.

37. Deut 28:15–68 expounds and expands on 4:26–28.

38. It derives from the same root as רֶחֶם, the word for "womb" (Isa 49:15; Jer 20:17). Cf. HALOT, 1216–18.

YHWH; but they may appeal to his great compassion (רַחֲמִים). Unlike the gods of wood and stone, YHWH is moved by the prayers of his people.

Second, YHWH will not abandon his people forever. From Moses' statement in v. 26 it had appeared that he would not withdraw his fury until he had "utterly destroyed" (הִשָּׁמֵד תִּשָּׁמֵדוּן) them. From what follows immediately, this is obviously hyperbolic speech, for he speaks of a remnant of the population surviving in exile. Presumably the absolute statement refers to the covenant triangle relationship, which must be demolished before YHWH can start over with his people. In v. 31 Moses expresses YHWH's fidelity to Israel with two expressions: he will not "drop" (הַרְפֶּה) them and he will not destroy them. In everyday speech the first is used of relaxing the hands so that one drops what one is holding (cf. 2 Sam 24:16 = 1 Chr 21:15). Here it signifies "to abandon" or "to release" from the relationship. The second expression seems to answer the hopelessness created by v. 26. Because YHWH is gracious, he will not destroy (הִשְׁחִית) them totally. The Israelites may be determined to destroy themselves (v. 16 and 31:29 use the same verb, הִשְׁחִית), but YHWH's compassion prevents him from totally annihilating them. In effect, through the exile he saves the Israelites from themselves.

Third, though Israel may forget YHWH's covenant with them (v. 23), YHWH cannot forget his covenant with the ancestors. The last phrase, "covenant of your ancestors" (בְּרִית אֲבֹתֶיךָ) raises the question: Which covenant does Moses have in mind? Although most scholars assume the Abrahamic covenant,[39] the issues are not that simple. First scholars are recognizing increasingly that a dichotomy between the [supposedly unconditional] Abrahamic covenant and the [supposedly conditional] Israelite covenant is false. Since all covenants involve relationships, the health of such relationships is always conditional, depending upon the disposition and actions of each party toward the other.[40] Second, the covenant made at Horeb was anticipated in Gen 17:7, and signified the establishment (הֵקִים) with Abraham's descendants of the very covenant that YHWH had first made (כָּרַת) with the ancestor (Gen 15:18). Third, although elsewhere we read of God's covenant "with" Abraham, outside this context "the covenant with the fathers," or "of the fathers," (בְּרִית אֲבֹתֶיךָ) never occurs.[41] Fourth, the argument based on Lev 26:42 is neutralized by verse 45, which, while referring to a "covenant with their predecessors" (בְּרִית רִאשֹׁנִים) explicitly identifies them as those "whom I brought out of Egypt in the sight of the nations to be their God."

---

39. Thus Merrill, *Deuteronomy*, 129; Weinfeld, *Deuteronomy 1–11*, 210; Mayes, *Deuteronomy*, 157. Three considerations may support this interpretation: (1) in previous occurrences of the expression, "which he swore to X," in Deuteronomy, the clause referred to YHWH's covenant promise of land to the patriarchs (1:8, 35), while the Sinai narratives never speak of YHWH "swearing" to Israel to keep the covenant; (2) biblical narratives frequently refer to the covenant with the patriarchs as God's covenant with Abraham, Isaac, and Jacob (Exod 2:24; cf. 6:4; Lev 26:42; 2 Kgs 13:23; 1 Chr 16:15–18 = Ps 105:8–11); (3) the covenant curses in Lev 26 base Israel's hope for renewal on God's covenant with the patriarchs.

40. So also, Brueggemann, *Theology of the Old Testament*, 199; Christopher Wright, *Knowing Jesus through the Old Testament*, 55–102.

41. The expression, "the covenant that I made with their/your ancestors" (הַבְּרִית אֲשֶׁר כָּרַתִּי אֶת־אֲבוֹתָם) occurs in Jer 31:32 and 34:13, but in both instances the ancestors are identified as the exodus generation.

Fifth, in Deut 4 generally and vv. 9–31 particularly the central issue is the covenant that YHWH made with Israel at Horeb.

On the other hand, there is no need to choose between the patriarchal covenant and the Israelite covenant; the distinct language is merely a matter of focus. Rather than emphasizing the land, which was the focus in the promise to the patriarchs, in verse 31 Moses' attention is on YHWH's relationship with his people: "He will neither fail *you* nor destroy *you*." Furthermore, the "return" spoken of in verses 29–31 is not to the land but to YHWH.[42] The issue in this chapter is much greater than land. Unlike the gods of the nations, who were primarily interested in territory and only secondarily concerned about people, YHWH's primary concern lies with his people and his relationship to them (cf. Gen 17:7). The covenant he remembers is the one made with Abraham, extended to his descendants at Horeb, and confirmed with this generation in Moab. In Deuteronomy the covenant with the fathers and their descendants is one.[43] In the future YHWH may suspend the benefits of the covenant (4:25–28; cf. Lev 26:14–39; Deut 28:15–68), but this will not affect the covenant itself.[44] On the contrary, both the judgment and the restoration are written into the covenant. In the end, when the Israelites come to their spiritual senses and repent of their rebellion (Lev 26:41; Deut 4:30; 30:6–10), YHWH will renew his covenant relationship with them.

Deuteronomy 30:1–10

Deuteronomy 30 represents the climax of the gospel Moses has proclaimed in this book. Much of the theological freight of this section is carried by key words. The most important of these is the root שׁוּב, "to return, turn back," which occurs seven times, with some variation in meaning.[45] Since four of the seven involve Israel as the subject (vv. 1, 2, 8, 10) and three involve YHWH (vv. 3a, 3b, 9), Israel's future restoration obviously requires a change in the disposition of both parties.[46] The subthemes interwoven throughout this passage exhibit an exquisite chiastic arrangement:[47]

---

42. Cf. the references to the "land" that he swore to the ancestors in 1:8, 35; 6:10; 7:13; 10:11; 11:9, 21; 26:3; 28:11; 30:20; 31:20.

43. For full discussion, see chapter 4, "Covenance: A Whole Bible Perspective," above, pp. 65–77, and Hwang *Rhetoric of Remembrance*, 187–207, 302–8.

44. On the eternality of God's covenant with Israel, see note 79 below.

45. For a full study of the word, see W. L. Holladay, *The Root* שׁוּב *in the Old Testament*.

46. The third occurrence of שׁוּב involves the idiom, שׁוּב שְׁבוּת, "to restore the fortunes" (v. 3a). For a more recent study of שׁוּב in this context, see Frisch, "Repentance and Return," 129–48 [Hebrew].

47. Cf. C. J. H. Wright, *Deuteronomy*, 289.

> A   When you and your children return (v. 2a)
>> B   and listen to his voice with all your heart and being (v. 2b)
>>> C   then YHWH will restore your fortunes and prosper you more than your ancestors (vv. 3–5)
>>>> D   *YHWH will circumcise your heart and the heart of your offspring,*
>>>> D' *so that you will love YHWH with all your heart and being, and live (v. 6)*[48]
>>> C' YHWH will delight in prospering you, as he took delight in your ancestors (vv. 8–9)
>> B' if you listen to the voice of the YHWH your God (v. 10a)
> A' and if you turn to YHWH your God with all your heart and with all your soul (v. 10b).

This is a gloriously holistic text, announcing the full restoration of the triadic covenantal relationships. Based on syntactical and conceptual markers, the text breaks down into three readily identifiable segments each of which describes a specific feature of Israel's "eschatological" future: (1) The restoration of the bilateral relationship between YHWH and Israel (vv. 1–3); (2) The divine restoration of the trilateral covenant relationship (vv. 4–8); (3) The environmental proof of the restoration (vv. 9–10).

The Restoration of the Bilateral Relationship Involving YHWH and Israel (vv. 1–3)

The way Moses begins suggests that vv. 1–10 expand on his earlier summary statement in 4:29–30. He does not refer to "the latter days," but the clause, "when all these words have come upon you" pushes the events into the distant future. Although most translations render כָּל־הַדְּבָרִים הָאֵלֶּה as "all these things," presumably the events predicted in 29:16–20[17–21],[49] his clarification, "the blessing and the curse," and the modifier, "which I have set before you" point back to the promises and threats of chapter 28.

Moses' description of the restoration of the bilateral relationship between deity and people divides into two parts: vv. 1b–2 highlight the change in Israel's disposition toward YHWH, and v. 3 highlights YHWH's change in disposition toward Israel. Concerning the former, among all the nations where YHWH their God has banished them, they will

---

48. Verse 7 is omitted because it deals with what YHWH will do to the nations, rather than Israel, though these actions will ultimately be for Israel's benefit.

49. In Deuteronomy and the Pentateuch generally the expression always means "all these words." Gen 20:8; 29:13; Exod 19:7; 20:1; 24:8; Num 16:31; Deut 4:30; 12:28; 30:1; 32:45.

(1) come to their senses,[50] (2) return (שׁוּב) to YHWH their God,"[51] and finally listen to the voice of YHWH (cf. 4:30).[52] The coordinate expression, "with all your heart and with all your being" (vv. 2, 6, 10), picks up an oft-repeated refrain from 4:29[53] that highlights the completeness of the people's "repentance."

Additional echoes of 4:29–31 are heard in verse 3 as Moses shifts his attention to YHWH's changed attitude and actions. First, YHWH's *intentions* concerning Israel will change: he will restore their fortunes[54] by lifting the judgment and restoring the relationship between the people of Israel and their land. Second, YHWH's *disposition* toward his people will change: he will show compassion to them (רִחַם, cf. 4:31), in response to Israel's listening to his voice and doing what is right in his sight (cf. 13:18[17]). Third, YHWH's *orientation* regarding Israel will change: he will "turn around."[55] Here שׁוּב expresses YHWH's fundamental reorientation: instead of turning from Israel and operating as their enemy, he will turn toward them and act on their behalf. Fourth, YHWH's *treatment* of Israel will change: Whereas previously he had scattered them among the nations, now he will gather them (cf. 4:27; 28:64). While we hear nothing yet of the restoration of the people to the land, this divine action represents a necessary first step in the reversal of their uprooting (29:27[28]).

The Restoration of the Trilateral Relationships Involving YHWH, Israel, and the Land (vv. 4–8)

The syntax of verse 4 signals a shift in flow, though the repetition of the verb, "to gather" suggests that verses 4–5 expand on the last clause in verse 3 and highlight the comprehensiveness of the restoration. Moses begins this paragraph by addressing the nation-land relationship of the triangle (vv. 4–5). His solution involves five elements, expressed with five verbs: he will gather (קִבֵּץ) Israel, take (לָקַח) them,[56] "bring" (הֵבִיא) them to the

50. In the clause rendered by *NIV* as "you take them to heart," the verb הֵשִׁיב, "to turn/bring x back," lacks an object. Assuming "all these words" (v. 1b) to be the object, in exile the Israelites will reverse their hardened disposition (cf. 29:18[19]) and in effect recast as a confession what Moses had presented as a third person interpretation in 29:24–27[25–28].

51. A verbatim quotation from 4:30. The statement signifies a reversal of past faithless behavior that included "abandoning" YHWH (28:20) or his covenant (29:24[25]), and turning aside from his way (9:12) or from him to serve other gods (11:16).

52. This clause serves as a refrain in the book: 4:30; 8:20; 9:23; 13:5, 19[4, 18]; 15:5; 21:18, 20; 26:14, 17; 27:10; 28:1–2, 15, 45, 62; 30:2, 8, 10, 20.

53. Deut 4:29; 6:5; 10:12–13; 11:13–15; 13:4[3]; 26:16.

54. This is the first of 25 occurrences of the idiom שׁוּב שְׁבוּת/שְׁבִית, in the First Testament, and its only occurrence in Deuteronomy. In Job 42:10 the expression involved restoration of the beleaguered man's original good fortune.

55. When used of YHWH, the verb שׁוּב, "to turn, return," reverses the hostile disposition reflected in expressions like, "he will turn away from you" (וְשָׁב מֵאַחֲרֶיךָ, 23:15[14]; 2 Chr 30:8) and verbs of divine abandonment, like עָזַב, or rejection, like מָאַס, or abhorrence, like גָּעַל. The latter two occur in the Leviticus version of the covenant curses (Lev 26:44).

56. The verb, "to take" is cryptic. The link with 4:20—the only other occurrence with YHWH as the subject and Israel as the object—suggests concrete affirmation of election; YHWH will claim Israel as his own possession once more.

land, ensure their well-being (הֵטִיב),⁵⁷ and multiply (הִרְבָּה) the population beyond anything their ancestors had known before the judgment.⁵⁸ Finally the physical and national ideals announced in the covenant with Abraham and confirmed when the Israelites were incorporated in this covenant at Horeb will be realized.

In verse 6 Moses addresses the heart of the problem: Israel's ruptured relationship with YHWH. Reintroducing a notion presented briefly in 10:16, where he had called upon the Israelites to circumcise their hearts, he now announces that YHWH will perform this spiritual surgery. The metaphor refers to removing all psychological, moral, and spiritual barriers to true devotion to YHWH, resulting in undivided love and obedience. This is not to say that this act happens here for the first time. There have always been individuals within Israel (like Abraham, Moses, Joshua, Caleb, David, the prophets), whose hearts were circumcised. What is new is that this will happen at the national scale: all Israel will be transformed from the inside out. While Moses observes that a positive disposition toward God is a prerequisite to restoration, he declares that permanent and total covenant commitment can be achieved neither by appealing to the people to get themselves right with YHWH nor by a mere return to the land. Apart from this divine surgery, national infidelity is not only inevitable, but also dangerous; it poses an ever-present threat to the current generation (5:29; 9:6, 13, 24; 13:3[2]; 31:16-18, 27-29).

But Moses has already declared that however certain Israel's failure may be, just as certain is the conviction that alienation from YHWH and exile must end (cf. 4:28–31). YHWH will secure permanent and total devotion through circumcising the hearts of the generation he restores and their descendants in perpetuity. The goal of this surgery is simple but profound: "to love YHWH your God." As elsewhere "love" denotes commitment demonstrated in actions that serve the interests and pleasure of one's covenant partner (cf. 6:4-5). This could not be achieved by legislation; it required a radical new surgical removal of the symbols of the old affections.⁵⁹ This heart surgery will seal the complete restoration of the covenantal triangle.

After a brief passing notice that in that day YHWH will repair Israel's standing among the nations and impose the sanctions that his own people had experienced (29:21-27[22-28]) on those who served as his agents of punishment (v. 7), verse 8 describes concretely the evidence that the new day has arrived. YHWH's people will demonstrate a new orientation, a new receptiveness, and a new obedience in compliance with Moses' teaching.

---

57. YHWH's original delight, expressed concretely in the blessings of 28:1-14, will return.

58. For references to Israel prospering in the land and multiplication of the population, see also 6:3; 7:13, and 30:16.

59. Since elsewhere Moses suggests this goal would be achieved through reading/hearing the Torah (17:19-20; 31:11-13), circumcising the heart is equivalent to implanting the Torah in peoples' hearts.

The Environmental Proof of the Restoration (vv. 9–10)

Expanding on verse 5, in vv. 9–10 Moses draws his hearers' attention back to YHWH, who causes the land to fulfill its role within the tripartite covenant relationship. In describing the physical evidences of this new order, he highlights Israel's special relationship with YHWH by what these two will do for each other. On the one hand YHWH will cause the Israelites to prosper in all they do. Echoing the blessing in 28:11, he cites three dimensions of this prosperity: in their own progeny, in the progeny of their livestock, and in the productivity of the ground. Reiterating his earlier promise, Moses declares that YHWH will "turn toward Israel"[60] with renewed delight over them (cf. 28:63). The promises made to the present generation (7:12–16; 8:11–13; 11:13–15; cf. 32:13–14), were not merely utopian dreams; they would one day be fully realized in all their physicality.

Moses concludes this section with one more reminder that although the triangular covenantal relationships will be fully restored, his people should not view these promises as unconditional predictions, overriding and trumping a rebellious disposition (v. 10). On the contrary, first, the Israelites must pay full attention to the voice of YHWH, which means ordering their conduct according to his commands and decrees as written in "this book of the Torah" (בְּסֵפֶר הַתּוֹרָה הַזֶּה), that is the transcript of Moses' addresses. Second, reversing the order of "hearing" and "returning" from v. 3, Moses declares that Israel must return to YHWH her God with all her heart/mind and her entire being. Introduced by the three-fold occurrence of the particle כִּי, "because," Moses declares the grounds and the certainty of Israel's newfound prosperity: YHWH will bless Israel because he will delight in her (v. 9b), because they will listen to his voice (v. 10a), and because they will return to him (v. 10b).[61] It seems the missing element in Israel's history had not been the ability to keep the will of YHWH—as if it placed impossible demands on them—but the will to do so, an issue resolved in the circumcision of the heart.

In Deut 30:1–10 Moses reiterates and expounds on his vision of Israel's future as summarized in 4:30–31 and envisioned in Lev 26:40–45. In the end, YHWH's mercy wins out over his fury and his eternal commitment to his people is confirmed. In this portrait of Israel's inevitable restoration Moses has planted numerous seeds that will sprout and grow in later texts. In Jeremiah's announcement (Jer 30:3) and in his vision of the new covenant (Jer. 31:27–37) we hear clear lexical and conceptual echoes of Deut 30:1–10.[62] Although Jeremiah does not use the language of heart circumcision here (cf. Jer 4:4; 9:25–26 [24–25]), his understanding of the divine inscription of the Torah on

---

60. As in vv. 3c and 8, NIV obscures the reference to reorientation by treating יָשׁוּב, "he will return," as an adverb, "again."

61. Cf. Aejmelaeus, "Function and Interpretation of *kî* in Biblical Hebrew," 428. Contra McConville, *Deuteronomy*, 428, syntactically, the temporal interpretation seems too reliant on theological assumptions regarding Israel's incapacity to turn to YHWH prior to his circumcision of their heart in 10:16.

62. "Restore [your] fortunes" (שׁוּב שְׁבוּת, cf. Deut 30:3); "Bring [them] back to the land" (Jeremiah uses הֵשִׁיב; Deut 30:5 uses הֵבִיא, "to bring"); the land (הָאָרֶץ) associated with the ancestors (אָבוֹת; Deut 30:5, "that your ancestors possessed"; Jer 30:3, "that I gave their ancestors"); the verb, יָרַשׁ, "to possess," used of the land (cf. Deut 30:5).

the hearts of the people and his vision for all Israel participating in the new order fall within the same theological field. Like Moses, Jeremiah was fully aware that there are two Israels: (1) the Israel that claims status before God and before the nations by virtue of descent from Abraham, their identification with the exodus from Egypt through the annual celebration of the Passover, and their possession of the Torah (Paul's "Israel after the flesh," Rom 4:1; 9:3, 5; Gal 4:23, 29)"; (2) true spiritual Israel, for whom the Shema (Deut 6:4–5) is the watchword, and who like Josiah turn to YHWH with their entire inner beings, their persons, and their resources (2 Kgs 23:25); like Caleb and Rahab and Ruth (who were gentiles by blood) they have a different spirit and follow YHWH fully (cf. Num 14:24; Deut 1:36; Josh 14:8); and like David they trust YHWH fully (2 Sam 22:2–51). Historically, times when the boundaries of these two Israels coalesced were rare (Fig. 15.2).

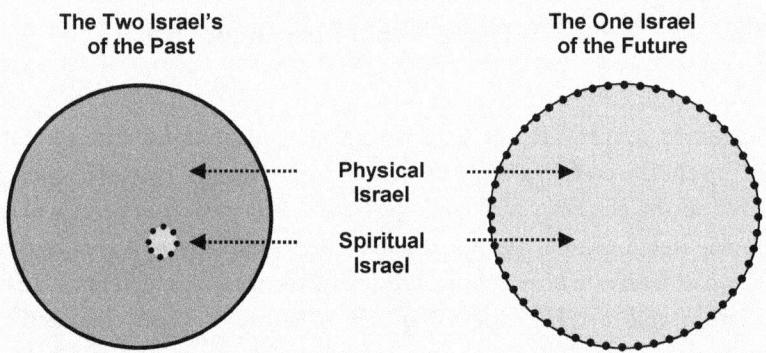

Figure 15.2
The Relationship between Physical Israel and Spiritual Israel As Perceived by Moses and Jeremiah

But the image envisioned here is different. As pictured on the right, Moses looks forward to a time when the boundaries of physical and spiritual Israel will be coterminous. All Israel will be circumcised of heart; all will love YHWH; all will listen to his voice and live according to the Torah of Moses; all will participate in YHWH's favor. Taking a page out of Moses' notebook, Jeremiah envisioned a future when the original Torah of YHWH would be internalized in the hearts of all Israel and all Israel would be freed to walk in the ways of YHWH.[63]

---

63. In context Jer 31:27–40 is entirely parochial; only Israel is in view here. Ezekiel did not use the language of heart circumcision, but replaced this metaphor with that of a heart transplant. Echoing Moses' ambivalence in Deuteronomy, in one moment he calls on the Israelites to get themselves a new heart and a new spirit (Ezek 18:31; cf. Deut 10:16), and in the next speaks of YHWH transplanting the peoples spirit and heart (Ezek 11:19; 36:24–34; cf. Deut 30:6). Like Moses, Ezekiel saw the proof of spiritual renewal to be obedience to the will of God.

Deuteronomy 32

Although the poem inserted in chapter 32 is commonly identified as "the Song of Moses," it should really be called "the Song of YHWH,"[64] because YHWH inspired it and apparently dictated it to Joshua and Moses in the Tent of Meeting (31:14–21). This is a complex composition, involving no fewer than four degrees of direct discourse.[65] Based on demarcations of the speeches and syntactical signals,[66] we may divide the song into sections and stanzas as follows:

A. The Exordium: A Call to Acknowledge the Perfections of YHWH (vv. 1–4)

B. The Recollection: A Call to Acknowledge the Imperfections of YHWH's People (vv. 5–18)

   Stanza I: The Thesis Statement (vv. 5–6)

   Stanza II: A Call to Remember YHWH's Grace (vv. 7–14)

   Stanza III: Trampling Underfoot the Grace of YHWH (vv. 15–18)

C. The Confession: A Call to Recognize the Justice of YHWH (vv. 19–35)

   Stanza I: YHWH's Justice in Dealing with His Own People (vv. 19–25)

   Stanza II: YHWH's Justice in Dealing with Israel's Enemies (vv. 26–35)

D. The Gospel: A Call to Treasure the Compassion of YHWH (vv. 36–42)

E. The Coda: A Call to Celebrate the Deliverance of YHWH (v. 43)

This song presents a sophisticated poetic review of Israel's history from Moses' perspective: past (vv. 1–12) and future (vv. 13–43). With reference to Israel's anticipated future the song speaks successively of (1) YHWH's blessing Israel with prosperity in the land (vv. 13–14), (2) Israel's revolt against their gracious God (vv. 15–18), (3) YHWH's outpouring of fury on his people (vv. 19–25), (4) YHWH's judgment on Israel's enemies (vv. 26–35), (5) YHWH's outpouring of restorative grace on his own people (vv. 36–42), and (6) the cosmic celebration of YHWH's full restoration of Israel and its land (v. 43). In accord with our previous observations, although "eschatological" vocabulary is missing, and phases 1–3 pertain to Israel's future from Moses' point of view (all having been fulfilled in the first millennium BCE), technically only phases 4–6 remain unfulfilled to this time and relate to Israel's distant future. Therefore, they may be considered eschatological.

Israel is not the focus of vv. 26–35, but like Ezekiel's oracles against the nations (Ezek 25–32) and the oracle against Gog (Ezek 38–39), this stanza offers hope for Israel,

---

64. "The song of Moses the servant of God, and the song of the Lamb" in Revelation 15:3 are often associated with this text, but the epithet may just as well refer to Exod 15, which explicitly celebrates YHWH's deliverance of the Israelites from their tyrannical Egyptian overlords, which is paradigmatic of the salvation provided by the Lamb.

65. Cf. Fokkelman, *Major Poems of the Hebrew Bible*, 58–62.

66. Contra prevailing perceptions, the particle כִּי serves fundamentally as a discourse marker, which may function causally ("because," v. 20), or temporally ("when," v. 36c), though neither is certain. For full discussion, see Follingstad, *Deictic Viewpoint in Biblical Hebrew Text*.

for here YHWH declares in unequivocal terms his determination to vanquish Israel's enemies. This stanza, which may be interpreted as a poetic commentary on 30:7, climaxes in a divine claim to the right to vengeance and retribution (נָקָם וְשִׁלֵּם), followed by an announcement of the imminence of the day of their doom (עֵד/עֲתִדֹת). However, the heart of the song's "eschatological" gospel occurs in 32:36–42, calling on Israel to treasure YHWH's amazing compassion.

This stanza opens with the voice of the poet, who announces the theme brilliantly:

> See, YHWH will champion the cause of his people
> and have compassion on his servants,
> when he sees that their power is gone
> and there is none remaining, neither ruler nor helper (v. 36).[67]

The first verb (דִּין) involves a legal expression, meaning "to judge,"[68] but in cases involving the oppressed it means "to champion the cause of."[69] The second involves a hithpael of the root נחם, "to be sorry, feel compassion," (cf. Ps 135:14; Num 23:19).[70] While both YHWH and Moses deem Israel's future infidelity and judgment to be inevitable (Deut 31:16–18, 20–21), already in 4:31 Moses had declared the present assertion of divine empathy to be rooted YHWH's compassion (רַחוּם). The second half of v. 36 sets the context of his change in disposition from the fury poured out in vv. 19–25. The expression, "Their strength is gone" (lit. "Their hand evaporates)," contrasts Israel's powerlessness with the boast of the enemies (v. 27c). But the song adds a profound detail: YHWH sees! In contrast to the foreign gods (4:28) and reversing the hiding of his face earlier (v. 20), YHWH observes that the Israelites have expended their resources.

In verses 37–38 YHWH's voice returns and carries on through verse 42. He begins by taunting the Israelites for having put their confidence in other gods. The rhetorical question (v. 37a) alludes to verses 15–18, ironically and sarcastically using the generic singular "rock." The gods the people have chosen are mere pebbles, in contrast to YHWH, the omnipotent and perfectly just Rock (v. 4). In verse 38 the mockery turns to idols themselves. Recognizing the importance of keeping gods satisfied, YHWH challenges the gods they have chosen to come to their aid by asking where the gods who accepted their devotees' sacrifices and libations are. The triad of action verbs reinforces the sarcasm: "Let them rise up and help you; let them be your protection." These expressions all play on the reference to the gods as "rock" in verse 37.

The unparalleled heaping up of attention-grabbing expressions in v. 39 signals the climax—"See! Now! Note! I! I am he!"[71]—and focuses hearers' attention on YHWH, who declares self-assuredly, "There is no God beside me." Whether we interpret עִמָּדִי as "with me" or "besides me," he alone controls the events of history; no one shares status

---

67. As translated by Block, "Power of Song," 183.

68. Often as an alternative to or correlative of שָׁפַט (e.g., Ps 7:9[8]; 9:9[8]). In Deut 17:8 the cognate noun refers to a lawsuit or legal case too difficult for local courts to resolve.

69. So NJPSV. Of God: Gen 30:6; Ps 54:3[1]; of human officials: Prov 31:9; Jer 5:28; 21:12; 22:16.

70. The niphal is used often to express God's sorrow or his change in disposition toward an object: Gen 6:6–7; Exod 32:12, 14; 1 Sam 15:11, 29, 35 Jon 3:9–10; 4:2.

71. רְאוּ עַתָּה כִּי אֲנִי אֲנִי הוּא. Cf. 1 Chr 28:10, רְאֵה עַתָּה כִּי, "See! Now! Note!"

or rank with him.⁷² The remainder of verse 39 and verses 40–42 elaborate on YHWH's exclusive control over the fates and fortunes of human beings. If Israel has suffered, this has indeed been the work of YHWH, but the switch to an imperfect verb turns this statement into a promise: YHWH will certainly heal (אֶרְפָּה) his people. The last line of verse 39 emphasizes that when he acts on Israel's behalf, no outside power—neither divine nor human—can stop him.

The final strophe (vv. 40–42) seals Israel's future. With a dramatic non-verbal gesture and an emphatic verbal declaration, YHWH assures Israel that he will deal with their enemies once and for all. The idiom "to lift the hand to heaven," followed by the oath formula, suggests a legal gesture of raising the hand in association with swearing an oath.⁷³ By adding "forever" to the oath (חַי אָנֹכִי לְעֹלָם) the certainty of YHWH's defeat of the enemy equals that of his oath to Abraham in Gen 22:16.

Verses 41 and 42 reinforce the substance of the divinely sworn affidavit, beginning with a reference to the context: when YHWH, the divine warrior, prepares his weapons for battle. The first line speaks literally of sharpening "the lightning of my sword." But YHWH's weapons of war are also weapons of judgment. Alluding back to verse 35, YHWH declares that he will repay his enemies, personally wielding the sword he had placed in the hands of Israel's enemies (v. 25). In verse 42 the picture turns grotesque, portraying YHWH's sword and arrows as carnivorous beasts that cannot get enough of human blood and human flesh.⁷⁴

Israel's anthem ends on a festive note, with a coda appealing to the nations and the host of heaven to join in the celebration of YHWH's gracious acts on behalf of Israel (v. 43). The reading is problematic, and scholars disagree in their assessment of the textual evidence for this verse, but the arguments for the eight-line reading of LXX are persuasive and serve as the base for our comments:⁷⁵

> Rejoice, O heavens with him,
> and bow down to him, all sons of God.
> Rejoice, O nations, with his people.
> And let all the messengers of God strengthen themselves.
> See, the blood of his sons he will avenge;
> and avenge and take vengeance on his enemies.
> He will pay back those who hate him,
> and atone for the land of his people.

The switch from first person forms in verse 42 to third person in verse 43 signals a shift in speaker from YHWH (vv. 37–42) to the poet. Lexical features keep the attention

---

72. The use אֲנִי הוּא, "I [alone] am he," in Isaiah confirms this: Isa 41:4; 43:9–13; 43:25; 46:3–4; 48:12; 51:12; 52:6.

73. For further attestation of and bibliography the idiom, see Block, *Deuteronomy*, 766.

74. While the notion of arrows drinking occurs only here, the image of a sword devouring its victims is common in the First Testament (2 Sam 2:26; 11:25; Isa 1:20; 34:5–6; Jer 46:10; etc.), and elsewhere (*ANET*, 540, ll. 635–36).

75. For discussion of and bibliography on the complex text-critical issues involved, see Block, "The Power of Song, 184," and "Excursus B: Text-Critical Issues in Deuteronomy 32:43," 185–88.

focused squarely on YHWH.[76] The way the coda refers to Israel reinforces this interpretation. Given the complete collapse of the relationship between deity and nation in verses 15–25, that the nation should be referred to as "his sons" (בָּנָיו)[77] and "his people" (עַמּוֹ) alone is cause for celebration, for it declares that the promise of verse 36a–b has been fulfilled.

The first four lines focus on the addressees, which consist of two categories: the heavenly host, identified as "the heavens" (הַשָּׁמַיִם), "all sons of God" (כָּל בְּנֵי אֱלֹהִים), and "envoys of God" (מַלְאֲכֵי אֱלֹהִים), on the one hand, and the "nations" (גּוֹיִם), on the other. The last reference is especially significant, for it has the nations celebrating together *with* (אֶת) "his people." Apparently, this indicates the realization of YHWH's goal declared in 26:19, "He will set you high above all nations that he has made, for [his] praise, fame, and honor, and that you might be a people holy to YHWH your God, as he promised."

The last four lines shift the focus from the celebrants to the targets and beneficiaries of YHWH's action. The middle pair of four lines arranged chiastically echo verse 41c–d and function as a shorthand expression for YHWH's fuller declaration of his defeat of his adversaries in verses 39–42. The statement is remarkable, for Israel's enemies have become YHWH's adversaries. The outside lines identify the beneficiaries of YHWH's actions. To be sure YHWH will defeat his enemies, but in doing so he will avenge the blood of his sons and make atonement for his land and his people.[78] The need for the land's atonement was created by human blood violently shed (Num 35:30–34) and unburied corpses (Deut 21:23) that defile the land—the effects of the slaughter of the Israelites (32:43c; cf. 25).

Viewed as a whole, verse 43 presents the hosts of heaven and the nations with three reasons to celebrate and pay homage to YHWH: (1) YHWH has restored his relationship with Israel; (2) YHWH has taken vengeance on Israel's (and his own) enemies; (3) YHWH has made atonement for the land. In so doing he has reversed the earlier dissolution of the tripartite relationship involving deity-nation-people that was precipitated by Israel's idolatry. This is cause for celebration not only by the Israelite beneficiaries of the divine action—as in this song—but also by the hosts of heaven and the nations; indeed, the entire universe rejoices.

Conclusion

On this magnificent note, we reach the climax of Deuteronomy's eschatological vision. The remarkable correspondence between Moses' anticipation of Israel's immediate future and the way events actually transpired up to the fall of Judah to Babylon gives readers confidence that the nation's ultimate destiny following the judgment will also follow the basic contours that the book establishes. Rooted in the covenant that YHWH made with Abraham (Gen 15, 17), established with their descendants at Horeb (Deut

---

76. The object of praise is not named, but YHWH is referred to at least twelve times, eight explicitly by means of pronominal suffixes on nouns, and four implicitly in third person singular verbs, to which we should add the phrases, "sons of *God*," and "messengers of *God*."

77. MT reads עֲבָדָיו, "his servants," as in v. 36.

78. The verb כִּפֶּר, "to atone for, to cleanse," occurs elsewhere in Deuteronomy only in 21:8.

4:9–24), and confirmed with the present generation on the Plains of Moab (cf. 26:16–19; 29:9–12[10–13]), the basic elements of Israel's eschatological hope were established. If the covenant secured the tripartite relationship involving YHWH, Israel, and the land he promised them, and if the nation's punishment involved the total disintegration of this triangular association, then the restoration must involve the reconstitution of this triangle. This would require the following critical elements: (1) the preservation of the physical seed of Abraham as an identifiable ethnic people, who would embody before the nations the transforming power of divine grace; (2) a change in YHWH's disposition so that he would look again on his people with compassion; (3) the return of Israel to the promised land.

Although many assume that the destruction of Judah and the deportation of its population in 586 BCE signaled the end of YHWH's covenant with Israel, and called for a new dispensation involving a spiritual people of God, this interpretation is unwarranted on several counts. First, as noted earlier, YHWH's covenant with Abraham and his descendants was repeatedly declared to be eternal, that is, irrevocable (לְעוֹלָם).[79] However, the same kind of language is used of the Israelite covenant.[80]

Second, as Daniel recognizes in his penitential prayer (9:7–14), both the curse for persistent infidelity (Lev 26:14–39; Deut 28:15–68) and the promise of ultimate restoration (Lev 26:40–45; Deut 4:29–31; 30:1–10) were written into the covenant. YHWH would have betrayed his covenant if he had not abandoned his people and brought in first the Assyrians and then the Babylonians to destroy what remained of Israel's attachment to the land.

Third, in fulfillment of Jeremiah's prediction (2 Chr 36:22–23; Ezra 1:1; cf. Jer 25:12; 29:10), and in response to Daniel's prayer (Dan 9:1–2, 20–23), the restoration of the remnant community in Jerusalem in the Persian era served as a deposit of Israel's ultimate full restoration.[81] However, this was only a partial (מְעַט) fulfillment; in contrast to the Mosaic and prophetic visions, (1) the population was small and numerable (Ezra

---

79. The eternality of the covenant made with Abraham is highlighted repeatedly in the Patriarchal Narratives with expressions like בְּרִית עוֹלָם (Gen 17:7, 13, 19; cf. 9:16) and assurances that specific promises have eternal force "to your seed forever" (עַד עוֹלָם, Gen 13:15; 17:8; 48:4; Exod 32:13; Ps 105:8–10; 1 Chr 16:15).

80. Exod 31:16–17 speaks of an eternal/irrevocable covenant for their generations (לְדֹרֹתָם בְּרִית עוֹלָם), with the seventh-day Sabbath functioning as a sign forever (אוֹת הִוא לְעֹלָם); Lev 24:8 characterized the covenant established at Horeb as an "everlasting covenant" (בְּרִית עֹלָם; so also Isa 24:4–5); in Judg 2:1 YHWH declares he will never break his covenant with Israel; Ps 111:5 declares YHWH will remember his covenant forever (לְעוֹלָם; cf. also v. 9); in Isa 54:4–10, YHWH speaks of his eternal חֶסֶד, places his covenant with Israel in the same irrevocable category as the cosmic covenant, and declares that "my covenant of peace" (בְּרִית שָׁלוֹם) will never be removed; Jer 31:35–37 declares that YHWH's commitment to Israel is as firm and irrevocable as the fixed order of the universe. Like the Isaiah text, here Jeremiah attaches the certainty of the cosmic order (as guaranteed in the Cosmic Covenant) to the Israelite covenant. Ezekiel characterizes YHWH's future "covenant of peace" (בְּרִית שָׁלוֹם) as an "eternal/irrevocable covenant" (בְּרִית עוֹלָם, 16:60; 37:26). This is the covenant that he remembers "from the days of your youth" (i.e., at Sinai), whose features in 34:25–30 deliberately echo the blessings built into the Israelite covenant in Lev 26:4–13. For discussion, see Block, *Ezekiel Chapters 25–48*, 303–6.

81. The prayer of confession in Neh 9:5–37 is laced with references to the covenant and assesses the present circumstances of the post-exilic community in the light of the covenant.

2; Neh 7); (2) they occupied only a small portion of the promised land in the vicinity of Jerusalem; (3) although YHWH's blessing was on the community initially, his temple was a mere shadow of the original (Hag 2).[82] Since this community represented only a fraction of the restoration celebrated in Deut 32:43, and in any case would be totally destroyed again in 70 CE, this was not the fulfillment Moses and YHWH had in mind in Deuteronomy.

Even so, the irrevocable divine covenantal commitments remain (Rom 9–11), and Paul looks forward to the day when "all Israel will be saved" and the ideals of YHWH's covenant will finally be realized (11:26). Although Paul's vision of Israel's future is refracted through the lens of Jer 31:31–40, the roots of this hope were established centuries earlier in the Torah of Moses and in Israel's national anthem.

---

82. Although not explicitly part of the Mosaic vision, the Davidic line was preserved, but the representative (Zerubbabel) was merely a governor, rather than a king ruling from David's throne.

16

The Spiritual and Ethical Foundations of Messianic Kingship

Deuteronomy 17:14–20[1]

Introduction

IT IS REMARKABLE THAT in Deuteronomy, the foundational theological document of the First Testament, explicit references to the Messiah are difficult to find. Although many interpret the promise that YHWH will raise up a prophet like Moses in 18:15 messianically,[2] in the context of vv. 9–22 Moses' concern is first, to assure Israel that after his own departure YHWH will continue to speak to his people through commissioned prophets (v. 18), and second, to challenge the people to listen to the prophet when he comes, or face extremely dire consequences (v. 19). As an addendum, he adds that the sentence of death hangs over any prophet who poses as an authorized prophet of YHWH, even though YHWH has never sent him (vv. 20–22; cf. Jer 23:16–22).[3] Both Peter (Acts 3:14–26) and Stephen (7:35–39, 51–53) condemn their audiences for rejecting Jesus, because in rejecting him they have rejected Moses and the train of prophets like Moses who spoke of him, the Messiah (3:21), the Servant of God (3:26), and "the Righteous One" (7:52).

Even if Deut 18:15 is not considered a messianic text, does Deuteronomy help us understand the role and mission of the Messiah? The answer comes in a brief text, located at the heart of Moses' third address (Deut 12–26, 28), namely in 17:14–20. Although concerned with the third of four provisions of leadership in the Israelite community (judges [Deut 16:18]; Levitical priests [Deut 17:8–13; 18:1–8]; the king [Deut 17:14–20]; prophets [Deut 18:9–22]), it occurs within the context of injunctions for the people,

---

1. This is a slightly modified version of an article forthcoming in *The Moody Handbook of Messianic Prophecy*, edited by Michael Rydelnik and Edwin A. Blum (Chicago: Moody Publishers). I am grateful to the editors for their suggestions for its improvement, and for their kind permission to republish it here.

2. For the messianic interpretation of Deut 18:15–19, see James Sibley, "Deuteronomy 18:15–19," forthcoming in *The Moody Handbook of Messianic Prophecy*.

3. For further discussion, see Block, "My Servant David, 26–32; also, *Deuteronomy*, 438–46.

whose watchword is "Righteousness, only righteousness *you* [the people] shall pursue" (16:20). Moses' instructions concerning the four public offices in 16:18—18:22 were not intended primarily for the officeholders, but for public consumption, that lay people might understand the roles their leaders played in the corporate pursuit of righteousness and justice. Accordingly, the people should know that judges are to be agents and administrators of righteousness, Levitical priests were to be guardians of and instructors in the way of righteousness, prophets would represent the conscience of righteousness, and kings would serve as paradigms of righteousness.

The Mosaic Paradigm of Kingship

The Request for a King (v. 14)

Deuteronomy 17:14–20 is logically constructed, beginning with a hypothetical wish expressed by an interlocutor who represents Israel as a nation after they have established themselves in the land that YHWH had promised to the ancestors and had now delivered into their hands: "I would like to set a king over me like all the nations around me" (author's translation). Remarkably, as was the case in 12:20, speaking for YHWH, Moses grants the people's request—even though the request is based on a non-Israelite model of kingship ("like all the nations around me"). This ready granting of permission must be understood in the light of earlier anticipations of kings among Abraham's descendants (Gen 17:6, 16; 35:11), Jacob's divinely inspired promise to Judah, that "The scepter will not depart from Judah, or the staff from between his feet, until he whose right it is comes and the obedience of the peoples belongs to Him" (Gen 49:10), and Balaam's prediction not only of a generally exalted king and kingdom, but also of his specific foresight:

> I see him, but not now;
> I perceive him, but not near.
> A star will come from Jacob,
> and a scepter will arise from Israel.
> He will smash the forehead of Moab
> and strike down all the Shethites (Num 24:17, CSB)

While the history of the monarchy in Israel would prove disastrous in many respects, no Israelite prophet and no biblical author rejected the monarchy in principle.

The Qualifications of the King (v. 15)

Having granted the Israelites permission to install a king over themselves, Moses set the parameters of kingship in Israel. First, he narrowed the field of candidates (v. 15), by declaring that the king must be an Israelite chosen by YHWH. The concept of divine election surfaces often in Deuteronomy. Elsewhere the verb בָּחַר, "to choose," with YHWH as subject applies to the election of Israel out of all the peoples on earth (4:37; 7:6, 7; 10:15; 14:2), of a place to establish his name (12:5, 14, etc.), and of the Levites as priests out of all the tribes (18:5; 21:5). The notion of divinity choosing a person to serve as his royal representative is widely attested in the ancient Near East, from as early as the eighteenth-century BCE to beyond the First Testament period.

Moses is even more emphatic about the second qualification—the king must be an Israelite, "from the midst of your brothers," and then excluding any outsider "who is not your brother."[4] Unlike the Egyptians, who were ruled by the Asiatic Hyksos from Avaris for more than a century (1650–1530 BCE),[5] the people of YHWH were to be ruled by a viceroy of YHWH chosen from their own ranks, not a strongman brought in from outside.

The Conduct of the King (vv. 16–20)

The remainder of this literary unit is taken up with instructions regarding the king's performance of his royal duties. The text continues in third person, reminding hearers that the purpose of this paragraph is not to provide the king with a manual for leadership, but to create in the minds of the Israelites an image of responsible leadership. In contrast to the office of judge, which the Israelites are to institute (16:18–20; 17:9), the office of priest, which YHWH had already instituted (17:9; 18:1–8), and the office of prophet, which YHWH will institute in the future (18:9–22), the office of king is presented as optional, subject to the desire of the people. To highlight the contrast with prevailing approaches to kingship in biblical times, Moses began with a triad of proscriptions designed to curb royal, self-interested abuse of power, the office that arises out of greed and ambition (vv. 16–17), and ended by prescribing an extraordinary spiritual and ethical standard for the king (vv. 18–20).

Moses' Negative Commands (vv. 16–17)

Although Moses' proscriptions consist of four main statements, they actually involve three prohibitions: excessive accumulation of horses, women, and precious metals, respectively. Since in the ancient Near East horses were used primarily for pulling chariots, the proscription on horses was intended to stifle militaristic impulses (cf. Deut 20:1; Josh 17:16–18; Judg 1:19). The intent of the prohibition on multiplying women in the court extended far beyond limiting the opportunities for the king to satisfy his sexual cravings with the most beautiful women in the kingdom.[6] Since marriages were often arranged to strengthen alliances with other states (cf. 1 Kgs 9:15–16; 16:31), the institution of the harem enabled a king to be allied simultaneously with many outside rulers (cf. 1 Kgs 11:1). Moreover, along with good-looking male courtiers (cf. Dan 1:3–4), these women served as decoration for the court to impress foreign visitors with the glory of the king

---

4. On נָכְרִי, "foreigner," see above on 14:21 and 15:3 (cf. also 23:21 and 29:20[21]). On the status of the נָכְרִי, see Block, "Sojourner, Alien, Stranger," 562.

5. Cf. Redford, 341–44.

6. Since in our world "wives" connotes a marital relationship, נָשִׁים is better rendered generically as "women," the reference being to the harem of a typical oriental king.

337

when they visited his court. But these are not Moses' primary concerns; he viewed the harem as a threat to spiritual fidelity to YHWH: the women would turn the king's heart away. The warning concerns defection into idolatry (cf. Deut 7:3–4), though in light of what follows it may involve defection from the Torah generally and the Supreme Command (Deut 6:5) in particular. The reference to "his heart" suggests such defection is not viewed primarily as an external act, but as a fundamental aspect of one's being (cf. 6:5). Like wine and strong drink, pursuing pleasure and status could be intoxicating and inhibit the proper exercise of the king's responsibilities (cf. Prov 31:3–9).[7]

In the prohibition of excessive accumulation of silver and gold, these precious metals function as shorthand for wealth and opulence in general. In the ancient Near Eastern political world this wealth was generally amassed at the expense of the people by taxing the citizens and demanding tribute from subject states.

Together these prohibitions of common royal behavior address three major temptations facing ancient rulers: lust for power, lust for status, and lust for wealth. The text does not prohibit the purchase of horses, or marriage, or the accumulation of some silver and gold. The threefold repetition of "for himself" (לוֹ) reflects the propensity of kings to exploit their office for personal gain.[8]

Moses' Positive Commands (vv. 18–20)

Moses' positive instructions for the king are even more remarkable than the prohibitions. This "standard for kingship"[9] involves three commands relating to the Torah, followed by a fourfold declaration of the rationale underlying the commands. First, Moses commanded the king to copy the Torah for himself. While scholars debate the significance of "this Torah" or "instruction" (הַתּוֹרָה הַזֹּאת, v. 18), given the way this and related expressions are used in the book, it seems best to understand "this Torah" minimally as Moses' second and third addresses (Deut 5–11; 12–26 + 28), and maximally as the collection of all the utterances preserved in Deut that he delivered as his farewell to his people, including the first address (1:6–4:40), the fourth address (29:1[2]—30:20), Israel's "national anthem" (32:1–43), and Moses' final benediction of the tribes (33:2–29). Deuteronomy 31:9–13, 24–26 notes that Moses wrote down "this Torah" ("this law," CSB) and instructed the Levitical priests to place it beside the ark of the covenant, in recognition of its immediate authority as Scripture. For the king, copying the Torah was a covenantal act performed in the presence of priests. This bound the king himself to all that these words promised and demanded. he hereby affirmed his spiritual subordination to the priests as guardians of the Torah and his subordination to the Torah itself as a symbol of the covenant that bound YHWH and Israel.

Second, the king was to "wear the Torah" (v. 19a). The two-word Hebrew sentence, וְהָיְתָה עִמּוֹ, "and-it-is-to-remain-with-him," declares that the king was not to treat the

---

7. Cf. the warning of Lemuel's mother in Prov 31:3–9.

8. For a superb discussion of the intent of this text generally to divest the king of exclusionary power, see Berman, *Created Equal*, 53–64.

9. Translating מִשְׁפַּט הַמֶּלֶךְ, literally "the judgment/standard of the king," in 1 Sam 8:11, but representing a positive model in contrast to the image Samuel presents.

Torah, a concrete expression of YHWH's covenant with Israel, as a museum piece or a good luck charm (cf. Jer 8:8). Instead it was to accompany him constantly, providing a written reminder of his personal vassal status before YHWH and his primary role as a model of covenant righteousness (cf. Prov 3:1–9).

Third, the king was to read the Torah all the days of his life (Deut 17:19b). The directive is simple, but its importance is highlighted by four infinitive purpose clauses arranged in a chiastic ABBA pattern, with the first and last beginning with "in order that [X happens]" (לְמַעַן + imperfect verb) and the middle two beginning with "in order that X does not happen (לְבִלְתִּי + infinitive construct). Whereas the first three identify specific responses that are dependent on the reading, the last announces the long-range reward for the king and his successors. Even so, all four statements echo earlier injunctions to the people that now become the spiritual and ethical foundations for Israel's monarchy.

First, faithful reading of the Torah is the key to a proper disposition toward YHWH, the divine suzerain. The king is to read it "that he may learn to fear YHWH his God." As is often the case in Deuteronomy and elsewhere, the fear of which he speaks is not terror, but trusting awe that inspires keeping "all the words of this Torah and these ordinances by doing them" (לַעֲשׂוֹתָם). The Torah of Moses provides repeated reminders of the gracious and trustworthy God who has fulfilled his promises to the ancestors by delivering his people from bondage, calling them to covenant relationship with himself, revealing to them his will, and delivering the land of the Canaanites into their hands (cf. 6:20–25).

Second, faithful reading of the Torah is the key to a proper disposition toward one's fellow members of the covenant community. The king is to read the Torah to keep his heart from rising above his brothers. With this warning, which includes a strong biblical idiom for pride, Moses responded explicitly to prevailing Near Eastern patterns of kings elevating themselves high above their people and acting as if they were the center of the universe. In the first clause of verse 20 Moses asserted that the king is not even the greatest among equals—he is one with his brothers. And here lies the paradox: he may have been chosen by YHWH and installed by the people as king over them, but he must resist every temptation to consider himself as essentially superior or of a different genre of humanity.

Third, faithful reading of the Torah is the key to the king's staying on course in his devotion to YHWH. The clause, "[that he not] turn aside from *the command* (הַמִּצְוָה) to the right or to the left,"[10] echoes 5:31–32. As elsewhere, the singular expression, "the command" refers to the Supreme Command (see 6:5); like the people, the king must demonstrate total covenant commitment to YHWH.

Fourth, faithful reading of the Torah is the key to a secure future, described here as lengthened days over his kingdom. Although the statement echoes earlier statements involving the people of Israel,[11] it anticipates a dynastic monarchy and applies to the

---

10. This is equivalent to "walking in his ways" (i.e., "the ways of YHWH"; Deut 8:6; 10:12; 11:22; 19:9; 26:17; 28:9; 30:16; 32:4).

11. For references to the Israelites lengthening their days, see Deut 4:26, 40; 5:33; 11:9; 22:7; 30:18; 32:47. For references to their days lengthening, see 5:16; 6:2; 25:15.

king's household the principle enunciated in the Decalogue: people's actions determine both their own well-being and the well-being of their households (cf. 5:9).

The Historical Significance of the Mosaic Paradigm of Kingship

Within its ancient Near Eastern context, the Mosaic vision of kingship is revolutionary in many respects.

1. Although the kings of other nations often gained power by force and at the expense of their rivals and their subjects, the Israelite kingship will be established in response to a democratic impulse and with the blessing of YHWH.

2. Although foreigners, either usurpers from the outside or imperial overlords, often governed other states, the Israelites were to be governed by one of their own under the imperial reign of YHWH.

3. Although elsewhere in the ancient world monarchs assumed responsibility for three primary administrative duties—defending their people against external threats by leading in battle, defending them against internal threats by administering justice, and defending them against threats from the gods by maintaining the national cult and building temples for the deities—in Israel the king had one primary role: to embody covenant righteousness as spelled out in the Torah, and in so doing act as the exemplary Israelite (cf. 1 Kgs 10:9; 2 Chr 9:8).

4. Although kings of other nations regularly used their office to satisfy their own lust for power, status, and wealth, Israelite kings were always to act as servants of YHWH and in the interests of their people.

5. Although other kings codified laws to protect their own interests and to regulate the conduct of subjects rather than themselves,[12] the Israelite laws were codified by YHWH, interpreted by his spokesman who had no vested interests in the kingship, and then required of the king himself.

6. Although the kings of other nations used epithets like "son of God" and "image of Bel/Shamash"[13] to elevate themselves above their subjects, Deuteronomy applies the former title to the people of Israel (14:1; 32:6, 18; cf. 1:31),[14] and the latter is

---

12. See especially the prologue to the Law Code of Hammurabi in Roth, *Law Collections from Mesopotamia and Asia Minor,* 76–81. This is not to deny extrabiblical evidence for comparable ideals for their kings. See "Advice to a Prince," in Lambert, *Babylonian Wisdom Literature* 113–15; the Ugaritic epic of *Kirta,* in Parker, ed., *Ugaritic Narrative Poetry,* 41, as well as Job 29:7–17 and Prov 31:1–9, which concern non-Israelite rulers.

13. See the characterization of Esarhaddon: "[T]he father of the king, my lord, was the very image of Bel, and the king, my lord, is likewise the image of Bel." See Parpola, *Letters from Assyrian Scholars,* 181 (§228:18–20).

14. Though later texts refer to Israel's kings as "the son of God." See 2 Sam 7:14; 1 Chr 22:10; Ps 89:27–28[26–27]. In these contexts, the "father-son" language functions as a metaphor for the suzerain-vassal relationship that existed between YHWH and the king. (cf. 2 Kgs 16:7). On "divine sonship" of kings in the ancient world see Fossum, "Son of God," 788–89.

missing altogether. Apart from "king" (מֶלֶךְ), the only epithet Israel's monarch may claim was "brother" (אָח) of his people.

The paradigm of kingship spelled out in Deut 17:14–20 should have secured the place of Israel's kings as the appointed rulers over God's people. Occasional echoes of this passage are heard in later texts. Although Joshua did not technically fit this royal paradigm—he was not a king (מֶלֶךְ) chosen by YHWH in response to the people's request and then installed by the people, as Moses' successor at the head of the Israelites—in Josh 1:8 YHWH required of him what this text demanded of the king (note the singular). Psalm 1 opens the Psalter by characterizing the blessed man as one who delights in the Torah and meditates on it day and night (v. 2). If the Psalter is indeed a fundamentally royal document, as some have argued,[15] this psalm serves particularly as a guide for the king on how to read the Torah (specifically Deut).[16]

Deuteronomy 17:14–20 is important for understanding Israel's political history. Several centuries later, when the elders demanded that Samuel install a king over them, their appeal echoed Deut 17:14: "We must have a king over us. Then we'll be like all the other nations" (1 Sam 8:19–20). Samuel seems to have composed his prior "pronouncement concerning the king" (מִשְׁפַּט הַמֶּלֶךְ) in 1 Sam 8:11–17 against the backdrop of Deut 17:16–17. He warned the people that the king they demanded would use his office for selfish ends and run roughshod over their interests. YHWH answered this request by giving them Saul, from the tribe of Benjamin, who had proved by deed and disposition to be like the lowest of the nations (Judg 19–21; cf. Gen 19). But Saul's rule was doomed from the outset, and he served ultimately primarily as a foil for the one YHWH had in mind from the beginning (1 Sam 13:14).[17] And when David prepared to pass the royal mantle to his son Solomon, he appealed to him to keep the charge of YHWH his God, "by walking in his ways, by keeping his ordinances, his commands, and his judgments [concerning covenant righteousness], and his testimonies, as it is written in the Torah of Moses," that he might prosper in all his activities (1 Kgs 2:3, author translation).

The paradigm of kingship established in Deut 17:14–20 provides the lens used by Israel's historians and prophets to evaluate their kings. This is most evident in the portrayal of Solomon. Although he famously constructed the temple for YHWH (David's project), he multiplied horses (1 Kgs 5:6–8[4:26–28]; 10:26–29) and wives (11:1–13), and amassed vast riches for the crown (10:23). To be fair, the historian did not condemn Solomon explicitly for multiplying wealth or horses, but he denounced him sharply for marrying foreign women (11:1–13), forcefully ruling over his countrymen (5:13–18[4:33–5:4]), and breaking the covenant (11:9–13, 33). Ultimately, responsibility for Israel's exile in 586 BCE rested on the shoulders of kings who abused the people and led the nation in apostasy (2 Kgs 24:3–4).[18]

15. Waltke, *Old Testament Theology*, 871–84.

16. Some suggest Psalm 1 anticipates the royal messianic king. See Cole, "Psalms 1–2," in *The Moody Handbook of Messianic Prophecy*, forthcoming.

17. Cf. Block, "My Servant David, 39; DeRouchie, "The Heart of YHWH and His Chosen One," 467–89.

18. On Deut 17:14–20 and the later evaluation of Solomon, see Knoppers, "Rethinking the Relationship between Deuteronomy and the Deuteronomistic History," 393–415.

The Messianic Significance of the Mosaic Paradigm of Kingship

Based on the history of the northern kingdom of Israel recounted in 1 Kgs 12–17 it is evident that the Torah of Moses generally and his vision of kingship specifically had no influence on that nation's kings. Their apostate spirit and political state are reflected in the ubiquitous assessment by the narrator: "They did *the* evil (הָרַע) in the eyes of YHWH."[19] In this expression the article on "the evil" is significant; it always refers primarily to violating the Supreme Command, that is, betraying YHWH and going after other gods (Deut 5:7; cf. 6:13; 10:20; 13:3–4[2–3]). Although David exhibited significant character flaws (acknowledged in 1 Kgs 15:5), the historian's overall assessment of his performance vis-à-vis the Mosaic vision was remarkable. Solomon recognized that David walked before YHWH "in faithfulness, righteousness, and integrity" with him (1 Kgs 3:6); YHWH himself acknowledged that David "walked [before me] . . . with integrity of heart and uprightness, doing according to all that I have commanded you, [and by keeping] my ordinances and my judgments" (1 Kgs 9:4; cf. 3:14, author's translation). As for the narrator's own assessment, unlike Solomon, whose foreign wives turned his heart away to other gods, David's heart was "wholly true" with YHWH his God (1 Kgs 11:4; cf. 15:3; 2 Chr 17:3) and was full after YHWH (11:6),[20] a fidelity that was demonstrated generally in "doing the right thing in the eyes of YHWH" (15:3; 2 Chr 17:3, author's translation) and specifically in obedience to the revealed will of YHWH (11:34, 38; 14:8; 15:5; 16:2; 2 Chr 7:17; 28:1; 29:2; 34:2).

When Solomon had completed all his construction projects (including the temple) YHWH appeared to him a second time at Gibeon and reminded him of David's paradigmatic faithfulness (1 Kgs 9:2–9), and the importance of following this model if he and his successors hoped to be secure on the throne. However, he also added a strong note of the kings' representative role before the people:

> If you or your sons turn away from following Me and do not keep My commands—My statutes that I have set before you—and if you go and serve other gods and worship them, I will cut off Israel from the land I gave them, and I will reject the temple I have sanctified for My name. Israel will become an object of scorn and ridicule among all the peoples. Though this temple is *now* exalted, every passerby will be appalled and will mock. They will say: Why did the Lord do this to this land and this temple? Then they will say: Because they abandoned the LORD their God who brought their ancestors out of the land of Egypt. They clung to other gods and worshiped and served them. Because of this, the LORD brought all this ruin on them (CSB).

---

19. 1 Kgs 15:34 (Baasha); 16:19, 25 (Omri); 16:30; 21:20, 25 (Ahab); 22:52 (Ahaziah); 2 Kgs 3:2 (Jehoram); 8:27 (Ahaziah); 13:2 (Jehoahaz); 13:11 (Jehoash); 14:24 (Jeroboam II); 15:9 (Zechariah); 15:18 (Menahem); 15:24 (Pekahiah); 15:28 (Pekah); 17:2 (Hoshea). Jeroboam I (son of Nebat) is identified as the paradigmatic apostate king (1 Kgs 15:34; 16:19; 22:52; 2 Kgs 13:2, 11; 14:24; 15:9, 18, 24, 28).

20. "To be full after YHWH" ("follow the LORD completely," CSB) is an awkward idiom, used elsewhere only of Caleb, in contrast to the rest of the Israelites (Num 32:11–12; Deut 1:36; Josh 14:8, 9, 14).

Samuel had warned Israel of the apparently inevitable administrative style of the kind of king they demanded, though without explicit reference to the kings' obligations to the Torah (1 Sam 8:11–18). This contrasts with YHWH's warning to Solomon in this text. Remarkably he said nothing about how well the kings administered justice in the land, or how successful they were in military conflicts with outsiders; his only declared concern was their fidelity to YHWH and to his covenant with Israel. On these counts, David set the royal standard for both the northern kingdom of Israel[21] and the southern kingdom of Judah (1 Kgs 9:4; 11:30–39; 2 Chr 7:17). With regard to the kings of Judah, where comparisons are drawn, some results are negative,[22] some are qualified,[23] and a handful are positive: Asa (1 Kgs 15:11), Jehoshaphat (2 Chr 17:3), Hezekiah (2 Kgs 18:3), Josiah (2 Kgs 22:2).

Solomon and Josiah present particularly interesting cases. Although Solomon began with deep covenant commitment (i.e., "love," Hebrew אָהֵב) for YHWH, demonstrated in imitating David ethically (1 Kgs 3:3), his extraordinary wisdom (1 Kgs 3:4–28; 5:9–14[4:29–34]; 10:1–25), and piety, and his faithful completion of David's temple project (note his dedication prayer in 1 Kgs 8), by the end of his life everything had changed. Preoccupied with private construction projects (1 Kgs 9:17–19, 24), and driven by the lure of wealth (9:26–28), he exploited and abused his own subjects (9:15, 20–22), leading to both human and divine resistance that resulted ultimately in the disintegration of the kingdom (11:9–43). While the narrator notes other features of his reign, his closing critique is scathing, noting particularly his violation of the three prohibitions in Deut 17:16–17: his excessive militarism, symbolized by the multiplication of horses (1 Kgs 10:26, 28–29; cf. Deut 17:16), his excessive multiplication of wives, who did indeed lead his heart astray (1 Kgs 11:1–8; cf. Deut 17:17a), and his accumulation of wealth (1 Kgs 9:26–28; 10:11–23).

The opening image of Solomon is impressive; he began as a humble son of David, awed by his new role as heir to the Davidic throne and kingdom and pleading with YHWH for a special gift of wisdom to rule well (3:3–9)—a prayer that YHWH answered immediately in superlative degree in the form of a dream (3:10–15). The concluding image is pathetic; Solomon ended as the consummate fool, driven by lust of every sort and setting the nation on a downward spiritual spiral from which it would never recover. Although the apostasy is characterized as personal and domestic, resulting in the disintegration of the Davidic hold on the throne (11:11–43), ultimately, as the king went, so went the kingdom. In 11:32–33 the narrator intentionally generalizes the resulting spiritual problem with plural forms, whose antecedent is "all the tribes of Israel" (11:32):

---

21. Compare Ahijah's detailed assessment of Jeroboam I in 1 Kgs 14:7–16, and the narrator's accusing Jeroboam of driving Israel away from YHWH and causing them to commit extreme sin (וְהֶחֱטִיאָם חֲטָאָה גְדוֹלָה) in 2 Kgs 17:21. Indeed, in contrast to David, the paradigmatic pursuer of righteousness (cf. Deut 16:20), Jeroboam is repeatedly identified as the paradigmatic pursuer of evil; those explicitly compared with Jeroboam include Baasha (1 Kgs 15:34; 16:2), Omri (16:19, 26), Ahab (16:31), Ahaziah (22:52), Jehoram (2 Kgs 3:3), Jehu (10:31), Jehoahaz (13:2), Jehoash (13:11), Jeroboam II (14:24), Zechariah (15:9), Menahem (15:18), Pekahiah (15:24), Pekah (15:28).

22. Solomon (1 Kgs 11:4, 6), Rehoboam (14:22), Abijam (15:3), Ahaz (2 Kgs 16:2; 2 Chr 28:1),

23. Solomon (1 Kgs 3:3), Amaziah (2 Kgs 14:3–4).

> For they [the tribes of Israel] have abandoned Me; they have bowed the knee to Ashtoreth, the goddess of the Sidonians, to Chemosh, the god of Moab, and to Milcom, the god of the Ammonites. They have not walked in My ways to do what is right in My eyes and to carry out My statutes and My judgments as his father David did (CSB).

Josiah represents the opposite kind of paradigm. The narrator's assessments of the man are thoroughly deuteronomic from beginning to end:

> He did what was right in YHWH's sight and walked in all the ways of his ancestor David; he did not turn to the right or the left. (2 Kgs 22:2).

> Before him there was no king like him, who turned to YHWH with all his heart/mind (לֵב), and with all his being (נֶפֶשׁ), and with all his resources (מְאֹד), according to all the Torah of Moses, nor did any like him arise after him (2 Kgs 23:25).[24]

As if to highlight the link between the narrative and Deut 17:14–20, the entire account (2 Kgs 22:1–23:30) is driven by the narrator's (and Josiah's) interest in the Torah document—the scroll of Deuteronomy—that his workers found in the temple. Although Josiah's life was headed in a positive direction even before the discovery of the scroll in the Temple (22:1–8), the discovery gave added impetus to his personal spiritual commitments and focus to his administration. With exemplary humility, upon hearing the Torah read, Josiah recognized the desperate spiritual state of his nation and immediately sought further guidance from YHWH regarding an appropriate response to the crisis (vv. 12–13). YHWH's answer was twofold: (1) Because of their history of apostasy, the doom of what remained of the nation of Israel had been irrevocably decreed (vv. 15–17). (2) Because Josiah's own heart was tender (רַךְ) and he humbled himself before YHWH his own future was guaranteed—he would die in peace and be spared the sight of the horrors to come. Unlike Solomon, who in the end embodied all that was wrong with his people, Josiah stood out as a paragon of righteousness in contrast to a thoroughly corrupted people. Almost as an Enoch figure, because he was spiritually out of step with his generation and more at home with God than with his countrymen, YHWH removed him before the disaster struck.

For Josiah knowledge of his personal destiny did not result in diminished deuteronomic fervor. On the contrary, not satisfied with refurbishing the Temple after generations of neglect and abuse sponsored by his predecessors, he arranged for a public covenant renewal ritual in Jerusalem (23:1–3) and oversaw the observance with unprecedented enthusiasm of the foundational national celebration, the Festival of Passover (vv. 21–23). He purged Jerusalem and Judah of all vestiges of pagan worship (23:24–25), and then extended the purge to the territories of what used to be the northern kingdom of Israel, even though at the time it was an Assyrian province (23:4–20). The only non-spiritual act reported by the narrator resulted in his death. With striking irony, while

---

24. Although the narrator changes the verb from אָהַב, "to love," to שׁוּב אֶל, "to turn to," the triad of expressions, "with all his heart/mind, and with all his being, and with all his resources" (בְּכָל־לְבָבוֹ וּבְכָל־נַפְשׁוֹ וּבְכָל־מְאֹדוֹ), derives verbatim from the Shema in Deut 6:4–5.

trying at Megiddo to intercept the Egyptian army, which was headed north to join the Assyrians in battle against the rising Babylonians, the man who had been promised a peaceful demise died a violent death, a victim of an apparently "random" arrow (23:28–30; cf. 2 Chr 35:20–27). Ironically, as an act of divine mercy, contrary to the promise of Deut 17:20, the life of the occupant of the Davidic throne who most fully embodied the Mosaic vision of royal righteousness while occupying the throne of David was cut short, rather than extended. Apparently, Jerusalem's appointment with destiny in 586 BCE had been written irrevocably on her calendar; not even the efforts of a righteous Josiah could halt fulfillment of the curses of Deuteronomy in all their divine fury.[25]

With Josiah's demise, it was only a matter of time before the nation would fall. The narrator characterized all of his successors as he had so many of the northern kings: "they committed *the evil* (הָרַע) in the eyes of YHWH according to all that their father/fathers had done."[26] If the northern kingdom fell to the Assyrians because of the people's persistent rebellion against YHWH (note the deuteronomic flavor of the narrator's interpretation in 2 Kgs 17:7–18), the narrator repeatedly blames the kings for having led them down this course.[27] Although, of the Judean kings the narrator explicitly holds only Manasseh responsible for leading the people down this sinful path (2 Kgs 21:11, 16, 17), with few exceptions they were equally guilty of sponsoring state and regional apostasy (cf. 2 Kgs 24:3–4). However, the demise of the nation and the Davidic dynasty in 586 BCE left the people wondering not only about the veracity of YHWH's promise of an eternal Davidic dynasty (2 Sam 7:13, 16, 29; 1 Kgs 2:33, 45; 9:5; 1 Chr 17:12, 14; 22:10; 28:4; Ps 89:30, 37[29, 36]; 132:12), but also about the relevance of Deut 17:14–20.

The ending to the books of Kings is auspicious: after the death of Zedekiah and with him the Davidic dynasty, all hope seemed lost (Ps 89:47–52[46–51])—except that mysteriously the king of Babylon released a 55-year-old Judean from prison, who happened to be the surviving link to the original house of David, and elevated him to a prominent position in the Babylonian court (2 Kgs 25:27–30). With Jehoiachin's release the royal hope was reignited, albeit as only a glimmering coal. However, the question remained: given the history of the monarchy in Israel, even if the Davidic dynasty would be restored, what would prevent it from going down the same path once again?

Enter the prophetic messianic hope. Like Deut 17:14–20, earlier psalmists had linked the Davidic throne with the pursuit of righteousness (Ps 45:1–8[1–7]; 89:30–38[29–37]), but it was left to the prophets to develop this theme. The eighth-century BCE prophet Isaiah looked forward to the birth of a child who would bear the throne names of "Wonderful Counselor, Mighty God, Eternal Father, Prince of Peace," and who would secure David's throne forever by pursuing "justice and righteousness" (מִשְׁפָּט וּצְדָקָה, Isa 9:5–6[6–7]; cf. 1 Kgs 10:9). This "branch" (נֵצֶר) from the stem/roots of Jesse would be

---

25. Cf. YHWH's rejection of Noah, Daniel, and Job as lightning rods to stave off his fury in Ezek 14:12–23.

26. The assessment for each is virtually identical, with slight variation in the identity of the models: Jehoahaz (2 Kgs 23:32, his fathers), Jehoiakim (23:37, his fathers), Jehoiachin (24:9, his father); Zedekiah (24:19, Jehoiakim).

27. With Jeroboam as the paradigmatic evil-doer who led Israel into sin: 1 Kgs 14:16; 15:26, 30, 34; 16:2, 13, 19, 26; 21:22; 22:52; 2 Kgs 3:3; 10:29, 31; 13:2, 6, 11; 14:24; 15:9, 18, 24, 28; 23:15.

girded with the belt of righteousness and faithfulness (אֵזוֹר צֶדֶק וֶאֱמוּנָה), and through his righteous administration of justice, peace will come not only to Israel, but also to the entire cosmos (Deut 11:1–10).[28] Later in Isaiah, the four Servant Songs (Isa 42:1–9; 49:1–6; 50:4–9; 52:13—53:12) characterize the Servant of YHWH (עֶבֶד יהוה), clearly a Davidic figure,[29] as the vassal of YHWH *par excellence*.

It is extremely significant that the word for "righteous"/"righteousness" (צֶדֶק/צְדָקָה), so significant in Deut 16:20, occurs in the first and last of these Servant Songs. Isaiah 42:6 portrays the call of the Servant as an act of divine righteousness (צֶדֶק); he always acts in accord with his covenant commitments. Indeed, he has appointed him as "a covenant for the people" (בְּרִית עָם) and "a light to the nations" (אוֹר גּוֹיִם). In the last Servant Song YHWH acknowledges that he is the embodiment of righteousness, identifying him as "the Righteous One, My Servant" (צַדִּיק עַבְדִּי, 53:11), who makes many righteous (יַצְדִּיק) by offering himself as a "restitution offering" (אָשָׁם, v. 10), and bearing their iniquities (עֲוֹנֹתָם הוּא יִסְבֹּל, v. 11). Far from his heart being lifted up above his countrymen (cf. Deut 17:20), he is portrayed in this Song as the good shepherd, who gives up his life for the sheep (John 10:15).

Jeremiah had less to say about the Messiah than Isaiah, but what little he says is directly related to the Mosaic vision of kingship in Deut 17:14–20. Speaking for YHWH, in Jer 23:1–6 he pronounced doom on the Davidic kings who, instead of caring for the sheep, had cared only for themselves, and in so doing had driven the flock away (he held them accountable for the exile, vv. 1–2). But he promised that YHWH would one day regather the sheep (Israel) and cause them to flourish again, and appoint over them shepherds who would actually care for (רָעָה) the flock and secure their well-being (vv. 3–4). This short oracle reaches its climax with YHWH's promise that he will raise up for David "a righteous Branch" (צֶמַח צַדִּיק), who will reign as king by acting justly and righteously" (וְעָשָׂה מִשְׁפָּט וּצְדָקָה). His effectiveness (הִשְׂכִּיל) will be demonstrated by Judah's salvation (ישׁע) and Israel's security (בֶּטַח). The Torah righteousness that he will embody and that he will secure for his people will be reflected in his title: "YHWH Our Righteousness" (יהוה צִדְקֵנוּ, vv. 5–6).

Although Ezekiel does not use the word "righteous" or "righteousness" in Ezek 34, it is obvious in this chapter that the exiled prophet had access to Jeremiah's prophecy and intentionally developed it further.[30] After pronouncing doom on the dynasty of David for having misused their role and abused their people (Ezek 34:1–10), YHWH promised to regather the scattered flock, bring them back to their homeland, and personally care for them, including ensuring that the sheep do not abuse each other (vv. 11–22). The oracle reaches its climax in vv. 23–24, where YHWH announced that he would set over his people "a single shepherd, my servant David," who will exercise his princely role by feeding and caring for the sheep. This would confirm YHWH's "covenant of peace" (בְּרִית שָׁלוֹם), which will secure for them eternal well-being and security in the land (vv. 25–31).

---

28. For fuller development of the Isaianic vision of the righteous messianic king, see Isa 32.

29. On the Servant of YHWH as a royal Davidic figure, see Block, "My Servant David," 49–55.

30. For discussion of the relationship between these two texts, see Block, *Ezekiel Chapters 25–48*, 275–77.

As David recognized in 2 Sam 7:18–26, the appointment of the Davidic king confirmed YHWH's commitment to Israel as his covenant people (cf. Ezek 34:24a, 31).

One more echo of these notions appears in Mic 5:1–4a[2–5a]. The prophet Micah foresaw the coming of a ruler from humble Bethlehem who would rise and shepherd his people, his "brothers" (אֶחָיו, the same expression used in Deut 17:20; "countrymen," CSB) in the strength and name of YHWH (Mic 5:1–4a[2–5a]). Although he would shepherd his own people, his greatness would be acknowledged to the ends of the earth. Indeed, he will secure universal well-being (שָׁלוֹם).

In the New Testament, it becomes clear that the Mosaic vision of kingship was ultimately fulfilled by Jesus the Messiah, the son of David. This is evident especially in the portrayal of Jesus as the suffering servant of Isa 53, echoes of which occur throughout the New Testament.[31] But it also appears in Jesus' own statement when, at the time of his baptism, he was introduced as the Messiah: he needed to be baptized "to fulfill all righteousness" (πληρῶσαι πᾶσαν δικαιοσύνην, Matt 3:15). Immediately thereafter the voice from heaven proclaimed the significance of this event: "This is my beloved Son. I take delight in Him!" (Matt 3:17; cf. Mark 9:7; Luke 3:22). This is not only a declaration of Jesus' membership within the Trinity, but also an announcement of his Davidic messianic status. All three expressions have messianic significance. "My Son" (i.e., "son of God") is used of the Davidic king in Ps 2:6–8 and 89:27–28[26–27]).[32] "Beloved" (ὁ ἀγαπητός) has its roots in the Hebrew verb, אָהַב, "to love," and probably alludes to YHWH's covenant commitment to the Davidic house. The verb is never used of David, but is used of Solomon with YHWH as subject in 2 Sam 12:24 and Neh 13:26.[33] "Take delight in" (εὐδοκέω) speaks of the special favor Jesus enjoyed with the Father, as in 1 Chr 29:23, "And Solomon sat on YHWH's throne as king in place of his father David, and he was favored/taken delight in" (LXX).[34] In short, Jesus is the Davidic king whom YHWH had in mind from the beginning (cf. Deut 17:15; 1 Sam 13:14). In fulfilling all righteousness, Jesus embodied perfectly the ideals of covenant relationship as represented in the Torah. He was the climax of the royal metanarrative underlying the entire First Testament and his kingdom is secure.

Jesus' declaration that he came not to abolish the Law and the Prophets, but to fulfill [them] (Matt 5:17) ought also to be viewed in relation to Deut 17:14–20. Based on the broader context this cannot mean that he came to terminate the authority or relevance of the First Testament Scriptures for his followers (cf. vv. 18–19). Although here the expression, ὁ νόμος ("the law") designates the entire Pentateuch—in keeping with custom by New Testament times—in Deut 17:18 and in most occurrences in the

---

31. Matt 8:17; Luke 22:37; John 6:45; 10:15; 12:38; Acts 8:32–33; 13:34; Rom 2:24; 10:15, 16; 15:21; 2 Cor 6:17; 1 Pet 2:22.

32. These texts are rooted in 2 Sam 7:14–15, where YHWH declares of Solomon, "I will be a father to him and he will be a son to me." This has long been acknowledged as an adaptation of the adoption formula. See Paul, 173–85, esp. 178. In Ps 89:28[27] the Davidic king is also called YHWH's "firstborn" (בְּכֹר).

33. When used of Abraham in Isa 41:8, אֹהֲבִי, usually translated "my friend," clearly refers to him as YHWH's vassal covenant partner (cf. vv. 9–10).

34. Here the passive form, εὐδοκήθη, translates Hebrew וַיִּצְלַח, "and he prospered/was effective."

First Testament (e.g., Josh 1:8; 1 Kgs 2:3; 2 Kgs 22:8–16; 23:25; Ezra 7:6; Neh 8:1–18; Ps 1:2; Jer 8:8; Dan 9:11, 13) הַתּוֹרָה (consistently rendered in LXX as *ho nomos*) refers primarily to the written version of the Torah that the king was to copy for himself in Deut 17:18, which is largely our book of Deuteronomy. For Jesus, the Messianic descendant of David, this book had special authority. In the context of the Sermon on the Mount, for him "to fulfill" the Torah meant in part to recover for his followers the spirit of Moses as declared in the latter's addresses in Deut and encapsulated especially in Deut 10:12–11:1. That Jesus quoted from and alluded to Deut more frequently than to any other book of the First Testament reinforces this conclusion.

At its heart the Torah is not merely about keeping the commands as a duty to God. Rather, keeping the Torah is essentially and primarily a matter of the heart—with awe and gratitude saying, "not my will, but yours be done" (Luke 22:42). In the words of Moses, for God's people it means to fear YHWH, to walk in all his ways, to demonstrate covenant love for him, to serve him with all one's being, and last, to keep his commands (Deut 10:12–13), in response to the favors he has lavished on them (Deut 10:14–11:1). This was the essence of the surpassing righteousness of which Jesus spoke in Matt 5:20, in contrast to the righteousness of the scribes and Pharisees, who were supercilious with their tithe, but had neglected the weightier matters of Torah: practicing justice, mercy, and faithfulness.[35] As the Messiah, Jesus' mission was not only to recover the essence of the Torah and to teach it to his followers, but also to embody and model it perfectly. When, at the time of his crucifixion the crowd in Jerusalem screamed, "We have no king but Caesar!" (John 19:15), tragically they flushed away a thousand years of Messianic hope. Nevertheless, one day, Israel will welcome her King, as Jesus foretold in Matt 23:37–39, "He who comes in the name of the Lord is the blessed One." Then Israel and all creation will finally experience the rule of the righteous King anticipated in Deut 17:14–20.

---

35. Here Greek κρίσις, ἔλεος, and πίστις correspond to Deuteronomy's מִשְׁפָּט, חֶסֶד, and אֱמוּנָה, respectively.

17

A Prophet Like Moses

Another Look at Deuteronomy 18:9–22[1]

Introduction

IT IS A LITTLE more than fifteen years since I first expressed publicly my preliminary interpretation of Moses' anticipation of "a prophet like me" (נָבִיא כָּמֹנִי) in the context of a broader study of ancient Israel's perceptions of the Messiah.[2] Since at that time I had not yet completed my commentary work on the book of Deuteronomy, my conclusions were exploratory. The time has come to return to the subject for a more focused study. After an evaluative survey of the history of the messianic interpretation, which prevails in many circles, especially among theologians and New Testament scholars, and among a few Hebrew Bible scholars, I shall take a closer look at Deut 18:9–22.

The Roots of the Messianic Interpretation of Deuteronomy 18:15

Although the boundaries among these interpretations blurred, historically, "A prophet like Moses" has been understood in four different ways.[3] First, most First Testament scholars assume a distributive sense for the singular verbs, יָקִים, "he will raise up" (v. 15) and אָקִים, "I will raise up" (v. 18), and the singular object, נָבִיא, "a prophet," in both statements. By this interpretation YHWH will continue the prophetic institution that he established in Israel through Moses, the paradigmatic prophet, by raising up prophets from time to time.[4]

---

1. I am grateful to my colleagues, M. Daniel Carroll Rodas and Carlos Sosa Siliezar for reading earlier drafts of this paper and for offering many helpful suggestions for its improvement. Carlos has been especially helpful in expanding my New Testament bibliographic horizons. Of course, any infelicities in presentation or flaws in argument are my own.

2. Block, "My Servant David," 26–32.

3. For summaries of the common interpretations and representatives of each, see Allison, *The New Moses*, 73–75; Yoon-Hee Kim, "The 'Prophet Like Moses,'" 86–100; Rydelnik, *The Messianic Hope*, 56–64.

4. See, for example, Driver, *Deuteronomy*, 226; Tigay, *Deuteronomy*, 175; McConville,

Second, beginning with Moses, and then carried on through Joshua and Samuel, YHWH would raise up a series of prophetic rulers over Israel. The third–fourth century CE Christian historian, Eusebius, wrote,

> Moses prophesied forty years; then Joshua, the son of Nun, prophesied thirty years. Joshua lived one hundred and ten years and pitched the holy tabernacle in Shiloh. After that, Samuel became a prophet. Then, by the will of God, Saul was chosen by Samuel to be king, and he died after ruling twenty one years. Then David his son ruled . . . .[5]

Third, linking Mal 3:1 and 3:23[4:5] with Deut 18:15, 18, some in the Qumran community responsible for the Dead Sea Scrolls developed the notion of an eschatological prophet, distinct from both the Davidic and priestly messiahs.[6]

Fourth, the dominant interpretation in Christian circles understands the prophet like Moses in Deut 18:15–18 as a singular eschatological figure, the Messiah. This interpretation is grounded especially in Peter's and Stephen's quotation of statements in Deut 18:15–19 in Acts 3:22–23 and 7:37, respectively. Although this essay will touch on the other interpretations, our goal here is primarily to assess this last view.

According to some, the Messianic interpretation of the prophet like Moses begins as early as the book of Deuteronomy itself. John Sailhamer asserts that a prophet was yet to come, and that the author who ended the Pentateuch understood Moses' words in Deut 18 precisely as NT authors did. The "Prophet like Moses" was indeed the expected Messiah—and he had not yet appeared.[7]

Assuming that Deut 34 reflects an exilic or post-exilic context, Sailhamer and others find confirmation of this interpretation in the account of Moses' death. He interprets the assessment in 34:10 ("Since then no prophet like Moses has arisen in Israel") to mean that none of the prophets in Israel's history has matched Moses. Accordingly, the comment calls on hearers to look forward to "the coming of an individual future prophet," whom he takes to be the Messiah.[8]

Many texts in the Hebrew Bible exhibit connections with Deut 18:9–22, especially in the characterization of prophets.[9] However, not a single First Testament text hints

---

Deuteronomy, 302–3.

5. As translated by C. R. Holladay, *Fragments from Hellenistic Jewish Authors*, vol. 1, *Historians*, 115. For discussion, see Meeks, *Prophet-King*, 149–52.

6. 1QS 9:11; 4Q175 *Testimonia*. The latter links Deut 18:18–20; 33:8–11; and Num 24:15–17. For the text in translation, see Martínez and Tigchelaar, *The Dead Sea Scrolls*, 1.357. All translations of Qumran texts derive from this publication in two volumes (1997, 1998). On the paucity of evidence for hope of an eschatological prophet at Qumran, see Bauckham, "Jewish Messianism," 212–15.

7. Sailhamer, "The Messiah and the Hebrew Bible," 5–23.

8. Sailhamer, *The Meaning of the Pentateuch*, 17–19. For similar interpretations, see Rydelnik, *The Messianic Hope*, 56–64; Y. Kim, "The 'Prophet Like Moses.'" See also Akin, "The Prophet Who is Like and Greater Than Moses, 485–94.

9. Note especially specific references to YHWH putting his words in the prophets' mouths or YHWH's words being from a prophet's mouth (Deut 18:18; cf. Num 22:38; 23:5, 12, 16; 1 Kgs 17:24; 2 Chr 36:21, 22; Isa 51:16; Jer 1:9; 5:14), and later prophets' portrayal of their conflicts with false prophets (Jer 23:16–22; Ezek 12:21—13:16).

at a messianic interpretation of "the prophet like Moses." Indeed, one could argue for the opposite. Everyone knows that the Hebrew word מָשִׁיחַ ("Messiah") derives from the root מָשַׁח, "to anoint." We also know that at least one prophet was anointed (1 Kgs 19:16).[10] However, although Deut 18:15-19 suggests that Moses was formally inducted into the prophetic office on "the day of the assembly" at Horeb (cf. Exod 19:9, 18-19; Deut 5:22-33),[11] the text is as silent on an anointing ritual for Moses as it is for Aaron, who was Moses' "prophet."[12]

The only possible hints of a messianic prophet, whether eschatological or otherwise, occur at the end of the prophetic line in Mal 3:1 ("See, I am sending my messenger, and he will prepare the way before me") and 3:23[4:5] ("See, before the great and fearful day of YHWH arrives I will send to you the prophet Elijah"). However, while in the first instance the prophet prepares the way for YHWH, and in the second he announces the day of YHWH, neither statement identifies him as an anointed one or even as the primary anticipated subject, and the links to Deut 18:15 are indirect at best. To be sure, the narrative of 1 Kgs 17:24 speaks of YHWH putting his words in Elijah's mouth (cf. Deut 18:18), and 1 Kgs 19:8-17 has him back at Horeb, the mountain of divine revelation to which Moses had brought the people, and where he had been inducted into the prophetic office. However, neither image is messianic or eschatological. Malachi's comment not only signaled the end of the prophetic institution as the Israelites had known it,[13] but also planted fresh seeds when he associated the name Elijah with an eschatological figure whose arrival would mark a new day in Israel's story. In any case, linking Mal 3:23[4:5] with "the prophet like me" creates tension with the preceding verse, which sees Moses as a figure from the past ("*Remember* the Torah of Moses"; 3:22[4:4]), in contrast to Elijah, who is clearly a future figure and whose anticipated role will differ significantly from the description in Deut 18:9-22.

The notion of an eschatological prophet surfaces occasionally in the intertestamental literature. Sirach 48:10 speaks of "an appointed time" when Elijah would "calm the

---

10. Otherwise First Testament evidence for prophecy as an office into which one could be inducted by anointing is extremely slight. Apart from 1 Kgs 19:16, Groningen (*Messianic Revelation*, 33), can cite only Ps 105:15 (= 1 Chr 16:22).

11. Kibbe (*Godly Fear or Ungodly Failure?*, 24-33) rightly argues that a significant purpose of YHWH's testing Israel at Sinai (cf. Exod 19:20) was to assess their confidence in Moses as the authorized mediator between himself and the people.

12. Although Miriam was a prophet (נְבִיאָה, Exod 15:20), Aaron is never identified as a prophet of YHWH; his role in relation to Moses was analogous to the role of a prophet (נָבִיא) in relation to God (Exod 7:1), that is, he functioned as Moses' mouthpiece. His role in relation to God was always priestly.

13. Compare Josephus' comment, "because of the failure of the exact succession of prophets" (διὰ τὸ μὴ γενέσθαι τὴν τῶν προφητῶν ἀκριβῆ διαδοχήν, *Against Apion* 1.41), and the rabbinic view reflected in *Tosefta Sotah* 13.2, "When the last prophets — Haggai, Zechariah, and Malachi died, the Holy Spirit ceased from Israel," with *Seder Olam Rabbah* 30, "Until then, the prophets were prophesying by means of [or in accordance with] the Holy Spirit. From then on, turn your attention to, and obey the sages." However, several have rightly noted that these comments did not mean the absolute end of prophecy in Israel. *Baba Bathra* 12a identifies that moment as the destruction of the Temple in Jerusalem. See further, R. Gray, *Prophetic Figures*, 7-34, developing further the views of Barton, *The Oracles of God*, 13-95; idem, "The Law and the Prophets," 4-7.

wrath of God before it breaks out in fury, to turn the hearts of parents to their children, and to restore the tribes of Jacob." In 1 Macc 14:41 "The Jews and their priests have resolved that Simon [Maccabee] should be their leader and high priest forever, until a trustworthy prophet should arise." Similar expectations are attested in the Qumran texts, as in 1QS 9:9-11:

> They should not depart from any counsel of the Torah in order to walk in complete stubbornness of their heart, but instead shall be ruled by the first directives which the men of the Community began to be taught until the prophet comes, and the Messiahs of Aaron and Israel.[14]

Remarkably this text appears to distinguish "the prophet" (נביא, without article) from "the Messiahs of Aaron and Israel" (משיחי אהרון וישראל).[15] 4Q558 also speaks of God sending Elijah, but it is too fragmentary to yield much additional information. Sometimes dubbed "Messianic Apocalypse," 4Q521 offers more promise:

> [. . . for the heav]ens and the earth will listen to his anointed one (משיחו), [and all th]at is in them will not turn away from the precepts of the holy ones. Strengthen yourselves, you who are seeking the Lord, in his service! Will you not in this encounter the Lord, all those who hope in their heart? For the Lord will consider the pious and call the righteous by name, and his spirit will hover upon the poor, and he will renew the faithful with his strength. For he will honor the pious upon the throne of an eternal kingdom, freeing prisoners, giving sight to the blind, straightening out the twis[ted.] And for[e]ver shall I cling to [those who h]ope, and in his mercy [. . .] and the fru[it of . . .] not be delayed. And the Lord will perform marvellous acts such as have not existed, just as he sa[id, for] he will heal the badly wounded and will make the dead live; he will proclaim good news to the poor and [. . .] he will lead the [. . .] and enrich the hungry. [. . .] and all [. . . .].[16]

The echoes of Ps 146 and Isa 61:1-2 (as well as 52:7) are obvious, and the expression, משיחו ("his anointed") links this "Messiah" with the anointed figure of Isa 61:1. Although many identify this person as an "anointed eschatological prophet," presumably an Elijah-like figure,[17] a fragment of column III of the same document, 4Q521 3:1-6, strengthens the link with Mal 3:24[4:6]:

> . . . and the law of your favour. And I will free them with [. . .] it is su[re:] The fathers will return towards the sons. [. . .] which the blessing of the Lord in his

---

14. As translated by Martínez and Tigchelaar, 1.92-93.
15. For discussion of this text, see Hurst, "Did Qumran Expect Two Messiahs?" 157-80.
16. Martínez and Tigchelaar, 2.1045.
17. Thus Collins, *The Scepter and the Star*, 117-22. Collins makes this identification despite admitting the paucity of evidence for the anointing of prophets in the Hebrew Bible, but with the support of CD 2:12 and 1QM 11:7, which refer to prophets of the past as "anointed ones."

good will [. . .] May the [ea]rth rejoice in all the plac[es . . .] fo[r] all Israel in the rejoicing of [. . .] and the [. . .].[18]

However, it seems best to interpret this text as referring to two different persons, a prophetic figure who serves as a new Elijah, and the royal Messiah, whose arrival he would announce.[19]

Given the verbal nature of the mission of the person anointed by YHWH in Isa 61:1, it is not surprising that most critical scholars identify the speaker here as a prophetic herald, who announces a message of good news,[20] and in so doing associate this person with the servant figure of Isa 40–55. I have no objection to the latter identification, but as John Oswalt has correctly noted, this person does not "simply hurl words at the poor." Rather, he inaugurates a reign of righteousness and justice, and he sets the captives free.[21] No prophet has this authority. And with the Spirit of YHWH upon him, this anointed person is to be linked with the shoot/branch from the stem/roots of Jesse on whom the Spirit of YHWH rests in Isa 11:1–5.[22] Some interpret the linking of this passage with the servant and the Messiah in Luke 4:17–21 as the early Christian church's "legitimate reader response" to Isa 61.[23] However, Jesus' appropriation of the role of the anointed one in this passage is based not merely on a new reading; it accords perfectly with a grammatical historical interpretation of the text itself. In any case, this text exhibits no links with Deut 18:9–22.

We find further evidence for the anticipation of an eschatological Elijah-like prophet (à la Malachi) in the New Testament Gospels. Following his account of the transfiguration of Jesus on a high mountain in the company of Elijah and Moses, in Matt 17:10–13 (// Mark 9:11–13) the evangelist records a snippet of a conversation between Jesus and his disciples:

> The disciples asked Jesus, "Why do the scribes say that Elijah must come first?"
>
> He replied, "Elijah is indeed coming and he will restore all things; but I tell you that Elijah has already come, and they did not recognize him. Instead, they did to him whatever they pleased. In the same way the Son of Man is about to suffer at their hands.

---

18. Martínez and Tigchelaar, 2.1045.

19. So also, Puech, "Some Remarks on 4Q246 and 4Q521, 559–61; Strathearn, "4Q521 and What It Might Mean for Q 3–7," 395–424. To these Second Temple Judaism texts we should also add the tradition of the Samaritans, for whom the notion of the restorer figure, the *Taheb,* who was the prophet like Moses, was rooted in Deut 18:15, 18. Significantly this figure was both prophet and king, though apparently, he was disconnected from the Davidic Messiah. Thus Bowman, "Samaritan Studies," 310. For further study on the Taheb in Samaritan thought, see 298–327; idem, "Early Samaritan Eschatology," 63–72; Meeks, *The Prophet-King,* 246–54. For an innovative approach to the relationship between Jesus as Messiah and the Messiahs in Second Temple Judaism, see Novenson, *Christ among the Messiahs.*

20. For further discussion, see Childs, *Isaiah,* 501–8.

21. Oswalt, *Isaiah Chapters 40–66,* 561–68.

22. So also, Oswalt, *Isaiah,* 564.

23. Thus Childs, *Isaiah,* 505.

Then the disciples understood that he was speaking to them about John the Baptist (NRSV).

Jesus' final comment is significant. Undoubtedly based on Malachi, he acknowledged that the scribes' anticipation of the arrival of the eschatological prophet was correct. But even more significant for the present discussion is the evangelist's affirmation of the disciples' identification of John the Baptist as that prophet. This obviously excludes Jesus from consideration for that role.

We may also find evidence for the anticipation of "an eschatological prophet" in Jewish circles in the Second Temple Period in the Gospel of John. In John 1:19–34 the evangelist reports a conversation between priests and Levites on the one hand and John the Baptist on the other:

> [19] This is the testimony given by John when the Jews sent priests and Levites from Jerusalem to ask him, "Who are you?"
>
> [20] He confessed and did not deny it, but confessed, "I am not the Messiah."
>
> [21] And they asked him, "What then? Are you Elijah?"
>
> He said, "I am not."
>
> "Are you the prophet?"
>
> He answered, "No."
>
> [22] Then they said to him, "Who are you? Let us have an answer for those who sent us. What do you say about yourself?"
>
> [23] He said, "I am the voice of one crying out in the wilderness, 'Make straight the way of YHWH,' as the prophet Isaiah said.
>
> [24] Now they had been sent from the Pharisees.
>
> [25] They asked him, "Why then are you baptizing if you are neither the Messiah, nor Elijah, nor the prophet?"
>
> [26] John answered them, "I baptize with water. Among you stands one whom you do not know, [27] the one who is coming after me; I am not worthy to untie the thong of his sandal."
>
> [28] This took place in Bethany across the Jordan where John was baptizing.
>
> [29] The next day he saw Jesus coming toward him and declared, "Here is the Lamb of God who takes away the sin of the world! [30] This is he of whom I said, 'After me comes a man who ranks ahead of me because he was before me.' [31] I myself did not know him; but I came baptizing with water for this reason, that he might be revealed to Israel."
>
> [32] And John testified, "I saw the Spirit descending from heaven like a dove, and it remained on him. [33] I myself did not know him, but the one who sent me

to baptize with water said to me, 'He on whom you see the Spirit descend and remain is the one who baptizes with the Holy Spirit.' ³⁴ And I myself have seen and have testified that this is the Son of God" (NRSV, modified).

This conversation is remarkable on several grounds. First, and most obviously, it confirms that the hope for the arrival of a prophet to announce the messianic age was in the air in Palestine, at least among the religious leaders of Jerusalem. Second, in the minds of some, the role of eschatological prophet and eschatological Messiah were closely linked if not blurred; apparently they could not tell whether John the Baptist was the Messiah (ὁ χριστός) or the Prophet (ὁ προφήτης, vv. 19–21). Third, whatever his reason for denying the role of "the Prophet," in claiming to be a voice of another person and in quoting Isa 40:3 to call the people to prepare the way of YHWH (v. 23), he fulfills precisely the role of the prophet predicted in Mal 3:1 and 3:23[4:5].[24] Fourth, the sequel to this event confirms his role as herald of the Messiah: (1) the evangelist explicitly characterizes his role as bearing witness (μαρτυρέω) to someone else (vv. 32, 34); (2) John identified himself as divinely sent;[25] (3) his role was preparatory—he baptized in water in preparation for the coming one who will baptize with the Holy Spirit (John 1:23); (4) he quoted the divine word by which the coming one would be identified— "the one upon whom the Holy Spirit would descend and on whom he would remain, v. 33);[26] (5) he introduced Jesus with two messianic epithets: "Son of God" (ὁ υἱὸς τοῦ θεοῦ, v. 34), Lamb of God (ὁ ἀμνὸς τοῦ θεοῦ, v. 36); (6) Andrew introduced Jesus to Peter as "the Messiah," which is translated as "the anointed one" (τὸν Μεσσίαν, ὅ ἐστιν μεθερμηνευόμενον χριστός, v. 41); (7) Philip introduced Jesus to Nathaniel as "[the one] of whom Moses in the Torah and the prophets wrote" (ὃν ἔγραψεν Μωϋσῆς ἐν τῷ νόμῳ καὶ οἱ προφῆται εὑρήκαμεν, v. 45); (8) to the messianic epithet, "Son of God," Nathaniel added "King of Israel" (σὺ βασιλεὺς εἶ τοῦ Ἰσραήλ, v. 49); (9) Jesus identified himself as "the Son of Man" (τὸν υἱὸν τοῦ ἀνθρώπου), whose messianic status would be visibly and divinely confirmed by the heavens opening and the envoys of God (τοὺς ἀγγέλους τοῦ θεοῦ) ascending and descending upon him (v. 51).

Although the opening chapter of John is clear on the distinction between the Messiah and the prophet who was sent to introduce him, and although believers in the book grasped that Jesus was not only greater than a prophet, but also the Messiah himself (7:31; 11:27; 20:31), in the minds of the Jewish leaders and the people as a whole at best Jesus was "the [eschatological] prophet" whom many were expecting.[27]

---

24. Cf. Luke's recognition of John the Baptist's role as "the prophet": Luke 1:76; 20:6.

25. ὁ πέμψας με, v. 33. Cf. ἐγὼ ἐξαποστέλλω τὸν ἄγγελόν μου in Mal 3:1 and ἐγὼ ἀποστέλλω ὑμῖν Ηλιαν τὸν Θεσβίτην in v. 23[4:5].

26. The divine word recalls the anointing of the first royal Messiah, whose status was confirmed by "the Spirit of YHWH coming mightily upon David [and remaining on him] from that day forward" (1 Sam 16:13). On the differences between the anointing of Saul and the anointing of David, see Block, "Empowered by the Spirit of God," 52–53.

27. John 4:19; 6:14; 9:17; but note the struggles concerning his messianic vs. prophetic status in 7:25–44. For a superb study on Johannine Messianism, see Bauckham, "Jewish Messianism according to the Gospel of John," 207–38. Bauckham rightly observes that in contrast to expectations at Qumran, in John 6:14 and 7:40 the crowds expected the Moses-like prophet to be a liberator and agent of

Having excluded any support for a messianic interpretation of "the prophet like Moses" in the Gospels, we are left with the only two texts in the New Testament that actually cite Deut 18:15, namely Acts 3:22–23 and 7:37. New Testament scholars are virtually unanimous in assuming that "the prophet like me" in both contexts refers to Jesus.[28] However, upon closer analysis, this turns out not to be the most natural reading.

The citation in Acts 3 occurs in the middle of a longer speech by Peter in response to the onlooker's amazement at the healing of a lame man at the "Beautiful Gate" of the Temple (vv. 12–26). The speech divides into three parts: vv. 12–16, 17–24, and 25–26, respectively. The first part is framed by Peter's explanation of the miracle: it was not his and John's power or piety that enabled the man who had been lame from birth to walk. Rather the key lay in faith in the name of Jesus. Admittedly the name of Jesus does not occur in the framework, but the two-fold reference to "his name" (τὸ ὄνομα αὐτοῦ) in v. 16 points back to Jesus, who is named in verse 13. But Peter was not satisfied with identifying him only by name. In verses 13–14 he used four epithets for Jesus: "the Servant (παῖς) of the God of the Fathers," "the Holy One" (ὁ ἅγιος), "the Righteous One" ([ὁ] δίκαιος), and "the Prince/Source of Life" (ὁ ἀρχηγός). This focus on Jesus must surely have added to the people's amazement, for everyone knew that he had died by crucifixion, which explains Peter's summary of what had happened to Jesus in the recent past; Jesus had been handed over and executed, but God had glorified him by raising him from the dead. The "Prince of Life" had not only been resurrected, but his life-giving power had also healed this man.

In this brief biographical note, Peter did not mince any words in declaring the people's culpability for the death of Jesus: "You handed over the Servant of the God of the Fathers"; "You rejected him"; "You disowned the holy and righteous One"; "You preferred to spare a murderer"; "You executed the Prince of Life." The people's role in the death of Jesus became the focus of the second part of this address (vv. 17–24). Peter began by acknowledging that the people and their leaders did not comprehend what they were doing when they executed Jesus. However, in no way did he excuse them; this was not an innocent act, but the nadir in the history of Israel's rejection of the revelation

---

miraculous signs, not a teacher, that is the mediator of divine revelation (p. 225). My colleague Carlos Sosa Siliezar helpfully reminds me that in John 11:51 the narrator attributes Caiaphas' prophecy that Jesus would die for the nation not to any link with the train of prophets since Moses, but to his high priestly office.

28. E.g., Jeremias, "Μωϋσῆς," 868—69; Haenchen, *Acts of the Apostles*, 209; Bruce, *Acts*, 92–93; Kistemaker, *Acts*, 136–37; Fitzmyer, *Acts of the Apostles*, 289; Bock, *Acts*, 178–79; Marshall, "Acts,", 547–48; Schnabel, *Acts,* 218. On Acts 2:22–23, Pervo writes (*Acts*, 108–9):

> This portion of the speech supports the claims that all has happened in accordance with God's plan by appeal to prophetic tradition, not however by siting an apocalyptic text, but through asserting the Jesus is the 'prophet like Moses' predicted in Deut 18:15.... Although a good deal of material from disparate sources suggests the development of a prophet with messianic features, Luke's 'prophetic Christology' follows a different path. For Luke (the earthly) Jesus is more prophet like Moses (and Elijah, etc.) than a messiah endowed with prophetic qualities.

On 7:37, Pervo writes (*Acts*, 188): "For Luke it is no embarrassment that Jesus is a 'prophet like Moses.' This suits his Christology."

that God had provided through his human mouthpieces, the prophets. While the quotation of Deut 18:15 and 19 in verses 22–23 preserves the singular of the source text (προφήτην, τοῦ προφήτου), a series of features of Peter's own comments that frame the citation of Moses demonstrate that he is concerned with the long succession of prophets, if not the prophetic institution itself: (1) the consistent use of the plural "prophets" (vv. 18c, 21d, 24a); (2) the reference to "all the prophets" (πάντων τῶν προφητῶν, vv. 18c, 24a); (3) the historical perspective represented by "long ago" (ἀπ' αἰῶνος, v. 21e); (4) the specific naming of Samuel; and (5) the reference to his successors (τῶν καθεξῆς, v. 24c). However, Peter's use of the singular for the organ of speech (στόματος) in verses 18 and 21 demonstrates that in his mind recent events have not caught God by surprise but represent the fulfilment of predictions God had made through his prophets through the centuries. At the heart of the prophetic pronouncements was the figure of the Messiah, whose mission was to restore all things (v. 21b), but the achievement of this goal would require the Messiah to suffer.[29] This part of the speech is framed by declarations that recent events have transpired exactly as predicted by all the prophets (vv. 18, 24).

This provides context for interpreting Peter's citation from Deut 18. He was not hereby introducing either a new eschatological messianic figure or a single figure in contrast to the succession of prophets of which he spoke in Acts 3:18–21 and 24. Rather he was providing background and reinforcement for statements he had already made. More than a millennium earlier Moses had reassured the Israelites that after his departure YHWH would not leave his people without access to his mind or his will. Although Moses was not the first person in their history designated as a נָבִיא (Greek προφήτης; cf. Gen 20:7), at Horeb he was cast and inaugurated as the founder and paradigm of the institution and the succession of professional mouthpieces for YHWH that he graciously provided for his people. Deuteronomy 18:9–22 not only highlights the distinctive nature of Israel's version of a common ancient Near Eastern phenomenon, but it also emphasizes the seriousness with which the Israelites were to treat Moses and his prophetic heirs. Not to listen to them was to refuse the word of YHWH, the height of rebellion, and apparently a capital crime.[30] While Peter's addition of verse 23 reinforced the gravitas of the prophetic office and the messages proclaimed by authentic prophets, in this context it is rhetorically shocking. He interprets the execution of the Messiah as a capital crime,

---

29. This paragraph recalls Peter's description of the role of the prophets in 1 Pet 1:10–12:

> [10] Concerning this salvation, the prophets who prophesied of the grace that was to be yours made careful search and inquiry, [11] inquiring about the person or time that the Spirit of Christ within them indicated when it testified in advance to the sufferings destined for Christ and the subsequent glory. [12] It was revealed to them that they were serving not themselves but you, in regard to the things that have now been announced to you through those who brought you good news by the Holy Spirit sent from heaven—things into which angels long to look! (NRSV)

30. Cast in YHWH's voice, Deut 18:19 declares cryptically "I will seek from him (אָנֹכִי אֶדְרֹשׁ מֵעִמּוֹ), which minimally means that YHWH will personally hold the rebels accountable for the rejection of his word, and maximally that he will demand their lives (cf. Gen 9:5). In Jewish tradition, this meant the death penalty. LXX rendered the idiom in this context ἐγὼ ἐκδικήσω ἐξ αὐτοῦ, "I will avenge, demand justice from." Peter changed it to ἐξολεθρευθήσεται ἐκ τοῦ λαοῦ, presumably equating the Hebrew expression in Deut 18:19 with the idiom, נִכְרְתָה מֵעַמֶּיהָ, "to be cut off from one's people," found in Lev 23:29.

not primarily because it was an act of murder, but because it signified the rejection of the message of the prophets, and with that a rejection of the God of the fathers, Abraham, Isaac, and Jacob (v. 13).[31]

In the conclusion to this speech (vv. 25-26) Peter declared in effect that the execution of the Messiah signified the people's rejection of their own special spiritual heritage and their divine mission of being a blessing to all the families of the earth. His earlier invitation to his audience to repent and turn from their sins that they might yet experience the presence and blessing of God (v. 19), had already sounded a note of God's incredible grace to this generation, a grace that is focused on Jesus, the Messiah, who was "appointed for you" (τὸν προκεχειρισμένον ὑμῖν). In the concluding statement, Peter reinforced the benefit that the resurrected Christ represented for his audience: "For you first, God raised up his Servant and sent him to bless you by turning each of you from your evil.[32] In this address Peter suggested that the prophetic institution was raised up especially to proclaim the coming of the Messiah. Remarkably, he also appeared to place himself in that train of prophets, and his hearers are admonished to listen to him, even as they should have listened to the prophets of old. Given the hardness of the Jewish leaders' hearts toward Jesus, their reaction to his address in the sequel (Acts 4:1-3) is not unexpected, though the apostles were undoubtedly encouraged by the 5000 men who believed in Jesus (v. 4).

We should be equally cautious about finding a reference to a prophetic Messiah in Stephen's citation of Deut 18:15 in Acts 7:37. As is the case with Acts 3:22, New Testament scholars generally see in "a prophet like me" a reference to Christ.[33] But this interpretation deflects from the overall thrust of the speech, whose purpose is to trace the history of Israel's spiritual obstinacy. A major portion of the speech is devoted to Moses, specifically reviewing his call to the ministry of deliverance (vv. 20-34), followed by a summary statement of the people's rejection of him despite his lofty standing with God and his status in the community (vv. 35-38), and ending with a prolonged indictment (vv. 39-43). The citation of Deut 18:15 occurs within verses 35-38, where the emphasis is clearly on the stature of Moses, the one sent by God to rule and deliver Israel (v. 35), the one who performed signs and wonders before them for forty years (v. 36), the paradigmatic prophet (v. 37), and the one who received the oracles from God and passed them on to the people.[34] We detract from Stephen's focus if we isolate the quotation in verse 37 and impose on it a Messianic significance. Stephen's attention was not on "a

---

31. Witherington (*Acts of the Apostles*, 188), rightly notes that the function of the warning represented by the quotation was not to condemn Israel, but to warn his audience of the dire consequences of not repenting of their actions against Jesus.

32. Although translations generally render ἀπὸ τῶν πονηριῶν ὑμῶν something like, "from your evil ways," given the deuteronomic base of this address, we should interpret "the evil" more particularly as a violation of the Supreme Command and a repudiation of YHWH as their God. In Deuteronomy and the deuteronomistic writings the idiom "to do evil in the sight of YHWH" the object of the verb always has the article: עָשָׂה הָרַע בְּעֵינֵי יְהוָה. Cf. Deut 4:25; 9:18; 17:2; 31:29; Judg 2:11; 3:7, 12; etc.

33. See for example, Witherington *Acts of the Apostles*, 271; Polhill, *Acts,* 199-200.

34. Note the five-fold repetition of the demonstrative pronoun, Τοῦτον τὸν Μωϋσῆν, "This Moses" (v. 35a), followed by τοῦτον ὁ, "this one whom . . . " (v. 35b), οὗτος, "this one" (v. 36), οὗτός ἐστιν ὁ Μωϋσῆς ὁ, "this is the Moses who. . ." (v. 37), οὗτός ἐστιν ὁ, "this is the one who . . ." (v. 38).

prophet like me," let alone the Messiah,[35] but on "me," that is Moses, who predicted that he is not the last prophet God will raise up. Nor would he or his message be the last to be rejected by his people. Stephen concludes his speech with a summary statement:

> [52] Which of the prophets did your ancestors not persecute? They killed those who foretold the coming of the Righteous One, and now you have become his betrayers and murderers. [53] You are the ones that received the law as ordained by angels, and yet you have not kept it.

If Stephen's address establishes any link between Moses and Jesus, it is analogical, inasmuch as the present rejection of Jesus fits Israel's longstanding pattern of rebellion against God, as supremely illustrated by their response to Moses, his agent of deliverance and revelation. Indeed, judging by the people's response to Stephen (vv. 54–60), Luke appears to insert this man into the line of prophets like Moses. This impression is reinforced by the notice that Stephen had direct visual access to the heavenly throne room (vv. 54–55) and the citation of his final intercessory prayer.[36].

Re-Viewing Deuteronomy 18:9–22

The foregoing exploration of the *Wirkungsgeschichte* (history of interpretation) of the motif of "the prophet like Moses" has established that in Second Temple Judaism a strong anticipation of an eschatological prophet had arisen on Palestinian soil. Based upon Malachi's predictions of the arrival of "my messenger" before the return of YHWH (Mal 3:1) and the appearance of Elijah the prophet before the coming of the fearful day of YHWH (3:23[4:5]), the expected prophet was often associated with the coming Messiah. However, this examination of New Testament texts also established that even if lay people or religious leaders identified the Messiah as a prophetic figure, neither the Gospels nor the speeches of Peter and Stephen in Acts provide any warrant for identifying Jesus the Messiah as the long expected "prophet like Moses" as he is presented in Deut 18:15–19. It remains for us to take another closer look at the textual roots of these perceptions. What is striking about the most ardent defences of the messianic interpretation of the prophet like Moses is their inattention to contextual, literary, rhetorical, and discourse grammatical features of Deut 18:9–22.[37]

---

35. Haenchen (*Acts of the Apostles*, 282) correctly observes that "the speaker does not come to the theme of Jesus until verse 52."

36. Luke also reinforces his sense of Stephen's prophetic role "like Moses" by having spoken earlier of the deacon being "full of grace and power, and performing great wonders and signs among the people" (Acts 6:8), which recalls the narrators comment on Moses in Deut 34:11. On the role of prayer in the ministry of a prophet, see Gen 20:7, 17–18. On Moses as the paradigmatic prophetic intercessor, see Exod 32:11–14, 31–34; Num 14:11–20; Deut 9:18–20, 25–29. For further discussion of Moses' intercessory prayers, see chapter 12, "Wrestling with God: A Study on Prayer in Deuteronomy," above, pp. 240–63.

37. For a helpful examination of the discourse grammar of this passage, see Jones, "Reconsidering the *Prophetengesetz*." The following textlinguistic discussion is indebted to Jones.

The Literary Context of Deuteronomy 18:9–22

Messianic interpretations of the prophet like Moses often begin with verse 15, paying scant if any attention to what precedes.[38] Since נָבִיא is the first word we encounter, without context the prophet is immediately thrust into the foreground, reinforcing preconceived understandings of the identity and role of this figure. However, this approach disregards embedded syntactical features, particularly the temporal clause signaled by כִּי in verse 9. As Robert Dooley and Stephen Levinsohn have observed, the starting point of a new literary unit is often marked by a "preposed expression, especially one of time."[39] In Deuteronomy the signal is often the particle כִּי followed by an imperfect verb, which sets the temporal context for what follows.[40] The כִּי clause in 18:9a signals a transition from the discussion of the people's responsibilities toward Levitical priests (vv. 1–8) to YHWH's provision for ongoing communication with his people through a prophet (vv. 9–22).

Within Moses' third address (12:1—26:19; 28:1–69[29:1]) Deut 18:9–22 concludes a more or less self-contained unit involving instructions concerning administrative and religious officials that extends from 16:18 to 18:22. Indeed, if we focus on the officers in the larger unit, we observe a chiastic structure:

    A   Instructions concerning communal judges (16:18–17:7)

        B   Instructions concerning the Levitical priests (17:8–13)

            D   Instructions concerning the king of Israel (17:14–20)

        B'   Instructions concerning the Levitical priests (18:1–8)

    A'   Instructions concerning prophets (18:9–22)

Scholars commonly interpret this section of Deuteronomy as a sort of administrative constitution for Israel.[41] However, not only is there is no evidence that these laws ever existed separately, apart from their incorporation into the book,[42] but this approach also overloads these sections with political freight, at the expense of more central issues, which are spiritual and religious. On first sight the opening statement—"Judges and officers you may/shall appoint in all your towns" (16:18)—seems to focus on the leaders, and invites us to expect instructions on how they were to execute their judicial functions (cf. 1:16–18). However, there is no shift in addressee from the previous section, as Moses insists that the pursuit of righteousness is everybody's business. This trajectory carries on throughout this section. None of the officials (judges, kings, priests, prophets) are

---

38. E.g., Akin, "The Prophet Who is Like and Greater Than Moses," 48–93.

39. Dooley and Levinsohn, *Analyzing Discourse*, 40.

40. E.g., Deut 4:25; 7:1; 12:20, 29; 17:14; 18:9; 19:1 20:1, 10, 19; 21:10; 22:8; 23:10[9]; 24:10, 19; 26:12. In 18:21 the form is וְכִי, signaling the beginning of a new sub-unit (paragraph); the topic continues to be the prophet and his message.

41. Thus Halpern, *The Constitution of the Monarchy*, 226–33; Rütersworden, *Von der politischen Gemeinschaft zur Gemeinde*, 89–90; McBride, "The Polity of the Covenant People," 229–44; Nelson, *Deuteronomy*, 212.

42. McConville, *Deuteronomy*, 281.

addressed directly. For the people's benefit, in 17:14–20 the focus is entirely on the king's role as a model of covenant righteousness as spelled out in "this Torah"; not a word is said of his performance of normal royal duties. Deuteronomy 18:1–8 says even less about priestly obligations within the social and administrative structures; the emphasis is on the Israelites' responsibilities to care for those whom YHWH chose to stand before him. A primary function of 18:9–22 is to clarify the role of the prophet of YHWH within Israel and to assist the people in discriminating between true and false prophets, so that they might carry out the policies required in 13:2–6[1–5].[43]

Throughout 16:18—18:22, the predominant concern is not merely "social justice" (מִשְׁפָּט), but righteousness in all its dimensions, demonstrated especially in the people's absolute fidelity to YHWH. Deuteronomy 16:20 provides the key to this entire section: צֶדֶק צֶדֶק תִּרְדֹּף, "Righteousness, righteousness you shall pursue." What follows is not a manual for judges, kings, priests, and prophets, but instructions for the people, particularly male heads of households, on their roles in the maintenance of righteousness in the nation. The officials to be identified will function as agents of the people and of YHWH, specifically appointed to assist the former in their maintenance of righteousness. The same applies to the instructions concerning the prophet in 18:9–22.

---

43. For a superb discussion of the people as the addressees and the democratizing intent of this section of text, see Berman, *Created Equal*, 51–80.

The Style and Structure of Deuteronomy 18:9–22

Figure 17.1
A Colometric Synopsis of Deuteronomy 18:9–22

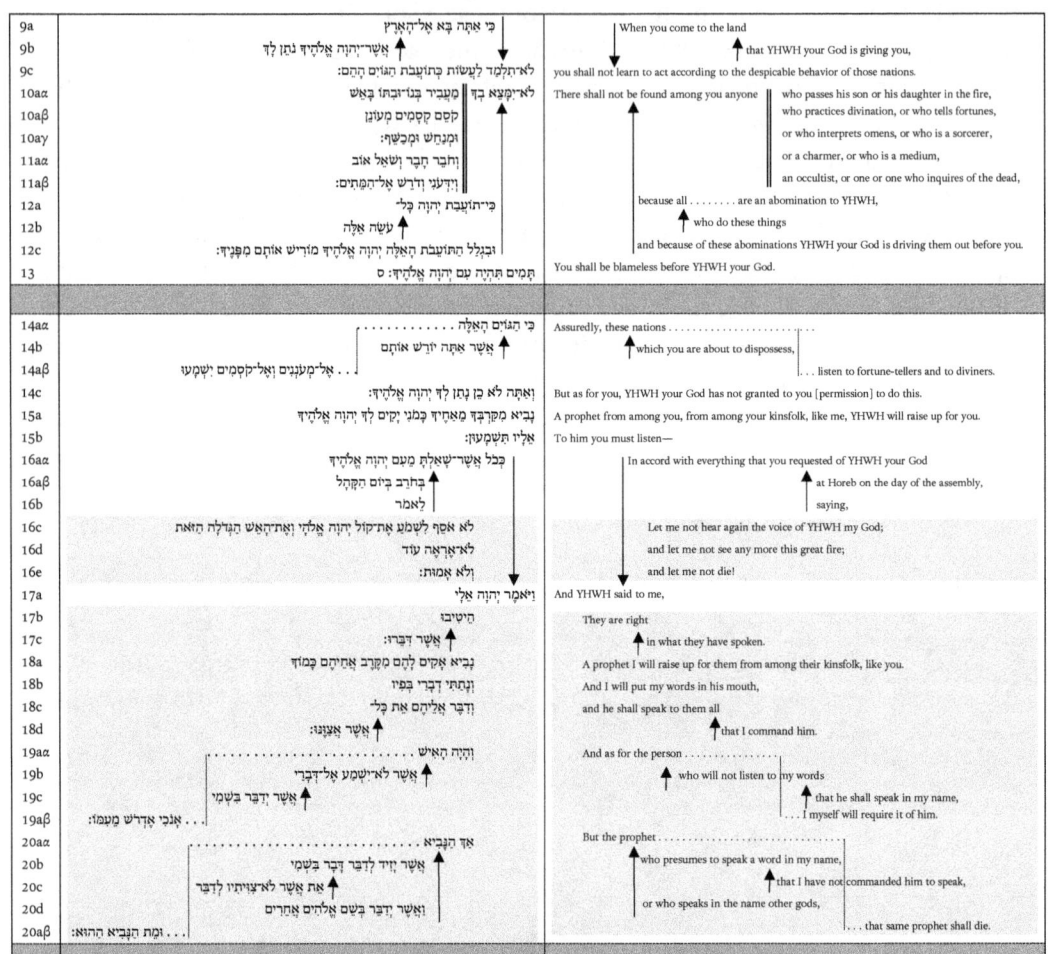

An examination of this text rightly begins with a visual portrayal of its discourse grammar (Figure 17.1). Like most others, in an earlier treatment I identified three sub-units in this passage, consisting of verses 9–14, 15–20, and 21–22 respectively.[44] However, upon closer attention to the discourse logic and grammar, verse 14 is best interpreted

---

44. Block, *Deuteronomy*, 434–38.

as the introduction to verses 15–20.[45] On the surface, verse 14 appears to summarize verses 9–13, exhibiting a similar A B structure, with A describing the practices of the nations and B demanding a different paradigm of revelatory communication from the Israelites (Table 17.1). The introductory particle כִּי in verses 12a and 14a seem to reinforce this approach.

Table 17.1
The Parallel Structures of Deuteronomy 18:9–13 and 14

When you come to the land that YHWH your God is giving you, you shall not learn to act according to the despicable behavior of those nations. There shall not be found among you anyone who passes his son or his daughter in the fire, who practices divination, or who tells fortunes, or who interprets omens, or who is a sorcerer, or a charmer, or who is a medium, an occultist, or one or one who inquires of the dead, because all who do these things are an abomination to YHWH, and because of these abominations YHWH your God is driving them out before you.	Assuredly, these nations, which you are about to dispossess, listen to fortune-tellers and to diviners.
You shall be blameless before YHWH your God.	But as for you, YHWH your God has not granted to you [permission] to do this.

However, several factors argue against this interpretation. First, and most obviously, in the Masoretic formatting the *setumah* (ס) inserted between verses 13 and 14 suggests the rabbis saw something that scholars often miss. Second, the כִּי particles at the beginning of verses 12 and 14 obviously function differently. In the first instance כִּי introduces a causal clause, an interpretation that is confirmed by the following differently constructed clause (v. 12c). In the second the כִּי functions deictically and assertively,[46] introducing a paradigm that replaces and corrects what precedes.[47] Third, this interpretation is reinforced by the emphatic fronting of וְאַתָּה ("But as for you"), in 14c, which corresponds to the fronting of הַגּוֹיִם הָאֵלֶּה ("these nations") in 14a, and intentionally forbids the Israelites from resorting to divinations and sorcery. Fourth, the repetition of the verb שָׁמַע ("to hear, listen") in 14aβ and 15b binds verses 14 and 15 inextricably and highlights the intended contrast and replacement motif; whereas the nations listen to fortune-tellers and diviners, Israelites are to listen to the prophet like Moses whom YHWH will raise up. The awkward but parallel construction of these sentences, with the verbs as the last element, strengthens the rhetorical intent:

---

45. So also, Jones ("Reconsidering the *Prophetengesetz*"), with a much more detailed presentation.

46. Follingstad, *Deictic Viewpoint in Biblical Hebrew Text*, 568. Contra Lundbom (*Deuteronomy*, 548), who argues that the initial כִּי v. 14 creates an inclusion with v. 9.

47. Following Jones, "Reconsidering the *Prophetengesetz*." On the use of כִּי to signal "modification of active information by replacement and correction," see Follingstad, *Deictic Viewpoint*, 561.

כִּי הַגּוֹיִם הָאֵלֶּה [אֲשֶׁר אַתָּה יוֹרֵשׁ אוֹתָם] . . . .
אֶל־מְעֹנְנִים וְאֶל־קֹסְמִים . . יִשְׁמָעוּ

וְאַתָּה [לֹא כֵן נָתַן לְךָ יְהוָה אֱלֹהֶיךָ: נָבִיא מִקִּרְבְּךָ מֵאַחֶיךָ כָּמֹנִי יָקִים לְךָ יְהוָה אֱלֹהֶיךָ]
אֵלָיו . . . . תִּשְׁמָעוּן

    Assuredly, <u>these nations</u> . . . <u>to fortune-tellers and to diviners</u> <u>they listen</u>.

    But as for <u>you</u>, ... <u>to him</u> [the prophet] . . . . <u>you must listen</u>.

Accordingly, having deprived the Israelites of pagan forms of divination, verses 14–15 together introduce them to YHWH's graciously provided alternative. Through the institution of prophecy YHWH will satisfy all the impulses that drive other peoples to their abhorrent (תּוֹעֵבָה) magical practices.[48] While he takes away one widely perceived benefit—access to supernatural knowledge via mediums—he replaces it with another, as we shall see more reliable gift, that is, access to himself via clear revelation through a prophet. In so doing he fleshes out what "blameless" (תָּמִים) communication with YHWH (cf. v. 13) looks like.

    Having established that verse 14 introduces a new subsection, which carries on through the divine speech in vv. 17b–20, the next discourse marker of a literary break occurs in verse 21a. The transition is signaled by וְכִי, which I have rendered as "Now," and the change to a verb with a second person subject, "you." Following a rhetorical strategy that is common in the book, Moses' own voice returns to introduce a hypothetical interlocutor who expresses verbally how the Israelites might respond in the future to competing claims to the office of prophet and the practice of the prophetic vocation.[49] Here he builds on chapter 13, where he had identified appealing to the people to go after other gods as one of the marks of a false prophet (13:2–6[1–5]). Now Moses focuses on predictive prophecy (which was the primary goal of the pagan divinatory practices listed in verses 10–11 and 14). The fact that Moses refers to people who [falsely] claim to speak for YHWH speaks to the ubiquity of fraudulent prophetic utterances in the ancient Near East.[50] It will obviously not suffice for a so-called prophet to preface, punctuate, or end a declaration with one of the common prophetic formulas, such as the citation formula (כֹּה אָמַר אֲדֹנָי יהוה, "Thus has Adonay YHWH declared"), or the divine signatory formula (נְאֻם אֲדֹנָי יהוה, "the declaration of Adonay YHWH").[51]

---

48. Labuschagne (*Deuteronomium*, 134) rightly argues for a fundamental difference between prophets, who proclaim the word of YHWH, and diviners, who predict the future. But these differences do not rule out similarities. For further discussion on the relationship between Israelite prophecy and divination see Overholt, *Channels of Prophecy*, 117–47; Barstad, "No Prophets," 47–49. On the relationship between prophecy and ecstasy see the still helpful study by Haller, *Charisma und Ekstasis*, 5–39.

49. As in Deut 7:17; 8:17; and 9:4, here the interlocutor happens to be talking to himself. The idiom, תֹּאמַר בִּלְבָבֶךָ, "you say in your heart," is euphemistic for "you think."

50. Cf. Jer 23:16–22; Ezek 12:21–13:16.

51. On these and other divine speech markers used by prophets, see Block, *Ezekiel Chapters 1–24*, 32–36.

The Identity and Function of the Prophet in Deuteronomy 18:14–20

Having established the literary and cultural context for Deut 18:9–22 it remains to examine more carefully verses 15–19, to see what, if any, light they shed on the identity and role of the prophet like Moses.

First, the opening temporal clause in verse 9 points to [the beginning of] the fulfillment of the promise of the prophet in the near future; it does no good to promise an eschatological figure when the temptation of pagan divination is just ahead: "When you enter the land." The form of the beginning links this periscope with the instructions concerning the king: "When you enter the land and possess it and live in it (17:14).

Second, the medium of divine revelation is called a נָבִיא. The word was encountered earlier in 13:2[1], in association with חֹלֵם חֲלוֹם, "dreamer of dreams." Although the First Testament refers to prophets by several designations, נָבִיא[52] is the most common designation. The etymology of this word remains uncertain, but it seems best to recognize a derivation from a hypothetical root, נָבָא, "to call,"[53] and to the interpret the form as an I-class passive, "one summoned by God."[54] Although some have understood the use of the singular, נָבִיא, rather than the plural, נְבִיאִים, to refer to a specific future prophet, nothing in this context points in that direction. Rather, in context the singular should be understood something like a prophet in each generation.[55] Moses hereby assures the people that they will never need to resort to manipulative divination, because YHWH is providing them with the gift of a succession of prophets, all of whom will command obedience.

Third, the prophet will be divinely chosen and installed. The verb הֵקִים, meaning "to raise up" and entrust with a commission, is used elsewhere of divinely appointed saviors (מוֹשִׁיעִים, Judg 3:9, 15), tribal chieftains (שֹׁפְטִים, Judg 2:16, 18), a king (מֶלֶךְ, 1 Kgs 14:14), a priest (כֹּהֵן, 1 Sam 2:35), sentries (צֹפִים, Jer 6:17), and shepherds (רֹעִים, Jer 23:4; Ezek 34:23; Zech 11:16). In the broader context of Deut 16:18—18:22 the direct appointment and installation by YHWH of the prophet represents a contrast to the judges and officials (שֹׁפְטִים וְשֹׁטְרִים) whom the people are to appoint (נָתַן) in all their towns when they have crossed the Jordan (16:18), and the king, whom YHWH will choose but whom the people will install (שִׂים in 17:15; הֵקִים in 28:36). Like the perfect הֵקִים in Judg 2:18, here the imperfect יָקִים should be interpreted in a distributive sense, referring not to a single appointment but to

---

52. רֹאִים, "seer"; חֹזִים, "visionary"; עַבְדֵי יהוה, "servants of YHWH"; מַלְאֲכֵי יהוה, "messengers/envoys of YHWH"; אִישׁ הָאֱלֹהִים, "man of God")

53. Cognate to Akkadian *nabu*, "to call, name." *AHw*, 697b, 699b. The verb occurs in the First Testament only in the reflexive stems (niphal, hithpael). *HALOT*, 659.

54. Analogous to many other official terms: מָשִׁיחַ, "anointed one, messiah"; נָגִיד, "promoted one, ruler"; נָשִׂיא, "raised one, prince"; נָזִיר, "consecrated one, Nazirite"; פָּקִיד, "appointed one, overseer"; שָׂכִיר, "hired one, hireling." For a defense of this interpretation of נָבִיא and a discussion of such forms, see Huehnergard, "On the Etymology and Meaning of Hebrew *nābîʾ*," 88*–93*. Cf. Fleming ("The Etymological Origins of the Hebrew *nābîʾ*," 217–24), who argues for an active meaning, "one who invokes the gods."

55. So also Perlitt, "Mose als Prophet," 596; Mayes, *Deuteronomy*, 282; Nelson, *Deuteronomy*, 228.

a series, that is, from time to time as needed.⁵⁶ This accords generally with the concern in 16:18—18:22 with administrative and religious offices and institutions, and more particularly with the instructions concerning the king in 17:12–20.

Fourth, this prophet will be raised up "from the midst" (מִקִּרְבְּךָ) and "from the brotherhood" (מֵאַחֶיךָ) of Israel. He will come from the same pool of candidates as the king (17:15). Since the one "from the midst of your brothers"⁵⁷ had been contrasted with the אִישׁ נָכְרִי ("a foreigner") as recently as 17:15, there is no need to specify more closely what is meant. By highlighting the Israelite origin of the prophet, he may have had in mind Balaam, the prophet for hire from Mesopotamia whom the Moabites had engaged to curse Israel (cf. 23:4–5[3–4]; Num 22–24). Since the prophet like Moses will be raised up from within Israel, he will have nothing in common with the diviners and magicians now in the land. In contrast to the kings, whom Gen 49:10 specifies as coming from the tribe of Judah, and the priestly functionaries, who are all Levites (Deut 17:9, 18; 18:1; 24:8; 27:9), the promise leaves open both the tribal source and the gender of prophets who will succeed Moses.

Fifth, this prophet will be like Moses. Grammatically כָּמֹנִי ("like me") functions as an attributive modifier of נָבִיא, "prophet," highlighting the fact that the one whom YHWH will raise up will be a prophet after the order of Moses.⁵⁸ As if to reinforce his own role as "mouthpiece" of YHWH, verse 18 puts the promise of a prophet into YHWH's own mouth and presents it as a benefit for the people that YHWH had made to Moses at Horeb. Except for some adjustments in word order and the shift from third to first person, YHWH's words in verse 18a largely repeat what Moses had expressed in verse 15 (Table 17.2).

---

56. Cf. Rashi, who saw in this text the promise of a succession of prophets (מנביא לנביא). See further Chiesa, "La Promessa di un Profeta," 17–26, esp. 20–23. Contra Y. Kim, "'The Prophet Like Moses,'" 89–94.

57. Note the stylistic variations in these two passages: 17:15, מִקֶּרֶב אַחֶיךָ, "from the midst of your brothers"; 18:15, מִקִּרְבְּךָ מֵאַחֶיךָ, "from your midst from your brothers."

58. Cf. Schüle, "Kāmokā—der Nächste wie Du," 118.

Table 17.2
Moses' and YHWH's Promises of a Prophet Like Moses

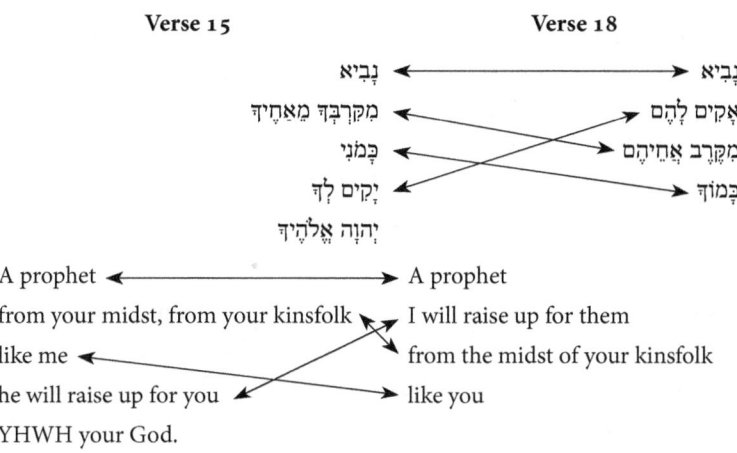

The prophetic institution receives surprisingly little attention in the Pentateuch. Indeed, the word נָבִיא appears only four times prior to Deut 13, and the cognate verb only twice (Num 11:25–26). In Gen 20:7, Abraham's prophetic role involved primarily intercession. Exodus 7:1 casts Moses' and Aaron's relationship as analogous to the relationship existing between a deity and his commissioned mouthpiece. Numbers 11:25–26 is intriguing, not only because of the seventy elders' ability to prophesy, but especially because they did so after a portion of the spirit (רוּחַ) had been taken from Moses and placed on the seventy. Numbers 12:6–8 is even more remarkable, because it explicitly contrasts Moses' role with that of prophets. Responding to Miriam and Aaron's claim that they had as much right to speak for YHWH as Moses did, God declared that even if they were prophets, their status was inferior to that of Moses. Whereas he (YHWH) speaks to prophets through visions and dreams, he speaks to Moses directly ("mouth to mouth"), clearly (מַרְאֶה) and unambiguously (לֹא בְחִידֹת, "not in riddles"). This paradigm of Mosaic prophecy suits the present context, which uses the divination of the nations as a foil; the latter is typically indirect, obscure, and ambiguous.

Verses 16–20 will clarify what Moses meant by a prophet "like me." In the first instance, they will be as inspired as Moses was: as YHWH had done to Moses, so he will do for his successor[s]. He will put his words in their mouths (v. 18b). Second, they will have the same commission Moses had: they shall declare the word of YHWH to the people (v. 18c–d). Third, they will come with the same authority as Moses: neither their status nor their experience will commend them; they will speak in the name of YHWH (v. 19c). Fourth, they will come with the same guarantee: YHWH will not leave it to them to secure the proper response of the audience; he will personally hold them accountable for rejecting the prophets' message (v. 19a). Moses reports this divine speech as having been addressed to him at Horeb (cf. v. 16a–b). However, as he recalled that moment on the Plains of Moab forty years later he may have had in mind the event reported in Num 12:1–15. When his own siblings, Miriam and Aaron challenged Moses' authority, YHWH personally called them to account.

In verse 20, YHWH reinforces this image of a prophet like Moses by digressing and describing a hypothetical prophet who is not like Moses: he speaks presumptuously without YHWH's authorization to speak in his name; he declares a word that YHWH has not put in his mouth; he speaks in the name of another deity. According to verses 21–22 the proof of a true prophet is that his prediction is always fulfilled.[59]

These comparisons with Moses speak only to the essential nature of true prophecy. They do not mean that all subsequent prophets, or the final ideal prophet—if one takes this text to anticipate an eschatological or Messianic figure—would be clones of Moses. On the contrary, in his eulogy on Moses the final author of Deuteronomy declared in unequivocal terms his uniqueness within the historical succession of prophets:

> [10] Never since has there arisen a prophet in Israel like Moses, whom YHWH knew face to face. [11] He was unequaled for all the signs and wonders that YHWH sent him to perform in the land of Egypt, against Pharaoh and all his servants and his entire land, [12] and for all the mighty deeds and all the terrifying displays of power that Moses performed in the sight of all Israel. (Deut 34:10–12, NRSV modified).

Contra Sailhamer and his followers, there is no need to date this epitaph to the exile or the post-exilic period, after the Israel's prophetic institution had been shut down.[60] All it requires is a protracted period of time, long enough for the appearance of several representatives, which is possible if one posits a date for the composition of the book of Deuteronomy more or less as we have it (and the Pentateuch as a whole) to the United Monarchy period (as I do). And whether one interprets וְלֹא־קָם . . . עוֹד as "never since" (NRSV), "since then" (NIV, NAS; cf. ESV), "never again" (NJPSV), or the entire clause as "No prophet like Moses ever came,"[61] this comment recognizes that even if Moses was the founder and paradigm of the entire line of true Israelite prophets, for his intimacy with YHWH (cf. Num 12:6–8), his performance of signs and wonders,[62] his mighty demonstrations of power (הַיָּד הַחֲזָקָה), and all his awesome deeds (כֹּל הַמּוֹרָא הַגָּדוֹל), he was in a class of his own. But this does not mean that there have been no prophets like Moses in other respects. While the expression "like Moses" (כְּמֹשֶׁה) in 34:10 links this text to 18:15 and 18, in no way does it suggest either the failure or

---

59. The narrative of Saul's consultation of the woman of Endor and the appearance of the prophet Samuel from the netherworld in 1 Sam 28:3–25 reinforces my insistence that this text focuses on YHWH's promised prophetic alternative to pagan means of communicating with the divine, and on the importance of future generations listening to those who speak for YHWH, rather than on the identity of some future eschatological prophet. For explorations of the relationship between this text and Deut 18:9–22, see Arnold, "Necromancy and Cleromancy in 1 and 2 Samuel," 199–213; Berman, "The Legal Blend in Biblical Narrative," 117–21.

60. Thus Sailhamer ("The Canon of the Hebrew Bible, 31), Rydelnik (*The Messianic Hope*, 61), and Y. Kim ("The 'Prophet Like Moses,'" 276–82).

61. Thus Sailhamer, *Introduction to Old Testament Theology*, 247–48; Rydelnik, *The Messianic Hope*, 62–63.

62. Remarkably this is the only place in Deuteronomy where הָאֹתוֹת וְהַמּוֹפְתִים, "the signs and wonders" are attributed to Moses; elsewhere they are always portrayed as divine acts. See 4:34; 6:22; 7:19; 11:3; 26:8; 29:2[3].

nonfulfillment of YHWH's and Moses' predictions of a prophet like Moses in Israel's past, or invite them to look forward to a new Messianic "Moses" who would speak with God face to face.[63] To claim this text as support for the view that the Torah points to a future Messiah is both gratuitous and tendentious. This image is entirely in the eye of the beholder, and represents the conclusion of a search for evidence for a conclusion pre-established on other grounds.

Concluding Reflections

The foregoing discussion represents a modest foray into a subject that cannot be resolved in one short essay. However, my observations and conclusions require a couple of further comments.

First, in my assessment, neither the First nor the New Testament offers any warrant for interpreting Deut 18:14–19 messianically, either in its expectation of a singular eschatological prophetic Messiah or in its anticipation of an ideal Prophet at the end of a succession of prophets. While the former should be clear from the discussion above, the latter, which is actually much more common that the former, calls for further comment. Many find a precedent for this view in the ordinance concerning the king in Deut 17:14–20. Although this text is not explicitly messianic, it presents an image of kingship in Israel that is both distinguished radically from prevailing contemporary ancient Near Eastern paradigms and is ultimately fulfilled in Jesus the Messiah.[64] Several of these have been hinted at above, but a summary of the links between these two texts might be helpful. (1) Both occur within the segment of Moses' fourth valedictory address devoted to administrative and religious functionaries (16:18—18:22). (2) Both begin with a temporal clause establishing the historical context of the fulfillment of both: after the Israelites have entered the land. (3) Both refer to the office holder with anarthrous singular forms (מֶלֶךְ, 17:15–16; נָבִיא, 18:15, 18), but which refer not to a single figure but to a succession of figures. (4) Both highlight YHWH's involvement in the elevation of the office-holder: YHWH will "choose" (בָּחַר) the king (17:15) and "raise up" (הֵקִים) the prophet (18:15, 18).

While these links are significant, they should not obscure the differences between the presentations of these two offices. First, whereas YHWH's choice of the king is presented as the divine response to the people's desire (17:14), the elevation of the prophet is redundantly characterized as an entirely divine act. Indeed, given the foil of humanly initiated mediums for gaining supernatural information (18:9–13), the prophetic arrangement expressly eliminates human initiative.

Second, whereas the instructions concerning the king anticipate a dynastic succession of office-holders (17:20), no such succession is anticipated for prophets. Indeed, judging by the biblical narratives, with respect to their background, prophets appear to have been appointed *ad hoc*. To be sure, we encounter the expression, "sons of the

---

63. Contra Rydelnik, *Messianic Hope*, 63–64.

64. For discussion of this matter, see chapter 16, "The Spiritual and Ethical Foundations of Messianic Kingship: Deuteronomy 17:14–20," above, pp. 335–48.

prophets" (בְּנֵי הַנְּבִיאִים), but the expression expresses membership in a guild, rather than genealogical descent.⁶⁵

With respect to the royal charter, the earliest concrete expressed anticipation of its fulfillment comes from the prayer/oracle of Hannah, whom the Targum rightly identifies as a prophet:

> YHWH will judge the ends of the earth.
> He will give power to his king (מַלְכּוֹ),
> And lift up the horn of his anointed (מְשִׁיחוֹ). (1 Sam 2:10, NRSV)

This sets the stage for the history of the monarchy. After the failed Saulide experiment in kingship, in 1 Sam 13:14 YHWH identifies David as the one whom he has had in mind from the beginning: "YHWH has sought out for himself the man⁶⁶ after his own heart (כִּלְבָבוֹ), and YHWH has commanded him to be prince (נָגִיד) over his people." The covenant that YHWH established with David and his household, i.e., descendants (בֵּיתוֹ), in 2 Sam 7 (// 1 Chr 17; cf. 2 Sam 23:5; Ps 89; 132) confirmed his eternal and irrevocable (עַד עוֹלָם) title to the throne of Israel. Indeed, in his response to this covenant in 2 Sam 7:19, David planted the seed for the universalization of what has previously been perceived as a purely national monarchical role: "You have also spoken about your servant's house with reference to the distant future, and this is the Torah of humanity, O Adonay YHWH!" (וַתְּדַבֵּר גַּם אֶל־בֵּית־עַבְדְּךָ לְמֵרָחוֹק וְזֹאת תּוֹרַת הָאָדָם אֲדֹנָי יְהוִה). Although, the demise of Judah, accompanied by the termination of the Davidic throne and the exile of Jehoiachin cast doubts on the veracity of the divine commitment (Ps 89:46–51[45–50]), even before this happened the Psalms and the prophets attest to a growing messianic hope focused on the rise of a Davidic king.⁶⁷ That Jesus is the fulfillment of this royal messianic hope is reflected in his titles: "son of David," "Christ" ("anointed one"), "king of Israel." Indeed, in his perfect fulfillment of the Mosaic royal charter (Deut 17:14–20) he is cast as the Ideal King."

Within the Scriptures no such traditions exist either for the prophets as a group or for an individual within that group. Of course, as the Qumran texts and the Gospels suggest, this did not prevent the Jewish people from developing all sorts of messianic hopes, focused on ideal eschatological [messianic] figures, whether didactic ("Teacher of Righteousness"), priestly (Aaronic), royal (Davidic), and yes, prophetic figures. However, to say that at the turn of the eons in Palestine hopes for an ideal prophetic figure were in the air does not mean they were actually rooted in the texts. We need to distinguish textual locutions (what texts say) and illocutions (what texts mean), on the one hand, from readerly/audience perlocutions (what hearers/readers take texts to mean), on the other.

---

65. 1 Kgs 20:35; 2 Kgs 2:3, 5, 7, 15; 4:1, 38; 5:22; 6:1; 9:1. In Acts 3:25, οἱ υἱοὶ τῶν προφητῶν denotes heirship to Israel's spiritual traditions.

66. Although אִישׁ lacks the article, the following clause and the context identify him as a specific individual. It is not that just any man could have emerged as a candidate. For starters, Gen 49:10 had guaranteed the royal scepter for the tribe of Judah, which meant that on this count YHWH was never seriously committed to the Saulide experiment. On this interpretation of 1 Sam 13:14, see, Block, "My Servant David," 39; and more fully, DeRouchie, "The Heart of YHWH and His Chosen One," 467–89.

67. Amos 9:11; Hos 3:5; Mic 5:1–4[2–5]; Isa 9:1–6[2–7]; 11:1–10; Jer 23:1–6; Ezek 34:23–24; 37:21–26.

In this regard, the portrayal of Jesus as Messiah in the New Testament matches First Testament portrayals perfectly; he is the royal descendant of David, and he embodies both royal and divine righteousness (John 1:14, 16–17).

Second, my skepticism about finding evidence for a "prophetic messianic hope" does not mean that in my view Jesus the Messiah did not perform prophetic functions. Among the correspondences between Jesus' ministry and the ministry of the prophets that preachers and scholars have cited many are trivial.[68] However, Daniel Akin has offered a helpful list of significant features of Deut 18:15–22 that are found in the New Testament's portrayal of Jesus:[69]

1. God's prophets speak at God's initiative.
2. God's prophets speak as God's mediators.
3. God gives the prophets the words to proclaim.
4. God expects his people to accept the prophet's message.
5. God's prophets speak truth for the one true God.

These are obviously all true of Jesus, and if this qualifies one to be a prophet, then he was indeed the ideal prophet. His prophetic function is reinforced by the forms his speeches take, many of which are rooted in the prophets (e.g., his "woe pronouncements" in Matt 11:21; 23:13–29; etc.). However, if Caiaphas could prophesy without holding the office of prophet (John 11:51), why could this not also have been true of Jesus? Furthermore, Jesus' rhetorical style was not borrowed only from the prophets. As illustrated by the Beatitudes (Matt 5:3–11) and his parables, he often cast his utterances in the form of a sage's instruction. Indeed his oral proclamation is most commonly identified as "teaching,"[70] though he is often also said to have "proclaimed" (κηρύσσω) his message.[71]

Inasmuch as Jesus appeared to operate like a prophet we might say he was one. However, this does not mean either that this was a legitimate *messianic* title or that Jesus was specifically and uniquely the one of whom Moses and YHWH spoke in Deut 18:15 and 18 respectively. Why do we not say the same of Caiaphas, or David, whom Peter and John characterized as speaking prophetically in Acts 4:25: "Through the mouth of our

---

68. Many lists are available on bloggers' websites. For example, John J. Parsons cites thirty ways in which Jesus' ministry resembled that of Moses. http://www.hebrew4christians.com/Articles/Like_Moses/Printer_Version/printer_version.html.

69. "The Prophet Who is Like and Greater than Moses," 487–92.

70. Using the root, διδάσκω: Matt 4:23; 5:2; 7:29; 9:35; 11:1; 13:54; 21:23; 22:16; 26:55; Mark 1:21–22; 2:13; 4:1–2; 6:2, 6, 34; 8:31; 9:31; 10:1; 11:17; 12:14, 35; 14:49; Luke 4:15, 31; 5:3, 17; 6:6; 11:1; 12:12; 13:10, 22, 26; 19:47; 20:1, 21; 21:37; 23:5; John 6:59; 7:14, 28, 35; 8:2, 20; 9:34; 18:20. People address Jesus as "Teacher" (διδάσκαλε) more than two dozen times in the Gospels (e.g., Matt 8:19; Mark 9:38; Luke 3:12; John 1:38 = Hebrew רַבִּי; cf. רַבּוּנִי in John 20:16), and often as "Rabbi" (רַבִּי, Matt 26:25, 49; Mark 9:5; 11:21; 14:45; John 1:38, 49; 3:2, 26; 4:31; 6:25; 9:2; 11:8).While many perceived Jesus as a prophet (Matt 14:5; 21:11, 46; Mark 6:15; Luke 7:16; John 4:19; 6:14; 7:40; 9:17), no one ever addressed him as "Prophet."

71. In the LXX κηρύσσω is usually used of official proclamations or sounds of alarm. It functions this way occasionally in the prophets (Hos 5:8; Mic 3:5; Joel 1:14; 2:1, 15; 4:9[3:9]; Jonah 1:2; 3:2, 4–5, 7; Zeph 3:14; Zech 9:9; Isa 61:1), but is never used of regular prophetic oracles.

father David, your servant, you said by the Holy Spirit, 'Why did the Gentiles rage, and the peoples plot in vain?'" Obviously, in the apostles' minds, God put the words in David's mouth a là Moses, but this did not mean that David occupied the prophetic office, and certainly not that he was the individual of whom Moses spoke. In some respects, Jesus may be viewed as one link in this prophetic chain of succession, but he was neither the only one in the New Testament nor the last. In Paul's *apologia* in Gal 1 the apostle intentionally cast himself in the mold of the Mosaic prophet.[72]

This entire discussion has extremely significant Christological implications. Indeed, it could be argued that the preoccupation with Mosaic prophetic typology actually reflects a low Christology.[73] In our zeal to equate Moses and Jesus we may overlook the fact that while Jesus is indeed the human descendant of David, he is also YHWH incarnate.[74] This means that rather than being the prophet in the divine human relationship, he is actually the embodiment of the one who puts his words into the mouths of the prophets, if not the embodiment of the prophets' words themselves. For this reason, John begins his gospel with "In the beginning was the Word, and the word was with God, and the word was God (John 1:1). In bearing witness to him, John the Baptist, the true eschatological Elijah, bore witness to him, the true light of the world (1:6–9). To receive eternal life people needed to receive him, and if they did, he gave them the right to become children of God. No prophet, not even Moses could ever do this (1:10–13). Indeed, in Jesus the Word was embodied, and dwelt among us. John continues that he and his apostolic colleagues beheld his glory, which was not a secondary glory, or the glory of another person reflecting off his face (cf. Exod 34:29–35); it was as intrinsic to him as it was to the Father (John 1:14). John's opening paean to Jesus the Messiah reaches a climax in verses 16–18:

> Indeed, from his fullness we have all received grace after grace. For the Torah (ὁ νόμος) was given through Moses (Μωϋσέως); Grace and truth (Heb חֶסֶד

72. For fuller discussion, see chapter 18, "Hearing Galatians with Moses: An Examination of Paul as a Second and Seconding Moses," below, pp. 374–404.

73. The extreme is represented by the Quran, which recognizes Jesus as Messiah (3:44; 4:157), but insists repeatedly that he was nothing more than a prophet:

> O People of the Book, exceed not the limits in your religion nor speak anything about Allah, but the truth. The Messiah, Jesus, son of Mary, is only a messenger of Allah and His word which He communicated to Mary and a mercy from Him. So believe in Allah and His messengers. And say not, Three. Desist, it is better for you. Allah is only one God. Far be it from His glory to have a son. To Him belongs whatever is in the heavens and whatever is in the earth. And sufficient is Allah as having charge of affairs. (4:171. Cf. also 2:136, 253; 3:83; 4:163; 61:6).

74. For full treatment of the development of the New Testament's high divine Christology, see Hurtado, *LORD JESUS CHRIST*. I am indebted to Carlos Sosa Siliezar for reminding me of Hurtado's work. In addition to his discussion of the development of the doctrine of Jesus as divine/God (pp. 627–48), see the remains of an early third century CE prayer chapel discovered on the grounds of a prison near Megiddo. The most impressive feature of the site is a beautiful tile floor whose mosaic includes the following inscription: "The God-loving Akeptous has donated the table to God Jesus Christ as a memorial." This is not only not only the earliest inscriptional reference to Jesus Christ, but also the earliest extra-biblical reference to Jesus Christ as God. For discussion, see Tzaferis, "Inscribed 'To God Jesus Christ,'" 38–49.

וַתְּאֱמֶת) happened through Jesus Christ (διὰ Ἰησοῦ Χριστοῦ ἐγένετο). No one has ever seen God. It is God the only Son, who is intimate with the Father (ὁ ὢν εἰς τὸν κόλπον τοῦ πατρός), who has revealed him (ἐκεῖνος ἐξηγήσατο).

Hebrews 1:1–2 presents Jesus as the climactic and eschatological agent of divine revelation. Significantly, the author of the latter text does not write, "Long ago God spoke to our ancestors in many and various ways by the prophets, but in these last days he has spoken to us by *the [supreme] Prophet*, whom he appointed heir of all things, through whom he also created the worlds" (NRSV modified). No, he has spoken "by a Son" (ἐν υἱῷ).

With hindsight we do indeed see analogical connections between the ministry of Jesus and the work of the prophets, and Jesus obviously performed many prophetic functions, but a generic gulf separated the prophetic institution from the Messiah. If John the Baptist was greater than a prophet because he directed the people to the One, whose coming the prophets had foretold (Matt 11:9–15), how much greater is this One to Whom John pointed? He is YHWH, for whom John the Baptist prepared the way (John 1:23). We need to keep this in mind when we read the only texts in all of Scripture that quote Deut 18:15. In Acts 3:22–23 and 7:37 Peter and Stephen respectively condemned the Jewish people because, in rejecting the Righteous One, the Messiah, they had rejected the One of whom the prophets had spoken "with one mouth," for God had put the words concerning Jesus into their mouths. Jesus is more than a prophet; simultaneously he is the Word the prophets spoke and the One who put his word in the prophets' mouths.

18

Hearing Galatians with Moses

An Examination of Paul as a Second and Seconding Moses[1]

Introduction

IN THE LAST THIRTY years we have witnessed a revolution in scholarly perspectives on Paul's understanding of the relationship between the faith of Israel and Second Temple Judaism, on the one hand, and between the faith of Israel and the Gospel of Jesus Christ, on the other. Especially in Protestant circles, it is widely accepted that the Hebrew Bible records the history of a failed system of life based on law in contrast to the effectual new covenant inaugurated by Jesus Christ and driven by the Spirit. Based on Rom 3–4 and Gal 3–4, some find an analogue to the New Testament way of faith in the Hebrew Bible by leapfrogging over almost a millennium of Israel's history as a nation back to Abraham, who modeled a righteousness based on faith, in opposition to a righteousness based on obedience to the law.[2]

Although the roots of this perspective date to the early centuries of Christianity, in the wake of the Reformation this approach has dominated Protestant scholarship. The forms of expression vary in different branches of Protestantism, but a generally negative view of Israel and of the Hebrew Bible itself has ruled the day for a long time—until the

---

1. This is a stylistically modified version of an essay that was originally produced for publication in *Sepher Torath Mosheh: Studies in the Composition and Interpretation of Deuteronomy*, edited by Daniel I. Block and Richard L. Schultz (Peabody, MA: Hendrickson, 2017), 338–74. I am grateful to the publishers for their kind permission to republish it here. Special thanks are due also to Jonathan Kline, the Hendrickson editor of this volume for his careful reading of the document and his many suggestions for its improvement, and to Nick Perrin, Seth Ehorn, Todd Wilson, and my brother George Block, for reading an earlier draft of this paper and for offering many helpful suggestions, particularly with respect to New Testament issues and bibliography. I also thank my students Jordan Brown, Michelle Knight, Daniel Lanz, Franklin Wang, and Meredith Morris for their assistance along the way, and lastly my colleague Richard Schultz for his helpful suggestions as I prepared the final draft. Of course, any infelicities in style and content are my own responsibility.

2. John Sailhamer, a Hebrew Bible scholar, interprets Exodus–Deuteronomy generically as a biography of Moses *sub lege* ("under the law") in contrast to the biography of Abraham, who lived *ante legem* ("before the law"). Abraham embodies the divinely approved pattern of a life of faith, while Moses demonstrates the inevitable failure of a life driven by law. See Sailhamer, *Introduction to Old Testament Theology*, 272–89.

emergence three decades ago of what in Pauline scholarship is called the "new perspective." Scholars such as E. P. Sanders, James Dunn, and N. T. Wright do not agree on all points. However, based on a fresh look at Second Temple evidence, their work reflects a more positive disposition toward Judaism and a much more sympathetic reading of the Hebrew Bible.[3]

As an outsider to the debates between representatives of the "new" and "old" perspectives, I am struck by several features of the discussions. First, Hebrew Bible scholars are completely absent. Magnus Zetterholm's eight-page bibliography (135 entries) at the end of his volume on recent scholarship on Paul lacks the name of a single recognizable Hebrew Bible scholar.[4]

Second, and probably related to the previous observation, is that historically the course of the debate has been determined by the direction in which one reads the Scriptures. Proponents of the "old" perspective tend to read the Scriptures backward and interpret the Torah generally and the law particularly in the light of the New Testament. This approach often results in muffling the Hebrew Bible's own voice, forcing interpretations on earlier biblical texts that overlook internal evidence and marginalize natural readings of the texts. Representatives of the new perspective at least appear to listen more closely to the Hebrew Bible's own voice and to read later writings in the light of the earlier before they read the earlier in light of the later.

Third, proponents of the "old" perspective often appear uninterested in or unaware of the tensions their arguments create for an orthodox view of Scripture. Taking Paul's statements about the law at face value creates an intolerable opposition to the Torah. The Hebrew Bible perceives the law as an unprecedented gift (Deut 4:5–8) to be celebrated (Pss 19:7–14[6–13]; 119). Obedience to it yields well-being and life (Deut 6:24), and results in the divine affirmation of law-observant Israelites: "You are righteous" (Deut 6:25; Ps 24:5; Ezek 18:9). But for Paul, the law brings (divine) wrath on people (Rom 4:13–15), animates sin (Rom 7:8–9), is associated with sin and death (Rom 8:2–4), is terminated in Christ (Rom 10:4–5), is/brings the curse (Gal 3:12–14), and imprisons and holds captive (Gal 3:21–24). In contrast to the Spirit, who animates (2 Cor 3:6), the letter (of the law) kills. If Moses and Paul were both inspired and their writings authoritative (as orthodox Christians believe), God appears minimally to speak out of both sides of his mouth and maximally to contradict himself.

I am admittedly a novice to the vast literature this discussion has spawned, and I present my response to these debates with considerable trepidation. However, having lived with Moses for three decades, I have often found myself wondering what Moses, the statesman and theological trailblazer of ancient Israel, might have thought of Paul. And what would Moses have thought of our interpretations of the writings attributed to him and those attributed to the New Testament apostle? Breaking with my own past and popular practice, rather than reading Moses in the light of Paul, in this paper I attempt to

---

3. For a helpful introduction to the debates on Pauline views of gospel and law, see Zetterholm, *Approaches to Paul: A Student's Guide to Recent Scholarship*; Barclay, *Paul and the Gift*, 79–182.

4. This impression is reinforced by recent collections of studies on Paul and the law, which rarely include Hebrew Bible scholars. See, for example, Dunn, ed., *Paul and the Mosaic Law*; Elliott et al., eds., *Galatians and Christian Theology*.

read Paul in the light of Moses. The challenge is huge, and this essay represents an initial foray into what must be a much larger project. John Barclay's recent work, *Paul and the Gift,* recognizes rightly that Paul's epistles to the Romans and Galatians are at the heart of the debate. Although Romans represents a fuller theological statement and reflects Paul's thinking at a later stage, I begin my work in Galatians because this is where Paul began,[5] and frankly as a matter of expediency; this epistle is much shorter than Romans.

I sometimes imagine Moses and myself being present in one of the churches in Galatia as this epistle was read.[6] Occasionally I lean over to him and ask, "Did you say that?" or "How can Paul say that?" or "What do you think of that?" And I imagine looks on his face ranging from puzzlement to incredulity and surprise, perhaps even consternation.[7] However, at the same time I sense there is much in Galatians that Moses would have affirmed—much more than many modern readers will expect.

I begin this paper with summary observations from Gal 1–2 that present a portrait of Paul not merely as a prophet in the tradition of Jeremiah and Isaiah, as many have observed,[8] but as "a prophet like Moses," *à la* Deut 18:15–22.[9] If this is so, then Paul should have affirmed and built on Moses' work, rather than debunking or subverting him or his teaching.[10] Testing this hypothesis will be a complex task that will involve exploration of many of the key themes in Galatians. The second half of this paper concerns a single critical issue: What would Moses' disposition have been toward the debate between Paul and his detractors on whether or not Gentile believers in Jesus needed to be circumcised?[11]

Paul's Status as "Prophet Like Moses"

Despite the absence of any explicit claims by Paul to the title "prophet" (Hebrew נָבִיא, Greek προφήτης), many New Testament scholars have recognized the prophetic nature

---

5. Scholars generally accept Galatians as Paul's earliest extant literary work, probably written prior to the Jerusalem Council (Acts 15), ca. 48 CE, though proponents of the North Galatian hypothesis suggest a date in the early 50s. See Longenecker, *Galatians,* lxxii–lxxxviii. The Epistle to the Romans was Paul's climactic literary work, produced in the mid-50s. See Dunn, *Romans 1–8,* xliii–xliv; idem, "Romans, Letter to the," 838.

6. Martyn (*Galatians,* 42) rightly calls on modern readers to imagine themselves in the world of Paul's original addressees and invites us to "take a seat in one of the Galatian congregations, in order—as far as possible—to listen to the letter with Galatian ears."

7. For an analogous rhetorical ploy, though from an unsympathetic perspective, see Neusner, *A Rabbi Talks with Jesus.*

8. See further below.

9. Cf. Aernie (*Is Paul Also among the Prophets?*, 184), who concludes, "Although it is possible to argue at one level that Paul is either the expected prophet like Moses, the fulfillment of the servant tradition in Isaiah, or a type of second Jeremiah, the combination of all these parallels within 2 Corinthians seems to favour the understanding that Paul's emphasis is not on his connection with each prophet individually, but with the prophetic tradition corporately."

10. For a fuller treatment of the use of Deuteronomy in Paul's letters, see Lincicum, *Paul and the Early Jewish Encounter with Deuteronomy,* 117–68.

11. In this essay, I refer to Moses as speaker because everyone involved in the original conversation would have assumed that in Deuteronomy we hear Moses speaking, even as we assume we hear Paul's voice in Galatians.

of his ministry.¹² In discussions of Paul as prophet some refer to Moses in passing, but the apostle's relationship to Israel's paradigmatic prophet has not received the attention it deserves. Several features in Galatians appear to portray Paul as one in a long succession of "prophets like Moses" (promised by YHWH to Israel in Deut 18:9–22),¹³ perhaps even as the new covenant Moses.¹⁴ Moses had played a foundational role in establishing Israel as the covenant people of YHWH, interpreting YHWH's great acts of salvation associated with Israel's exodus and serving as an agent of divine revelation. In the wake of the "new exodus" that Jesus accomplished through his atoning work (cf. Matt 1:21), Paul functioned similarly to Moses. Indeed, we may perceive Paul as a "second" and "seconding Moses" who attempted to recover the heart of the faith of Israel's great leader.¹⁵ Romans 7:12 declares Paul's default disposition: "So then, the Torah is holy, and the command is holy, righteous, and good" (cf. v. 16; 1 Tim 1:8).¹⁶ While the subject demands an entire volume on its own, I offer a brief summary of features in Paul's *apologia* in Gal 1–2 that suggest he perceived himself as a Mosaic prophet.

1. Paul's Self-Designation as "Apostle" (ἀπόστολος) of Jesus Christ (Gal 1:1)

In Gal 1:1 Paul introduces himself with his favorite title, an "apostle" called through Jesus Christ and God the Father.¹⁷ Ἀπόστολος is a passive verbal adjective of the verb

---

12. The vast literature on the subject is represented by Evans, "Paul and the Prophets, 115–28; Nicklas, "Paulus—der Apostel als Prophet," 77–104; and fuller studies by Sandnes, *Paul—One of the Prophets*, and Aernie, *Is Paul Also among the Prophets?* (n. 9 above). In an otherwise robust placement of Paul in the tradition of Israel's prophets (rooted in Isa 49:1 and Jer 1:5), Susan Eastman remarkably never mentions Moses or Deut 18:15–22, the foundational reference for a biblical understanding of the prophetic movement. See the chapter, "Paul among the Prophets" in Eastman, *Recovering Paul's Mother Tongue*, 63–88.

13. Against prevailing New Testament scholarship, I interpret Deut 18:9–22 as a promise of a succession of future prophets to carry on Moses' work, rather than a messianic prediction. See generally Block, *Deuteronomy*, 433–47. For more detailed argument, especially my interpretation of Acts 3:12–26 and 7:20–43, two critical New Testament texts often cited in the discussion, see my article "'My Servant David,'" 26–32; and chapter 17, "A Prophet Like Moses," above, pp. 356–59.

14. A notion suggested by Bammel ("Paulus, der Moses des Neuen Bundes," 399–408), though Bammel concludes that Paul cannot have viewed himself as the προφήτην . . . ὡς ἐμὲ, "the prophet . . . like me" (Deut 18:15 LXX). On Paul as the minister of the new covenant, see further Aernie, *Is Paul Also among the Prophets*, 161–66, and more fully Hafemann, *Paul, Moses, and the History of Israel*.

15. Secondary literature often suggests that in Galatians Paul has cast off his Jewish roots. See Zetterholm, *Approaches to Paul*, 69–94.

16. Cf. N. T. Wright, "The Letter to the Galatians: Exegesis and Theology," 211–12; For a provocative discussion of what this might mean, see Eisenbaum, "On the Contrary, We Uphold the Law," 208–39. Unless otherwise noted, all translations of biblical texts in this essay are my own.

17. Cf. the fuller expressions ἀπόστολος Χριστοῦ Ἰησοῦ (1 Cor 1:1; 2 Cor 1:1; Eph 1:1; Col 1:1; 1 Tim 1:1; 2 Tim 1:1) and ἀπόστολος Ἰησοῦ Χριστοῦ (Titus 1:1; Peter prefers the latter in 1 Pet 1:1; 2 Pet 1:1). Paul also uses the word of other leaders in the early church in Gal 1:17, 19; cf. 1 Cor 9:5). Elsewhere it is used of Jesus' twelve disciples (Matt 10:2; Mark 3:14; 6:30; Luke 6:13; 9:10; 17:5; 22:14; 24:10; Acts 1:2, 26; 2:37, 43; 4:33, 36; 5:12, 18, 29, 40; etc.), and in Acts 14:14 it is applied to other leaders (Paul and Barnabas; cf. 1 Cor 9:5). In 1 Cor 15:5–11 Paul suggests that a key qualification for the title was the claim to having encountered the risen Christ.

ἀποστέλλω, "to send, commission," used as a noun.[18] The word has long been understood as the Greek rendering of Hebrew שָׁלִיחַ, "envoy, commissioned officer," from ש-ל-ח, "to send, commission."[19] By definition, apostles do not speak on their own initiative, but in response to a superior's commissioning. In Rom 1:1 Paul claims to have been "called" (κλητός) and "selected" (ἀφορίζω) to proclaim "the Gospel of God" (εὐαγγέλιον θεοῦ). Picking up on the former notion, in 1 Cor 1:1 he adds that he was called (κλητός) as an "apostle" of Christ Jesus by the will of God (διὰ θελήματος θεοῦ). Assuming the latter notion in Gal 1:15, Paul declares that he was "selected" (ἀφορίζω) before his birth and privileged to receive the revelation of God's Son that he might proclaim him among the gentiles (ἵνα εὐαγγελίζωμαι αὐτὸν ἐν τοῖς ἔθνεσιν).[20]

The Hebrew Bible offers little direct help in understanding Paul's preference for this professional epithet. The word ἀπόστολος appears only once in the LXX, translating the Hebrew participle שָׁלוּחַ, "sent," in an obscure variant reading of 1 Kgs 14:6.[21] While the absence of the lexeme ἀπόστολος from the First Testament is striking, the notion of "envoy, messenger" is represented by Hebrew מַלְאָךְ, which the LXX translators regularly rendered as ἄγγελος, "angel."[22] The frequent linkage of this noun to the verb ש-ל-ח, "to send, commission," reinforces the status of a מַלְאָךְ as a commissioned agent.[23] Moses is never identified as a מַלְאָךְ or a שָׁלוּחַ, but the frequent use of the verb ש-ל-ח with YHWH as subject and Moses as object suggests that YHWH and the biblical writers perceived him as "the apostle" *par excellence* (cf. Deut 34:11). Although other human agents were also divinely commissioned,[24] with YHWH as subject the verb ש-ל-ח overwhelmingly involves prophets,[25] and Moses appears as the object of this verb more frequently than

---

18. Thus de Boer, *Galatians*, 21. For lexical studies of the noun and the verb, see BDAG, 122–22; Bühner, "ἀποστέλλω *apostellō* send forth," 140–42; idem, "ἀπόστολος *apostolos* delegate, apostle," 142–46; Silva, "ἀποστέλλω (*apostellō*), to send . . . ," and "ἀπόστολος (*apostolos*), envoy, ambassador, apostle . . . ," 365–76; Rengstorf, "ἀποστέλλω," 398–447.

19. The *i*-class passive form is not attested in Biblical Hebrew (cf. *u*-class שְׁלוּחָה in Gen 32:19[18]; Ezek 2:9). Aramaic-speaking Christians would probably have referred to the apostles as שְׁלִיחִין, a corresponding (plural) noun from the root ש-ל-ח. On *i*-class passive forms common in Hebrew titular nouns, see Huehnergard, "On the Etymology and Meaning of Hebrew *nābîʾ*," 88*–93*.

20. Cf. also Rom 1:5, and especially Paul's declaration in 11:13: "I am the apostle of the Gentiles" (εἰμὶ ἐγὼ ἐθνῶν ἀπόστολος).

21. Hebrew וְאָנֹכִי שָׁלוּחַ אֵלַיִךְ קָשָׁה, "But I *have been sent* to you with bad news." The Greek text reads καὶ ἐγώ εἰμι ἀπόστολος πρός σε σκληρός, "and I am to you *an apostle* of bad news." See Rahlfs, ed., *Septuaginta* 1:668. For further discussion of this text, see Rengstorf, "ἀποστέλλω," 413–14. Since Ahijah is explicitly identified as a prophet (נָבִיא, 1 Kgs 14:2) and described as delivering a divine message to Jeroboam, here ἀπόστολος bears the technical sense of prophetic messenger of God.

22. Applied to agents of human authorities, see Gen 32:4, 7[3, 6]; Num 20:14, 21:21; 22:5; Judg 11:12–19; etc. Applied to envoys of God, see Gen 16:7–11; Exod 3:2; 32:34; Num 22:22–35; etc. For further references, see *DCH* 5:284–87. The New Testament uses ἄγγελος ("angel") for human envoys (Matt 11:10; Mark 1:2; Luke 7:24, 27; 9:52; Jas 2:25), but Paul never claims this title.

23. More than seventy times. For references see *DCH* 5:285–86.

24. "Judge" deliverers: Judg 6:14; 1 Sam 12:11; King Saul: 1 Sam 15:18, 20; YHWH's servant: Isa 42:19; Aaron and Miriam, along with Moses: Josh 24:5; 1 Sam 12:8; Ps 105:26; Mic 6:4.

25. Prophets generally: Jer 25:4; 26:6; 35:15; 44:4 (cf. 29:19, where YHWH sends [ש-ל-ח] his "word" [דָּבָר] by his servants the prophets). Individual prophets: Samuel (1 Sam 15:11), Nathan (2 Sam 12:1), Isaiah (Isa 6:8), Jeremiah (Jer 1:7; 25:15; 8:17; 26:12, 15), Ezekiel (Ezek 2:3, 4).

all other prophets combined.[26] Paul's claim to the title ἀπόστολος locates him firmly in the prophetic train of Moses.[27]

2. Paul's Self-Designation as "Servant" (δοῦλος) of Jesus Christ (Gal 1:10)

Although ἀπόστολος was Paul's favorite titular epithet for himself, δοῦλος was a close second.[28] In the Greek world of Paul, this word and its cognate verbs were commonly used of slaves and their service, and Paul occasionally used it this way (Gal 3:28; 4:7, 22, 23, 30, 31).[29] However, given the conceptual and lexical legacy of the Hebrew Bible and the inscriptional use of the Semitic root ע-ב-ד in the ancient Near East, it is misleading to render the word δοῦλος as "bond-slave" or "bond-servant" when Paul applies it to himself.[30] In royal circles, עֶבֶד הַמֶּלֶךְ, "servant of the king," was an honorific title designating persons equivalent to cabinet ministers in modern governments (2 Sam 18:29; 2 Kgs 22:12 [// 2 Chr 34:20]; 25:8). The expression occurs often in the Hebrew Bible,[31] but its courtly significance is confirmed by the plethora of ancient seals from Israel and its environs bearing epithets like עֶבֶד הַמֶּלֶךְ, "servant of the king,"[32] or more specifically, "servant of RN," where RN represents a royal name. Even more impressive is a recently discovered Anatolian monument erected by a "servant of the king."[33] No slave would have had the resources, authority, or the chutzpah to erect a monument like this.

However, Paul's identification of himself as the δοῦλος of God and Christ involves a profoundly theological claim, probably rooted in Israelite tradition rather than in

---

26. Exod 3:10, 12, 13, 14, 15; 4:28; 5:22; 7:16; Num 16:28, 29; Deut 34:11; Josh 24:5; 1 Sam 12:8; Mic 6:4; Ps 105:26.

27. Similarly Sandnes, *Paul—One of the Prophets?*, 68–69. On the tradition of Moses as apostle in Second Temple Judaism and in the book of Hebrews, see Lierman, *The New Testament Moses*, 71–78.

28. Rom 1:1; Gal 1:10; Phil 1:1; Titus 1:1. The title was also claimed by James (Jas 1:1), Peter (2 Pet 1:1), and Jude, the brother of James (Jude 1:1), and applied to John (Rev 1:1) and Moses (Rev 15:3).

29. On the use of δοῦλος and cognates in the Greek world, see LSJ, 446–47; Rengstorf, "δοῦλος," 261–65; BDAG, 259–60, ("pert. to being under someone's total control, *slavish, servile, subject*" [259; italics original]); Spiqc, "δοῦλος," 380–86 ("The word *slave* refers above all to a legal status, that of an object or property [Latin *res mancipt*]. . . . A slave is an article of property that one buys, sells, leases, gives, or bequeaths, that one can possess jointly" [381]); Weiser, "δουλεύω," 349–50 ("In the Greek world and in Hellenism the word group has, because of the high valuation of personal freedom, almost exclusively a demeaning, scornful significance" [350]).

30. NAS renders the word "bond-servant" in Luke 2:29; Rom 1:1; Gal 1:10; Phil 2:7; Col 1:7; 4:7; 2 Tim 2:24; Titus 1:1; Jas 1:1; 2 Pet 1:1; Jude 1:1; Rev 1:1; 15:3.

31. The word עֶבֶד occurs frequently in construct with names of specific kings: e.g., Saul (1 Sam 29:3); Solomon (1 Kgs 11:26; 2 Chr 13:6); the king of Babylon (2 Kgs 25:8). Note also the personal name, עֶבֶד-מֶלֶךְ in Jer 38:7–13; 39:15–18.

32. For example, the Edomite seal inscribed "belonging to Qaws'anal, servant of the king" (לקוסענל עבד המלך) from Tell el-Kheleifeh (Bartlett, *Edom and the Edomites,*, 151–57); the seal "belonging to Shema, servant of Jeroboam" (לשמע עבד ירבעם) from Megiddo (see Cogan and Tadmor, *II Kings*, plate 12a); and the unprovenanced seal that reads "belonging to Obadiah, servant of the king" (לעבדיהו עבד המלך) (Gibson, *Hebrew and Moabite Inscriptions*, 62, 64).

33. For translation and discussion of the text, see Pardee, "A New Aramaic Inscription from Zincirli," 51–71.

his Greek socio-political environment. The frequency of theophoric names involving עֶבֶד plus the name of a deity in Israel[34] and in the world beyond demonstrates how widespread the notion of humans as "servants" of a deity was in the ancient Near East.[35] While biblical authors and characters in the narratives apply the epithet עֶבֶד יהוה/עֶבֶד אֱלֹהִים, "servant of YHWH/God," to many significant figures engaged in divine service,[36] for understanding Paul's status as δοῦλος of Christ/God, the treatment of prophets, often identified collectively as "my/his/your servants the prophets,"[37] is most important.[38] In these contexts עֶבֶד does not refer to a menial role, but designates one specially commissioned by YHWH and invited to stand in his council (סוֹד, Jer 23:16–22).

In contexts involving specific humans as servants of God, the LXX used five different expressions to translate עֶבֶד: in descending order of frequency, δοῦλος, παῖς, θεράπων,[39] ἄνθρωπος (2 Chr 24:6), and οἰκέτης (Deut 34:5). Δοῦλος occurs more than twice as often as all the others combined, and is preferred to παῖς by a 2:1 ratio.[40] Remarkably, outside the Gospels, in the New Testament παῖς occurs only in Acts, four times referring to Jesus (3:13, 26; 4:27, 30), once to David (4:25),[41] and once to a young lad (20:12). Why Paul avoided the word when identifying himself as "the servant" is unclear. Was it to avoid identification with the "servant" in the book of Isaiah whom the

---

34. The name Obadiah ([וֹ]עֹבַדְיָה, "servant of YHWH") is ascribed to at least a dozen individuals in the Hebrew Bible and is frequently attested in Hebrew seals and inscriptions. See Dobbs-Allsopp et al, *Hebrew Inscriptions*, 611–12. On the name itself, see Fowler, *Theophoric Personal Names*, 116, 353.

35. For Ugaritic, see Gröndahl, *Die Personennamen*, 104-6; for Punic and Phoenician, Benz, *Personal Names in Phoenician and Punic Inscriptions*, 369-72; for Edomite, Bartlett, *Edom*, 203, 205-6, 211; for Ammonite, Aufrecht, *A Corpus of Ammonite Inscriptions*, 371; for Aramaic and Canaanite, Layton, *Archaic Features of Canaanite Personal Names*, 122, 130-31. To these we should add Old Arabic, Akkadian, and Amorite names involving [w]ardu, their word for "servant." Cf. *CAD 1/II*, 250.

36. Abraham (Gen 26:4; Ps 105:42), Jacob/Israel (1 Chr 16:23; Isa 41:8; etc.); Moses (Deut 34:5; Josh 1:1; etc.), Joshua (Josh 24:29; Judg 2:8), Caleb (Num 14:24), David (on which see Block, "My Servant David," 45–49), Hezekiah (2 Chr 32:16; Zerubbabel (Hag 2:23), and the Messianic Branch (Zech 3:8). Note also non-Israelites like Job (Job 1:8; 2:3; 42:7, 8) and Nebuchadnezzar (Jer 25:9; 27:6).

37. For "my servants the prophets," see 2 Kgs 9:7; 17:13; Jer 7:25; 26:5; 29:19; 35:15; 44:4; Ezek 38:17; Zech 1:6; for "his servants the prophets," see 2 Kgs 17:23; 21:10; 24:2; Jer 25:4; Dan 9:10; Amos 3:7; Rev 10:7; 22:6; for "your servants the prophets," see Ezra 9:11; Dan 9:6; Rev 11:18.

38. Note also the common identification of individual prophets as YHWH's servant: Ahijah (1 Kgs 14:18; 15:29), Elijah (2 Kgs 9:36; 10:10), Jonah (2 Kgs 14:25), Isaiah (Isa 20:3). This expression was especially useful for distinguishing true prophets from charlatans who claimed to speak for YHWH but whom he disowned (Ezek 12:21–13:23).

39. Used primarily of Moses (Exod 14:31; Num 11:11; 12:7, 8; Josh 1:2; 9:2; 1 Chr 16:40, though עֶבֶד is lacking in Hebrew; cf. Heb 3:5), but also used of Job (Job 2:3; 42:7, 8), as an alternative to παῖς (1:8).

40. While never used exclusively, the concentration of παῖς in Joshua, 1 and 2 Chronicles, and Isaiah suggests the choices reflected translators' preferences rather than deep-seated convictions regarding distinction between the two expressions. This conclusion is reinforced by the variation in readings of Dan 9:6 and 17; Vaticanus renders עֶבֶד as δοῦλος, while Theodotian prefers παῖς. The translator of Jeremiah generally preferred δοῦλος, but in references to prophets as "my servants" (26:5; 35:15; 44:4) he preferred παῖς (but see δοῦλος in 7:25 and 25:4).

41. The use of παῖς here reflects the same impulse that led the editors to use this word in the superscription of Ps 18 (LXX Ps 17). The heading to Ps 36 uses δοῦλος. Nowhere else is David identified as the παῖς of God.

New Testament views as Jesus? By claiming the epithet δοῦλος, Paul identified himself with a long list of human beings whom YHWH had called into his service. But this was not menial service. Like Moses and the prophets of Israel, he served as a member of the heavenly council, received divine revelation, and spoke and wrote for God.

3. Paul's Call to Divine Service (Gal 1:15–16)

Paul's recollection of his call to divine service in Gal 1:15–16 is much sketchier than the classical "prophetical call narratives" of the Hebrew Bible, particularly the call of Moses (Exod 3–4)[42]—or than Luke's accounts of Paul's call in Acts (see Table 18.1).[43]

Table 18.1
The Structure of Biblical Prophetic Appointment Accounts

Elements	Moses (Exodus)	Paul (Acts)	Samuel (1 Samuel)	Isaiah (Isaiah)	Jeremiah (Jeremiah)	Ezekiel (Ezekiel)
(1) Divine Confrontation	3:1–4a	9:1–4a 22:3–7 26:9–14		6:1–4	1:4	1:1–28
(2) Introductory Word (and Response)	3:4b–9	9:4b–5a 22:8–9 26:15	3:2–10	6:5–7	1:5	2:1–2 3:12–15, 22–24
(3) Divine Commission	3:10	9:5b–6a 22:10, 14–15 26:16, 18	3:11–14	6:8–13	1:10	2:3–5a 3:4–6, 10–11, 22–27
(4) Objections	3:11, 13 4:1, 10, 13				1:6	[2:6–8a] [3:16–21][44]
(5) Divine Assurance	3:12, 14–22 4:2–9, 11–12, 14–17	9:10–17 26:17			1:7–9, 17–19	3:7–9
(6) The Sign	4:2–9, 17	9:18–19 22:9, 11–13			1:11–16	2:8b–3:3

---

42. Cf. the call narratives of Samuel (1 Sam 3:2–14), Isaiah (Isa 6:1–13), Jeremiah (Jer 1:3–16), and Ezekiel (Ezek 1:1–3:27). For discussion of calls in the Hebrew Bible and the significance of the "Mosaic pattern" in establishing the authority of prophets, see Hafemann, *Paul, Moses, and the History of Israel*, 47–62. Although Paul's calling takes him in different directions, according to Hafemann, the apostle's allusion to Moses in 2 Cor 3:4–6 "is motivated by his conception of the parallels in function between his own ministry and the ministry of Moses" (p. 109).

43. Though commonly interpreted as Paul's conversion experience, in all accounts this issue has been subordinated to the commission. On this event as a call to mission, see Stendahl, *Paul among Jews and Gentiles*, 7–23; Hays, "The Letter to the Galatians," 212–17.

44. The square brackets suggest objections are implied, rather than explicitly declared.

Nevertheless, Werner Stenger has identified four elements of a prophetic call in Gal 1:15–16 (see Table 18.2):[45]

Table 18.2
Elements of a Prophetic Call in Galatians 1:15–16

15a, 16aα	The Appointment (*Einsetzung*)	Ὅτε δὲ εὐδόκησεν [ὁ θεὸς] ἀποκαλύψαι τὸν υἱὸν αὐτοῦ ἐν ἐμοί,	But when [God] ... was pleased to reveal his Son in me,
15b	The Divine Calling (*Berufungswort*)	ὁ ἀφορίσας με ἐκ κοιλίας μητρός μου καὶ καλέσας διὰ τῆς χάριτος αὐτοῦ	... who had set me apart before I was born and called me through his grace ...
16aβ	The Commission (*Dienstanweisung*)	ἵνα εὐαγγελίζωμαι αὐτὸν	so that I might proclaim him
16aβ	The Context of the Mission (*Zuständigkeitsbereich*)	ἐν τοῖς ἔθνεσιν.	among the gentiles.

Paul's being set apart "while in my mother's womb" alludes most obviously to Jeremiah's call (Jer 1:5).[46] However, the reference to God's revelation of his son in Paul recalls the revelatory purpose of the signs and wonders associated with the exodus (Deut 4:32–35), the theophany at Sinai (4:10–14, 36), and YHWH's revelation to Moses personally (Exod 33:11–34:7; cf. 34:29–35).[47]

4. Paul's Message (Gal 1:16)

Paul's Christocentric mission of proclaiming "the good news of him [Jesus]" is shorthand for the salvation from sin accomplished through Jesus' death and resurrection. While the word εὐαγγελίζω (Hebrew בִּשֵּׂר) is missing in Exod 3–4 LXX,[48] conceptually the notion corresponds to Moses' word of rescue for his people enslaved in Egypt (Exod 3:14–22).[49] Paul's focus on Jesus in the proclamation[50] answers to Moses' focus on YHWH as Israel's deliverer throughout Exod 3:6–22 and the specific event announced

---

45. The scheme is adopted by Sandnes, *Paul*, 59, and Ciampa, *The Presence and Function of Scripture in Galatians 1 and 2*, 112–13.

46. But see also the Jewish tradition of a foreordained mission assigned to Moses in Assumption of Moses 1:14, according to which God "has devised and invented me [Moses], I who have been prepared from the beginning of the world to be the mediator of his covenant" (as translated by Tromp, *The Assumption of Moses*, 7; for commentary on this statement, see pp. 142–43).

47. While an instrumental use of the preposition ἐν in ἐν ἐμοί (Gal 1:16aα) is not excluded (cf. 2 Cor 3:13), Paul later highlights the transforming effect of the revelation of the glory of the Lord (v. 18).

48. The word is used in Isaiah with reference to the good news of Israel's return from exile, which was a new exodus (Isa 40:9; 52:7; cf. also 61:1).

49. Cf. Isa 52:7, which identifies the proclamation of "peace" (שָׁלוֹם) and "salvation" (יְשׁוּעָה) as "gospel/good news" (εὐαγγελίζω).

50. In Gal 1:7 he calls it τὸ εὐαγγέλιον τοῦ Χριστοῦ. Cf. Rom 1:16–17; 10:13–16; 15:16–20; 1 Cor 1:17–18; 15:1–8; but especially his summary of the gospel for gentiles in Eph 1–3.

in Exod 14:13 and celebrated in the Song of the Sea (15:1–18). Many have found in Galatians a "cosmological apocalyptic theology," according to which the Christ-event signals God's intervention in the cosmos, liberating humankind from sin, which has enslaved it, and inaugurating a new age and resulting in a new creation.[51] While Moses' ministry could scarcely be characterized either as "eschatological" or "cosmological apocalyptic," as far as Israel was concerned he certainly announced the dawn of a new age and the birth of a new creation. Indeed, if the critical question for the Galatians was "What time is it?"[52] this was also the critical question for Moses and the Israelites. The narrative preamble to the call of Moses ends on a puzzling note:

> The Israelites groaned under their slavery, and they cried out. And their cry for help because of their slavery rose up to God. God heard their groaning, and God remembered his covenant with Abraham, Isaac, and Jacob. God saw the Israelites, and God knew (וַיֵּדַע אֱלֹהִים). (Exod 2:23b–25)

The last clause in the final sentence is incomplete. By omitting an object or a modifier, the narrator invites hearers to fill in the blank. Most translations assume the Israelites are the object, completing the sentence with something like "God took notice *of them*" (NRSV, NJPSV; cf. NIV). However, the reference to the ancestral covenant in verse 24 suggests otherwise. The cry of the people signaled to God that the time had come to act in fulfillment of his promises in Gen 15: (1) the Israelites had become an innumerable host (Gen 15:5–6); (2) they had been aliens (גֵּר) in a foreign land for four hundred years (v. 13); (3) they had been enslaved (v. 13); and (4) the depravity of the Amorites (עֲוֹן הָאֱמֹרִי) had reached an intolerable level (v. 16). The time had come for YHWH to break into Israel's world, to defeat the forces of oppression in Egypt and of evil in Canaan, and to usher in a new era involving a new people in a new land.[53] The paradigmatic significance of this event for New Testament portrayals of the Christ-event is well documented.

5. Paul's Inspiration (Gal 1:11–12)

The Torah presents Moses as having received his revelation of YHWH directly from God himself (Exod 3:1—4:17; 33:7—34:9), without a human mediator. Although Paul was aware of later tradition that had inserted angels into the process (Gal 3:19),[54] by

---

51. See especially de Boer, "Paul and Jewish Apocalyptic Theology," 169–90; Martyn, "The Apocalyptic Gospel in Galatians," 246–66.

52. Thus Martyn, *Galatians*, 104–5.

53. Note the announcement of the chronological significance of the timing of the exodus in Exod 12:2 and the subsequent emphasis on the timing of the event (Exod 13:4; 23:14; 34:18; Deut 16:1).

54. Although the angel of YHWH (מַלְאַךְ יהוה) would figure as a guardian (Exod 14:9), guide (23:20–23; 32:34), and advance force for the Israelites in their battles for Canaan (33:2), in the remainder of the narratives of Exodus–Deuteronomy after Moses' original commission (Exod 3:2; cf. Acts 7:35) no angelic figure ever interacts with Moses. The tradition of the Torah being mediated through angels first appears in the Second Temple period: Deut 33:2 LXX; Josephus, *Ant.* 15.136; Philo, *Dreams* 1.140–44; Jubilees 1:27–2:1; Pseudo-Philo 11:5; cf. Gal 3:19; Acts 7:38, 53; Heb 2:2. Though without foundation in the Hebrew Bible, by New Testament times Jewish tradition claimed that prophecies generally were received through angelic mediators (cf. Gal 3:19; Acts 7:53; Heb 2:2).

emphasizing that he had received his message directly through a revelation of Jesus Christ (δι' ἀποκαλύψεως Ἰησοῦ Χριστοῦ, 1:12c; cf. v. 16), he actually reinforced the linkage with Moses. In Gal 1:11–22 the apostle claimed that neither was he auto-inspired nor had he derived his gospel from any other human. Since it came directly from God himself, if his detractors rejected his message they would account to God and not to him. Paul makes this point repeatedly,[55] and in so doing he sounds particularly Mosaic. After the declaration of the Decalogue (Exod 19:16—20:21; Deut 4:9–15, 35; 5:1–27), all revelation at Sinai was given directly to Moses,[56] with whom YHWH spoke "face to face like someone speaks to a friend" (Exod 33:11; cf. Deut 34:10). In Deuteronomy both Moses and the narrator note that even his final speeches were delivered as YHWH had commanded him;[57] indeed, Moses occasionally equated his instructions/commands with the commands/voice of YHWH himself.[58] YHWH's defense of Moses in response to Aaron and Miriam's dispute over his monopoly of divine revelation (Num 12:1–9) is particularly pointed:

> Listen to my words:
> "When there are prophets among you,
> I, YHWH, reveal myself to them in visions;
> I speak to them in dreams.
> Not so with my servant Moses:
> In my whole household he is faithful.
> With him I speak mouth to mouth,
> clearly and not in riddles;
> he gazes at the form of YHWH.
> Then why were you not afraid
> to speak against my servant Moses?" (vv. 6–8)

By declaring that he received his gospel directly from God, Paul claimed Moses-like privilege and reinforced the seriousness with which people needed to take his message. Cast in the roles of Aaron and Miriam, his detractors had set themselves up as the targets of divine fury.

---

55. (1) The gospel he preached was not a human message (1:11). In the phrase κατὰ ἄνθρωπον, the preposition marks a norm or standard, that is, "according to" human logic or imagination. Similarly, Barclay, *Paul and the Gift*, 355–56. (2) He did not receive his gospel from another human being (1:12a). (3) He was not taught this gospel (1:12b). (4) He received his gospel directly through a revelation of Jesus Christ (δι' ἀποκαλύψεως Ἰησοῦ Χριστοῦ, 1:12c). (5) After his call to prophetic service, Paul cut himself off from the apostles for three years (1:16b–17).

56. The formula וַיְדַבֵּר יְהוָה אֶל־מֹשֶׁה לֵּאמֹר occurs seventy times between Exod 20:22 and Num 35:9. The clause וַיֹּאמֶר יְהוָה אֶל־מֹשֶׁה לֵּאמֹר occurs an additional five times.

57. The narrator: Deut 1:3; 28:69[29:1]; Moses: 4:5, 14; 6:1, 25.

58. Deut 4:2, 40; 6:2; 8:1, 11; 10:13; 11:27, 28; 12:28; 13:19[18]; 15:5; 26:13–14; 28:1, 13, 15; 30:2, 8, 16; 31:29.

6. Paul's Retreat to Arabia (Gal 1:17–18a)

Paul's enigmatic reference in Gal 1:17–18a to his three-year stay in Arabia raises all sorts of questions, especially since the narratives in Acts never allude to this journey. Against the prevailing view that Paul launched into his gospel mission immediately after his call and spent three years evangelizing the Nabateans,[59] N. T. Wright reads Ἀραβία as a cipher for Sinai/Horeb (cf. 4:25),[60] and argues that the purpose of his time spent there was to redirect his Phinehas- and Elijah-like zeal for Judaism to the mission of the crucified and risen Christ.[61] Wright is on the right track, but Paul returned from Arabia as more than an Elijah figure; he had been transformed into a second Moses, who had himself been transformed through his encounter with YHWH at this place.[62] If the exodus from Egypt had signaled the dawn of a new era in *Heilsgeschichte*,[63] how much more had this been the case with the coming of Christ. Paul would declare Christ to be the redeemer of humankind, not in opposition to Moses, but as the climax and fulfillment of YHWH's grand covenantal plan. For Paul to understand this required reconsidering the "ancestral traditions" (αἱ πατρικαί μου παραδόσεις, Gal 1:14), abandoning his Judaizing agenda,[64] recovering the spirit of Moses and the heart of covenant theology, and grasping the cosmic significance of the new revelation. Like Moses (and Israel months later), Paul needed this divine appointment at Horeb (cf. Exod 3:12; 19:1–3) to experience personally the truth of Exod 19:4–5, to grasp anew YHWH's missionary vision for Israel, and to rediscover the spiritual foundations for his own mission, bringing people from every tribe and nation into the covenant community.[65]

---

59. On this view, see Schnabel, *Paul and the Early Church*, 1032–45; Hengel and Schwemer, *Paul between Damascus and Antioch*, 110–13; Murphy-O'Connor, "Paul in Arabia," 732–37; Schreiner, *Galatians*, 102–103; Moo, *Galatians*, 106–7.

60. N. T. Wright, "Paul, Arabia, and Elijah (Galatians 1:17)," 683–92.

61. Ibid., 687–92.

62. Suggesting that if the road to Damascus was the site of Paul's spiritual conversion, his theological conversion occurred at Sinai. For a Jewish perspective on conversion generally, and Paul's conversion specifically, see Segal, *Paul the Convert*, 72–149.

63. This is hinted at in the enigmatic ending to Exod 2:25, which fails to specify what God knew when he heard the groaning of the Israelites under the weight of the Egyptian bondage. The reference to the covenant with the ancestors in the previous verse suggests that God knew the time had come to rescue his people as promised in Gen 15:13–14 and to confirm (הָקִים) his covenant made with the ancestors as promised in Gen 17:7–8.

64. With Novenson ("Paul's Former Occupation in *Ioudaïsmos*," 24–39), and contra BDAG, 479, I understand Ἰουδαϊσμός in 1:13–14 not to refer to Judaism as a religion or set of beliefs but to a sectarian political program in defense of traditional Jewish practices. Neither in Galatians nor elsewhere does Paul give up the fundamentals of the Jewish/Israelite religion (summarized in Rom 9:4–5). While his former Ἰουδαϊσμός involved the defense of Jewish ancestral traditions within his own ethnic group (which the new "Christian" sect was undermining), in Galatians Judaizers insist on imposing traditional Jewish practices on gentile believers in Jesus. Novenson has rightly reined in Mason's contention ("Jews, Judaeans, Judaizing, Judaism," 457–512) that the word Ἰουδαϊσμός nominalizes the verb ἰουδαΐζω, "to behave like a Jew," and that it signifies actions only non-Jews can take.

65. While Paul's involvement in the gentile mission undoubtedly shaped his rhetoric in Galatians (and Romans), contra Barclay (*Paul and the Gift*, 361, 481, 487, 541, 570), as noted above, he received his message (which includes his theology) directly from God.

7. Paul's Absolute Authority (Gal 1:6–9)

Although Paul's vocabulary differs from that of Moses (LXX), after the cordial opening to Galatians (1:1–5), conceptually Paul's denunciation of his detractors in 1:6-9 is thoroughly Mosaic. His reference to his detractors' divine election (τοῦ καλέσαντος ὑμᾶς ἐν χάριτι) recalls Moses' emphasis on YHWH's unmerited election of Israel, grounded in his love for the ancestors (Deut 4:32–38) and their descendants (Deut 7:6–8).[66] His astonishment that they had deserted (μετατίθημι) their God for a different gospel (Gal 1:6) recalls Moses' references to Israel abandoning (עָזַב) YHWH in favor of alien gods (Deut 28:20; 31:16; cf. 29:24[25]).[67] Most dramatically, in style and essence his denunciation of the Judaizers in Gal 1:8–9 appears to have been inspired by Deut 13,[68] where Moses imagines three scenarios involving false teachers who would invite YHWH's people to serve other gods.[69] Moses pronounced the death penalty over all who would lead the people astray, and in the third scenario (13:13–19[12–18]) condemned to חֵרֶם towns that would abandon YHWH and go after other gods (13:16–19[15–18]).[70] LXX renders Moses' command of "utter destruction" (הַחֲרֵם) emphatically as ἀναθέματι ἀναθεματιεῖτε, "you shall anathematize as an anathema" (13:16[15]; cf. v. 19[18]).[71] Paul employed the words of Moses to curse the Judaizers and highlight the exclusive nature of his gospel of Jesus Christ.[72]

Paul's invective against those who preach another gospel appears also to have been rooted in Deut 18:15–22. After sternly warning against refusing to listen to his authentic prophetic successors (vv. 18–19), Moses pronounced the death sentence on any prophet who falsely claimed to speak for YHWH or spoke by the authority of another deity (v. 20). The nature of Paul's condemnation of the Judaizers (Gal 1:8–9) suggests he perceived himself to be within this Mosaic prophetic train.

---

66. Except for Deut 7:6 (προαιρέω); 21:5 (ἐπιλέγω); and 23:17[16] (missing), LXX renders בָּחַר with ἐκλέγομαι, "to choose," rather than καλέω, "to call." However, this word often means by extension "to choose for the receipt of a special benefit or experience" (BDAG, 503). Paul uses the word with this sense in Gal 1:15–16 and 5:13.

67. This conceptual echo is reinforced by Paul's reference to "another" gospel (ἕτερον εὐαγγέλιον). Except for 31:18 and 20, which have θεοὺς ἀλλοτρίους, in Deuteronomy LXX always renders the adjective in the phrase אֱלֹהִים אֲחֵרִים with a form of ἕτερος (sixteen of eighteen times; 5:7; 6:14; etc.). In 1 Kgs 9:9 (// 2 Chr 7:22) Solomon linked the motifs of abandoning (עָזַב) YHWH, the "gospel" (אֲשֶׁר הוֹצִיא אֶת־אֲבֹתָם מֵאֶרֶץ מִצְרָיִם), and clinging to other gods (וַיַּחֲזִקוּ בֵּאלֹהִים אֲחֵרִים).

68. Cf. the discussions in Sandnes, *Paul*, 70–73; Ciampa, *Presence and Function*, 83–90.

69. Paul's reference to himself or "an angel from heaven" in Gal 1:8 answers to "a prophet or dreamer of dreams" in the first scenario, who declares, "'Let us go after other gods,' which you have not known, 'and let us serve them'" (13:2–3[1–2]).

70. Paul's pronouncement of ἀνάθεμα (vv. 8, 9) links his opponents' fate with that of the Canaanites (Deut 20:17), but more particularly with Israelites guilty of apostasy (הַתּוֹעֵבָה, Deut 13:14–15[13–14]).

71. LXX renders הַחֲרֵם consistently as ἀνάθεμα in Joshua, where the policy of Deut 20:17 is executed against the Canaanites (Josh 6:17, 18[3x]; 7:1[2x], 11, 12[2x], 13[2x]; 22:20).

72. While Paul used the term ἀνάθεμα elsewhere in Rom 9:3 and 1 Cor 12:3 and 16:22, his invocation of a curse (ἀνάθεμα) on anyone who does not love the Lord in the last reference bears the strongest link to our text.

Moses and Paul on Circumcision

Having argued that in Galatians Paul functions as a second and seconding Moses,[73] I turn now to explore how this works out in the argument of the book. The issue is extremely complex, but because of space constraints I must limit my discussion to a single symbol of the gulf separating Paul and his opponents: whether or not gentile believers in Jesus needed to be circumcised. It seems that Paul never expected Jewish believers to give up circumcision as a cultural practice; indeed, Luke reports that apparently for the sake of the ministry to Jews in Lystra and Iconium he circumcised his protégé Timothy, whose father was Greek but whose mother was Jewish (Acts 16:1–3).[74] But in Galatia the issues were different. Whereas the Judaizers insisted that circumcision was required of gentile converts for their salvation and admission to the "inner circle" represented by Jewish Christians, Paul argued that the boundaries of the people of God transcend race (physical descent from Abraham) and that faith in Jesus Christ, rather than circumcision, is now the badge of membership in the covenant community.

The question for us is, if Moses had been an observer or participant in these debates, whose side would he have taken? Although the "circumcision party"[75] would have grounded their position in Gen 17,[76] as others of their persuasion did prior to the Jerusalem Council, they probably invoked the name of Moses to support their case:

> Unless you are circumcised according to *the custom of Moses* (τῷ ἔθει τῷ Μωϋσέως), you cannot be saved. (Acts 15:1)

> It is necessary to circumcise them [gentile believers in Jesus] and to order them to keep the law of Moses (τὸν νόμον Μωϋσέως). (Acts 15:5)

However, if we compare the biblical evidence for Moses' and Paul's treatments of the subject we discover the opposite: Moses would probably have sided with Paul.

The frequency with which the words περιτέμνω ("to circumcise"), περιτομή ("circumcision"), and ἀκροβυστία ("uncircumcision") appear in Paul's writings reflects the significance of circumcision in his thinking,[77] which contrasts with Moses' marginal-

---

73. I do not hereby claim that he was the only "prophet like Moses," but that he viewed himself within this tradition, which suggests that by definition his message could not contradict Moses.

74. Remarkably, this event shows Paul to have been more zealous about physical circumcision than Moses. On this event, see Schreiner, "Circumcision," 139.

75. The phrase οἱ ἐκ περιτομῆς, "those of the circumcision," occurs in Acts 10:45; 11:2.

76. Cf. Stephen's reference to "the covenant of circumcision" (διαθήκη περιτομῆς, Acts 7:8). If we must distinguish between the Abrahamic and Israelite covenants (which seems unwise to me), strictly speaking this refers to the Abrahamic covenant, rather than to the covenant established at Sinai. Presumably because the word בְּרִית occurs thirteen times in Gen 17, Maimonides concluded that God made thirteen covenants with Abraham. See Maimonides, "Laws of Circumcision," chapter 3.7–8 (165a).

77. περιτέμνω, "to circumcise": 1 Cor 7:18[2x]; Gal 2:3; 5:2, 3; 6:12, 13[2x]; Col 2:11; περιτομή, "circumcision": Rom 2:25–29[6x]; 3:1, 30; 4:9–12[6x]; 15:8; 1 Cor 7:19; Gal 2:7–9[3x], 12; 5:6, 11; 6:15; Eph 2:11; Phil 3:3, 5; Col 2:11; 3:11; 4:11; Titus 1:10; ἀκροβυστία, "foreskin, [state of] uncircumcision, uncircumcised person": Rom 2:25–27[4x]; 3:30; 4:9–12[6x]; 1 Cor 7:18, 19; Gal 2:7; 5:6; 6:15; Eph 2:11; Col 2:13; 3:11. For more detailed discussion of the relationship of circumcision and the covenant

ization of the physical rite. Physical circumcision figures prominently in the Abraham narratives (Gen 17:10–27; 21:4; 34:14–25) but is rarely mentioned in Exodus–Deuteronomy. The verb מול, "to circumcise," never occurs in the Moses narratives,[78] and "foreskin" (עָרְלָה) appears only in Exod 4:25.[79] Since YHWH had declared that non-Israelite slaves (עֲבָדִים) and aliens (גֵּרִים) who wanted to participate in the original Passover event needed to be circumcised first (Exod 12:44–48), and that the same ordinance (תּוֹרָה) applied to native Israelites and aliens alike (v. 49), the descendants of Abraham who left Egypt were probably circumcised.

Given the foundational covenantal significance of circumcision in the patriarchal narratives, it is striking that in all of Israel's laws reference to the physical rite occurs only in Lev 12:3. In the context of regulations concerning female ritual cleanness, as a passing comment YHWH reiterated his command in Gen 17:3 that all male children be circumcised on the eighth day (Lev 12:3). Moses would undoubtedly have uttered the words relating to circumcision when he declared these divine ordinances to the people, but this would have been cast as divine speech, rather than his own. He never picked up the topic himself.

Apart from the absence of speech about physical circumcision, three striking facts reflect Moses' personal indifference to the practice. First, Exod 4:24–26 reports that YHWH would have killed him had not his Midianite wife instinctively circumcised their son. While this text is difficult at many levels, it raises questions regarding how God could have chosen Moses to be his agent of deliverance for his people when he had neglected the fundamental covenant rite applying to all Abraham's descendants.

Second, having noted that the Israelites had left Egypt as a circumcised multitude, in Josh 5:2–9 the narrator reports that the rite had been suspended during their four decades of wandering in the desert.[80] Either Moses intentionally neglected it because YHWH had rejected the exodus generation as the covenant people (cf. Deut 5:1–5),[81] or he simply did not deem it important. Ironically, the generation that had come out of Egypt and that bore the physical brand of the covenant would not enjoy the fulfillment of YHWH's covenant promises; they died in the desert (Deut 1:26–2:1). Meanwhile, despite the uncircumcised state of its males, the generation that stood before Moses was

---

in Paul, see Lincicum, *Paul and the Early Jewish Encounter with Deuteronomy*, 147–53.

78. In Exod 4:25 the narrator uses the verb כָּרַת, "to cut off."

79. עָרְלָה occurs in Gen 17:11, 14, 23, 24, 25; 34:14; עָרֵל, "having a foreskin," in Gen 17:14; מוּל in Gen 17:10–14[6x], 23–27[5x]; 21:4; 34:15, 17, 22[2x], 24. Cf. Lev 19:23, which metaphorically characterizes forbidden fruit as עָרְלָה.

80. YHWH's command to circumcise the Israelites "a second time" (שֵׁנִית, v. 2) is puzzling. LXX omits the word. Since this ritual (Josh 5:2–9) apparently preceded the first Passover celebration in the promised land (5:10–11), the natural impulse is to view the "first" circumcision as the rite that apparently preceded the original Passover event (Exod 12:44, 48). Thus Hubbard, *Joshua*, 181; Howard, *Joshua*, 148. However, some suggest that the individuals were circumcised a second time because their previous circumcision had been according to the Egyptian practice, which did not involve the complete removal of the foreskin. Thus Sasson, "Circumcision in the Ancient Near East," 473–76. For further discussion, see Hess, *Joshua*, 118–19; DeRouchie, "Circumcision in the Hebrew Bible and Targumim," 186–89. In light of Josh 5:7, the present argument is not affected by the interpretation one prefers.

81. Note the narrator's reference to the people's resistance to the voice of YHWH in Josh 5:6.

formally accepted as YHWH's covenant people (5:1–5; 26:16–19; 27:9–10; 29:9–12[10–13]), and as such it would claim the land promised to the patriarchs.[82]

Third, in Deuteronomy Moses never speaks of physical circumcision, not even as a prerequisite to participation in Israel's annual festivals (cf. Exod 12:48).[83] In Deut 31:12 he charges the Levitical priests to read the Torah publicly (before men, women, children, and "your alien" [גֵּרְךָ]) at the central sanctuary every seventh year, when they assembled for the covenant renewal ritual. This was the "assembly of YHWH" (קְהַל יְהוָה) from which Ammonites and Moabites were permanently barred, but to which Edomites and Egyptians would eventually be welcomed (23:4–9[3–8]). Whatever the Israelites' physical state, the Torah they were to hear (presumably Moses' addresses in Deuteronomy) said nothing about the physical mark of the covenant.

Since Moses could use the metaphors "uncircumcised of lips" (עֲרַל שְׂפָתַיִם, Exod 6:12, 30) and "circumcision of the heart" (Deut 10:16; 30:6),[84] his neglect, both as a character in the narratives and as the speaker in Deuteronomy, of the physical rite obviously did not arise out of ignorance. Although Israel's covenant relationship with YHWH is front and center in the entire book, physical circumcision is never identified as *an* or *the* Israelite identity marker. Nevertheless, as the book of Judges suggests, it did not take long for the Israelites to treat this as *the* distinguishing mark of their ethnic identity and to disconnect the external rite from internal spiritual realities.[85] On the one hand, we may note the pejorative characterization of Philistines as "the uncircumcised" (הָעֲרֵלִים),[86] and on the other, we notice that Samson, who must have been circumcised, embodied all that was wrong with Israel and had himself become a virtual Philistine at heart (cf. 15:11; 16:30).[87]

---

82. Both YHWH and Moses expressed pessimism about Israel's fidelity in the long run (Deut 4:25–28; 5:29; 29:17–27[18–28]; 31:16–21, 27–29; 32:15–27), but on several occasions Moses commended this generation for its fidelity to YHWH (4:4; 5:1–6, 29).

83. Deuteronomy 16 invites all sons and daughters, male and female servants, resident Levites, and the triad of alien, fatherless, and widow to participate in Shabuoth and Sukkoth. On aliens (הַגֵּר) participating in worship at the central sanctuary, see also 14:29; 26:11–13; 31:12. Moses' silence on physical circumcision might suggest that he simply assumed it. However, given its centrality in Gen 17, on the one hand, and Moses' personal neglect of the rite and his frequent identification of the fundamental covenant requirements in spiritual and ethical terms, on the other, this interpretation is unlikely.

84. Note the graphic and physical nature of 10:16, וּמַלְתֶּם אֵת עָרְלַת לְבַבְכֶם, lit., "And you shall circumcise the foreskin of your heart" (similarly Jer 4:4). In 30:6 the reference to "foreskin" is dropped.

85. At this point I have only one quarrel with Lincicum's observation that Paul essentially divorces the "physical observance from the demand of the law in order to claim that true circumcision is an eschatological state determined by the Spirit that enables one to fulfill the law—regardless of whether one is physically circumcised" (*Paul and the Early Jewish Encounter with Deuteronomy*, 149). The problem here is the word "eschatological." It is true that Deut 30:1–10 and Ezek 36:26–27 envision the circumcision/transplant of Israel's collective heart as an eschatological reality, but nothing precludes this from having transpired in the hearts of individual Israelites in Moses' day or thereafter.

86. Judg 14:3; 15:18. Cf. 1 Sam 14:6; 17:26, 36; 31:4; 2 Sam 1:20; 1 Chr 10:4. Cf. also Isa 52:1; Jer 9:25–26[24–25]. On Israelite and Philistine dispositions toward circumcision, see most recently Faust, "The Bible Archaeology, and the Practice of Circumcision," 253–71. On the (un)circumcision of Philistines in the Hebrew Bible, see Thiessen, *Contesting Conversion*, 44–46.

87. Cf. Block, *Judges, Ruth*, 392. Jeremiah addresses the incongruity of physical circumcision apart from heart/spirit circumcision in Jer 9:23–25[22–24].

Moses' neglect of physical circumcision in speech and practice raises serious questions about the Judaizers' comment in Acts 15:1: "Unless you are circumcised according to the custom of Moses, you cannot be saved" (NRSV). The elevation of external identity markers above internal spiritual realities may have been traditional and customary (ἔθος) in Paul's day, but this development did not derive from Moses.[88] The association of Moses with circumcision was probably rooted in the fact that he (and Aaron) would have had to implement the rite as outlined in Exod 12:43–50, or in the notion that the entire Pentateuch came from him.[89]

If Not Circumcision, Then What?

In light of the foregoing discussion, a question arises inevitably: If physical circumcision was not *the* critical identity marker of the covenant people for Moses, then what was? Deuteronomy provides several potential answers.

1. True Israelites claimed the Shema as the fundamental declaration of Israelite identity: wholehearted and full-bodied covenant commitment to YHWH.

> Hear, O Israel: YHWH is our God, YHWH alone. You shall demonstrate love for YHWH your God with all your heart/mind (לֵב), and with all your being (נֶפֶשׁ), and with all your resources (מְאֹד). (Deut 6:4–5)[90]

Rather than functioning merely as a verbal badge of identity,[91] this declaration functions as a thesis statement for the segment of Moses' second address that is framed by two שְׁמַע's (6:4; 9:1) and highlights the importance of unreserved and unqualified commitment to YHWH. While this commitment was obviously to be public (worn on the forehead and hands and inscribed on doors and gates, 6:8–9), in what follows the actual marks of identity include exclusive devotion to YHWH (6:10–15), doing what is right and good in his eyes (6:18, 24–25; 7:10–11; 8:1–5), repudiating all that is pagan (7:1–26), and blessing YHWH alone as the source of their well-being (8:7–20).

The commentary on the שְׁמַע offered by Deut 10:12–11:1 reinforces this interpretation. In catechetical style Moses poses a question, and then provides a three-part answer, with two literal appeals (vv. 12b–13, 20) sandwiching a metaphorical call for covenant loyalty (v. 16; see Table 18.3, page 391). All three are grounded doxologically in YHWH's transcendent sovereignty and his immanent grace.[92]

---

88. A fact overlooked by Schreiner ("Circumcision," 138), who cites this text without comment under the heading "The Scriptures."

89. Given Paul's focus on Abraham and God's covenant with him, it is ironic that *the sign* of the Abrahamic covenant should have become the premier symbol of the "cultural capital" (cf. Barclay, *Paul and the Gift*, 362–65) associated with Moses and the law that Paul rejected.

90. On the interpretation presented here, see Block, "How Many Is God?" 193–212. On Hebrew אָהֵב as "demonstrate love," see n. 127 below.

91. For detailed instruction on the recitation/reading of the Shema, see Maimonides, "Laws of Reading the Shema," 94a–97b.

92. For fuller discussions of this text, see Block, *Deuteronomy*, 268–79; idem, "In Spirit and in Truth," 290–93.

Table 18.3
The Structure of Deuteronomy 10:12–11:1

The Issue	So what does YHWH your God ask (שֹׁאֵל) of you? (10:12a)		
	I (vv. 12b–15)	II (vv. 16–19)	III (vv. 20–22)
The Requirement	You shall fear YHWH your God, walk in all his ways, demonstrate love for him, and serve YHWH your God with all your heart and with all your being, and keep the commands and statutes of YHWH, which I am commanding you today for your good. (10:12b–13)	Circumcise therefore the foreskin of your heart, and be no longer stubborn. (10:16)	You shall fear YHWH your God. You shall serve him and hold fast to him, and by his name you shall swear. (10:20)
The Doxology	Look, to YHWH your God belong heaven and the heaven of heavens, the earth with all that is in it. (10:14)	For YHWH your God is God of gods and Lord of lords, the great, the mighty, and the awesome God, who is not partial and takes no bribe. (10:17)	He is your praise. He is your God, who has done for you these great and terrifying things that your eyes have seen. (10:21)
The Basis of the Requirement / **The Application**	Yet YHWH set his heart in love on your fathers and chose their offspring after them, you above all peoples, as you are this day. (10:15)	He executes justice for the fatherless and the widow, and demonstrates love for the sojourner, giving him food and clothing. So demonstrate love for the sojourner, for you were sojourners in the land of Egypt. (10:18–19)	Your fathers went down to Egypt seventy persons, and now YHWH your God has made you as numerous as the stars of heaven. (10:22)
The Summary Conclusion	You shall therefore demonstrate love for YHWH your God and keep his charge, his statutes, his rules, and his commands always. (11:1)		

The center of gravity in each answer involves deep internal spiritual and dispositional commitments. In the first answer Israel's identity is marked with five verbs: fearing YHWH, walking in his ways, loving him, serving him wholeheartedly, and obeying his commands (vv. 12b–13); the second calls for a circumcision of the heart, and the third for exclusive devotion to YHWH. The text is silent on the sorts of markers Judaizers were imposing on Gentile believers in Galatians.

2. True Israelites received the story of Israel's redemption and the gift of the promised land as their story, and they responded to YHWH's grace demonstrated in these formative events with grateful obedience.

This disposition is reflected in two celebrative texts, which we may identify as the "Domestic Catechism" (6:20–25) and the "Little Creed" (26:1–11). While both statements prescribe a particular verbal response, the recitations themselves were not to be the identity marker, any more than merely reciting the שְׁמַע was to be. The point is receiving YHWH's salvation and the promised land as gracious gifts, rather than as entitlements (cf. 9:4–24), and responding to the privilege of being YHWH's people with overflowing gratitude and righteous living. Elsewhere the divine requirement is summarized as צֶדֶק צֶדֶק תִּרְדֹּף ("Righteousness, only righteousness, you shall pursue," 16:20). For Moses and Paul (and for Jesus, Matt 23:23), the primary badges of covenant relationship with God did not involve observance of rites and rituals but the weightier matters of Torah.

3. True Israelites were marked by deep-seated and reverential trust in YHWH.

This discussion will be more complex than the preceding, but it is particularly necessary if we would understand Paul's identification of "faith working through love" (πίστις δι' ἀγάπης ἐνεργουμένη) as the true identity marker for the Christian community in Gal 5:6. Πίστις/πιστεύω words are scarce in LXX Deuteronomy, but conceptually Paul's statement is thoroughly Deuteronomic. The verb πιστεύω (used for הֶאֱמִין in Gen 15:6) occurs twice in LXX Deuteronomy, but only 9:23 is relevant.[93] Here Moses interprets Israel's refusal to listen to YHWH's voice and enter Canaan from Kadesh-barnea as rebellion and unbelief.[94] When referring to this event in the first address, Moses had used the Hebrew word הֶאֱמִין: "But in spite of this,[95] you would not trust (אֵינְכֶם מַאֲמִינִם) in

---

93. Deuteronomy 28:66 uses the verb non-theologically of people losing confidence in life itself.

94. וַתַּמְרוּ אֶת־פִּי יְהוָה אֱלֹהֵיכֶם וְלֹא הֶאֱמַנְתֶּם לוֹ וְלֹא שְׁמַעְתֶּם בְּקֹלוֹ. The Greek renders both מָרָה, "to rebel," and הֶאֱמִין, "to believe, trust," with "faith" words: καὶ ἠπειθήσατε τῷ ῥήματι κυρίου τοῦ θεοῦ ὑμῶν καὶ οὐκ ἐπιστεύσατε αὐτῷ καὶ οὐκ εἰσηκούσατε τῆς φωνῆς αὐτοῦ. While ἀπειθέω means primarily "to be disobedient," in the New Testament it occasionally refers to unbelievers: John 3:36; Acts 14:2; Rom 15:31.

95. Hebrew וּבַדָּבָר הַזֶּה, which LXX translates literally, καὶ ἐν τῷ λόγῳ τούτῳ. The expression is shorthand for (1) YHWH's promise to fight for Israel (1:30); (2) the reminder of his salvation in Egypt (v. 30b); (3) the experience of his care in the desert (v. 31).

YHWH your God" (1:32). However, instead of πιστεύω LXX renders הֶאֱמִין here with the rare but related word ἐμπιστεύω.[96]

The noun πίστις occurs in Deuteronomy only in 32:20, where YHWH characterizes Israel as "a perverse generation, sons utterly lacking in faithfulness,"[97] which contrasts starkly with YHWH, whom 7:9 and 32:4 characterize as θεὸς πιστός (Heb. הָאֵל הַנֶּאֱמָן and אֵל אֱמוּנָה, respectively).[98] If YHWH's faithfulness involved the divine Suzerain's actions in accord with his promises in the covenant, Israel's faithfulness would have involved the vassal's actions in keeping with the covenant to which they had committed themselves, first at Horeb and now on the Plains of Moab.

Although this accounts for all the πίστις words in Deuteronomy, it does not mean that the notion of "faith"/"belief" is unimportant in the book. Indeed, יָרֵא, which normally means "to be afraid, to fear," often functions as a substitute for הֶאֱמִין.[99]

This usage is evident already in the narratives that precede Deuteronomy. In Gen 15:6, the classic text for this conversation, Greek πιστεύω renders Hebrew הֶאֱמִין (cf. Gal 3:6; Rom 4:3), as expected. Although this is the last occurrence of the root א-מ-ן in a theological context in Genesis,[100] it does not mean this was the last time Abraham's faith was tested. In 22:1 the narrator announces formally that what follows was designed as a divine test. Despite the absence of הֶאֱמִין in this context, YHWH's demand to sacrifice Isaac (22:2) obviously tested whether or not he could trust YHWH to keep his promise to multiply his descendants *through Isaac* (21:8–12). However, the divine envoy used a different word in his assessment of Abraham's response: "Now I know that you are a God-fearer (כִּי־יְרֵא אֱלֹהִים אַתָּה; cf. LXX, ὅτι φοβῇ τὸν θεὸν σύ),[101] seeing you have not withheld your son, your only son, from me" (v. 12). Although יָרֵא means fundamentally

---

96. ἐμπιστεύω is rare even outside the Greek Bible. See LSJ, 545. The word is common in the Apocrypha, but in translating the Hebrew Bible LXX employs this lemma only in Judg 11:20; 2 Chr 20:20 [3x]; Jonah 3:5.

97. Hebrew, כִּי דוֹר תַּהְפֻּכֹת הֵמָּה בָּנִים לֹא־אֵמֻן בָּם; Greek, ὅτι γενεὰ ἐξεστραμμένη ἐστίν υἱοὶ οἷς οὐκ ἔστιν πίστις ἐν αὐτοῖς.

98. Deuteronomy 7:9

הָאֵל הַנֶּאֱמָן	θεὸς πιστός
שֹׁמֵר הַבְּרִית וְהַחֶסֶד	ὁ φυλάσσων διαθήκην καὶ ἔλεος
לְאֹהֲבָיו וּלְשֹׁמְרֵי מִצְוֹתָו	τοῖς ἀγαπῶσιν αὐτὸν καὶ τοῖς φυλάσσουσιν τὰς ἐντολὰς αὐτοῦ
לְאֶלֶף דּוֹר	εἰς χιλίας γενεάς
אֵל אֱמוּנָה	θεὸς πιστός
וְאֵין עָוֶל צַדִּיק וְיָשָׁר הוּא	καὶ οὐκ ἔστιν ἀδικία δίκαιος καὶ ὅσιος κύριος

The adjective πιστός recurs in 28:59, but there the word characterizes maladies as "persistent."

99. For full discussion, see chapter 14, "The Fear of YHWH: The Theological Tie that Binds Deuteronomy and Proverbs," above, pp. 283–302.

100. In Gen 42:20 and 45:26 the word involves believing in another human being.

101. Contra LXX and virtually all English translations, which render יְרֵא with a finite verb, this is a verbless clause of classification. Cf. Speiser (*Genesis*, 163), "You are a God-fearing man." As Abraham and Job (Job 1:1, 8; 2:3) demonstrate, יְרֵא represents trusting awe demonstrated in righteous living and specific obedience to God's command. Although this statement appears to be overlooked, for discussion of verbless clauses of classification, see Andersen, *The Hebrew Verbless Clause*, 42–45. The phrase יְרֵא אֱלֹהִים occurs elsewhere in Deut 25:18 (negatively of Amalek) and Eccl 7:18.

"to be afraid, to fear, to revere," here it connotes "trusting awe," or "awed trust," demonstrated by obedience.

The midwives' fear of God in Exod 1:17 and 21 may also be interpreted as trust in God to defend them against the fury of Pharaoh.[102] However, the sense of "belief" for יָרֵא is nearer the surface in Exod 9:20, where the narrator notes that after Moses' announcement of impending hail, those Egyptian officials who "feared" (i.e., "believed") YHWH's word hastily removed their slaves and livestock to a secure place. Exodus 14:31 conjoins יָרֵא and הֶאֱמִין in a single statement: in the wake of YHWH's annihilation of Pharaoh's army "the people feared (יָרֵא) YHWH; they believed (הֶאֱמִין, LXX ἐπίστευσαν) in him and his servant Moses."[103] This characterization reinforces Walter Moberly's proposal that in the Hebrew Bible "the fear of God" is the primary expression for the appropriate response to him:

> The First Testament use of "fear of God" is thus more or less equivalent *in function* to the New Testament's use of various forms of "believe/trust" and "have faith" (*pisteuō* and *pistis*) to depict appropriate human response to God; so in terms of function a Christian way of conveying the tenor of "one who fears God" might be "a believer," "a person of faith."[104]

The forty plus occurrences of יָרֵא in Deuteronomy testify both to its breadth of meaning and significance in the book (Fig. 18.1). It often bears the common sense of fright or terror,[105] and the awesome/awe-inspiring character of YHWH's name and actions are represented by the cognate words הַנּוֹרָא (7:21; 10:17, 21; 28:58) and מוֹרָא (4:34; 26:8).[106] However, given the revelatory intention of these "signs and wonders,"[107] YHWH's awesome deeds should also have prompted the Israelites to trust him. The phenomena that precipitate this response offer clues to the nature of "fear": (1) the great fire and the sound of YHWH's voice at Horeb (4:10; 5:5, 29); (2) YHWH's signs and wonders in Egypt (4:34; 10:21; 26:8; cf. 34:12); (3) the judgment in criminal cases (13:12[11]; 17:13; 19:20; 21:21); (4) eating in the presence of YHWH at the central sanctuary (14:23); (5) hearing the words of the Torah (17:19; 31:12–13; cf. 28:58). How the first four of these might prompt fear in the form of fright (##1, 3) or awe (##2, 4) is readily grasped, but how reading the Torah promotes either is not so clear—unless one follows LXX, which renders תּוֹרָה pervasively as νόμος, "law," in which case the word may refer to fear of punishment.

---

102. Weinfeld (*Deuteronomy and the Deuteronomic School*, 274) interprets יָרֵא here as moral restraint; similarly, Gen 20:11; 42:18; Lev 19:14, 32; 25:17, 36, 43; and Deut 25:18. According to Tigay (*Deuteronomy*, 47; cf. 352 n. 40) the word "is virtually a synonym for ethical behavior and fear of sin (cf. Deut 5:26; 25:18)." Cf. Moberly, *The Old Testament of the Old Testament*, 189. For Gregory Smith (*The Testing of God's Sons*, 81–82), יָרֵא involves action in obedience to the will of YHWH, demonstrated loyalty.

103. With NJPSV, interpreting the *waw* on וַיַּאֲמִינוּ explicatively.

104. Moberly, *Old Testament Theology*, 245 (italics his).

105. Without distinguishing the cause of the fright: 1:19, 21, 29; 2:4, 25; 11:25 (מוֹרָא); etc. In 1:19 and 8:15 the desert is characterized as "terrifying" (הַנּוֹרָא).

106. In 34:12 the narrator exceptionally attributes these "awesome deeds" (הַמּוֹרָא הַגָּדוֹל) to Moses.

107. Note the recurring recognition formula "They/you will know that I am YHWH" in Exodus: 6:7; 7:5, 17; 8:18[22]; 10:2; 14:4, 18; 16:12; 29:46.

Figure 18.1
The Semantic Spectrum of ירא Words in Deuteronomy

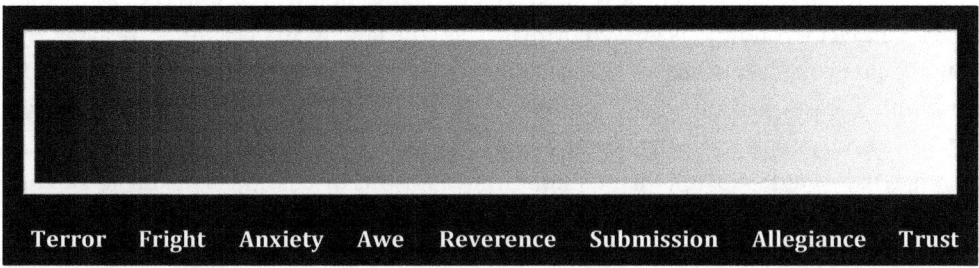

Terror | Fright | Anxiety | Awe | Reverence | Submission | Allegiance | Trust

Although Deuteronomy often links יָרֵא with obedience and righteous living,[108] important clues to its meaning are found particularly in the sequence of verbs scattered within the book: reading—hearing—learning—fearing—obeying—living well (Table 18.4).

Table 18.4
The Importance of Hearing the Torah

Reference	Reading	Hearing	Learning	Fearing	Obeying	Living well
1. 4:10		✓	✓	✓		
2. 5:23–29		✓		✓	✓	✓
3. 6:1–3			✓	✓	✓	✓
4. 17:13		✓		✓	✓	
5. 17:19–20	✓	[✓]	✓	✓	✓	✓
6. 19:20		✓		✓	✓	
7. 31:11–13	✓	✓	✓	✓	✓	

For our purposes, the fifth and seventh texts, which involve encounters with YHWH through the hearing of the Torah, are especially significant.[109] Whereas Israel's encounter with YHWH at Horeb had terrified the people (4:9–14, 36; 5:5, 23–33; 18:16),

---

108. Deut 5:29; 6:2; 8:6; 10:12–13; 13:5[4]; 17:19; 28:58; 31:12.

109. In the first three the sound of YHWH's voice accompanied by awesome theophanic visual phenomena at Horeb evoked severe fright in the people. The fourth and sixth cases involve warnings against disregarding the divinely rendered decisions in criminal cases (17:13) or repeating the crime (19:20).

Deuteronomy portrays worship at the place where YHWH would establish his name as confident, intimate, and celebrative.[110]

The Torah itself answers how the verb יָרֵא fits this picture. If הַתּוֹרָה (i.e., Moses' addresses in Deuteronomy) is viewed primarily as "the law," as many assume, hearing "the law" could evoke fear of negative consequences analogous to the effect hearing verdicts in criminal cases had on the community (13:12[11]; 17:13; 19:20; 21:21). However, if הַתּוֹרָה is understood as "instruction," whose goal is the promotion of יָרֵא in the sense of "faith, trust" (Paul's πίστις), then its significance for this discussion is readily apparent.

But how does hearing the Torah promote faith in YHWH? This preliminary essay cannot offer a full discussion of the issue, but we may begin by observing Deuteronomy's characterization of YHWH.

First, Deuteronomy portrays YHWH in gloriously transcendent terms, pointing to a trustworthy deity. By itself this image could evoke fright/awe, but in context it is intended to promote confidence (cf. Isa 40:12–31). The concluding "Song of YHWH" opens by ascribing greatness (גֹּדֶל) to him (32:3), a theme that had been declared in earlier doxological descriptions.

7:21	כִּי־יְהוָה אֱלֹהֶיךָ בְּקִרְבֶּךָ אֵל גָּדוֹל וְנוֹרָא	YHWH your God is in your midst, a great and awesome God
10:17	יְהוָה אֱלֹהֵיכֶם הוּא אֱלֹהֵי הָאֱלֹהִים וַאֲדֹנֵי הָאֲדֹנִים הָאֵל הַגָּדֹל הַגִּבֹּר וְהַנּוֹרָא	YHWH your God is God of gods and Lord of lords, the great, the mighty, and the awesome God.
28:58	לְיִרְאָה אֶת־הַשֵּׁם הַנִּכְבָּד וְהַנּוֹרָא הַזֶּה אֵת יְהוָה אֱלֹהֶיךָ	That you may fear this glorious and awesome name, YHWH your God.

YHWH's transcendent power and glory were demonstrated particularly through the "signs and wonders" performed against the Egyptians (4:34; 10:21; 26:8) and for Israel's benefit.[111]

Second, the Torah portrays YHWH in graciously personal terms. Although explicit verbal characterizations of YHWH as gracious are rare in Deuteronomy,[112] Israel's confidence in future restoration after judgment was based on his compassionate character (כִּי אֵל רַחוּם יְהוָה אֱלֹהֶיךָ, 4:31) and his change of heart toward his wayward people (וְעַל־עֲבָדָיו יִתְנֶחָם, 32:36). But Moses laced his recollections of past events with stories of divine grace: YHWH revealed his will to Israel (4:1–8; cf. 5:1–22; 6:20–25; 30:11–20); he invited Israel to assemble in his presence at Horeb and established his covenant with them there (4:9–31; cf. 5:2–3); he rescued his people from Egypt (4:32–40; cf. 5:6 et passim); he

---

110. Signaled by the verb שָׂמַח ("to celebrate, rejoice"), in 12:7, 12, 18; 14:26; 16:11, 14–15; 26:11 (cf. Lev 23:40). On the contrast between Israel's terrifying, one-time encounter with YHWH at Horeb and Israel's confident, regular meetings with him at the central sanctuary, see chapter 7, "A Place for My Name," above, pp. 126–51.

111. Deuteronomy 11:2–7 includes YHWH's care for the Israelites in the desert and his punishment of Dathan and Abiram among "all the great acts of YHWH that he executed" (כָּל־מַעֲשֵׂה יְהוָה הַגָּדֹל אֲשֶׁר עָשָׂה). Cf. Exod 15:11.

112. The root חֵן occurs only in 24:1, which notes its absence in a man with a needy wife.

loved the ancestors and elected their descendants for his favor out of all the peoples on earth (4:37; cf. 7:6-7; 10:15; 14:2); he spared Israel and renewed the covenant at Horeb (9:19; 9:25-10:5); he cared for Israel in the desert (1:31; 8:1-5); he gave them a fruitful homeland (1:7-8; 6:10-11, 23; 8:7-10; 11:9-12; 26:9, 15; 27:3; 32:13-14); he provided leadership in the forms of king (17:14-20), prophets (like Moses; 18:9-20), and Levitical priests (10:8-9; 18:1-8; 21:5; 33:8-11); he confirmed the covenant with the present generation in Moab (26:16-19; 27:9; 28:69[29:1]; 29:11[12]; etc.); he invited Israel to worship and celebrate in his presence (12:1-14; 14:1-21, 26; 16:11-14; 26:1-11); and his ultimate goal was Israel's well-being (11:18-25; 12:7, 18; 15:10; 23:21[20]; 28:1-14; 30:11-20). Even threats of punishment (e.g., the covenant curses in 28:15-68) represent overtures of grace, reminding the people how passionately YHWH treasured his relationship with them and warning in advance of the consequences of apostasy. Hearing the Torah would remind the people of all these graces, hopefully evoking in them, not fear in the sense of fright and awe, but especially the sense of confidence in the one who had chosen them to be his treasured people.

Third, the Torah portrays YHWH as faithful to his word. The exordium to the "Song of YHWH" (ch. 32) begins by proclaiming YHWH's greatness (32:3), but the next strophe focuses on his faithfulness:

הַצּוּר תָּמִים פָּעֳלוֹ	The Rock, his work is perfect;
כִּי כָל־דְּרָכָיו מִשְׁפָּט	See, all his ways are justice.
אֵל אֱמוּנָה וְאֵין עָוֶל	A God of faithfulness and without iniquity,
צַדִּיק וְיָשָׁר הוּא	Righteous and upright is he (32:4).

While אֵל אֱמוּנָה conveys the notion of trustworthiness explicitly, this quality is also reflected in the last line: צַדִּיק וְיָשָׁר הוּא. In Deuteronomy "righteousness" (צֶדֶק/צְדָקָה) means "conduct in accord with an objective standard," which is established by YHWH within the covenant that he made with his people. Moses celebrated YHWH's perfect embodiment of this trait doxologically in 7:9:[113]

יְהוָה אֱלֹהֶיךָ הוּא הָאֱלֹהִים	YHWH your God is God,
הָאֵל הַנֶּאֱמָן	the faithful God
שֹׁמֵר הַבְּרִית וְהַחֶסֶד	who maintains covenant loyalty
לְאֹהֲבָיו וּלְשֹׁמְרֵי מִצְוֹתָיו (ereQ)	with those who love him and keep his command,
לְאֶלֶף דּוֹר	to a thousand generations.

While this summary declaration is covenantal from beginning to end, the Torah of Deuteronomy proclaims the faithfulness of YHWH with repeated reminders of how he has kept the promises associated with his covenant made with the ancestors, established with their descendants at Horeb,[114] and renewed with this generation:[115] (1) YHWH has

---

113. Cf. Exod 34:6; Ps 86:15.

114. Cf. Gen 17:6-8; Exod 6:2-8; 19:4-6; Deut 4:9-31.

115. On "the covenant with the fathers," see Hwang, *The Rhetoric of Remembrance*, 178-232.

multiplied the population like the stars of the sky;[116] (2) as predicted in Gen 15:13, after centuries in a foreign land, ending in slavery, YHWH rescued them from their oppressors;[117] (3) now, after the failure of the exodus generation (1:35; 4:25), YHWH is about to deliver the promised land of Canaan into their hands.[118] But YHWH's fidelity to his word is also reflected in his oath with which he guarantees the fulfillment of the imprecations for his people's infidelity built into the covenant (11:13–28; 28:1–69[29:1]). However, building on Lev 26:40–45,[119] Moses declared that however horrendous the punishment for rebellion might be (4:26–28; 28:15–68; 29:19–27[20–28]), the judgment would not be the last word. With compassionate heart and true to his commitments, YHWH would bring his people back from exile and reestablish them in the land promised to the ancestors (4:30–31; 30:1–10; 32:43). Both Moses and YHWH anticipated that the Israelites would soon forget their commitments by going after other gods (4:23; 6:12; 8:11, 14, 19; 31:16–18, 26–29), but YHWH would never forget his covenant (4:31). For this generation, YHWH guaranteed his people's future with his promise (32:36–43) and his oath.[120]

I return to the issue raised at the beginning of this lengthy excursus, namely, the importance of hearing the Torah in community. In addition to stimulating reverent awe (יָרֵא), hearing the reminders of YHWH's compassion toward his people in the past and his declarations of his faithfulness to his words, his covenant, and his people in the future should evoke in hearers the faith that Abraham exhibited in Gen 15:6 and 22:1–12. Since this confidence in YHWH represents part of the fuller meaning of יָרֵא in Deuteronomy, hearing the Torah would be critical for maintaining Israel's faith. At the festival of Sukkoth, the priests were to "read" the Torah, that the people might "hear," that they might "learn" to "fear" (i.e., trust) YHWH, that they might "obey," that they might "live" (Deut 31:9–13).[121] We now understand why the five markers of Israel's identity in Deut 10:12–13 begin with "fear/trusting awe" and then move successively through walking in the ways of YHWH, demonstrating love for him, and wholehearted and full-bodied service, and finally to obedience to the commands. Borrowing from Deuteronomy, the wisdom writers had it right:

---

116. Deut 1:10; 10:22; 26:5; cf. Gen 15:5; 22:17; 26:4.

117. Deut 4:37; 5:6; 6:12, 21–23; 7:8; 8:14; 13:6, 11[5, 10]; 26:6–8.

118. References to the covenant oath involving the land occur a dozen times in the book: 1:8, 35; 4:21; etc.

119. Assuming Lev 26 antedates Deut 4:25–31; 11:13–28; 28:1–69[29:1]. See now Kilchör, "The Direction of Dependence between the Laws of the Pentateuch," 1–14; idem, *Mosetora und Jahwetora*; contra Stackert, who argues that while using the language of Deuteronomy the authors of the Holiness Code (which includes Lev 26) intentionally superseded, subverted, and supplanted the Deuteronomic Law. See his *Rewriting the Torah*; idem, "The Holiness Code," 389–96.

120. Cf. the references to "a covenant . . . with an oath" in 29:11, 13, 20[12, 14, 21].

121. This sequence reinforces Sarna's contention (*Exodus*, 75) that "faith" in the Hebrew Bible "refers to trust and loyalty that find expression in obedience and commitment."

| תְּחִלַּת חָכְמָה יִרְאַת יְהוָה | The fear of [trusting awe in] YHWH is the first principle of wisdom |
| וְדַעַת קְדֹשִׁים בִּינָה | And knowledge of the Holy One is understanding. (Prov 9:10)[122] |

And now we also understand the conclusion to the book of Malachi, and indeed to the First Testament.[123] In a series of oracles from the Persian period responding to the absence of fear/trust in YHWH in the restored community in Jerusalem, Malachi prescribes the solution: "Remember the Torah of Moses my servant whom I charged at Horeb [to teach] ordinances and judgments for all Israel" (Mal 3:22[4:4]).[124]

Based on the formulaic sequence, reading—hearing—learning—fearing—obeying—living well, I imagine Moses standing beside me as the epistle to the Galatians is being read and asking, "How shall they live, if they do not obey? How shall they obey, if they do not have faith in YHWH? How shall they have faith, if they have not learned of him? How shall they learn of him, if they do not hear the Torah? How shall they hear the Torah, if no one reads it for them?"[125]

With this conclusion, we may have encountered another conceptual link between Paul in Galatians and Moses in Deuteronomy. In Gal 3:2, Paul asks, "Did you receive the Spirit by works of the law or by *hearing* with faith?" (ἐξ ἔργων νόμου τὸ πνεῦμα ἐλάβετε ἢ ἐξ ἀκοῆς πίστεως;). Just as Paul's proclamation of the gospel produced faith, so in an earlier time hearing the Torah of Moses should have produced faith. Although they refused to trust YHWH, the exodus generation did not need this Torah, for they had experienced firsthand YHWH's transcendent power, his gracious deliverance, and his confirmation of his word. Nevertheless, they failed YHWH and the covenant on this very count. Moses proclaimed the Torah for the present and future generations, to provide constant reminders of YHWH's grace and faithfulness (חֶסֶד וֶאֱמֶת) and to inspire awed trust in him, yielding righteous living (16:20) and securing his favor (6:25).

For Moses, circumcision was not the primary badge of the Israel of God.[126] For him, as for Paul, "The only thing that counts is faith expressing itself through love" (NIV; Greek, ἀλλὰ πίστις δι' ἀγάπης ἐνεργουμένη). Although the nuance of "faith/trust" is more explicit in Greek πίστις (Gal 5:6) than in Hebrew יָרֵא (Deut 17:18-19; 31:11-13), the apostle's statement reflects the Deuteronomic understanding of "love" (Hebrew אָהַב, Greek ἀγάπη)—"covenant commitment demonstrated in action in the interest of the

---

122. Cf. Prov 1:7; 15:33; Job 28:28; Ps 111:10. On "fear" and its relation to wisdom, see Moberly, *Theology of the Old Testament*, 265-77. On the relationship of יָרֵא in Deuteronomy and Proverbs, see chapter 14, "The Fear of YHWH: The Theological Tie that Binds Deuteronomy and Proverbs," above, pp. 283-311.

123. As arranged in LXX and all Christian translations. The Hebrew Bible concludes with 2 Chronicles.

124. Malachi echoes Deut 4:1 and 4:14. Cf. also 6:1.

125. My own adaptation of the words of Paul in Rom 10:14-15, which, of course, would not have been accessible to Moses, since the epistle to the Romans would not be written for another millennium.

126. The expression "Israel of God" (Ἰσραὴλ τοῦ θεοῦ) occurs only in Gal 6:16 and finds no equivalent in the Hebrew Bible. With Eastman ("Israel and the Mercy of God," 367-95), I interpret the phrase to refer, not to Christians as the new covenant community, but to the people of Israel (Paul's physical kin), for whom the apostle pleads for divine mercy. Similarly, Barclay, *Paul and the Gift*, 420-21, 445. Cf. Sanders, *Paul, the Law, and the Jewish People*, 176.

other person."¹²⁷ While the supreme command recognized both vertical and horizontal dimensions of covenant love,¹²⁸ in Gal 5:13–15 Paul's primary concern was its horizontal expression (cf. Rom 13:8–9).

In Gal 5:16–26 Paul describes the reverse side of this badge of Christ followers—walking by the Spirit. The Hebrew Bible rarely uses such language to speak of faithful living, but we see it embodied by persons like Caleb, whom Moses characterized as "full after God" (1:36),¹²⁹ but whom YHWH identified as "my servant" and credited with "a different spirit" (הָיְתָה רוּחַ אַחֶרֶת עִמּוֹ; ἐγενήθη πνεῦμα ἕτερον ἐν αὐτῷ, Num 14:24). Whether or not this association is valid, the trajectory of Paul's ethic represented by "walking by the Spirit" (Gal 5:16) and "the fruit of the Spirit" (vv. 22–23) is certainly at home in Deuteronomy, and Paul's prioritizing of heart over physical circumcision is neither as innovative nor as radical as some suggest.¹³⁰ Correspondingly, Moses might have employed Paul's list of "deeds of the flesh" (vv. 19–21) to characterize the Canaanites. Paul's note that "those who practice such things will not inherit the kingdom of God" (v. 21b) is at home with the ubiquitous references in Deuteronomy to Israel possessing (יָרַשׁ, Greek κληρονομέω) the land, identified as their divine grant (נַחֲלָה, Greek κλῆρος).¹³¹

Returning to the issue of circumcision, when Moses spoke of circumcision, he—like Paul—was concerned with circumcision of the heart (Deut 10:16). Following YHWH's lead in Lev 26:41 (לְבָבָם הֶעָרֵל), for him this was the badge of the true Israel. Individuals like Caleb and Joshua and Josiah (cf. 2 Kgs 23:25) were circumcised of heart, but Deut 30:6–8 envisions the day when YHWH will circumcise the hearts of all Israel. Then they will collectively demonstrate covenant commitment to him (אָהַב, "love") with complete obedience.

Paul does not use the metaphor of heart circumcision in Galatians, but he develops it fully in Rom 2:25–29. His conviction that circumcision of the heart is the only kind that matters is entirely Mosaic and explains why the physical rite was a focal point in Paul's debate with the Judaizers over the nature of the new covenant community. In Gal 2:12 he identifies those who insisted that gentile believers in Jesus needed to submit to external Jewish identity markers as "the circumcision faction" (NRSV; Greek, περιτομή). For Paul, Peter's caving in to their pressure (2:11–14) nullified the grace of God (vv. 15–21). In 5:2–12 he declares that circumcising gentile believers neutralizes the work of Christ on their behalf (v. 2), obligates them to the fine print of the entire Law (νόμος, v. 3), cuts them off from Christ (v. 4a), and shows they have fallen away (ἐκπίπτω) from grace (v. 4b). At the end of this paragraph he declares physical circumcision to be

---

127. On אָהַב, "love," as active demonstration of commitment to the well-being of the next person, see Malamat, "'You Shall Love Your Neighbor as Yourself,'" 111–15.

128. Matt 22:37–39; Mark 12:30–31; Luke 10:27.

129. Hebrew מִלֵּא אַחֲרֵי יְהוָה, rendered periphrastically by LXX as προσκεῖσθαι αὐτὸν τὰ πρὸς κύριον, "attached to the LORD."

130. Contra Lincicum (*Paul and the Early Jewish Encounter with Deuteronomy*, 150): "Paul's innovation is to radically prioritize circumcision of the heart over physical circumcision, at the same time effectively accusing Christ-believing Jews of an 'ethical epispasm' that has rendered their physical circumcision null and void."

131. Various forms of the verb κληρονομέω occur forty-nine times in LXX Deuteronomy.

irrelevant for gentiles and affirms the true identity marker for the Christian community: faith working through love (5:13–22; cf. v. 6).

Conclusion

Scholars debate whether Paul's *apologia* in Gal 1 was intended to defend himself and his gospel against the attacks of Judaizers,[132] or whether he was painting a self-portrait to contrast with the portrait of the agitators mentioned in the book.[133] However we answer the question, we should remember that Paul viewed the Galatian Christians to be his pastoral charge. Rather than being self-interested, his defense of himself was driven by his passion for his people and the gospel. In both respects, he resembles Moses.

The table of Christian fellowship, particularly the question of who is welcome there, symbolized the problem in Galatia (Gal 2:11–14). By focusing on external cultural identity markers that had eclipsed the badges of true Israelites as defined by Moses, the Judaizers promoted a two-tier Christianity. Apparently, they did not deny Jesus the Messiah, but to faith in him they added "the works of the law" (2:16; 3:10), that is, the external markers of Judaism: circumcision, observing kosher dietary laws, and celebrating Jewish festivals.[134] By this standard, the new people of God consisted of Jews who believed in Jesus and gentile believers in Jesus who submitted to Jewish identity markers, which meant converting to Judaism and ceasing to be gentiles. In short, to gain access to the table gentiles needed to become Jews first.

These agitators could have learned from Moses the marks of the true Israel of God. Remarkably, Moses begins his own version of "table talk" in Deut 14:1–21 by describing those who are invited to YHWH's table (vv. 1–2, rearranged):

בָּנִים אַתֶּם לַיהוָה אֱלֹהֵיכֶם	You are children belonging to YHWH your God....
כִּי עַם קָדוֹשׁ אַתָּה	Indeed you are a holy people
לַיהוָה אֱלֹהֶיךָ	belonging to YHWH your God,
וּבְךָ בָּחַר יְהוָה	and YHWH has chosen you
מִכֹּל הָעַמִּים אֲשֶׁר עַל־פְּנֵי הָאֲדָמָה	out of all the peoples who are on the face of the earth
לִהְיוֹת לוֹ לְעַם סְגֻלָּה	to belong to him as a treasured people.

Moses hereby summarizes the prerequisites to table fellowship in the presence of YHWH: (1) being adopted as God's sons and daughters; (2) being sanctified by God; (3) being engaged with God in covenant relationship; (4) being chosen by God from

---

132. Thus Schreiner, *Galatians*, 34; Barclay, "Mirror-Reading a Polemical Letter," 73–93, esp. 87.

133. Hardin ("Galatians 1–2 without a Mirror," 302) concludes, "Paul's narrative aim was to provide himself as a foil to the agitators in an effort to persuade his dear children not to fall prey any longer to the Judaizing message of the agitators." Similarly, Anton Fridrichsen ("Die Apologie des Paulus Gal. 1," 173), who argues that Paul was not defending himself but campaigning against the threatening apostasy in Galatia.

134. Cf. Dunn, "Works of the Law and the Curse of the Law (Galatians 3:10–14)," 523–42; Segal, *Paul the Convert*, 124–25.

all the peoples on earth; and (5) being treasured by YHWH as his crown jewel (סְגֻלָּה). Fellowship with YHWH is a gift. This is precisely the ideal that Paul tried to establish in Galatia and all his churches. But the scope of invitees to the table had changed. Whereas in the past YHWH had called out for himself a people from among the nations (Israel) and set them high above the nations as lights of the world (Deut 4:5–8; 26:19), now Jesus Christ, the embodiment of divine χάριτος καὶ ἀληθείας (חֶסֶד וֶאֱמֶת, John 1:14), has called out for himself people from all the nations. This is the new covenant community, invited to fellowship and to celebrate in the presence of God. And this characterizes Paul's vision for the churches of Galatia.

Postscript: While early Christian biblical scholarship and art tended to contrast Paul and Moses, the complementarity of the two figures is occasionally represented, as in a fourth-century Ravenna sarcophagus sculpture (Fig. 18.2) and an early twelfth-century capital sculpture in the Church of St. Madeline, in Vezelay, France (Figure 18.3).

Figure 18.2[135]

Twelve Apostles Sarcophagus
with Sculpture of the Traditio Legis
Sant'Apollinare in Classe
Ravenna, Italy
(Fifth Century CE)

The figure on the right is the Apostle Peter. He has received the cross from Jesus Christ, enthroned in the center. The figure on the left is the Apostle Paul, who carefully receives a scroll from the hand of Jesus, presumably to treasure and use as the base of his own teaching. The object received may have been the entire Pentateuch, or more likely, the Torah scroll of Deuteronomy. Judging from the frequency of Jesus' citations from this book and allusions to it in the Gospels, it was most formative in his ministry. The size of the scroll also favors the latter.

135. Photograph courtesy of Mary Ann Sullivan, Bluffton University. Used with permission. According to Lincicum (*Paul and the Early Jewish Encounter with Deuteronomy*, 200–201), the scroll may be Deuteronomy, "given to the apostle to nourish the Gentile church and to make known the God of Israel's revelation in Jesus Christ: *Dominus Deuteronomium dat.*" For discussion of the sculpture, see Klausern, *Frühchristliche Sarkophage in Bild und Wort*, 82–84. For discussion of the *traditio legis* ("transmission of the law") motif, see Hvalvik, "Christ Proclaiming the Law to the Apostles," 403–37. Hvalvik interprets the scroll as "the new law of Christ," which replaces the Mosaic law.

Figure 18.3[136]

Mystic Mill Capital
Benedictine Abbey
Church of Sainte-Marie-Madeleine
Vézelay, France
(Twelfth Century, CE)

The figure on the left is Moses, who pours grain into a small mill. He stands in shadow since he belongs to the First Testament. The figure on the right is Paul, who carefully receives the flour. He stands in the light since he belongs to the New Testament. A wheel with cross-shaped spokes drives the mill, which implicitly stands for Christ, who extracts the life-giving essence of the Torah and transforms it into the renewed message of the New Testament.

136. Photo © Adrian Fletcher, Used with permission. For discussion, see Moffatt, "The Mystic Mill from Vézelay," 215–17; Ambrose, *The Nave Structure of Vézelay*, 71–72.

Bibliography

Ackerman, Susan. "Who is Sacrificing at Shiloh? The Priesthoods of Ancient Israel's Regional Sanctuaries." In *Levites and Priests in Biblical History and Tradition*, edited by M. Leuchter and J. M. Hutton, 25–43. Ancient Israel and Its Literature 9. Atlanta: Scholars Press, 2011.

Aejmelaeus, A. "Function and Interpretation of *kî* in Biblical Hebrew." *Journal of Biblical Literature* 105 (1986) 202–8.

Aernie, Jeffrey W. *Is Paul Also among the Prophets? An Examination of the Relationship between Paul and the Old Testament Prophetic Tradition in 2 Corinthians*. Library of New Testament Studies 467. New York: T&T Clark, 2012.

Aharoni, Miriam. "Arad: The Israelite Citadels." In *The New Encyclopedia of Archaeological Excavations in the Holy Land*, edited by Ephraim Stern, 1:82–87. New York: Simon & Schuster, 1993.

Akin, Daniel L. "The Prophet Who is Like and Greater Than Moses: A Sermon on Deuteronomy 18:15–22." In *For Our Good Always: Studies on the Message and Influence of Deuteronomy in Honor of Daniel I. Block*, edited by Jason S. DeRouchie, Jason Gile, and Kenneth J. Turner, 485–94. Winona Lake, IN: Eisenbrauns, 2013.

Albertz, Rainer. *A History of Israelite Religion in the Old Testament Period*. Translated by J. Bowden. Old Testament Library. 2 vols. Louisville: Westminster John Knox, 1994.

Albright, W. F. "The List of Levitical Cities." In *Louis Ginzberg Jubilee Volume* (English section), 49–73. New York: American Academy for Jewish Research, 1945.

Alexander, T. D. "Genesis 22 and the Covenant of Circumcision." *Journal for the Study of the Old Testament* 25 (1983) 17–22.

Allegro, John M. *Qumrân Cave 4, I [4Q158–4Q186]*. Discoveries in the Judaean Desert 5. Oxford: Clarendon, 1968.

Allen, David L. *Hebrews*. New American Commentary 35. Nashville: Broadman and Holman, 2010.

Allender, Dan B. *Sabbath*. Nashville: Thomas Nelson, 2009.

Allis Oswald T. *The Five Books of Moses*. Eugene, OR: Wipf & Stock, 2001 (republished 1943 edition).

Allison, Dale C. Jr. *The New Moses: A Matthean Typology*. Minneapolis: Fortress, 1993.

Alt, Albrecht. "The Origins of Israelite Law." In *Essays on Old Testament History and Religion*. Translated by R. A. Wilson, 101–171. Garden City: Doubleday, 1967.

Ambrose, Kirk. *The Nave Structure of Vézelay: The Art of Monastic Viewing*. Toronto: Pontifical Institute of Mediaeval Studies, 2006.

Andersen, Francis I. *The Hebrew Verbless Clause in the Pentateuch,* Journal of Biblical Literature Monograph Series 14. Nashville: Abingdon, 1970.

Anderson, Cheryl B. "Audience of the Ten Commandments." Accessible at http://www.bibleodyssey.org/tools/video-gallery/a/audience-of-the-ten-commandments-anderson.aspx.

Anderson, Gary A. "Sacrifices and Sacrificial Offerings: Old Testament." In *Anchor Bible Dictionary,* edited by D. N. Freedman, 5:878–79. Garden City: Doubleday, 1992.

———. "What about the Canaanites?" In *Divine Evil?: The Moral Character of the God of Abraham,* edited by M. Bergmann, et al., 27–72. Oxford: Oxford University Press, 2013.

Ansberry, Christopher B. *Be Wise, My Son, and Make My Heart Glad: An Exploration of the Courtly Nature of the Book of Proverbs.* Beihefte zur Zeitschrift für die alttestamentliche Wissenschaft 422. Berlin: de Gruyter, 2011.

Arand, Charles P. "Luther's Radical Reading of the Sabbath Commandment,. In *Perspectives on the Sabbath: 4 Views,* edited by edited by C. J. Donato, 216–61. Nashville: Broadman & Holman, 2011.

Archer, Gleason. *A Survey of Old Testament Introduction.* Rev. ed. Chicago, IL: Moody Press, 2007.

Arnold, Bill T. "Necromancy and Cleromancy in 1 and 2 Samuel." *Catholic Biblical Quarterly* 66 (2004) 199–213.

———. "The Love-Fear Antinomy in Deuteronomy 5–11." *Vetus Testamentum* 61 (2011) 552–62.

Arzi Abraham. "Tikkun Sopherim." In *Encyclopaedia Judaica,* edited by Fred Skolnik, 19:723. 2nd ed. Farmington Hills, MI: Gale, 2007.

Assmann, Jan. "Altorientalische Fluchinschriften und das Problem performativer Schriftlichkeit: Vertrag und Monument als Allegorien des Lesens." In *Schrift,* edited by H. U. Gumbrecht and K. L. Pfeiffer, 233–56. Materialität der Zeichen A/12. Munich: Fink, 1993.

Aufrecht, W. E. *A Corpus of Ammonite Inscriptions.* Ancient Near Eastern Texts and Studies 4. Lewiston: Edwin Mellen, 1989.

Auld, A. Graeme. "The 'Levitical Cities': Texts and History." *Zeitschrift für die alttestamentliche Wissenschaft* 91 (1979) 194–206.

Ausloos, Hans. "The 'Proto-Deuteronomist': Fifty Years Later." *Old Testament Essays* 26 (2013) 531–58.

Avalos, Hector. "The Letter Killeth: A Plea for Decanonizing Violent Texts." *Journal of Religion, Conflict, and Peace* 1 (2007). http://religionconflictpeace.org/volume-1-issue-1-fall-2007/letter-killeth.

Averbeck, Richard E. "שלם." In *New International Dictionary of Old Testament Theology & Exegesis,* edited by Willem VanGemeren, 4:130–43. Grand Rapids: Zondervan, 1997.

Avi-Yonah, M. "Gezer." In *Encyclopedia of Archaeological Excavations in the Holy Land,* edited by Michael Avi-Yonah, 2:429–43. Jerusalem: Israel Exploration Society and Masada Press, 1975.

Baab, Lynne M. *Sabbath Keeping: Finding Freedom in the Rhythms of Rest.* Downers Grove: InterVarsity, 2005.

Baden, Joel S. *The Composition of the Pentateuch: Renewing the Documentary Hypothesis.* Anchor Yale Bible Reference Library. New Haven: Yale University Press, 2012.

Balentine, Samuel E. *Prayer in the Hebrew Bible: The Drama of Divine-Human Dialogue.* Overtures to Biblical Theology. Minneapolis: Augsburg, 1993.

Bammel, Ernst. "Paulus, der Moses des Neuen Bundes." *Theologia* 54 (1983) 399–408. Reprinted in idem, *Judaica et Paulina: Kleine Schriften II*, 205–14. Wissenschaftliche Untersuchungen zum Neuen Testament 91. Tübingen: Mohr Siebeck, 1997.

Barclay, John M. G. "Mirror-Reading a Polemical Letter: Galatians as a Test Case." *Journal for the Study of the New Testament* 31 (1987) 73–93.

———. *Paul and the Gift*. Grand Rapids: Eerdmans, 2015.

Barker, Paul A. "The Theology of Deuteronomy 27." *Tyndale Bulletin* 49 (1998) 277–303.

———. *The Triumph of Grace in Deuteronomy: Faithless Israel, Faithful Yahweh in Deuteronomy*. Paternoster Biblical Monographs. Eugene, OR: Wipf & Stock, 2007.

Barrett, Rob. *Disloyalty and Destruction: Religion and Politics in Deuteronomy and the Modern World*. The Library of Hebrew Bible/Old Testament Studies 511. London: T&T Clark, 2009.

Barrick, William D. "The Mosaic Covenant." *The Masters Seminary Journal* 10 (1999) 213–32.

Barstad, Hans M. "No Prophets? Recent Developments in Biblical Prophetic Research and Ancient Near Eastern Prophecy." *Journal for the Study of the Old Testament* 57 (1993) 39–60.

Bartlett, John R. *Edom and the Edomites*. Journal for the Study of the Old Testament Supplement Series 77. Sheffield: Journal for the Study of the Old Testament, 1989.

Barton, John. "Covenant in Old Testament Theology." In *Covenant as Context: Essays in Honour of E. W. Nicholson*, edited by A. D. H. Mayes and R. B. Salters, 23–38. Oxford: Oxford University Press, 2003.

———. "'The Law and the Prophets.' Who are the Prophets?" In *The Old Testament: Canon, Literature and Theology: Collected Essays of John Barton*, 5–18. Society for Old Testament Studies Monographs. New York: Routledge, 2016 (reprint of 2007 Ashgate publication).

———. *The Oracles of God: Perceptions of Ancient Prophecy in Israel after the Exile*. London: Darton, Longman & Todd, 1986.

Bates, Matthew W. *Salvation by Allegiance Alone: Rethinking Faith, Works, and the Gospel of Jesus the King*. Grand Rapids: Baker, 2017.

Bauckham, Richard. "Jewish Messianism according to the Gospel of John." In *The Testimony of the Beloved Disciple: Narrative, History, and Theology in the Gospel of John*, 207–38. Grand Rapids: Baker, 2007. Originally published in *Historical and Literary Studies in John: Challenging Current Paradigms*, edited by P. M. Head and J. Lierman, 34–68; WUNT 2. Tübingen: Mohr Siebeck, 2007.

———. "Sabbath and Sunday in the Protestant Tradition." In *From Sabbath to Lord's Day*, edited by D. A. Carson, 311–42. Eugene, OR: Wipf & Stock, 1999.

Beale, G. K. *A New Testament Biblical Theology: The Unfolding of the Old Testament in the New*. Grand Rapids: Baker, 2011.

Becker, Joachim. *Gottesfurcht im Alten Testament*. Analecta Biblica 25. Rome: Pontifical Biblical Institute, 1965.

Beckman, Gary. *Hittite Diplomatic Texts*. 2nd ed. Society of Society of Biblical Literature Writings of the Ancient World Series 7. Atlanta Scholars Press, 1999.

Beckwith, Roger T. "The Unity and Diversity of God's Covenants." *Tyndale Bulletin* 38 (1987) 93–118.

Begg, C. "The Cisjordanian Altar(s) and their Associated Rites According to Josephus." *Biblische Zeitschrift* 41 (1997) 192–211.

Ben Zvi, Ehud. "The List of the Levitical Cities." *Journal for the Study of the Old Testament* 54 (1992) 77–106.

Benz, F. L. *Personal Names in Phoenician and Punic Inscriptions.* Studia Pohl 8. Rome: Pontifical Biblical Institute, 1972.

Berman, Joshua. *Created Equal: How the Bible Broke with Ancient Political Thought.* Oxford: Oxford University Press, 2008.

———. "CTH 133 and the Hittite Provenance of Deuteronomy 13." *Journal of Biblical Literature* 131 (2011) 25–44.

———. "Historicism and Its Limits: A Response to Bernard M. Levinson and Jeffrey Stackert." *Journal of Ancient Judaism* 4 (2013) 297–309.

———. "The History of Legal Theory and the Study of Biblical Law." *Catholic Biblical Quarterly* 76 (2014) 19–39.

———. "The Legal Blend in Biblical Narrative (Joshua 20:1–9, Judges 6:25–31, 1 Samuel 15:2, 28:3–25, 2 Kings 4:1–7, Jeremiah 34:12–17, Nehemiah 5:1–12)." *Journal of Biblical Literature* 134 (2015) 105–25.

———. "Measuring Writing Style: Introducing the Tiberias Project." https://www.youtube.com/watch?v=MDjx99KTMto.

Biddle, Mark E. *Deuteronomy.* Smyth & Helwys Bible Commentary. Macon, GA: Smyth & Helwys, 2003.

Blenkinsopp, Joseph. *The Pentateuch: An Introduction to the First Five Books of the Bible.* Anchor Bible Reference Library. New York: Doubleday, 1992

———. *The Pentateuch: An Introduction to the First Five Books of the Bible.* Anchor Bible Reference Library; New York: Doubleday, 1992.

Block, Daniel I. "Bearing the Name of the Lord with Honor." In *How I Love Your Torah, O LORD! Studies in the Book of Deuteronomy*, 61–72. Eugene, OR: Cascade Books, 2011.

———. *The Book of Ezekiel Chapters 1–24.* NICOT. Grand Rapids: Eerdmans, 1997.

———. *The Book of Ezekiel Chapters 25–48.* NICOT. Grand Rapids: Eerdmans, 1998.

———. "Covenance: A Whole Bible Perspective." Paper presented to the Evangelical Theological Society in Baltimore, November, 2013.

———. "Unspeakable Crimes: The Abuse of Women in the Book of Judges." *The Southern Baptist Theological Journal* 2 (1998) 46–55.

———. "The Decalogue in the Hebrew Scriptures." In *The Decalogue through the Centuries: From the Hebrew Scriptures to Benedict XVI*, edited by J. P. Greenman and T. Larsen, 1–28. Louisville: Westminster John Knox, 2012.

———. "Deuteronomic Law." In *The Oxford Encyclopedia of the Bible and Law*, edited by Jeffrey Stackert and Brent A. Strawn, 1:182–95. New York: Oxford University Press, 2015.

———. *Deuteronomy.* NIV Application Commentary. Grand Rapids: Zondervan, 2012.

———. "Deuteronomy 17:14–20: The Spiritual and Ethical Foundations of Messianic Kingship." In *Moody Dictionary of Messianic Prophecy*, edited by Michael Rydelnik. Chicago: Moody Press, forthcoming.

———. "The Doctrine of the Future and Moses: 'All Israel Shall Be Saved.'" In *Eschatology: Biblical, Historical, and Practical Approaches*, edited by D. Jeffrey Bingham and Glenn R. Kreider, 107–34. Grand Rapids: Kregel, 2016.

———. "Eden: A Temple? A Reassessment of the Biblical Evidence." In *From Creation to New Creation: Biblical Theology and Exegesis.* Essays in honor of G. K. Beale, edited by D. M. Gurtner and B. L. Gladd, 3–32. Peabody, MA: Hendrickson, 2013.

———. "Empowered by the Spirit of God: The Holy Spirit in the Historiographic Writings of the Old Testament." *The Southern Baptist Theological Journal* 1 (1997) 42–61.

———. "The Fear of YHWH: A Call for Allegiance to YHWH Alone." In *Interpreting the Old Testament Theologically: Essays in Honor of Willem A. VanGemeren*, edited by Andrew T. Abernethy. Grand Rapids: Zondervan, forthcoming.

———. *For the Glory of God: Recovering a Biblical Theology of Worship*. Grand Rapids: Baker, 2014.

———. *The Gods of the Nations: A Study in Ancient Near Eastern National Theology*. 2nd ed. Eugene, OR: Wipf & Stock, 2013. Reprint of Baker, 2000 edition, with added Appendix.

———. *The Gospel according to Moses: Theological and Ethical Reflections on the Book of Deuteronomy*. Eugene, OR; Cascade Books, 2012.

———. "The Grace of Torah: The Mosaic Prescription for Life (Deut 4:1–8; 6:20–25)." In *How I Love Your Torah, O LORD! Studies in the Book of Deuteronomy*, 1–20. Eugene, OR: Cascade Books, 2011.

———. "Hearing Galatians with Moses: An Examination of Paul as a Second and Seconding Moses." In *Sepher Torath Mosheh: Studies in the Composition and Interpretation of Deuteronomy*, edited by Daniel I. Block and Richard L. Schultz, 338–74. Peabody, MA: Hendrickson, 2017.

———. "How Can We Bless YHWH? Wrestling with Divine Violence in Deuteronomy" In *Wrestling with the Violence of God: Soundings in the Old Testament*, edited by M. Daniel Carroll R. and J. Blair Wilgus, 31–50. Bulletin for Biblical Research Supplement Series 10. Winona Lake, IN: Eisenbrauns, 2015.

———. *How I Love Your Torah, O LORD!: Studies in the Book of Deuteronomy*. Eugene, OR: Cascade Books, 2012)

———. "How Many is God? An Investigation into the Meaning of Deuteronomy 6:4–5." In *How I Love Your Torah, O LORD! Studies in the Book of Deuteronomy*, 61–72. Eugene, OR: Cascade Books, 2012.

———. "'In Spirit and in Truth': The Mosaic Vision of Worship." In *The Gospel according to Moses: Theological and Ethical Reflections on the Book of Deuteronomy*, 272–98. Reprinted in *Rediscovering Worship: Past, Present, and Future*, edited by Wendy J. Porter, 1–26. Eugene, OR: Pickwick, 2015.

———. "In the Tradition of Moses: The Conceptual and Stylistic Imprint of Deuteronomy on the Patriarchal Narratives." In *Exploring the Composition of the Pentateuch*, edited by K. Berglund and R. Gane. Bulletin for Biblical Research Supplements. Winona Lake, IN: Eisenbrauns, forthcoming.

———. "The Joy of Worship: The Mosaic Invitation to the Presence of God (Deut 12:1–14)." In *How I Love Your Torah, O LORD! Studies in the Book of Deuteronomy*, 131–49. Eugene, OR: Cascade Books, 2011.

———. *Judges, Ruth*. New American Commentary. Nashville: Broadman & Holman, 1999.

———. "Leader, Leadership, Old Testament." In *New Interpreter's Dictionary of the Bible*, edited by Katherine Doob Sakenfeld, 3:620–26. Nashville: Abingdon, 2008.

———. "Marriage and Family in Ancient Israel." In *Marriage and Family in the Biblical World*, edited by K. Campbell, 33–102. Downers Grove, IL: InterVarsity, 2003.

———. "'The Meeting Places of God in the Land': Another Look at the Towns of the Levites." In *Current Issues in Priestly and Related Literature: The Legacy of Jacob Milgrom and Beyond*, edited by Roy E. Gane and Ada Taggar-Cohen, 93–121. Resources for Biblical Study 82. Atlanta: Society of Biblical Literature, 2015.

———. "My Servant David: Ancient Israel's Vision of the Messiah." In *Israel's Messiah in the Bible and the Dead Sea Scrolls*, edited by R. S. Hess and M. D. Carroll R., 17–56. Grand Rapids: Baker, 2003.

———. "No other Gods: Bearing the Name of YHWH in a Polytheistic World." In *The Gospel according to Moses: Theological and Ethical Reflections on the Book of Deuteronomy*, 237–71. Eugene, OR: Cascade Books, 2012.

———. "Other Religions in Old Testament Theology." In *The Gospel according to Moses: Theological and Ethical Reflections on the Book of Deuteronomy*, 200–36. Eugene, OR: Cascade Books, 2012.

———. "'A Place for My Name': Horeb and Zion in the Mosaic Vision of Israelite Worship." *Journal of the Evangelical Theological Society* 58 (2015) 221–47.

———. "Reading the Decalogue Right to Left: The Ten Principles of Covenant Relationship in the Hebrew Bible." In *How I Love your Torah, O LORD! Studies in the Book of Deuteronomy*, 21–55. Eugene, OR: Cascade Books, 2011.

———. "Recovering the Voice of Moses: The Genesis of Deuteronomy." In *The Gospel according to Moses: Theological and Ethical Reflection on the Book of Deuteronomy*, 21–51. Eugene, OR: Cascade, 2012.

———. *Ruth: The King is Coming*. Zondervan Exegetical Commentary on the Old Testament. Grand Rapids, MI: Zondervan, 2015.

———. "Sojourner; Alien; Stranger." In *International Standard Bible Encyclopedia*. Rev. ed., edited by G. W. Bromiley, 4:561–64. Grand Rapids: Eerdmans, 1988.

———. "'That They May Hear': Biblical Foundations for the Oral Reading of Scripture in Worship." *Journal for Spiritual Formation & Soul Care* 5 (2012) 5–23.

———. "The Power of Song: Reflections on Ancient Israel's National Anthem (Deuteronomy 32)." In *How I Love Your Torah, O LORD! Studies in the Book of Deuteronomy*, 162–88. Eugene, OR: Cascade Books, 2011.

———. The Privilege of Calling: The Mosaic Paradigm for Missions (Deut 26:16–19)." In *How I Love Your Torah, O LORD! Studies in the Book of Deuteronomy*, 140–61. Eugene, OR: Cascade Books, 2011.

———. "The View from the Top: The Holy Spirit in the Prophets." In *Presence, Power and Promise: The Role of the Holy Spirit in the Old Testament*, edited by David G. Firth and Paul D. Wegner, 175–207. Nottingham: Apollos, 2011.

———. "To Serve and to Keep: Toward a Biblical Understanding of Humanity's Responsibility in the Face of the Biodiversity Crisis." In *Keeping God's Earth: The Global Environment in Biblical Perspective*, edited by Daniel I. Block and Noah J. Toly, 116–42. Downers Grove: InterVarsity, 2010.

———. "What Do These Stones Mean? The Riddle of Deuteronomy 27." *Journal of the Evangelical Theological Society* 56 (2013) 17–41.

———. What has Delphi to do with Samaria? Ambiguity and Delusion in Israelite Prophecy." In *Writing and Ancient Near Eastern Society: Papers in Honour of Alan R. Millard*, edited by P. Bienkowski, C. Mee, and E. Slater, 189–216. New York/London: T&T Clark, 2005.

———. Who do Commentators say 'the Lord' is? The Scandalous Rock of Romans 10:13." In *On the Writing of New Testament Commentaries: Festschrift for Grant R. Osborne on the Occasion of his 70th Birthday*, edited by S. E. Porter and E. J. Schnabel, 173–92. Texts and Editions of New Testament Study 8. Leiden: Brill, 2012.

———. "Will the Real Moses Please Rise? An Exploration into the Role and Ministry of Moses in the Book of Deuteronomy." In *The Gospel according to Moses: Theological and*

Ethical Reflections on the Book of Deuteronomy, 68–103. Eugene, OR: Cascade Books, 2012.

———. "'You shall not covet your neighbor's wife': A Study in Deuteronomic Domestic Ideology." *Journal of the Evangelical Theological Society* 53 (2010) 449–74. Republished in *The Gospel according to Moses: Theological and Ethical Reflections on the Book of Deuteronomy*, 137–168. Eugene, OR: Cascade, 2012.

Blomberg, Craig L. "The Sabbath as Fulfilled in Christ." In *Perspectives on the Sabbath: 4 Views*, edited by C. J. Donato, 305–58. Nashville: Broadman & Holman, 2011.

Blum, Erhard. *Die Komposition der Vätergeschichte*. Wissenschaftliche Monographien zum Alten und Neuen Testament 57. Neukirchen: Neukirchener Verlag, 1984.

———. *Studien zur Komposition des Pentateuch*. Beihefte zur Zeitschrift fur die alttestamentliche Wissenschaft 189. Berlin: Walter de Gruyter, 1990.

Bock, Darrell L. *Acts*. Baker Exegetical Commentary on the New Testament. Grand Rapids: Baker, 2007.

Boda, Mark J. "Prayer." In *Dictionary of the Old Testament: Historical Books*, edited by Bill T. Arnold and H. G. M. Williamson, 806–11. Downers Grove: InterVarsity, 2005.

de Boer, Martinus C. *Galatians: A Commentary*. New Testament Library. Louisville: Westminster John Knox, 2011.

———. "Paul and Jewish Apocalyptic Theology." In *Apocalyptic and the New Testament: Essays in Honor of J. Louis Martyn*, edited by J. Marcus and M. L. Soards, 169–90. Sheffield: Sheffield Academic, 1989.

Boling, Robert G. "Levitical Cities: Archaeology and Texts." In *Biblical and Related Studies Presented to Samuel Iwry*, edited by A. Kort and S. Morschauser, 23–32. Winona Lake, IN: Eisenbrauns, 1985.

Bohmbach, Karla G. "Names and Naming in the Biblical World." In *Women in Scripture: A Dictionary of Names and Unnamed Women in the Hebrew Bible, the Apocryphal/Deuterocanonical Books, and the New Testament*, edited by C. Meyers, T. Craven, and R. S. Kraemer, 33–40. Boston: Houghton Mifflin, 2000.

Bonhéme, Marie-Ange. "Kingship." In *The Oxford Encyclopedia of Ancient Egypt*, edited by D. B. Redford, 2.238–45. Oxford: Oxford University Press, 2001.

Bottéro, Jean. *Religion in Ancient Mesopotamia*. Translated by T. L. Fagan. Chicago: University of Chicago Press, 2001.

Bowman, John. "Early Samaritan Eschatology." *Journal of Jewish Studies* 6 (1955) 63–72.

———. "Samaritan Studies." *Bulletin of the John Rylands Library* 40 (1958) 298–327.

Braulik, G., and N. Lohfink. "Deuteronomium 1,5 באר את־התורה הזאת: 'er verlieh dieser Tora Rechstkraft.'" In *Textarbeit: Studien zu Texten und ihrer Rezeption aus dem Alten Testament und der Umwelt Israels: Festschrift für Peter Weimar zur Vollendung seines 60. Lebensjahres mit Beiträgen von Freunden, Schülern und Kollegen*, edited by K. Kiesow and T. Meurer, 35–51. Alter Orient und Altes Testament 294. Münster: Ugarit Verlag, 2003.

Braulik, Georg. "'Weisheit' im Buch Deuteronomium." In *Weisheit ausserhalb der kanonischen Weisheitsschriften*, edited by B. Janowski, 39–69. Veröffentlichungen der Wissenschaftlichen Gesellschaft für Theologie 8. Gütersloh; Gütersloher Verlagshaus, 1996 (Reprinted in Georg Braulik, *Studien zum Buch Deuteronomium* 24, 225–71. Stuttgart: Verlag Katholisches Bibelwerk, 1997.)

———. "Commemoration of Passion and Feast of Joy." In *The Theology of Deuteronomy: Collected Essays of Georg Braulik*, 67–85. Translated by U. Lindblad. Bibal Collected Essays 2. N. Richland Hills, TX: Bibal, 1994.

———. "The Joy of the Feast." In *The Theology of Deuteronomy: Collected Essays of Georg Braulik*, 27–65. Translated by U. Lindblad. Bibal Collected Essays 2. N. Richland Hills, TX: Bibal, 1994.

Brekelmans, Chris H. W. "Die sogenannten deuteronomischen Elemente in Gen.-Num: Ein Beitrag zur Vorgeschichte des Deuteronomiums." In *Volume du Congrés Genève 1965*, 90–96. Supplements to Vetus Testamentum. Leiden: Brill, 1966.

Brenneman, J. E. "True and False Prophecy." In *Dictionary of the Old Testament Prophets*, edited by Mark J. Boda and J. Gordon McConville, 781–88. Downers Grove: InterVarsity, 2012.

Brockelmann, Carl. *Grundriss der vergleichenden Grammatik der semitischen Sprachen*, 1:522. Berlin: Verlag von Reuther & Reichard, 1908.

Brown, M. L. "'Is It Not?' or 'Indeed!': HL in Northwest Semitic." *Maarav* 4 (1987) 201–19.

Bruce, F. F. *The Book of the Acts*. New International Commentary on the New Testament. Grand Rapids: Eerdmans, 1986.

Brueggemann, Walter. *Great Prayers of the Old Testament*. Louisville: Westminster John Knox, 2008.

———. *Theology of the Old Testament: Testimony, Dispute, Advocacy*. Minneapolis: Fortress, 2013.

Bühner, J. A. "ἀποστέλλω *apostellō* send forth." In *Exegetical Dictionary of the New Testament*, edited by H. Balz and G. Schneider, 1:140–42. Grand Rapids: Eerdmans, 1990.

———. "ἀπόστολος *apostolos* delegate, apostle." In *Exegetical Dictionary of the New Testament*, edited by H. Balz and G. Schneider, 1:142–46. Grand Rapids: Eerdmans, 1990.

Burton, Keith. "Denouncing Sabbath Worship." *Spectrum* (July 2, 2009), accessible at http://spectrummagazine.org/article/column/2009/07/02/denouncing-sabbath-worship.

Carr, David M. *Reading the Fractures of Genesis: Historical and Literary Approaches*. Louisville: Westminster John Knox, 1996.

———. *Writing on the Tablet of the Heart: Origin of Scripture and Literature*. Oxford: Oxford University Press, 2005.

Carson, D. A. ed., *From Sabbath Day to Lord's Day*. Eugene, OR: Wipf & Stock, 1999.

Cassian, John. *Conferences*, Translated by C. Luibheid. Classics of Western Spirituality. New York: Paulist Press, 1985.

Chiesa, B. "La Promessa di un Profeta (Deut 18,15–20)." *Bibliotheca Orientalis* 15 (1973) 17–26.

Childs, Brevard S. *Introduction to the First Testament as Scripture*. Minneapolis: Augsburg, 2001.

———. *Isaiah*. Old Testament Library. Louisville: Westminster John Knox, 2001.

Clarke, E. G., translator. *Targum Pseudo-Jonathan: Deuteronomy*. Aramaic Bible 5B. Edinburgh: T&T Clarke, 1998.

Clements, Ronald E. *In Spirit and in Truth: Insights from Biblical Prayers*. Atlanta: John Knox, 1985.

Clines, David J. A. "What Does Eve Do to Help? And Other Irredeemably Androcentric Orientations in Genesis 1–3." Chapter 1, in *What Does Eve Do to Help? And Other*

Readerly Questions to the Old Testament, 25–48. Journal for the Study of the Old Testament Supplement Series 94. Sheffield: Sheffield Academic Press, 1990.

———. "The Ten Commandments, Reading from Left to Right." In *Words Remembered, Texts Renewed: Essays in Honour of John F. A. Sawyer*, edited by J. Davies, G. Harvey, and W. G. E. Watson, 97–112. Journal for the Study of the Old Testament Supplement Series 195. Sheffield: Sheffield Academic Press, 1995.

Cody, Aelred. *A History of the Old Testament Priesthood*. Analecta Biblica 35. Rome: Pontifical Biblical Institute, 1969.

Cogan, Mordechai, Hayim Tadmor. *II Kings: A New Translation with Introduction and Commentary*. Anchor Bible 11. New York: Doubleday, 1988.

Cole, Robert L. "Psalms 1–2." In *The Moody Handbook of Messianic Prophecy*, edited by Michael Rydelnik and Edwin A. Blum. Chicago: Moody Publishers, forthcoming.

Colenso John W. *The Pentateuch and the Book of Joshua Critically Examined*, Part III. 2nd ed. London: Longman, 1879.

Collins, John J. *The Scepter and the Star: The Messiahs of the Dead Sea Scrolls and Other Ancient Literature*. New York: Doubleday, 1995.

———. "The Zeal of Phinehas: The Bible and the Legitimation of Violence." *Journal of Biblical Literature* 122 (2003) 3–21.

Conrad, J. "שָׁחַת, šaḥat." In *Theological Dictionary of the Old Testament*, edited by G. J. Botterweck, H. Ringgren, and H.-J. Fabry, and translated by J. T. Willis, G. W. Bromiley, and D. E. Green, 14:583–95. 15 vols. Grand Rapids: Eerdmans, 2004.

Cook, Stephen L. *The Social Roots of Biblical Yahwism*. SBL Studies in Biblical Literature 8. Atlanta: Society of Biblical Literature, 2004.

Cooke, G. A. *A Critical and Exegetical Commentary on Ezekiel*. International Critical Commentary. Edinburgh: T&T Clark, 1936.

Cooper, A., and B. R. Goldstein. "The Cult of the Dead and the Theme of Entry into the Land." *Biblical Interpretation* 3 (1993) 292.

Craigie, Peter C. *The Book of Deuteronomy*. New International Commentary on the Old Testament. Grand Rapids: Eerdmans, 1976.

Creach, Jerome F. D. *Violence in Scripture*. Interpretation. Louisville: Westminster John Knox, 2013.

Cribb, Bryan. *Speaking on the Brink of Sheol: Form and Message of Old Testament Death Stories*. Piscataway, NJ: Gorgias, 2009.

Crouch, Carly. *Israel and the Assyrians: Deuteronomy, the Succession Treaty of Esarhaddon, and the Nature of Subversion*. Ancient Near Eastern Monograph 8. Atlanta: Society of Biblical Literature, 2014.

Crüsemann, Frank. *The Torah: Theology and Social History of Old Testament Law*, translated by Allan W. Mahnke. Minneapolis: Fortress, 1996.

Dandamaev, Muhammad A. *Slavery in Babylonia: From Nabopolassar to Alexander the Great (626–331 B.C.)*, edited by M. A. Powell and D. B. Weisberg. Translated by V. A. Powell. DeKalb, IL: Northern Illinois University Press, 1984.

Davidson, Richard M. "Theology of Sexuality in the Song of Songs: Return to Eden." *Andrews University Seminary Studies* 27 (1989) 1–19.

Davidson, Richard M. *The Flame of Yhwh: Sexuality in the Hebrew Bible*. Peabody, MA: Hendrickson, 2007.

Davies, John A. *A Royal Priesthood: Literary and Intertextual Perspectives on an Image of Israel in Exodus 19.6*. Journal for the Study of the Old Testament Supplement Series 395. London: T&T Clark, 2004.

Davis, Ellen F. and Richard B. Hays, editors. *The Art of Reading Scripture*. Grand Rapids: Eerdmans, 2003.

Dawn, Marva J. *Keeping the Sabbath Wholly: Ceasing, Resting, Embracing, Feasting*. Grand Rapids: Eerdmans, 1989.

Day, John. "Why Does God 'Establish' rather than 'Cut' Covenants in the Priestly Source." In *Covenant as Context: Essays in Honor of E. W. Nicholson*, edited by A. D. H. Mayes and R. B. Salters, 91–109. Oxford: Oxford University Press, 2003.

Del Monte, G. F. "The Hittite *Ḥērem*." In *Memoriae Igor M. Diakonof, Annual of Ancient Near Eastern, Old Testament, and Semitic Studies*, edited by L. Kogan, 21–45. Babel und Bibel 2. Orientalia et Classica 8. Winona Lake, IN: Eisenbrauns, 2006.

Demsky, Aaron. "When the Priests Trumpeted the Onset of the Sabbath." *Biblical Archaeology Review* 12/6 (November-December, 1986) 50–52.

DeRouchie, Jason S. "Circumcision in the Hebrew Bible and Targumim: Theology, Rhetoric, and the Handling of a Metaphor." *Bulletin for Biblical Research* 14 (2004) 175–203.

———. "The Heart of YHWH and His Chosen One in 1 Samuel 13:14." *Bulletin for Biblical Research* 24 (2014) 467–89.

———. "Counting the Ten: An Investigation into the Numbering of the Decalogue." In *Four Our Good Always: Studies in the Message and Influence of Deuteronomy in Honor of Daniel I. Block*, edited by J. S. DeRouchie, J. Gile, and K. J. Turner, 93–126. Winona Lake: Eisenbrauns, 2013.

Dershowitz, Idan, Navot Akiva, Moshe Koppel, and Nachum Dershowitz. "Computerized Source Criticism of Biblical Ttexts." *Journal of Biblical Literature* 134 (2015) 253–71.

Dion, Paul E. "Deuteronomy 13: The Suppression of Alien Religious Propaganda in Israel during the Late Monarchical Era." In *Law and Ideology in Monarchic Israel*, edited by B. Halpern and D. W. Hobson, 147–216. Journal for the Study of the Old Testament Supplement Series 124. Sheffield: Sheffield Academic, 1991.

Dobbs-Alsopp, F. W., J. J. M. Roberts, C. L. Seow, and R. E. Whitaker. *Hebrew Inscriptions: Texts from the Biblical Period of the Monarchy with Concordance*. New Haven: Yale University Press, 2005.

Donato, Christopher John, ed. *Perspectives on the Sabbath: 4 Views*. Nashville: Broadman & Holman, 2011.

Dooley, Robert A., and Stephen H. Levinsohn. *Analyzing Discourse: A Manual of Basic Concepts*. Dallas, TX: SIL International, 2001.

Dorsey, David A. *The Roads and Highways of Ancient Israel*. Baltimore: Johns Hopkins University Press, 1991.

Douglas, Mary. *Purity and Danger: An Analysis of the Concepts of Pollution and Taboo*. London: Routledge, 2002 (reprint of 1966 edition).

Dressler, Harold P. "The Sabbath in the Old Testament." In *From Sabbath Day to Lord's Day.*, edited by D. A. Carson, 21–42. Eugene, OR: Wipf & Stock, 1999.

Driver, S. R. *Deuteronomy*. International Critical Commentary. 3rd ed. Edinburgh: T&T Clark, 1916.

Duke, Rodney. "Punishment or Restoration: Another Look at the Levites of Ezekiel 44:6–16." *Journal for the Study of the Old Testament* 40 (1988) 61–81.

Dumbrell, W. J. *Covenant and Creation: A Theology of the Old Testament Covenants*. London: Paternoster, 1984.

Dunn. James D. G. *Jesus, Paul, and the Law: Studies in Mark and Galatians* (Louisville, KY: Westminster John Knox, 1990.

———. *Romans 1–8*. Word Biblical Commentary 38. Dallas: Word, 1988.

———. "Romans, Letter to the." In *Dictionary of Paul and His Letters,* edited by G. F. Hawthorne, R. P. Martin, and D. G. Reid, 838–50. Downers Grove, IL: InterVarsity, 1993.

———. "Works of the Law and the Curse of the Law (Galatians 3:10–14)." *New Testament Studies* 31 (1985) 523–42.

Dunn, James D. G., ed. *Paul and the Mosaic Law*. Grand Rapids: Eerdmans, 1994.

Earl, Douglas S. "Holy War and חרם: A Biblical Theology of חרם." In *Holy War in the Bible: Christian Morality and the Old Testament Problem,* edited by H. A. Thomas, J. Evans, and P. Copan, 152–78. Downers Grove, IL: InterVarsity, 2013.

Eastman, Susan Grove. "Israel and the Mercy of God: A Re-reading of Galatians 6:16 and Romans 9–11." *New Testament Studies* 56 (2010) 367–395.

———. *Recovering Paul's Mother Tongue: Language and Theology in Galatians*. Grand Rapids: Eerdmans, 2007.

Ebeling, Jennie. "Tel Hazor Excavations: Highlights from Recent Seasons." http://www.bibleinterp.com/articles/hazor358002.shtml.

Egger-Wenzel, Renate. "'Faith in God' Rather Than 'Fear of God' in Ben Sira and Job: A Necessary Adjustment in Terminology and Understanding." In *Intertextual Studies in Ben Sira and Tobit: Essays in Honor of Alexander A. Di Lella, O.F.M,* edited by Jeremy Corley and Vincent Skemp, 211–26. Catholic Biblical Quarterly Monograph Series 38. Washington: Catholic Biblical Association, 2005.

Eirikh, Anna, Hamoudi Khalaily and Shua Kisilevitz. "Temples and sacred vessels from Biblical times discovered at Tel Motza." http://www.mfa.gov.il/mfa/israelexperience/history/pages/temple_vessels_biblical_tel_motza_26-dec-2012.aspx.

Eisenbaum, Pamela. "On the Contrary, We Uphold the Law." In *Paul Was Not a Christian: The Original Message of a Misunderstood Apostle,* 208–39. New York: HarperOne, 2009.

Eissfeldt, O. "Gilgal or Shechem." In *Proclamation and Presence,* edited *by* J. I. Durham and J. R. Porter, 90–101. Richmond: John Knox, 1970.

Elliott, Mark W., et al., eds. *Galatians and Christian Theology: Justification, the Gospel, and Ethics in Paul's Letter*. Grand Rapids: Baker, 2014.

Evans, Craig A. "Paul and the Prophets: Prophetic Criticism in the Epistle to the Romans (with Special Reference to Romans 9–11)." In *Romans and the People of God: Essays in Honor of Gordon D. Fee on the Occasion of His 65th Birthday,* edited by K. Soderlund and N. T. Wright, 115–28. Grand Rapids: Eerdmans, 1999.

Fales, Evan. "Comments on 'Canon and Conquest.'" In *Divine Evil?: The Moral Character of the God of Abraham,* edited by Michael Bergmann, et al., 309–13. Oxford: Oxford University Press, 2013.

Faust, Avraham. "The Bible. Archaeology, and the Practice of Circumcision in Israelite and Philistine Societies." *Journal of Biblical Literature* 134 (2015) 253–71.

Ferguson, Kathy E. "Patriarchy." In *Views from the Sciences,* vol. 1 of *Women's Studies Encyclopedia,* edited by Helen Tierney, 265–67. New York: Greenwood, 1989.

Fishbane, Michael. *Biblical Interpretation in Ancient Israel*. Oxford: Clarendon, 1985.

———. *Sacred Attunement: A Jewish Theology*. Chicago: University of Chicago Press, 2008.

Fisher, Aaron. "Sabbath for Those Who Serve: An Examination of the Practices and Perceptions of the Sabbath for People of Faith Serving in Under-Resourced Contexts." PsyD diss. Wheaton College, 2012.

Fisher, David H. *Historians' Fallacies: Toward a Logic of Historical Thought*. New York: Harper & Row, 1970.

Fitzmyer, Joseph A. S.J. *The Acts of the Apostles: A New Translation with Introduction and Commentary*. New York: Doubleday, 1997.

Fleming, Daniel E. "The Etymological Origins of the Hebrew *nābîʾ*: The One Who Invokes God." *Catholic Biblical Quarterly* 55 (1993) 217–24.

Fokkelman, J. P. *Major Poems of the Hebrew Bible, at the Interface of Prosody and Structural Analysis*, vol. 1, *Exod 15, Deut. 32, and Job 3*. Studia Semitica Neerlandica. Assen: Van Gorcum, 1998.

Follingstad, Carl Martin. *Deictic Viewpoint in Biblical Hebrew Text: A Syntagmatic and Paradigmatic Analysis of the Particle* כי. Dallas, TX: SIL International, 2001.

Foster, Benjamin R. *Before the Muses: An Anthology of Akkadian Literature*. 2nd ed. Potomac, MD: CDL, 1996.

Fossum, J. "Son of God." In *Dictionary of Deities and Demons in the Bible*, edited by K. van der Toorn, B. Becking, and P. van der Horst, 288–89. Rev. ed. Leiden: Brill, 1999.

Fowler, Jeaneane D. *Theophoric Personal Names in Ancient Hebrew: A Comparative Study*, Journal for the Study of the Old Testament Supplement Series 49. Sheffield: Sheffield Academic, 1988.

Franke, John R., ed. *Joshua, Judges, Ruth, 1–2 Samuel*. Ancient Christian Commentary on Scripture 4. Downers Grove: InterVarsity, 2005.

Freedman, D. N., and J. Lundbom, "חָנַן." In *Theological Dictionary of the Old Testament*, edited by G. J. Botterweck, H. Ringgren, and H.-J. Fabry, and translated by J. T. Willis, G. W. Bromiley, and D. E. Green, 5:22–36. 15 vols. Grand Rapids: Eerdmans, 2004.

Fretz, Mark. "*Herem* in the Old Testament: A Critical Reading." In *Essays on War and Peace: Bible and Early Church*, edited by W. M. Swartley, 7–44. Occasional papers 9. Elkhart, IN: Institute of Mennonite Studies, 1986.

Fridrichsen, Anton. "Die Apologie des Paulus Gal. 1." In *Exegetical Writings: A Selection*, translated and edited by Chrys C. Caragounis and Tord Fornberg. Tübingen: Mohr Siebeck, 1994 (reprint of 1920 article).

Friedman, Richard E. *Commentary on the Torah: With a New English Translation*. San Francisco: Harper, 2001.

Frisch, A. "Repentance and Return—A Literary-Theological Study of Three Biblical Texts (Deut 30:1–10; I Kings 8:46–51; II Chronicles 30:6–9)." In *Studies in Bible and Exegesis 4*, edited by B. Kasher, Y. Sefati, and M. Zipor, 129–48. Ramat Gan: Bar-Ilan University, 1997 [Hebrew].

Fuhs, H. F. "יָרֵאʾ *yārēʾ*; יָרֵאʾ *yārēʾ*; יִרְאָה *yirʾâ*; מוֹרָאʾ *môrāʾ*." In *Theological Dictionary of the Old Testament*, edited by G. J. Botterweck and H. Ringgren, and translated by D. E. Green, 6:290–315. 15 vols. Grand Rapids: Eerdmans, 1990.

Garfinkel, Yosef. "Three Shrines from Khirbet Qeiyafa: Judean Cult at the Time of King David." Paper presented to the Society of Biblical Literature in Chicago, 18 November 2012.

Garret, Duane. *Rethinking Genesis: The Source and Authorship of the First Book of the Pentateuch*. Grand Rapids: Baker, 2001.

Geeraerts, Dirk. "Introduction: A Rough Guide to Cognitive Linguistics." In *Cognitive Linguistics: Basic Readings*, edited by Dirk Geeraerts, René Dirven, John Taylor, and Ronald W. Langacker, 1–28. Cognitive Linguistics Research 34. Berlin: de Gruyter Mouton, 2006.

Geeraerts, Dirk, René Dirven, John Taylor, eds., and honorary editor Ronald W. Langacker. *Cognitive Linguistics: Basic Readings*. Cognitive Linguistics Research 34. Berlin: Walter de Gruyter, 2006.

Gentry, Peter J., and Stephen J. Wellum. *Kingdom through Covenant: A Biblical-Theological Understanding of the Covenants*. Wheaton: Crossway, 2012.

Gibson, John C. L. *Hebrew and Moabite Inscriptions*. Textbook of Syrian Semitic Inscriptions, vol. 1. Oxford: Clarendon, 1971.

Goff, Matthew J. *Discerning Wisdom: The Sapiential Literature of the Dead Sea Scrolls*. Supplements to Vetus Testamentum 116. Leiden: Brill, 2007.

Gordon, R. P. "Where Have All the Prophets Gone? The 'Disappearing' Israelite Prophet Against the Background of Ancient Near Eastern Prophecy." *Bulletin for Biblical Research* 5 (1995) 78–85.

Grant, Jamie. *The King as Exemplar: The Function of Deuteronomy's Kingship Law in the Shaping of the Book of Psalms*. SBL Academia Biblica Series 17. Atlanta: Society of Biblical Literature, 2004.

Grant, Peter, and Rosemary Grant. *40 Years of Evolution: Darwin's Finches on Daphne Major Island*. Princeton, NJ: Princeton University Press, 2104.

Graves, Michael. "The Public Reading of Scripture in Early Judaism." *Journal of the Evangelical Theological Society* 50 (2007) 467–87.

Gray, G. B. *Sacrifice in the Old Testament*. New York: KTAV, 1971.

Gray, Rebecca. *Prophetic Figures in Late Second Temple Jewish Palestine: The Evidence from Josephus*. Oxford: Oxford University Press, 1993.

Greenberg, Moshe. "On the Political Use of the Bible in Modern Israel: An Engaged Critique." In *Pomegranates and Golden Bells: Studies in Biblical, Jewish, and Near Eastern Ritual, Law, and Literature in Honor of Jacob Milgrom*, edited by D. P. Wright, D. N. Freedman, and A. Hurvitz, 461–71. Winona Lake, IN: Eisenbrauns, 1995.

———. *Biblical Prose Prayer as a Window to the Popular Religion of Ancient Israel*. Berkeley: University of California Press, 1983.

Grisanti, Michael A. "Deuteronomy." In *The Expositor's Bible Commentary*, vol. 2, *Numbers to Ruth*. Rev. ed, edited by Tremper Longman III and David E. Garland. Grand Rapids: Zondervan, 2012.

———. "Josiah and the Composition of Deuteronomy." In *Sepher Torath Mosheh: Studies in the Composition and Interpretation of Deuteronomy*, edited by Daniel I. Block and Richard L. Schultz, 110–38. Peabody, NJ: Hendrickson, 2017.

Gröndahl, F. *Die Personennamen der Texte aus Ugarit*. Studia Pohl 1. Rome: Biblical Institute, 1967.

Groningen, Gerard van. *Messianic Revelation in the Old Testament*. Grand Rapids: Baker, 1990.

Groß, Walter. *Zukunft für Israel: Alttestamentliche Bundeskonzepte und die aktuelle Debatte um den Neuen Bund*. Stuttgarter Bibelstudien 176. Stuttgart: Katholisches Bibelwerk, 1998.

Groves, J. A. "Zion Traditions." In *Dictionary of the Old Testament: Historical Books*, edited by B. T. Arnold and H. G. M. Williamson, 1019–25. Downers Gove: InterVarsity, 2005.

Gruber, Mayer I. *Aspects of Nonverbal Communication in the Ancient Near East*. Studia Pohl 12/1. Rome: Biblical Institute Press, 1980.

Guest, Steven Ward. "Deuteronomy 26:16–19 as the Central Focus of the Covenantal Framework of Deuteronomy." PhD diss., Southern Baptist Theological Seminary, 2009.

Gunneweg, A. J. H. *Leviten und Priester: Hauptlinien der Traditionsbildung und Geschichte des israelitisch-jüdischen Kultpersonals*. Forschungen zur Religion und Literatur des Alten und Neuen Testaments 89. Göttingen: Vandenhoeck & Ruprecht, 1965.

Hackett, JoAnn. *The Balaam Text from Deir ʿAllah*. Havard Semitic Monographs 19. Atlanta: Scholars, 1984.

Haenchen, Ernst. *The Acts of the Apostles: A Commentary*. Philadelphia: Westminster, 1971.

Hafemann, Scott J. *Paul, Moses, and the History of Israel: The Letter/Spirit Contrast and the Argument from Scripture in 2 Corinthians 3*. Paternoster Biblical Monographs. Milton Keynes: Paternoster, 2005.

Haller, Eduard. *Charisma und Ekstasis: Die Erzählung von dem Propheten Micha ben Imlah 1. Kön. 22,1–28a*. Theologische Existenz Heute 82. Munich: Chr. Kaiser, 1960.

Hallo, William W., ed. *Canonical Compositions from the Biblical World*. Vol. 2 of *The Context of Scripture*. Leiden: Brill, 1997.

Halpern, Baruch. *The Constitution of the Monarchy in Israel*. Harvard Semitic Monographs 25. Chico, CA: Scholars, 1981.

Haran, Menahem. "Studies in the Account of the Levitical Cities. Part I: 'Preliminary Considerations.'" *Journal of Biblical Literature* 80 (1961) 45–54.

Haran, Menahem and S. David Sperling. "Holiness Code." In *Encyclopaedia Judaica*, 2nd edition, edited by F. Skolnik, 9:318–321. New York: Thomson Gale, 2007.

———. "Studies in the Account of the Levitical Cities. Part II: 'Utopia and Historical Reality.'" *Journal of Biblical Literature* 80 (1961) 156–65.

Hardin, Justin. "Galatians 1–2 without a Mirror: Reflections on Paul's Conflict with the Agitators." *Tyndale Bulletin* 65 (2014) 275–303.

Harnack, Adolf von. *Marcion: The Gospel of the Alien God*. Translated by J. E. Steely and L. D. Bierma. Durham, NC: Labyrinth, 1990.

Hauer, Chris Jr. "David and the Levites." *Journal for the Study of the Old Testament* 23 (1982) 33–54.

Hawkins, Ralph K. *The Iron Age Structure on Mt. Ebal: Excavation and Interpretation*. Bulletin for Biblical Research Supplement 6. Winona Lake, IN: Eisenbrauns, 2012.

Hays, Richard B. "The Letter to the Galatians: Introduction, Commentary, and Reflections." In *The New Interpreter's Bible*, edited by Leander Keck, 11:299–310. 12 vols. Nashville: Abingdon, 2000.

Hengel, Martin, and Anna Maria Schwemer. *Paul between Damascus and Antioch: The Unknown Years*. Translated by J. Bowden. Louisville: Westminster John Knox, 1977.

Herodotus. *Histories*. Translated by A. D. Godley. 4 vols. LCL 117–120. Cambridge, MA: Harvard University Press, 1931, 1932.

Herr, Larry G. "Plaster." In *International Standard Bible Encyclopedia*. Rev. ed., edited by G. W. Bromiley, 3:883. Grand Rapids: Eerdmans, 1986.

Heschel, Abraham Joshua. *The Sabbath: Its Meaning for Modern Man*. New York: Noonday Press, 1951.

Hess, Richard S. *Israelite Religions: An Archaeological and Biblical Survey*. Grand Rapids: Baker, 2007.

———. *Joshua: An Introduction and Commentary.* Tyndale Old Testament Commentaries. Downers Grove: InterVarsity, 1996.

———. "Second Millennium BC Cuneiform from the Southern Levant and the Literature of the Pentateuch." In *Exploring the Composition of the Pentateuch*, edited by K. Berglund and R. Gane. Bulletin for Biblical Research Supplements. Winona Lake, IN: Eisenbrauns, 2017, forthcoming.

Hill, Andrew E. "The Ebal Ceremony as Hebrew Land Grant." *Journal of the Evangelical Theological Society* 31 (1988) 399–406.

Hoffmeier, James K. "Some Egyptian Motifs Related to Warfare and Enemies and their Old Testament Counterparts." In *Egyptological Miscellanies: A Tribute to Professor Ronald J. Williams*, edited by J. K. Hoffmeier and E. S. Meltzer, 53–70. Ancient World 6. Chicago: Ares, 1983.

———. "The Arm, of God Versus the Arm of Pharaoh in the Exodus Narratives." *Biblica* 67 (1986) 378–87.

Hoftijzer, Jacob, and Karen Jongeling. *Dictionary of the North-West Semitic Inscriptions.* 2 vols. Leiden: Brill, 1995.

Hoftijzer, Jacob, and G. van der Kooij. *Aramaic Texts from Deir ʿAllah.* Documenta et Monumenta Orientis Antiqui 19. Leiden: Brill, 1976.

———. *The Balaam Text from Deir ʿAllah Re-evaluated: Proceedings of the International Symposium Held at Leiden 21–24 August 1989.* Leiden: Brill, 1991.

Holladay, C. R. *Fragments from Hellenistic Jewish Authors*, vol. 1, *Historians*. Society of Biblical Literature Texts and Translations 20, Pseudepigrapha 10. Chico: Scholars Press, 1983.

Holladay, W. L. *The Root שוב in the Old Testament (with Particular References to Its Usage in Covenantal Contexts).* Leiden: Brill, 1958.

Houtman, C. *Exodus*, vol. 3, *Chapters 20–40*. Historical Commentary on the Old Testament. Leuven: Peeters, 2000.

Howard, David M. *Joshua.* New American Commentary. Nashville: Broadman & Holman, 1998.

Hubbard, Robert L. *Joshua.* NIV Application Commentary. Grand Rapids: Zondervan, 2009.

Huehnergard, J. "On the Etymology and Meaning of Hebrew *nābîʾ*." *Eretz Israel* 26 (1999) 88*–93*.

Hugenberger, Gordon. *Marriage as a Covenant: Biblical Law and Ethics as Developed from Malachi.* Biblical Studies Library. Winona Lake: Eisenbrauns, 1998.

Hundley, Michael. "To Be or Not to Be: A Reexamination of the name Language in Deuteronomy and the Deuteronomistic History." *Vetus Testamentum* 59 (2009) 533–55.

Hurowitz, Victor. *"I Have Built You an Exalted House": Temple Building in the Bible in the Light of Mesopotamian and Northwest Semitic Writings.* Journal for the Study of the Old Testament Supplement Series 115. Sheffield: Sheffield Academic, 1992.

Hurst, L. D. "Did Qumran Expect Two Messiahs?" *Bulletin for Biblical Research* 9 (1999) 157–80.

Hurtado, Larry W. *Lord Jesus Christ: Devotion to Jesus in Earliest Christianity.* Grand Rapids: Eerdmans, 2003.

Hutton, Jeremy M. "The Levitical Diaspora (I) A Sociological Comparison with Morocco's Ahansal." In *Exploring the Longue Durée: Essays in Honor of Lawrence E. Stager*, edited by J. D. Schloen, 223–34. Winona Lake, IN: Eisenbrauns, 2009.

———. "The Levitical Diaspora (II) Modern Perspectives on the Levitical Cities Lists (A Review of Opinions)." In *Levites and Priests in Biblical History and Tradition*, edited by Mark Leuchter and Jeremy Michael Hutton, 45–81. Atlanta: Society of Biblical Literature, 2011.

Hvalvik, Reidar. "Christ Proclaiming the Law to the Apostles: The Traditio Legis-Motif in Early Christian Art and Literature." In *The New Testament and Early Christian Literature in Greco-Roman Context*, edited by John Fotopoulos, 405–37. Novum Testamentum Supplements 122. Leiden: Brill, 2006.

Hwang, Jerry. *The Rhetoric of Remembrance: An Investigation of the "Fathers" In Deuteronomy*. Siphrut 8. Winona Lake, IN: Eisenbrauns, 2012.

Imes, Carmen Joy. *Bearing YHWH's Name at Sinai: A Re-Examination of the Name Command of the Decalogue*. Bulletin for Biblical Research Supplements 19. Winona Lake, IN: Eisenbrauns, forthcoming.

Ishida, Tomoo. "The Structure and Historical Implications of the Lists of Pre-Israelite Nations." *Biblica* 60 (1979) 461–90.

Jackson, Bernard S. "Law in the Ninth Century: Jehoshaphat's 'Judicial Reform.'" In *Understanding the History of Ancient Israel*, edited by H. G. M. Williamson, 269–97. Proceedings of the British Academy 143; Oxford: Oxford University Press, 2007.

Japhet, Sara. *I & II Chronicles*. Old Testament Library. Louisville: Westminster/John Knox, 1993.

Jastrow, Marcus *Dictionary of the Targumim, Talmud Babli, Yerushalmi and Midrashic Literature*. New York: Judaica Press, 1971.

Jenni, Ernst, and Claus Westermann, eds. *Theological Lexicon of the Old Testament*, translated by Mark E. Biddle. 3 vols. Peabody, MA: Hendrickson, 1997.

Jeremias, Joachim. "Moses." In *Theological Dictionary of the New Testament*, edited by G. Kittel, and translated by G. W. Bromiley, 4:848–73. Grand Rapids: Eerdmans, 1964.

Jones, Jennifer B. "Reconsidering the *Prophetengesetz*: A Text Linguistic Approach to Deuteronomy 18:9–22." Unpublished seminar paper, Wheaton College, 2014.

Josberger, Rebekah Lee. "Between Rule and Responsibility: The Role of the ʾAB as Agent of Righteousness in Deuteronomy's Domestic Ideology." Ph.D. dissertation, The Southern Baptist Theological Seminary, Louisville, 2007.

Josephus, Flavius. *Jewish Wars*. Translated by H. St. J. Thackeray, Loeb Classical Library. Cambridge, MA: Harvard University Press, 1927.

Kaminsky, Joel S. "Joshua 7: A Reassessment of the Israelite Conceptions of Corporate Punishment." In *The Pitcher is Broken: Memorial Essays for Gösta W. Ahlström*, edited by S. W. Holloway and L. K. Handy, 315–46. Journal for the Study of the Old Testament Supplement Series 190. Sheffield: Sheffield Academic Press, 1995.

Kaufmann, Yehezekel. *The Biblical Account of the Conquest of Canaan*. Jerusalem: Magnes/Hebrew University Press, 1953.

Keil, C. F. *Genesis und Exodus*. Giessen: Brunnen, 1983.

Keneally, Thomas. *Moses the Lawgiver*. New York: Harper & Row, 1975.

Kibbe, Michael. *Godly Fear or Ungodly Failure? Hebrews 12:18–29 and the Sinai Theophanies*. Beihefte zur Zeitschrift für die neutestamentliche Wissenschaft 216. Berlin: Walter de Gruyter, 2016.

Kilchör, Benjamin. "The Direction of Dependence between the Laws of the Pentateuch: The Priority of a Literary Approach." *Ephemerides Theologicae Lovanienses* 89 (2013) 1–14.

———. *Mosetora und Jahwetora: Das Verhältnis von Deuteronomium 12-26 zu Exodus, Levitikus, und Numeri*. Beihefte zur Zeitschrift für altorientalische und biblische Rechtsgeschichte 21. Wiesbaden: Harrassowitz, 2015.

Kim, Brittany. "'Enlarge the Place of Your Tent'": The Metaphorical World of Israel's Household in the Book of Isaiah." Ph.D. diss., Wheaton College, 2014.

Kim, Yoon-Hee. "The 'Prophet Like Moses': Deut 18:15-22 Reexamined within the Context of the Pentateuch and in Light of the Final Shape of the TaNaK." Ph.D. diss. Trinity Evangelical Divinity School, 1995.

King, L. W. *The Code of Hammurabi*. Whitefish, MT: Kessinger, 2004 (reprint of 1910 edition).

Kistemaker, Simon J. *Acts*. New Testament Commentary. Grand Rapids: Baker, 1990.

Kitchen, Kenneth A. *On the Reliability of the Old Testament*. Grand Rapids: Eerdmans, 2003.

Kitchen, Kenneth A., and Paul J. N. Lawrence. *Treaty, Law and Covenant in the Ancient Near East*. 3 vols. Wiesbaden: Harrassowitz, 2012.

———. *Treaty, Law and Covenant in the Ancient Near East*. Part 3, *Overall Historical Survey*. Wiesbaden: Harrassowitz, 2012.

Klausern, Theodor. *Frühchristliche Sarkophage in Bild und Wort*. Beiheft zur Halbjahresschrift Antike Kunst 3. Olten: Urs Grav-Verlag, 1966.

Klingbeil, Gerald. "Looking at the End from the Beginning: Studying Eschatological Concepts in the Pentateuch." *Journal of the Adventist Theological Society* 11 (2000) 174-87.

Knoppers, Gary N. *I Chronicles 1-9: A New Translation with Introduction and Commentary*. Anchor Bible 12. New York: Doubleday, 2003.

———. "Ancient Near Eastern Royal Grants and the Davidic Covenant: A Parallel?" *Journal of the American Oriental Society* 116 (1996) 670-97.

———. "Projected Age Comparisons of the Levitical Townlists: Divergent Theories and Their Significance." *Textus* 22 (2005) 21-63.

———. "Rethinking the Relationship between Deuteronomy and the Deuteronomistic History: The Case of Kings." *Catholic Biblical Quarterly* 63 (2002) 393-415.

Köstenberger, Andreas J., with David W. Jones. *God, Marriage and Family: Rebuilding the Biblical Foundation*. Wheaton: Crossway, 2004.

Köstenberger, Andreas J., and Margaret E. Köstenberger. *God's Design for Man and Woman: A Biblical-Theological Survey*. Wheaton: Crossway, 2014.

Kruger, Thomas. "Law and Wisdom according to Deut 4:5-8." In *Wisdom and Torah: The Reception of "Torah" In the Wisdom Literature of the Second Temple Period*, edited by Bernd U. Schipper and D. Andrew Teeter, 35-54. Journal for the study of Judaism Supplement Series 163. Leiden: Brill, 2013.

Kugler, Robert, and Patrick Hartin. *An Introduction to the Bible*. Grand Rapids: Eerdmans, 2009.

Labuschagne, C. J. *Deuteronomium*. 2 parts. De Prediking van het Oude Testament. Nijkerk: Uitgeverij Callenbach, 1990.

Lambert, Wilfred G. *Babylonian Wisdom Literature*. Oxford: Clarendon, 1960.

Lasine, Stuart. "Fiction, Falsehood, and Reality in Hebrew Scripture." *Hebrew Studies* 25 (1984) 24-40.

Lauinger, Jacob. "Some Preliminary Thoughts on the Tablet Collection in Building XVI from Tell Tayinat." *The Canadian Society for Mesopotamian Studies* 6 (2011) 5-14.

Layton, S. C. *Archaic Features of Canaanite Personal Names in the Hebrew Bible*. Harvard Semitic Monographs 47. Atlanta: Scholars Press, 1990.

Lee, Won W. "The Exclusion of Moses from the Promised Land." In *The Changing Face of Form Criticism for the Twenty-First Century*, edited by Marvin A. Sweeney, and Ehud Ben Zvi, 217–39. Grand Rapids: Eerdmans, 2003.

LeFebvre, Michael. *Collections, Codes, and Torah: The Re-characterization of Israel's Written Law*. Library of Hebrew Bible/Old Testament Studies 451. New York: T&T Clark, 2006.

Lehne, Susanne. *The New Covenant in Hebrews*. Journal for the Study of the New Testament Supplement Series 44. Sheffield: Sheffield Academic, 1990.

Leibert, Julius. *The Lawgiver*. New York: Exposition, 1953.

Leprohon, Ronald L. "Royal Ideology and State Administration in Pharaonic Egypt." In *Civilizations of the Ancient Near East*, edited by J. M. Sasson, 1:273–87. Peabody, MA: Hendrickson, 2000.

Lerner, Gerda. *The Creation of Patriarchy*. New York: Oxford University Press, 1986.

Leuchter, Mark. "'The Levite in Your Gates': The Deuteronomic Redefinition of Levitical Authority." *Journal of Biblical Literature* 126 (2007) 417–36.

Levenson, Jon D. *Inheriting Abraham: The Legacy of the Patriarch in Judaism, Christianity, and Islam*. Princeton: Princeton University Press, 2012.

———. *The Love of God: Divine Gift, Human Gratitude, and Mutual Faithfulness in Judaism*. Princeton: Princeton University Press, 2016.

Levin, Christoph. "Righteousness in the Joseph Story." In *The Pentateuch: International Perspectives on Current Research*, edited by Thomas B. Dozeman, Konrad Schmid, and Baruch J. Schwartz, 223–40. Forschungen zum Alten Testament 78. Tübingen: Mohr Siebeck, 2011.

Levine, Baruch. *In the Presence of YHWH*. Leiden: Brill, 1974.

Levine, Lee I. *The Synagogue: The First Thousand Years*. New Haven: Yale University Press, 2000.

Levinson, Bernard M. *"The Right Chorale": Studies in Biblical Law and Interpretation*. Winona Lake, IN: Eisenbrauns, 2011.

———. *Deuteronomy and the Hermeneutics of Legal Innovation*. Oxford: Oxford University Press, 1998.

Levinson, Bernard M., and Jeffrey Stackert. "Between the Covenant Code and Esarhaddon's Succession Treaty." *Journal of Ancient Judaism* 3 (2012) 123–140.

Levy, D., and Jacob Milgrom, "עֵדָה ʿēdâ." In *Theological Dictionary of the Old Testament*, edited by G. J. Botterweck and H. Ringgren, and translated by J. T. Willis, G. W. Bromiley, and D. E. Green, 10:466–80. 15 vols. Grand Rapids: Eerdmans, 1986.

Lewis, Theodore J. "Baal-Berith." In *Anchor Bible Dictionary*, edited by D. N. Freedman, 1:550–51. Garden City, NY: Doubleday, 1992.

Lieberman, Joe. *The Gift of Rest: Rediscovering the Beauty of the Sabbath*. New York: Howard Books, 2011.

Lierman, John. *The New Testament Moses: Christian Perceptions of Moses and Israel in the Setting of Jewish Religion*. Wissenschaftliche Untersuchungen zum Neuen Testament 2/173. Tübingen: Mohr Siebeck, 2004.

Lim, Johnson Teng Kok. "The Sin of Moses in Deuteronomy." *Asia Journal of Theology* 17/2 (2001) 250–66.

Lincicum, David. *Paul and the Early Jewish Encounter with Deuteronomy*. Wissenschaftliche Untersuchungen zum Neuen Testament 2/284. Tübingen: Mohr Siebeck, 2010.

Lincoln, Andrew T. "From Sabbath to Lord's Day: A Biblical and Theological Perspective." In *From Sabbath to Lord's Day*, edited by D. A. Carson, 343–412. Eugene, OR: Wipf & Stock, 1999.

Lohfink, Norbert, and Georg Braulik. "Deuteronomium 4,13 und der Horebbund." In *Für immer verbündet: Studien zur Bundestheologie der Bibel*, edited by C. Dohmen and C. Freud, 27–36. Stuttgarter Bibelstudien 211. Stuttgart: Katholisches Bibelwerk, 2007.

Lohfink, Norbert. "Die These vom 'deuteronomischen' Dekalog-anfang: Ein fragwürdiges Ergebnis atomistischer Sprachstatistik." In *Student zum Pentateuch: Walter Kornfeld zum 60. Geburtstag*, edited by Georg Braulik, 99–109. Vienna/Freiburg/Basel: Herder, 1963.

———. "Fortschreibung? Zur Technik von Rechtsrevisionen im deuteronomischen Bereich, erörtert an Deuteronomium 12, Ex 21,2–11 und Dtn 15,12–18." In *Das Deuteronomium und seine Querbeziehungen*, edited by T. Veijola, 133–181. Schriften der Finnischen Exegetischen Gesellschaft 62. Göttingen, Germany: Vandenhoeck & Ruprecht, 1996.

———. "חָרַם, ḥāram." In *Theological Dictionary of the Old Testament*, edited by G. J. Botterweck and H. Ringgren, and translated by J. T. Willis, G. W. Bromiley, and D. E. Green, 5:180–99. 15 vols. Grand Rapids: Eerdmans, 1986.

———. *Das Hauptgebot: Eine Untersuchung literarischer Einleitungsfragen zu Dtn 5–11*. Analecta Biblica 20. Rome: Pontificio Instituto Biblico, 1963.

Longenecker, Richard N. *Galatians*. Word Biblical Commentary 41. Nashville: Thomas Nelson, 1990.

Longman, Tremper III. *Proverbs*. Baker Exegetical Commentary. Grand Rapids: Baker, 2006.

Lundbom, Jack R. *Deuteronomy: A Commentary*. Grand Rapids, MI: Eerdmans, 2013.

Lyons, Michael. *From Law to Prophecy: Ezekiel's Use of the Holiness Code*. Library of Hebrew Bible/Old Testament Studies 507. New York: T&T Clark, 2009.

McCarty, Skip. "The Seventh Day Sabbath." In *Perspectives on the Sabbath: 4 Views*, edited by C. J. Donato, 9–72. Nashville: Broadman & Holman, 2011.

MacDonald, Nathan. *Deuteronomy and the Meaning of Monotheism*. Forschungen zum Alten Testament 2/1. Tübingen: Mohr Siebeck, 2003.

Maimonides. "Laws of Circumcision." In *Mishneh Torah: The Book of Adoration*, translated by Moses Hyamson. Jerusalem: Feldheim, 1981.

———. "Laws of Reading the Shema." In *Mishneh Torah: The Book of Adoration*, translated by Moses Hyamson. Jerusalem: Feldheim, 1981.

Malamat, Abraham. "'You Shall Love Your Neighbor as Yourself': A Case of Misinterpretation?" In *Die Hebräische Bibel und ihre Nachgeschichte*, Rendtorff Festschrift, edited by E. Blum, Christian Macholz, and Ekkehard Stegemann, 111–15. Neukirchen/Vluyn: Neukirchener Verlag, 1990.

Martínez, Florentino Garcia, and Elbert J. C. Tigchelaar. *The Dead Sea Scrolls: Study Edition*. Vol. 1, *1Q1–4Q273*. Grand Rapids: Eerdmans, 2000.

Martyn, J. Louis. "The Apocalyptic Gospel in Galatians." *Interpretation* 54 (2000) 246–66.

———. *Galatians: A New Translation with Introduction and Commentary*. Anchor Bible 33A. New York: Doubleday, 1997.

Mason, Steven. "Jews, Judaeans, Judaizing, Judaism: Problems of Categorization in Ancient History." *Journal for the Study of Judaism in the Persian, Hellenistic, and Roman Periods* 38 (2007) 457–512.

Matlock, Michael D. *Discovering the Traditions of Prose Prayers in Early Jewish Literature*. Library of Second Temple Studies. New York: T&T Clark, 2012.

Mayes, A. D. H. *Deuteronomy*. New Century Bible. Grand Rapids: Eerdmans, 1981.

———. *The Story of Israel between Settlement and Exile: A Redactional Study of the Deuteronomistic History*. London: SCM, 1983.

Mazar, Amihai. *Archaeology of the Land of the Bible 10,000–586 B.C.E*. New York: Doubleday, 1990.

Mazar, Benjamin. "The Cities of the Priests and Levites." In *Congress Volume Oxford 1959*, edited by G. W. Anderson, 193–205. Supplements to Vetus Testamentum 7. Leiden: Brill, 1960.

McBride, S. Dean. "The Polity of the Covenant People: The Book of Deuteronomy." *Interpretation* 41 (1987) 229–244.

———. "The Deuteronomic Name Theology." PhD dissertation, Harvard University, 1969.

McCarthy, C. *Deuteronomy, BHQ*, 5. Stuttgart: Deutsche Bibelgesellschaft, 2007.

———. *The Tiqqune Sopherim and Other Theological Corrections of the Masoretic Text of the Old Testament*. Orbis biblicus et orientalis. Freiburg: Universitätsverlag/Göttingen: Vandenhoeck & Ruprecht, 1981.

McComiskey, Thomas E. *The Covenants of Promise: A Theology of the Old Testament Covenants*. Grand Rapids: Baker, 1985.

———. *Reading Scripture in Public: A Guide for Preachers and Lay Leaders*. Grand Rapids: Baker, 1991.

McConville, J. G. *Deuteronomy*. Apollos Old Testament Commentaries 5. Downers Grove: InterVarsity, 2002.

———. "Deuteronomy's Unification of Passover and *Maṣṣôt*: A Response to Bernard M. Levinson." *Journal of Biblical Literature* 119 (2000) 47–58.

———. *Law and Theology in Deuteronomy*. Journal for the Study of the Old Testament Supplement Series 33. Sheffield: Sheffield Press, 1984.

———. "Singular Address in the Deuteronomic Law and the Politics of Legal Administration." *Journal for the Study of the Old Testament* 97 (2002) 19–36.

———. "Time, Place, and the Deuteronomic Altar-Law." In *Time and Place in Deuteronomy*, by J. Gordon McConville and J. G. Millar, 89–139. Journal for the Study of the Old Testament Supplement Series 179. Sheffield: Sheffield Academic, 1994.

———. "Wisdom and Torah in Deuteronomy." In *Sepher Torath Mosheh: Studies in the Composition and Interpretation of Deuteronomy*, edited by Daniel I. Block and Richard L. Schultz, 261–76. Peabody, MA: Hendrickson, 2017.

McConville, J. Gordon, and J. Gary Millar, *Time and Place in Deuteronomy*. Journal for the Study of the Old Testament Supplement Series 179. Sheffield Academic Press, 1984.

McKane, William M. *Proverbs: A New Approach*. Old Testament Library. Philadelphia: Westminster, 1975.

McLean, Max, and Warren Bird. *Unleashing the Word: Rediscovering the Public Reading of Scripture*. Grand Rapids: Zondervan, 2009.

McNamara, M. *Targum Neofiti 1: Deuteronomy*. Aramaic Bible 5A. Edinburgh: T&T Clark, 1997.

Marshall, I. Howard. "Acts." In *Commentary on the New Testament Use of the Old Testament*, edited by G. K. Beale and D. A. Carson, 513–606. Grand Rapids: Baker, 2007.

Martin, Ralph P. *Worship in the Early Church*. Grand Rapids: Eerdmans, 1975.

Martínez, Florentino Garcia, and Eibert J. C. Tigchelaar. *The Dead Sea Scrolls: Study Edition*, 2 vols. Grand Rapids: Eerdmans, 1997, 1998.

Meeks, Wayne A. *Prophet-King: Moses Traditions and the Johannine Christology*, Novum Testamentum Supplements 14. Leiden: Brill, 1967.

Melville, Herman. *Moby Dick*. Oxford: Oxford University Press, 2008.

Mendenhall, George. "The Conflict between Value Systems and Social Control." In *Unity and Diversity: Essays on the History, Literature, and Religion of the Ancient Near East*, edited by J. J. M. Roberts, 169–180. Baltimore: Johns Hopkins University Press, 1975.

Merendino, R. P. "Dt 27:1–8: Eine literarkritische und Überlieferungsgeschichtliche Untersuchung." *Biblische Zeitschrift* 24 (1980) 194–207.

Merrill, Eugene H. "The Case for Moderate Discontinuity." In *Show Them No Mercy: Four Views on God and Canaanite Genocide*, C. S. Cowles et al., 61–110. Grand Rapids: Zondervan, 1978.

———. *Deuteronomy*. New American Commentary. Nashville: Broadman & Holman, 1994.

Meyers, Carol L. "Every Day Life: Women in the Period of the Hebrew Bible." In *The Women's Bible Commentary*, Expanded Edition with Apocrypha, edited by C. A. Newsome and S. H. Ringe, 251–59. Westminster/John Knox, 1992.

———. "The Family in Early Israel." In *Families in Ancient Israel*, edited by L. G. Perdue, J. Blenkinsopp, J. J. Collins, and C. Meyers, 1–47. Louisville: Westminster John Knox, 1997.

Milgrom, Jacob. "The Levitical Town: An Exercise in Realistic Planning." *Journal of Jewish Studies* 33 (1982) 185–88.

———. *Leviticus 1–16: A New Translation with Introduction and Commentary*. Anchor Bible 3. New York: Doubleday, 1991.

———. *Leviticus 17–22: A New Translation with Introduction and Commentary*. Anchor Bible 3A. New York: Doubleday, 2000.

———. *Leviticus 23–27: A New Translation with Introduction and Commentary*. Anchor Bible 3B; New York: Doubleday, 2001.

———. *Numbers*. Jewish Publication Society Torah Commentary. Philadelphia: Jewish Publication Society, 1990.

Milgrom, Jacob and Daniel I. Block. *Ezekiel's Hope: A Commentary on Ezekiel 38–48*. Eugene, OR: Cascade, 2012.

Millar, Gary. "Living at the Place of Decision: Time and Place in the Framework of Deuteronomy." In *Time and Place in Deuteronomy*, by J. Gordon McConville and J. G. Millar, 15–88. Journal for the Study of the Old Testament Supplement Series 179. Sheffield: Sheffield Academic, 1994.

———. *Calling on the Name of the Lord: A Biblical Theology of Prayer*. New Studies in Biblical Theology. Downers Grove: InterVarsity, 2016.

Miller, Patrick D. "'Moses My Servant': The Deuteronomic Portrait of Moses." *Interpretation: A Journal of Bible and Theology* 41 (1987) 245–55.

———. *They Cried to the Lord: The Form and Theology of Biblical Prayer*. Minneapolis: Fortress, 1994.

———. *The Religion of Ancient Israel*. Library of Ancient Israel. Louisville: Westminster John Knox, 2000.

Miller, P. D., P. D. Hanson, and S. D. McBride, eds. *Ancient Israelite Religion: Essays in Honor of Frank Moore Cross*. Philadelphia: Fortress, 1987.

Miller, Pavla. "Patriarchy." In *The Oxford Encyclopedia of Women in World History*, edited by Bonnie G. Smith, 3:419–24. Philadelphia: Oxford University Press, 2010.

Moberly, R. W. L. "Toward an Interpretation of the Shema." In *Theological Exegesis: Essays in Honor of Brevard S. Childs*, edited by C. Seitz and K. Greene-McCreight, 124–44. Grand Rapids: Eerdmans, 1999.

———. *At the Mountain of God: Story and Theology in Exodus 32–34*. Journal for the Study of the Old Testament Supplement Series 22. Sheffield: Journal for the Study of the Old Testament, 1983.

———. *Old Testament Theology: Reading the Hebrew Bible as Christian Scripture*. Grand Rapids: Baker, 2013.

———. *The Old Testament of the Old Testament: Patriarchal Narratives and Mosaic Yahwism*. Minneapolis: Augsburg, 1992.

Moffatt, Marian. "The Mystic Mill from Vézelay." In *A World History of Architecture*, edited by Michael Fazio, Marian Moffat, and Lawrence Wodehouse, 2nd edition, 215–17. London: McGraw-Hill, 2008.

Monroe, Lauren "Israelite, Moabite and Sabaean War-*ḥērem* Traditions and the Forging of National Identity: Reconsidering the Sabaean Text RES 3945 in Light of Biblical and Moabite Evidence." *Vetus Testamentum* 57 (2007) 318–41.

Moo, Douglas J. *Galatians*. Baker Exegetical Commentary on the New Testament. Grand Rapids: Baker, 2013.

Moore, Russell D. "After Patriarchy, What? Why Egalitarians Are Winning the Gender Debate." *Journal of the Evangelical Theological Society* 49 (2006), 569–76.

Morschauser, Scott. "'Do Not Look to Egypt?': On an Alternative to Joshua Berman's 'CTH 133 and the Hittite Provenance of Deuteronomy 13.'" Unpublished essay.

Mulder, M. J. "Baal-Berith." In *Dictionary of Deities and Demons in the Bible*, edited by K. van der Toorn, B. Becking, and P. van der Horst, 141–42. Rev. ed. Leiden: Brill, 1999.

Murdock, D. M. a.k.a Acharya S. *Did Moses Exist? The Myth of the Israelite Lawgiver*. Seattle, WA: Stellar, 2014.

Murphy, Roland K. *Proverbs*. Word Biblical Commentary 22. Nashville: Thomas Nelson, 1998.

Murphy-O'Connor, Jerome. "Paul in Arabia." *Catholic Biblical Quarterly* 55 (1993) 732–37.

Naʿaman, N. "Shechem and Jerusalem in the Exilic and Restoration Period." *Zion* 58 (1993) 7–32 (Hebrew).

———. "The Law of the Altar in Deuteronomy and the Cultic Site Near Shechem." In *Rethinking the Foundations: Historiography in the Ancient World and the Bible*, edited by S. McKenzie, John Van Seters, T. Römer, and Hans Heirich Schmid, 141–61. Beihefte zur Zeitschrift für die alttestamentliche Wissenschaft 294; Berlin: de Gruyter, 2000.

Najman, Hindy. *Seconding Sinai: The Development of Mosaic Discourse in Second Temple Judaism*. Journal for the Study of Judaism Supplement Series 77. Leiden: Brill, 2003.

Nelson, Richard D. *Deuteronomy: A Commentary*. Old Testament Library. Louisville: Westminster John Knox, 2002.

———. *Joshua: A Commentary*. Old Testament Library. Louisville: Westminster John Knox, 1997.

———. *Raising Up a Faithful Priest: Community and Priesthood in Biblical Theology*. Louisville: Westminster John Knox, 1993.

Neusner, Jacob. *A Rabbi Talks with Jesus*. Rev. ed. Montreal: McGill-Queens University Press, 2000.

Nicholson, Ernest. *Deuteronomy and Tradition: Literary and Historical Problems in the Book of Deuteronomy*. Philadelphia: Fortress, 1967.

Nicklas, Tobias. "Paulus—der Apostel als Prophet." In *Prophets and Prophecy in Jewish and Early Christian Literature*, edited by Joseph Verheyden, Korinna Zamfir, and Tobias

Nicklas, 77–104. Wissenschaftliche Untersuchungen zum Neuen Testament 2/286. Tübingen: Mohr Siebeck, 2010.

Nielsen, E. *Deuteronomium*. Handbuch zum Alten Testament 6. Tübingen: J. C. B. Mohr, 1995.

———. "A Note on Zechariah 14,4-5." In *In the Last Days: On Jewish and Christian Apocalyptic and Its Period*, edited by K. Jeppesen, K. Nielsen, and B. Rosendal, 33–7. Aarhus: Aarhus University Press, 1997.

Noth, Martin. *The Deuteronomistic History*. Translated by D. Orton. Journal for the Study of the Old Testament Supplement Series 15. Sheffield: JSOT Press, 1981.

———. *Überlieferungsgeschichtliche Studien*. 2nd ed. Tübingen: Max Niemeyer, 1957.

Novenson, Matthew V. *Christ among the Messiahs: Christ Language in Paul and Messiah Language in Ancient Judaism*. Oxford: Oxford University Press, 2012.

———. "Paul's Former Occupation in *Ioudaismos*." In *Galatians and Christian Theology*, edited by Mark W. Elliott et al., 24–39. Grand Rapids: Baker, 2014.

O'Brien, Mark A., O.P., "The Story of Abraham and the Debate over the Source Hypothesis." *Australian Biblical Review* 38 (1990) 1–17.

O'Donovan, Oliver. "The Reading Church: Scriptural Authority in Practice." A lecture delivered at St. Mary, Islington, April 2009, http://www.fulcrum-anglican.org.uk/page.cfm?ID=422.

O'Dowd, Ryan. *The Wisdom of Torah: Epistemology in Deuteronomy and the Wisdom Literature*. Forschungen zur Religion und Literatur des Alten und Neuen Testaments 225. Göttingen: Vandenhoeck & Ruprecht, 2009.

Old, Hughes Oliphant. *The Reading and Preaching of the Scriptures in the Worship of the Early Church*. Vol. 1, *The Biblical Period*. Grand Rapids: Eerdmans, 1998.

———. *The Reading and Preaching of the Scriptures in the Worship of the Christian Church*. Vol. 2, *The Patristic Age*. Grand Rapids: Eerdmans, 1998.

Olyan, Saul M. "Why an Altar of Unfinished Stones? Some Thoughts on Ex 20,25 and Dtn 27,5-6." *Zeitschrift für die alttestamentliche Wissenschaft* 108 (1996) 161–71.

Oswalt, John N. *The Book of Isaiah Chapters 40-66*. New International Commentary on the Old Testament. Grand Rapids: Eerdmans, 1998.

Otto, Eckart. "Aspects of Legal Reforms and Reformulations in Ancient Cuneiform and Israelite Law." In *Theory and Method in Biblical and Cuneiform Law: Revision, Interpolation and Development*, edited by B. M. Levinson, 160–196. Journal for the Study of the Old Testament Supplement Series 181. Sheffield: Sheffield Academic, 1994.

———. "Rechtsformen in Deuteronomium xii–xxvi und im Mittelassyyrischen Kodex der Tafel A (KAV 1)." In *Congress Volume: Paris 1992*, edited by J. A. Emerton, 239–273. Leiden, The Netherlands, and New York: Brill, 1995.

———. "Revisions in the Legal History of Covenant Code, Deuteronomy, Holiness Code and the Legal Hermeneutics of the Torah." Paper delivered to the Society of Biblical Literature, New Orleans, November 23, 2009.

———. "Treueid und Gesetz: Die Ursprünge des Deuteronomiums im Horizont neuassyrischen Vertragrechts." *Zeitschrift für altorientalische und biblische Rechtsgeschichte* 2 (1996) 1–52.

———. *Deuteronomium 1–11*. Vol. 1, *Deuteronomium 1,1–4,43*. Herders Theologischer Kommentar zum Alten Testament. Stuttgart: Herders, 2012.

Otto, Rudolph. *The Idea of the Holy*. Translated by John W. Harvey. Oxford: Oxford University Press, 1923.

Overholt, Thomas W. *Channels of Prophecy: The Social Dynamics of Prophetic Activity.* Minneapolis: Fortress, 1989.

Pajunen, Mika S. "4QSapiential Admonitions B (4Q185) Unsolved Challenges of the Hebrew Text." In *The Mermaid and the Partridge: Essays from the Copenhagen Conference on Revising Texts from Cave Four,* edited by George J. Brooke and Jesper Høgenhaven, 191–220. Studies on the Texts of the Desert of Judah 96. Leiden: Brill, 2011.

Pakkala, Juha. "The Date of the Oldest Edition of Deuteronomy." *Zeitschrift für die Alttestamentliche Wissenschaft* 121 (2009) 388–401.

Pardee, Dennis. "A New Aramaic Inscription from Zincirli." *Bulletin of the American Schools of Oriental Research* 356 (2009) 51–71.

Parker, Simon B. ed. *Ugaritic Narrative Poetry.* Society of Biblical Literature Writings from the Ancient World 9. Atlanta: Scholars Press, 1997.

Parpola, Simo. *Letters from Assyrian Scholars.* State Archives of Syria 10 (Helsinki: Helsinki University Press, 1993.

Parsons, John J. "Moses' Prophecy of the Messiah: Jesus as the Prophet Like unto Moses." http://www.hebrew4christians.com/Articles/Like_Moses/like_moses.html.

Patai, Raphael. *Family, Love and the Bible.* London: Macgibbon & Kee, 1960.

Paul, Shalom. "Adoption Formulae: A Study in Cuneiform and Biblical Legal Clauses." *Maarav* 2 (1978–80) 173–85,

Pearce, Laurie E., and Cornelia Wunsch. *Documents of Judean Exiles and West Semites in Babylonia in the Collection of David Sofer.* Cornell University Studies in Assyriology and Sumerology 28. Bethesda, MD: CDL, 2014.

Pedersen, Johannes. *Israel: Its Life and Culture.* Atlanta: Scholars Press, 1991. Reprint of the 1926 edition.

Perlitt, Lothar. "Mose als Prophet." *Evangelische Theologie* 31 (1971) 588–608.

———. "Sinai und Horeb." In *Beiträge zur alttestamentlichen Theologie: Festschrift für Walther Zimmerli zum 70. Geburtstag,* edited by H. Donner et al., 303–22. Göttingen: Vandenhoeck & Ruprecht, 1977.

Pervo, Richard I. *Acts.* Hermeneia. Minneapolis: Fortress, 2009.

Peter C. Craigie, *Deuteronomy.* New International Commentary on the Old Testament. Grand Rapids: Eerdmans, 1976.

Peterson, John L. "A Topographical Surface Survey of the Levitical 'Cities' of Joshua 21 and 1 Chronicles 6: Studies on the Levites in Israelite Life and Religion." ThD diss., Chicago Institute for Advanced Theological Studies, Seabury-Western Theological Seminary, 1977.

Pettegrew, Larry D. "The New Covenant." *The Master's Seminary Journal* 10 (1999) 251–70.

Pfeiffer, Robert H. "The Fear of God." *Israel Exploration Journal* 5 (1955) 41–48.

Plath, Siegfried. *Furcht Gottes: Der Begriff* ירא *im Alten Testament.* Stuttgart: Calwer Verlag, 1962.

Polhill, John B. *Acts.* New American Commentary 26. Nashville: Broadman, 1992.

Pressler, Carolyn. *The View of Women Found in the Deuteronomic Family Laws.* Beihefte zur Zeitschrift für die alttestamentliche Wissenschaft 216. Berlin/New York: de Gruyter, 1993.

Pritchard, J. B. *The Ancient Near East in Pictures Relating to the Old Testament.* Princeton: Princeton University Press, 1954.

Pritchard, J. B., ed. *Ancient Near Eastern Texts Relating to the Old Testament.* 3rd ed. Princeton: Princeton University Press, 1969.

Puech, Émile. "Some Remarks on 4Q246 and 4Q521 and Qumran Messianism." In *The Provo International Conference on the Dead Sea Scrolls: Technological Innovations, New Texts, and Reformulated Issues*, edited by Donald W. Parry and Eugene Ulrich, 559-61. Leiden: Brill, 1999.

Rabin, Chaim. "Linguistic Aspects." In *Genesis: An Authorship Study in Computer-Assisted Statistical Linguistics*, by Yehuda T. Raddy et al., 218-24. Analecta Biblica 103. Rome: Pontifical Institute, 1985.

Rad, Gerhard von. *Deuteronomy: A Commentary*. Old Testament Library. Philadelphia: Westminster, 1966.

———. *The Problem of the Hexateuch and Other Studies*. London: SCM, 1966.

———. *Studies in Deuteronomy*. Translated by D. Stalker. Studies in Biblical Theology 1/9. Chicago: Henry Regnery, 1953.

Radday, Yehuda T., and Haim Shore. *Genesis: An Authorship Study in Computer-Assisted Statistical Linguistics*. Analecta Biblica 103. Rome: Pontifical Institute, 1985.

Rahlfs, A., ed. *Septuaginta*. 2 vols. Stuttgart: Württembergische Bibelanstalt, 1935.

Redford, Donald B. "Hyksos." In *Anchor Bible Dictionary*, edited by D. N. Freedman, 4:341-48. Garden City: Doubleday, 1992.

Rehm, M. D. "Levites and Priests." In *Anchor Bible Dictionary*, edited by D. N. Freedman, 4:297-310. Garden City: Doubleday, 1992.

Rendsburg, Gary. "A New Look at Pentateuchal *HW*?." *Biblica* 63 (1982) 351-69.

Rendtorff, Rolf. *Studien zur Geschichte des Opfers im alten Israel*. Wissenschaftliche Monographien zum Alten und Neuen Testament 24. Neukirchen-Vluyn: Neukirchener Verlag des Erziehungsvereins, 1967.

———. *The Old Testament: An Introduction*. Minneapolis: Fortress, 1991.

———. *The Problem of the Process of Transmission in the Pentateuch*. Translated by John J. Scullion. Journal for the Study of the Old Testament Supplement Series 89. Sheffield: Journal for the Study of the Old Testament, 1990.

Rengstorf, K. H. "ἀποστέλλω." In *Theological Dictionary of the New Testament*, edited by G. Kittel, and translated by G. W. Bromiley, 1:398-447. Grand Rapids: Eerdmans, 1964.

Rich, Tracey R. "Shabbat." http://www.jewfaq.org/shabbat.htm.

Richter, Sandra L. "The Place of the Name in Deuteronomy." *Vetus Testamentum* 57 (2007) 342-66.

———. *The Deuteronomistic History and the Name Theology: lešakkēn šĕmô šām in the Bible and the Ancient Near East*. Beihefte zur Zeitschrift für die Alttestamentliche Wissenschaft 318. Berlin: de Gruyter, 2002.

Ridderbos, J. *Deuteronomy*. Translated by E. M. van der Maas. Bible Student's Commentary. Grand Rapids: Zondervan, 1984.

Ringgren, H. et al. "עָבַד *'ābad*; עֶבֶד *'ebed*; עֲבֹדָה." In *Theological Dictionary of the Old Testament*, edited by G. J. Botterweck and H. Ringgren, and translated by J. T. Willis, G. W. Bromiley, and D. E. Green, 10:376-405. 15 vols. Grand Rapids: Eerdmans, 1999.

———. *Israelite Religion*. Translated by D. E. Green. Philadelphia: Fortress, 1966.

Robertson, O. Palmer. *The Christ of the Covenants*. Phillipsburg, NJ: Presbyterian & Reformed, 1980.

Rodd, Cyril S. *Glimpses of a Strange Land: Studies in Old Testament Ethics*. Old Testament Studies. Edinburgh: T. & T. Clark, 2001.

Römer, Thomas. "Deuteronomy in Search of Origins." In *Reconsidering Israel and Judah: Recent Studies in the Deuteronomistic History*, edited by G. N. Knoppers and G. J.

McConville, 112–138. Sources for Biblical and Theological Study 8. Winona Lake, IN: Eisenbrauns, 2000.

———. *Dark God: Cruelty, Sex, and Violence in the Old Testament*. Mahwah, NJ: Paulist, 2013.

Rose, Martin. *5. Mose: 12–25. Einführung und Gesetze*. Zürcher Bibelkommentare, AT. Zurich: Theologischer Verlag, 1994.

Ross, J. P. "The 'Cities of the Levites' in Joshua XXI and I Chron VI." PhD Diss., University of Edinburgh, 1973.

Roth, Martha T. *Law Collections from Mesopotamia and Asia Minor*. 2nd ed. Society of Biblical Literature Writings from the Ancient World Series 6. Atlanta: Scholars Press, 1997.

Rowland, C. "A Summary of Sabbath Observance in Judaism at the Beginning of the Christian Era." In *From Sabbath to Lord's Day*, edited by D. A. Carson, 43–56. Eugene, OR: Wipf & Stock, 1999.

Rüterswörden, Uwe. *Von der politischen Gemeinschaft zur Gemeinde: Studien zu Dt 16,18–18,22*. Bonner biblische Beiträge 65. Frankfurt-am-Main: Athenäum, 1987.

Rydelnik, Michael. *The Messianic Hope: Is the Hebrew Bible Really Messianic?* NAC Studies in Bible and Theology. Nashville: Broadman & Holman, 2010.

Rydelnik, Michael, and Edwin A. Blum, eds. *The Moody Handbook of Messianic Prophecy*, Chicago: Moody Publishers, forthcoming.

Sailhamer, John H. "The Canon of the Hebrew Bible: A Wisdom Redaction?" Paper presented to the Society of Biblical Literature, Washington, D.C., November, 1993.

———. "The Messiah and the Hebrew Bible." *Journal of the Evangelical Theological Society* 44 (2001) 1–22.

———. *Introduction to Old Testament Theology: A Canonical Approach*. Grand Rapids: Zondervan, 1995.

———. *The Meaning of the Pentateuch: Revelation, Composition and Interpretation*. Downers Grove: InterVarsity, 2009.

———. *The Pentateuch as Narrative: A Biblical-Theological Commentary*. Grand Rapids: Zondervan, 1992.

———. Appendix B: "Compositional Strategies in the Pentateuch." In *Introduction to Old Testament Theology: A Canonical Approach*, 272–89. Grand Rapids: Zondervan, 1999.

Sanders, E. P. *Paul, the Law, and the Jewish People*. Philadelphia: Fortress, 1983.

Sanday, Peggy Reeves. "Matriarchy." In *Oxford Encyclopedia of Women in World History*, edited by Bonnie G. Smith, 3:192–95. 4 vols. Oxford: Oxford University Press, 2008.

———. *Women at the Center: Life in a Modern Matriarchy*. Ithaca: Cornell University Press, 2002.

Sandnes, Karl Olav. *Paul—One of the Prophets?* Wissenschaftliche Untersuchungen zum Neuen Testament 2/43, Tübingen: Mohr Siebeck, 1991.

Sandy, Brent. *Plowshares & Pruning Hooks: Rethinking the Language of Biblical Prophecy and Apocalyptic*. Downers Grove: InterVarsity, 2002.

Sarna, Nahum. *Exodus*. Jewish Publication Society Torah Commentary. Philadelphia: Jewish Publication Society, 1991.

Sasson, Jack. "Circumcision in the Ancient Near East." *Journal of Biblical Literature* 85 (1966) 473–76.

Satterthwaite, Phillip. E., and David W. Baker. "Nations of Canaan." In *Dictionary of the Old Testament: Pentateuch*, edited by T. D. Alexander and D. W. Baker, 596–605. Downers Grove: InterVarsity, 2003.

Schaper, J. "The 'Publication' of Legal Texts in Ancient Judah." In *The Pentateuch as Torah: New Models for Understanding Its Promulgation and Acceptance*, edited by G. N. Knoppers and B. M. Levinson, 225–36. Winona Lake, IN: Eisenbrauns, 2007.

———. *Priester und Leviten im achämenidischen Juda: Studie zur Kult- und Sozialgeschichte Israels in persischer Zeit.* Forschungen zum Alten Testament 31. Tübingen: Mohr Siebeck, 2000.

Schipper, Bernd U. "When Wisdom is not Enough! The Discourse on Wisdom and Torah and the Composition of the Book of Proverbs." In *Wisdom and Torah: The Reception of "Torah" In the Wisdom Literature of the Second Temple Period*, edited by Bernd U. Schipper and D. Andrew Teeter, 55–79. Journal for the Study of Judaism Supplement Series 163. Leiden: Brill, 2013.

Schipper, Bernd U. and D. Andrew Teeter, eds. *Wisdom and Torah: The Reception of "Torah" In the Wisdom Literature of the Second Temple Period.* Journal for the study of Judaism Supplement Series 163. Leiden: Brill, 2013.

Schloen, J. David. *The House of the Father as Fact and Symbol: Patrimonialism in Ugarit and the Ancient Near East.* Winona Lake: Eisenbrauns, 2001.

Schmid, Hans H. *Der sogenannte Jahwist: Beobachtungen und Fragen zur Pentateuchforschung.* Zürich: Theologischer Verlag, 1976.

Schmitt, Clayton J. *Public Reading of Scripture: A Handbook.* Nashville: Abingdon, 2002.

Schnabel, Eckhard J. *Acts.* Zondervan Exegetical Commentary on the New Testament. Grand Rapids: Zondervan, 2012.

———. *Early Christian Mission: Paul and the Early Church.* Downers Grove, IL: InterVarsity, 2004.

Schreiner, Thomas R. "Circumcision." In *Dictionary of Paul and His Letters,* edited by G. F. Hawthorne, R. P. Martin, and D. G. Reid, 137–39. Downers Grove, IL: InterVarsity, 1993.

———. *Galatians.* Zondervan Exegetical Commentary on the New Testament. Grand Rapids: Zondervan, 2010.

———. "Good-bye and Hello: The Sabbath Command for New Covenant Believers." In *Progressive Covenantalism: Charting a Course between Dispensational and Covenant Theologies*, edited by S. J. Wellum, and B. W. Parker, 159–88. Nashville: Broadman & Holman, 2016.

Schüle, Andreas. "*Kāmokā*—der Nächste wie Du. Zur Philologie des Liebesgebotes von Lev 19,18.34." *Kleine Untersuchungen zur Sprache des Alten Testaments un seiner Umwelt* 2 (2001) 97–129.

Schultz, Richard "פלל." In *New International Dictionary of Old Testament Theology & Exegesis*, edited by Willem VanGemeren, 3:627–28. Grand Rapids: Zondervan, 1997.

———. "Unity or Diversity in Wisdom Theology? A Canonical and Covenantal Perspective." *Tyndale Bulletin* 48 (1997) 271–306.

Schunck, K.-D. "עֶבְרָה *'ebrâ*." In *Theological Dictionary of the Old Testament*, edited by G. J. Botterweck and H. Ringgren, and translated by J. T. Willis, G. W. Bromiley, and D. E. Green, 10:425–30. 15 vols. Grand Rapids: Eerdmans, 1999.

Seebass, H. "Garazim und Ebal als Symbole von Segen und Fluch." *Biblica* 63 (1982) 22–31.

Segal, Alan F. *Paul the Convert: The Apostolate and Apostasy of Saul the Pharisee.* New Haven: Yale University Press, 1990.

Seibert, Eric A. *Disturbing Divine Behavior: Troubling Old Testament Images of God.* Minneapolis: Fortress, 2009.

———. *The Violence of Scripture: Overcoming the Old Testament's Troubling Legacy.* Minneapolis: Fortress, 2012.

Seitz, Christopher. "Canon and Conquest: The Character of the God of the Hebrew Bible." In *Divine Evil?: The Moral Character of the God of Abraham*, edited by M. Bergmann, et al., 294–308. Oxford: Oxford University Press, 2013.

Seitz, Gottfried. *Redaktionsgeschichtliche Studien zum Deuteronomium.* Beihefte zur Wissenschaft vom Alten und Neuen Testament 93. Stuttgart: Kohlhammer, 1971.

Sheppard, Gerald T. *Wisdom as a Hermeneutical Construct: The Sapientializing of the Old Testament.* Beihefte zur Zeitschrift für die alttestamentliche Wissenschaft 151. Berlin: de Gruyter, 1980.

Sibley, James. "Deuteronomy 18:15–19." In *The Moody Handbook of Messianic Prophecy*, edited by Michael Rydelnik and Edwin A. Blum. Chicago: Moody Publishers, forthcoming.

Silva, Moises. "ἀποστέλλω (*apostellō*), to send . . . ," and "ἀπόστολος (*apostolos*), envoy, ambassador, apostle . . . ." In *New International Dictionary of New Testament Theology*, edited by M. M. Silva, 1:398–447. Grand Rapids: Zondervan, 2014.

Singer, Itamar. *Hittite Prayers.* Society of Biblical Literature Writings from the Ancient World 11. Atlanta: Society of Biblical Literature, 2002.

Slanski, Kathryn E. *The Babylonian Entitlement narûs (kudurrus): A Study in their Form and Function.* American Schools of Oriental Research Books 9. Boston: American Schools of Oriental Research, 2003.

Smith, Bonnie G., ed. *The Oxford Encyclopedia of Women in World History.* 4 vols. Philadelphia: Oxford University Press, 2010.

Smith, Gregory S. *The Testing of God's Sons: The Refining Faith as a Biblical Theme.* Nashville: Broadman and Holman, 2014.

Smith, Morton. "Jewish Religious Life in the Persian Period." In *The Cambridge History of Judaism.* Volume One, *Introduction; the Persian Period*, edited by W. D. Davies and Louis Finkelstein, 219–78. Cambridge: Cambridge University Press, 1984.

Snaith, N. H. *The Distinctive Ideas of the Old Testament.* London: Epworth, 1944.

Sohn, Seock-Tae. *The Divine Election of Israel.* Grand Rapids: Eerdmans, 1991.

———. "'I Will Be Your God and You Will Be My People': The Origin and Background of the Covenant Formula." In *Ancient Near Eastern, Biblical, and Judaic Studies in Honor of Baruch A. Levine*, edited by R. Chazan, W. W. Hallo, and L. H. Schiffman, 355–72. Winona Lake, IN: Eisenbrauns, 1999.

Sokoloff, Michael. *A Dictionary of Jewish Palestinian Aramaic.* 2nd ed. Baltimore, MD: Johns Hopkins University Press, 2002.

Sonnet, Jean-Pierre. *The Book within the Book: Writing in Deuteronomy.* Biblical Interpretation Series 14. Leiden: Brill, 1997.

Sparks, Kenton L. "The Egalitarian Spirit in Biblical Law." *Sapientia Logos* 1 (2008) 99–121.

———. *Ancient Texts for the Study of the Hebrew Bible: A Guide to the Background Literary.* Peabody, MA: Hendrickson, 2005.

Speiser, E. A. *Genesis: Introduction, Translation, and Notes.* Anchor Bible 1. Garden City, NY: Doubleday, 1964.

Spencer, John R. "Priestly Families (or Factions) in Samuel and Kings." In *The Pitcher is Broken: Memorial Essays for Gösta Ahlström*, edited by S. W. Holloway and L. K. Handy,

387–400. Journal for the Study of the Old Testament Supplement Series 190. Sheffield: Sheffield Press, 1995.

———. "The Levitical Cities: A Study of the Role and Function of the Levites in the History of Israel." PhD diss., University of Chicago, 1980.

Spiqc, C. "δοῦλος." In *Theological Lexicon of the New Testament*, translated by J. D, Ernest, 1:380–86. 3 vols. Peabody, MA: Hendrickson, 1994.

Stackert, Jeffrey. "The Elohist Source: The End of Israelite Prophecy." Chapter 3 in *A Prophet like Moses: Prophecy, Law, and Israelite Religion*, 70–125. Oxford: Oxford University Press, 2014.

———. "The Holiness Code." In *The Oxford Encyclopedia of the Bible and Law*, edited by Brent Strawn, 1:389–96. Oxford: Oxford University Press, 2015.

———. "The Holiness Legislation and Its Pentateuchal Sources." In *The Strata of the Priestly Writings: Contemporary Debate and Future Directions*, edited by S. Shectman and J. S. Baden, 187–204. Zürich: Theologischer Verlag, 2009.

———. "The Treaty of/and Deuteronomy Once Again." Paper presented to the Society of Biblical Literature, Chicago, 17 November 2012.

———. *Rewriting the Torah: Literary Revision in Deuteronomy & the Holiness Legislation*. Forschungen Zum Alten Testament 52. Tübingen, Germany: Mohr Siebeck, 2007.

Stähli, H.-P. "ירא yrʾ to fear." In *Theological Lexicon of the Old Testament*, edited by E. Jenni and C. Westermann, and translated by M. E. Biddle, 2:568–78. 3 vols. Peabody, MA: Hendrickson, 1997.

Stavrakopoulou, F. and J. Barton, eds. *Religious Diversity in Ancient Israel and Judah*. London: T&T Clark, 2010.

Stein, Robert H. *The Synoptic Problem: An Introduction*. Grand Rapids: Baker, 1987.

Stendahl, Krister. *Paul among Jews and Gentiles*. Philadelphia: Fortress, 1976.

Stern, P. D. *The Biblical Herem: A Window on Israel's Religious Experience*. Brown Judaic Studies 211. Atlanta: Scholars Press, 1991.

Stoebe, H. J. "חנן ḥnn to be gracious." In *Theological Lexicon of the Old Testament*, edited by E. Jenni and C. Westermann, and translated by M. E. Biddle, 1:439–47. 3 vols. Peabody, MA: Hendrickson, 1997.

Strathearn, Gaye. "4Q521 and What It Might Mean for Q 3–7." In *Bountiful Harvest: Essays in Honor of S. Kent Brown*, edited by Andrew C. Skinner, D. Morgan Davis, and Carl Griffin, 395–424. Provo, UT: Brigham Young University, 2012.

Strugnell, John. "Notes en marge du volume V des 'Discoveries in the Judaean Desert of Jordan.'" *Revue de Qumran* 7 (1970) 163–276.

Surls, Austin. *Making Sense of the Divine Name in Exodus: From Etymology to Literary Onomastics*. Bulletin for Biblical Research Supplements 17. Winona Lake, IN: Eisenbrauns, 2017.

Swanson, Dwight D. "'A Covenant Just Like Jacob's': The Covenant of 11QE 29 and Jeremiah's New Covenant." In *New Qumran Texts and Studies: Proceedings of the First Meeting of the International Organization for Qumran Studies, Paris 1992*, edited by George J. Brooke, 273–86. Leiden: Brill, 1994.

Taggar-Cohen, Ada. "Covenant Priesthood: Cross-cultural Legal and Religious Aspects of Biblical and Hittite Priesthood." In *Levites and Priests in Biblical History and Tradition*, edited by M. Leuchter and J. M. Hutton, 11–24. Ancient Israel and Its Literature 9. Atlanta: Scholars Press, 2011.

Talmon, Shemaryahu. "The Community of the Renewed Covenant: Between Judaism and Christianity." In *The Community of the Renewed Covenant: The Notre Dame Symposium on the Dead Sea Scrolls*, edited by E. Ulrich and J. VanderKam, 3–24. Christianity and Judaism in Antiquity Series 10. Notre Dame, IN: Notre Dame Press, 1994.

Targum Palaestinense in Pentateuchum, vol. 5, *Deuteronomium*, 94–5. Biblia Polyglotta Matritensia IV; Madrid: 1980.

Tawil, Hayim Ben Yosef. *An Akkadian Lexical Companion for Biblical Hebrew: Etymological-Semantic and Idiomatic Equivalents with Supplement on Biblical Aramaic*. Jersey City, NJ: KTAV, 2009.

Taylor, William M. *Moses: The Law-Giver*. Bible Biographies Series. Grand Rapids: Baker, 1961.

Thiessen, Matthew. *Contesting Conversion: Genealogy, Circumcision, and Identity in Ancient Judaism and Christianity*. Oxford: Oxford University Press, 2011.

———. "The Form and Function of the Song of Moses (Deuteronomy 32:1–43)." *Journal of Biblical Literature* 123 (2004) 407–24.

Thompson, John A. *Deuteronomy: An Introduction and Commentary*. Tyndale Old Testament Commentaries. Downers Gove: InterVarsity, 1974.

Tierney, Helen, ed. *Women's Studies Encyclopedia*. 2nd edition. 3 vols. Westport, CT: Greenwood, 1999.

Tigay, Jeffrey H. *Deuteronomy*. Jewish Publication Society Torah Commentary. Philadelphia: Jewish Publication Society, 1990.

———. "Parashat Terumah." In *Learn Torah With . . .* , edited by S. Kelman and J. L. Grishaver, 141–47. Los Angeles: Alef Design Group, 1996.

Tooman, William A. "Wisdom and Torah at Qumran: Evidence from the Sapiential Texts." In *Wisdom and Torah: The Reception of "Torah" In the Wisdom Literature of the Second Temple Period*, edited by Bernd U. Schipper and D. Andrew Teeter, 203–32. to the Journal for the Study of Judaism Supplement Series 163. Leiden: Brill, 2013.

Tov, Emanuel. *Textual Criticism of the Hebrew Bible*. 3rd ed. Minneapolis: Fortress, 2012.

Trible, Phyllis. *Texts of Terror: Literary Feminist Readings of Biblical Narratives*, Overtures to Biblical Theology. Philadelphia: Fortress, 1984.

Tromp, Johannes. *The Assumption of Moses: A Critical Edition with Commentary*. Leiden: Brill, 1992.

Tzaferis, Vassilios. "Inscribed 'To God Jesus Christ': Early Christian Prayer Hall Found in Megiddo Prison." *Biblical Archaeology Review* 33/2 (Mar/Apr 2007) 38–49.

van der Merwe, Christo H. J., Jackie A. Naudé, and Jan H. Kroeze. *A Biblical Hebrew Reference Grammar*. Biblical Languages: Hebrew 3. Sheffield: Sheffield Academic, 2004.

van der Toorn, Karel. *Family Religion in Babylonia, Syria and Israel: Continuity and Change in the Forms of Religious Life*. Studies in the History and Culture of the Ancient Near East 7. Leiden: Brill, 1996.

———. *Scribal Culture and the Making of the Hebrew Bible*. Cambridge, MS: Harvard University Press, 2007.

Van Pelt, Miles. V. and Walter C. Kaiser, Jr., "ירא." In *New International Dictionary of Old Testament Theology & Exegesis*, edited by Willem VanGemeren, 2:527–33. Grand Rapids: Zondervan, 1997.

van Wolde, Ellen. "Cognitive Linguistics and the Hebrew Bible: Illustrated with a Study of Job 28 and Job 38." In *The Professorship of Semitic Languages at Uppsala University 400 years, Jubilee Volume from a Symposium held at the University Hall, 21-23 September

2005, edited by B. Isaksson, M. Eskhult, and G. Ramsay, 247–77. Acta Universitatis Upsaliensis: Studia Semitica Upsaliensis 24. Uppsala: Uppsala University, 2007.

———. "Does ʿinnâ Denote Rape? A Semantic Analysis of a Controversial Word." *Vetus Testamentum* 52 (2002) 528–44.

———. *Reframing Biblical Studies: When Language and Text Meet Culture, Cognition, and Context*. Winona Lake, IN: Eisenbrauns, 2009.

Vang, Carsten. "When a Prophet Quotes Moses: On the Relationship between the Book of Hosea and Deuteronomy." *Sepher Torath Mosheh: Studies in the Composition and Interpretation of Deuteronomy*, edited by Daniel I. Block and Richard L. Schultz, 277–303. Peabody, MA: Hendrickson, 2017.

Vanhoozer, Kevin J. *Is There a Meaning in This Text?: The Bible, the Reader, and the Morality of Literary Knowledge*. Grand Rapids: Zondervan, 1998.

de Vaux, Roland. *Ancient Israel*, vol. 2, *Religious Institutions*. New York: McGraw-Hill, 1965.

Verhoef, P. A. "Prayer." In *New International Dictionary of Old Testament Theology & Exegesis*, edited by Willem VanGemeren, 4:1060–61. Grand Rapids: Zondervan, 1997.

Vetter, D. "ראה *rʾh* to see." In *Theological Lexicon of the Old Testament*, edited by E. Jenni, with assistance from C. Westermann. Translated by M. E. Biddle, 3:1179–80. Peabody, MA; Hendrickson, 1997.

Vogt, Peter T. "'These Are the Words Moses Spoke': Implied Audience and a Case for Pre-Monarchic Dating of Deuteronomy." In *For Our Good Always: Studies on the Message and Influence of Deuteronomy in Honor of Daniel I. Block*, edited by Jason S. DeRouchie, Jason Gile, and Kenneth J. Turner, 61–80. Winona Lake, IN: Eisenbrauns, 2013.

———. *Deuteronomic Theology and the Significance of Torah: A Reappraisal*. Winona Lake, IN: Eisenbrauns, 2006.

von Waldow, H. Eberhard. "The Concept of War in the Old Testament." *Horizons in Biblical Theology* 6 no. 2 (1984) 27–48.

Waltke, Bruce K. "The Fear of the Lord: The Foundation for a Relationship with God." In *Alive to God: Studies in Spirituality* presented to James Houston, edited by J. I. Packer and Loren Wilkinson, 17–33. Downers Grove: InterVarsity, 1992.

———. *The Book of Proverbs Chapters 15–31*. New International Commentary on the Old Testament. Grand Rapids: Eerdmans, 2005.

Waltke, Bruce K., and M. O'Connor. *An Introduction to Biblical Hebrew Syntax*. Winona Lake, IN: Eisenbrauns, 1990.

Waltke, Bruce K. with Charles Yu. *An Old Testament Theology*. Grand Rapids: Zondervan, 2007.

Walton, John H. *Ancient Near Eastern Thought and the Old Testament: Introducing the Conceptual World of the Hebrew Bible*. Grand Rapids: Baker, 2006.

Wanke, Günther. "φόβος and φοβέομαι in the Old Testament." In *Theological Dictionary of the New Testament*, edited by G. Kittel, and translated by G. W. Bromiley, 9:197–205. Grand Rapids: Eerdmans, 1971.

Weeks, Stuart. "Fear God and Keep His Commandments": Could Qohelet Have Said That? In *Wisdom and Torah: The Reception of "Torah" In the Wisdom Literature of the Second Temple Period*, edited by Bernd U. Schipper and D. Andrew Teeter, 101–18. Journal for the Study of Judaism Supplement Series 163. Leiden: Brill, 2013.

Weinfeld, Moshe. "The Covenant of Grant." *Journal of the American Oriental Society* 90 (1970) 184–83.

———. "The Decalogue: Its Significance, Uniqueness, and Place in Israel's Tradition." In *Religion and Law: Biblical-Judaic and Islamic Perspectives*, edited by E. B. Firmage, B. G. Weiss, and J. W. Welch, 3–48. Winona Lake, IN: Eisenbrauns, 1990.

———. "The Origin of Apodictic Law." *Vetus Testamentum* 23 (1973) 63–75.

———. "The Pattern of the Israelite Settlement in Canaan." In *Congress Volume Jerusalem 1986*, edited by J. A. Emerton, 270–83. Supplements to Vetus Testamentum 40. Leiden: Brill, 1988.

———. *Deuteronomy 1–11: A New Translation with Introduction and Commentary*. Anchor Bible 5. New York: Doubleday, 1991.

———. *Deuteronomy and the Deuteronomic School*. Winona Lake, IN: Eisenbrauns, 1992.

Weiser, A. "δουλεύω." In *Exegetical Dictionary of the New Testament*, edited by H. Balz and G. Schneider, 1:349–50. Grand Rapids: Eerdmans, 1990.

Wellhausen, Julius. *Die Komposition des Hexateuchs und der historischen Bücher des Alten Testaments*. 3rd ed. Berlin: G. Reimer, 1899.

———. *Prolegomena to the History of Ancient Israel*. Translated by Allan Menzies and J. Sutherland Black. New York: Meridian Books, 1957.

Wells, Bruce. "The Covenant Code and Near Eastern Legal Traditions: A Response to David Wright." *Maarav* 13, no. 1 (2006) 85–118.

Wenham, Gordon J. "Deuteronomy and the Central Sanctuary." *Tyndale Bulletin* 22 (1971) 103–18.

———. *Genesis 1–15*. Word Biblical Commentary 1. Waco, TX: Word, 1987.

———. *Genesis 16–50*. Word Biblical Commentary 2. Waco, TX: Word, 1987.

Westbrook, Raymond. "Prohibition on Restoration of Marriage in Deuteronomy 24:1–4." In *Studies in Bible 1986*, edited by Sara Japhet, 387–405. Scripta Hierosolymitana 31. Jerusalem: Magnes, 1986.

Westermann, Claus. *Genesis 12–36: A Commentary*. Translated by John J. Scullion S.J. Minneapolis: Augsburg, 1985.

Whybray, R. N. *The Making of the Pentateuch: A Methodological Study*. Journal for the Study of the Old Testament Supplement Series 53. Sheffield: Journal for the Study of the Old Testament, 1994.

Williams, Stephen N. "Could God Have Commanded the Slaughter of the Canaanites?" *Tyndale Bulletin* 63 (2012) 161–78.

———. "Holy War and the New Atheism." In *Holy War in the Bible: Christian Morality and the Old Testament Problem*, edited by H. A. Thomas, et al., 312–31. Downers Grove, IL: InterVarsity, 2013.

Williamson, Paul R. "Covenant." In *Dictionary of the Old Testament: Pentateuch*, edited by T. D. Alexander and D. W. Baker, 142–43. Downers Grove: InterVarsity, 2003.

———. *Sealed with an Oath: Covenant in God's Unfolding Purpose*. New Studies in Biblical Theology 23. Downers Grove: InterVarsity, 2007.

Willis, T. M. "'Eat and Rejoice Before YHWH': The Optimism of Worship in the Deuteronomic Code." In *Worship and the Hebrew Bible: Essays in Honour of John T. Willis*, edited by Rick R. Marrs, 276–94. Journal for the Study of the Old Testament Supplement Series 284. Sheffield: Journal for the Study of the Old Testament Press, 1999).

———. *The Elders of the City: A Study of the Elders-Laws in Deuteronomy*. Society of Biblical Literature Monograph Series 55. Atlanta: Society of Biblical Literature, 2001.

Wilson, Gerald H. *Psalms*. vol. 1. NIV Application Commentary. Grand Rapids: Zondervan, 2002.

Wilson, Ian. "Central Sanctuary or Local Settlements? The Location of the Triennial Tithe Declaration (Dtn 26,13–15)." *Zeitschrift für die alttestamentliche Wissenschaft* 120/3 (2008) 323–40.

———. *Out of the Midst of the Fire: Divine Presence in Deuteronomy*. Society of Biblical Literature Dissertation Series 151. Atlanta: Scholars Press, 1995.

Winter, Irene J. "Trees on the Mountain: Landscape and Territory on the Victory Stela of Naram Sin of Agade." In *Landscapes: Territories, Frontiers and Horizons in the Ancient Near East: Papers Presented to the XLIV Rencontre Assyriologique Internationale, Venezia, 7–11 July 1997 Part I*, edited by L. Milano et al., 63–72. Rencontre Assyriologique Internationale 44. Padova: Sargon, 1999.

Wirzba, Norman. *Living the Sabbath: Discovering the Rhythms of Rest and Delight*. Grand Rapids: Brazos, 2006.

Wise, Michael, Martin Abegg Jr., and Edward Cook. *The Dead Sea Scrolls: A New Translation*. San Francisco: HarperCollins, 2005.

Wiseman, Donald J. "Abraham in History and Tradition, Part 1: Abraham the Hebrew." *Bibliotheca Sacra* 134 (1977) 126.

———. "Abraham Reassessed." In *Essays on the Patriarchal Narratives*, edited by A. R. Millard and D. J. Wiseman, 141–60. Leicester: InterVarsity, 1980.

Witherington, Ben III. *The Acts of the Apostles: A Socio-Rhetorical Commentary*. Grand Rapids: Eerdmans, 1998.

Wolterstorff, Nicholas. "Comments on 'What about the Canaanites?'" In *Divine Evil?: The Moral Character of the God of Abraham*, edited by M. Bergmann, et al., 283–88. Oxford: Oxford University Press, 2013.

Wright, C. J. H. *Knowing Jesus through the Old Testament*. Downers Grove: InterVarsity, 1995.

———. *Deuteronomy*. New International Biblical Commentary. Peabody, MA: Hendrickson, 1996.

———. *The God I Don't Understand: Reflections on Tough Questions of Faith*. Grand Rapids: Zondervan, 2008.

———. *God's People in God's Land*. Grand Rapids: Eerdmans, 1990.

Wright, David P. *Inventing God's Law: How the Covenant Code of the Bible Used and Revised the Laws of Hammurabi*. Oxford: Oxford University Press, 2009.

Wright, G. Ernest. "The Levites in Deuteronomy." *Vetus Testamentum* 4 (1954) 325–30.

Wright, N. T. "The Letter to the Galatians: Exegesis and Theology." In *Between Two Horizons: Spanning New Testament Studies and Systematic Theology*, edited by Joel B. Green and Max Turner, 205–36. Grand Rapids: Eerdmans, 2000. Reprinted in N. T. Wright, *Pauline Perspectives: Essays on Paul, 1978–2013*, 191–215. Minneapolis: Fortress, 2013.

———. *The New Testament and the People of God: Christian Origins and the Questions of God*. Minneapolis: Fortress, 1992.

———. "Paul, Arabia, and Elijah (Galatians 1:17)." *Journal of Biblical Literature* 115 (1996) 683–92.

Wyatt, Nicholas. "A Royal Garden: The Ideology of Eden." *Scandinavian Journal of the Old Testament* 28 (2014) 19–22.

Young, Edward J. *An Introduction to the Old Testament*. Revised edition. Grand Rapids: Eerdmans, 1989.

Younger, K. Lawson. "Some Recent Discussion on the ḥērem." In *Far from Minimal: Celebrating the Work and Influence of Philip R. Davies*, edited by D. Burns and J. W. Rogerson, 505–22. London: T&T Clark, 2012.

Zehnder, Markus. "Building on Stone? Deuteronomy and Esarhaddon's Loyalty Oaths (Part 1) Some Preliminary Observations." *Bulletin for Biblical Research* 19, no. 3 (2009a) 348–351.

———. "Building on Stone? Deuteronomy and Esarhaddon's Loyalty Oaths (Part 2) Some Additional Observations." *Bulletin for Biblical Research* 19, no. 4 (2009b) 511–530.

Zertal, Adam. "An Early Iron Age Cultic Site on Mount Ebal: Excavation Seasons 1982–1987." *Tel Aviv* 13–14 (1986–1987) 105–65.

———. "Ebal, Mount." In *Anchor Bible Dictionary*, edited by D. N. Freedman, 2:255–58. Garden City: Doubleday, 1992.

———. "Has Joshua's Altar Been Found on Mount Ebal?" *Biblical Archaeology Review* 11 (1985) 26–44.

Zetterholm, Magnus. *Approaches to Paul: A Student's Guide to Recent Scholarship*. Minneapolis: Fortress, 2009.

Zevit, Ziony. *The Religions of Ancient Israel: A Synthesis of Parallactic Approaches*. London: Continuum, 2001.

Index of Modern Authors

Abegg, Martin, 302n71
Ackerman, Susan, 191n63, 195, 195n75
Aejmelaeus, A., 327n61
Aernie, Jeffrey W., 376n9, 377n12, 377n14
Aharoni, Miriam, 193n69
Akin, Daniel L., 350n8, 360n38, 371
Akiva, Navot, 107n21
Albertz, Rainer, 186n42
Albright, W. F., 180n11, 186n43
Alexander, T. D., 67n23
Allegro, John M., 301n71
Allen, David L., 84n54
Allender, Dan B., 199n3
Allis Oswald T., 105n3,
Allison, Dale C. Jr., 349n3
Alt, Albrecht, 92
Ambrose, Kirk, 403n136
Andersen, Francis I., 296n49, 306n99, 393n101
Anderson, Cheryl B., 232n29
Anderson, Gary A., 166n56, 265n5, 268n14
Ansberry, Christopher B., 1n1, 306n95
Arand, Charles P., 209n43, 209n44
Archer, Gleason, 105n3
Arnold, Bill T., 286n15, 294n43, 295, 368n59
Arzi, Abraham, 244n21
Assmann, Jan, 168n64
Aufrecht, W. E., 380n35
Auld, A. Graeme, 177n4
Ausloos, Hans, 106n6
Avalos, Hector, 275, 275n41
Averbeck, Richard E., 166n56
Avi-Yonah, M., 161n37

Baab, Lynne M., 199n3
Baden, Joel S., 106n8, 107n18
Baker, David W., 268n12
Balentine, Samuel E., 245n22, 246n28
Bammel, Ernst, 377n14

Barclay, John M., G. 81n50, 375n3, 384n55, 385n65, 390n89, 399n126
Barker, Paul A., xivn1, 156n25, 163n45
Barrett, Rob, 269n16
Barrick, William D., 76n41
Barstad, Hans M., 364n48
Bartlett, John R., 255n57, 379n32, 380n35
Barton, John, 62n9, 186n42, 351n13
Bates, Matthew W., 295n45
Bauckham, Richard, 209n43, 350n6, 355n27
Beale, G. K., 82n52
Becker, Joachim, 283n5, 284n7, 287n18, 304n86, 308n100
Beckman, Gary, 154n9
Beckwith, Roger T., 78n45
Begg, C., 154n10
Ben Zvi, Ehud, 186n43
Benz, F. L., 380n35
Berman, Joshua, 9n26, 42n16, 57, 57n76, 95n29, 107n19, 338n8, 361n43
Biddle, Mark E., 155n17
Bird, Warren, 33n48
Blenkinsopp, Joseph, 72n35, 106, 106n9
Block, Daniel I., xviin3, 2n6, 6n13, 10n30, 11n32, 19n2, 21n12, 23n20, 33n50, 37n4, 39n7, 41n10, 43n17, 43n18, 53n65, 53n67, 58n78, 59n80, 60n3, 64n18, 72n33, 76n42, 79n47, 84n56, 85n57, 88n59, 88n60, 100n45, 105n5, 110n40, 117n87, 121n111, 124n124, 126n2, 131n16, 138n50, 140n58, 146n66, 149n78, 169n69, 172n77, 178n8, 180n13, 183n24, 184n35, 189n57, 191n64, 192n66, 204n19, 204n20, 209n41, 210n46, 210n47, 212n50, 214n53, 221n73, 225n3, 227n12, 229n20, 231n28, 233n31, 240n4, 241n5, 242n8, 242n14, 256n63, 262n78, 263n79, 263n80, 266n7, 271n23, 273n28, 274n33, 274n35, 291n34, 292n35,

Block, Daniel I. (*continued*), 292n36, 293n39, 294n40, 295n45, 296n48, 312n3, 313n4, 317n22, 319n31, 330n67, 331n73, 331n75, 333n80, 335n3, 337n4, 341n17, 346n29, 346n30, 249n2, 355n26, 363n44, 364n51, 370n66, 374n1, 377n13, 380n36, 389n87, 390n90, 390n92
Blomberg, Craig L., 199n5, 211, 211n48, 216n65
Blum, Erhard, 72n35, 106n9, 107n18, 118n95, 123n122
Bock, Darrell L., 356n28
Boda, Mark J., 250n37
Bohmbach, Karla G., 227n13
Boling, Robert G., 195n74
Bonhéme, Marie-Ange, 55n73
Bottéro, Jean, 270n19
Bowman, John, 353n19
Braulik, G., 130n13, 140n58, 168n63, 302, 302n75, 311n112
Brekelmans, Chris H. W., 105n6, 106n6
Brenneman, J. E., 242n11
Brockelmann, Carl, 139n52
Bruce, F. F., 356n28
Brueggemann, Walter, 245n22, 322n40
Bühner, J. A., 378n18
Burton, Keith, 199n2

Carr, David M., 72n35, 163n43, 187n46 187n47
Carson, D. A., 199n5
Cassian, John, 33, 34n51
Chiesa, B., 366n56
Childs, Brevard S., 353n20, 353n23
Clements, Ronald E., 245n22, 311n111
Clines, David J. A., 225, 232n30
Cody, Aelred, 178n7
Cogan, Mordechai, 255n57, 379n32
Cole, Robert L., 341n16
Colenso John W., 106n9, 108n23
Collins, John J., 275n39, 352n17
Conrad, J., 251n41
Cook, E., 302n71
Cook, Edward, 302n71
Cook, Stephen L., 187n49
Cooke, G. A., 166n56
Craigie, Peter C., 132n20, 319n32
Creach, Jerome, F. D., 275n43
Cribb, Bryan, 313n8
Crüsemann, Frank, 90n3

Dandamaev, Muhammad A., 291n34
Davidson, Richard M., 60n4
Davies, John A., 61n5, 63n12, 69, 69n28, 70n31
Davis, Ellen F., 31n44
Dawn, Marva J., 199n3

Day, John, 64n19
de Boer, Martinus C., 378n18, 383n51
de Vaux, Roland, 166n56, 186n42
Del Monte, G. F., 277n55
Demsky, Aaron, 207n36
DeRouchie, Jason S., 209n41, 232n28, 341n17, 370n66, 388n80
Dershowitz, Idan, 107n21
Dershowitz, Nachum, 107n21
Dion, Paul E., 94n24
Dirven, René, 285n11
Dobbs-Alsopp, F. W., 241n5, 380n34
Donato, Christopher John, 199n5
Dooley, Robert A., 360n39
Dorsey, David A., 175n83
Douglas, Mary, 165n53
Dressler, Harold P., 199n5
Driver, S. R., 108n23, 284n31, 349n4
Duke, Rodney, 178n8
Dumbrell, W. J., 63n16, 69, 69n29
Dunn, James D. G., 217n66, 375, 375n4, 376n5, 401n134

Earl, Douglas S., 275, 276n51, 277n52, 280n64
Eastman, Susan Grove, 81n50, 377n12, 399n126
Ebeling, Jennie, 93n20
Egger-Wenzel, Renate, 301, 301n68
Eirikh, Anna, 192n65
Eisenbaum, Pamela, 377n16
Eissfeldt, O., 155n17
Elliott, Mark W., 375n4
Evans, Craig A., 377n12

Fales, Evan, 278n57, 282n65
Faust, Avraham, 389n86
Ferguson, Kathy E., 226n7
Fishbane, Michael, 313n5
Fisher, Aaron, 200n6
Fisher, David H., 180n11
Fitzmyer, Joseph A. S.J., 356n28
Fleming, Daniel E., 364 5n54
Fletcher, Adrian, 404n136
Fokkelman, J. P., 329n65
Follingstad, Carl Martin, 329n66, 363n47
Fossum, J., 340n14
Foster, Benjamin R., 240n3
Fowler, Jeaneane D., 380n34
Franke, John R., 275n45
Freedman, D. N., 254n52
Fretz, Mark, 280n63
Fridrichsen, Anton, 401n132
Friedman, Richard E., 257n65
Frisch, A., 323n46
Fuhs, F., 285n10

Garfinkel, Yosef, 192n65
Garret, Duane, 123n123
Geeraerts, Dirk, 285n11, 286, 286n14
Gentry, Peter J., 62n10, 63n16, 63n17, 63n18, 67n23
Gibson, John C. L., 255n57, 379n32
Goff, Matthew J., 301n71
Gordon, R. P., 242n10
Grant, Jamie, 20n6, 47n35
Grant, Peter, 285n13
Graves, Michael, 26n29
Gray, G. B., 166n56
Gray, Rebecca, 351n31
Greenberg, Moshe, 245n22, 275n38
Grisanti, Michael A., 105n4
Gröndahl, F., 380n35
Groningen, Gerard van, 351n10
Groß, Walter, 69n30
Groves, J. A., 137n42
Gruber, Mayer I., 247n30
Guest, Steven Ward, 39n7
Gunneweg, A. J. H., 178n7

Hackett, JoAnn, 170n74
Haenchen, Ernst, 356n28
Hafemann, Scott J., 377n14, 381n42
Haller, Eduard, 364n48
Halpern, Baruch, 360n41
Haran, Menahem, 186n43, 193, 193n72
Hardin, Justin, 401n133
Harnack, Adolf von, 275n40
Hauer, Chris Jr., 186n43
Hawkins, Ralph K., 165n53, 166n56, 188n52
Hays, Richard B., 31n44, 381n43
Hengel, Martin, 385n59
Herr, Larry G., 162n42
Heschel, Abraham Joshua, 199n4, 205
Hess, Richard, 123n120, 173n79, 186n42, 388n80
Hill, Andrew E., 11n47, 156
Hoffmeier, James K., 256n63, 267n9
Hoftijzer, Jacob, 170n74
Holladay, C. R., 350n5
Holladay, W. L., 323n45
Houtman, C., 246n27
Howard, David M., 388n80
Hubbard, Robert L., 388n80
Huehnergard, J., 365n54, 378n19
Hugenberger, Gordon, 237n42
Hundley, Michael, 129, 170n73
Hurowitz, Victor, 138n48
Hurst, L. D., 352n15
Hurtado, Larry W., 372n74
Hutton, Jeremy M., 177n5
Hvalvik, Reidar, 403n135

Hwang, Jerry, 16n47, 73, 111n46, 130n13, 160n31, 300n61, 313n7, 323n43, 397n115

Imes, Carmen Joy, 219n67, 291n34, 292n35
Ishida, Tomoo, 113n64

Jackson, Bernard S., 184n34, 186n40
Japhet, Sara, 177n4, 182n21, 191n63
Jastrow, Marcus, 167n62
Jeremias, Joachim, 356n28
Jones, David W., 225n4
Jones, Jennifer B., 359n37, 363n45, 363n47
Josberger, Rebekah Lee, 231n26

Kaiser, Walter C. Jr., 285n10
Kaminsky, Joel S., 277n52
Kaufmann, Yehezekel, 186n43, 188
Keil, C. F., 246n28
Keneally, Thomas, 2n5
Khalaily, Hamoudi, 192n65
Kibbe, Michael, 126n1, 134n27, 135n30, 135n31, 151n79, 243n12, 351n11
Kilchör, Benjamin, 113n64, 122, 300n65, 398n119
Kim, Brittany, 149n78,
Kim, Yoon-Hee, 349n3, 350n8, 366n56, 368n60
King, L. W., 163n44
Kisilevitz, Shua, 192n65
Kistemaker, Simon J., 356n28
Kitchen, Kenneth A., 57n76, 90n5, 92n11, 93n16, 94n28, 154n12, 165n53
Klausern, Theodor, 403n135
Klingbeil, Gerald, 318n24, 318n26
Knoppers, Gary N., 63n12, 177n4, 177n5, 341n18
Kooij, G. van der, 170n74
Koppel, Moshe, 107n21
Köstenberger, Andreas J., 225n4
Kroeze, Jan H., 160n29
Kruger, Thomas, 302n76

Labuschagne, C. J., 132n20, 364n48
Lambert, Wilfred G., 340n12
Lasine, Stuart, 265n6
Lauinger, Jacob, 94n25
Lawrence, Paul J. N., 90n5, 92n11, 93n16, 94n28, 154n12
Layton, S. C., 380n35
Lee, Won W., 260n71
LeFebvre, Michael, 95n35
Lehne, Susanne, 79n46, 82n51, 82n52
Leibert, Julius, 2n5
Leprohon, Ronald L., 55n73

Lerner, Gerda, 236n40, 237n41
Leuchter, Mark, 182, 182n20, 182n21, 182n22, 185n37
Levenson, Jon D., 56n74, 110n31, 121n109, 122n115, 212n51, 294n43, 299n58
Levin, Christoph, 107n16
Levine, Baruch, 166n56
Levine, Lee I., 196n82
Levinsohn, Stephen H., 360n39
Levinson, Bernard M., 95n32, 95n35, 96n37, 99n44, 101n50, 188n51, 189n58
Levy, D., 185n39
Lewis, Theodore J., 61n5
Lieberman, Joe, 199n4
Lierman, John, 379n27
Lim, Johnson Teng Kok, 260n71
Lincicum, David, 388n77, 389n85, 400n130, 403n135
Lincoln, Andrew T., 210n47
Lohfink, Norbert, 95n32, 106n6, 130n13, 136n36, 168n63, 275n43
Longenecker, Richard N., 376n5
Longman, Tremper, III, 305n91
Lundbom, J., 254n52, 363n46,
Lundbom, Jack R., 254n52, 363n46

MacDonald, Nathan, 274n33, 275n46
Maimonides, 45, 387n76, 390n91
Malamat, Abraham, 212n51, 294, 294n43, 400n127
Margaret E. Köstenberger, 225n4
Marshall, I. Howard, 356n28
Martin, Ralph P., 27n33
Martínez, Florentino Garcia, 301n71, 350n6, 352n14, 352n16, 353n18
Martyn, J. Louis, 383n51, 383n52
Mason, Steven, 385n64
Matlock, Michael D., 245n22
Mayes, A. D. H., 106n9, 155n15, 185n36, 322n39, 365n55
Mazar, Amihai, 161n37
Mazar, Benjamin, 180n11, 182n21, 186n43
McBride, S. Dean, 101n49, 139n52, 186n42, 360n41
McCarthy, C., 43n18, 139n52, 244n21
McCarty, Skip, 216n65, 217n65
McComiskey, Thomas E., 32n48, 62n11
McConville, J. G., 102n52, 138n45, 138n49, 154n13, 178n8, 183n27, 191, 193n72, 235n36, 273n31, 302n72, 302n77, 327n61, 349n4
McKane, William M., 304n89
McLean, Max, 33n48
Meeks, Wayne A., 350n5, 353n19

Melville, Herman, 19n3
Mendenhall, George, 98n42
Merendino, R. P., 155n18
Merrill, Eugene H., 105n3, 132n20, 135n31, 254n52, 277n56, 322n39
Meyers, Carol L., 227n13, 230n22
Milgrom, Jacob, 68n26, 124n128, 166n56, 178n8, 181, 181n16, 181n19, 182n21, 185n39, 188, 188n53, 189, 189n58, 189n59, 197
Millar, J. Gary, 138n45, 245n22, 314n10
Miller, Patrick D., 46n30, 186n42, 187n45, 245n22, 250n36, 252n46, 252n48, 255n61, 260n72
Miller, Pavla, 226n7
Moberly, R. W. L., 17n53, 246n28, 274n36, 275n46, 296, 296n50, 394, 394n102, 399n122
Moffatt, Marian, 403n136
Monroe, Lauren, 277, 277n54
Moo, Douglas J., 385n59
Moore, Russell D., 225n5
Morschauser, Scott, 95n30
Mulder, M. J., 61n5
Murdock, D. M., 2n5
Murphy, Roland K., 304n89, 305n91
Murphy-O'Connor, Jerome, 385n59

Naʿaman, N., 155n18, 156n18
Najman, Hindy, 967n39
Naudé, J., Jackie A., 160n29
Nelson, Richard D., 101n49, 155n15, 178n7, 183n26, 187n45, 235n36, 360n41, 365n55
Neusner, Jacob, 51n57, 376n7
Nicholson, Ernest, 93n18
Nicklas, Tobias, 377n12
Nielsen, E., 153n4, 155n18
Noth, Martin, 89, 89n2, 124, 124n126
Novenson, Matthew V., 353n19, 385n64

O'Brien, Mark A., O.P., 106n9
O'Donovan, Oliver, 30, 30n43
O'Dowd, Ryan, 283n3, 284n6, 305n94, 310n108
Old, Hughes Oliphant, 32n45, 277n33
Olyan, Saul M., 165n53
Oswalt, John N., 353, 353n22
Otto, Eckart, 90, 94n24, 95n32, 95n35
Otto, Rudolph, 287n18
Overholt, Thomas W., 364n48
Pajunen, Mika S., 301n71

Pakkala, Juha, 41, 41n13, 98n40, 125n130, 137n44
Pardee, Dennis, 255n58, 379n33

INDEX OF MODERN AUTHORS

Parker, Simon B., 340n12
Parpola, Simo, 340n13
Parsons, John J., 371n68
Patai, Raphael, 229n15, 229n18
Pearce, Laurie E., 241n5,
Pedersen, Johannes, 230, 230n23
Perlitt, Lothar, 128n9, 365n55
Pervo, Richard I., 356n28
Peter C. Craigie, 132n20, 319n32
Peterson, John L., 178n9, 180n11, 195, 195n74
Pettegrew, Larry D., 79n48
Pfeiffer, Robert H., 291n30
Plath, Siegfried, 283n5, 292n37, 304n86, 307n98
Polhill, John B., 358n33
Pressler, Carolyn, 235n37, 237n42
Puech, Émile, 353n19

Rabin, Chaim, 107n15
Rad, Gerhard von, 93n12, 03n17, 314n11
Radday, Yehuda T., 107, 107n14, 107n19, 122n116
Redford, Donald B., 337n5
Rehm, M. D., 183n27
Rendsburg, Gary, 109n26, 109n27, 109n28
Rendtorff, Rolf, 106, 106n10, 166n56
Rengstorf, K. H., 378n18, 378n21, 379n29
Rich, Tracey R., 199n4
Richter, Sandra L., 139n52, 140n56, 169, 169n67, 169n70, 189n55
Ridderbos, J., 132n20
Ringgren, H., 186n42, 255n55
Roberts, J. J. M., 241n5
Robertson, O. Palmer, 62n11
Rodd, Cyril S., 271n25
Römer, Thomas, 268n13, 275, 275n44
Rose, Martin, 94, 95n31
Rosemary Grant, 285n13
Roth, Martha T., 236n39, 340n12, 90n5
Rowland, C., 203n18
Rütersworden, Uwe, 360n41
Rydelnik, Michael, 317n22, 335n1, 349n3, 350n8, 368n60, 368n61, 369n63

Sailhamer, John H., 47n31, 121, 121n110, 135n31, 312n2, 317n19, 350, 350n7, 350n8, 368, 368n60, 368n61, 374n2
Sanday, Peggy Reeves, 226n11
Sanders, E. P., 81n50, 375, 399n126
Sandnes, Karl Olav, 377n12, 379n27, 382n45, 386n68
Sandy, Brent, 9, 10n29
Sarna, Nahum, 17n52, 301n67, 398n121
Sasson, Jack, 388n80
Satterthwaite, Phillip. E., 268n12

Schaper, J., 168n63, 178n7, 182n21
Schipper, Bernd U., 284n6, 302n72, 309n105
Schloen, J. David, 229n16
Schmid, Hans H., 106, 106n11
Schmitt, Clayton J., 33n48
Schnabel, Eckhard J., 356n28, 385n59
Schreiner, Thomas R., 199n5, 211, 211n49, 215n57, 216, 216n65, 385n59, 387n74, 390n88, 401n132
Schüle, Andreas, 366n58
Schultz, Richard, 250n37, 305n94, 374n1
Schunck, K.-D., 257n65
Schwemer, Anna Maria, 385n59
Seebass, H., 155n17
Segal, Alan F., 385n62, 401n134
Seibert, Eric A., 266n8, 275, 275n42
Seitz, Christopher, 264n3, 265n4, 282n65
Seow, C. L., 241n5
Sheppard, Gerald T., 302n73
Shore, Haim, 107, 107n14, 107n19, 122n116
Sibley, James, 335n2
Silva, Moises, 378n18
Singer, Itamar, 240n2
Slanski, Kathryn E., 156n20, 156n22 156n24
Smith, Bonnie G., 226n9
Smith, Gregory S., 135n29, 296n50, 394n102
Smith, Morton, 196n82
Snaith, N. H., 254n53
Sohn, Seock-Tae, 149n78
Sokoloff, Michael, 167n62
Sonnet, Jean-Pierre, 38n5, 98n41, 153n6
Sparks, Kenton L., 100n46, 161n33
Speiser, E. A., 296n49, 393n101
Spencer, John R., 178n7
Spiqc, C., 379n29
Stackert, Jeffrey, 94n26, 95n35, 96n37, 180n14, 300n65, 398n119
Stähli, H.-P., 285n10
Stavrakopoulou, F., 186n42
Stein, Robert H., 27n34
Stendahl, Krister, 381n43
Stern, P. D., 277n53
Stoebe, H. J., 254n52
Strathearn, Gaye, 353n19
Strugnell, John, 301n71
Sullivan Mary Ann, 403n135
Surls, Austin, 4n10, 148n74, 255n60
Swanson, Dwight D., 68n25

Tadmor, Hayim, 255n57, 379n32
Taggar-Cohen, Ada, 177n1, 195n78
Talmon, Shemaryahu, 79n48, 80n48
Tawil, Hayim Ben Yosef, 191n61
Taylor, William M., 285n11

INDEX OF MODERN AUTHORS

Teeter, D. Andrew, 284n6, 302n72
Thiessen, Matthew, 35n1, 389n86
Thompson, John A., 57n76, 154n8
Tierney, Helen, 236n40
Tigay, Jeffrey H., 25n26, 26n30, 26n31, 102n52, 132n20, 139n53, 148n73, 175n84, 296n50, 319n32, 349n4, 394n102
Tigchelaar, Elbert J. C., 301n71, 350n6, 352n14, 352n16, 353n18
Tooman, William A., 301n71
Tov, Emanuel, 117n86, 139n54, 157n28, 192n66, 244n21
Trible, Phyllis, 229n19
Tromp, Johannes, 382n46
Tzaferis, Vassilios, 372n74

van der Merwe, Christo H., 160n29
van der Toorn, Karel, 183n25, 186n42, 229n16
Van Pelt, Miles, 285n10
van Wolde, Ellen, 285n11, 114n58, 235n36
Vang, Carsten, 42n14, 125n129, 125n130
Vanhoozer, Kevin J., 91n8, 93n13
Verhoef, P. A., 250n37
Vetter, D., 148n73
Vogt, Peter T., 96n38, 105n5, 140n56, 189n58
von Waldow, H. Eberhard, 279n59

Waltke, Bruce K., 20n6, 47n33, 287n18, 303n79, 303n82, 305n90, 305n91, 341n15
Walton, John H., 270n19
Wanke, Günther, 285n10
Weeks, Stuart, 304n88, 305n92, 311n111, 311n113
Weinfeld, Moshe, 23n18, 50n55, 61n6, 63n12, 92n11, 93n16, 93n19, 99n43, 99n44, 101n50, 102n51, 103n53, 105n1, 108n23, 115n71, 118n95, 124n125, 132n20, 135n33, 136n36, 139n56, 140n58, 162, 162n40, 184n28, 194, 195n73, 234n34, 283, 283n3, 287n18, 296n50, 302, 302n73, 302n74, 311, 311n112, 322n39, 394n102
Weiser, A., 379n29
Wellhausen, Julius, 106n7, 178, 178n6
Wells, Bruce, 94n23
Wellum, Stephen J. 62n10
Wenham, Gordon J., 105n5, 138n49
Westbrook, Raymond, 237n42
Westermann, Claus, 113n64, 118n95
Whitaker, R. E., 241n5
Whybray, R. N., 106, 107n13, 124
Williams, Stephen N., 276, 276n49, 278n57
Williamson, Paul R., 64n19, 67n23
Willis, T. M., 140n58, 185n39
Wilson, Gerald H., 1n221n8, 45n26
Wilson, Ian, 101n48, 129n10, 139n54, 140n56, 141n62
Winter, Irene J., 161n33
Wirzba, Norman, 199n3
Wise, Michael, 301n71
Wiseman, Donald J., 115n75
Witherington, Ben III, 358n31, 358n33
Wolterstorff, Nicholas, 275n46
Wright, C. J. H., 132n20, 238n43, 278n58, 322n40, 323n46
Wright, David P., 94n22, 95n34, 195n74
Wright, G. Ernest, 180n11
Wright, N. T., 217n66, 375, 377n16, 385, 385n60, 385n61
Wunsch, Cornelia, 241n5
Wyatt, Nicholas, 61n7

Young, Edward J., 105n3
Younger, K. Lawson, 277n53
Yu, Charles, 20n6

Zehnder, Markus, 57n76, 94n27, 95n29
Zertal, Adam, 165n53, 188n52
Zetterholm, Magnus, 375, 375n3, 377n15
Zevit, Ziony, 186n42

Index of Selected Subjects

Aaron/Aaronic/Aaronid, 125n30, 141n64, 142, 146n69, 147, 178, 178n7, 189, 190, 191, 194197, 243, 246, 250, 257, 262n76, 351, 351n12, 352, 367, 370, 378n24, 384, 390
Aaronic benediction/blessing, 31
Abraham, xiii, 15n39, 17, 32, 63–74, 79, 81, 84, 105–25, 149, 76, 99, 106–25, 127, 130n14, 135n29, 149, 160n31, 164, 168, 175, 205n24, 208, 214, 215, 216, 227, 229n19, 244–45, 244n21, 245n34, 246, 247, 252–60, 278, 282, 295–96, 300, 313, 314, 315, 317, 326, 331, 347n33, 358, 367, 374, 374n2, 388, 393, 393n101, 398
Abrahamic covenant, 61, 62n11, 63, 65–74, 77, 78, 80, 82n51, 114n70, 121, 122, 149, 149n76, 167, 168, 214n56, 215, 281, 313, 315, 322, 322n39, 323, 326, 332, 333, 333n79, 383, 387n76, 390n89
Adam, 63–64, 84–87, 224
Adoption [divine], 10n31, 59, 60, 82, 82n51, 149, 270, 281, 317, 347n32, 401,
Advice to a Prince, 340n12
Anthem [national] (Song of YHWH/Moses[sic]), xiv, 15, 16, 33n49, 38, 39, 40, 43, 53, 57, 124, 187, 266, 269, 274, 298, 299, 312, 313, 319, 331, 334, 338, 329, 396, 397
Ark of the covenant, 13, 36, 75, 96, 137, 186, 190, 201n13, 214, 338
Asherah, 143, 189, 193n69
Atonement, xiv, 7n23, 183n24, 332

Baal, 61n5, 143, 161
Balaam, 105n2, 162, 318n27, 366
Bearing the name of YHWH, 138–39, 138n50, 139n55, 169, 171, 219, 231, 282, 292, 292n35, 232, 302, 317
Book of the Covenant/Covenant Document, 23, 23n19, 39n8, 57, 74n39, 78, 89, 90, 93–96, 122, 132, 148n71, 166, 167n58, 170, 209n42, 210, 234, 311, 312
Booths, Festival of (Sukkoth), 11, 13n35, 24, 24, 27, 37, 42, 76, 101, 140, 140n57, 141n65, 153, 170, 194, 234, 298

Caleb, 5, 6n11, 79, 79n47, 153n7, 180, 181, 216n60,326, 328, 342n20, 380n36, 400
Circumcision [of the heart], 216n60, 327–28, 328n63, 389, 392, 400, 400n130
Circumcision, 28, 61, 67, 73, 73n38, 121, 121n113, 168, 205, 211, 216n60, 220, 327–28, 328n63,387–90, 399, 400, 401
Cosmic covenant, 63–65, 74, 78, 333n80
Covenance, 60–88
Covenant blessing[s], 5, 6, 9, 21n12, 46, 57, 61–62, 64n20, 65, 72, 73n37, 75, 76, 76n42, 80n48, 85, 90, 91, 100, 141, 154, 155, 171–73, 215, 217, 260, 274, 283, 324, 326n57, 327, 329, 333n80,
Covenant curse[s], 64n20, 75, 46, 57, 61–62, 64n20, 65, 73n37, 75, 76, 76n42, 80n48, 85, 90, 91, 100, 153n3, 155, 171–73, 215, 283, 324
Covenant triangle, 75, 76, 78, 85, 88, 141n65, 168–170, 172, 272, 292, 315–16, 3219, 320, 322, 325, 326 333

Daniel (the statesman), 26n28, 62, 77, 260n70, 321, 333, 345n25
David, 24, 25, 42, 47, 79, 86–88, 100, 125, 137, 138n48, 141n64, 161n38, 186n43, 190, 202, 227, 229n19, 244, 260n70, 279n61, 317n23, 326, 329, 341, 342, 343, 343n21, 344, 347, 355n26, 370, 371, 372, 380, 380n36
Davidic covenant, 61, 62, 62n11, 63, 63n12, 86–88, 214, 214n56

445

INDEX OF SELECTED SUBJECTS

Davidic house/dynasty, 78, 95, 137, 276, 283, 317, 334n82, 345, 346, 347, 370, 371

Decalogue (Ten Words), 7n22, 11, 12, 22, 23, 38–39, 39n8, 48, 54, 74n39, 76, 78, 89, 90, 96–97, 99, 100, 105, 110n38, 111n42, 119n101, 122, 124, 130n13, 131, 131n16, 132–33, 135, 136n36, 148n71, 163, 166, 201, 203, 209–14, 209n40, 209n41, 220, 227, 231–33, 232n29, 236n40, 239, 280, 290n28, 292n35, 293, 302, 312, 315, 320, 340, 384

Deir ʿAlla Inscriptions (Ammonite), 162, 170, 170n74

Eden, 49, 61, 75, 83, 84n56, 86, 160, 223, 281
El, 61n5, 67, 112, 164, 289, 299, 321
Election/Choice [divine], 12n34, 16, 49, 50, 56–57m 59, 82n51, 87, 101, 102, 120, 115, 120, 121, 137–38, 137n39, 137n40, 142, 146, 147, 146, 166, 169, 189, 190, 241, 245n24, 252, 255, 274, 281, 299, 317, 325n56, 336, 337, 339, 341, 361, 365, 386, 388, 397, 401

Ezekiel (the prophet), 72, 77, 82, 128n8, 182, 189, 247n29, 328, 329, 333, 346, 378n25, 381

Faith (אֱמוּנָה/הֶאֱמִין, *pistis*), 5, 15, 17, 80–81, 116n82, 121, 295–97, 308, 358, 392–94, 392n94

Father [God as], 84, 340n14, 347n32
Fear (יָרֵא) [of YHWH]. xiv, 1, 7, 7n20, 8, 10–17, 24, 29–30, 50, 59, 71, 92–93, 97, 101, 116, 116n81, 121n112, 129, 135–36, 136n35, 140, 148, 273, 273n30, 283–311, 339, 348, 391, 393–99

Gerizim and Ebal (Mounts), 23, 41, 76, 90, 111, 112n49, 146, 153n7, 154, 155, 157, 162–65, 171–75, 183, 191n63, 315, 315n17

Hammurabi/Hammurabi Law Code 58, 93, 164n44, 34n12

Hezekiah, 89, 94, 137, 155n18, 180n11, 190, 244n19, 260n70, 317n23, 343, 380n36
Hittite Laws, 93, 236n39
Hittite/Hittites, 36, 93, 94, 97, 112, 113n64, 118, 154, 236, 240, 268, 277n55
Holy people (הוהיל הודק סע), 3, 50, 97, 102, 142, 147, 149, 153n3, 204n22, 205n24, 206n28, 219, 226, 270, 271, 273, 274, 278–79, 281, 291, 332, 401
Holy Spirit/Spirit of YHWH/God, 6n12, 22, 27, 28, 30, 34, 79, 79n47, 80, 302, 351n13, 353–55, 357, 372, 374, 389n85, 399, 400

Horeb/Sinai (Mount), 5–6, 7n23, 10, 15, 15n41, 15n42, 16, 25, 38, 68, 96, 125, 126–36, 138n45, 141n64, 142–51, 153n5, 154n14, 160, 166, 168, 170, 208, 215, 243, 245, 251, 252, 253, 258, 260, 263, 286–88, 297, 297n54, 298–301, 309, 310, 313–15, 322–23, 332n80, 351, 357, 366, 367, 385, 393, 394, 395–97

Hosea (the prophet), 42, 125, 187

Instructions on Holiness/Holiness Code, 23n19, 68, 74n39, 89, 90, 94, 95, 122, 123, 125, 209n42, 210, 290n28, 312, 300n65, 398n119

Isaac, 15n39, 68, 68n25, 99, 108, 109n30, 111, 111n41, 112n51, 114n68, 116n77, 118, 120, 122n115, 124n127, 160n31, 227, 247, 252, 259, 296, 302n71, 313, 314, 322n39, 358, 383, 393

Isaiah (the prophet), 26n28, 80, 82, 137, 200, 242, 345, 346, 354, 376, 378n25, 380n38, 381

Israelite covenant, 61, 63, 63n18, 65–88, 167, 214–17, 214n56, 322–23, 333

Jacob, 53, 54, 61, 68, 68n25, 69, 98, 99, 108, 109, 109n30, 111, 112, 112n50, 114, 115, 116, 118, 120, 122n115. 124, 124n127, 150, 160n 31, 161n38, 164–64, 167, 175, 243, 247, 252, 259, 250n70, 311, 313, 314, 318n27, 322n39, 336, 352, 380n36, 383

Jeremiah (the prophet), 26n28, 43, 72, 77–80, 82n52, 88, 193, 216, 221, 242, 247n29, 327, 328, 333, 333n80, 346, 376, 378, 380–82, 389n87

Jesus, Jesus Christ, xvi, xix, 6, 19, 22, 26n32, 27, 28, 29, 31, 48, 49, 51, 59, 65, 80–81, 83, 84, 87–88, 104, 125, 141n60, 151, 203, 205n27, 208, 211–12, 215, 216, 217, 219, 222–24, 230n24, 243n14, 276, 280, 317, 335, 34748, 353–56, 358–59, 369, 371–73, 374, 376–382, 384–87, 392, 400–404

Jewish leaders, 203, 223, 355, 358,
Jewish tradition, 21, 23, 46, 48, 205, 221, 222, 357n30, 379, 379n27, 382n46, 383n54, 385, 385n64, 387n73, 390,

Jonah (the prophet), 25, 31, 295n45. 380n38
Joshua, 5, 6n11, 18, 24, 38, 46–47, 80n49, 38n49, 142, 147, 153n7, 155, 162, 167, 171, 172, 173–76, 177, 187, 257, 259, 277, 313, 315, 326, 329, 341, 350, 380n36, 400

Josiah, 24, 42, 45, 79, 89, 90, 94, 95, 103, 125, 137, 182n21, 188, 190–91, 196, 275, 317n23, 328, 343–45, 400

INDEX OF SELECTED SUBJECTS

Kirta Epic, 340n12

Levites/Levitical priests, 2, 9, 11, 13, 16, 18, 23–24, 29, 36, 37, 42, 76, 90, 92–93, 98, 99, 100–103, 117, 123–24, 130n14, 140, 142, 146–47, 153–53, 155, 163, 167, 170–71, 177–97, 204n22, 206n32, 253, 259, 298, 299, 310, 335, 336, 338, 354, 360, 366, 389n83, 397
Levitical towns, 2, 11n33, 12, 42, 102, 137, 177–97
Love (אָהַב), 7, 8, 11, 16, 17, 24, 26, 36, 50–51, 51n58, 56, 92, 97, 99, 100, 104, 109, 109n30, 119, 121, 121n108, 135, 204, 211–13, 212n51, 218, 221, 239, 252, 253, 262, 262n78, 270, 293, 294, 294n43, 297, 300, 301, 309, 310, 314, 316, 324, 326, 328, 343, 344n24, 347–48, 386, 390, 390n90, 391, 392, 397–401, 400n127

Maimonides, 45, 387n76, 390n91
Marriage, 60, 73, 79, 102, 149, 228, 231, 231n28, 233, 235, 236, 237, 238, 269, 271, 337, 338
Megiddo Prison Mosaic Inscription, 372n74
Mesha Inscription (Moabite), 181n16, 277
Messiah, 27, 80, 87, 88, 243n14, 312, 317, 317n22, 335–48, 349, 350, 349–59, 369–73, 401

New covenant; see "new/renewed Israelite covenant" below.
New/renewed Israelite covenant, 63, 77–84, 79n48, 88, 151, 211, 215–16, 216n61, 327–28, 374, 377, 377n14, 399n126, 400, 402
Noachian covenant, 63, 86
Noah, 63–64, 72, 86, 210n12, 230n23, 345n25

Passover, Festival of (Pesach), 11, 13n35, 23, 27, 101, 110n35, 140, 140n57, 172, 194, 221, 234, 328, 344, 388, 388n80
Paul, xiii, xv, 18, 22, 28, 30, 31, 32, 49, 49n54, 51, 65, 81–83, 216–17, 217n66, 301n71, 302, 334, 18–404
Peter, 30, 65, 335, 350, 355, 356–59, 371, 373, 377n17, 379n28, 400, 403
Pharisees, 28, 203, 205n27, 224, 348, 354
Prayer to Every God, 59n80, 240
Prophet/prophecy, 2n6, 25, 37, 41, 93, 100, 110, 137, 138, 139n51, 187, 187n48, 191, 191n63, 216, 242–45, 262, 317n22, 335–37, 345, 346, 347, 349–73, 376–87

Qumran, Qumran scrolls, 27, 43, 79n48, 301n71, 350, 350n6, 352, 355n27, 370

Rahab, 79, 276, 280, 282, 328
Righteous/Righteousness (צֶדֶק/צְדָקָה), xvi, 3–6, 9, 11, 12, 14, 15, 16, 18, 20, 22, 30, 38, 46, 47, 56, 59, 62, 64–65, 67, 70, 70n32, 73, 76, 79, 80, 82–84, 86–88, 92, 96–99, 112, 117, 119n104, 120–22, 129, 135n33, 139n54, 151, 183, 185, 195, 208, 215, 217, 244, 248, 252–53, 262, 263, 267, 269–71, 280n64, 282, 292, 296n49, 297, 299, 310, 310–12, 315n16, 316–17, 335–36, 339–48, 352, 353, 356, 360–61, 371, 373, 374–75, 377, 392, 393n101, 395, 397, 399
Ruth, 79, 328

Sabbath/sabbaths, 27, 61, 70, 74, 98, 188, 198–224, 232, 266n8, 333n80
Samaritan Pentateuch, 157n28, 184, 253n49
Samaritans, 80, 81, 353n19
Servant [of YHWH/Christ] (עֶבֶד, δοῦλος), 18, 87, 88, 255, 261, 329n64, 335, 346, 347, 379–81
Shema (Deut 6:4–5), 11, 42, 104, 163, 255n57, 274, 274n33, 294, 294n40, 328, 344n24, 379n32, 390, 390n91
Stephen, 335, 350, 35859, 373, 387n76

Tablets of the covenant, xiii, 12, 23, 39, 74, 75, 78—79, 96, 131, 133, 136, 147, 209, 210n45, 213, 246, 250, 253
Torah [of Moses], xv, xvi, xix, 2n6, 3, 3n8, 10–18, 20–26, 29–30, 33, 36–59, 68, 76, 80, 79n46, 78, 82, 82n51, 83, 86, 90, 96, 98, 101–104, 121, 124, 125, 129, 205n27, 208, 211, 216, 218, 229, 270n18, 283–84, 292, 294n42, 294n44, 334, 338, 342–44, 346, 372, 375, 377, 383, 383n54, 392
Torah of Deuteronomy/Deuteronomic Torah, 47, 70n32, 92, 119n101, 140, 147, 148, 152–55, 158–63, 167–68, 171–72, 183, 185, 187, 203, 204, 205, 206n32, 209n42, 210, 211, 234, 239, 261, 270n18, 290, 296–97, 299–304, 304n89, 309–11, 312, 314, 317, 326n59, 327–28, 338–41, 347–48, 355, 361, 369, 389, 394–401, 403
Treasured possession (סְגֻלָּה), 16, 36, 50, 56–57, 61 n5, 97, 102, 147, 149, 251n43, 253, 270, 274, 281, 299, 317, 397, 401, 402
Treaties [ancient], 57, 85, 90, 91, 161
   Hittite, 36, 94, 97, 154
   Neo-Assyrian, 36, 94, 97

447

INDEX OF SELECTED SUBJECTS

Urim and Tummim, 184, 184n35

Victory Stela (Naram-sin), 161n33

Weeks, Festival of (Shavuoth), 11, 13n35, 23, 101, 124, 140, 140n57, 141n65, 194, 234

Zadok/Zadokite, 178, 178n7, 189, 191, 194, 197

Zion/Mount Zion, 26, 83, 126, 128n8, 136–51, 204n21, 297n55

Index of Biblical References

First Testament

Genesis

Genesis–Revelation	61
Genesis–Deuteronomy	125
Genesis–Numbers	44, 106, 106n9
Genesis, book of	xiii, 3n8, 44, 68n25, 72, 73, 105n5, 107, 109, 110, 110n38, 112, 113, 115n72, 117, 118n99, 119, 121, 123, 164, 208, 393
1–3	63, 201, 225
1–2	64, 84, 85, 86
1:1—2:4	107n22, 108n22
1	202n15
1:22	64n20
1:26–31	276n50
1:26–28	84, 85
1:28	64n20
1:31	64, 202, 204
2	84, 85
2:1–3	203, 221
2:1–2	202
2:2–3	208
2:3	203
2:4	123n121
2:7	6n12, 30n42
2:9	64n20
2:15	64n20, 85, 219, 276n50
2:16–17	85
3	64, 64n20
3:9	230
3:15	312, 317n21
3:16	230n21, 239
3:17–18	219
4–9	86
4:4	64, 86n58
4:11	171n75
4:12	171n75
4:26	64, 86n58
5	84, 229n14
5:1	123, 123n121
5:22–24	64, 86n58
6–9	279
6:1–8	86
6:1–5	63n14
6:6–7	330n70
6:8	63n14, 86n58
6:9	63n14, 86n58, 118n93, 123n121
6:11–13	63n14
6:12	113n64, 134n25
6:13–22	86n58
6:13	134n25
6:17	134n25
6:18	63, 64, 86
6:19	134n25
7:1	63n14, 118n93, 230n23
7:7	230
7:13	230n23
8:9	201n13
8:13–22	231
8:21	65
8:22	201n9
9	63, 64, 86
9:1–7	64, 86
9:5–6	65
9:5	357n30
9:8–11	64
9:12–17	61, 64
9:13–16	74
9:15	115n71, 118n95
9:16	64, 70, 115n71, 214, 333n79
9:17	220

449

Genesis (continued)

Reference	Pages
10	229n14
10:1	123n121
11:10	123n121
11:27—35:29	108
11:27—25:11	32, 108
11:27	123n121
11:28	112n51
11:30	110
12:1–3	66, 125, 149
12:1	67, 15n39, 112n51, 230
12:2	67, 115, 115n74
12:3	67, 115, 317n18
12:4	67
12:5	112n48
12:6	111, 112, 175
12:7	111, 244, 260
12:7–8	231
12:10–20	119, 119n104, 120, 227, 229n19, 244
12:10	111
12:13	111
12:27–Deut 34:12	124n127
13:1–13	230
13:7	112
13:10	112, 113
13:14–17	111
13:15	70, 333n79
13:16	67, 115n72, 119
13:17	115
14:2	109n27, 112
14:5	113
14:6	113
14:8	112
14:20	110
15	66, 67, 74, 281, 313, 332, 383
15:1–21	67, 113
15:1	115
15:5–6	383
15:5	67, 17n48, 300n62, 398n116
15:6	17, 67, 116, 117, 117n92, 117n93, 120, 121, 295, 392, 393, 398
15:7–21	111, 168
15:7	72n34, 114
15:13–14	119, 119n103, 385n63
15:13	17, 115, 300, 383, 398
15:13–21	69, 123. 167
15:14	119n105
15:16	112, 278, 383
15:18–21	278
15:18	111, 113, 114, 322
15:19–21	113
16:2—19:22	118n95
16:7–11	378n22
16:10	105
16:11	111, 111n44
17	66, 67, 68n25, 69n27, 69n30, 73, 107n18, 118n95, 281, 313, 332, 387, 387n76, 389n83
17:1	67, 70, 83, 112n53, 116, 120, 121, 124n127, 244, 244n19
17:3	388
17:4–8	167
17:4–6	67
17:6	67, 86, 336
17:6–8	16n46, 215, 300n60, 397n114
17:7–10	69n30
17:7–8	114, 124, 385n63
17:7	67, 68, 69, 70, 73, 78, 81, 114, 115, 125, 127, 149, 214, 251, 313, 323, 333n79
17:8	70, 114, 160n31, 333n79
17:9–14	61, 67
17:9–10	69, 118, 118n95
17:9	69n30, 121
17:10–27	388
17:10–14	121, 388n79
17:10	67
17:11	67, 220, 388n79
17:13	67, 70, 78, 214, 333n79
17:14	118, 388n79
17:16	67, 86, 336
17:19	67, 70, 78, 115, 125, 214, 333n79
17:20	110, 115n73
17:21	115
17:22–27	67
17:23–27	388n79
17:23	121n113, 388n79
17:24	388n79
17:25	388n79
18	116, 245, 282
18:2	117n88
18:3	244n20
18:6–33	244
18:7	246
18:10	117n93
18:14	110
18:16–33	121
18:17–19	105
18:17	244

INDEX OF BIBLICAL REFERENCES

18:18–19	70, 244	22:1–12	17, 398
18:18	67, 115, 317n18	22:1	67, 118, 120, 135n29, 296, 393
18:19	67, 115, 117, 120, 121, 215, 244, 245n24	22:2	296, 393
18:20–21	244	22:5	117, 120, 295
18:22	116, 116n86, 130n14	22:12	67, 15n39, 116, 120, 121, 215, 291n29, 291n31, 296, 393
18:23–28	118n93		
18:23–25	244n20	22:16–18	105
18:23	117n92	22:16–17	119
18:25	117, 117n92, 244, 278	22:16	331
18:27	244n20	22:17	17n48, 67, 110, 115, 115n72, 300n62, 317n21, 320n35, 398n116
18:28	110		
18:30	244n20		
18:31	244n20	22:18	67, 69, 115, 116, 120. 317n18
18:32	244n20		
19	341	23	107n18
19:1	117n88	23:3–9	112
19:2	113n58	23:7	117n88
19:8	109, 229n19	23:10	113
19:13–14	110	23:12	117n88
19:19	111	23:17–18	111
19:20	109n27	23:18	113
19:21	109	24:3	112, 112n51, 116, 118, 120
19:22	112	24:4	112n51
19:23	112	24:6	118
19:25	109	24:7	112n51, 115
19:27	130n14	24:12	111
19:29	109	24:14	111
19:30	112	24:20	120
20	245	24:27	220n68
20:1–18	112, 227, 244	24:28	233
20:2	112	24:37	112n51
20:4	118n93	24:40	116, 244n19
20:5–6	112	24:48	117, 120
20:5	109n27	24:49	111, 220n68
20:7	110, 250, 357, 359n36, 367	24:60	115
20:8	324n49	24:67	109n30
20:11–13	112	25:12	123n121
20:11	116, 291n29, 291n31, 296n50, 309n104, 394n102	25:19—35:29	108
		25:19–34	99
20:13	111	25:19	123n121
20:17–18	359n36	25:20–21	124n127
21:1–7	230	25:20	113
21:4	388, 388n79	25:23–24	116
21:8–12	296, 393	25:28	109n30
21:8	115n73	25:29	202n14
21:10–13	119n104	26:2–5	68, 208
21:22	115	26:3	67, 109, 115, 168
21:23–24	116n84	26:4–5	72, 105, 215
21:23	111	26:4	67, 17n48, 109, 110, 111, 115, 119, 300n62, 317n18, 380n36, 398n116
21:27	68n25, 114n69		
21:32	68n25, 114n69		
22	135n29		
22:1–19	33		

Genesis (continued)

26:5	69, 74, 79, 105n8, 116, 118, 120, 121, 122, 216n60
26:6	67
26:7–11	227
26:7	109n27
26:22	111
26:24	67, 68, 105, 110, 114, 115
26:28–29	115
26:28	68n25, 114n69
26:34–35	118
27:4	109n30
27:9	109n30
27:14	109n30
27:28	110, 111
27:29	115, 117n88
27:37	110, 115
27:39	111
27:46—28:9	107n18
27:46	118
28:1	118, 120n107
28:3	110
28:5	113
28:13–15	68
28:13	67, 111, 114, 115n74
28:14–15	67
28:14	67, 115, 115n72, 119
28:15	105
28:18	161n38
28:20–22	110
28:22	161n38
29:13	324n49
29:18	109n30
29:30–32	109
29:32	109n30
30:6	330n69
30:30	115
30:33	117n92, 117n93
31:1–55	230
31:3	112n51
31:13	112n51
31:20	113
31:24	113, 118
31:42	116n77, 301n71
31:43–55	61
31:44	68n25, 110, 114n69
31:45	161n38
31:48	110
31:52	110
31:53	301n71
31:54	141n63
32:3[2]	116
32:4[3]	378n22
32:7[6]	378n22
32:9[8]	260n70
32:10[9]	112n51, 255n61
32:10–13[9–12]	250n40
32:11[10]	111
32:12[11]	115n72, 119
32:19[18]	378n19
33:3	117n88
33:6	117n88
33:7	117n88
33:18–20	112, 165
33:18	112
33:20	112
34	114
34:2	112
34:3	109n30
34:8	109, 299n58
34:9–10	118, 120
34:14–25	388
34:14	388n79
34:15	388n79
34:16–17	118
34:16	118
34:17	388n79
34:18	112n48
34:20	113
34:21	118
34:22	388n79
34:24	388n79
34:30	110, 112, 320n35
35:1–4	105
35:1	230
35:2–15	231
35:2–4	122n115
35:2	110
35:4	110, 165
35:5	116
35:9–15	107n18
35:10–12	68
35:11	67, 86, 115n73, 336
35:12	111
35:14	161n38
35:22	114
36	229n14
36:1	123n121
36:9	123n121
36:16	113n64
36:20	113
36:21	113
36:29	113
36:30	113
36:43	111n45
37–50	119, 120, 124
37:2	123n121

37:3	109n30
37:4	109n30
37:7	117n88
37:9	117n88
37:10	117n88
38:25	109n27
38:26	117, 117n91, 117n93
38:36	112
39:14	171n76
40:10	109n27
40:14	111
41:46	116n85
41:49	320n35
41:57	253n49
42:6	117n88
42:18	116, 291n29, 291n31, 296n50, 394n102
42:20	393n100
42:21	254n54
43:15	116n85
43:18	247n30
43:26–34	141n64
43:26	117n88
43:28	117n88
43:32	109n29, 109n30, 110n37
43:33	141n64
44:16	117n93
44:20	109n30, 110n37
45:26	393n100
46:1–7	120
46:3	67, 115
46:3–4	53, 67, 68
46:4	67
46:6–7	115
46:27	119
46:34	109n29
47:7	116n85
47:9–28	124n127
47:13	171n75
47:29	111
47:31	117n88
48:3–7	107n18
48:4	70, 333n79
48:12	117n88
48:15	244n19
49:1	318n27
49:3–4	114n65
49:5–7	114
49:8–12	317n21
49:8	117n88
49:10	86, 336, 366, 370n66
49:15	201n13
50:11	112
50:24	115n74

Exodus

Exodus–Deuteronomy	121, 124n127, 374n2, 383n54, 388
Exod 1:1–Deut 34:12	124n127
Exod 19:1–Lev 27:34	124n127
Exod 19–Lev 26	124
Exodus–Numbers	109, 110n35, 110n38, 110n39, 112n56, 113n57, 113n60, 116n63, 115n73, 117, 118n99, 245
Exodus–Leviticus	58
Exodus, book of	3n8, 4, 44, 111n42, 119, 146n69, 147, 205, 209, 212, 213, 220, 223, 233, 237, 252n48, 266n8, 290n26, 381, 394n107
1–18	124
1:1–4	54
1:5	54
1:7	119
1:16	109n27
1:17	116n80, 291n29, 291n31, 296, 394
1:21	116n80, 291n29, 291n31, 296, 394
2:22	115n76
2:23–25	68–69, 383
2:23–24	54
2:24	115n71, 123, 322n39, 383
2:25	68, 69n27, 385n63
2:28	119n103
3–4	250, 381, 382
3:1—4:17 3833:1	127n5
3	129
3:1–6	204n21
3:1–4	381
3:2	378n22, 383n54
3:4–9	381
3:5	144, 146, 206n30
3:6–22	382
3:6–10	256
3:6	114n68
3:7	111n44
3:8	113n64, 160n31, 168, 253, 256, 278, 313n6
3:9	123
3:10	379n26, 381
3:11	381
3:12–15	148
3:12	23n16, 124, 253n50, 379n26, 381, 385
3:13–15	xv
3:13	114n68, 379n26, 381

Exodus (continued)

3:14–22	381, 382
3:14	379n26
3:15–16	114n68
3:15	379n26
3:17	113n64, 160n31, 313n6
3:20	110n34
4:1	116n82, 381
4:2–9	381
4:5	114n68, 116n82
4:7–8	129
4:8	116n82
4:9–15	129
4:9	116n82
4:10	381
4:11–12	381
4:13	381
4:14–17	381
4:17	381
4:21	266
4:23	23n16, 149n75, 253n50
4:24–26	388
4:25	388, 388n78
4:28	379n26
4:31	116n82, 309
5:1–33	129
5:22	244n19, 379n26
5:24	244n19
6:2–9	256
6:2–8	16n46, 75, 168, 255, 300n60, 397n114
6:2–7	251
6:4–8	74
6:4–7	69, 125
6:4	115n71, 322n39
6:6–8	123
6:6–7	79
6:7	81, 114, 114n67, 251, 290n26, 394n107
6:8	160n31, 278
6:9	118n93, 244n19
6:12	389
6:16–26	93
6:20	125n130
7:1	110n32, 118n93, 243, 351n12, 367
7:3	263n76, 266
7:5	79, 290n26, 394n107
7:7	5
7:16	23n16, 149n75, 253n50, 379n26
7:17	79, 290n26, 394n107
7:26[8:1]	23n16, 149n75, 253n50
8:6[10]	4n10
8:16[20]	23n16, 149n75
8:18[22]	4n10, 79, 290n26, 394n107
8:22[26]	109n29
8:24[28]	253n50
9:1	23n16, 149n75m 253n50
9:13	23n16, 149n75, 253n50
9:14	4n10
9:20	296, 394
9:27	117n90, 117n91
9:29	4n10
10:1	266
10:2	4n10, 79, 290n26, 394n107
10:3	23n16, 149n75, 253n50
10:7–8	253n50
10:7	23n16, 149n75
10:8	23n16
10:11	23n16, 253n50
10:12	290n28
10:24	23n16, 253n50
10:26	23n16, 253n50
11:7	4n10
11:24	74
12:2	149, 383n53
12:7	244n18
12:12	55
12:13	110n35
12:16	206n29, 221
12:23	110n35
12:31	23n16, 253n50
12:41	124n127
12:43–50	390
12:43–49	73
12:44–48	388
12:44	388n80
12:48	388n80, 389
12:49	388
13:3	54n71
13:4	383n53
13:5	113n64, 115n74, 160n31, 313n6
13:9	21n9, 46n27
13:10	118n99
13:14	54n71
13:21	149
13:22	149
14	329
14:4	79, 266, 290n26, 394n107
14:9	383n54
14:11–12	253
14:13	383
14:15	248n35
14:18	79, 290n26, 394n107
14:19	149

INDEX OF BIBLICAL REFERENCES

14:24	149	19:6	205n24, 243
14:31	296, 380n39, 394	19:7	243, 324n49
15	329n64	19:8	23, 74, 78, 244n17
15:1–18	383	19:9–24	204n21
15:2	114n68	19:9	116n82, 243, 244n17, 351
15:11	16n43, 298n56, 396n111	19:10–24	146
15:13	144	19:10–16	145, 147
15:16	116n78	19:11	127n6
15:20	351n12	19:12–13	145, 147, 287n17
15:25	118, 248n35	19:16—20:21	384
15:26	105n8	19:16–17	25n24
16	208	19:16	131n15
16:1	208	19:17	32
16:3	135n32	19:18–19	351
16:4	118, 220	19:18	127n6
16:12	290n26, 394n107	19:20	127n6, 351n11
16:15	208, 208n38	19:21–24	145, 147
16:22–30	203	19:22–24	146n69
16:23–29	208	19:22	144
16:23–24	201n13	19:23	127n6, 287n17
16:23	201	19:24	144
16:28	118, 121, 203	20	74, 210
16:29	203, 208	20:1–21	74n39, 209n42
16:31	208n38	20:1–17	23, 39
17:2	118	20:1	209, 324n49
17:6	127n5	20:2–17	23n17, 23n19, 89, 122, 312
17:8–14	153n7	20:2	54n71, 74, 114n67, 209
17:14	123	20:2–6	149n77
18:1	23	20:3–6	280n62
18:3	115n76	20:3	110n38
18:4	114n68	20:4–6	217
18:12	141n64	20:4	101, 118n93
18:13–23	100	20:6	109, 111
18:15	184, 184n34	20:7	138n50
18:19	184, 184n34	20:8–11	205, 212–13
18:21	291n29	20:9–11	203
18:22	184	20:9–10	208
18:23–28	118n93	20:10	182n23
18:25	184	20:11	98, 201, 203, 209
18:26	184n35	20:12	111n42, 209, 320n33
19–24	23, 57, 63n15, 66, 126n1, 128, 147, 205n24, 215, 281	20:17	233
		20:18	287n16
19–20	243	20:19–21	243
19	145, 147	20:19–20	134n28
19:1–3	385	20:19	133, 134n28
19:1	124n127, 208	20:20	24, 118, 134, 135, 135n33, 287n18, 291n29
19:3–25	244		
19:3	243	20:21	131n15
19:4–6	61, 74, 75, 16n46, 145, 147, 149, 300n60, 317n18, 397n114	20:22	39n8, 384n56
		20:22—23:19	74, 74n39, 89, 122, 209n42, 210, 312
19:4–5	385	20:24–26	102, 166, 188
19:5–6	74, 125, 215, 313	20:24–25	102, 165n53, 196
19:5	69, 69n30, 152n3	20:24	139n51, 166n57, 188

455

Exodus (continued)

20:25	165, 188
21–23	234
21:1—23:19	23n17, 23n19, 39n8, 129
21:1	90
21:2–11	234
21:5	109
21:6	184n29
21:14	193
21:15	266n8
21:16	266n8
21:17	266n8
21:21	48n52
21:27	114n69
21:32	114n69
22:7–8[8–9]	184n29
22:15[16]	236
22:20[21]	116n76
23:7–8	117n90, 117n91
23:9	116n76
23:12	201, 202
23:13	110n38
23:14–27	194
23:14–19	189
23:14–17	234
23:14	383n53
23:17	148n73
23:19	137n43
23:20–31	123
23:20–23	74, 383n54
23:23	113n64
23:26	110n33
23:27	116n78
23:31	113n60
23:32	114n70
24	69n30, 74, 76, 148n71
24:1–11	135n30, 145, 146n69, 147, 166, 168, 170
24:1	144
24:3	23, 74, 78, 148n71
24:4	122, 161, 166
24:5–11	141n63
24:5	102, 144, 166n57
24:6–8	67n23
24:6	74
24:7–8	79
24:7	23, 39, 39n8, 74, 78, 89, 148n71, 167, 209n42
24:8	114n70, 148n71, 324n49
24:9–11	75, 134, 142, 144
24:9	144
24:10–11	141n64, 148n71
24:11	144
24:12–18	132
24:12	23, 75, 119n101, 166
24:13	153n7
24:16	127n6
25:1—30:10	202n15
25:8–9	143
25:16	214
26:28	114n69
26:33–34	210
27:1–8	188
28:2	291
28:30	148n73, 184n35
28:31	280n64
28:35	148n73
28:36	102, 145, 204n22, 291
28:40	291
29	204n22
29:45	79, 216n61
29:46	114n67, 394n107
30:11–16	202n15
30:17–21	202n15
30:22–33	202n15
30:34–38	202n15
31:1–11	202n15
31:1–5	221n71
31:8	23
31:12–17	202n15, 203, 217, 214
31:14–15	217
31:15–17	61
31:15	201, 208, 266n8
31:16–17	70, 74, 333n80
31:16	214
31:17	202
31:18	75, 122, 132, 209, 213
31:44	114n69
32–34	136
32	5, 263, 282
32:1	251
32:4	114n67
32:6	166n57
32:10–14	245n23
32:10	115n73, 246, 246n26
32:11–14	248n35, 249, 250, 359n36
32:11–13	247n31, 248
32:11	250n39
32:12	252n48, 330n70
32:13	70, 115n72, 115n74, 252, 333n79
32:14	248, 250, 253, 330n70
32:15	213
32:17	153n7
32:30–34	259, 7n23

INDEX OF BIBLICAL REFERENCES

32:31–34	359n36
32:32–33	151n81
32:34	378n22, 383n54
33:1	115n74
33:2	113n64, 383n54
33:3	160n31, 313n6
33:6	127n5
33:7—34:9	383
33:11—34:7	382
33:11	153n7, 384
33:13	79, 216n62, 281
33:19	136
33:21	117n89
33:30–35	247n31
34:1–28	75
34:2	127n6
34:3–4	78
34:4	127n6
34:6–7	78, 79, 136, 255, 258, 280n62, 321
34:6	16n45, 220n68, 299n59, 397n113
34:7	78
34:9	216n63, 247n31
34:10	110n34, 114n70
34:11	113n64, 181n16
34:12	114n70
34:14	110n38
34:15–16	118n94
34:15	114n70
34:18	383n53
34:23	194, 234
34:24	111
34:26	137n43
34:27	63n15, 114n70
34:28–29	122
34:28	23, 209n40, 210
34:29	127n6, 213
34:29–35	372, 382
34:32	127n6
35:1	201
35:3	222
35:31	221n71
38:1–7	188
38:24	221n71
38:26	6n11
39:10	204n22
39:22	280n64
39:30	291
39:43	221n71
40:20	75

Leviticus

Leviticus–Numbers	118n97
Leviticus, book of	39, 75, 110, 177n2, 266n8, 325n55
1–16	23n19
1:3	165
4:1—6:7	xiii
4:20	xiv, 79, 216n63
4:26	xiv, 79, 216n63
4:31	xiv, 79, 216n63
4:35	xiv, 79, 216n63
5:6	xiv
5:10	xiv, 79, 216n63
5:11	109n27
5:13	xiv, 79, 216n63
5:16	xiv, 79, 216n63
5:18	xiv, 79, 216n63
5:26[6:7]	xiv, 79, 216n63
6:15–16[22–23]	280n64
7:11–18	166n55
7:38	127n6
8	184n35, 204n228
8:35	118n97
11:39	109n27
11:45	114n67
12	188
12:3	73, 388
12:6	188
13–14	188
13:6	109n27
13:10	109n27
13:21	109n27
14:11	188
14:23	188
14:33–57	188
14:34	74
15	188
15:14	188
15:29	188
16	123n119
16:2	210
16:31	109n27, 201, 201n8
17:1	123, 123n118
17–26	23n19, 74, 74n39, 89, 2123, 09n42, 210, 312
18:1	123n118
18:4	118n99
18:5	118n99
18:19–30	271
18:22–30	109n29
18:25	171n75
18:26	118n99
18:27	109n25

457

Leviticus (continued)

18:28	171n75
18:30	118n97
19	117n90
19:1	123n118
19:2	205n24, 206n31
19:3	233, 233n33, 290n28
19:4	116n76
19:5	130n14
19:12	116n84
19:14	116n79, 296n50, 394n102
19:15	117n90, 117n91
19:18	104, 109
19:19	58n79, 118n99
19:22	79, 216n63
19:23	388n79
19:30	201n8, 290n27, 292
19:32	116n79, 296n50, 394n102
19:34	109
19:36	114n67, 117n90, 117n91
19:37	118n99
20:1	123n118
20:8	118n99
20:10	266n8
20:13	109n29, 266n8
20:15–16	266n8
20:17	109n27
20:18	109n27
20:22	118n99, 171n75
20:24	160n31, 313n6
20:27	266n8
21:1–15	123n118
21:1	123n118
21:9	109n27
21:16	123n118
22:1	123n118
22:9	118n97
22:16	123n118
22:17	123n118
22:21	110n34
22:33	114n67
23:1	123n118
23:2–4	206n29
23:3	203, 206, 207, 208
23:4	207
23:7–8	206n29
23:9	123n118
23:11–16	203
23:21	206n29
23:23	123n118
23:24	206n29, 207
23:26	123n118
23:27	206n29, 207
23:29	357n30
23:32	201, 201n8
23:33	123n118
23:35–37	206n29
23:37–38	201n8
23:39	201n8
23:40	15n42, 141, 142n65, 297n55, 396n110
24:1	123n118
24:8	70, 74, 78, 203, 214, 333n80
24:13	123n118
24:16	266n8
24:17	266n8
25:1	123n118, 127n6
25:2–6	201
25:4	201
25:9	207, 207n33
25:15	116n79
25:17	296n50, 394n102
25:23	172, 180
25:32–34	177, 177n3, 180, 181
25:36	116n79, 296n50, 394n102
25:38	74, 114n67
25:42	114n67
25:43	116n79, 296n50, 394n102
25:55	114n67, 251n44
26	61, 77, 300n65, 398n119
26:1–39	75
26:2	201n8
26:3	290n27, 292
26:4–13	64n18, 72, 333n80
26:9	115n71
26:10	319n31
26:12	74, 79, 114, 216n61
26:13	114n67
26:14–39	73, 323, 333
26:15	118n96
26:30	110n36
26:31	188
26:34–35	201
26:34	171n75, 202n17
26:38	171n75
26:40–46	75
26:40–45	17, 77, 300, 327, 333, 398
26:41	73, 216n60, 323, 400
26:42	68n25, 115n71, 322, 322n39
26:43	171n75, 201, 202n17
26:44	78, 118n96, 325n55
26:45	114n67, 115n71, 322
26:46	76n42, 123, 124n128, 127n6
27:1	123n118

INDEX OF BIBLICAL REFERENCES

27:2	110n34
27:3–5	6n11
27:21–29	276
27:28	277
27:30–32	110
27:34	124n128, 127n6

Numbers

Numbers, book of	4, 39, 44, 110, 177n2, 254,
1:3	6n11
1:18–45	6n11
1:53	118n97
3:1	123n121, 127n6
3:7	118n97
3:8	118n97
3:28	118n97
3:38	118n97
4:6	280n64
4:30	204n22
5:11–31	183n27
5:13	109n27
5:14	109n27
6:2	110n34
8:26	118n97
9:19	118n97
9:23	118n97
10:10	166n57
10:11	124n127, 380n39
11:2	248n35
11:3	5
11:25–26	367
11:27	161n32
11:28	153n7
11:29	110n32, 135n32
11:34	5
12:1–15	367
12:1–9	384
12:6–8	243, 367, 368, 384
12:6	110n32
12:7	380n39
12:8	380n39
12:13–14	248n35
12:14	238n44
13–14	78
13:16	80n49, 125n130, 153n7
13:27	313n6
13:29	113n64
13:32	171n75
14	263, 282
14:3	5
14:6	153n7
14:8	161n32, 313n6
14:11–20	359n36
14:11	116n82
14:12–19	245n23
14:12	115n73
14:13–20	248n35
14:13–19	248, 249, 250
14:13	250n39
14:14–16	252n48
14:16	115n74
14:19	216n63, 250
14:20	216n63, 250
14:22	118
14:24	79, 216n60, 328, 380n36
14:29	6n11
14:30	153n7
14:31	5
14:38	153n7
15:3	110n34
15:8	110n34, 166n57
15:18	216n63
15:22	216n63
15:23	216n63
15:41	114n67
16:3	206n31
16:13–14	313n6
16:13	161n32
16:14	161n32
16:28	379n26
16:29	379n26
16:30	171n75
16:31	324n49
18:1–32	189
18:12	111
18:15	134n25
18:20	180n15
18:21–32	180
18:21–28	110
20:1–13	261
20:1–12	254
20:2–3	206
21:7–9	248n35
21:7	250
20:12	116n82, 257, 260
20:14	378n22
21:21	378n22
22–24	366
22:5	378n22
22:22–35	378n22
22:38	350n9
23:5	350n9
23:10	318n27
23:12	350n9
23:16	350n9
23:19	330

459

Numbers (continued)

24:9	317n21
24:14	318n27
24:15–17	350n6
24:17	18, 317n21, 336
25:1–5	10
26:2	6n11
26:4	6n11
27:12–14	254
27:18–23	153n7
28:6	127n6
28:9–10	203, 206, 221
28:18	206n29
28:25–26	206n29
29:1	206n29
29:7	206n29
29:12	206n29
30:6	216n63
30:9	216n63
30:13	216n63
31	279
31:6	207
31:30	118n97
31:47	118n97
32:3	181
32:11–12	342n20
32:11	6n11
33:2	123
33:3–4	55
33:50—34:29	180
33:52	110n36
34	138n49
34:12	267
35:1–8	102, 177, 180
35:1–5	178, 186n42
35:6–8	180
35:9–34	180
35:9–15	185n39
35:9	384n56
35:30–34	332

Deuteronomy

1–26	163n45
1–4	90, 91, 170
1:1–5	39, 40, 41, 57, 317n20
1:1–4	39, 41
1:1–2	144
1:1	2n6, 6, 7n25, 91, 152n2, 175n81
1:2	127n4, 128
1:3	6, 38, 91, 96, 124n127, 152n2, 242, 265, 384n57
1:4	39, 157n27, 265, 267, 315
1:5	2n6, 3, 6, 39, 41, 91, 119n101, 127, 152n2, 163n45, 167, 168, 170, 175n81, 314n12
1:6—30:20	41
1:6—4:44	57
1:6—4:40	38, 40, 41, 91, 312, 338
1:6—3:22	6
1:6–8	242
1:6	128, 257n66
1:7–8	16, 299, 397
1:8	17n50, 99, 115, 138n46, 300n64, 313, 314n14, 322n39, 323n42, 398n118
1:9–18	283
1:9–12	128, 260n73
1:10	17n48, 38n6, 115, 300n62, 398n116
1:13–16	184
1:15–17	185
1:15	133n22
1:16–18	360
1:16	4, 98, 117n91, 117n92, 117n93
1:17	113, 184, 184n35, 284
1:18	91
1:19	127, 128, 284, 285, 288, 315, 394n105
1:19–46	5, 138n45, 245n23
1:20–29	315
1:21	116, 138n46, 284, 284n8, 285, 287, 394, 394n105
1:23	111n42
1:25	128n7
1:26—2:1	388
1:26	5
1:27–28	5
1:27	110, 110n36, 265, 269, 54n69
1:28–29	268
1:28	289n24
1:29	284, 284n8, 285, 287, 394n105
1:30–33	315
1:30	5, 138n45, 295, 313, 392n95
1:31	5, 16, 56, 138n45, 295, 299, 340, 392n95, 397
1:32–46	315
1:32	5, 120, 295, 393
1:33	5
1:34–40	5

INDEX OF BIBLICAL REFERENCES

1:35	17, 17n50, 138n46, 168n65, 300, 300n64, 314n14, 322n39, 323n42, 398, 398n118	3:14	38n6, 314n9
		3:18–22	274n37, 315
		3:18	91, 157n27
		3:20	174n81, 267n11
1:36	328, 342n20, 400	3:21	157n27
1:37	257n65, 260, 313	3:22	247n30, 284n8, 285, 288
1:38–39	315	3:23–29	6, 245, 254, 258–59, 313
1:45	139n54	3:23	254, 255
		3:24	254, 256n63, 260, 263
2:1–23	267	3:25	174n81, 254, 257
2:1–2	315	3:26–28	257
2:1	242	3:26	260
2:2–23	268, 314	3:27	261n74
2:3	257n66	3:28	315
2:4	7n15, 284n8, 285, 288, 394n105	3:33	316
2:5	269, 278	4–5	136
2:7	127, 221, 245	4	4, 52, 57, 90, 302, 323
2:8	99	4:1–31	6
2:9–11	278	4:1–8	16, 52, 58, 299, 396
2:9	267, 269	4:1–2	42, 58, 265
2:10–13	319n31	4:1	2n6, 7n14, 18n55, 36, 38, 91, 114n68, 138n46, 242, 301n70, 315n16, 399n124
2:10–12	41		
2:11	113		
2:12	110n36, 111n45, 113, 278	4:2	10, 163, 167, 183, 261, 317n20, 384n58
2:14–15	315		
2:19–21	278	4:3–4	10, 58, 99, 261
2:19	269	4:3	269
2:20–23	41	4:4	38n6, 41, 97, 389n82
2:20–21	113	4:5–8	58, 96, 218, 274, 282, 292, 317, 375, 402
2:20–11	113		
2:20	113	4:5	2n6, 36n1, 38, 91, 96, 315n16, 317n20, 384n57
2:21	110n36		
2:22	38n6, 110n36, 113, 265, 278, 314n9	4:6–8	3, 115, 226, 241, 252, 263, 302
2:23	110n36	4:6	4, 6, 97, 283
2:24—3:17	274n37, 315	4:7–8	115, 129, 240, 321
2:24—3:11	267	4:7	241, 255
2:24	267	4:8	38n6, 91, 97, 119n101, 270n18, 314, 314n12, 315n16
2:25	38n6, 116, 265, 284, 284, 285, 288, 314n9, 394n105		
		4:9–24	333
2:29	267n11	4:9–15	128, 129, 138n45, 384
2:30	265, 268, 314n9	4:9–14	6, 15, 57, 96, 297, 315, 395
2:32–35	266	4:9–13	38, 240
2:33–35	266	4:9–10	ix, 10n31, 129, 130
2:33	266	4:9	2n6, 7n15, 7n18, 118, 131, 242, 252n47
2:34–35	268		
3:2	127n4, 266, 284n8, 285, 288	4:9–31	16, 16n46, 52, 57, 124n127, 299, 300n60, 323, 396, 397n114
3:3	266		
3:9	41	4:10–14	130, 382
3:11	12, 41, 113, 130, 174n80	4:10–13	38, 131
3:13	113		

461

Deuteronomy (continued)

4:10	2n6, 14, 24, 36n3, 116, 116n81, 120, 127, 129, 130, 131, 131n14, 132, 135, 139n54, 144, 145, 147, 160, 273, 284n8, 285, 297, 298, 309, 394, 395
4:11–14	132
4:11	132, 133, 145, 147, 148
4:12	131, 132, 132n18, 133
4:13–14	133, 145, 147
4:13	12, 39, 56n75, 57, 91, 122, 130n13, 131, 132, 145, 147, 148n71, 209n40, 213, 315
4:14	2n6, 18n55, 38, 91, 96, 130, 131, 242, 301n70, 315n16, 317n20, 384n57, 399n124
4:15–24	57, 136, 221
4:15	7n15, 127, 131, 132, 132n18, 160
4:16	252n47, 273n32, 274, 322
4:19	252n47, 273
4:20–31	xiv
4:20	54, 54n69, 56, 57, 97, 148, 251n42, 270n20, 314n9, 325n56
4:21–22	128n7, 313
4:21	17n50, 257n65, 260, 267n11, 300n64, 398n118
4:23	17, 7n15, 7n18, 56n75, 91, 114, 118, 252n47, 273n32, 274, 300, 322, 398
4:24	134n2, 316
4:25–31	57, 75, 300n65, 398n119
4:25–29	77
4:25–28	316, 320, 323, 389n82
4:25–27	318
4:25	17, 100, 247, 273n32, 274, 300, 319, 358n32, 360n40, 398
4:26–28	17, 300, 320, 321n37, 398
4:26–27	269n15
4:26	38n6, 57, 110n36, 322, 339n11
4:27	265, 319, 320n34, 325
4:28–31	326
4:28	134, 221n70, 241, 273n32, 319, 320, 330
4:29–31	78, 110n36, 319, 320, 323, 325, 333
4:29–30	316, 321, 324
4:29	321, 325, 325n53
4:30–31	17, 77, 300, 327, 398
4:30	73, 116, 120, 152n3, 318, 321, 323, 324n49, 325, 325n51, 325n52
4:31	16, 17, 56n75, 57, 59, 91, 99, 115n71, 115n74, 251, 299, 313, 316, 322, 323, 325, 330, 396, 398
4:32–40	6, 16, 49n53, 52, 55, 99, 252, 256, 261, 263, 274, 299, 396
4:32–39	148
4:32–38	386
4:32–36	96
4:32–35	382
4:32–34	55
4:32–33	4
4:32	6, 314, 318
4:33	6, 128, 129, 132, 132n19, 133, 144, 145, 147, 287, 289, 313
4:34	6, 15, 138n45, 256n63, 262n76, 265, 267, 270n20, 270n21, 284, 285, 289, 298, 313, 315, 368n62, 394, 396
4:35	5, 55, 134
4:36	6, 15, 128, 129, 132, 145, 147, 297, 382, 395
4:37–38	274n37
4:37	6, 16, 17n49, 54n69, 56, 97, 109, 115, 120, 252, 253, 270n22, 299, 300n63, 313, 314, 336, 397, 398n117
4:38	265, 268, 314n9
4:39	5, 7n16, 38n6, 55, 129, 134, 139, 289, 290
4:40	5, 38n6, 55, 111, 111n42, 136n35, 310n109, 310n110, 320n33, 339n11, 384n58
4:41—5:1	7n25
4:41–44	40
4:41	152n2, 175n81
4:42	109
4:44—26:19	32
4:44—25:11	32
4:44—11:32	32n46, 124n127
4:44–45	39, 90
4:44	2n6, 39, 91, 119n101, 152n2, 314
4:45—11:32	57
4:45—6:1	41
4:45—5:1	40
4:45	2n6, 36n1, 90, 91, 152n2, 242, 265, 315n16

4:46–47	175n81	5:8	273n32
4:46	152n2, 315	5:9	117, 120, 229, 265, 269, 269n15, 340
5–28	66	5:10	97, 109, 111
5–27	169	5:11	138n50
5–26	74, 90, 91, 152, 170, 209n42, 210, 312	5:12–15	98, 212–13
		5:12–14	201
5:1—26:19	40, 91, 312	5:13–15	203
5:1—11:32	2n6, 38, 40, 154	5:13–14	208
5–11	7n25, 90, 91, 92, 96, 100, 338	5:14	182n23
		5:15	7n17, 54n69, 99, 119n102, 201, 223, 232, 256n63, 270n21, 315n15
5:1–6:3	6		
5	74, 99, 130, 131, 210	5:16	111n42, 233, 233n33, 290n28, 310n109, 310n110, 320n33, 339n11
5:1–33	57, 128, 129		
5:1–27	384		
5:1–22	16, 299, 396		
5:1–6	389n82	5:19	395n108
5:1–5	6, 10, 91, 128, 132, 388, 389	5:21	233
		5:22–6:3	132
5:1–2	315	5:22–33	131, 154, 243
5:1	2n6, 7n14, 7n19, 36n1, 36n3, 38, 38n6, 90, 91, 131, 132, 152n2, 304n89, 315n16	5:22–31	132, 145, 148
		5:22–30	132
		5:22–23	134, 351
		5:22	36n3, 57, 132, 133, 144, 145, 147, 171n76
5:2–33	7n23		
5:2–5	2n6, 131, 261, 313	5:23–33	15, 261, 297, 395
5:2–3	16, 132, 145, 147, 299, 396	5:23–29	14, 24n21, 297, 395
5:2	56n75, 114, 127, 128, 131n17, 138n45	5:23–27	132, 133, 144
		5:23–26	286, 287, 304
5:3	38n6, 56n75, 99, 114, 131, 132, 313	5:23	153n5
		5:24–27	134n28
5:4	132, 147	5:24	133, 256n62, 314n9
5:5	15, 17n49, 132, 132n19, 144, 145, 147, 148, 149, 284n8, 285, 286, 297, 304, 394, 395	5:25–26	133
		5:25	134
		5:26	134, 287, 394n102
		5:27	133, 134, 155, 243
5:6—26:19	91	5:28–32	132
5:6–27	145, 147	5:28–31	7n22, 92, 134
5:6–22	23, 122	5:28–29	10
5:6–21	11, 39, 90, 131, 210, 227, 232	5:28	134, 243
		5:29	15n40, 111n42, 116n81, 135, 135n30, 273, 284n8, 285, 294n41, 297n53, 316, 326, 389n82, 394
5:6–11	302		
5:6–10	136, 149n77, 221		
5:6–7	10		
5:6	16, 54, 54n69, 54n71, 99, 114, 119n102, 232, 240, 270n21, 299, 300n63, 315n15, 396, 398n117	5:31–32	339
		5:31	36n1, 38, 91, 136, 155, 243, 304n89, 315n16
		5:32—6:3	132
5:7–11	280n62	5:32	7n19, 185
5:7–10	274, 320	5:33	7n21, 97, 117, 120, 270, 310n109, 320n33, 339n11
5:7	110n38, 274n34, 342, 386n67		
5:8–10	217	6–26	23
5:8–9	274	6–11	91, 99, 136n36

Deuteronomy (continued)

6:1–3	14, 24n21, 297, 310, 395
6:1–2	293, 311
6:1	2n6, 18n55, 36n1, 38, 91, 96, 136n36, 301n70, 304n89, 315n16, 317n20, 384n57, 399n124
6:2	7n20, 15n40, 36n2, 97, 116n81, 118, 121, 136n35, 273n30, 284n8, 285, 294n42, 297n53, 310n109, 320n33, 339n11, 384n58, 395n108
6:3	7n19, 111n42, 114n68, 138n46, 160n30, 171n75, 310n110, 313, 326n58
6:4—11:32	6
6:4–9	7
6:4–6	390
6:4–5	xi, 11, 42, 43, 49, 100, 103, 204, 274, 294, 326, 328, 344n24
6:4	6, 7n14, 48n51, 283, 390
6:5	7, 7n20, 97, 109, 321n36, 325n53, 338, 339
6:6–9	187
6:6–7	304n89
6:6	38n6, 79, 216n60
6:7	10, 10n31
6:8–9	390
6:9	162
6:10–15	390
6:10–11	16, 261, 299, 316, 397, 138n46
6:10	99, 115n74, 168n65, 313, 314n14, 323n42
6:10	99, 115n74, 168n65, 313, 314n14, 323n42
6:12	7n15, 7n18, 7n21, 17, 17n49, 54n69, 54n71, 99, 118, 119n102, 149, 252n47, 270n21, 300, 300n63, 315n15, 398, 398n117
6:13	97, 116, 116n81, 120, 284n8, 285, 294, 298, 342
6:14–15	274
6:14	97, 110n38, 274n34, 386n67
6:15	110n36, 252n47, 269n15
6:16	7n23, 49n53, 118, 138n45
6:17	315n16
6:18–19	274n37
6:18	111n42, 115n74, 128n7, 138n46, 168n65, 310n110, 314n14, 390
6:19	265
6:20–25	10n31, 11, 16, 54, 58, 59, 96, 232, 240, 256, 261, 274, 299, 339, 392, 396
6:20–21	7n24
6:20	36n1, 59, 315n16
6:21–23	6, 17n49, 59, 300n63, 398n117
6:21–22	55, 267n9
6:21	54n69, 99, 119n102, 138n45, 149, 255, 256n63, 270n21, 313, 315n15
6:22	262n76, 315, 368n62
6:23	16, 54n69, 54n70, 138n46, 168n65, 261, 270n21, 299, 314n14, 397
6:24–25	208, 390
6:24	6, 7n20, 59, 97, 116n81, 136n35, 273n30, 284n8, 285, 298, 310, 314n9, 375
6:25	4, 7n19, 59, 97, 117, 117n89, 117n92, 117n93, 120, 122, 136n36, 139n54, 215, 302, 310, 375, 384n57, 399
7	275, 280
7:1–26	316, 390
7:1–11	274n37
7:1–5	101, 280
7:1	113, 268, 279, 360n40
7:2–5	279
7:2–4	118, 118n94, 120
7:2	56n75, 266, 277
7:3–5	122n115
7:3–4	338
7:4	110n36, 110n38, 269n15, 274n34
7:5	161, 273n32
7:6–11	261
7:6–10	254
7:6–9	56, 253
7:6–8	281, 386
7:6–7	16, 56, 115, 120, 299, 397
7:6	56, 97, 145, 149, 205n24, 206n28, 251n43, 270, 273, 274, 291, 317, 336, 386n66
7:7	109, 270n22, 299, 336
7:8	17n49, 53, 53n68, 54n69, 54n71, 55, 56, 99, 109, 115n74, 119n102, 149,

INDEX OF BIBLICAL REFERENCES

	256n63, 270n21, 270n22, 300n63, 315n15, 398n117	8:7–10	16, 127, 256, 299, 316, 397
		8:7	128n7
7:9	7n16, 16, 56n75, 78, 97, 109, 111n43, 118, 299, 300, 393, 393n98, 397	8:10	128n7
		8:11–29	220
		8:11–18	56
7:10–11	390	8:11–17	319n31
7:10	265	8:11–13	327
7:11	36n1, 38n6, 91, 136n36, 315n16	8:11–12	7n21, 252n47
		8:11	7n18, 17, 36n1, 36n2, 38n6, 91, 118, 118n99, 300, 384n58, 398
7:12–16	6, 261, 316, 327		
7:12	7n19, 56n75, 97, 99, 111n43, 115n74	8:12–13	261
		8:13–18	45
7:13	97, 109, 110, 115n74, 138n46, 168n65, 270n22, 314n14, 323n42, 326n58	8:14–16	7n23
		8:14	7n18, 17, 17n49, 54n69, 54n71, 99, 119n102, 149, 270n21, 300, 300n63, 315n15, 398, 398n117
7:14	110		
7:16	110n37, 118, 266		
7:17–26	274n37	8:15–16	138n45, 261, 315
7:17–18	7n24	8:15	284, 285, 288, 394n105
7:17	266, 364n49	8:16	111n42, 118, 120, 310n110, 318n28, 318n30
7:18–19	267n9		
7:18	7n17, 55, 284n8, 285, 288	8:17–18	7n24, 254
7:19	6, 54n69, 54n70, 256n63, 262n76, 284, 285, 288, 315, 368n62	8:17	7n21, 364n49
		8:18	7n17, 56, 56n75, 99, 115, 115n74, 313, 314n9
7:21	15, 115, 284, 285, 289, 298, 396	8:19–20	269n15
		8:19	17, 38n6, 97, 110n38, 117, 274n34, 300, 398
7:22–26	161		
7:22	7n21, 109, 252n47	8:20	116n83, 152n3, 152n3, 265, 274n37, 325n52
7:23	110n36, 265		
7:24	110n36, 266		
7:25–26	274, 277, 280		
7:25	7n21, 109n29, 252n47, 273n32	9:1—10:11	57, 315
		9	5, 128, 252, 269, 282
7:26	109n29	9:1–24	279
		9:1–23	254
8	6, 49n53	9:1–6	274n37
8:1–6	315	9:1	7n14, 38n6, 266, 268, 283, 390
8:1–5	16, 261, 299, 390, 397		
8:1	7n19, 7n21, 38n6, 115n74, 136n36, 138n46, 168n65, 314n14, 384n58	9:3–6	5
		9:3	7n16, 38n6, 110n36, 265, 266
8:2–16	99	9:4–24	392
8:2–6	138n45	9:4–6	117n92, 117n93
8:2–4	6, 7n23	9:4–5	7n24, 117n92, 252
8:2	7n17, 118, 120, 245	9:4	265, 278, 364n49
8:4	245	9:5–6	56
8:5	6, 56, 97, 129	9:5	99, 115n74, 138n46, 313, 314n14
8:6	6n12, 15n40, 97, 116n81, 117, 120, 270, 284n8, 285, 293, 297n53, 339n10, 395n108		
		9:6—10:11	7n23, 75
		9:6	7n16, 56, 127, 128n7, 326
		9:7—10:11	7n23
8:7–20	390	9:7–26	99
8:7–14	261	9:7–21	5, 128, 138n45, 313

465

Deuteronomy (continued)

9:7-14	333
9:7-8	248
9:7	7n17, 7n18, 56, 128, 135n30, 136
9:8—10:11	128, 136
9:8-21	6, 110n32
9:8	56, 110n36, 127, 128
9:9-15	74
9:9	7n23, 56n75, 114, 131, 213, 247, 247n31, 252
9:10	36n3, 128, 144, 146, 209
9:11	56n75, 96, 131, 213
9:12-14	7n22, 92
9:12	54n69, 56, 144, 147, 251, 273n32, 325n51
9:13	56, 252, 326
9:14	110n36, 246, 259n69, 265
9:15-17	246
9:15	56n75, 96, 131, 213
9:16	56, 273n32
9:17	246
9:18-22	56
9:18-20	360
9:18-19	245, 245n23, 246, 247, 248, 250, 258-59
9:18	56, 100, 139n54, 247, 247n31, 248n35, 250, 260, 263, 358n32
9:19	7n23, 16, 110n36, 248, 250, 253, 284, 299, 397
9:20	110n36, 146n69, 250, 251n42
9:21	246
9:22-24	138n45, 248
9:22	313
9:23	116, 116n83, 120, 152n3, 295, 325n52, 392
9:24	135n30, 136, 326
9:25—10:11	258-59
9:25—10:5	16, 128, 138n45, 299, 397
9:25-29	110n32, 245, 245n23, 246-47, 248, 250, 360
9:25-26	250
9:25	7n23, 110n36, 139n54, 260, 263
9:26-29	249, 250
9:26	53, 54n69, 56, 247n30, 250, 253, 254, 256n62, 260, 270n21
9:27	99, 250, 251, 252, 313
9:28	7n21, 54, 54n69, 54n70, 252, 265
9:29	54n69, 54n70, 56, 253
10:1-10	75
10:1	15
10:1-10	75
10:1-8	96
10:1-5	12, 122, 136, 250, 253
10:1-4	57
10:1-2	7n22, 92
10:4	36n3, 39, 128, 131, 144, 145, 146, 147, 148n71, 209, 209n40
10:6-9	11
10:8-9	16, 253, 299, 397
10:8	13, 16, 38n6, 56n75, 116, 120, 130n14, 139n54, 140, 144, 145, 146, 147, 183n27, 186, 187, 187n44, 210, 314n9
10:9	98
10:10	247n31, 253
10:11	7n22, 92, 138n46, 168n65, 253, 261, 314n14, 323n42
10:12-11:1	ix, x, xi, 7, 8, 11, 11n32, 38, 49, 204, 215, 293, 348, 390, 391
10:12-22	101, 140, 145
10:12-15	8, 391
10:12-13	8, 11, 15n40, 17, 50, 70n32, 100, 135n33, 292, 297, 297n53, 301, 309, 310, 325n53, 348, 390, 392, 395n108, 398
10:12	7, 7n20, 8, 97, 109, 116n81, 117, 270, 273n30, 283, 284n8, 285, 293, 294, 298, 299, 309, 321n36, 339n10, 391
10:13	36n2, 38n6, 118n99, 384n58
10:14—11:1	11, 348
10:14	8, 294, 391
10:15	8, 16, 56, 97, 109, 115, 120, 261, 270, 270n22, 299, 314, 314n9, 336, 391, 397
10:16-19	8, 391
10:16	8, 135, 216n60, 326, 327n61, 328n63, 389, 389n84, 390, 391, 400
10:17-19	8, 270
10:17-18	234
10:17	8, 55, 116n81, 284, 285, 289, 298, 391, 394, 396
10:18-19	98, 117, 391

INDEX OF BIBLICAL REFERENCES

10:18	97, 99, 109, 229n17, 234
10:19	99, 109, 115, 119
10:20–22	8
10:20	7n20, 8, 97, 116, 116n81, 120, 273n30, 285, 294, 298, 342, 390, 391
10:21	8, 15, 284, 285, 289, 298, 391, 394, 396
10:22	8, 17n48, 53, 54, 99, 114, 115, 119, 138n45, 300n62, 314, 320n35, 398n116
11	41, 91, 119
11:1–10	346
11:1	7n20, 8, 36n1, 91, 97, 109, 118, 118n99, 121, 348, 391
11:2–7	15n43, 298n56, 396n111
11:2–6	7n23
11:2–4	55, 99, 261, 267
11:2	38n6, 256n62, 256n63
11:3	138n45, 315, 368n62
11:4	38n6, 314n9
11:5–6	99
11:8–17	316
11:8–15	316
11:8	38n6, 136n36
11:9–12	16, 256, 261, 299, 397
11:9–10	41
11:9	7n21, 115, 115n74, 138n46, 160n30, 168n65, 171n75, 310n109, 314n14, 320n33, 323n42, 339n11
11:10–12	128
11:10	164n48
11:12	139n53, 171n75, 318n28
11:13–28	17, 300n65, 398, 398n119
11:13–25	6
11:13–15	261, 325n53, 327
11:13	7, 7n20, 38n6, 97, 100, 109, 321n36
11:14	110
11:16–17	274
11:16	7n15, 7n21, 110n38, 117, 118, 274n34, 316, 325n51
11:17	128n7, 171n75, 269n15, 300
11:18–25	299, 397
11:18–19	304n89
11:18	7, 384n58
11:19–20	10
11:20	10n31, 162
11:21–25	316
11:21	115n74, 138n46, 168n65, 314n14, 323n42
11:22	97, 109, 117, 118n98, 136n36, 270, 339n10
11:23–25	274n37
11:23	266, 268
11:24–25	171
11:24	113, 115
11:25	116, 284, 285, 288, 394n105
11:26–32	xi, 7n25, 41, 90, 155
11:26–28	21n12, 38, 46, 138n45, 155, 157, 283,
11:26	38n6
11:27	38n6, 384n58
11:28–25	16
11:28	97, 110n38, 274n34, 316, 38n6
11:29–32	170, 174, 277n55, 315
11:29–31	41, 155
11:29–30	155
11:30–31	174n81
11:30	38n6, 111, 112, 174
11:31–32	155
11:31	267n11
11:32	7n19, 36n1, 90, 155, 315n16
12:1—28:69[29:1]	154
12–28	97
12–26	7, 7n25, 9, 89, 90, 91, 92, 99, 233, 335, 338
12:1—26:15	154
12–18	91
12–16	100, 209n4
12:1—26:19	2n6, 32n46, 38, 40, 57, 124n127, 360
12	41, 95, 101, 166
12:1–14	6, 16, 147, 299, 397
12:1–13	142
12:1–4	274
12:1–3	101
12:1	7n19, 7n25, 36n1, 41, 90, 91, 92, 99, 114n68, 138n46, 315n16, 316
12:2—26:15	90
12:2–14	9, 140
12:2–3	101
12:3	180, 273n32
12:4	140
12:5–14	9, 142
12:5–12	101
12:5–10	137
12:5–7	140–41

Deuteronomy (continued)

12:5	12n34, 95, 128, 138, 138n47, 144, 145, 146, 166, 189n55, 316, 336
12:6	110, 141, 144, 145, 147, 166
12:7	15n42, 16, 101, 139n54, 141n65, 144, 145, 146, 147, 165, 297n55, 299, 396n110, 397
12:8–9	140
12:8	10, 38n6, 135n30
12:10	102, 267n11, 295
12:11	12n34, 95, 101, 110, 128, 138n47, 141, 141n61, 144, 145, 146, 147, 166, 189n55, 316
12:12	7n21, 13, 15n42, 101, 102, 139n54, 140, 141n65, 142, 144, 145, 146, 147, 147n70, 182n23, 190, 194, 195n76, 195n77, 234, 297n55, 396n110
12:13–14	101, 140, 166
12:13	7n15, 7n19, 92, 102, 118
12:14–19	142
12:14	12n34, 95, 128, 138n47, 144, 316, 336
12:15–28	6
12:15–27	102
12:15–16	261
12:15	7, 92, 189
12:16	145, 147. 189
12:17	110, 144
12:18	15n42, 16, 101, 102, 128, 138n47, 139n54, 141n65, 142, 144, 145, 146, 147, 147n70, 165, 182n23, 190, 195n76, 195n77, 234, 297n55, 299, 316, 396n110, 397
12:19	7n15, 7n19, 7n21, 92, 118, 195n77
12:20–28	142, 190
12:20–25	261
12:20–23	9
12:20–22	92
12:20	7n24, 92, 111, 336, 360n40
12:21	12n34, 91, 138n47, 166, 189, 189n55, 316
12:22	189
12:23–25	189
12:25	7n21, 92, 111n42, 189, 310n110
12:26–27	101
12:26	12n34, 128, 138n47, 141n61, 316
12:27	166
12:28—13:19[18]	6, 261
12:28	7n19, 7n21, 92, 111n42, 189, 310n110, 324n49, 384n58
12:29—13:19[18]	100
12:29–32	274
12:29–31	278–79
12:29	265, 360n40
12:30	7n15, 7n19, 7n21, 92, 110n36, 118
12:31	271
13	51, 93, 100, 364, 367, 386
13:1[12:32]	7n19, 42, 92, 183, 261
13:2–19[1–18]	269, 274
13:2–6[1–5]	110, 361, 364
13:2–3[1–2]	386n69
13:2[1]	262n76, 365
13:3–4[2–3]	342
13:3[2]	97, 110n38, 120, 262n76, 274n34, 321n36, 326
13:4–5[3–4]	100
13:4[3]	xvi, 7n20, 92, 97, 109, 118, 152n3, 294, 325n53
13:5[4]	15n40, 92, 97, 116n81, 116n83, 118, 121, 284n8, 285, 294, 297n53, 298, 325n52, 395n108
13:6–7[5–6]	274n34
13:6[5]	17n49, 53, 53n68, 54n69, 54n71, 99, 101, 114, 117, 119n102, 149, 266, 270, 270n21, 271, 271n24, 300n63, 315n15, 398n117
13:7–12[6–11]	288n21
13:7[6]	98, 110n38
13:8[7]	318
13:9[8]	110n37, 266, 273
13:10[9]	266, 318n30
13:11[10]	7n20, 17n49, 54n69, 54n71, 99, 119n102, 149, 266, 270n21, 300n63, 315n15, 398n117
13:12–17[11—16]	280
13:12[11]	15, 92, 273, 284n8, 285, 288, 297, 394, 396
13:13–19[12–18]	386
13:14–15[13–14]	386n70

INDEX OF BIBLICAL REFERENCES

13:14[13]	110n38, 274n34	15	234
13:15[14]	184, 271	15:1–18	98
13:16–19[15–18]	101, 386	15:1	318
13:16–17[15–16]	280	15:2–3	98
13:16[15]	266, 386	15:3	98, 337n4
13:17[16]	166n54, 280n64	15:5	7n19, 136n36, 152n3, 325n52, 384n58, 38n6
13:18[17]	7n21, 92, 325	15:6	92
13:19[18]	7n19, 38n6, 92, 116n83, 118n98, 152n3, 325n52, 384n58, 386	15:7	92, 98
		15:9–10	92
		15:9	7n15, 7n19, 7n21, 7n24, 92, 98, 116n83, 118, 241
14:1–21	6, 16, 102, 142, 147, 166n56, 189, 299, 397, 401	15:10	16, 221, 270n22, 299, 397
14:1–2	50, 145, 281, 317, 401	15:11–12	98
14:1	49n53, 56, 59, 97, 147, 149n78, 206n28, 270, 340	15:11	157n27
		15:12	234
14:2	16, 56, 97, 102, 115, 120, 149, 205n24, 206n28, 251n43, 270, 273, 274, 291, 299, 336, 397	15:15	7n17, 38n6, 53, 53n68, 92, 99, 119n102, 270n21, 315n15
		15:16	109
14:3	271	15:19–23	101, 142, 194
14:20–23	143	15:19–20	144
14:21–27	142n65	15:19	145, 147
14:21	56, 97, 149, 205n24, 206n28, 270, 273, 274, 281, 291, 337n4	15:20	12n34, 101, 138n47, 139n54, 145, 147, 316
		15:21	165, 272n27
14:22—16:17	6		
14:22–29	142, 182n22, 194	16	389n83
14:22–27	101	16:1–17	11, 140, 189
14:22–19	143	16:1–8	13n35, 101, 140n57, 145
14:22	110	16:1–5	223
14:23–25	101, 189n55	16:1	54n69, 99, 313, 383n53
14:23	7n20, 7n21, 12, 12n34, 92, 97, 101, 110, 116n81, 138n47, 139n54, 140, 144, 145, 146, 147, 148n72, 273n30, 284n8, 285, 298, 309, 310, 316, 394	16:2	12n34, 101, 138n47, 144, 146, 316
		16:3	7n17, 92
		16:6–7	101, 316
		16:6	12n34, 138n47, 144, 146
		16:7	12n34, 138n47
14:24–27	190	16:9–12	13n35, 101, 140n57, 142n65, 145
14:24–26	9		
14:24	12n34, 138n47	16:10–11	145, 147
14:25	12n34, 138n47	16:11–14	16, 299, 397
14:26	15n42, 16, 101, 139n54, 141n65, 142, 144, 145, 147, 297n55, 299, 396n110, 397	16:11–12	101
		16:11	12n34, 13, 15n42, 98, 99, 101, 102, 138n47, 139n54, 140, 141n65, 142, 144, 145, 146, 147n70, 182n23, 190, 194, 195n76, 195n77, 229n17, 234, 297n55, 396n110
14:27–29	13, 101, 140, 142, 144, 145, 147n70, 180		
14:27	102, 182n23, 190, 195n76		
14:28	110, 318		
14:29	7n21, 98, 99, 101, 102, 182n23, 190, 195n76, 195n77, 221, 229n17, 389n83	16:12	7n17, 7n19, 92, 99, 119n102, 138n45, 313, 315n15,

469

Deuteronomy (continued)

16:13–17	13n35, 101, 140n57, 142n65, 145
16:14–15	15n42, 141n65, 297n55, 396n110
16:14	98, 99, 101, 102, 142, 144, 146, 147n70, 182n23, 190, 195n76, 195n77, 229n17, 234
16:15–16	101, 145, 147, 316
16:15	12n34, 138n47, 221
16:16–17	194
16:16	12, 12n34, 101, 138, 138n47, 139, 140, 144, 145, 148, 148n73, 234
16:18—18:22	6, 99, 184n35, 336, 361, 365, 366, 369
16:17—17:13	99
16:18—17:7	360
16:18–20	11, 183, 337
16:18	97, 99, 100, 117n92, 117n93, 182, 360, 365
16:19	182
16:20	4, 7n21, 9, 97, 99, 117, 117n93, 120, 121, 185, 215, 227, 270, 302, 311, 336, 343n21, 346, 361, 392, 399
16:21—17:7	97
16:21	102, 189
17	153
17:1–7	274
17:1	271
17:2–7	100, 183, 266, 269
17:2	56n75, 91, 358n32
17:3	110n38, 117, 273, 274n34
17:4	184, 271
17:5–7	185, 271
17:5	183n24
17:6	266
17:7	266, 271, 271n24, 318n30
17:8–13	13, 101, 100, 140, 144, 145, 146, 147, 183, 185, 288, 335, 360
17:8–9	183, 185
17:8	12n34, 101, 110, 138n47, 182, 183n27, 184, 184n35, 316
17:9	183, 183n27, 184, 184n34, 184n35, 187, 187n44, 337, 366
17:10–12	183, 184
17:10	7n19, 12n34, 138n47, 184, 184n35, 316
17:11	119n101, 184n35, 185
17:12–20	366
17:12–13	269
17:12	139, 184n35, 185, 187, 271, 271n24
17:13	7n20, 14, 15, 15n41, 24n21, 92, 273, 284n8, 285, 297, 297n54, 394, 395, 395n109, 396
17:14–20	viii, xxii, 16, 20, 46, 47, 86, 91, 92, 95, 98, 99, 100, 232, 261, 263, 299, 310, 317, 335–48, 335, 336, 341, 341n18, 344, 345, 346, 347, 348, 360, 361, 369, 370, 397
17:14–15	9
17:14	7n24, 92, 316, 336, 341, 360n40, 365, 369
17:15–16	369
17:15	86, 98, 137, 336, 347, 365, 366, 366n57, 369
17:16–20	337
17:16–17	337, 341, 343
17:16	7n22, 92, 343
17:17	92, 343
17:18–20	11, 47n35, 337, 338
17:18–19	24, 42, 310, 314n12, 347, 399
17:18–13	183
17:18	23, 39, 119n101, 162, 183, 187, 187n44, 338, 347, 348, 366
17:19–20	14, 24n21, 92, 98, 136n35, 297, 310, 326n59, 395, 7n21
17:19	7n19, 7n20, 15n40, 92, 97, 116n81, 118, 119n101, 121, 273n30, 284n8, 285, 294n42, 297n53, 298, 309, 338, 339, 394, 395n108
17:20	136n36, 185, 310n109, 320n33, 345, 346, 347, 369
18	357
18:1–8	9, 16, 99, 100, 177n3, 180, 183, 191, 195, 299, 335, 337, 360, 360, 397
18:1–2	180n15
18:1	183n27, 187n44, 366
18:2	92, 98
18:3	30, 183n27

INDEX OF BIBLICAL REFERENCES

18:4	110	18:21–22	363, 368
18:5–8	144, 146	18:21	7n24, 92, 360n40, 364
18:5	11, 116, 120, 168n65, 187, 337	18:22	284, 360
18:6–8	9, 13, 101, 140, 145, 191, 195	19–25	36, 91
		19:1—25:19	6
18:6–7	145, 147	19:1–13	269
18:6	12n34, 101, 102, 138n47, 182, 182n23, 190, 195n76, 316	19:1	265, 316, 360n40
		19:6	7n21
		19:8–13	185n39
18:7	98, 130n14, 139n54, 187	19:8	92, 99, 111, 138n46, 168n65
18:9–22	viii, x, 9, 99, 100, 243, 243n14, 335, 337, 349–73, 350, 351, 353, 357, 359, 359–69, 360, 361, 362, 365, 368n59, 377, 377n13	19:9	7n19, 38n6, 97, 109, 117, 118n98, 136n36, 270, 339n10
		19:10	92
18:9–20	16, 299	19:11–13	266
18:9–19	243	19:11	109, 272n27
18:9–14	243n15, 269n17, 363	19:12–22	13
18:9–13	xi, 363, 369	19:13	110n37, 271, 271n24, 273
18:9–12	274n37	19:14	283
18:9	269n17, 360, 360n40, 363n46, 365	19:15–21	184, 185, 288
		19:15–19	350
18:10–11	364	19:17–19	99
18:12	269n17, 278, 363	19:17	139n54, 183n27, 184, 184n30, 185, 187, 187n44
18:13	363, 364		
18:14–20	365	19:18–21	266
18:14–19	369	19:19	271, 271n24
18:14	xi, 363, 363n46, 364	19:20	7n20, 14, 15, 15n41, 24n21, 273, 284n8, 285, 297, 297n54, 394, 395, 395n109, 396
18:15–22	12, 38, 110, 242, 261, 376, 377n12, 386		
18:15–20	363	19:21	110n37, 273
18:15–19	243n15, 335n2, 351, 359, 365	20	268, 274n37
18:15–18	144, 146, 350	20:1–4	183
18:15	2n6, 93, 98, 242, 335, 349, 350, 351, 356, 356n28, 357, 358, 363, 366, 366n57, 367, 369, 371, 373, 377n14	20:1	53, 99, 114n67, 284n8, 285, 288, 337, 360n40
		20:2	183n27, 187n44
18:16–20	367	20:3–4	115
18:16	6, 15, 36n3, 128, 127, 128, 138n45, 144, 145, 146, 148, 287n16, 287n18, 297, 367, 395	20:3	7n24, 38, 92, 284, 284n8, 285, 287
		20:4	52
		20:5–7	7n21
18:17–20	364	20:5	234
18:17	357	20:6	234
18:18–20	350n6	20:7	234
18:18–19	386	20:8	285, 289
18:18	38, 93, 98, 349, 350, 335, 144, 351, 366, 367, 369	20:10–18	279
		20:10–17	268
18:19	335, 357n30, 367	20:10–15	267n10
18:20–22	243, 243n16, 335	20:10	360n40
18:20	110n38, 261, 269, 274n34, 368, 386	20:13	265, 266
		20:14	280

471

Deuteronomy (continued)

20:15	268
20:16–18	280
20:17	92, 113, 268n12, 386n70, 386n71
20:19	360n40
20:22	391
21:1–9	183, 185n39
21:5	16, 183n27, 187, 187n44, 299, 337, 386n66, 397
21:8–9	183n24
21:8	53, 56, 99, 270n21, 332n78
21:9	271, 271n24
21:10–14	98, 227, 235, 237
21:10	360n40
21:11	109
21:12–13	7n20
21:14	235
21:15–17	228, 235
21:15–16	109
21:16	110n37
21:18–21	185n39, 228, 233n33, 235, 266, 269, 271, 288
21:18	116n83, 266, 325n52
21:19	113n59
21:20	116n83, 325n52
21:21	7n20, 15, 227, 271, 271n24, 273, 284n8, 285, 297, 394, 396
21:22–23	272
21:22	266, 272n27, 299n58
21:23	332
21:29	113
22:1–4	98
22:5	271
22:6–7	97
22:7	7n21, 111n42, 310n109, 310n110, 316, 320n33, 339n11
22:8	360n40
22:9	7n21
22:13–21	185n39, 228, 235
22:13–19	235
22:15	113
22:18	266
22:19	110n37, 236
22:20–24	266
22:20–21	228, 235, 269, 271
22:21	227, 271, 271n24
22:22–29	228
22:22	227, 228, 271
22:23–29	236
22:23–27	228
22:23–24	236, 270
22:24	113, 227, 271, 271n24
22:25–27	236
22:25	113n59, 270
22:27	52n64
22:28–29	237n41
22:29	110n37
23:2–4[1–3]	144, 147
23:4–9[3–8]	389
23:4–7[3–6]	120
23:4–5[3–4]	92, 366
23:6[5]	97, 109, 270n22
23:7[6]	116
23:8–9[7–8]	120
23:8[7]	99, 115n76, 120
23:9[8]	144, 147
23:10[9]	7n19, 360n40
23:15[14]	204n21, 325n55
23:16–17[15–16]	99
23:16[16]	52n63, 316
23:17[16]	386n66
23:18–19[17–18]	271
23:18[17]	98
23:19[18]	95, 137n43, 147
23:20–21[19–20]	98
23:21[20]	7n21, 16, 145, 299, 337n4, 397
23:24[23]	7n19
24	155
24:1–5	97, 98
24:1–4	228, 237, 273
24:1	53n68, 98, 16n44, 242, 298n57, 396n112
24:3	318n30
24:4	110n37, 139n54, 271
24:5	142n65, 234
24:7	98, 271, 271n24
24:8	7n19, 7n17, 183, 183n27, 187, 187n44, 366
24:9	92
24:10	49n53, 360n40
24:11	119n102
24:13	4, 97, 117n92, 117n93, 139n54
24:14	99, 182n23
24:16	117n92, 266
24:17–22	97, 98
24:17	98, 182
24:18	7n17, 53, 92, 99, 119n102, 138n45, 270n21, 313, 315n15

INDEX OF BIBLICAL REFERENCES

24:19–21	99, 229n17	26:7	111, 114
24:19	7n21, 221, 360n40	26:8	15, 54n69, 99, 256n63, 262n76, 265, 267n9, 284, 285, 289, 298, 315, 368n62, 394, 396
24:22	7n17, 92, 99, 119n102, 315n15		
25:1–3	266	26:9	16, 160n30, 171n75, 261, 299, 397
25:1	4, 117, 117n91, 117n92, 117n93, 120	26:10	50, 57, 117, 120, 139n54
25:3	7n21	26:11	15n42, 101, 141n65, 142, 144, 146, 297n55, 396n110
25:5–10	98, 185n39, 228, 238		
25:5–9	98	26:11–13	182n23, 195n77, 389n83
25:5–6	231	26:12–13	98, 99, 144, 147n70, 180, 229n17
25:5	48n45		
25:7–10	266	26:12	13, 101, 102, 110, 140, 145, 190, 195n76, 360n40
25:7	238		
25:8	238	26:13–15	7n24, 92
25:11–12	228, 266, 273n31	26:13–14	384n58
25:12	110n37, 228	26:13	139n54
25:13–16	97, 283	26:14	116n83, 152n3, 325n52
25:15	4, 7n21, 117n91, 117n92, 117n93, 310n109, 320n33, 339n11	26:15	16, 56, 99, 138n46, 144, 146, 160n30, 168n65, 171n75, 299, 314n14, 397
25:16	271	26:16—26:69[29:1]	xi, 154
25:17–19	92, 268	26:16–28:68	155
25:17–18	92, 290	26:16–19	9, 16, 39n7, 41, 75, 76n42, 90, 138n45, 152n3, 153n3, 154, 157, 168, 172, 299, 333, 389, 397
25:17	7n17		
25:18	7n20, 116, 116n81, 284n8, 285, 291, 291n29, 296n49, 296n50, 309n104, 393n101, 394n102		
		26:16–18	7n19
		26:16–17	315n16
25:19	7n18	26:16	36n1, 38n6, 90, 91, 92, 172, 314n9, 321n36, 325n53
26	41, 90, 100, 152, 152n3	26:17–19	114
26:1–15	6, 9, 143	26:17–18	96
26:1–11	13, 16, 101, 140, 142n65, 145, 194, 274, 299, 392, 397	26:17	38n6, 81, 97, 116, 117, 118n98, 120, 152n3, 270, 325n52, 339n10
26:1	12n34	26:18–19	92, 145, 317
26:2–10	54–55	26:18	38n6, 56, 118n98, 149, 251n43, 270, 273, 274
26:2–3	145, 147		
26:2	101, 138n47, 145, 316	26:19	3, 49, 49n53, 56, 115, 149, 153n3, 205n24, 206n28, 220, 226, 270, 274, 218, 281, 290, 291, 317, 332, 402
26:3–4	144, 146		
26:3	7n24, 92, 99, 115n74, 138n46, 143, 144, 168n65, 314n14, 323n42		
26:4	183n27		
26:5–10	7n24, 92, 99, 143	27–28	90
26:5–9	92, 256	27	vii, xi, xxi, 41, 76, 90, 119, 138n49, 146, 152–76, 154, 154n10, 154n12, 155, 156, 163, 168, 170, 171, 172, 173, 174,
26:5–8	138n45, 261		
26:5	17n48, 53, 111, 113, 115, 139n54, 300n62, 314, 320n35, 398n116		
26:6	315	27:1–26	40, 155, 277n55, 315
26:6–8	17n49, 300n63, 398n117		

473

Deuteronomy (continued)

27:1–8	ix, 23, 41, 90, 12, 142n65, 152, 152n1, 153n7, 156, 156n26, 157, 158, 169
27:1	2n6, 38n6, 118n98, 136n36, 152, 155n18, 157, 158, 160
27:2–8	154, 168
27:2–4	156, 172
27:2–3	ix, 155, 155n18, 158, 159, 160, 161, 267n11
27:2	157, 160, 161, 162n41, 174
27:3	16, 114n68, 119n101, 138n46, 153, 155n18, 156, 160, 160n30, 299, 313, 314n12, 397
27:4–8	ix, 154n10, 158, 159, 161, 163
27:4–7	155, 156n21
27:4–5	157n28, 170
27:4	38n6, 154, 155n18, 157, 162n41, 163n45, 163n46, 174,
27:5–7	102, 156
27:5–6	155n18, 165
27:5	155n18
27:6–7	165
27:7	139n54, 141n65, 145, 155n18, 166n54, 170
27:8	119n101, 153, 155n18, 156, 163n45, 163n46, 167, 168, 314n12
27:9–26	183
27:9–10	90, 114, 152, 156, 156n26, 160, 171, 183n27, 389
27:9	2n6, 16, 38, 38n6, 152, 171, 183n27, 187, 187n44, 299, 314n9, 366, 397
27:10	76, 116n83, 153n3, 325n52, 38n6
27:11–26	41, 90, 152, 156, 156n26, 157, 171
27:11–13	155, 171
27:11	152, 157
27:12–13	156, 161, 171
27:12	155, 157, 172, 174
27:13	157
27:14–26	155, 171, 173
27:14	171, 173, 187
27:15–26	156, 171, 173
27:15	221n70, 273n32, 274
27:19	229n17
27:26	119n101, 314n12
28	7n25, 41, 61, 74, 77, 89, 90, 91, 93, 100, 152, 152n3, 153, 154, 171, 209n42, 210, 266, 269, 312, 324, 335, 338
28:1–69[29:1]	17, 32n46, 38, 40, 57, 124n127, 155, 300n65, 360, 398, 398n11928:1–68 91, 312
28:1–14	3, 6, 9, 16, 41, 90, 153n3, 16, 172, 261, 274, 299, 316, 326n57, 397
28:1–8	40
28:1–4	136n35
28:1–2	116, 120, 325n52
28:1	7n19, 38n6, 57, 115, 152n3, 153n3, 172, 384n58
28:2	153n3
28:5	15
28:6	141n60
28:7	291
28:8–10	219
28:8	291
28:9–10	172, 282, 317
28:9	7n19, 56, 57, 92, 97, 117, 118n98, 153n3, 270, 339n10
28:10	115, 139n51, 284n8, 285, 291
28:11–12	291
28:11	115n74, 138n46, 168n65, 314n14, 323n42, 327
28:12	221
28:13	7n19, 38n6, 115, 291, 384n58
28:14	9, 38n6, 97, 110n38, 172, 185, 274n34
28:15–69[29:1]	6
28:15–68	2n6, 9, 17, 24, 73, 90, 103, 274, 290,299, 300, 312, 316, 319, 320, 321n37, 323, 333, 397, 398
28:15	7n19, 36n2, 38n6, 116n83, 118n99, 153n3, 325n52, 384n58
28:18	63n18
28:19	141n60
28:20–29	266
28:20	110n36, 265, 274, 325n51, 386
28:22	265
28:24	110n36
28:26	284, 303

INDEX OF BIBLICAL REFERENCES

28:27–28	265	29:3[4]	38n6, 135n34, 314n9
28:29	52	29:4–5[5–6]	99, 315
28:31	52	29:4[5]	245
28:35–37	266	29:6–7[7–8]	315
28:35	265	29:8–17[9–18]	168
28:36	110n38, 273n32, 274n34, 365	29:8[9]	56n75, 91, 118, 121
28:37	265	29:9–12[10–13]	333, 389
28:45	7n19, 36n2, 110n36, 116n83, 118n98, 118n99, 153n3, 325n52	29:9–10[10–11]	153
		29:9[10]	38n6, 118n95, 131n14, 133n22, 139n54
28:46	262n76	29:11[12]	16, 17n51, 56n75, 114, 299, 300n66, 38n6, 397, 398n120
28:47	5, 97		
28:48	110n36	29:12[13]	56, 99, 313
28:49	318, 318n30	29:13–20[14–21]	274
28:51	110, 110n36	29:13–14[14–15]	313
28:52	295	29:13[14]	17n51, 56n75, 300n66, 398n120
28:55–66	266		
28:58–59	290	29:14–27[15–28]	77
28:58	7n19, 7n20, 39, 15n40, 116n81, 119n101, 284, 284n8, 285, 294n44, 297n53, 298, 314n12, 394, 395n108, 396	29:14[15]	38n6, 131n14, 139n54
		29:15–16[16–17]	313, 313n4
		29:16–20[17–21]	324
		29:16–17[17–18]	315
		29:16[17]	273n32
28:59	110n34, 393n98	29:17[18]	38n6
28:60	248n34, 284	29:17–27[18–28]	316, 319, 389n82
28:61	13, 39, 103, 110n36, 119n101, 314n12	29:18[19]	56n75, 325n50
		29:19–27[20–28]	17, 300, 398
28:62	115, 116n83, 153n3, 325n52	29:19[20]	39, 216n63, 265
		29:20[21]	13n37, 17n51, 39, 103, 119n101, 300n65, 337n4, 398n120
28:63	110n36, 111n42, 327		
28:64	110n38, 265, 274n34, 318, 325	29:21–27[22–28]	326
		29:22[23]	109, 113
28:65	135n34, 201n13, 265	29:24–27[25–28]	325n50
28:66–67	116n78	29:24[25]	54n69, 56n75, 97, 99, 114, 114n68, 313, 325n51, 386
28:66	284, 392n93		
28:67	135n32, 265, 284	29:25[26]	110n38, 117, 274n34
28:68	255	29:26[27]	13n37, 39
28:69—29:20[29:1–21]	138n45	29:27[28]	314n9, 325
28:69—29:1[29:1–2]	7n25	29:28[29]	119n101, 314n12
28:69[29:1]	16, xvi, 39n9, 40, 41, 56n75, 76n42, 91, 114, 138n45, 211, 299, 384n57, 397		
		30	78, 323
		30:1–20	6
		30:1–10	xiv, 17, 57, 59, 82, 216, 319, 321, 323, 324, 333, 389n85, 398
29–30	76n42, 90		
29:1[2]—30:20	38, 40, 41, 91, 157, 312, 338		
		30:1–3	316, 324
29	77	30:1–2	324
29:1–28[2–29]	6	30:1	91, 136n36, 314, 316, 323, 324n49, 325n50
29:1–27[2–28]	57		
29:1–2[2–3]	6, 262n76, 267n9	30:2	116n83, 153n3, 265, 321n36, 323, 324, 325, 325n52, 384n58, 38n6
29:1[2]	2n6, 36n3m 38, 40, 55		
29:2[3]	315, 368n62		

Deuteronomy (continued)

30:3–5	316, 324
30:3	265, 316, 323, 323n46, 324, 325, 327, 327n60, 327n62
30:4–8	324, 325
30:4–5	325
30:4	270n20, 318, 325
30:5	138n46, 310n110, 313, 327, 327n62
30:6–10	73, 323
30:6–8	400
30:6	73, 97, 109, 135, 216n60, 321n36, 324, 325, 326, 328n63, 389, 389n84
30:7	324n48, 326, 330
30:8–9	324
30:8	38n6, 116n83, 153n3, 323, 325n52, 326, 327n60, 384n58
30:9–10	324, 327
30:9	313, 323, 327
30:10–14	59
30:10	13n37, 39, 103, 116n83, 118n98, 118n99, 119n101, 153n3, 300, 314, 321n36, 323, 324, 325, 325n52, 327
30:11–20	7n25, 16, 138n45, 299, 396, 397
30:11–14	240, 24n22
30:11	38n6, 110, 136n36, 304n89
30:14	304n89
30:15–20	21n12, 38, 41, 46, 57
30:15	38n6, 91, 314
30:16	36n1, 36n2, 38n6, 97, 109, 110, 117, 118n98, 118n99, 270, 326n58, 339n10, 384n58
30:17	110n38, 117, 274n34
30:18	38n6, 310n109, 320n33, 339n11
30:19	38n6, 91, 283, 314
30:20	97, 99, 109, 115n74, 116n83, 138n46, 153n3, 168n65, 313, 314n14, 316, 323n42, 325n52
31:1—34:12	138n45
31	10, 77, 153, 157n27, 163
31:1–29	57
31:1–8	40, 153n7
31:1	2n6, 91
31:2	2n6, 38n6, 313
31:3–8	315
31:3	110n36, 274n37
31:4	110n36, 265
31:5	136n36
31:6	115, 284, 284n8, 285, 288
31:7	2n6, 115n74, 138n46, 168n65
31:8	115, 284, 284n8, 285, 287
31:9–13	1, 11, 13, 13n35, 17, 29, 37, 42, 45, 57, 76101, 105, 122, 140, 145, 147, 153, 153n4, 154, 167, 170, 183, 187, 276n48, 301, 310, 338, 398
31:9–11	183n27
31:9	39, 57, 96, 119n101, 133n22, 144, 153, 183n27, 186, 187, 187n44, 210, 314n12
31:10–13	298
31:10–12	124, 142
31:10	24, 2n6, 157n27, 318
31:11–13	14, 23, 25, 206n32, 297, 326n59, 395, 399
31:11–12	314n12
31:11	12, 12n34, 101, 119n101, 138, 138n47, 139, 140, 145, 148, 148n73, 316
31:12–13	116, 120, 273n30, 394
31:12	15n40, 36n3, 116n81, 119n101, 144, 147n70, 182n23, 234, 284n8, 285, 294, 294n41, 297n53, 310, 389, 389n83, 395n108
31:13	116n81, 148n72, 284n8, 285, 310
31:14–23	40
31:14–22	38
31:14–21	329
31:14–20	316
31:14–16	313
31:16–21	314, 389n82
31:16–20	57
31:16–18	10, 17, 77, 300, 326, 330, 398
31:16	97, 909, 114, 110, 118, 138n46, 145, 274, 287, 313, 386
31:17–18	316, 320
31:17	36n3
31:18	110n38, 274n34, 386n67
31:19–22	187
31:19	39, 91, 122, 154
31:20–21	314n14, 330
31:20	97, 99, 118, 138n46, 160n30, 168n65, 274,

INDEX OF BIBLICAL REFERENCES

	274n34, 316, 323n42, 386n67	32:16	271
		32:17	284
31:21	38n6, 110, 115, 168n65	32:18	340
31:22	2n6, 39, 91, 122	32:19–35	329
31:23	157n27, 168n65, 314n14, 315	32:19–25	274, 316, 319, 329, 330
		32:19–22	269
31:24–29	153n7, 157, 314	32:20	318n29, 329n66, 330, 393
31:24–26	37, 124, 153, 183n27, 338	32:22–25	279
31:24	39, 119n101, 314n12	32:23–27	266
31:25–26	96	32:25	265, 284, 331, 332
31:25	2n6, 57, 157n27, 210	32:26–35	329
31:26	13n37, 39, 57, 103, 110, 119n101, 210, 214n54	32:27	284, 330
		32:29	21n12, 318
31:26–29	17, 300, 398	32:32	113
31:27–29	10, 77, 153, 316, 319, 326	32:35	331
31:27–19	389n82	32:36–43	17, 300, 319, 398
31:27	38n6, 318n30	32:36–42	316, 329, 330
31:28–30	40	32:36	16, 56, 119, 299, 316, 329n66, 330, 332, 332n77, 396
31:28	36n3, 57, 133n22, 153		
31:29	153, 154, 318, 318n29, 318n30, 319, 322, 384n58	32:37–42	331
		32:37–38	330
31:30	36n3	32:37	330
		32:38	330
32	xiv, 16, 33n49, 38, 39, 43, 91, 269, 299, 329–32, 397	32:39–42	332
32:1–48	154	32:39	265, 330, 331
32:1–43	vii, 6, 10, 11, 35, 38, 39, 40, 312, 338	32:40–42	331
		32:41	331, 332
32:1–18	77	32:42	330, 331
32:1–14	274	32:43	xi, 17, 43n18, 44, 300, 317, 329, 331, 332, 334, 398
32:1–12	329		
32:1–4	329	32:44–47	40
32:2–5	127	32:44–46	187
32:3	15, 16, 256n62, 298, 299, 396, 397	32:44	2n6
		32:45	2n6, 324n49
32:4	4, 16, 78, 97, 117n92, 263n80, 270, 299, 330, 339n10, 393, 397	32:46–47	10n31
		32:46	38n6, 119n101, 314n12
		32:47	310n109, 320n33, 339n11
32:5–18	329	32:48—33:2	40
32:5–6	329	32:48–52	245, 260, 261, 313
32:6	2n6, 340	32:48	38n6, 314n9
32:7–14	329	32:49–52	260
32:7	7n17	32:49	172, 261n74
32:8–9	251	32:50	56
32:8	43	32:51	261, 263
32:9	56, 97, 251n42	32:52	261n74
32:10	315		
32:11	144	33	39
32:12	110	33:1–26	6, 38, 313
32:13–43	329	33:1	2n6, 261
32:13–14	16, 299, 327, 329, 397	33:2–29	40, 338
32:15–27	389n82	33:2	127, 144, 383n54
32:15–25	332	33:3	56, 270n22
32:15–18	316, 329, 329, 330	33:4	119n101

477

Deuteronomy (continued)

33:5	57
33:6	114
33:7	56, 110n36
33:8–11	11, 16, 299, 350n6, 397
33:8–10	185
33:8	118
33:9–10	2, 23, 42
33:9	118, 121
33:10	18n56, 47n36, 102, 119n101, 185, 187, 204n22, 280n64
33:12	295
33:13	111, 171n75
33:18	142n65
33:19	4, 117n93
33:21	117n89, 117n92, 117n93
33:26	57
33:27	265, 266
33:28	110, 110n40, 111, 295
33:29	46, 53
34	350
34:1–12	40, 245
34:1–8	41
34:1–3	112, 261
34:1	257, 261
34:2	318n30
34:4	99, 115, 261, 314n14
34:5–12	254
34:5	261, 380
34:6	263, 314n9, 38n6
34:7	124n127
34:9–12	41
34:10–12	263, 368
34:10	2n6, 93, 110, 242, 263, 350, 368, 384
34:11	55, 315, 359n36, 378, 379n26, 380n36
34:12	256n63, 284, 285, 289n25, 394, 394n106

Joshua

Joshua, book of	275n45, 350, 380n40, 386n71
1:1	380n36
1:2	380n39
1:3	171
1:4	113n60
1:7–8	20, 21
1:8	3n8, 47, 47n35, 341, 348
2:8–11	280
3:3–14	214n54
3:10	113
4:1–24	172
4:1–9	161
4:19—5:12	155, 175
4:20	155
5:1–9	172
5:2–9	388, 388n80
5:2	388n80
5:6	388n81
5:7	388n80
5:10–12	172
5:10–11	388n80
5:12	208
6:5	207n33
6:6	214n54
6:15–25	276
6:17–20	277
6:17	386n71
6:18	386n71
6:20	207n33
7	174, 276
7:1	174, 386n71
7:2–3	174
7:6–26	280
7:9	173
7:11–13	174
7:11	174, 386n71
7:12	386n71
7:13	386n71
8	171
8:1–29	173
8:15	175
8:30–35	76, 138n49, 154n10, 162, 167, 173, 277n55
8:30–32	173
8:31–32	103
8:31	45n21, 165n51, 166n57
8:32	45n21
8:33–35	173
8:33	153n7, 173
8:35	173
9:1–2	173
9:1	113n64, 173
9:2	380n39
9:3–21	173
9:27	12n34, 138n47
10:1–43	175
10:1–5	173
10:6–43	173
10:6	246n26
10:8	175
10:42	175
11:1–15	175

11:3	113n64	2:7–12	18
11:20	175	2:8	380n36
12:8	113n64	2:10–12	192
12:21	191n63	2:10	24, 187, 216n62
13:33	180n15	2:11	358n32
14–19	138n49	2:16	365
14:4	190	2:18—3:21	103
14:8	328, 342n20	2:18	365
14:9	171, 342n20	2:22	70n32
14:14	342n20	3:5	113n64
15:29	164n48	3:7	103, 358n32
17:16–18	337	3:9	365
19:3	164n48	3:12	358n32
20:7–8	193n67	3:15–25	33
21	177, 186, 186n42, 190	3:15	365
21:1–45	178	4:5	184n33
21:1–42	102, 177	6:7–10	187n48
21:9	178	6:11–12	125n130
21:11	181, 193n67	6:14	378n24
21:12	180	6:24	103, 192n65
21:16	180	6:25–32	192n65
21:17	195	6:25–27	103
21:18	180, 193	6:25	192n65
21:21	193n67	7:1	111n47
21:22	180, 180n12	7:3–4	103
21:27	180, 193n67	7:5	103
21:32	193n67	7:6	103
21:34	180n12	7:8	103
21:36	193n67	7:9–10	103
21:38	193n67	7:12	103
22	267n11	7:17	103
22:19	102	9:11–14	103
22:20	386n71	10:11–14	187n48
22:23	166n57	10:16	110n38, 122n115
22:27	166n57	11:12–29	378n22
23:6	45n21, 103	11:20	295n46, 393n96
24	138n49, 162, 167	11:34–40	229n19
24:2–15	167n59	13:1–23	230n25
24:5	378n24, 379n26	13:12	184n33
24:11	113	14:3	389n86
24:14	122n115	15:11	389
24:16–24	167n59	15:18	389n86
24:23	110n38, 122n115	16:30	389
24:26–27	161n38	17–21	192
24:29	380n36	17–20	191, 191n63, 195n79
		17–18	103
		17	193

Judges

Judges, book of	29, 103, 193, 227, 229n20, 319n31, 389,	17:1–5	192
1:19	337	17:4	193
2:1–5	187n48	17:5	193
2:1	70, 78, 118n96, 215, 333n80	17:6	193
		17:7	192
		17:8	192
		17:9	192

Judges (continued)

17:10–13	192
18:1	193
18:3–4	192
18:5–6	192
18:19	192
18:27–31	192
18:30	103, 192, 319n31
19–21	341
19–20	193
19:1—20:7	193
19:1	193
19:27—20:6	193
20:1	163n48
20:13	271n24
20:26–27	138n49
20:26	166n57
20:27	214n54
20:40	280n64
21:4	166n57
21:6–23	193
21:19–24	229n19
21:19–21	138n49
21:25	193

Ruth

Ruth, book of	27, 33n50
1:8	233
1:9	201n13
2:10	296
3:1	201n13
4:5	231
4:10	231

1 Samuel

1 Samuel, book of	381
1–4	193n71
1–3	138n49
1:1	191, 191n63
1:10	250n38
1:19	191n63
2:10	86, 370
2:12–13	184n33
2:12	216n62
2:18—3:21	103
2:25	250n37
2:30	244n19
2:35	365
4:4–5	214n54
4:17	52n61

5:6–22	231
5:8–10	231
5:11	231
5:13–14	231
5:14	231
5:21	231
6:20	130n14
7:3–4	103, 191
7:3	110n38, 122n115
7:5	103, 191, 250
7:6	103, 191
7:8	103, 191
7:9–11	191
7:9–10	103
7:9	280n64
7:10	171n76
7:12	103, 161n38, 191
7:15–18	182
7:15–16	191
7:17	103, 191
8:1–5	182
8:10–11	184n33
8:11	338n9
8:11–18	343
8:11–17	341
8:19–20	341
9:11–14	103, 191
9:12–14	191n61
9:22–24	191
10:5	191n61
10:13	191n61
12–26	231
12:8	378n24, 379n26

2 Samuel

1:20	52n61, 52n62, 389n86
2:6	220n68
2:26	331n74
3:1	24
3:2–14	381n42
3:2–10	381
3:2–5	227
3:7	216n62
3:10	163n48
3:11–14	381
3:19–21	191
3:20	163n48
4:10	52n61, 52n62
4:11	271n24
5:7	137, 137n41
5:17–25	279n61
6:2	137
6:15	207n33

INDEX OF BIBLICAL REFERENCES

7	86, 370
7:1	137
7:11–16	86
7:13	138n50, 345
7:14–15	347n32
7:14	62, 86, 340n14
7:16	345
7:18–26	347
7:18–24	255n56
7:19	87, 370
7:23–27	87
7:23	53n66
7:27	250n38
7:29	345
8:15	117n89
11–12	227
11:1–27	229n19
11:13	141n64
11:25	331n74
12:1	378n25
12:11	378n24
12:23	247n29
12:24	347
13:1–19	229n19
13:14	341, 347, 370, 370n66
14:3	193n71
14:6	389n86
15:11	330n70, 378n25
15:12	161n38
15:18	378n24
15:20	378n24
15:23	253n49
15:24	214n54
15:29	193n71
15:29	330n70
15:35	330n70
16:1–5	103, 192
16:13–14	202
16:13	355n26
17:11	163n48
17:26	389n86
17:27–29	202
17:36	389n86
17:46	253n49
18:18	161n38
18:19–20	52n61, 52n62
18:20	52n61
18:22	52n61
18:25	52n61
18:26	52n61, 52n62
18:27	52n61
18:29	255, 379
18:31	52n61, 52n62
22:2–51	328
22:19–20	193n71
22:21	231
22:22	70n32
23:3	291n29
23:5	86, 214, 370
24:2	163n48
24:15	163n48
24:16	251n41, 322
24:18–25	103, 138n48, 192n65
24:18–22	231
24:25	166n57
28:3–25	368n59
28:12	171n76
29:3	255n56, 379n31
31:4	389n86
31:9	52n62
33:21	117n89

1 Kings

1:25	141n64
1:42	52n61, 52n62
1:51	193
2:2–4	18n59, 47n39, 125
2:3	3n8, 45n23, 341, 348
2:26	193
2:28–29	193
2:33	345
2:45	345
3:2	138n50
3:3–9	343
3:3	343, 343n23
3:4–28	343
3:4	103, 191n61, 192n65, 195
3:6	244n19, 342
3:9	135n34
3:10–15	343
3:12	135n34
3:14	342
3:16	130n14
4:10	271n24
5:6—8[4:26–28]	341
5:9–14[4:29–34]	343
5:13–18[4:33–5:4]	341
5:17–19[3–5]	138n50
6:7	165n51
8	343
8:1	137, 137n41
8:5	201n13
8:9	127n5
8:15	255n56
8:17–20	138n50
8:23	139n55
8:25	244n19

1 Kings (continued)

8:30	139n55, 216n63, 250n38
8:32	139n55
8:33	254n54
8:34	139n55, 216n63
8:35	250n38
8:36	139n55, 216n63
8:42	250n38
8:43	139n51, 139n55
8:44	138n50, 250n38
8:45	139n55
8:47	254n54
8:48	138n50, 250n38
8:49	139n55
8:50	216n63
8:51	54n72
8:59	254n54
9:1	109n31, 299n58
9:2–9	342
9:3	254n54
9:4	244n19, 342, 343
9:5	345
9:9	386n67
9:15–16	337
9:15	343
9:17–19	343
9:19	109n31, 299n58
9:20–22	343
9:24	343
9:25	166n57
9:26–28	343
10:1–25	343
10:9	340, 345
10:11–23	343
10:19	117n89
10:23	341
10:26–29	341
10:26	343
10:28–29	343
11:1–13	341
11:1–8	343
11:1	337
11:4	342, 343n22
11:6	342, 343n22
11:9–43	343
11:9–13	341
11:11–43	343
11:26	255n56, 379n31
11:30–39	343
11:32–33	343
11:32	343, 343–44
11:33	341
11:34	342
11:38	342
12–17	342
12:8	130n14
12:32–33	103, 192n65
13:1–5	103, 192n65
13:32	103, 192n65
14:2	378n21
14:5	184n32
14:6	378
14:7–16	343n21
14:8	342
14:14	365
14:16	345n27
14:18	380n38
14:22	343n22
15:3	342, 343n22
15:5	342
15:11	343
15:20	164n48
15:26	345n27
15:29	380n38
15:30	345n27
15:34	342n19, 343n21, 345n27
16:2	342, 343n21, 345n27
16:13	345n27
16:19	342n19, 343n21, 345n27
16:25	342n19
16:26	343n21, 345n27
16:30	342n19
16:31	337, 343n21
17:1	130n14
17:24	350n9, 351
18:15	130n14
18:30–35	103, 192n65
19:8–17	351
19:8	127n5
19:10	103, 192n65
19:11	130n14
19:14	103, 192n65
19:16	351n10
20:35	370n65
21:20	342n19
21:22	345n27
21:25	342n19
22:5	184n32
22:21	130n14
22:52	342n19, 343n21, 345n27
33:21	117n89

2 Kings

2 Kings, book of	45,
1:16–17	262n75
2:3	370n65

INDEX OF BIBLICAL REFERENCES

2:5	370n65	19:31	137
2:7	370n65	21:3–5	103, 192n65
2:15	370n65	20:3	244n19
3:2	342n19	21:7	12n34, 138n47
3:3	343n21, 345n27	21:10	380n37
3:14	130n14	21:11	345
4:1	370n65	21:16	345
4:12	130n14	21:17	345
4:23	201n8, 208	22:1—23:30	344
4:38	370n65	22:1–8	344
5:15	130n14	22:1	18n59
5:16	130n14	22:2	343, 344
5:18	216n63	22:8–16	348
5:22	370n65	22:8	44, 45
6:1	370n65	22:10	24
7:9	52n61	22:11	45, 47n39
8:9	130n14	22:12–13	344
8:27	342n19	22:12	255, 379
9:1	370n65	22:15–17	344
9:7	380n37	23:1–20	42
9:36	380n38	23:1–7	190, 196
10:10	380n38	23:1–3	344
10:29	345n27	23:3–16	125
10:31	46n27, 21n9, 343n21, 345n27	23:4–20	344
11:5–9	208	23:5	190, 191
13:2	342n19, 343n21, 345n27	23:8–20	3n8, 24, 89
13:6	345n27	23:8–9	190, 196
13:11	342n19, 343n21, 345n27	23:9	190
13:23	322n39	23:10–14	190
14:3–4	343n23	23:15–20	190
14:6	18n59, 45n21, 47n39, 104	23:15	345n27
14:24	342n19, 343n21, 345n27	23:20	190
14:25	380n38	23:21–23	344
15:9	342n19, 343n21, 345n27	23:24–25	344
15:18	342n19, 343n21, 345n27	23:24	45
15:24	342n19, 343n21, 345n27	23:25	45n23, 47n39, 18n59, 104, 328, 344, 348, 400
15:28	342n19, 343n21, 345n27		
15:29	164n48	23:27	12n34, 138n47
16:2	343n22	23:28–30	345
16:4	103, 192n65	23:32	345n26
16:7	61, 84, 340n14	23:37	345n26
16:10–16	192n65	24–25	77
16:28	208	24:2	380n37
17	77	24:3–4	341, 345
17:2	342n19	24:4	216n63
17:7–18	345	24:9	345n26
17:13	380n37	24:19	345n26
17:21	343n21	25:8	255n56, 379n31
17:23	380n37	25:23	241n5
18:3	343	25:27–30	345
19:15–19	250n40, 260n70	25:29	141n64
19:15	255n56		
19:18	221n70		
19:21	137		

1–2 Chronicles, books of 95, 380n40

1 Chronicles

3:1–9	227
4:29	164n48
6	177, 186, 186n42, 190
6:18–23[33–38]	191
6:18[33]	182
6:39–66[54–81]	102, 177, 178
6:39–41[13–15]	196n80
6:50[65]	178
6:53[68]	180n12
8:6	109n31
8:13	201n8
9:2	177n3
10:11–13	260n70
10:4	389n86
10:9	52n61, n62
11:5	137n41
13:1—16:43	32n47
13:1–3	177n3
13:2	102, 190
15:3	47n36
15:24–29	214n54
15:28	207n33, 207n34
16:1	166n57
16:15–18	78, 214, 322n39
16:15	70, 333n79
16:22	351n10
16:23	52n62
16:40	21n9, 46n27, 380n39
17	370
17:12	345
17:14	345
17:21	53n66
18:3	161n38
19:8	47n36
19:23	347
21:15	322
21:18	138n48
21:26	166n57
22:10	340n14, 345
22:12	46n27
22:15	221n71
23:18	45n23
23:31	201n8
26:29–32	177n3, 182
28:2	201n13
28:4	345
28:9[8]	216n62
28:10	330n71
28:21	221n71
29:1	221n71
29:10–29	250n40
30:16	45n23

2 Chronicles

2 Chronicles, book of	380n40
2:3	201n8
4:1	188
5:2	137n41, 214n54
5:10	127n5
6:21	216n63
6:25	216n63
6:27	216n63
6:30	216n63
6:39	216n63
7:14	139n51, 216n63, 250n38, 321n36
7:17	342, 343
7:22	386n67
8:6	109n31, 299n58
8:13	201n8
9:8	340
9:32	206
10:8	130n14
11:13–17	177n3
11:13–14	190
11:14	190
12:1	21n9, 46n27
13:6	255n56, 379n31
13:12	207n34
15:3	18n56
15:14	207n33, 207n34
16:4	164n48
16:6	214n54
17	86
17:3	342, 343
17:7–9	177n3
17:9	21n9, 46n27
18:4	184n32
18:20	130n14
19:4–11	177n3, 185n40
19:4–7	185n40
19:8–11	185n40
20:7	121n108
20:13	131n14
20:20	295n46, 393n96
23:1–11	190
23:2	190
23:4–8	208
24:6	380
25:4	45n22
25:8	255, 379
28:1	342, 343n22

INDEX OF BIBLICAL REFERENCES

29–31	180n11	8:1–8	348
29:2	342	8:1	25, 44, 45n21, 103
30:8	325n55	8:2	25
31:3–4	21n9, 46n27	8:3	45
31:3	201n8	8:5	32
31:13	201n8	8:8	206n32
31:17–20	177n3	8:9–13	25
31:19	190	8:13–18	25, 45
32:16	380n36	9:1—10:39	25
32:19	221n70	9:1	25
33:15	110n38, 122n115	9:2	25
34:2	342	9:3	21n9, 25, 46n27, 247n30
34:14	21n9, 45n24, 46n27	9:4	25
34:15	45n24	9:5–37	333n81
34:20	255, 379	9:5–9	25
35:6	45n25	9:10	263n76
35:12	45n22	9:13	127n6
35:20–27	345	9:38–39	25
35:26	46n27	10:21	206n30
36:21	202n17, 350n9	10:34	201n8
36:22–23	333	11:1	204n21
36:22	350n9	11:18	204n21
		13	200
		13:1	45n22
		13:26	347
		13:30	221n71

Ezra

1:1	333
2	334
3:2	45n23
6:12	12n34, 138n47
7:1–5	196n80
7:10	18n56, 21n9, 25, 31, 33, 46n27, 47n36
7:6	45n23, 348
9:11	380n37
9:15	130n14
10:1	247n30
10:16	184n32

Esther

Esther, book of	27

Job

1:1	291n29, 291n31, 296n49, 393n101
1:4–5	231
1:8	291n29, 291n31, 296n49, 309n104, 380n36, 380n39, 393n101
1:9	291n29, 291n31
2:3	291n29, 296n49, 309n104, 380n36, 380n39, 393n101
3:13	319n31
4:6	308n99
6:8	135n32
9:35	291n29
11:5	135n32
13:5	135n32
14:4	135n32
17:6	238n44
18:21	216n62
19:23	135n32
23:3	135n32

Nehemiah

1:9	12n34, 138n47
1:10	53n66
4:9	221n71
4:16	221n71
5:9	291n29
5:15	291n29
5:16	221n71
6:3	201n9, 221n71
6:9	221n71
7	334
7:2	291n29
8	3n8, 25, 45
8:1–18	125

Job (continued)

23:11	70n32
24:12	216n62
27:4	22n15
28:28	1, 27n1, 305n93, 306, 399n122
29:7–17	340n12
30:10	238n44
34:15	30n42
37:24	291n29
39:25	207n33
40–41	202n16
42:7	380n36, 380n39
42:8	250, 380n36, 380n39
42:10	325n54

Psalms

Psalms, book of (Psalter)	1n2, 20, 21, 22, 27, 29, 32, 45, 46, 46n29, 47, 49, 50, 104, 137, 220n68, 245n25, 257n65, 341, 370
1–41	46
1	18, 20, 46, 47, 47n35, 59, 341n16
1:1–3	51, 87
1:1–2	45, 47
1:1	20, 47n34, 291n29, 291n31, 296n49, 393n101
1:2	3n8, 20, 21, 22n15, 46, 341, 348
1:4–5	231
1:8	291n29, 291n31, 296n49, 309n104, 380n36, 380n39, 393n101
1:9	291n29, 291n31
2	20, 26, 87
2:3	291n29, 296n49, 309n104, 380n36, 380n39, 393n101
2:6–8	347
2:6	205n23
2:7	86
3–7	26
3:13	319n31
6:8	135n32
7:9[8]	330n68
8	84, 276n50
8:7[6]	220n69
9:9[8]	330n68
11:10	1
13:4	319n31
14:6	308n101
15	26
15:1	130n14
17 [LXX 18]	380n41
17:6	238n44
18:2[1]	22n14
18:22[21]	70n32
19	21, 46, 59
19:2[1]	220n69
19:7–13[6–12]	216n60
19:7–14[6–13]	18n57, 20, 47n37, 51, 375
22	26
23:1–2	202
23:2	201n13
23:3	135n32
23:4–6	134
23:11	70n32
24	26
24:3	130n14
24:5	375
24:12	216n62
25:10	220n68
25:11	216n63
26:6	112n54
28:5	220n69
29:7–17	340n12
30:9[8]	254n54
32	59
32:13–14	137
32:28	22n15
33	26
33:11	29
33:12	303n80
36	380n41
36:6[5]	220n68
36:11[10]	216n62
37:24	291n29
37:30	22n15
37:31	20n5, 216n60
37:34	70n32
39:10	52n61
39:25	207n33
40–41	202n16
40:8[7]	216n60
40:9[8]	20n5
40:10[9]	52n62
40:11[10]	220n68
42:10	325n54
42–72	46
42:7	380n36, 380n39
42:8	250, 380n36, 380n39
44	26
45	26
45:2–8[1–7]	345
46	26
46:2[1]	308n101

INDEX OF BIBLICAL REFERENCES

47	26	89:28[27]	347n32
47:6	207n33	89:30–38[29–37]	345
48	26	89:30[29]	345
50	26	89:31[30]	20n5
50:7	210n46	89:34[33]	220n68
51	26	89:37[36]	345
51:12[10]	216n60	89:46–51[45–50]	370
51:21[19]	280n64	89:47–52[46–51]	345
54:3[1]	330n69	89:50[49]	220n68
55:20[19]	291n29	90–106	46
56:14[13]	244n19	90:17	223
61:4[3]	308n101	91:2	308n101
62:8–9[7–8]	308n101	91:9	308n101
62:9[8]	308n101	91:14	109n31, 299n58
66	26	92	220
66:16	291n29	92:1–10[9]	220
67	26, 317n18	92:1	220
67:12	52n61	92:3[2]	220, 220n68
68:12[11]	52n62	92:5[4]	220n69
69:29[28]	151n81	92:6[5]	220n69
71:24	22n15	92:11–12[10–11]	220
71:7	308n101	92:13[12]	220
72	26, 87	92:16[15]	220
73–89	46	93	26
73:13	112n54	94:12	20n5
73:28	308n101	94:22	308n101
74	196	95–99	26
74:4	196n83	95	21, 26
74:8	177, 196	95:2	52n61
75	26	95:7–11	21
76	26	96:2	52n62
78:42	53n66	97	22
78:43	263n76	97:2	131n15
78:54	205n23	98	33
78:60	138n49	98:3	220n68
78:69–71	137n39	100	26
79:6	216n62	100:5	220n68
80	26	102:26[25]	220n69
81:11[10]	210n46	103:3	216n63
84	26	104	202n16
84:6[5]	303n82	104:29–30	30n42
84:13[12]	303n82	105–106	301n71
86:11	308n103	105	26
86:15	16n45, 397n113	105:12	320n35
86:25	299n58n59	105:15	351n10
87	26	105:25	54
87:4	216n62	105:26	378n24, 379n26
88:12[11]	220n68	105:27	263n76
89	26, 86, 370	105:42	380n36
89:2[1]	220n68	105:8–11	78, 214, 322n39
89:3[2]	220n68	105:8–10	70, 333n79
89:6[5]	206n31	106:19–23	245
89:25[24]	220n68	106:19	127n5
89:27–28[26–27[	86, 340n14, 347	106:23	130n14

487

Psalms (continued)

107–150	46
107	26
107:23	221
110	26, 87
111:2–9	70–71
111:5	215, 333n80
111:9	215, 333n80
111:10	305n93, 309n107, 399n122
115	26
115:2–8	241
115:4	221n70
115:7	22n15
116:1	22n14
116:9	244n19
119	18n57, 20, 21, 22, 26, 46, 47, 47n37, 51, 59, 375
119:11	79, 216n60
119:113	22
119:127	22
119:159	22
119:163	22
119:165	22
121	26
122	26
132	26, 86, 137n40, 370
132:12	62, 345
135:9	263n76
135:13–18	241n6
135:14	330
135:15	221n70
136	26, 33
137	33
142:6[5]	308n101
143:5	220n69
144:15	303n80
146–50	26
146	352

Proverbs

Proverbs, book of	1n1, 6, 15n39, 20n5, 233n32, 257n65, 283, 284, 286, 302–311, 399n122
1–9	304n88, 311n111
1:2–7	6
1:2–6	283
1:7	1, 283, 303n85, 304, 305, 307, 309, 399n122
1:26	303, 304
1:27	303, 304
1:29	283, 303n85, 304, 306
1:33	303, 304
2	306
2:5	291n29, 303n85, 304, 306
2:10	283
2:17	60
3:1–9	339
3:1–7	216n60
3:5	308
3:6	216n62
3:7	303, 304, 305, 306, 308
3:24	303, 304n87
3:25	303
3:25	304
3:31	283
3:32	283, 283n2
4:7	283
5:16	233n33
5:28	22n15
6:16–19	306n97
6:16	283n2
7:3	216n60
8:7	22n15, 283n2
8:9	221
8:13	303n85, 304, 305, 306, 306n97
8:15–16	283
8:32	70n32
9:9	283
9:10	1, 17, 283, 303n85, 304, 305, 309, 399
10:1	233n32
10:14–15	303n80
10:27	303n85, 304, 307
10:29	303n80
11:1	283n2
11:20	283n2
12:22	283n2
12:28	283
13:3	303n80
13:13	303n84, 304, 305, 307
13:14	283, 308n100
13:19	283n2
14:2	303n84, 304, 305, 306
14:6	304
14:15	308n102
14:16	303, 305
14:26–27	308
14:26	283n2, 303n85, 304, 307, 308n99
14:27	283, 303n85, 304, 307, 308n100, 308n100
14:28	303n80
15:8	283n2
15:9	283n2
15:16	303n85, 304, 307

15:20	233n32	2:8	221n70
15:33	1, 303n85, 304, 306, 310, 399n122	2:18	280n64
		5:8–30	33
16:5	283n2	5:8	215
16:6	303n85, 304, 306	5:12	220n69
16:12	283n2	5:24	18n58, 21n9, 46n27, 47n38
16:20	304, 308	6	242
17:15	283n2	6:1–13	381n42
18:7	303n80	6:1–4	381
18:21	283	6:5–7	381
19:23	303n85, 304, 307	6:8–13	381
19:26	233n32	6:8	378n25
20:2	303, 304	8:18	263n76
20:10	283, 283n2	8:20	18n58, 47n38
20:20	233n32	9:1–6[2–7]	370n67
20:23	283n2	9:5–6[6–7]	345
21:15	303	11:1–10	370n67
21:27	283n2	11:1–9	87
22:4	303n85, 304, 307	11:1–5	353
22:10	201n9	11:9	205n23
22:28	283	11:10	139n53
22:29	221	14:4	201n9
23:17	303n85, 304, 307	15:5	112n56
23:22	233n32	18:7	138n50
23:25	233n32	19:21	216n62
24:9	283n2	20:3	263n76, 380n38
24:21	303, 304, 305	21:4	109n31, 299n58
26:25	283n2, 308n102	24:4–5	71, 333n80
28:4	20n5	24:5	214
28:7	20n5	27:9	82n52
28:9	20n5, 283n2	28:12	201n13
28:14	303, 308	30:9	18n58, 47n38
28:24	233n32	32	346
28:25	308	32:1–8	87
29:15	233n32	33:8	201n9
29:18	20n5	33:9	171n75
29:25	303, 308	33:12	162n41
29:27	283n2	34:2	276
31:1–9	340n12	34:5–6	331n74
31:3–9	338. 338n7	34:14	201n13
31:9	330n69	37:19	221n70
31:10–31	233n32	37:22	137
31:21	303, 304	37:32	137
31:30	303n84, 304, 307	38:3	244n19
		38:17	109n31, 299n58
		40–55	353

Isaiah

Isaiah, book of	26n32, 27, 37n4, 78, 331n72, 346, 380, 380n40, 381, 382n48,	40:1–11	33
		40:3	353
		40:5	134n25
1:10	18n58, 47n38	40:6	134n25
1:13	201n8	40:8	29
1:20	331n74	40:9	52n61, 52n62, 382n48
2:1–4	151, 26n28	40:12–31	15, 298
		40:12–21	396

489

Isaiah (continued)

40:28–29	202
41:4	331n72
41:8	121n108, 347n33, 380n36
41:9–10	347n33
41:27	52n62
42:1–9	346
42:6	346
42:19	378n24
43:9–13	331n72
43:25	331n72
44:5	138n50, 216n62
44:12–20	241n6
46:3–4	331n72
48:2	204n21
48:10	54n72
48:12	331n72
48:14	121n108
49:1–6	346
49:1	377n12
49:15	321n38
50:4–9	346
51:7	18n58, 47n38, 216n60
51:12	331n72
51:13	303
51:16	350n9
52:1	204n21, 389n86
52:6	331n72
52:7	52n61, 52n62, 352, 382n48, 382n49
52:13—53:12	88, 346
53	28, 48, 87, 347
53:10	346
53:11	346
54:4–10	71–72, 333n80
54:9–10	64, 77, 215
55:3	77
55:7	216n63
55:8–9	281
56:1–8	217–18, 221
56:2	200, 221
56:3–8	200
56:4	221
59:3	22n15
59:12	82n52
59:13	22n15
60:6	52n61, 52n62
61	353
61:1–2	27, 352
61:1	52n61, 52n62, 352, 353, 371n71, 382n48
61:8	77
62:12	205n24
63:18	205n24
63:19	139n51
64:8	220n69
64:9	205n23
65:17	65
66:1	201n13
66:22	65
66:23	201n8

Jeremiah

Jeremiah, book of	43, 77, 380n40, 382
1	242
1:1	193
1:3–16	381n42
1:4	381
1:5	377n12, 381, 382
1:6	381
1:7–9	381
1:7	378n25
1:9	350n9
1:10	381
1:11–16	381
1:16	221n70
1:17–19	381
2:8	216n62
3:19–20	149n78
4:4	216n60, 327, 389n84
4:19	207n33
4:22	216n62
5:1	216n63
5:7	216n63
5:14	350n9
5:28	330n69
6:17	365
7–34	78
7:9	210n46
7:10	139n51
7:11	139n51
7:12–14	138n49
7:12	12n34, 138n47
7:14	139n51
7:25	380n37, 380n40
7:30	139n51
8:8	21n9, 46n27, 339, 348
8:17	378n25
9:2[3]	216n62
9:6[5]	216n62
9:23–25[22–24]	389n87
9:24[23]	216n62
9:25–26[24–25]	327, 389n86
10:3	221n70

INDEX OF BIBLICAL REFERENCES

10:9	221n70	31	66
10:25	216n62	31:2	79
11:54	54n72	31:15–22	80n48
12:4	171n75	31:21–22	79
12:11	171n75	31:23–40	77
14:4	171n75	31:23	205n23
15:1	131n14	31:25	202, 202n14
15:19	130n14	31:27–40	66, 77, 151, 328n63
17:19–27	200, 217, 221	31:27–37	327
17:24	221	31:27–34	215
17:27	221, 222	31:31–40	83, 334
18:6–10	278	31:31–37	82
18:18	18n56, 47n36	31:31–34	82, 88
18:20	247n29	31:31	77
19:24–26	217	31:32	78, 80n48, 82n52, 322n41
19:24	217	31:33–34	30
20:15	52n61, 52n62	31:33	78, 81n52
20:17	321n38	31:34	78, 79, 82n34, 216, 216n63
21:12	330n69	31:35–37	64, 72, 215, 333n80
22:16	330n69	32	78
22:29	171n75	32:7–9	193
23:1–8	26n28	32:20	263n76
23:1–6	346, 370n67	32:21	263n76
23:1–2	346	32:26–35	78
23:3–4	346	32:34	139n51
23:4	365	32:38–41	30
23:5–6	346	32:39	135n34
23:9–40	242n11	32:40	77
23:16–22	335, 350n9, 380	33:1–13	78
23:16–18	364n50	33:8	216n63
23:18	242n10	33:14–26	78
23:21–22	242n10	33:20	78
24:7	135n34, 216n61, 216n62	33:25	78
25:4	378n25, 380n37, 380n40,	34:13	322n41
25:9	276, 380n36	34:15	139n51
25:12	333	35:3	241n5
25:15	378n25	35:15	378n25, 380n37, 380n40
25:29	139n51	35:19	130n14
26:5	380n37, 380n40	36:3	216n63
26:6	378n25	38:7–13	255n56, 379n31
26:12	378n25	39:15–18	255n56, 379n31
26:15	378n25	40:8	241n5
26:18	26n28	42:1	241n5
27:6	380n36	44:4	378n25, 380n37, 380n40
28:1–17	242n11	44:28	320n35
29:1–23	242n11	46:10	331n74
29:10	333	48:13	112n56
29:13	321n36	50:5	77
29:19	378n25, 380n37	50:20	216n63
30:1—33:26	77	51:47	171n75
30:3	78, 327, 327n62	51:59	201n13
30:8–11	78	52:33	141n64
30:22	81		

Lamentations

Lamentations, book of	27, 32,
1:3	201n13
2:6	201n8
2:15	280n64
3:42	216n63
5:14	201n9

Ezekiel

Ezekiel, book of	29, 37n4, 77, 346, 381,
1:1—3:27	381n42
1:1–28	381
1:1–3	37
1:28—2:1	32
2:1–2	381
2:1	25n24
2:3–5	381
2:3	378n25
2:4	378n25
2:6–8	381
2:8—3:3	381
2:9	378n19
3:4–6	381
3:7–9	381
3:10–11	381
3:12–15	381
3:16–21	381
3:22–27	381
3:22–24	381
3:26	247n29
4–24	279
5:13	73n37
5:15	73n37
5:17	73n37
7:26	18n56, 47n36
8:11	241n5
8:18	240n5
11:1	241n5
11:10	135n34
11:19	328n63
12:21—13:23	380n38
12:21—13:16	350n9, 364n50
14:12–23	345n25
14:13	171n75
16:1–14	149n77
16:6	6n12
16:14	280n64
16:52	250n37
16:60	63n18, 72, 77, 214, 333n80
16:62	63n18
17:21	73n37
17:24	73n37
18:9	375
18:31	328n63
19:17	32
20:40	205n23
21:22	73n37
21:37	73n37
22:14	73n37
22:30	131n14
23:25–31	346
24:14	73n37
24:16	xviiin1
25–32	329
26:14	73n37
27:3	280n64
28:12	280n64
28:14	206n30
30:12	73n37
34	346
34:1–10	346
34:11–22	346
34:12	131n15
34:23–24	346, 370n67
34:23	365
34:24	73n37, 347
34:25	63n18, 73, 77, 202n17
34:25–30	64n18, 72, 333n80
34:31	347
36:22–32	73
36:24–34	328n63
36:26–28	30
36:26–27	6n12, 389n85
36:26	72, 135n34
36:28	81
36:36	73n37
37:14	73n37
37:15–18	73
37:21–26	370n67
37:26	63n18, 77, 333n80
38–39	329
38:16	216n62
38:17	380n37
43:13–17	188
43:27	166n57
44:1–27	189
44:3	141n64
44:15	130n14
44:24	201n8
44:28	180n15
45–46	190
45:1–5	177n3
45:17	201n8
46:1	200, 201n8, 221
46:3	201n8
46:4	200

46:12	200
48	190
48:8–22	177n3
48:14	182
48:35	190

Daniel

1:3–4	337
1:4	244n19
7:10	131n14
9	321n36
9:1–27	250n40
9:1–19	62, 77
9:1–2	26n28, 333
9:4	78, 247n30, 250n38, 255n56, 260n70
9:6	380n37, 380n40
9:7–14	77
9:10	380n37
9:11	45n23, 104, 348
9:13	45n23, 104, 348
9:16	205n23
9:17	380n40
9:18	321
9:19	216n63
9:20–23	333
9:20	205n23
9:24	204n21
9:27	201n9
11:32	216n62
11:38	216n62
12:1	151n81
12:7	205n24

Hosea

Hosea, book of	42n14, 125, 125n129
1–3	149n77
2:11	201n8
2:13	201n8
2:22[20]	216n62
3:5	370n67
4:2	210n46
5:4	216n62
5:8	371n71
8:2	216n62
13:2	221n70
13:4	216n62, 221n70

Joel

1:14	371n71
2:1	205n23, 371n71
2:15	371n71
2:21	171n75
2:25	202n17
3:5	52n61
4:9[3:9]	371n71

Amos

2:1	162n41
2:2	207n33
2:4	21n9, 46n27
3:7	380n37
5:5	139n53
7	282
7:1–9	247n29
7:2	216n63
8:5	200, 201n8
8:11–14	30
9:7	281
9:11	370n67
9:12	139n51

Obadiah

1:16	205n23

Jonah

1:2	371n71
1:9	291n29, 291n31, 295n45
2	25, 31
3–4	263
3:4–5	371n71
3:5	295n46, 393n96
3:7	371n71
3:9–10	330n70
4:2	330n70

Micah

3:5	371n71
4:1–8	150–51
4:1–3	26n28
4:13	277
5:1–4[2–5]	87, 347, 370n67
5:12	221n70
6:4	53n66, 378n24, 379n26
6:8	244n19

Nahum

2:1	52n61, 52n62

Habakkuk

2:2	167n61

Zephaniah

1:16	207n33
3:14	371n71

Haggai

Haggai, book of	95
2	334
2:23	380n36

Zechariah

Zechariah, book of	95
1:6	380n37
2:12	205n23
3:1	130n14
3:8	380n36
8:3	205n23
9:9	371n71
11:16	365
14:31	276

Malachi

Malachi, book of	1n2, 17, 22, 24, 47n31, 96, 136n35, 301, 353, 354, 399,
1:2	24
1:6–12	24
1:13	24
1:14	24
2:1–9	24, 195n79
2:6	18n56, 47n36, 244n19
2:9	18n56, 47n36, 70n32
2:10–12	24
2:13–16	24
2:14	60
2:17	24
3:1	350, 351, 355, 359
3:5	24, 48n52
3:8–9	24
3:13–15	24
3:22[4:4]	3n8, 18, 25, 127n5, 301, 351, 399
3:22[4:4]	47n31, 45n23
3:23[4:5]	350, 351, 355, 355n25, 359
3:24[4:6]	352

New Testament

Matthew

Matthew, book of	80, 230n24
1:1	87
1:5	276, 280
1:21	xiv, 80n49, 377
3:15	347
3:17	347
4:4	30
4:23	28n40, 371n70
5:2	371n70
5:3–11	371
5–7	6
5:14–16	226
5:17	48n49, 104, 317, 347
5:20	348
6:9–13	49n53
7:12	48n49
7:29	371n70
8:4	48n44
8:17	347n31
8:19	371n70
9:35	371n70
10:2	377n17
11:1	28n40, 371n70
11:9–15	373
11:10	378n22
11:13	48n49
11:21	371
11:28	141n60, 219
12:1–8	222
12:6–8	203
12:14	203
13:54	371n70
17:10–13	353
19:7	48n44
19:8	48n44
21:9	87
21:23	371n70
22:16	371n70
22:24	48n44

22:37–39	49
22:37	48n51, 104
22:39	104
22:40	48n49
23:13–39	205n27
23:13–29	371
23:23	25, 49, 392
23:34	84n55
23:35	84
23:37–39	348
26:55	371n70
26:67	238n44
27:30	238n44
27:46	31
28:18–19	87
28:19–20	80

Mark

Mark, book of	29, 52n60
1:1	378n22
1:2	378n22
1:14–15	28n40
1:21–22	371n70
1:31	28n40
1:38–39	28n40
1:44	48n44
2:13	371n70
2:23–26	223
2:27	208, 222
3:14	377n17
4:1–2	371n70
6:2	371n70
6:6	371n70
6:30	377n17
6:34	371n70
7:10	48n44
8:31	371n70
9:7	347
9:11–13	353
9:31	371n70
9:38	371n70
10:1	371n70
10:3	48n44
10:4	48n44
10:19	48
10:34	238n44
10:47	87
11:17	371n70
12:14	371n70
12:26	48n42
12:29–32	48n51
12:29–31	104
12:30–31	49, 74, 210, 400n128
12:35	371n70
14:39	371n70
14:65	238n44

Luke

1:6	82n53
1:33	355n25
1:76	355n24
2:22	48n40
2:29	379n30
3:12	371n70
3:22	347
3:32	87
3:38	87
4:14–15	27
4:15	371n70
4:16–20	26n32, 27
4:17–21	353
4:31	371n70
4:38	84
5:3	371n70
5:14	48n44
5:17	371n70
6:1–11	203
6:6	371n70
6:13	377n17
7:24	378n22
7:27	378n22
9:10	377n17
9:52	378n22
10:27	104, 211, 400n128, 48n51, 49
11:1	371n70
11:2–4	49n53
11:37–52	205n25
11:42	25
11:51	84
12:12	371n70
12:48	263
13:10	371n70
13:22	371n70
13:26	371n70
14:1–4	223
14:5	223
16:16	48n49
16:29	48n41
16:31	48n41
17:5	377n17
18:32	238n44
18:39	87
19:47	371n70
20:1	371n70
20:6	355n24

495

Luke (continued)

20:21	371n70
20:28	48n45
21:37	371n70
22:14	377n17
22:20	84, 88
22:37	347n31
22:42	348
23:5	371n70
24:10	377n17
24:13–33	27
24:44	3n8, 21, 45, 28n40, 48n49, 104, 125

John

John, book of	354, 355, 372,
1:1–2	87
1:1	372
1:6–9	372
1:10–13	372
1:14–18	19
1:14	xiv, 371, 372, 402
1:16–18	372
1:16–17	xix, 59, 371
1:19–34	354–55
1:19–21	355
1:23	355, 373
1:32	355
1:33	355, 355n25
1:34	355
1:36	355
1:38	371n70
1:41	355
1:45	48n49, 355
1:49	355, 371n70
1:51	355
3:2	371n70
3:16	65
3:26	371n70
3:36	295n47, 392n94
4:19	355n27, 371n70
4:31	371n70
5:45	48n41
5:46	48n41
5:47	48n43
6:14	355n27, 371n70
6:25	371n70
6:45	347n31
6:59	371n70
7:14	371n70
7:23	48n40
7:25–44	355n27
7:28	371n70
7:31	355
7:35	371n70
7:37	141n60
7:40	355n27, 371n70
8:2	371n70
8:5	48n44
8:20	371n70
9:2	371n70
9:17	355n27, 371n70
9:34	371n70
10:11	88
10:15	346, 347n31
11:8	371n70
11:27	355
11:50	272
11:51	356n27, 371
12:1–9	32n47
12:20–36	32n47
12:38	347n31
13:1–38	32n47
14:9	19
18:1–19:30	32n47
18:20	371n70
19:15	348
20:16	371n70
20:31	355

Acts

Acts, book of	27, 28n40, 80, 359, 380, 381, 385
1:16	22n13, 27n35, 47n32
1:2–3	27n36
1:2	377n17
1:26	377n17
2:4	80, 81
2:17–21	27n38
2:24	27n36
2:25	22n13, 47n32
2:30	27n36
2:33–36	27n37
2:33	27n36, 80, 81
2:34	22n13, 47n32
2:37	377n17
2:38	28n39, 80, 81
2:42	28
2:43	377n17
3	356
3:12–26	356, 377n13
3:12–16	356
3:13–14	356
3:13	27n37, 356, 358, 380
3:14–26	335

3:14	27n35	8:32–33	347n31
3:15	27n36	9:1–4	381
3:16	356	9:4–5	381
3:17–24	356	9:5–6	381
3:18–21	357	9:10–17	381
3:18	27n35, 357	9:18–19	381
3:19	28n39, 358	10:9–16	211
3:21	335, 357, 357	10:37–39	27n36
3:22–23	350, 356, 357, 373	10:43	27n35, 28n39
3:22	358	10:44–48	27n38, 81
3:23	357	10:44	81
3:24	357	10:45	387n75
3:25–26	356, 358	11:2	387n75
3:25	370n65	11:15–16	81
3:26	335, 380	11:16	81
4:1–3	358	12:5–17	263
4:4	358	13:12	28
4:11	27n37	13:15	48n49
4:25	22n13, 47n32, 371, 380	13:17–41	27n35
4:27	380	13:22	87
4:30	380	13:34	347n31
4:33	377n17	13:39	48n40
4:36	377n17	14:2	295n47, 392n94
5:12	377n17	14:14	377n17
5:18	377n17	15	376n5
5:28	28	15:1–21	28
5:29	377n17	15:1–20	211
5:30	27n36, 27n37	15:1	387, 390, 48n40
5:32	27n38	15:5	387, 48n40
5:40	377n17	15:8	28n39
5:42	28n40	16:1–3	387
6:8	359n36	17:10–15	28
6:11	48n41	18:24–26	28
6:14	48n44, 48n47	18:27–28	27n35
7:8	387n76	18:31	27n36
7:20–43	377n13	19:1–7	27n38
7:20–34	358	19:6	81
7:30	127n6	20:12	380
7:35–39	335	21:21	48n41
7:35–38	358	22:3–7	381
7:35	358, 358n34, 383n54	22:3	28
7:36	358, 358n34, 359	22:8–9	381
7:37	350, 356, 356n28, 358, 358n34, 373	22:9	381
		22:10	381
7:38	127n6, 358n34, 383n54	22:11–13	381
7:39–43	358	22:14–15	381
7:51–53	335	24:14	48n49
7:52–53	359	26:9–14	381
7:52	335, 359n35	26:15	381
7:53	383n54	26:16	381
7:54–60	359	26:17	381
7:54–55	359	26:18	381
8:14–24	27n38	26:22	48n41
8:14–17	80, 81	28:23	48n40, 48n49, 104
8:26–38	28	28:31	28n40

Romans

Romans, book of	xviii, xix, 49, 376, 386n65, 399n125
1:1	51n60, 378, 379n28, 379n30
1:3	87
1:5	378n20
1:16–17	382n50
2:16	51n60
2:24	347n31
2:25–29	387n77, 400
2:25–27	387n77
3–4	374
3:1	387n77
3:20	217n66
3:21	48n49, 104
3:28	217n66
3:30	387n77
4:1	328
4:3	393
4:9–12	387n77
4:13–15	375
5:14–19	87
7:8–9	375
7:12	377
7:16	377
8:2–4	375
8:18–25	88
8:19–23	85
8:20–22	65
8:28–29	87
9–11	81, 82n51, 334
9:3	386n72
9:4–5	82, 385n64
9:26–27	82n52
9:30—10:13	82n51
10:4–5	375
10:5	48n46
10:13–16	382n50
10:13	88
10:14–15	301n71, 399n125
10:15	347n31
10:16	347n31
10:19	48n46
11:9	22n13, 47n32
11:13	378n20
11:25–32	82
11:26–27	216
11:26	334
12:1–2	204
12:1	49
13:8–9	400
15:8	387n77
15:10	43n18
15:12	87
15:16–20	382n50
15:16	51n60
15:19	51n60
15:21	347n31
15:31	295n47, 392n94
16:25	51n60

1 Corinthians

1–3	30
1:1	377n17, 378
1:15	87
1:17–18	382n50
1:45	87
4:15	51n60
7:18	387n77
7:19	387n77
9:5	377n17
9:9	48n40, 48n48
9:12	51n60
11:25	84, 88
12:3	386n72
14:26	29, 31
15:1–8	382n50
15:5–11	377n17
16:22	386n72

2 Corinthians

2 Corinthians, book of	376n9
1:1	377n17
2:12	52n60
3:4–6	381n42
3:6	375
3:13	382n47
3:15	48n41
3:18	382n47
4:4	51n60
5:17	88
6:16	81, 216n61
6:17	347n31
9:13	52n60
10:14	51n60

Galatians

Galatians, book of	xviii, xix, 49, 217, 303, 374–404, 376, 377, 383, 385n64, 385n65, 386, 387, 392, 399, 400

1–2	376, 377
1:1–5	386
1	372
1:1	377
1:6–9	261, 386
1:6	51n60, 386
1:7	52n60, 382n50
1:8–9	386
1:8	51, 386n69, 386n70
1:9	386n70
1:10	379, 379n28, 379n30
1:11–22	384
1:11–12	383
1:11	384n55
1:12	384, 384n55
1:14	385
1:15–16	xi, 382, 386n66
1:15	378, 381
1:16–17	384n55
1:16	382, 382n47, 384
1:17–18	385
1:17	377n17
1:19	377n17
2:3	387n77
2:7–9	387n77
2:7	387n77
2:11–14	400, 401
2:12	387n77, 400
2:15–21	400
2:16	217n66, 401
3–4	374
3:2	217n66, 302, 399
3:5	217n66
3:6	393
3:10–14	217n66, 375
3:10	217n66, 401
3:19	383, 383n54
3:21–24	375
3:28	379
4:7	379
4:22	379
4:23	328, 379
4:24–25	127n6
4:25	385
4:29	328
4:30	379
4:31	379
5:2–12	400
5:2	387n77, 400
5:3	387n77, 400
5:4	400
5:6	387n77, 392, 399, 401
5:11	387n77
5:13–22	401
5:13–15	400
5:13	386n66
5:16–26	400
5:16	400
5:19–21	400
5:21	400
5:22–23	400
6:12	387n77
6:13	387n77
6:15	387n77
6:16	81n50, 399n126

Ephesians

Ephesians, book of	32
1–3	382n50
1:1	377n17
1:4	84n55
2:11	387n77
3:6	51n60
4:11	xiii, 28n40
4:12	28n40
5:18–19	29
5:25–33	239

Philippians

1:1	379n28
1:27	51n60
2:7	379n30
2:15	83n53
3:3	387n77
3:5	387n77
3:6	83n53

Colossians

Colossians, book of	28,
1:1	377n17
1:7	379n30
1:15	87
1:16–17	87, 88
1:18–20	87
1:20	88
1:28	28n40
2:11	387n77
2:13	387n77
3:11	387n77
3:16	xvi
3:17	29
4:7	379n30
4:11	387n77
4:16	28

1 Thessalonians

3:2	51n60
3:13	83n53
5:27	28

2 Thessalonians

1:8	52n60
2:14	51n60

1 Timothy

1:1	377n17
1:8	377
2:7	28n40
4:13	28
5:18	48

2 Timothy

1:1	377n17
1:10	51n60
1:11	28n40
2:8	51n60, 87
2:24	379n30
3:15–17	28
3:16–17	22, 30
3:16	18
4:2—4	28n40

Titus

1:1	377n17, 379n28, 379n30
1:10	387n77

Hebrews

Hebrews, book of	xvi, 30, 82, 83, 151, 216, 379n27
1:1–2	373
1:2–4	87
1:2	xix
2:2	383n54
3:5	380n39
4:3	84n55
4:4	213
4:6	216n64
4:7	22n13, 47n32
4:9	216
4:12	30
8:10–13	151
8:11	216
8:6–13	82
8:7–12	215
8:7	82
8:8–13	88
8:8	83
9:4	214n54
9:15	xvi, 83
10:26	216n64
10:28	48n40
11:4	84
12	126n1, 151n79
12:22–24	83, 151

James

James, book of	xiii, 28, 29, 49
1:1–2	379n30
1:1	379n28
2:25	378n22
5:13	29
5:16	248, 263

1 Peter

1 Peter, book of	49
1:1	377n17
1:10–12	357n29
1:16	205n24
1:19–20	88
1:20	84n55
1:23	6n12, 30
2:9–10	57
2:22	347n31

2 Peter

1:1	377n17, 379n28, 379n30
1:20–21	22
3:10–13	65
3:15–16	28

1 John

1 John, book of	49

Jude

1:1	379n28, 379n30

Revelation

Revelation, book of	xiv, 32, 61, 65, 87, 279, 329n64
1:1	379n30
1:3	28
1:12	379n28
3:4	244n19
5:5	87
10:7	380n37
11:4	131n14
11:18	380n37
13:8	84n55
15:3	329n64, 379n28, 379n30
17:8	84n55
19–21	87
21:1–4	65
21:3	216n61
22:6	380n37
22:16	87

Index of Ancient Extracanonical Literature

Deuterocanonical Books and Pseudepigrapha

Sirach (Ecclesiasticus)

1:11	311n114
1:12	311n114
1:14	405n93
1:16	405n93
1:18	311n114, 405n93
1:20	405n93
1:27	311n114, 405n93
1:28	311n114
1:30	311n114
2:10	311n114
2:16b	301
9:16	311n114
10:22	311n114
16:2	311n114
19:20	311n114, 405n93
21:11	311n114, 405n93
23:27	311n114
25:6	311n114
25:11	311n114
25:23–29	311
27:3	311n114
40:2	288n22
40:26	311n114
40:27	311n114
44:19–20	122
44:20	121n112, 296, 311n114
45:23	311n114
48:10	351

Baruch

3:36—4:4	122n115, 311

1 Maccabees

14:41	352

Jubilees

1.27—2:1	383n54

Genesis Apocryphon

21:29	113n62

Assumption of Moses

1:14	382n46

Dead Sea Scrolls and Related Documents

1QM 11:7	352n17	4Q246	353n19
1QS 9:11	350n6,	4Q521	352, 353n19
1QS 9:9–11	352	4Q558	352
4Q175 *Testimonia*	350n6	11Q29:10	68n25
4Q185 ["Sapiential Admonitions B"]	301n71	11Q29:10	68n25
4Q186	301n71	Cairo Damascus Document	2:12

Ancient Jewish Writers

Josephus

Antiquities of the Jews
4.308	154n10
15.136	383n54

Jewish Wars
4.9.12	207n36

Against Apion
1.41	351n13

Philo

Dreams
1.140–44	383n54

Pseudo-Philo
11.5	383n54

Rabbinic Works

Mishna, Talmud, and Related Literature

Mishnah Middot 3:4	165n52
Mishnah Shabbat 7	221n72
Tosefta Sotah 13.2	351n13
Baba Bathra	
12a	351n13
14b	105n2
b. Berakot 32a	246n27
Yerushalmi Hagigah 1:7	25n26
Eikhah Rabbati Proem 2	25n26
Pesikta de Rav Kahana 15	25n26
Genesis Rabbah 49.7	116n86, 244n21
Seder Olam Rabbah 30	351n13

Deuteronomy Targums

Targum Neofiti	246n27
Targum Onqelos	246n27
Targum Pseudo-Jonathan	246n27

Early Christian Writers

Justin Martyr, *First Apology* 67	29n41
Eusebius	350

Greco-Roman Literature

Herodotus, *Histories* 4.117–120	107n12

www.ingramcontent.com/pod-product-compliance
Lightning Source LLC
Chambersburg PA
CBHW060416300426
44111CB00018B/2865